HABITATS OF

AUSTRALIA, NEW GUINEA, AND THE SOLOMONS

HABITATS OF AUSTRALIA, NEW GUINEA, AND THE SOLOMONS

A Field Guide for Birders, Naturalists, and Ecologists

Iain Campbell, Charley Hesse, and Phil Gregory

Special Contributors
Giselle Velastegu, Pablo Cervantes, and Sam Woods

PRINCETON UNIVERSITY PRESS
PRINCETON AND OXFORD

Copyright © 2026 by Princeton University Press

Princeton University Press is committed to the protection of copyright and the intellectual property our authors entrust to us. Copyright promotes the progress and integrity of knowledge created by humans. By engaging with an authorized copy of this work, you are supporting creators and the global exchange of ideas. As this work is protected by copyright, any reproduction or distribution of it in any form for any purpose requires permission; permission requests should be sent to permissions@press.princeton.edu. Ingestion of any PUP IP for any AI purposes is strictly prohibited.

Published by Princeton University Press
41 William Street, Princeton, New Jersey 08540
99 Banbury Road, Oxford OX2 6JX

press.princeton.edu
GPSR Authorized Representative: Easy Access System Europe - Mustamäe tee 50,
10621 Tallinn, Estonia, gpsr.requests@easproject.com

All Rights Reserved
ISBN (pbk.) 978-0-691-26057-0
ISBN (e-book) 978-0-691-26887-3

British Library Cataloging-in-Publication Data is available

Editorial: Robert Kirk and Megan Mendonça
Production Editorial: Karen Carter
Typesetting and Design: D & N Publishing, Wiltshire, UK
Cover Design: Wanda España
Production: Steven Sears
Publicity: Matthew Taylor and Caitlyn Robson-Iszatt
Copyeditor: Amy K. Hughes
Cover illustrations by Christine Elder

This book has been composed in Cambay Devanagari

Printed in China

10 9 8 7 6 5 4 3 2 1

CONTENTS

List of Figures and Sidebars 6

INTRODUCTION 7

Preface 7

The Area and Scope of This Book 8

How to Use This Book 9

How Does *Habitats of the World* Complement Other Global Habitat Classification Systems? 10

What Is a Distinct Habitat? 12

First Nations People and the Pleistocene–Holocene Anthropogenic Habitats 13

Habitat Distribution Maps 14

Types of Habitat Boundaries and Ecotones 14

The Köppen Climate Classification and the Climate Graphs 16

Biomes of Australia, New Guinea, and the Solomon Islands 19

Taxonomy, Common and Scientific Names 21

Useful Habitat Terminology 21

NatureServe and the IVC 23

Acknowledgments 23

Abbreviations 24

Bibliography 24

OUTSIDERS' GUIDE TO AUSTRALIA, NEW GUINEA, AND THE SOLOMON ISLANDS 27

HABITATS OF AUSTRALIA

DESERTS 41

- Au2A Dune Spinifex Desert 41
- Au2B Dunecrest Canegrass 46
- Au2C Rocky Spinifex Desert 49
- Au2D Chenopod Shrubland 54
- Au2E Gibber Chenopodland 60
- Au2F Samphire Flat 64

HUMID BROADLEAF FORESTS 69

- Au4A Australasian Lowland Rainforest 69
- Au4B Australian Subtropical Rainforest 76
- Au4C Australasian Tropical Montane Rainforest 82
- Au4D New Guinea Hill Forest 88
- Au4E New Guinea High-Montane Rainforest 92
- Au4F Nothofagus Forest 97
- Au4G Australian Temperate Rainforest 102
- Au4H Australasian Littoral Rainforest 106
- Au4I Australasian Swamp Forest 110

TROPICAL DRY DECIDUOUS FORESTS 117

- Au5A Australian Dry Vineforest 117
- Au5B Australasian Monsoon Vineforest 122
- Au5C Brigalow 128

SAVANNAS 133

- Au6A Open Eucalypt Savanna 133
- Au6B Spinifex Eucalypt Savanna 141
- Au6C Tetrodonta Woodland Savanna 147
- Au6D Shrubby Eucalypt Savanna 153
- Au6F Northern Acacia Savanna 159
- Au6G Melaleuca Savanna 165
- Au6H Melaleuca Riverine Forest 170

GRASSLANDS 177

- Au7A Tropical Tussock Grassland 177
- Au7B Temperate Tussock Grassland 182
- Au7C Australian Montane Grassland 187

MEDITERRANEAN SHRUBLANDS 193

- Au8A Wallum and Ausbos 193
- Au8B Arid Heathland 201
- Au8C Tropical Heathland 206
- Au8D Kwongan Heathland 210
- Au8F Montane Heathland 215

SCLEROPHYLL WOODLANDS AND FORESTS 221

- Au9A Grassy Wet Sclerophyll Forest 221
- Au9B Rainforest Wet Sclerophyll Forest 226
- Au9C Karri Forest 232
- Au9D Grassy Dry Sclerophyll Forest 236
- Au9E Heathy Dry Sclerophyll Forest 242

Au9F Jarrah-Marri Forest 249
Au9G Ironbark-Box Woodland 254
Au9H Inland Riverine Woodland 260
Au9I Sheoak Riparian Forest 265
Au9J Subalpine Eucalypt Woodland 269
Au9K Inland Rocky Shrubby Woodland 274
Au9L Mixed Sandplain Woodland 279
Au9M Heathy Mallee 286
Au9N Shrubby and Chenopod Mallee 291
Au9O Spinifex Mallee 296
Au9P Western Eucalypt Woodland 301
Au9Q Grassy Mulga 306
Au9R Spinifex Mulga 311
Au9S Yilgarn Mixed Woodland 315
TUNDRAS 321
Au10A Australian Alpine Tundra 321
Au10B Austroparamo 325
FRESHWATER HABITATS 329
Au11A Australasian Tropical Freshwater Wetland 329
Au11B Australian Temperate Wetland 334
Au11C Lignum Swamp 337
Au11D Montane Bog and Fen 342
SALINE HABITATS 344
Au12A Australasian Tropical Mangrove Forest 344
Au12B Australian Temperate Mangrove 351
Au12C Australasian Sandy Beach 354
Au12D Australasian Sandy Cay 357
Au12E Australian Salt Pan 359
Au12F Australian Coastal Salt Marsh 362
Au12G Australasian Tidal Mudflat 365
Au12H Australasian Rocky Headland 368
Au12I Australasian Tropical Pelagic Waters 372
Au12J Australian Temperate Pelagic Waters 376
POST-COLONIAL ANTHROPOGENIC HABITATS 379
Au13A Australasian Cropland 379
Au13B Australasian Bananas and Sugarcane 382
Au13C Australian Open Grazing Land 385
Au13D Australasian Intensive Pasture 387
Au13E Australasian Urban Environments 389
Au13F Australasian Tree Plantations 392
APPENDIX 394
Soil Groups and Habitats 394
Common Canopy Leaf Types and the Forests Where You May Find Them 396
INDEX 397

LIST OF FIGURES AND SIDEBARS

FIGURES

Fig. 1. The region covered by this book 8
Fig. 2. Comparison of global ecosystem, habitat, and vegetation classification systems 11
Fig. 3. Comparison of biota taxonomy and habitat typology 12
Fig. 4. Types of habitat boundaries and ecotones 15
Fig. 5. Sample climate graphs 17
Fig. 6. The regions and biomes of the Australia–New Guinea region 27

SIDEBARS

What Are Key Biodiversity Areas, and Why Do They Matter? 101
The Extinct Australian Pleistocene Megafauna 140
Seamounts of Eastern Australia 375

INTRODUCTION

PREFACE

This book is part of a series of seven continental books and one global book in the Habitats of the World series. The authors of all the books have had a lifelong fascination with biogeography and wildlife ecosystems. Like the vast majority of other passionate travelling naturalists, they were most interested in birds and larger mammals, while also paying some attention to reptiles, amphibians, butterflies, and other groups. We were frustrated by the approach to habitat/ ecosystem classification used in most books and the complete absence of habitat information in many vertebrate field guides. The first book in this series, *Habitats of the World* (2021), limited in scope, had enough space for just 189 habitats to be delineated and described. What became apparent was that taking a slightly more detailed approach, with around 545 habitats divided among the seven continents, we could delineate habitats at a scale that mirrored the regional level of world vegetation but reclassify them using bird assemblages along with vegetation, and make a system that is functional for botanists, intuitive for ecologists, and accessible to naturalists. To do this required series creator Iain Campbell to undertake a PhD to align major world vegetation mapping systems, create bird assemblages for all habitats, and test whether bird assemblages better predict habitats than vegetation mapping alone. So, employing this common language and collaborating with a broader group of experts from the professional nature guiding and conservation world, we are creating these regional books that break down the habitats at a finer resolution than the original book. In this book, we present our view of Australian wildlife habitats (ecosystems). We have also created online resources, such as a bird-assemblage habitat database, listing all global habitats along with the indicator bird species, which will allow users to search via birds or habitats to find and understand their relationships (www.habitatsoftheworld.org/birdassemblages).

There are many lenses through which planet Earth's habitats can be assessed. Geology, geography, and botany are all critically important. But we don't view any of them as the final word on habitats, and much of what these models prioritise is of little immediate relevance to travelling naturalists or ecologists. A specialist in entomology or herpetology will apply a different, and fascinating, lens to the world. Our reason for prioritising the bird (and to a lesser extent mammal) 'lens' is that we look at the world primarily through this lens, and so do most of the world's travelling naturalists. A handful of specialists seek out moths in the mountains of New Guinea, whereas millions of tourists visit Kakadu National Park in the Northern Territory of Australia to see crocodiles and glamorous birds or visit the Royal National Park near Sydney for very casual birding, even if they don't realise that is what they are doing. Our presentation at first glance may lack the apparent clarity of a botanical approach to the world's habitats, but by using bird assemblages in conjunction with botany, we provide truly ecological mapping of habitats. At the scale we present it, our classification has far greater utility to most world travellers, regional ecologists, and conservationists than any other previous perspective on habitats.

In its attempt to cover the wildlife habitats of the entire continent of Australia, this is an ambitious book, in which difficult decisions had to be made about what to include and exclude based on botanical and bird assemblages. We freely admit that deep oceanic habitats, and to a lesser extent, surficial aquatic habitats, are worthy of far more detailed coverage using fish and invertebrate assemblages than we have given in this volume; we will get around to filling in these gaps in a global marine and aquatic volume once the terrestrial and surficial habitats are described. At this time, the habitats are almost all based on botany and aquatic habitats as they relate to birds and, to a lesser extent, mammals and reptiles. Our approach is certain to alienate some, but we firmly believe it will be both enjoyable and useful to most ecologists, conservationists, and global naturalists like us.

THE AREA AND SCOPE OF THIS BOOK

Australia has a large range of unique ecosystems, but they are poorly understood by the general public and government decision makers. This book, as part of the global Habitats of the World (HotW) series, allows botanists, ecologists, and conservationists to share a common language that is intuitive, easy to understand, and enticing to non-scientists. In the series, we describe ecosystems around the world and explain their relationships with the wildlife that lives in them, and how these ecosystems relate to surrounding ecosystems. We use the term 'habitat' to describe this vegetation, its environment, and its wildlife, so it is synonymous with the term 'ecosystem' used in other works. This book covers all of continental Australia and includes the islands of New Guinea (comprising Indonesian New Guinea in the west and Papua New Guinea in the east), New Britain, New Ireland, Bougainvillea, and the Solomon Islands (fig. 1). An argument could easily be made to include New Caledonia and New Zealand, as there are some associations with Australasian habitats. However, we chose to include those islands and their habitats in the forthcoming guide to the habitats of Antarctica and nearby ocean islands. Indonesia's Lesser Sunda Islands, which are very complex, with both strong Asian and Australasian influences, will also be covered in that book. Australia's many subantarctic islands, which are very similar to the islands south of Africa or South America, with near-identical bird and plant assemblages, are best described with them, also in the forthcoming Antarctica book.

Fig. 1. The region covered by this book includes the Solomon Islands but not New Caledonia, New Guinea but not the Moluccas, and Australia but not New Zealand or Macquarie Island. These areas are covered in other books in the series.

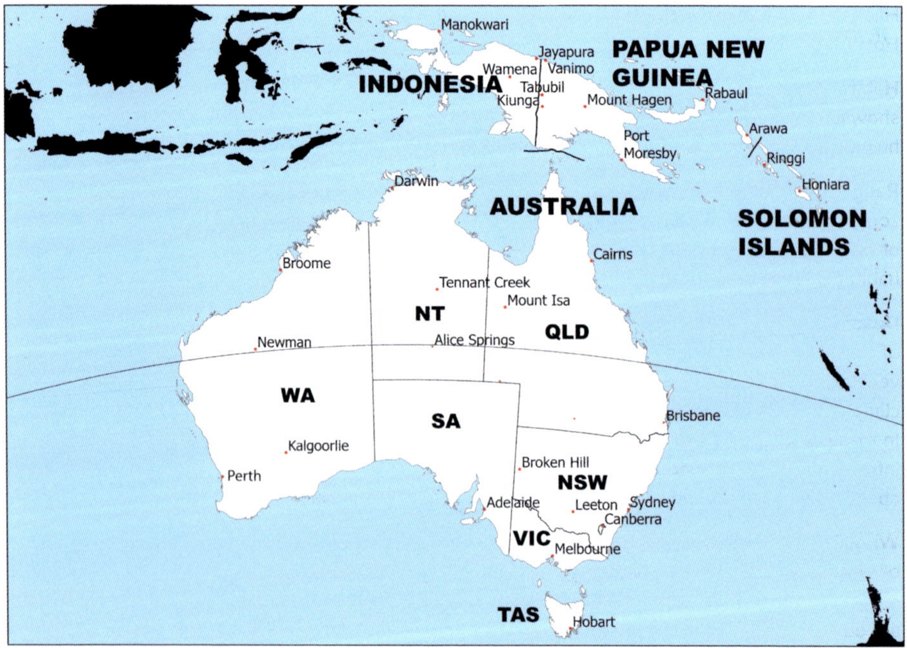

HOW TO USE THIS BOOK

The bulk of this book consists of habitat accounts, organised by biomes. While some habitats could reasonably be classified under multiple biomes, each is described only once. The introduction to each of the biomes includes a dendrogram illustrating how the Australian habitat relates to similar habitats within the global *Habitats of the World* book. For much more detailed explanations and dendrograms, readers are referred to the Habitats of the World website (www.habitatsoftheworld.org).

Each of the habitat accounts includes the following sections and elements.

In a Nutshell: A succinct explanation of what makes the habitat distinctive and worthy of separation from other habitats.

Global Habitat Affinities: Habitats from other continents that are structurally similar, providing a cross-reference to habitats that may be familiar to you, helping you to understand the unfamiliar habitat covered.

Continental Habitat Affinities: Habitats from elsewhere in Australia that are structurally similar. For these cross-references to other habitats within this book, we drop the broad regional designation and name just the habitat; for example, we list LOWLAND RAINFOREST rather than AUSTRALASIAN LOWLAND RAINFOREST.

Species Overlap: The habitats that have the most similar assemblages of birds (predominantly) and mammals. These are ranked from the most similar habitat to the least. The vast majority of these are habitats within the same zoogeographic region as the habitat covered. As with Continental Habitat Affinities, for habitats within Australia and New Guinea, we do not include the regional designation in the name.

Full Bird Assemblage: A link is provided to the full bird assemblage for each habitat on the Habitats of the World website. Users will be able to generate lists and input species lists to predict HotW habitat type.

Habitat Silhouette: These silhouettes are designed to give a quick visual snapshot of a habitat, showing some of its distinctive plant shapes and its overall height and structure. They include a human silhouette for scale.

Range Map: These are visual representations of a habitat's occurrence within a given zoogeographic region. Dark shading is used for areas where the habitat is the predominant habitat or one of the predominant habitats. In some maps, pale shading is used to indicate areas where the habitat is found only locally.

Description: This section explains what makes a habitat distinctive and its basic ecology. Some of the commonly included information is the height and composition of the various layers of vegetation, the overall gestalt and accessibility, local temperature, and rainfall. The accompanying climate graphs are discussed below, in The Köppen Climate Classification and the Climate Graphs. In these descriptions, we have purposefully chosen not to always include exactly the same information or to present it in the same order. This allows us to both stress what is most important about a given habitat and simply vary these sections to keep them interesting for readers.

Wildlife: This section may be the most interesting for a typical reader. Beyond the nuts and bolts of what makes a habitat distinctive and what makes it work, most visitors are keen to learn about and to find its wildlife. Throughout this book, when considering wildlife, birds and larger mammals are our primary focus, but in many accounts we go well beyond this to feature a broad array of vertebrates and some invertebrates. Species that are restricted to a certain habitat (endemics) are given special weight, as finding these will be the priority for many visitors.

Conservation: This section provides a quick summary of the conservation status of the habitat and major issues it is facing.

Distribution: This section and the accompanying range map indicate where the habitat occurs within a given zoogeographic region. The elevations at which it is found are sometimes mentioned, though this information may also be in the Description.

Where to See: These are places that you can visit to experience a given habitat. In general, these are the most readily or frequently visited places, in the most accessible regions.

Photos: Photos are included that illustrate both the habitat itself and some of its charismatic wildlife. Some photos are chosen because they effectively show both the habitat and some of its wildlife.

HOW DOES *HABITATS OF THE WORLD* COMPLEMENT OTHER GLOBAL HABITAT CLASSIFICATION SYSTEMS?

The understanding and correct classification of habitats is crucial to the development of representative and viable nature-reserve systems, as is knowing what wildlife occurs in threatened habitats within them. Currently, there is no system to classify all the world's habitats at a level that can be applied by most naturalists, birders, conservationists, and ecologists. There are reasons for this, such as, but not limited to, systems and typologies being overly hierarchical by design, and the challenges of trying to integrate different national mapping systems. The Global Ecosystem Typology (GET) system developed by the International Union for Conservation of Nature (IUCN) and the International Vegetation Classification (IVC), mainly developed through NatureServe, both have excellent ecosystem classifications that aim to define and protect ecological communities. These systems are very useful in principle, but neither works globally at a scale that conservation groups, birders, or ecologists can easily use, because they do not yet have all habitats described at a level that is convenient to use and understand (see fig. 2). However, on a global scale we do use the IVC/NatureServe Group levels to build our system, with the IVC Macrogroups as a starting point. Our Habitats of the World (HotW) system works as a Rosetta Stone that relates the GET and IVC habitat classification systems at a global scale with national and state mapping systems. A complete walk-through from the HotW system to the IVC, GET, Australian National Vegetation Information System (NVIS), and Australian state mapping systems is available online: www.habitatsoftheworld.org/intotheweedstypology/Australia.

As illustrated in figure 1, the GET system jumps from 108 global (described) units at the Group level to between 3500 and 3700 (undescribed) units at the Regional Ecotype level. Similarly, the IVC system jumps from 76 (described) units at Division level to 1196, often undescribed, units at Macrogroup level. Neither system describes the animals living in the habitats. It will be many years before either system has the coverage required for global or Australian use at the most detailed scale.

The HotW system has global coverage and includes 545 mainly terrestrial habitats worldwide (74 in Australia and northern islands), covering those home to almost all the world's birds and much of the other wildlife. At this level, it becomes much easier for the non-botanist to discern one habitat from another, understand how they differ, and develop the understanding and criteria to be able to comprehend how the ecology of these systems differs. The HotW system should make it easier to incorporate habitats into conservation planning, mapping, and ecological work.

Fig. 2. Comparison of global ecosystem, habitat, and vegetation classification systems. The Habitats of the World (HotW), International Vegetation Classification (IVC), and the IUCN's Global Ecosystem Typology (GET) are all systems for global habitat classification. The chart shows that although the GET system will be comprehensive, it is still in the very rudimentary stages, with only the 108 Groups defined. The IVC system is much more developed, with about half the 1196 Macrogroups defined and described. The HotW system is almost complete, with most of the 545 regional habitats classified and described. The shaded area shows the number of units that are comprehensive enough to describe variations of the world habitats but sufficiently general to be understood and learnt for the whole planet.

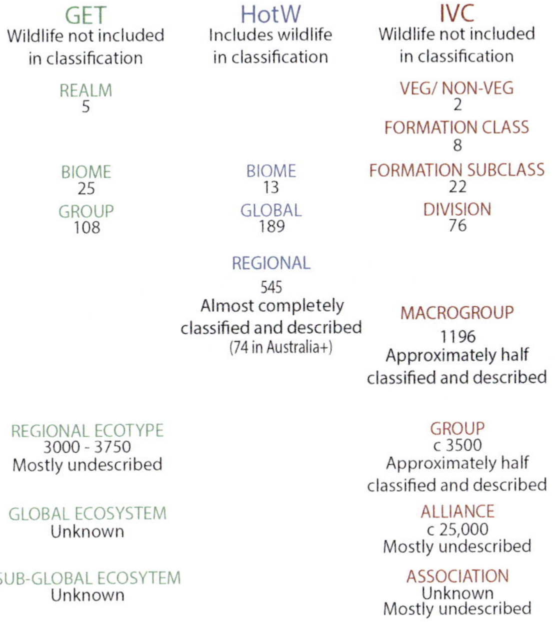

Habitats (sometimes called 'vegetation types') are amalgamations of various species of plants and animals under specific environmental conditions with artificial, human-imposed boundaries delineating them from adjacent similar habitats in what is almost always a gradual boundary at some scale. They are not taxonomic entities the way animals and plants are. Organisms have a distinct genetic code and evolutionary history that infers relatedness, which can be detailed in a strict dendrogram form (fig. 3). However, all the habitat classification systems use a hierarchical typology that just doesn't fit this rigid structure. As you will see in the breakdowns of different biomes in the Biomes of Australia section below, the dendrograms are helpful in showing relationships, but many habitats are crossovers or can easily be classified in multiple biomes. The relationships are not hierarchical but often more weblike. Examples include MELALEUCA SAVANNA, which is mainly a savanna but is inundated and could be regarded as an ephemeral wetland in the Freshwater Habitats biome; or SPINIFEX EUCALYPT SAVANNA, which may be described as both a desert and a savanna. These are not either/ors but both/ands.

One reason there are so many more birders than bat, rat, or beetle enthusiasts is that birds are readily identifiable animals of a limited number, around 11,000 species worldwide. It is possible to learn most of the world's bird species, to identify them, and to catalogue them (i.e., to keep lists), as so many birders are prone to do. This then becomes a meaningful contribution to citizen-science projects like iNaturalist or Cornell's eBird, which can be used to analyse global trends in species distribution and occurrence. In contrast, there are roughly 400,000 known species of beetles, a number that prevents observers from making easy identifications or discerning relationships among those that have been identified. Bats and rodents suffer the problem of being usually nocturnal, often cryptic, and extremely difficult to identify, which results in a dearth of bat and rodent

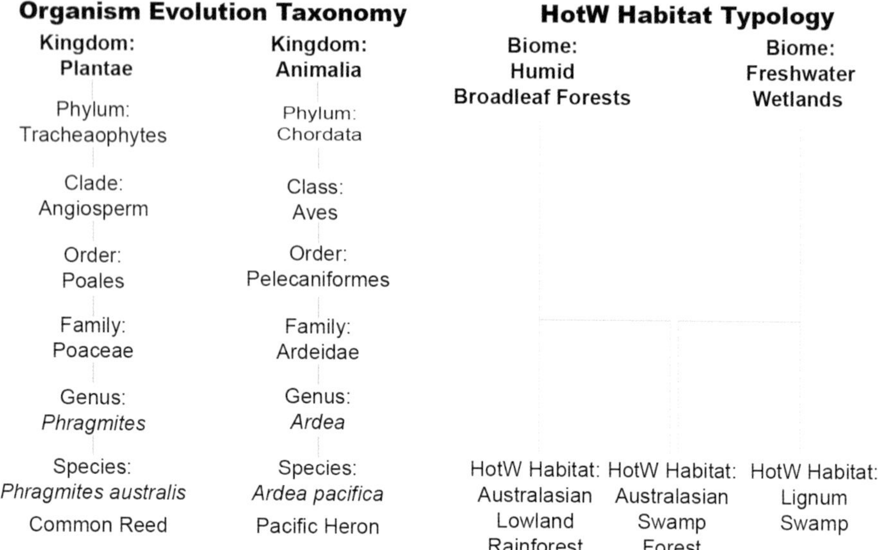

Fig. 3. Comparison of biota taxonomy and habitat typology. Species of flora and fauna, such as the Common Reed and the Pacific Heron, have clearly defined phylogenetic taxonomic classifications, each following a hierarchical Linnaean lineage encompassing phylum, class (or clade), order, family, genus, and species. Conversely, habitats present more complexity; some habitats, like Lignum Swamp, can belong to a single biome, yet others, such as Australasian Swamp Forest, integrate elements from multiple biomes, something not found in plants or animals. Consequently, with multi-biome habitats and ecotones between habitats, we can create a topology of habitats, but applying a pseudo-Linnaean phylogenetic taxonomy to habitats is illogical.

enthusiasts and, consequently, much less knowledge on these groups and their use in habitat delineation. The Habitats of the World system employs the 'Goldilocks principle', which makes it 'just right': detailed enough to be valuable but easy enough for anyone to understand. When trying to develop a system of understanding habitats that allows conservationists, ecologists, and planners to communicate across continents, we are left with similar problems, where the systems are either so broad as to be of little use at the birder and conservationist scale, or so detailed and difficult to separate that most users, including conservationists, don't understand them.

WHAT IS A DISTINCT HABITAT?

We use the word 'habitat' as a synonym for 'ecosystem'. We understand that anywhere an animal exists is its individual habitat, but we refer to broadly similar ecosystems with similar animal assemblages as habitats.

The habitat distribution was delineated using the existing Australia National Vegetation Information System's Major Vegetation Subgroups (NVIS-MVS) as a first-pass review. Because this mapping system is based on structure and floristics and is an amalgamation of the broad vegetation units within each state, and because the criteria for classification of those units differed so greatly between states, we went to the basal level of the 10,000-odd Australian state mapping units to reinterpret those units with the Habitats of the World (HotW) system. In this way we were able to 'realign' existing mapping polygons to create ours. For other areas to the north of

Australia, we relied on existing mapping undertaken by the Commonwealth Scientific and Industrial Research Organisation (CSIRO) and national mapping schemes.

We evaluate habitats based on two main criteria: (1) Their visual distinctiveness, which can be easily assessed by a casual observer and usually relates to the types of structure (e.g., forest vs. shrubland) and the species of plants present, which is a very similar approach to other ecosystem-mapping systems; and (2) their assemblage of wildlife—primarily birds, but we also considered other vertebrates—in a significant departure from any existing global or regional ecological mapping system. Each habitat is described with a suite of obligate and indicator bird species, available online at www.habitatsoftheworld.org/birdassemblages, and an individual link is given with every account. An example is Spinifex Eucalypt Savanna, which is quite distinct in appearance from other savanna habitats and supports a distinctive set of wildlife, including multiple grasswrens that are restricted to this habitat. But in some cases, one or the other criterion is of predominant importance. Except to the eye of a trained botanist, Australia's Chenopod Shrubland is not very different from other chenopod shrublands around the world such as Succulent Karoo of Africa or Succulent Puna of South America, but its bird assemblage is very different, not only from these analogous habitats but also from the surrounding habitats in Australia, so it is considered a distinct habitat.

Examples of the opposite case include Sheoak Woodland and Callitris Woodland, both subhabitats of Mixed Sandplain Woodland. Callitris Woodlands are characterised by the dominance of trees (*Callistris* spp., or cypress-pines) that look similar to juniper trees of the Northern Hemisphere and are very distinctive and easily recognizable, even as they lack a bird assemblage very different from surrounding Mixed Sandplain Woodland. Some species such as Yellow Thornbill are more common in this subhabitat, but a bird list alone cannot easily distinguish this environment. Having said that, the (very valid) case can be made that if we were to use the full suite of vertebrate assemblages, including amphibians and fishes, the distinction between this habitat and surrounding ones would be extremely obvious. The great strength of our system of using bird assemblages to refine habitat delineation also shows its weakness, compared to what could be, and we think should be, done with the use of other vertebrate and invertebrate groups. If readers have readily identifiable animals that we can use to make our system better, please contact us, and let's see how we can incorporate them into the algorithms we are building.

FIRST NATIONS PEOPLE AND PLEISTOCENE-HOLOCENE ANTHROPOGENIC HABITATS

For tens of thousands of years before colonial times, First Nations people in Australia and New Guinea managed the land using fire, in a practice often referred to as cultural burning or fire-stick farming. While these controlled burns were used to clear undergrowth, promote the growth of certain plants, and create a mosaic of habitats, the long-term impacts were not positive for the wildlife that occurred at the time of arrival of the first humans at least 50,000 years ago and possibly much earlier. Frequent burning likely transformed dense forests into more open woodlands and grasslands, altering ecosystems in ways that may have reduced biodiversity. Although this practice supported fire-adapted species, its ecological consequences were complex and not uniformly beneficial. The legacy of these transformations can still be seen in many of Australia's ecosystems today.

For this reason, the distinction between colonial anthropogenic habitats and 'natural' pre-colonial anthropogenic habitats has to be made, and for sheer convenience we treat the habitats at the time of colonisation as natural.

HABITAT DISTRIBUTION MAPS

Most of the habitats in this book have a map of the region showing the range of the habitat. The mapping differs from traditional vegetation maps in that we map both probable (usually confirmed) occurrence and possible occurrence. A habitat such as Spinifex Mallee may be mapped in pale green in regions where the woodlands have been destroyed for farming yet exist in tiny remnants lining roads or remaining in small reserves, and mapped in dark green for areas with extensive areas of habitat and where it is most likely to be encountered. Vegetation maps tend to have just one possibility mapped, yet the occurrence of one vegetation type does not preclude the occurrence of a different habitat, often from a completely different biome.

This world project is not a vegetation mapping exercise, and we did not want to reinvent the wheel. Where possible, we used existing boundaries of vegetation mapping units that match our classification. Ideally, we would have used the very detailed mapping employed by the International Vegetation Classification (IVC) system, which we have used for Africa, South America, and North America; however, only a few of Australia's habitats have been classified using this system, so we needed a different starting point. We did attempt to pre-empt the IVC work in Australia by adopting its approach to the broader vegetation classification of all Australian habitats and using this as a conceptual base before adapting it with wildlife.

For Australasia, we started at an extremely broad scale with the existing National Vegetation Information System's Major Vegetation Subgroups (NVIS-MVS). Because this mapping system is based on structure and floristics, it is an amalgamation of the broad vegetation units within each Australian state. Unfortunately, each state uses vastly different criteria for the classification of those vegetation units, and there are many units for each state. For example, in New South Wales, the basal unit is the Plant Community Type (PCT), while in Queensland the basal unit is the Regional Ecosystem Description Database (REDD), both of which have more than 1000 units. Consequently, we had to assess the many thousands of units throughout Australia to reinterpret them within the criteria of the Habitats of the World (HotW) system. In this way we were able to integrate existing vegetation criteria to create our base for mapping Australia. However, and this is a big caveat, because of the differing criteria on which the units were described in each state, the mapping units between states don't match perfectly. While we have been able to reconcile most of Queensland, New South Wales, Victoria, Tasmania, and Western Australia, there are still mismatches between those states and Northern Territory and South Australia, which still rely on the NVIS system. That being said, the reorganisation of the basal units with this system creates far more continuity between states than the existing NVIS system. With few exceptions, such as Dunecrest Canegrass, a habitat limited to the tops of inland sand dunes, we have made the decision to leave the map polygons in the state mapping system as they are and use pale green (possible) in the areas where we suspect the state mapping is incorrect.

In New Guinea and the Solomon Islands, there are no comparable vegetation systems, and so we relied on existing mapping undertaken by the CSIRO and national mapping schemes.

TYPES OF HABITAT BOUNDARIES AND ECOTONES

An ecotone is a place where two or more biomes meet, usually possessing traits of both. For example, mangrove is an ecotone between marine systems and terrestrial systems; savannas are an ecotone between tropical rainforests and deserts; and monsoon forests are ecotones between savannas and rainforests. So, most locales are ecotones at some scale. We try to avoid overuse of this confusing term in the book and prefer to treat zones between defined habitats as boundaries, where the ends of the transitions are different habitats with different bird assemblages. Sometimes the transitions are extremely **sharp**, especially where natural forests abut anthropogenic farmlands or wetland systems sit in otherwise arid terrains (fig. 4). **Mosaics** have distinct patches of different habitats in one area. This type of transition is very common in coastal forests and savanna edges. In a **mélange**, distinct systems intertwine in a complex manner across a broad zone. This pattern is very common in mountainous areas with complex geomorphology and geology and complex microclimates. The fourth kind of transition is **nebulous**, where the changes are so gradual that it is difficult to determine which habitat you are in. The bird and animal assemblages mix in this type of ecotone, and it can be difficult to determine the habitat based on either plant or animal assemblages; in a finer-scale habitat typology, these nebulous transition zones might be split out as a different habitat.

There are also regions where habitats **intrude** into one another, such as moist forests that extend far into arid terrains along waterways. The opposite exists where dry and heath-type habitats can extend as **outliers** in very humid environments along ridgelines with nutrient-deficient rocks such as granites. To further confuse things, another system exists on mountains that are high enough to become cold and/or attract orographic rainfall. Here the system flips, and wetter forests can occur on mountains, such Mt. Windsor, Queensland, where they are surrounded by Open Eucalypt Savanna.

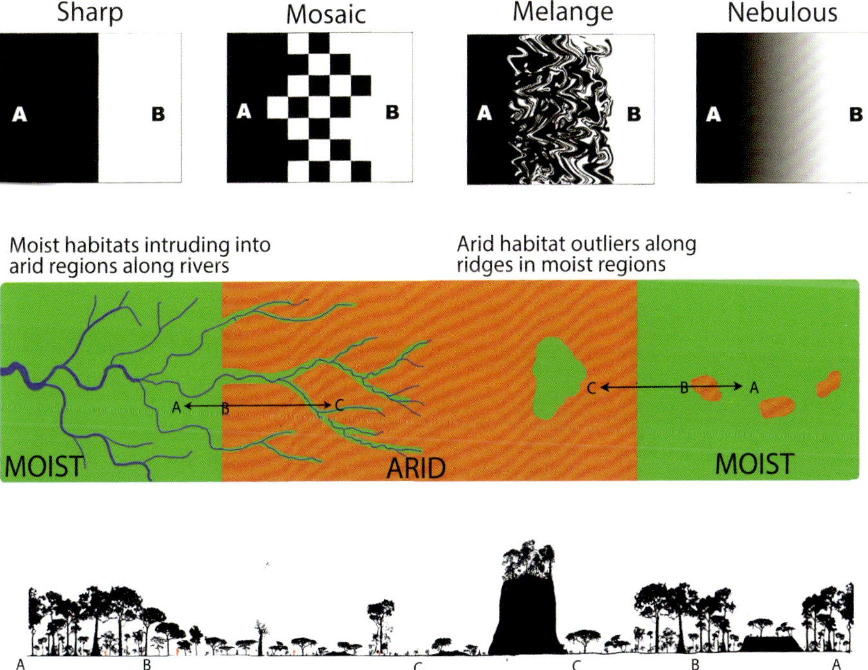

Fig. 4. Types of habitat boundaries and ecotones. Top: There are four types of habitat boundaries. In sharp and mosaic habitat boundaries, the bird assemblages between the different habitats remain separated. The habitats are separate in mélange boundaries, but the bird assemblage overlaps because the two habitats are so intertwined. Nebulous boundaries are ecotonal, where the exact change from one habitat to another is very diffuse, with a clinal change in bird assemblages. Bottom: Habitats can occur as outliers in other habitats, such as where wetter habitats intrude into arid environments along rivers, or where arid habitats occur in wet environments along ridgelines with poor soils.

THE KÖPPEN CLIMATE CLASSIFICATION AND THE CLIMATE GRAPHS

Throughout the book, each habitat description includes a brief overview of the climate (often with the Köppen climate code; discussed below) and a heavily adapted version of the Walter-Lieth climate graph, which create a powerful tool when combined. Looking at habitat distributions and their relationships to not only temperature and rainfall but also distribution of rainfall through the year, it became apparent that this annual rainfall distribution is often a more important factor in vegetation type than average precipitation alone. To help illustrate these variations through the year, we have created climate graphs for each habitat, based on the original work of Walter and Lieth, though we have heavily modified them to make them easier to read and interpret.

Reading these graphs may seem intimidating at first, but when their relevance is explained, they become more scrutable (fig. 5). When temperature and precipitation are plotted together, and where each 20 mm (0.8 in.) of precipitation is compared to each 10°C (18°F), some extremely interesting patterns emerge. When the precipitation plot drops below the temperature plot, the area is in a period of water stress (drought) because transpiration rates (the rate at which plants lose water) are higher than precipitation level. We have coloured these drought periods in orange. When the precipitation plot lifts above the temperature line, the area has a surplus of water, and plant growth is strong; these periods are coloured light blue. However, once the precipitation exceeds 100 mm (4 in.) a month, there is an extreme surplus of water, and regardless of the temperature, most water runs off and is not used by plants; we have coloured these periods in dark blue. Because the whole method makes sense only when used with the metric system, we have included temperature only in Celsius and rainfall in millimetres on the graphs.

The Köppen climate classification system is the most widely used global method to classify and categorise different climatic regions. Each climate is assigned a simple two- or three-letter code.

The first letter denotes the average temperature (B is an exception).

A: Tropical climate, with year-round average temperatures above 18°C (64°F).
B: Arid climate with low precipitation.
C: Mid-latitude climate with mild to cool temperatures.
D: Mid-latitude climate with cold winters and mild to cool summers.
E: Polar or alpine climates with extremely cold temperatures.

The second letter denotes when most precipitation occurs:

f: Year-round rainfall pattern, with precipitation evenly distributed throughout the year.
m: Monsoonal, with a pronounced wet season and a dry season.
w: Dominant dry winter season.
s: Dominant dry summer season.
T: Lacks a true summer.

The third letter denotes maximum and minimum temperatures, or cold/hot desert:

a: Hot summers, with the warmest month having an average temperature above 22°C (71.6°F).
b: Mild summers, with the warmest month averaging below 22°C (71.6°F) but above 10°C (50°F).
c: Cool summers, with the warmest month averaging below 10°C (50°F) but above 0°C (32°F).
d: Very cold winters, with the coldest month averaging below 0°C (32°F).
e: Cold summers, with the warmest month averaging below 10°C (50°F).
h: Hot desert.
k: Cold desert.

Australasia encompasses a wide range of temperature zones from Tasmania to the tropical zone of New Guinea and the Solomon Islands. Simultaneously, there are also varying rainfall regimes, resulting in everything from hot deserts to steamy rainforests and pretty much everything in between. Using the Köppen system, we have assigned the environments the following codes. When used in conjunction with the climate graphs explained earlier, these Köppen codes can explain why most habitats occur where they do.

1. Tropical humid climate (**Afa**, **Afb**): Areas with this climate type receive high amounts of rainfall and have high temperatures throughout the year. Habitats are moist forests such as AUSTRALASIAN LOWLAND RAINFOREST.
2. Tropical monsoonal climate (**Awa**, **Awb**): These regions have distinct wet summer and dry winter seasons. Some locations would have sufficient precipitation to support rainforest if the rain were distributed more evenly throughout the year. The main habitats are moist savannas, tropical grasslands, and monsoon forests; typical habitats are AUSTRALASIAN MONSOON VINEFOREST and TETRODONTA WOODLAND SAVANNA. They are prevalent in tropical Australia.
3. Mediterranean climate (**Csa**, **Csb**): These climates occur in the temperate zone of the Western Australia coast and in the Riverina area of South Australia, Victoria, and New South Wales. They are categorised by hot, dry summers and mild, wet winters. The main habitats are SPINIFEX MALLEE, SHRUBBY AND CHENOPOD MALLEE, and HEATHY MALLEE.
4. Desert (**Bwh**, **Bwk**): These regions are characterised by extremely low annual precipitation, high temperatures, and little vegetation. They include the GIBBER CHENOPODLAND, DUNECREST CANEGRASS, and ROCKY SPINIFEX DESERT.
5. Semiarid climate (**Bsh**, **Bsk**): These areas receive more rain than deserts but not enough rain in the wet season to allow the development of lush savanna. The main habitats are GRASSY MULGA and MIXED SANDPLAIN WOODLAND.
6. Temperate climate (**Cfa**, **Cfb**): These areas have mild winters that get cold but not freezing for long periods, and mild summers that are not hot for too long. The main habitats are AUSTRALIAN TEMPERATE RAINFOREST and NOTHOFAGUS FOREST.

Fig. 5. Sample climate graphs *(continued overleaf)*

Monsoon Forest: Awa

>Temperature hot much of the year

>Dry conditions for some months in winter

>Very intense monsoonal summer rains

>Significant overlap with savanna climate

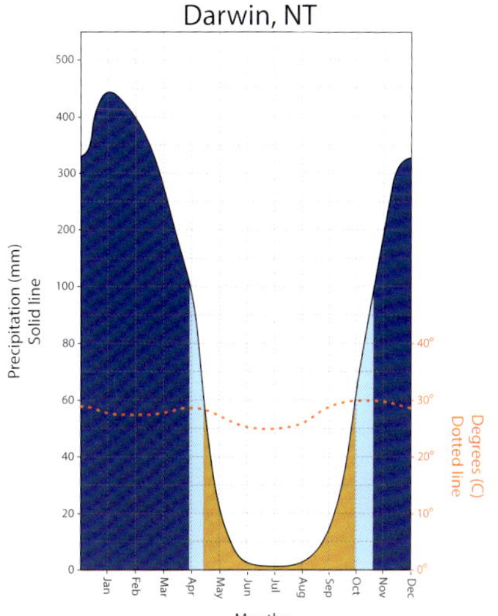

Fig. 5. Sample climate graphs *(continued)*

Savanna: Awa, Awb

>Temperature hot throughout the year

>Drought conditions in winter

>Very intense monsoonal summer rains

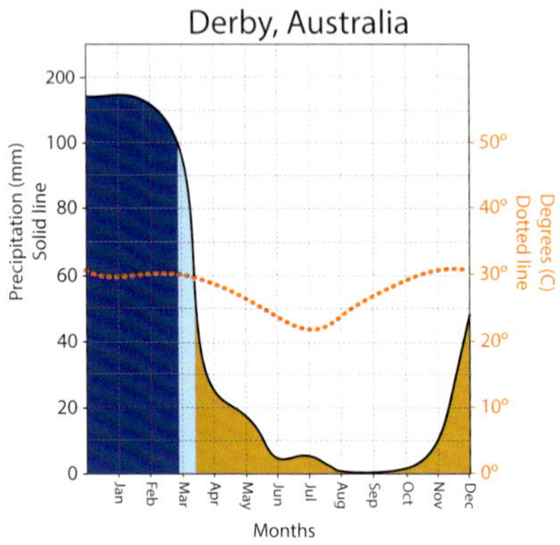

Lowland Rainforest: Afa, Afb

>Temperature hot throughout the year

>Abundant precipitation throughout the year

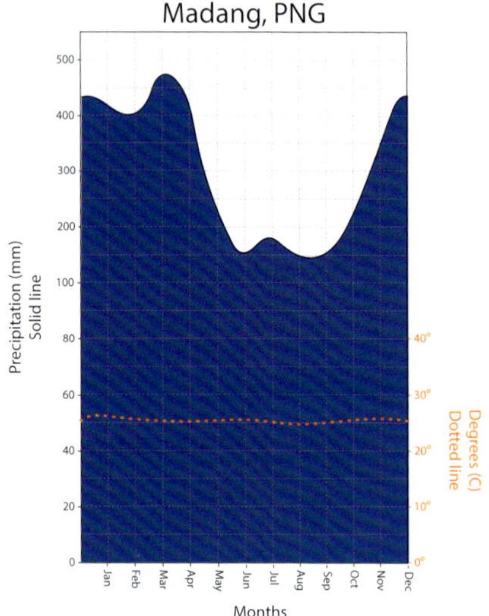

Mediterranean Scrub: Csa, Csb

>Cold winters, warm summers

>Wet winters

>Moderately dry summers

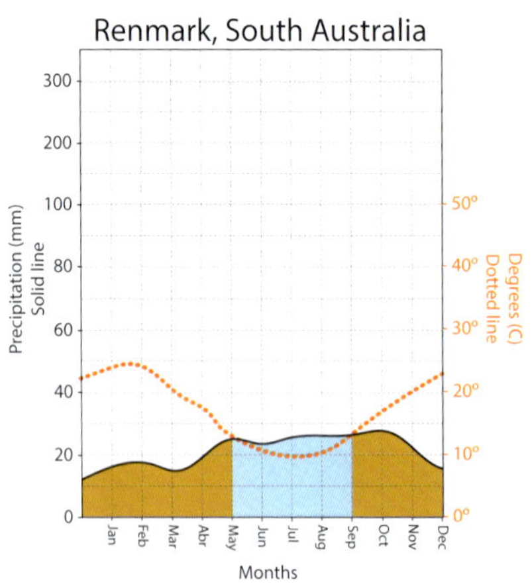

Warm Desert: Bwh

>Dry and hot throughout the year

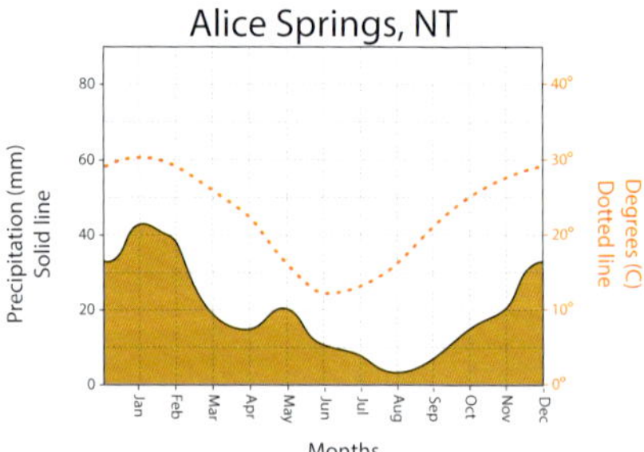

BIOMES OF AUSTRALIA, NEW GUINEA, AND THE SOLOMON ISLANDS

Multiple biomes, or ecological communities, are described in this book. All the regions covered in this book are within the Australasian biogeographical realm. The broad habitat categories and subcategories used are briefly explained in this section; the example habitats listed can be located in the table of contents. Refer to Useful Habitat Terminology for further explanations of most of the terms used here.

The broad habitat categories and subcategories used in this book are clustered by biomes (major ecological community types), and each has been given a unique code. For example, all deserts globally belong to HotW biome 2, deserts, and each regional habitat within that biome has its own code, such as Au2E for Gibber Chenopodland. Not all biomes are found in the Australasia region; we do not have biome 1, conifers; or biome 3, temperate deciduous forests.

CONIFER FORESTS (HotW BIOME 1): Not found in Australia. Forests made up of coniferous trees (which generally don't seasonally lose their leaves, with the exception of larches and a few others). Australia has some conifers with Northern Hemisphere affinities, such as *Callitris* (e.g., Black Cypress-Pine), but in contrast with all other continents, conifers of Australia are usually part of a woodland plant assemblage from a different biome. In a few places there are near-monotypic stands of *Callitris*, but these are regarded as a subhabitat of **Au9L Mixed Sandplain Woodland**. Australia also has conifers, such as *Araucaria* (e.g., Norfolk Island Pine), with distinctly Gondwanan origins, which have close relatives in New Zealand and South America.

DESERTS (HotW BIOME 2): Very dry and either unvegetated or sparsely vegetated habitat.

Deserts and Arid Scrubs: Arid areas with little plant growth.
Example: **Au2B Dunecrest Canegrass**

Desert and Semi-desert Shrublands: Open arid areas with small shrubs with generally small leaves; cacti or euphorbias can be present and may be large.
Example: **Au2E Gibber Chenopodland**

TEMPERATE DECIDUOUS FORESTS (HotW BIOME 3): Not found in Australia. Forests of broadleaf trees that, in the Northern Hemisphere, lose their leaves in winter, though some are evergreen. Australia's Nothofagus Forest could be regarded as a temperate forest, but because it is also a rainforest and not deciduous, it is placed in biome 4.

HUMID BROADLEAF FORESTS (HotW BIOME 4): Quintessential warm and wet rainforest-type environments.

Lowland Rainforest: Wet, tall, evergreen forest with thick full canopy cover and open undergrowth.
Example: **Au4A Australasian Lowland Rainforest**

Montane/Subtropical Evergreen Forest: Warm, wet forests with almost closed canopy of evergreen or partially deciduous trees.
Example: **Au4G Australian Temperate Rainforest**

TROPICAL DRY DECIDUOUS FORESTS (HotW BIOME 5): Warm forests that lose most of their leaves in dry periods. Fire-intolerant.

Example: **Au5A Australian Dry Vineforest**

SAVANNAS (HotW BIOME 6): Habitats with an open canopy, lots of grass or shrubbery, and a strongly seasonal (usually wet-summer/dry-winter) climate. Most habitats in this category are heavily influenced by fire.

Example: **Au6A Open Eucalypt Savanna**

GRASSLANDS (HotW BIOME 7): Habitats dominated by grasses, with or without shrubs and flowers, and with few or no trees. Fire-dependent.

Example: **Au7B Temperate Tussock Grassland**

MEDITERRANEAN SHRUBLANDS (HotW BIOME 8): Thick scrub in areas with climates defined by cold, wet winters and dry, hot summers.

Example: **Au8A Wallum and Ausbos**

SCLEROPHYLL WOODLANDS AND FORESTS (HotW BIOME 9): Thick scrub and forests in areas with climates defined by cold, wet winters and dry, hot summers, though they also occur as tall forests in cold wet and wet tropical climates.

Example: **Au9O Spinifex Mallee**

TUNDRAS (HotW BIOME 10): Habitat of very low vegetation, dominated by mosses and many lichens, found at extreme latitudes or elevations, where temperatures, snow cover, or exposure to wind prohibit the growth of trees.

Example: **Au10B Austroparamo**

FRESHWATER HABITATS (HotW BIOME 11): Non-forested habitats whose most important aspect is that they are seasonally or permanently flooded with fresh water.

Example: **Au11A Australasian Tropical Freshwater Wetland**

SALINE HABITATS (HotW BIOME 12): Habitats where the dominant force is the presence of high levels of salt in the water or soil.

Mangrove: A specialised forest that grows in tidally flooded coastal areas.
Example: **Au12A Australasian Tropical Mangrove Forest**

Salt Pan: Areas in which evaporation or volcanic activity has produced extremely high salt concentrations in the soil. Mostly unvegetated, though algae grow quickly when floods occur.
Example: **Au12E Australian Salt Pan**

Salt Marsh: Habitat of salt-tolerant marsh vegetation that grows in sheltered coastal areas periodically flooded with seawater.
Example: **Au12F Australian Coastal Salt Marsh**

Tidal Mudflats: Nutrient-rich areas of mud that are frequently flooded with seawater, usually in estuaries.
Example: **Au12G Australasian Tidal Mudflat**

Rocky Coastline and Sandy Beach: Nutrient-poor sandy and rocky beaches, cliffs, and other coastline types.
Example: **Au12H Australasian Rocky Headland**

Pelagic Waters: Marine environments with deep water.
Example: **Au12J Australian Temperate Pelagic Waters**

POST-COLONIAL ANTHROPOGENIC HABITATS (HotW BIOME 13): The primary force in shaping these habitats is the presence of humans.

Cultivated Lands: Areas cultivated by humans for the production of crops.
Grazing Lands: Areas that are heavily grazed by domestic animals.

TAXONOMY, COMMON AND SCIENTIFIC NAMES

For birds we follow the eBird-Avilist taxonomy. It is up to date, carefully maintained, and is the most popular global taxonomy for birders using eBird, post 2025. We found iNaturalist to be largely (but not perfectly) consistent and up to date for the groups that we know intimately well, giving us confidence that other groups are covered similarly. There is very little discrepancy between taxonomies for both birds and mammals, with both groups having very well-established common names. In an effort to keep the text flowing, we use only common names for most species of birds and mammals mentioned, adding scientific names where there may be confusion. For other taxa where taxonomy is not as well defined and some species lack common names, such as reptiles and amphibians, we always provide the scientific name as well as the common name if available. Because the taxonomy of plants is so varied, with no widespread agreement on common names, all plants have the scientific names and common names as available.

USEFUL HABITAT TERMINOLOGY

The following definitions will help the reader to understand some of the most important terms used in naming and defining habitats. These terms appear over and over in the book.

- **Aeolian.** Transported and/or deposited by wind.
- **Alluvial.** Referring to material (**alluvium**) transported and/or deposited by flowing water.
- **Alternative stable state.** A form of habitat based in the concept that habitats can persist under a variety of environmental conditions and that a single set of environmental conditions can support multiple, very different (i.e., alternative) stable habitats.
- **Alpine.** A life zone found in mountainous regions above the tree line. Vegetation is low, and the climate is harsh.
- **Austral.** Of the Southern Hemisphere.
- **Azonal.** Describes a habitat whose occurrence is not directly related to climate but is determined by local factors such as soil type or fire regime.
- **C3 grasses.** Grasses, typically from temperate climates, that use the most common form of plant photosynthesis, known as the C3 photosynthetic pathway.
- **C4 grasses.** Grasses, typically from tropical climates, that use an uncommon form of plant photosynthesis known as the C4 photosynthetic pathway.
- **Calcareous.** Refers to alkaline soils formed from rocks rich in calcium carbonate such as limestone and marble.
- **Chenopod.** A plant belonging to the Chenopodioideae, a subfamily comprising mostly shrubs and herbaceous plants that are often halophytic (salt-tolerant).
- **Colluvial.** Referring to deposits (**colluvium**) that have accumulated on the slope or at the base of a hill due to gravity, not flowing water.
- **Desert.** Very dry and either unvegetated or sparsely vegetated habitat.
- **Emergent.** A tree whose crown extends above the main canopy of a forest, often much higher than the surrounding trees.
- **Endemic.** Limited or native to only a specific geographic area.
- **Eucalypt.** A tree belonging to the genus *Eucalyptus*, *Corymbia*, or *Angophora*. Eucalypts are known by various common names, including box, mallee, gum, ironbark, stringybark.
- **Felsic.** A silica-rich (mostly quartz) rock; the origin of the rock is less important than the mineralogy.

- **Ferricrete.** A hardpan soil formed from an accumulation of iron oxides; associated with but not limited to laterites.
- **Forb.** An herb (nonwoody plant) other than grass.
- **Forest.** A stand of trees over 15 ft. (5 m) tall with a closed canopy of interlocking trees or an open canopy with over 70% cover.
- **Gondwanan.** Refers to flora and fauna with an ancient origin or lineage that can be traced back to the ancient supercontinent Gondwana (comprising South America, Australia, India, Antarctica, Africa, and Madagascar), before it started to split 180 MYA.
- **Grassland.** Habitat dominated by grasses with few shrubs or trees.
- **Halophytic.** Refers to a plant or organism that can grow in highly saline environments.
- **Heath/Heathland.** Shrubland dominated by waxy, thick-leaved sclerophyllous members of the protea family (Proteaceae) and fine-leaved evergreen members of the erica family (Ericaceae).
- **Indicator species.** A species whose presence or relative abundance is closely tied to the presence of specific habitat factors.
- **Laterite.** Concentrations of iron and aluminium oxides in a soil, formed through intense chemical weathering, in warm, humid tropical to subtropical climates.
- **Lignotuber.** A swollen, woody root ball at the base of certain plants, often trees and shrubs of fire-prone areas; containing both nutrients and dormant buds, it can sprout new growth after fire has damaged the rest of the plant.
- **Macropods.** Members of the Macropodidae family of terrestrial herbivorous marsupials with large hind legs, long tails, and a hopping locomotion, such as wallabies and kangaroos.
- **Mafic.** A type of rock rich in magnesium and iron but relatively low in silica.
- **Mallee.** A subset of *Eucalyptus* trees with a growth form of multiple stems arising from a woody underground lignotuber. Can also refer to a habitat dominated by these trees.
- **Mallee-form.** A plant growth form characterised by multiple stems arising from a woody underground lignotuber. Not restricted to mallee species or mallee habitats.
- **Montane.** A life zone within mountainous regions, above the lowlands and below the tree line. Often forested or with meadows.
- **Mulga.** Both a species of acacia (*Acacia aneura*) found through much of c. Australia, and the regions and habitats dominated by this tree and closely related species.
- **Obligate.** Refers to species that are found or breed only within a specific habitat and can be used as an indicator of that habitat.
- **Orographic rainfall.** Precipitation caused when moist air is forced to rise over a mountain range, cools, and falls as rain on the windward side of the range. The leeward side of the range often develops a rain shadow, where very little precipitation occurs.
- **Pelagic.** Referring to offshore waters, a zone also described as 'open ocean'. The transition from coastal waters to pelagic waters is usually gradual and varies from place to place, depending on factors such as underwater features (e.g., a continental shelf).
- **Phyllode.** A flattened leaf stalk that has replaced the traditional leaf in form and function.
- **Rainforest.** Lush forest that receives abundant moisture.
- **Samphire.** Halophyte (salt-tolerant plant) in the family Amaranthaceae with jointed stems and small scale-like leaves.
- **Savanna.** A lightly wooded or treeless tropical grassland with prominent wet and dry seasons.
- **Sclerophyll.** Plant with hard, desiccation-resistant leaves; the leaves are often, but not exclusively, small.
- **Semi-evergreen forest.** Forest that has rainforest structure but in which some trees lose at least some of their leaves at some point during the year.

- **Silcrete.** A duricrust, hardpan, or nodule formed by the precipitation of silica (SiO_2) within a soil profile that can become very resistant to erosion.
- **Spinifex.** Worldwide, refers to *Spinifex*, a genus of beach-loving grasses. In Australia, it is the widely used name for the hummock grasses of the genus *Triodia*, ubiquitous in certain habitats of the country's interior; these habitats are also called spinifex.
- **Sympatric.** Occupying the same geographical range.
- **Wetland.** Habitat that is frequently or permanently flooded.
- **Woodland.** Habitat with abundant trees, forming a nearly interlocking canopy, but in which sun still reaches the ground, allowing the growth of an understorey such as shrubs, grasses, or forbs.

NATURESERVE AND THE IVC

For most of the world, we used NatureServe International Vegetation Classification (IVC) delineations as the starting point to assign habitats based on bird assemblages. NatureServe has been the authoritative source for biodiversity data and the central coordinating organisation for a network of over 60 member programs throughout North America and around the world. Because the NatureServe IVC mapping is still limited in Australia at the time of writing, we are not able to use its mapping, but the units we have delineated have been put into a living matrix on the website www.habitatsoftheworld.org, which aligns our habitat and the Australian state mapping units to the IVC system and will be modified as IVC mapping progresses. As this series is an ongoing project, we will continue to do walk-throughs from the Australian HotW classification and the IVC classification as its Australian Macrogroup mapping develops.

ACKNOWLEDGMENTS

Our families have provided amazing support as we have created this book, and it would not have been possible without them. Thank you, Cristina, Gabriel, and Amy, for putting up with Iain's numerous outbursts when things didn't go as planned. Gabriel Campbell joined Iain for many ground-truthing trips through Australia for a science undergraduate's perspective, and his input was very helpful in making the habitat descriptions relatable. Charley would like to thank his wife, Ronell, and son, Felix, for their endless support and patience. Phil would like to thank his wife, Sue, for her patience, and grandchildren Kainde and Aleisha Gregory, who kept him entertained and interrupted as the work was in progress. Other bird experts who helped in ground-truthing the classification and bird assemblages included Ken Behrens, Keith Barnes, Gunnar Engblom, Jeremey Robertson, Rob Hynson, Clive Barker, Shane Kennedy, and Sam Woods.

Giselle Velastegui and Pablo Cervantes were instrumental in the creation of the maps and climate graphs for the book. Keith Barnes and Nick Athanas gave Iain the time away from Tropical Birding Tours to work on the project. Angela Moles from the University of New South Wales, Iain's PhD supervisor, guided him through the conceptualisation of the project and engaged in many important and lively discussions over proper experimental design.

A huge thank-you too to all those who helped read chapters and acted as sparring partners. Some of those that stand out include Jeremy Robertson, Keith Barnes, Sam Woods, and Shane Kennedy.

ABBREVIATIONS

Directions (north, south, east, west, central) are abbreviated only when they directly precede a geographical place name.

ACT	Australian Capital Territory
aka	also known as
c.	central
cw.	central-western
cm	centimetre
e.	east/eastern
ft.	foot/feet
GET	Global Ecosystem Typology
ha	hectare
HotW	Habitats of the World book series
in.	inch/inches
IND	Indonesia
IS	indicator species
IUCN	International Union for the Conservation of Nature
IVC	International Vegetation Classification
KBA	Key Biodiversity Area
kg	kilogram
km	kilometre
km^2	square kilometre
lb.	pound
m	metre
MYA	million years ago
mi.	mile
mm	millimetre
n.	north/northern
nc.	north-central
ne.	northeastern
NGO	non-governmental organisation
NSW	New South Wales
NT	Northern Territory
NVIS	National Vegetation Information System
nw.	northwestern
PNG	Papua New Guinea
QLD	Queensland
s.	south/southern
SA	South Australia
sc.	south-central
se.	southeastern
sp.	species (singular)
spp.	species (plural)
sq. mi.	square mile
subsp.	subspecies
sw.	southwestern
TAS	Tasmania
VIC	Victoria
w.	west/western
wc.	west-central
WA	Western Australia

BIBLIOGRAPHY

We are indebted to a great many wonderful databases, books, and papers on the habitats, plants, and wildlife of Australia. We debated citing sources through the text in a more academic fashion; however, the plant and animal lists would have made this text extremely laborious to read and defeat the purpose of the book. We opted instead to list the sources we used to write the text.

Archer, S. R., and F. E. Smeins. 1991. 'Ecosystem-Level Responses to Grazing in Semi-Arid Grasslands'. *Journal of Range Management* 44(5):398–403.

Australian Bureau of Statistics. 2021. 'National Land Account, Experimental Estimates'. https://www.abs.gov.au/statistics/environment/environmental-management/national-land-account-experimental-estimates/latest-release.

AviList Core Team. 2025. *AviList: The Global Avian Checklist, v2025*. https://doi.org/10.2173/avilist.v2025

Beehler, B. M., and T. K. Pratt. 2016. *Birds of New Guinea: Distribution, Taxonomy, and Systematics*. Princeton University Press.

Biello, D. 2012. 'Big Kill, Not Big Chill, Finished Off Giant Kangaroos'. *Scientific American*, March 22.

BirdLife International. 2021. Michaelmas Cay Site Assessment. https://datazone.birdlife.org/site/factsheet/michaelmas-cay-iba-australia.

Bowman, D.M.J.S. 2003. 'Australian Landscape Burning and Its Impacts on Habitats'. *Global Ecology and Biogeography* 12(6):482–89.

Brack, C. 2002. 'Eucalypt Plantations in Australia'. *Australian Forestry* 65(2):81–92.

Brisbane City Council. 2025. 'Koalas Conservation'. https://www.brisbane.qld.gov.au/environment-and-water/wildlife-and-conservation/koala-conservation.

Campbell, I., K. Behrens, C. Hesse, and P. Chaon. 2021. *Habitats of the World: A Field Guide for Birders, Naturalists, and Ecologists*. Princeton University Press.

Campbell, I., S. Woods, and N. Leseberg. 2014. *Birds of Australia: A Photographic Guide*. Princeton University Press.

City of Sydney. 2024. 'Living with Local Wildlife'. https://www.cityofsydney.nsw.gov.au/guides/living-with-local-wildlife.

Clarke, R., and T. Dolby. 2014. *Finding Australian Birds: A Field Guide to Birding Locations*. CSIRO.

Clements, J. F., P. C. Rasmussen, T. S. Schulenberg, M. J. Iliff, T. A. Fredericks, J. A. Gerbracht, D. Lepage, et al. 2024. *The eBird/Clements Checklist of Birds of the World*, v2024. https://www.birds.cornell.edu/clementschecklist.

Coates, B. J. 1985. *The Birds of Papua New Guinea*. Vol. 1: *Non-passerines*. Dove.

Coates, B. J. 1990. *The Birds of Papua New Guinea*. Vol. 2: *Passerines*. Dove.

Cogger, H. G. 2015. *Reptiles and Amphibians of Australia*. CSIRO.

Cobden, R., C. Clarkson, G. J. Price, B. David, J.-M. Geneste, J.-J. Delannoy, B. Barker, et al. 2017. 'The Identification of Extinct Megafauna in Rock Art Using Geometric Morphometrics: A *Genyornis newtoni* Painting in Arnhem Land, Northern Australia?' *Journal of Archaeological Science* 87:95–107. https://doi.org/10.1016/j.jas.2017.09.013.

Comer, P. J., D. Faber-Langendoen, R. Evans, S. C. Gawler, C. Josse, G. Kittel, S. Menard, et al. 2003. *Ecological Systems of the United States: A Working Classification of U.S. Terrestrial Systems*. NatureServe.

Costin, A. B., M. Gray, C. J. Totterdell, and D. J. Wimbush. 2000. *Kosciuszko Alpine Flora*. CSIRO.

Cushing, C. E., and J. D. Allan. 2001. *Streams: Their Ecology and Life*. Academic Press.

Dickman, C., and R. W. Ganf. 2007. *A Fragile Balance: The Extraordinary Story of Australian Marsupials*. Craftsman House.

Finlayson, C. M., and A. G. van der Valk. 2012. *Wetlands and Climate Change: Impacts and Management*. Springer.

Flannery, T. F. 1990. 'Pleistocene Faunal Loss: Implications of the Aftershock for Australia's Past and Future'. *Archaeology in Oceania* 25(2):45–55. https://doi.org/10.1002/j.1834-4453.1990.tb00232.x.

Fraser, H., C. E. Hauser, L. Rumpff, G. E. Garrard, and M. A. McCarthy. 2017. 'Classifying Animals into Ecologically Meaningful Groups: A Case Study on Woodland Birds'. *Biological Conservation* 214:184–94.

Fraser, H., J. S. Simmonds, A. S. Kutt, and M. Maron. 2019. 'Systematic Definition of Threatened Fauna Communities Is Critical to Their Conservation'. *Diversity and Distributions* 25(3):462–77.

Gill, F., D. Donsker, and P. Rasmussen, eds. 2024. *IOC World Bird List*, v.14.2. https://www.worldbirdnames.org/new/ioc-lists/crossref/.

Gillanders, B. M., S. E. Travis, I. A. Halliday, G. P. Jenkins, J. B. Robins, and F. J. Valesin. 2011. 'Potential Effects of Climate Change on Australian Estuaries and Fish Utilising Estuaries: A Review'. *Marine and Freshwater Research* 62(9):1115–31.

Gregory, P., and J. Matsui. 2024. *A Field Guide to the Birds of Far North Queensland*. 2nd ed. Reed New Holland.

Gregory, P. 2017. *Birds of New Guinea, Including Bismarck Archipelago and Bougainville*. Lynx Edicions.

Gregory, P. 2019. *Birds of Paradise and Bowerbirds*. Pica Press/Bloomsbury.

Gregory, P. 2024. *A Checklist of the Birds of Australia and Its Island Territories*. 4th ed. Sicklebill.

Gregory, P. 2024. *Checklist of the Birds of the Solomon Islands, inc. Bougainville*. 3rd ed. Sicklebill.

Gregory, P. 2024. *A Checklist of the Birds of New Guinea and Associated Islands*. 5th ed. Sicklebill.

Groombridge, B., and M. D. Jenkins. 1998. *Freshwater Biodiversity: A Preliminary Global Assessment*. World Conservation Monitoring Centre.

Hesp, P. A. 2000. 'Coastal Sand Dunes: Form and Function'. *Journal of Coastal Research* 16(1): 111–16.

Higgins, P., et al., eds. 1991–2006. *Handbook of Australian, New Zealand, and Antarctic Birds*. 7 vols. Oxford University Press.

iNaturalist. 2025. https://www.inaturalist.org.

Keating, B., and P. J. Sands. 2015. *Sustainable Management of Plantations in Australia*. CRC for Forestry.

Keith, D. A. 2004. *Ocean Shores to Desert Dunes: The Native Vegetation of New South Wales and the ACT*. Department of Environment and Conservation (NSW).

Keith, D. A., ed. 2017. *Australian Vegetation*. Cambridge University Press.

Keith, D. A., J. R. Ferrer-Paris, E. Nicholson, M. J. Bishop, B. A. Polidoro, E, Ramirez-Llodra, M. G. Tozer, et al. 2022. 'A Function-Based Typology for Earth's Ecosystems'. *Nature* 610(7932):513–18.

Kirkpatrick, J. B., and K. L. Bridle. 1998. 'Environment and Floristics of Ten Sphagnum-Dominated Bogs in Tasmania'. *Australian Journal of Botany* 46(4):465–74.

Kirkpatrick, J. B., and J. Glasby. 1981. *Salt Marshes and Wetlands in the Australian Region*. Elsevier.

McComb, A. J., and P. S. Lake. 1988. *The Conservation of Australian Wetlands*. Surrey Beatty and Sons.

McKeon, G. M., et al. 2009. *Climate Change Impacts on Northern Australian Rangelands*. CSIRO.

Menkhorst, P., et al. 2017. *The Australian Bird Guide*. CSIRO.

Menkhorst, P., and F. Knight. 2010. *A Field Guide to the Mammals of Australia*. 3rd ed. Oxford University Press.

Miller, G. H. 2005. 'Ecosystem Collapse in Pleistocene Australia and a Human Role in Megafaunal Extinction'. *Science* 309(5732):287–90. https://doi.org/10.1126/science.1111288.

Mitsch, W. J., and J. G. Gosselink. 2015. *Wetlands*. 5th ed. Wiley.

Murray, P., and G. Chaloupka. 1984. 'The Dreamtime Animals: Extinct Megafauna in Arnhem Land Rock Art'. *Archaeology in Oceania* 19(3):105–16. doi:10.1002/j.1834-4453.1984.tb00089.x.

Paijmans, K., ed. 1976. *New Guinea Vegetation*. Australian National University.

Phillips, B., and K. Müller. 2006. *Ecological Character Descriptions: Wetlands of International Importance*. Ramsar Convention Secretariat.

Pratt, T. K., and B. M. Beehler. 2014. *Birds of New Guinea: Including Bismarck Archipelago and Bougainville*. Lynx Edicions.

Pressey, R. L., and V. S. Logan. 1998. 'Size of Selection Units for Future Reserves and Its Influence on Actual vs. Targeted Representation of Features: A Case Study in Western New South Wales'. *Biological Conservation* 85(3):305–19.

Reid, N.C.H., and J. Landsberg. 2000. 'Tree Decline in Agricultural Landscapes: What We Stand to Lose'. *Agriculture, Ecosystems and Environment* 77(1):89–98.

Roberts, R. G., T. F. Flannery, L. K. Ayliffe, H. Yoshida, J. M. Olley, G. J. Prideaux, G. M. Laslett, et al. 2001. 'New Ages for the Last Australian Megafauna: Continent-Wide Extinction about 46,000 Years Ago'. *Science* 292(5523):1888–92. https://doi.org/10.1126/science.1060264.

Roberts, R., and Z. Jacobs. 2008. 'The Lost Giants of Tasmania'. *Australasian Science* 29(9):14–17.

Saltré, F., M. Rodríguez-Rey, B. W. Brook, C. N. Johnson, C.S.M. Turney, J. Alroy, A. Cooper, et al. 2016. 'Climate Change Not to Blame for Late Quaternary Megafauna Extinctions in Australia'. *Nature Communications* 7:10511. https://doi.org/10.1038/ncomms10511.

Schubert, H., P. White, S. Saatchi, and J. Chave. 2022. *The World Atlas of Trees and Forests: Exploring Earth's Forest Ecosystems*. Princeton University Press.

Tozer, M. G., K. Turner, D. A. Keith, D. Tindall, C. Pennay, C. Simpson, B. MacKenzie, et al. 2010. 'Native Vegetation of Southeast NSW: A Revised Classification and Map for the Coast and Eastern Tablelands'. *Cunninghamia* 11(3):359–406.

Turner, J., and M. Lambert. 2016. 'Pine Plantations in Australia: Economics and Ecology'. *Forest Ecology and Management* 361:55–65.

Turney, C.S.M., T. F. Flannery, R. G. Roberts, et al. 2008. 'Late-Surviving Megafauna in Tasmania, Australia, Implicate Human Involvement in Their Extinction'. *Proceedings of the National Academy of Sciences USA* 105(34):12150–53. https://doi.org/10.1073/pnas.0801360105.

Wahren, C.-H.A., W. A. Papst, and R. J. Williams. 1999. 'Post-fire Regeneration in Victorian Alpine and Sub-alpine Vegetation'. *Australian Journal of Botany*47(5):451–70.

Whinam, J., and G. S. Hope, 2005. 'The Peatlands of the Australasian Region'. In *Peatlands and Climate Change*, ed. M. Strack, 119–48. International Peat Society.

Whitehead, P. J., and R. Chatto. 1996. *Habitats and Populations of Waterbirds in Northern Australia*. CSIRO.

Wroe, S., J. H. Field, M. Archer, D. K. Grayson, G. J. Price, J. Louys, J. Tyler Faith, et al. 2013. 'Climate Change Frames Debate over the Extinction of Megafauna in Sahul (Pleistocene Australia–New Guinea)'. *Proceedings of the National Academy of Sciences USA* 110(22):8777–81. https://doi.org/10.1073/pnas.1302698110.

OUTSIDERS' GUIDE TO AUSTRALIA, NEW GUINEA, AND THE SOLOMON ISLANDS

Australia may be the smallest continent, but it contains a huge variety of habitats ringing the deserts of the interior. The vast majority of people visiting the region see a few iconic areas, such as the rainforests of Queensland and the heathlands of Kangaroo Island, but miss the many environments that really set Australia apart from the rest of the world. A little exploration of areas even close to the beaten path will give a very different perspective on Australian wildlife, vegetation, and biogeography. Australia and the northern islands, including New Guinea and the Solomon Islands, can be divided into a few broad areas for ease of description.

Fig. 6. The regions and biomes of the Australia–New Guinea region.

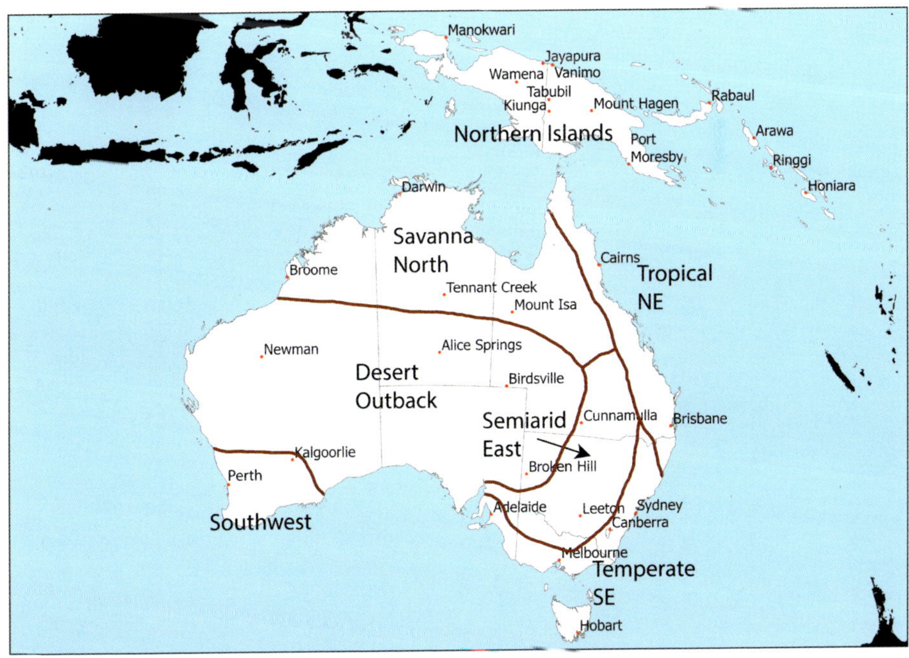

Below, each region is illustrated with a 'habitat niche' diagram; please note that these diagrams are representative of the relative niches of major habitats only—there is no space for minor habitats. Habitats that are completely azonal and occur over many climates, such as coastlines, are not represented on these diagrams. In the niche diagrams, blue-coloured type in the names of habitats indicates a habitat that is colder relative to others because it is in a montane region (i.e., cold because of elevation rather than latitude). Orange type indicates a habitat that is dominated by fire and that in the absence of fire may revert to a different habitat. A pink dotted line represents habitats that grow with other habitats but on nutrient-poor, sandy soils.

THE TROPICAL AND SUBTROPICAL NORTHEAST OF AUSTRALIA

The first stop for many visitors to Australia is n. Queensland. People come to this region for the Great Barrier Reef and the tropical rainforests, but most ignore the **Au6C** TETRODONTA WOODLAND SAVANNA of w. and n. Cape York Peninsula, part of the savanna system that extends from just west of Cairns all the way to Broome in Western Australia. The Great Barrier Reef, the world's largest coral reef system, stretches along the Queensland coast. This tropical marine environment supports an extraordinary diversity of sea life, such as tropical fish, sea turtles, and marine mammals. Some travellers venture to the reef habitat **Au12D** AUSTRALASIAN SANDY CAY, visiting places such as Michaelmas Cay, a large breeding colony of several species of seabirds.

The tropical rainforests of the Wet Tropics region of Queensland comprise a UNESCO World Heritage Site and are often touted as the oldest rainforests on earth. This may be the case, but the desire to hype the habitat tends to detract from its real grandeur—whether the forests are the oldest or the youngest, what matters is that the remnants are now well protected and easy to access. The Daintree Rainforest, which skirts the coastal area north of Cairns, is **Au4A** AUSTRALASIAN LOWLAND RAINFOREST, whilst the rainforest on the Atherton Tableland in sites

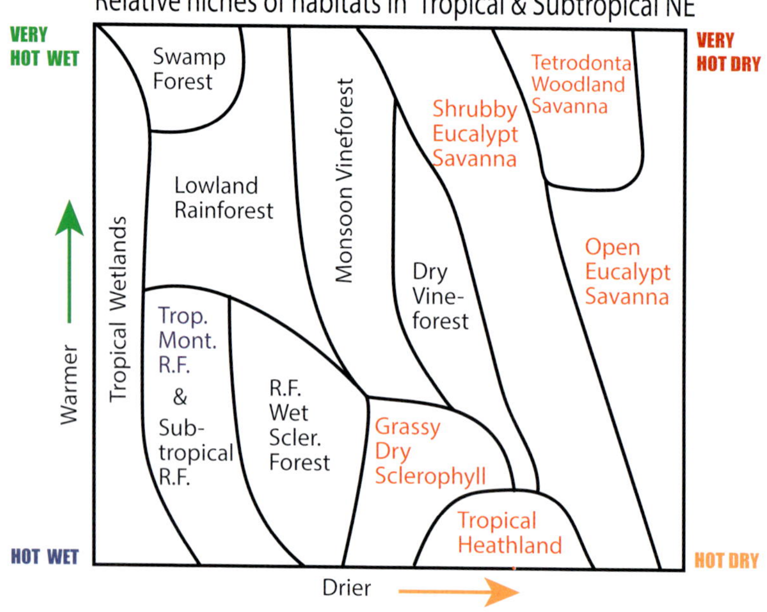

Macleay's Honeyeater is a bird typical of the understorey in the tropical rainforests of ne. Australia.
© IAIN CAMPBELL, TROPICAL BIRDING TOURS/UNSW E&ERC

such as Mt. Hypipamee is **Au4C** AUSTRALASIAN TROPICAL MONTANE RAINFOREST. These forests give people access to wildlife not found in other parts of the world, such as Southern Cassowary, birds-of-paradise, and tree-kangaroos.

The lowlands around Cairns also have **Au4I** AUSTRALASIAN SWAMP FOREST, such as the examples at Centenary Lakes in Cairns Botanic Garden. **Au12A** AUSTRALASIAN TROPICAL MANGROVE FOREST around Cairns is some of the most accessible mangrove forest in the world, and a visit to the Jack Barnes Bicentennial Mangrove Boardwalk off Airport Avenue can be a fascinating experience when the tides are high in the early morning. The rainforests are concentrated along the coastline, and not far inland the habitats change from rainforests to eucalypt forests such as **Au9B** RAINFOREST WET SCLEROPHYLL FOREST (yes, the name seems redundant, but it is a wet sclerophyll forest with a rainforest understorey) around Ravenshoe.

Queensland's climate varies from tropical in the north to subtropical in the south around Brisbane. In the Brisbane area visitors can experience **Au9D** GRASSY DRY SCLEROPHYLL FOREST with tall eucalypts (which provide Koala habitat) and a grassy understorey. West of the city, Lamington National Park protects **Au4B** AUSTRALIAN SUBTROPICAL RAINFOREST, where most visitors are astounded by how confiding the wildlife is around places such as O'Reilly's Rainforest Retreat.

THE TEMPERATE SOUTHEAST OF AUSTRALIA

Over two-thirds of the Australian population lives in the temperate regions of se. Australia, encompassing parts of Victoria, New South Wales, South Australia, Australian Capital Territory, and Tasmania. With the major draw of cities such as Sydney (New South Wales) and Melbourne (Victoria), most visitors to Australia predictably also visit this region, where some fantastic environments are right on these urban doorsteps.

The Blue Mountains, covering an area of nearly 3 million ac. (1.2 million ha) just to the west of Sydney, are named for the blue haze created by the vast **Au9E** HEATHY DRY SCLEROPHYLL FOREST that dominates the landscape. This World Heritage–listed area is characterised by steep cliffs, deep valleys, and cascading waterfalls. The many other nearby habitats include **Au8F** MONTANE HEATHLAND on the ridgelines.

The southern edge of Sydney abuts Royal National Park, one of the oldest national parks in the world, which, combined with adjoining reserves, encompasses over 46,000 ac. (18,600 ha). This is an amazing area of protected land considering the ever-present development pressures from Australia's biggest city. There are extremely few places in the world that have not succumbed to this pressure, and this resistance is something Australians should be immensely proud of (spoiler—not enough are). The park's coastline features dramatic **Au12H** AUSTRALASIAN ROCKY HEADLAND, **Au8A** WALLUM AND AUSBOS moorlands, **Au9E** HEATHY DRY SCLEROPHYLL FOREST, and even areas of **Au4B** AUSTRALIAN SUBTROPICAL RAINFOREST. Patches of **Au12B** AUSTRALIAN TEMPERATE MANGROVE line Sydney Harbour and Botany Bay.

Near Melbourne, **Au4G** AUSTRALIAN TEMPERATE RAINFOREST, **Au9A** GRASSY WET SCLEROPHYLL FOREST, and in the Otway Ranges, absolutely towering **Au9B** RAINFOREST WET SCLEROPHYLL FOREST are a highlight, offering a lush, green environment. The Great Ocean

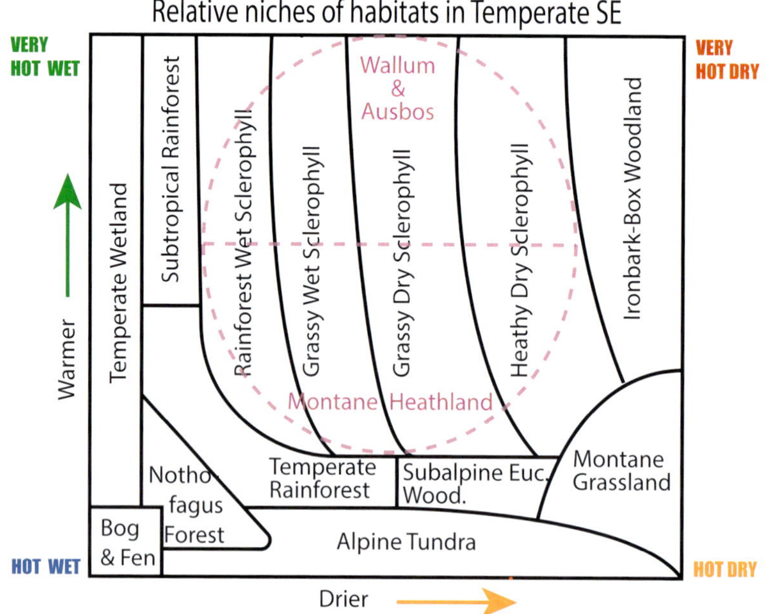

Despite the dense population (by Australian standards) of the east coast, remote beaches can still be found where wildlife such as Emu can roam. © IAIN CAMPBELL, TROPICAL BIRDING TOURS/UNSW E&ERC

Road winds through this region, traversing forests, coastline, and **Au8A** WALLUM AND AUSBOS heathland on the way to the famous Twelve Apostles limestone sea stacks.

Tasmania has the feel of Scotland in the cleared areas and towns, but its forests include **Au4G** AUSTRALIAN TEMPERATE RAINFOREST and **Au4F** NOTHOFAGUS FOREST. Most of the east of the state is dominated by **Au9D** GRASSY DRY SCLEROPHYLL FOREST and **Au9E** HEATHY DRY SCLEROPHYLL FOREST. A short trip to Mt. Wellington overlooking Hobart affords great access to **Au9J** SUBALPINE EUCALYPT WOODLAND and **Au10A** AUSTRALIAN ALPINE TUNDRA. People visiting Bruny Island off se. Tasmania pass through most of the preceding habitats along with extensive areas of **Au8A** WALLUM AND AUSBOS heathland and **Au9B** RAINFOREST WET SCLEROPHYLL FOREST on the taller hills.

The Australian Alps of Victoria and New South Wales, including their ski fields, are dominated by **Au9J** SUBALPINE EUCALYPT WOODLAND, **Au8F** MONTANE HEATHLAND, and **Au10A** AUSTRALIAN ALPINE TUNDRA.

Adelaide (South Australia) is situated at the boundary of the southeastern temperate climate and the semiarid interior of the country. The Adelaide Hills are a mix of dry sclerophyll forests and eucalypt woodlands. A short drive north of Adelaide the habitat changes to the semiarid woodlands described in the next section.

SEMIARID EASTERN AUSTRALIA

This region, which is unvisited by the vast majority of both visitors and city-dwelling Australians, encompasses the Brigalow Belt in Queensland, the Western Plains of New South Wales, and the mallee regions of nw. Victoria. These areas experience a semiarid climate with hot summers, mild winters, and moderate rainfall.

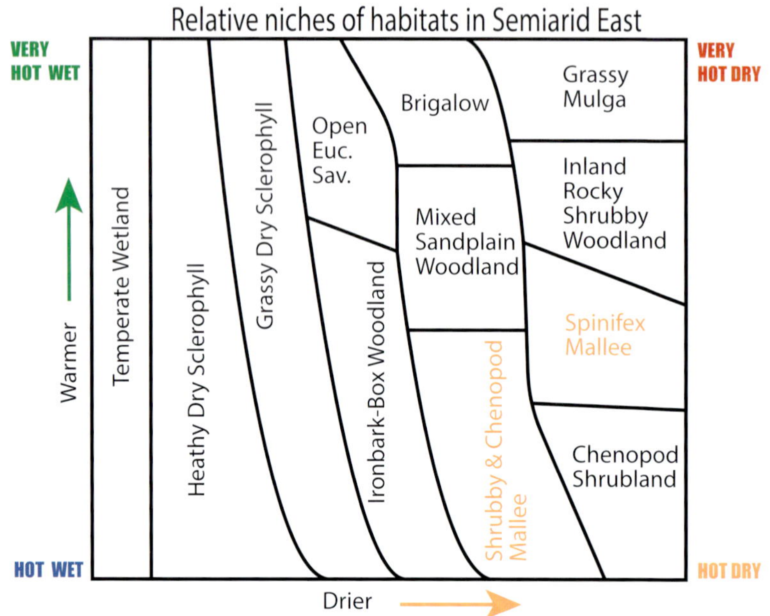

The Brigalow Belt is named for the now sadly depleted thick acacia savanna/forest known as **Au5C** BRIGALOW (also the name of its dominant tree, *Acacia harpophylla*). This area features a mosaic of other habitats such as **Au6A** OPEN EUCALYPT SAVANNA, **Au7A** TROPICAL TUSSOCK GRASSLAND, and **Au9D** GRASSY DRY SCLEROPHYLL FOREST. Surprisingly, this semiarid region contains **Au5A**

Visitors are often surprised by how open the Australian 'forests' can be, with almost complete light penetration to the ground layers. © IAIN CAMPBELL, TROPICAL BIRDING TOURS/UNSW E&ERC

AUSTRALIAN DRY VINEFOREST, which is an extension of rainforest and the closest thing Australia has to the dry tropical forests of other parts of the world. A little to the west of the Brigalow Belt, another acacia (*Acacia aneura*) becomes dominant in the **Au9Q** GRASSY MULGA shrublands.

The Western Plains of New South Wales, Australian Capital Territory, and inland Victoria are dominated by open woodlands such as **Au9G** IRONBARK-BOX WOODLAND, which, like BRIGALOW, was destroyed by early settlers, and only a fraction remains. The semiarid areas less suitable for farming have been spared. In low ridges are extensive areas of **Au9L** MIXED SANDPLAIN WOODLAND, which features plants of many different families and contains extensive groves of sheoaks (*Casuarina* and *Allocasuarina* spp.) and cypress-pines (*Callitris* spp.).

In nw. Victoria, sw. New South Wales, and e. South Australia, the mallee regions, characterised by their distinctive multi-stemmed eucalypts, are unlike any other habitats in the world. There are three kinds of mallee habitats: **Au9M** HEATHY MALLEE and **Au9N** SHRUBBY AND CHENOPOD MALLEE grow on poor- to medium-nutrient soils and have thicker understoreys. **Au9O** SPINIFEX MALLEE is the hardiest and least welcoming of the habitats with its spiky spinifex grass (*Triodia* spp.) understorey formed on palaeo-sand dunes that make farming near impossible—all of which makes this one of the world's most fascinating habitats.

THE SOUTHWEST OF AUSTRALIA

Southwestern Australia is renowned for its Mediterranean climate, characterised by hot, dry summers and cool, wet winters. Home to unique plant life, this region is a floral biodiversity hotspot, surpassed only by the Cape Floral Province of South Africa. Amazingly, the birdlife does not match the flora in diversity, and although there are some 15 regional endemics, the birds are usually generalists.

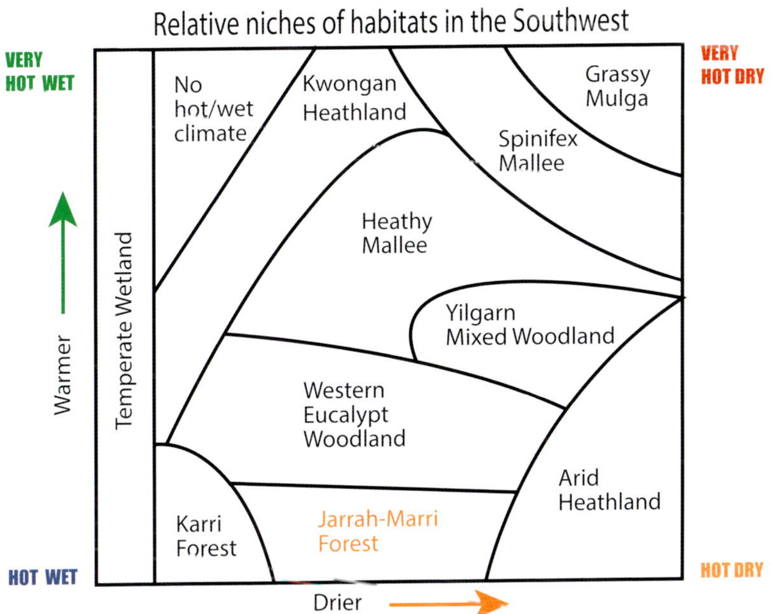

Quokka is a small macropod that has become very confiding on Rottnest Island.
© KEITH BARNES, TROPICAL BIRDING TOURS

Most of the Western Australia population lives in or to the south of Perth, which sits at the northern boundary of this region. The extreme southwestern habitats here include the towering eucalypt **Au9C** KARRI FOREST, which surpasses heights of 200 ft. (61 m), and farther north, the **Au9F** JARRAH-MARRI FOREST, the western equivalent of the **Au9E** HEATHY DRY SCLEROPHYLL FOREST of e. Australia.

Inland from the forests, the environment becomes semiarid. The woodlands of this region have been destroyed for wheat production in the Avon wheat belt. The remaining **Au9P** WESTERN EUCALYPT WOODLAND is concentrated in a few large pockets; those around Dryandra Woodland National Park give an impressive indication of how magnificent these woodlands must have been once. Farther east, on the Yilgarn Block (aka Yilgarn Craton), some of the oldest (and gold-rich) rock on the earth's surface, the woodlands become very complex and interesting with the eucalypts joined by wattles, sheoaks, and melaleucas in the **Au9S** YILGARN MIXED WOODLAND. This woodland has avoided widespread destruction because the climate is dry and the soils, some of which are millions (yes, millions) of years old, are just so unattractive to farmers. Inland from these woodlands, the habitats change to **Au9M** HEATHY MALLEE and **Au9N** SHRUBBY AND CHENOPOD MALLEE, which extend to e. Australia. North of the Yilgarn Mixed Woodland, the habitat changes to the acacia-dominated **Au9Q** GRASSY MULGA, which covers most of the eastern part of the state.

Coastal areas in s. Western Australia, such as those around Two Peoples Bay and Cheynes Beach, are dominated by **Au8D** KWONGAN HEATHLAND, a short coastal heathland that grows on poor soils in a Mediterranean climate. Farther inland these heathlands merge into **Au8B** ARID HEATHLAND, which extends through much of Australia.

THE SAVANNA NORTH

The savanna north of Australia is a massive area from Broome in Western Australia, across the Top End of the Northern Territory, and along the Gulf of Carpentaria to w. Cape York Peninsula in Queensland. However, the vast majority of this area is under-visited by birders, as most do just the Darwin-to-Kakadu circuit. The region is characterised by a tropical savanna climate with distinct wet and dry seasons. The wet season, from November to April, brings heavy monsoonal rains and high humidity, while the dry season, from May to October, is marked by lower humidity and much lower to nil rainfall.

Kakadu National Park, in the Top End region of the Northern Territory, is a UNESCO World Heritage Site that showcases the region's dramatic seasonal changes. During the wet season the floodplains, such as the vast Yellow Water, fill with water and come to life, greatly expanding the extent of **Au11A** AUSTRALASIAN TROPICAL FRESHWATER WETLAND. The flatlands here support a mix of **Au6A** OPEN EUCALYPT SAVANNA, **Au6G** MELALEUCA SAVANNA, and **Au6C** TETRODONTA WOODLAND SAVANNA. Farther inland, and on the rugged Arnhem Land escarpment, the tussock grassland cover of the savanna is replaced by very hardy spinifex grasses (*Triodia* spp.), and the habitat becomes **Au6B** SPINIFEX EUCALYPT SAVANNA.

The savannas of n. Australia hold some spectacular parrots such as this Hooded Parrot of the Northern Territory. © IAIN CAMPBELL, TROPICAL BIRDING TOURS/UNSW E&ERC

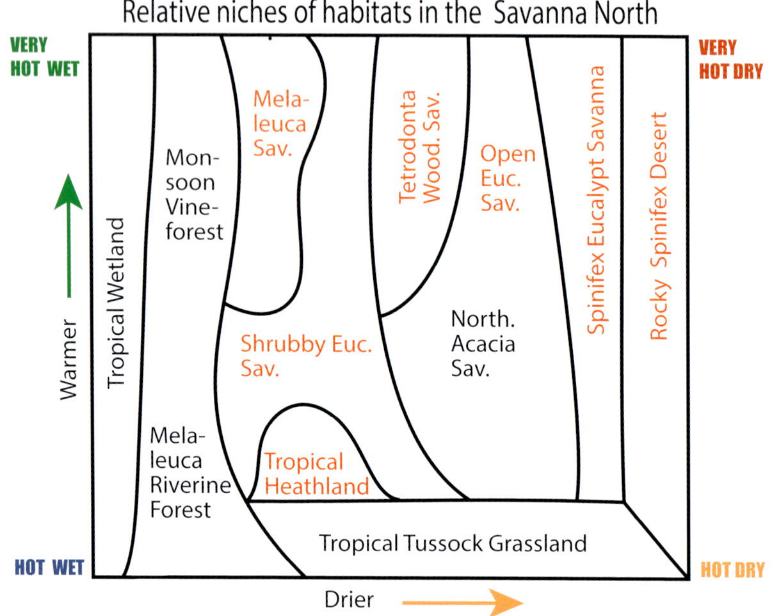

THE DESERT OUTBACK

The arid interior of Australia, often referred to as the Outback, encompasses immense desert regions and semiarid landscapes. Very few people live here, and you can cover vast distances without encountering anyone else—that is, unless you visit Uluru and Alice Springs (s. Northern Territory), in which case you will be surrounded by tourists. The Alice Springs area is encircled by **Au2C** ROCKY SPINIFEX DESERT and **Au6B** SPINIFEX EUCALYPT SAVANNA, with smaller areas of **Au9R** SPINIFEX MULGA. Southwest of Alice Springs, Uluru–Kata Tjuta National Park is home to Uluru (Ayers Rock), a massive red arkosic sandstone monolith, and Kata Tjuta (the Olgas), a series of domed rock formations; both are the sides of a massive anticline where softer surrounding rocks eroded away, leaving the resistant arkose and conglomerate masses standing isolated. The habitat of this area is **Au2C** ROCKY SPINIFEX DESERT with plains of sandy **Au2A** DUNE SPINIFEX DESERT dotted with Desert Sheoak (*Allocasuarina decaisneana*).

The Simpson Desert (se. Northern Territory, ne. South Australia, and sw. Queensland) is much less visited; however, it is spectacular, with huge areas of **Au2A** DUNE SPINIFEX DESERT and **Au2B** DUNECREST CANEGRASS, characterised by iconic red sand dunes that comprise one of the largest sand dune deserts in the world. The main town is Birdsville, sw. Queensland, usually accessed by the Birdsville Track, which runs through hundreds of miles of stony desert habitat called **Au2E** GIBBER CHENOPODLAND and, to the south, areas of **Au2D** CHENOPOD SHRUBLAND, which looks remarkably like the SUCCULENT KAROO of South Africa. These plains are interspersed with ephemeral wetlands such as **Au11C** LIGNUM SWAMP and **Au12E** AUSTRALIAN SALT PAN.

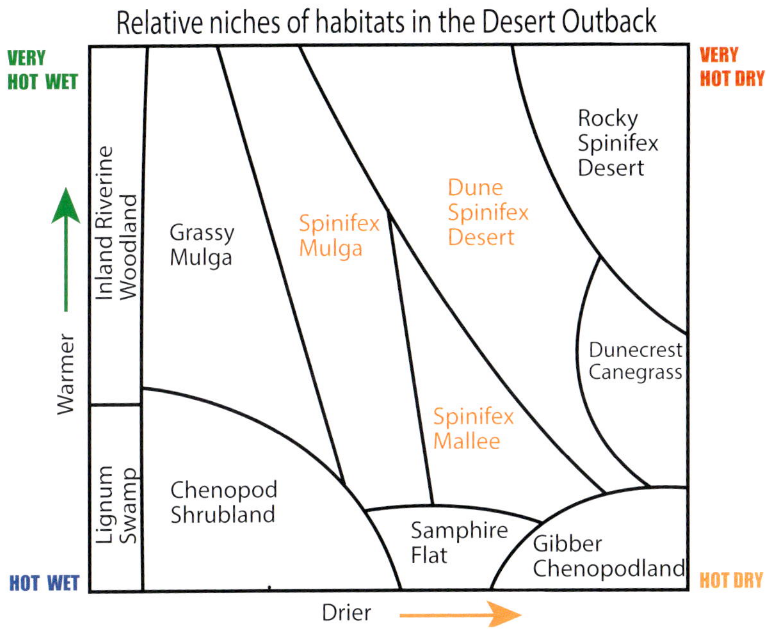

Much of c. Australia is home to extremely old soils that have lithified into resistant rocks such as ferricrete and silcrete, forming residual lateritic plateaus. © IAIN CAMPBELL, TROPICAL BIRDING TOURS/UNSW E&ERC

THE NORTHERN ISLANDS: NEW GUINEA TO THE SOLOMONS

The massive island of New Guinea lies north of Australia and is divided roughly down the middle, with the country of Papua New Guinea and its offshore islands occupying the eastern half and Indonesia's Papuan provinces (which we refer to as Indonesian New Guinea) the western. To the east and southeast of New Guinea lie numerous islands, including those of the Solomon Archipelago, which includes the Solomon Islands nation and other islands. This whole region is more tropical than Australia, with a less monsoonal climate and its rainfall spread more evenly throughout the year. Considering the massive mountain chain that runs east–west across the island, it is not surprising that the habitats found there are governed more by elevational temperature variation and less by rainfall than mainland Australia.

Au4A AUSTRALASIAN LOWLAND RAINFOREST is found around most of the northern and eastern coastline of New Guinea and its surrounding islands, such as New Ireland and New Britain, as well as the lowlands of the Solomon Islands. In the wettest areas and in regions with restricted drainage, **Au4I** AUSTRALASIAN SWAMP FOREST is the dominant humid forest. In the drier areas in the lowlands of the south, there are massive expanses of **Au6G** MELALEUCA SAVANNA in the regularly inundated areas and **Au6A** OPEN EUCALYPT SAVANNA in the better-drained areas. In regions that are wetter than the other savannas but with distinct savanna fire regimes, such as the area around Port Moresby (Papua New Guinea), the taller eucalypts form **Au6C** TETRODONTA WOODLAND SAVANNA. Where fire is retarded, this niche is filled by **Au5B** AUSTRALASIAN MONSOON VINEFOREST and blends into **Au4A** AUSTRALASIAN LOWLAND RAINFOREST. Around the coastline, **Au12A** AUSTRALASIAN TROPICAL MANGROVE FOREST covers the shoreline of most shallow bays and estuaries, though in steeper areas the savannas and forests can come right to the coast, meeting **Au12C** AUSTRALASIAN SANDY BEACH or **Au12H** AUSTRALASIAN ROCKY HEADLAND.

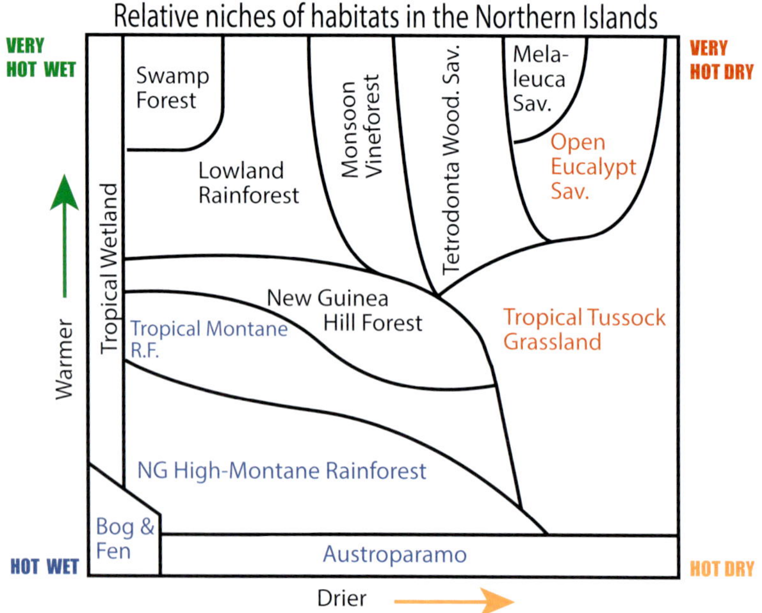

On the lower elevations of New Guinea's mountain ranges is **Au4D** NEW GUINEA HILL FOREST, which is found only to the north of Australia; yet above it is **Au4C** AUSTRALASIAN TROPICAL MONTANE RAINFOREST, a habitat also found in the Atherton Tableland of mainland Australia. Still higher on the mountain ranges is **Au4E** NEW GUINEA HIGH-MONTANE RAINFOREST, though much of this misty cloud forest has been cleared from the central highlands. The tops of the mountains have a tropical alpine tundra called **Au10B** AUSTROPARAMO because it is equivalent to the very well-known paramos of South America. In the drier parts of the central highlands, and in extensively cleared areas, **Au7A** TROPICAL TUSSOCK GRASSLAND dominates the landscape.

Few species conjure up the image of New Guinea more than Wilson's Bird-of-Paradise, which converts a bit of forest understorey into its dance floor. © KEITH BARNES, TROPICAL BIRDING TOURS

Australian Deserts Dendrogram (Biome 2)

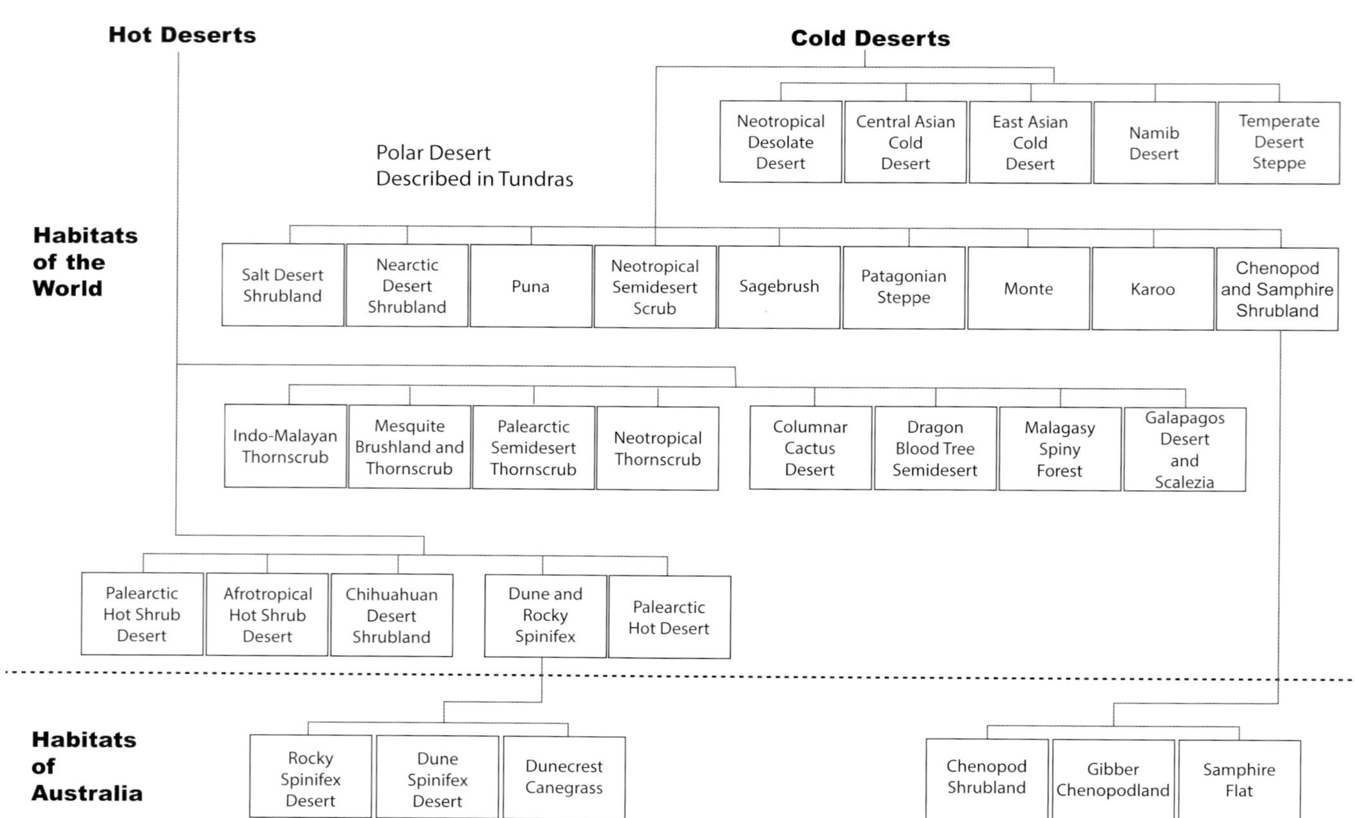

Au2A DUNE SPINIFEX DESERT

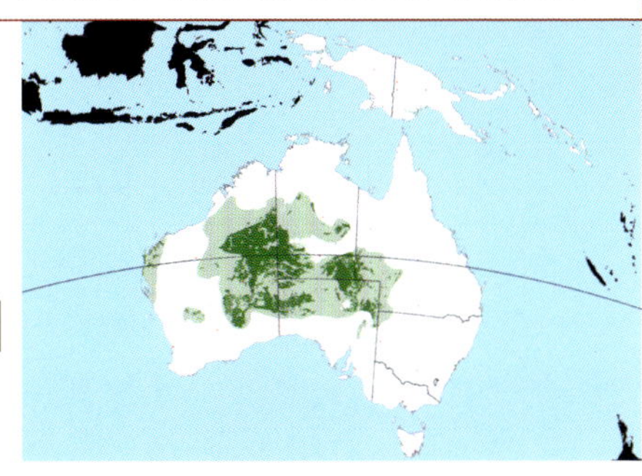

IN A NUTSHELL: A spiky, low grassland that can be nearly impenetrable, occurring on palaeo-sand dunes and sandy interdune swales in arid c. Australia. **Global Habitat Affinities:** None; spinifex grasslands are unique to Australia. **Continental Habitat Affinities:** ROCKY SPINIFEX DESERT; DUNECREST CANEGRASS. **Species Overlap:** ROCKY SPINIFEX DESERT; DUNECREST CANEGRASS; TROPICAL TUSSOCK GRASSLAND; NORTHERN ACACIA SAVANNA. **Full Bird Assemblage:** habitatsoftheworld.org/Au2A.

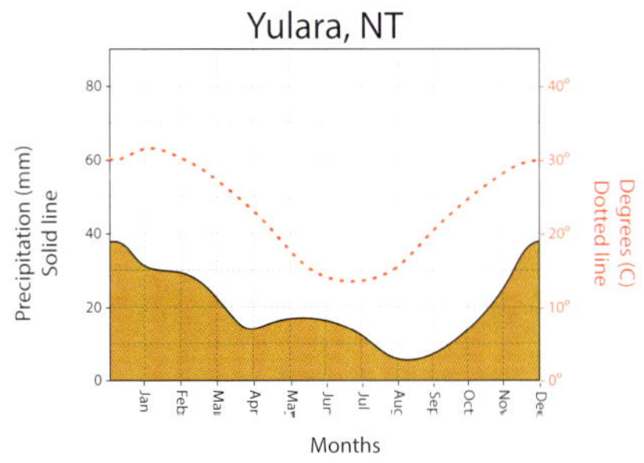

DESCRIPTION: These hummock grasslands are dominated by the *Triodia* genus of grasses, known, rather confusingly, by the common name spinifex, shared with grasses of the genus *Spinifex*. In c. Australia, and especially the Great Sandy Desert, the landscape is dominated by huge seas of linear sand dunes that were very active during the drier glacial periods, but most have been stable for around 20,000 years. The stabilised longitudinal dunes can be over 100 mi. (160 km) long and 60 ft. (20 m) high, although they are often much lower than that. The dunes all align, and the different strikes (directions) within the dune fields can indicate the prevalent wind direction of the time just prior to dune stabilisation. The longitudinal dunes, distinct from the crescent-shaped (barchan) sand dunes of Africa and Asia, are a result of more uniform wind direction and reduced amounts of sand.

Thinner sheets of aeolian (wind-blown) sand can blanket the landscape as sand plains, but these do not have a marked obvious structure, displaying only limited relief over thousands of acres/hectares. Although such sand plains are widespread, they tend to be ignored in favour of the more dramatic dune landscape. Loess deposits, more common in the Northern Hemisphere, are slightly different: they are sheets of extremely fine aeolian silt, much finer than the sand, and are laid down from silt clouds, much like ash from a volcano. Loess deposits do occur to a limited extent in s. Australia but rarely form the substrate of Dune Spinifex Desert. In the longitudinal dunes, and on the vast swales between dunes covered in sandy colluvium (gravity-transported material) and alluvium (water-transported material), spinifex forms the main sand-binding habitat. Spinifex is also found in rocky terrains, and although the grass systems and indeed many of the spinifex

Dune Spinifex Desert is the dominant habitat in the vast plain surrounding Uluru (Ayers Rock) in Northern Territory. © IAIN CAMPBELL, TROPICAL BIRDING TOURS/UNSW E&ERC

species are similar, Dune Spinifex Desert and ROCKY SPINIFEX DESERT habitats have different animal communities.

The dunes are covered with widely spaced spinifex tussocks with a curious and unique growth form of large, low hummocks, usually not more than 3 ft. (1 m) high but up to 5 ft. (1.5 m) wide, with the centre of the plant dead, so the hummocks grow into rings. The roots are stiff, and the stems of many grasses of the spinifex habitats are infused with silica at the tips, which makes the plants very rigid. The dominant spinifex species on the dunes are Feathertop Spinifex (*Triodia schinzii*) and Hard Spinifex (*Triodia basedowii*). Very widely dispersed trees such as Sandhill Bloodwood (*Corymbia chippendalei*) eke out an existence in the extremely nutrient-deficient soils.

In the swales between dunes and where the dunes are much lower and older and have more soil development, Hard Spinifex and Feathertop Spinifex can occur, but the very pugnacious and widespread Soft Spinifex (*Triodia pungens*) becomes dominant. Soft Spinifex is also the dominant grass species in most of the spinifex-related habitats. Desert Sheoak (*Allocasuarina decaisneana*) is a very iconic and distinctive tree of c. Australia. Its often flat top and long drooping leaves give the impression of a cross between an Umbrella Thorn (*Vachellia tortilis*) of Africa and a Weeping Willow (*Salix babylonica*) of China. Very slow-growing trees, Desert Sheoaks rarely create more than 20% canopy cover, usually representing only around 5% canopy cover. They are the main tree over much of the sandy plains and feature in many photographs around Uluru (Ayers Rock). In

Scarlet-chested Parrot is a beautiful, though rare and seldom-seen, inhabitant of the southern portions of Dune Spinifex Desert habitat. © PETE MORRIS

some large interdune swales, very open, low stands of Mulga (*Acacia aneura*) and Kariku Sheoak (*Casuarina pauper*) can occur, usually under 15 ft. (4.5 m) high and often associated with Hard Spinifex. Where the Mulga becomes denser than 40% canopy cover, and in some places forms a closed canopy, the dynamics of the habitat change, allowing many more animal species to survive, and the habitat is classified as SPINIFEX MULGA. In a few areas, the Dune Spinifex Desert merges with DUNECREST CANEGRASS, where the dunes are less stabilised and the dominant plant is Sandhill Canegrass (*Zygochloa paradoxa*) rather than spinifex (*Triodia*). At a distance the habitats seem very similar, but the Dune Spinifex Desert areas have more ground cover.

WILDLIFE: The grasses of spinifex habitats are spiny and nutrient-poor and therefore unattractive to grazing mammals such as the kangaroos so common through most of Australia. The few mammals that once lived in this habitat, such as the Greater Bilby or Rufous Hare-Wallaby, have been devastated, not only by a change in the fire regime of the region but also by the introduction of the food competitor European Rabbit and the predatory feral cat. Without large herbivores and their predators, the main herbivores are termites, and the food web builds from there. Although of limited use as a food source, spinifex cover forms a very important refuge for sheltering birds, lizards, and mammals.

The Dune Spinifex Desert has few birds, and very few are limited to it. Sandhill Grasswren is associated mainly with this habitat, and the rare Princess Parrot and Scarlet-chested Parrot, which both have very broad distributions through c. Australia, are largely centred around the Dune

Zebra Finch is a widespread and gregarious species that occurs in many inland habitats, including Dune Spinifex Desert. © IAIN CAMPBELL, TROPICAL BIRDING TOURS/UNSW E&ERC

Spinifex Desert, the former among Desert Sheoaks, and the latter among low eucalypts. With the trees so widely spaced, few of the small woodland birds such as thornbills or gerygones survive here, although ground-feeding species such as the Purple-backed Fairywren, Yellow-rumped Thornbill, and Southern Whiteface do occur. Zebra Finch is the only finch regularly found here, poised to take advantage when mass-seeding of spinifex occurs, when it is joined by Crested Pigeon, Diamond Dove, Mulga Parrot, and Budgerigar. Because the flowering tree and shrub cover is so limited, most of the blossom nomads (nectivorous birds that follow flower blooms) of surrounding habitats are missing. Singing, White-plumed, Grey-headed, and even the much rarer Pied Honeyeaters can be found occasionally in this habitat. The open plains and occasional tree for nesting provide a favourable environment for raptors such as Black-breasted Kite, Wedge-tailed Eagle, and Brown Falcon. Rainbow Bee-eater is the main perch-hawking insectivore, while White-backed Swallow hunts insects from the sky.

The populations of many lizards fluctuate greatly in a cyclical manner, and even species found in the same habitat vary in their microhabitat preferences, which are regulated by fire regimes and rain cycles. This means that species described in field guides as uncommon may be abundant in some years and rare in others. Some of the lizards you can hope to see here are the spectacular and bizarre-looking Thorny Devil (*Moloch horridus*); the large Sand Goanna (*Varanus gouldii*); Rusty Desert and Short-tailed Monitors (*Varanus eremius* and *Varanus brevicauda*); Long-nosed Dragon (*Gowidon longirostris*); Central Netted and Military Dragons (*Ctenophorus nuchalis* and *Ctenophorus isolepis*); Northern Spiny-tailed Gecko (*Strophurus ciliaris*); and Smooth Knob-tailed Gecko (*Nephrurus laevissimus*). Snakes present in this habitat (all venomous to varying degrees) include Mulga Snake (*Pseudechis australis*), Western Brown Snake (*Pseudonaja mengdeni*), Ringed Brown Snake (*Pseudonaja modesta*), Northern Desert Banded Snake (*Simoselaps anomalus*), and Narrow-banded Shovel-nosed Snake (*Brachyurophis fasciolatus*). Many Australian snakes are deadly, and some are very difficult to distinguish from harmless species—as a safety measure, do not approach any snakes. Frogs are few and far between, but the enigmatic Desert Spadefoot Frog (*Notaden nichollsi*) can be found here.

CONSERVATION: Dune Spinifex Desert is so inhospitable to agriculture that it has largely avoided widespread conversion to farming, though some areas are subjected to light grazing and

The colourful Rainbow Bee-eater, a widespread species in Australia, is most often seen hawking insects on the wing from a prominent perch. © BEN KNOOT

planting for improved pasture. The majority of the threats to this habitat are from introduced plants, introduced herbivores such as Dromedary Camel, and mammal predators such as feral cats. The reason so many of the small inland mammals have gone extinct is not fully understood, as it appears that some of them went extinct before cats had arrived in the centre of Australia.

DISTRIBUTION: Dune Spinifex Desert habitat is common from extreme sw. Queensland, all the way across the country to the tropical Western Australia coast. Any visitor to Australia's arid interior is likely to come across spinifex—e.g., on the Birdsville and Strzelecki Tracks (South Australia), around Alice Springs and Uluru (Northern Territory), and near Mt. Isa (Queensland).

WHERE TO SEE: Uluru, Northern Territory, Australia; Great Sandy Desert, Western Australia.

Au2B DUNECREST CANEGRASS

IN A NUTSHELL: Mainly barren longitudinal sand dunes with clumps of Sandhill Canegrass and a bit of spinifex. **Global Habitat Affinities:** SAHARAN ERG DESERT; NAMIB SAND DESERT. **Continental Habitat Affinities:** DUNE SPINIFEX DESERT. **Species Overlap:** TROPICAL TUSSOCK GRASSLAND; DUNE SPINIFEX DESERT. **Full Bird Assemblage:** habitatsoftheworld.org/Au2B.

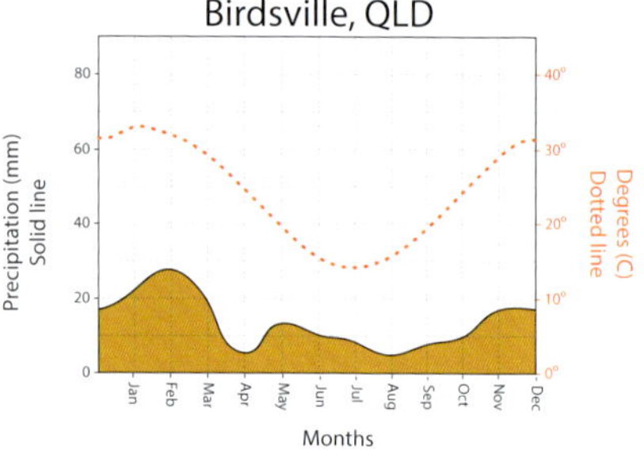

DESCRIPTION: This is the sparse, sandy habitat that forms on the crests of the younger longitudinal sand dunes of c. Australia. These longitudinal dunes tend to be higher than those dominated by spinifex, with Big Red, the easternmost of over 1000 sand dunes in the Simpson Desert, standing over 120 ft. (36.5 m) high. The dunes of the Simpson Desert are very young, some having been deposited as recently as 10,000–8000 years ago, and align along a strike (direction) parallel to the prevalent wind direction of the time, just prior to dune stabilisation. These longitudinal dunes are different from the crescent-shaped (barchan) sand dunes of Africa and Asia, where the dunes form perpendicular to the prevailing winds, are far more mobile and smaller, and usually have more sand with fewer swales between them. Dunecrest Canegrass habitat forms on aeolian sands in hot desert climates (Köppen **Bwh**) with 6.5 in. (170 mm) annual rainfall and summer temperatures reaching 120°F (50°C). Due to the desiccating climate and lack of organic material, the soils are usually devoid of any horizon development, being little more than unconsolidated original sand deposits. The red colour of some of the sands is caused by the very minor component of iron oxides, such as hematite, in the otherwise almost pure quartz of the sands.

Sandhill Canegrass (*Zygochloa paradoxa*) is a dense, green, bushy perennial grass that superficially resembles the spinifex grasses (*Triodia*; see DUNE SPINIFEX DESERT), in that it grows in hummocks 5 ft. (1.5 m) tall and 3 ft. (1 m) wide. It differs from spinifex in not being spiky and in having a horizontal rhizomatous stem sending out new shoots rather than the circular growth form of the spinifex rings. Sandhill Canegrass is the dominant grass on many of the dunes, although Erect Kerosene Grass (*Aristida holathera*) and Woollybutt Grass (*Eragrostis eriopoda*) often occur. Small hummocks of Hard Spinifex (*Triodia basedowii*) are almost always interspersed within the Sandhill Canegrass and may dominate along the lower edges of the sand dunes. Forbs are present, and after rains the dunes can be flush with green and yellow blossoms of Green Birdflower (*Crotalaria cunninghamii*) and Bluebush Pea (*Crotalaria eremaea*). Small widely spaced shrubs such as Sandhill Wattle (*Acacia ligulata*) and Sandhill Grevillea (*Grevillea stenobotrya*) are uncommon but contrast with the bare sand and, because they can grow to 6 ft. (2 m) tall in these sands, are obvious when present. Especially in dry years, the dunes can be devoid of any shrubby vegetation.

Simpson Desert is home to more than 1000 parallel dunes, the most famous of which is Big Red near the town of Birdsville in sw. Queensland, which stands 120 ft. (36.5 m) high. © SAM WOODS, TROPICAL BIRDING TOURS

Dunecrest Canegrass is not a fire-tolerant habitat, and fires in summer kill the canegrass and forbs resulting in the expansion of Hard Spinifex and Feathertop Spinifex (*Triodia schinzii*) at the expense of Sandhill Canegrass, so the habitat changes to Dune Spinifex Desert.

WILDLIFE: Because life on the top of a sand dune is so harsh, Dunecrest Canegrass is understandably characterised by its lack of wildlife, although Eyrean Grasswren is an endemic and obligate species here. This enigmatic small bird is both range-restricted and difficult to find,

Dunecrest Canegrass is a very localised habitat, occurring on the top of longitudinal dunes, deep within the Outback of c. Australia. © SAM WOODS, TROPICAL BIRDING TOURS

usually glimpsed running mouselike between clumps of Sandhill Canegrass, and unlike most other grasswrens, which will occasionally call from low branches of trees or shrubs, this species almost never leaves the ground or grass. Ground-feeding pigeons are surprisingly well represented, with Crested Pigeon and Diamond and Peaceful Doves regularly present, and even the rare Flock Bronzewing occasionally visiting the dunes after good rains. Purple-backed and White-winged Fairywrens are both present, in contrast with DUNE SPINIFEX DESERT, where White-winged Fairywren is much rarer. Both Crimson and Orange Chats are found here feeding on the ground, and the Cinnamon Quail-thrush, a medium-sized, skulking, ground-feeding species that is usually associated with chenopod-dominated habitats, can also be found in this habitat.

The threatened Crest-tailed Mulgara, a nocturnal, medium-sized marsupial that looks like a guinea pig with a stumpy, bushy tail, rests in burrows under Sandhill Canegrass hummocks. The vulnerable and range-restricted Dusky Hopping Mouse is a small nocturnal rodent that resembles a miniature South African Springhare; it is a communal animal, living in a series of connected burrows. One of the commonest reptiles found in this habitat is Central Bearded Dragon (*Pogona vitticeps*); some other species include Wedgesnout Ctenotus (*Ctenotus brooksi*), Canegrass Two-lined Dragon (*Diporiphora winneckei*), Painted Dragon (*Ctenophorus pictus*), Central Netted Dragon (*Ctenophorus nuchalis*), Ribbon Ctenotus (*Ctenotus taeniatus*), and Eastern Tree Dtella (*Gehyra versicolor*).

CONSERVATION: Dunecrest Canegrass is nearly impossible to farm. The majority of the threats to this habitat are from introduced plants, introduced herbivores such as Dromedary Camel, and mammal predators such as feral cats. Many of the smaller mammals here are under extreme threat, but the reasons for the plummeting numbers are not clearly understood.

DISTRIBUTION: Please note that where Dunecrest Canegrass occurs, it is almost invariably surrounded by DUNE SPINIFEX DESERT lower on the dunes; this makes it so limited it is not mappable with the units used in the various state mapping systems—thus the dark green areas of probable distribution on the map for this account do not match with state systems. Dunecrest Canegrass is centred on the Simpson and Strzelecki Deserts in sw. Queensland, n. South Australia, and s. Northern Territory. In the west and north, it is replaced by Dune Spinifex Desert, and to the south, it merges with the GIBBER CHENOPODLAND.

WHERE TO SEE: 'Big Red' sand dune near Birdsville, Queensland, Australia; Mungeranie, Birdsville Track, South Australia.

Eyrean Grasswren is an elusive habitat specialist of Dunecrest Canegrass. Its presence is sometimes revealed by the presence of its footprints within open sandy areas between clumps of grass. © SAM WOODS, TROPICAL BIRDING TOURS

Au2C ROCKY SPINIFEX DESERT

IN A NUTSHELL: A spiky, low grassland of very arid c. Australia that can be near impenetrable. **Global Habitat Affinities:** Unique; there are no grasslands like spinifex outside of Australia. **Continental Habitat Affinities:** DUNE SPINIFEX DESERT. **Species Overlap:** SPINIFEX EUCALYPT SAVANNA; TROPICAL TUSSOCK GRASSLAND; DUNE SPINIFEX DESERT. **Full Bird Assemblage:** habitatsoftheworld.org/Au2C.

DESCRIPTION: The word 'spinifex' usually refers to a genus of grasses (*Spinifex*) found in coastal areas around the world, but in Australia 'spinifex' is the name of desert habitat that includes hummock grasses (also known as spinifex) of the genera *Triodia* and, to a lesser extent, *Plectrachne*. The spinifex landscape described here is the quintessential habitat of the arid inland and, in various forms, covers large tracts of desert Australia. In contrast with the tussock grasses of Australia and almost all other grasses in the world, spinifex plants are extremely spiky, and some plants have leaves infused with silica at the tips, making them very rigid and dagger-like. Where this habitat occurs in warm monsoonal and savanna

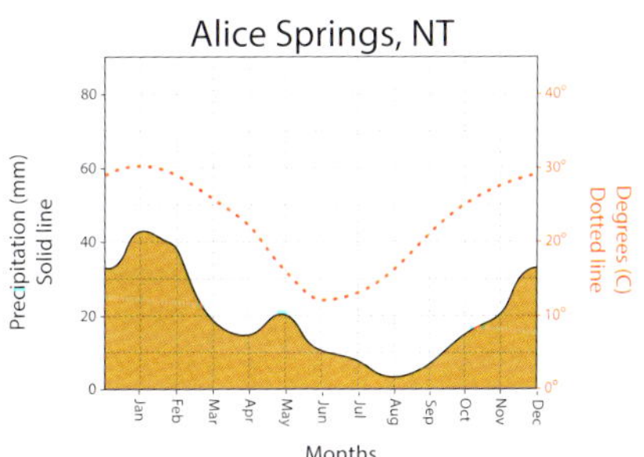

Rocky Spinifex Desert lines the hills of both lateritic outcrops and rocky swales in c. Australia. © IAIN CAMPBELL, TROPICAL BIRDING TOURS/UNSW E&ERC

climates (Köppen **Awa**, **Awb**) with long periods of plant stress, they are associated with extremely inert shallow soils over sandstone plateaus and escarpments. They are most common in desert climates (Köppen **Bwh**) with as little as 6 in. (150 mm) of annual rainfall. This usually precludes large trees from growing, so the few trees that do occur are limited to mallee-form (with most branches sprouting from the tree base) eucalypts such as Finke River Mallee (*Eucalyptus sessilis*), Blue-Leaved Mallee (*Eucalyptus gamophylla*), and Kingsmill's Mallee (*Eucalyptus kingsmillii*), and other desert eucalypts like Snappy Gum (*Eucalyptus leucophloia*). Pindan Wattle (*Acacia tumida*) is scattered through this habitat in the northwest of the country and can become concentrated into groves where the habitat is reclassified as NORTHERN ACACIA SAVANNA.

Rocky Spinifex Desert is found in rocky environments such as lateritic plateaus, where ancient iron-rich but nutrient-poor soils predominate, sandstone plateaus, breakaways (the edges of minor escarpments), and rocky ridgelines. The soils on the colluvial slopes (the edges of the steep rocky ridges) and sandstone plateaus are lithosols that are very sandy, very nutrient-deficient, and without much profile development. In these erosional and depositional environments, there is the near-ubiquitous Soft Spinifex (*Triodia pungens*), but the slopes are usually dominated by Giant Grey Spinifex (*Triodia longiceps*), Weeping Spinifex (*Triodia brizoides*), and Porcupine Grass (*Triodia molesta*)—the common and scientific names of which tell you all you need to know about wandering in this habitat! In the northwest of the country, Soft Spinifex and Limestone Spinifex (*Triodia wiseana*) reign supreme, with only minor incursions of Weeping Spinifex and Porcupine Grass. Rocky Spinifex Desert also forms on tops of lateritic plateaus that resemble the mesas of the sw. United States, where the residual soils are either iron-infused caps (ferricretes or laterites)

Rufous-crowned Emuwren is usually very shy, but when calling it comes to the top of spinifex hummocks. © PETE MORRIS

or silica-infused caps (silcrete), and although they have soil profiles that may have developed over millions of years, they also are extremely nutrient deficient.

The grass systems are similar in DUNE SPINIFEX DESERT and Rocky Spinifex Desert, but the two have very different suites of animals, so are treated as different habitats. The grasses are usually widely spaced and have a curious and unique growth form: large, low hummocks that are usually not very high but may be up to 5 ft. (1.5 m) wide, with each stem growing from the same node as the root, so that the stems have independent sources for nutrients. In this habitat, one of the harshest of environments in Australia, competition from other grasses or shrubs is limited, but the competitive strategy for the spinifex is to have mass seedings during good seasons but for the seeds to have delayed sprouting. In periods of fire, which usually occur about once a decade, some of the original spinifex grasses may be burnt back to the base and resprout, and the seeds may sprout with the next rain. As the individual plants age, undergo fires, and resprout after fires, the perimeter ring of the hummock continues to grow, so that rings often extend to 15 ft. (5 m) wide, and plants live for decades. After good rains, and if there has not been a fire for some decades, the spinifex grasses risk getting smothered by other grasses such as Red Spathe Grass (*Schizachyrium fragile*), various *Aristida* grasses, forbs such as Fragrant Streptoglossa (*Streptoglossa odora*), and a variety of shrubs such as Silver Senna (*Senna artemisioides*), *Eremophila*, and *Maireana* chenopod shrubs.

WILDLIFE: The spiny and nutrient-poor grasses of spinifex habitats are unattractive to grazing mammals such as the kangaroos so common through most of Australia. Without large herbivores and their predators, the main herbivores are termites, and the food web builds from there. Although of limited use as a food source, spinifex cover forms a very important refuge for

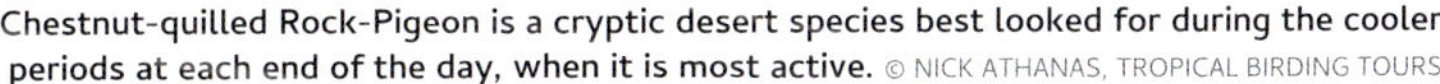

Chestnut-quilled Rock-Pigeon is a cryptic desert species best looked for during the cooler periods at each end of the day, when it is most active. © NICK ATHANAS, TROPICAL BIRDING TOURS

Spinifex Pigeon is the quintessential bird of spinifex habitats in n. Australia.
© IAIN CAMPBELL, TROPICAL BIRDING TOURS/UNSW E&ERC

sheltering birds, lizards, and small mammals.

Birds typical of Rocky Spinifex Desert areas include most of the grasswrens, such as Pilbara Grasswren, Black Grasswren, and Opalton Grasswren. Other birds using the spinifex for cover include Rufous-crowned Emuwren, Spinifexbird, Painted Firetail, Spinifex Pigeon, and the very rare (once thought extinct) Night Parrot. Chestnut-quilled and White-quilled Rock-Pigeons are both obligates to this habitat, living on the spinifex-covered sandstone escarpments of Arnhem Land (Northern Territory) and the Kimberley (Western Australia), respectively. Overhead, this is the favourite habitat of the rarest of all Australian raptors, Grey Falcon.

Rock-wallabies are the typical mammals of this habitat, with various species depending on location. Although macropods (members of the kangaroo family), they are adapted to this landscape with the seeming agility of mountain goats. Yellow-footed Rock-Wallaby from the Flinders Range North of Adelaide, for example, cohabits the rocky terrain with more widespread kangaroos such as Common Wallaroo and Red Kangaroo. Small marsupial mice such as Fat-tailed False Antechinus occur, and the ubiquitous neo-native (introduced only 8000 years ago) Dingo is a very regular visitor to this environment.

The populations of many lizards fluctuate greatly in a cyclical manner, and even species found in the same habitat vary in their microhabitat preferences, which are regulated by fire regimes and rain cycles. This means that species described in field guides as uncommon may be abundant in some years, and vice versa. Some of the lizards you can hope to see are Long-nosed Dragon (*Gowidon longirostris*), Slater's Ring-tailed Dragon (*Ctenophorus slateri*), Central Bearded Dragon (*Pogona vitticeps*), Centralian Rough Knob-tailed Gecko (*Nephrurus amyae*), Black-headed Monitor (*Varanus tristis*), Perentie (*Varanus giganteus*), and Central Clawless Gecko (*Crenadactylus horni*). Snakes are less obvious than lizards, but typical snakes include Centralian Carpet Python (*Morelia bredli*), Curl Snake (*Suta suta*), Mulga Snake (*Pseudechis australis*), and Central Whipsnake (*Demansia cyanochasma*). The latter three are venomous, but all snakes in Australia should be avoided.

CONSERVATION: This is a very widespread habitat throughout c. Australia, the majority of it well away from intense human activity, and most of it protected on Aboriginal lands. This is the habitat over most of the uranium deposits of the Northern Territory, so there is mining pressure on accessible parts of w. Arnhem Land.

DISTRIBUTION: Rocky Spinifex Desert is common from extreme sw. Queensland all the way across the country to the tropical Western Australia coast. It is prevalent in the sandstone escarpments of Arnhem Land (Northern Territory) and the Kimberley (Western Australia) and is very widespread in the Pilbara region (Western Australia).

WHERE TO SEE: MacDonnell Ranges, Northern Territory, Australia; Lark Quarry near Winton, Queensland, Australia; Marble Bar, Western Australia; Mt. Isa, Queensland, Australia.

Yellow-footed Rock-Wallaby is a striking but scarce and local dweller of rock outcroppings in this habitat, generally shying away from populated areas. © BEN KNOOT

Au2D CHENOPOD SHRUBLAND

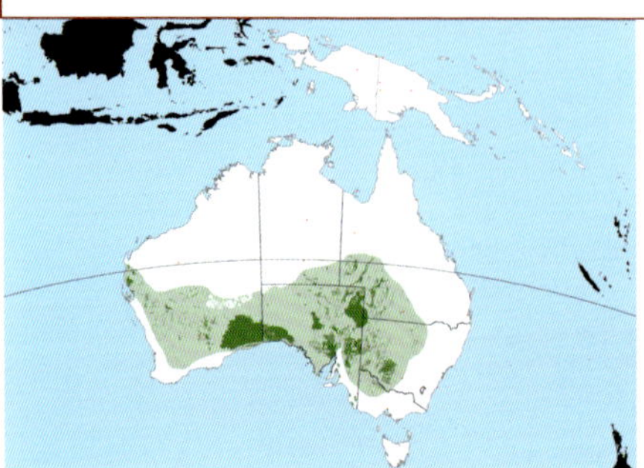

Chenopod Woodland subhabitat

IN A NUTSHELL: Very low, sparse shrubland tolerant of salt and aridity that can have occasional low trees in some areas. **Global Habitat Affinities:** SUCCULENT KAROO; SUCCULENT PUNA; NORTH AMERICAN SAGEBRUSH SHRUBLAND. **Continental Habitat Affinities:** GIBBER CHENOPODLAND. **Species Overlap:** GIBBER CHENOPODLAND; GRASSY MULGA. **Full Bird Assemblage:** habitatsoftheworld.org/Au2D.

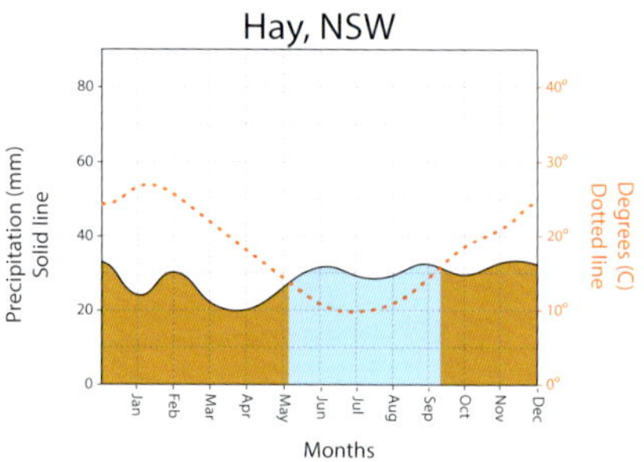

DESCRIPTION: The first impression an international visitor may have of the Hay Plain of w. New South Wales or the Nullarbor Plain of South Australia and Western Australia is just how similar the plant life looks to that of the South African SUCCULENT KAROO, Andean SUCCULENT PUNA, or the North American SAGEBRUSH SHRUBLAND. This 'cold' desert and semi-desert environment is dominated by succulent plants of the saltbush (Chenopodioideae) subfamily (of the amaranth family), which have succulent leaves, salt-excreting mechanisms, and granular foliage to help them conserve water and manage high salt concentrations. Chenopod Shrubland forms in regions with good soils and semiarid to Mediterranean arid climates (Köppen **Bsk–Csa**) with rainfall generally between 8 and 16 in. (200—400 mm) per year, falling mainly in the winter months. Winter nighttime temperatures can drop below freezing, and the summer daytime highs can be a scorching 104°F (40°C).

The best-known and most extreme examples of this habitat are on the Nullarbor Plain, a massive area straddling the South Australia–Western Australia

The seemingly uniform Chenopod Shrubland of the Nullarbor Plain, stretching for 300 mi. (500 km), contains localised hotspots for the Nullarbor Quail-thrush. © IAIN CAMPBELL, TROPICAL BIRDING TOURS/ UNSW E&ER

The vast Nullarbor Plain (77,000 sq. mi/200,000 km^2) of s. Australia is home to the largest expanses of Chenopod Shrubland. © IAIN CAMPBELL, TROPICAL BIRDING TOURS/UNSW E&ERC

border near, and occasionally abutting, the southern coastline of Australia. Similar habitats exist over many aeolian (wind-blown) silt deposits, alluvial plains, and soils derived from underlying limestone parent material. This region is defined by the apparent scarcity of plant life; it is an open habitat where trees struggle to take hold, and its vegetation consists mainly of low, open shrubs, only 1–3 ft. (30–100 cm) tall, dominated by the chenopods Pearl Bluebush (*Maireana sedifolia*), Rosy Bluebush (*Maireana erioclada*), Black Bluebush (*Maireana pyramidata*), Berry Saltbush (*Atriplex semibaccata*), Toothed Saltbush (*Atriplex acutibractea*), and Bladder Saltbush (*Atriplex vesicaria*), especially on clay soils; and Black Bluebush (*Maireana pyramidata*) on very calcareous soils. The best-known and largest of all the chenopods is the extremely hardy Old Man Saltbush (*Atriplex nummularia*), which is even more halophytic (salt-tolerant) than the bluebushes (*Maireana* spp.) and also does well in highly alkaline conditions. It is the largest species of Australian saltbush, growing to 9 ft. (3 m) high and 12 ft. (4 m) wide, and looks very similar to salt cedar (*Tamarix*) stands of the African Sahel. Not all succulent-looking plants are chenopods, and visitors can be fooled by Bluebush Daisy (*Cratystylis conocephala*), which looks remarkably like the dominant bluebushes and is found throughout Chenopod Shrubland.

Between the chenopod shrubs, the ground can be bare for months, or in some cases years, supporting only a few perennial grasses such as Tall Feathergrass (*Austrostipa elegantissima*), but after rains, the red earth is covered with ephemeral forbs such as Sturt's Desert Pea (*Swainsona formosa*), Pygmy Sunray (*Rhodanthe pygmaea*), Showy Daisy-Bush (*Olearia pimeleoides*), and Poached-egg Daisy (*Myriocephalus stuartii*), which can form a thick blanket of yellows and whites.

A prominent subhabitat of Chenopod Shrubland is **Chenopod Woodland**, which although distinct in appearance from the treeless plains, has a near-identical animal and shrub-layer plant assemblage. It differs in that it has very scattered emergent trees, generally species such as Western Myall (*Acacia papyrocarpa*), Mulga (*Acacia aneura*), and Sugarwood (*Myoporum platycarpum*), which grow to 15 ft. (5 m) tall, and the occasional Kariku Sheoak (*Casuarina pauper*), which can reach 24 ft. (8 m) and at a distance resembles Desert Sheoak (*Allocasuarina decaisneana*) from the hotter regions of c. Australia. However, most spectacular are the areas with Western Myall, with its short trunk, rounded, dense, and often lopsided crown, drooping branches with phyllodes (expanded leaf stalks) rather than true leaves nearly touching the ground, and the underlying bluebushes, giving the impression of a landscape in East Africa.

Chenopod Woodland, as on this slope, is a conspicuous subhabitat with taller, emergent trees that provide an important component for nesting parrots and raptors. The ground cover is a mixture of true chenopods such as bluebushes and pseudo-chenopods such as Bluebush Daisy. © IAIN CAMPBELL, TROPICAL BIRDING TOURS/UNSW E&ERC

Chenopod Shrubland can be of both natural origin and anthropogenic, derived through the clearing of semiarid habitats such as SHRUBBY AND CHENOPOD MALLEE and GRASSY MULGA, and much of the Hay Plain that is now treeless shrublands could have originally been the e. Australian equivalent of the Western Myall–dominated Chenopod Woodland subhabitat. Within Chenopod Shrubland there is degradation through overgrazing, with some areas that were once dominated by Old Man Saltbush and Bladder Saltbush becoming replaced by less palatable (to the sheep at least) Giant Red Burr (*Sclerolaena tricuspis*), Galvanised Burr (*Sclerolaena birchii*), and Australian Boxthorn (*Lycium austral*). Other plants, such as Round-leaved Pigface (*Disphyma crassifolium*), found in the chenopod habitats of both Australia and South Africa, are becoming more common with rising soil salinity.

WILDLIFE: While the overall number of bird species is quite low in Chenopod Shrubland compared to more wooded habitats, it has far more species than other open terrain habitats such as GIBBER CHENOPODLAND and many more than TEMPERATE TUSSOCK GRASSLAND. A high percentage of the species present are specialists to this habitat, such as Thick-billed Grasswren, Nullarbor Quail-thrush, Cinnamon Quail-thrush, Inland Dotterel, Plains-wanderer, Chestnut-breasted Whiteface, Banded Whiteface, and Redthroat. Other ground birds include Banded Lapwing, Little Buttonquail, Australian Pratincole, Orange Chat, and Brown Songlark.

White-winged Fairywren, widespread across arid and semiarid s. Australia, is particularly common in Chenopod Shrubland. Singing Honeyeater and Spiny-cheeked Honeyeater eke out an existence on plants such as *Eremophila* spp., but honeyeaters are not well represented in this habitat because many of the chenopods are wind-pollinated and do not provide the vast amount of nectar provided by species of *Grevillea*, *Banksia*, or *Melaleuca* in other shrublands and heathlands.

In the Chenopod Woodland subhabitat, the widespread emergent trees provide important habitat for the obligate Naretha Bluebonnet, as well as nesting sites for Scarlet-chested and Mulga Parrots. Raptors also require trees for nesting, and although they hunt over the shrubland, it is in these trees that diurnal raptors such as Black-shouldered Kite, Brown Falcon, Nankeen Kestrel, and Wedge-tailed Eagle build nests, and in their hollows that the nocturnal Australian Owlet-nightjar roosts and nests. A suite of arboreal birds such as Black-faced Cuckooshrike, Black-faced Woodswallow, and Dusky Woodswallow also require the trees. Blossom nomads, typical of mallee habitats, are not common in Chenopod Woodland or other Chenopod Shrubland, as the tree density is not high enough to provide an adequate food source.

Orange Chat is a widespread Outback species that is especially abundant in Chenopod Shrubland. © BEN KNOOT

Left: **Lizards, such as this Central Bearded Dragon, are a conspicuous feature of Chenopod Shrubland, along with other dragon species like Nullarbor Earless, Gibber Earless, and Claypan Dragons.**
© JUN MATSUI, SICKLEBILL SAFARIS

Opposite: **Plains-wanderer is a rare enigmatic species (and monotypic bird family) that is a target for birders in Chenopod Shrubland.**
© SAM WOODS, TROPICAL BIRDING TOURS

Most of the mammals that exist here are small marsupial mice or bats. The larger mammals include Euro (a subspecies of Common Wallaroo), Red Kangaroo, and Dingo. Unfortunately, feral cats have thrived in this habitat and seriously depleted native mammal and reptile populations.

Lizards are the most abundant animals of Chenopod Shrubland. Amid the samphire (salt-tolerant plants in the family Amaranthaceae) and chenopod shrubs, expect to find lizards like Central Bearded Dragon (*Pogona vitticeps*), Saltbush Slender Bluetongue (*Cyclodomorphus venustus*), Claypan Dragon (*Ctenophorus salinarum*), and Nullarbor Earless Dragon (*Tympanocryptis houstoni*).

CONSERVATION: Despite being in an arid part of Australia, the chenopods here are an incredibly rich resource for sheep farming, and it has been said that Adelaide (South Australia) was essentially built on the back of sheep and saltbush. This is not without serious consequence, and when travelling through this part of Australia, it is difficult to find areas that have not been seriously overgrazed. Outside of the Nullarbor Plain, there are few vast expanses where this habitat is protected properly.

DISTRIBUTION: Chenopod Shrubland is found across arid and semiarid s. Australia, from the Yilgarn region of Western Australia to the Hay Plain of w. New South Wales. It occurs in small patches in Queensland and Northern Territory but is predominantly south of the central deserts. The biggest single block is the Nullarbor Plain, which is 77,000 sq. mi. (200,000 km^2) of seeming emptiness (with just a few hundred people) abutting the Great Australian Bight.

The Chenopod Woodland subhabitat is found scattered through sw. New South Wales and within the Nullarbor Plain and exists as a massive arc around the north and west of the plain, where it forms the boundary between Chenopod Shrubland and the GRASSY MULGA woodlands of Western Australia and South Australia.

WHERE TO SEE: CHENOPOD SHRUBLAND—Booroorban, New South Wales, Australia; Eucla, Western Australia; Nullarbor Roadhouse, South Australia. CHENOPOD WOODLAND—Madura, Western Australia; between Hay and Deniliquin, New South Wales, Australia.

Au2E GIBBER CHENOPODLAND

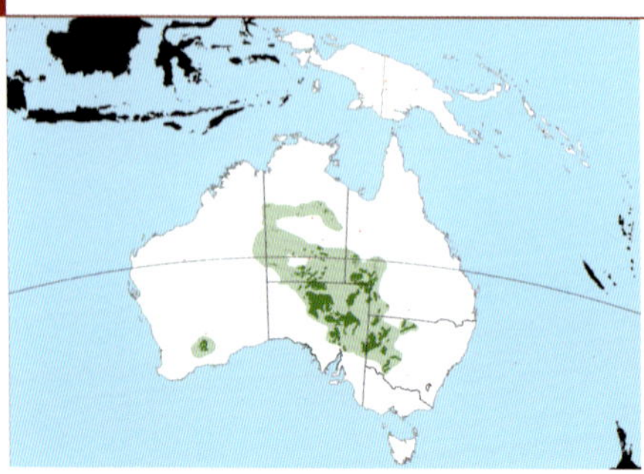

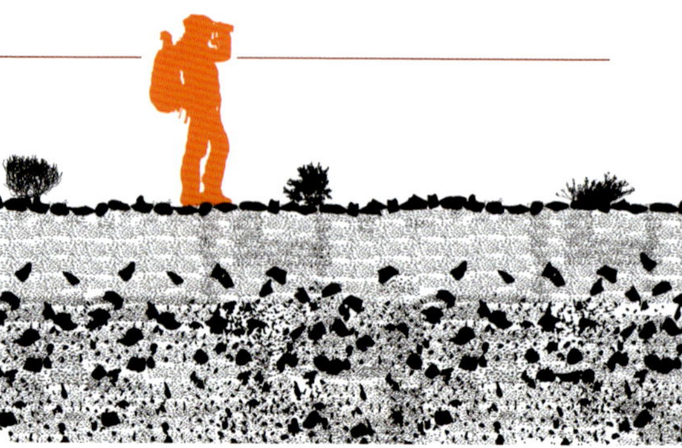

IN A NUTSHELL: An extremely sparse, seemingly barren, rocky desert landscape that springs to life after very intermittent rains. **Global Habitat Affinities:** SAHARAN REG DESERT; CENTRAL MIDDLE EASTERN REG DESERT. **Continental Habitat Affinities:** CHENOPOD SHRUBLAND. **Species Overlap:** ROCKY SPINIFEX DESERT; DUNE SPINIFEX DESERT; CHENOPOD SHRUBLAND. **Full Bird Assemblage:** habitatsoftheworld.org/Au2E.

DESCRIPTION: Gibber Chenopodland is both a landform and a habitat type, formed over desert pavement, the Australian equivalent of SAHARAN REG DESERT of Africa. These pavements form in areas where deflation from winds has eroded most of the finer sands and silts, winnowing small pebbles and cobbles (gibbers) so that they are left covering the ground, protecting the underlying material from erosion. Hypersaline waters in the desert transport calcium and silica and can deposit a patina (thin film) of silica mixed with iron oxides (magnetite and hematite) on the gibbers, which can become varnished with silica, giving them a shiny, smooth texture approaching a glassy black sheen.

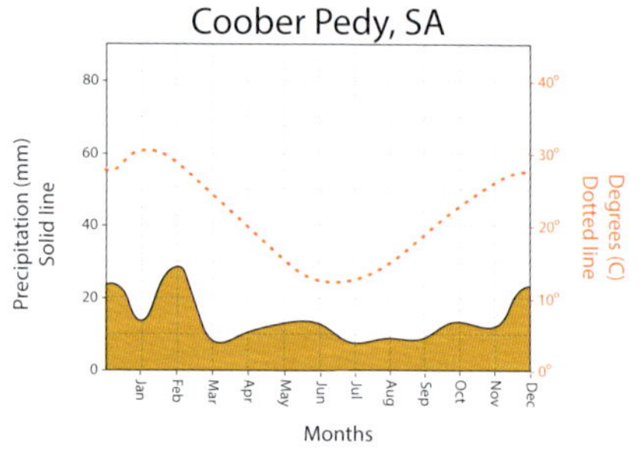

In some places, such as the Strzelecki Track, it is possible to see no trees or large shrubs and, in dry periods, very few forbs or grasses. This habitat can appear to be one of the most hostile places on the planet, with shimmering light reflecting from the polished gibbers. The rare permanent trees are dominated by desert species such as Bastard Mulga (*Acacia sibirica*), Mulga (*Acacia aneura*), and Kariku Sheoak (*Casuarina pauper*), growing as stunted bushes and trees less than 12 ft. (4 m) tall, with taller Coolabah (*Eucalyptus coolabah*) and River Red Gum (*Eucalyptus camaldulensis*) trees indicating an inland drainage system. After rains, the whole impression changes as the area bursts into life: chenopods such as Pearl Bluebush (*Maireana sedifolia*), Low Bluebush (*Maireana astrotricha*), Bladder Saltbush (*Atriplex vesicaria*), Pop Saltbush (*Atriplex holocarpa*), and Hedge Saltbush (*Rhagodia spinescens*) thicken and grow to 3 ft. (1 m) tall, and perennial grasses such as Feathertop Wiregrass (*Aristida latifolia*) and Roebourne Plains Grass (*Eragrostis xerophila*) grow rapidly. In the 'good' (wet) years, ephemeral grasses such as Pretty Wanderrie Grass (*Eriachne pulchella*) can form blankets that give the impression of a short desert grassland of Asia, and in other areas forbs such as Common White Sunray (*Rhodanthe floribunda*) and Erect Yellowheads (*Gnephosis arachnoidea*) rapidly grow and bloom to give the impression of ASIAN FLOWER STEPPE of w. Asia.

Gibber Chenopodland appears barren and lifeless, but it can erupt with a flush of birdlife following heavy rains. Very strong winds can whip up sandstorms (making doing a podcast near impossible). © GABRIEL CAMPBELL, TROPICAL BIRDING TOURS

Small, burnt red pebbles and cobbles (gibber) with a distinctive, varnished appearance are characteristic of the desert floor of Gibber Chenopodland. They accumulate on the surface through wind erosion of the surrounding fine sands and silts. Once enough have accumulated, they form a protective cap stopping further erosion. © IAIN CAMPBELL, TROPICAL BIRDING TOURS/UNSW E&ERC

Gibberbird is an indicator species for Gibber Chenopodland, although it is never abundant and is very thinly distributed within these vast plains. © BEN KNOOT

WILDLIFE: Those birds that occur are special species highly restricted to gibber desert habitats, including Gibberbird and Inland Dotterel. Chenopod and samphire specialists include Chestnut-breasted Whiteface, Orange Chat, Plains-wanderer, and White-fronted Chat. Where the chenopods are low, widely spaced, and close to spinifex, the Night Parrot can use this habitat. Cinnamon Quail-thrush is another species found in Gibber Chenopodland, especially where there are small patches of spinifex (*Triodia*) in the mix of chenopods

Most of the mammals that exist here are small marsupial mice or bats. The larger mammals are the Euro (a subspecies of Common Wallaroo), Red Kangaroo, and Dingo. Smaller mammals living here include Kultarr, Long-haired Rat, and various hopping mice (*Notomys* spp.).

Because these shrublands appear to support few birds and mammals, lizards are the most abundant vertebrates. Amid the samphire and chenopod shrubs, expect to find lizards like the Sand Goanna (*Varanus gouldii*), Eastern Tree Dtella (*Gehyra versicolor*), Saltbush Slender Bluetongue (*Cyclodomorphus venustus*), Claypan Dragon (*Ctenophorus salinarum*), and Nullarbor Earless Dragon (*Tympanocryptis houstoni*). In the gibber plains even more specialised lizards include the Gibber Gecko (*Lucasium byrnei*), Gibber Dragon (*Ctenophorus gibba*), Gibber Earless Dragon (*Tympanocryptis intima*), and the bizarre looking Goldfields Pebble Dragon (*Tympanocryptis pseudopsephos*). Snakes include the venomous Shield-snouted Brown Snake (*Pseudonaja aspidorhyncha*).

CONSERVATION: Although this landscape can look untouched by modern humans, feral cats have thrived in this habitat and seriously depleted native mammal and reptile populations. Farming is very limited, but massive pastural leases are held, and it is possible to see large flocks of sheep in what initially looks completely barren. Much of the grazing is on ephemeral growth after rare rains, so the sheep have to be moved around frequently to find viable livestock fodder.

DISTRIBUTION: Gibber Chenopodland occurs from e. Western Australia to nw. New South Wales and is most prevalent in n. South Australia. It is the main habitat of the Sturt Stony Desert (New South Wales) and Gibson Desert (Western Australia). It also occurs along the Strzelecki (South Australia) and Birdsville (Queensland–South Australia) Tracks; around Coober Pedy (South Australia); and in far sw. Queensland.

WHERE TO SEE: Coober Pedy, South Australia; Mungeranie, South Australia; Birdsville, Queensland, Australia.

Inland Dotterel is another indicator species for Gibber Chenopodland; it is very inconspicuous as it is most active after nightfall. © SAM WOODS, TROPICAL BIRDING TOURS

Au2F SAMPHIRE FLAT

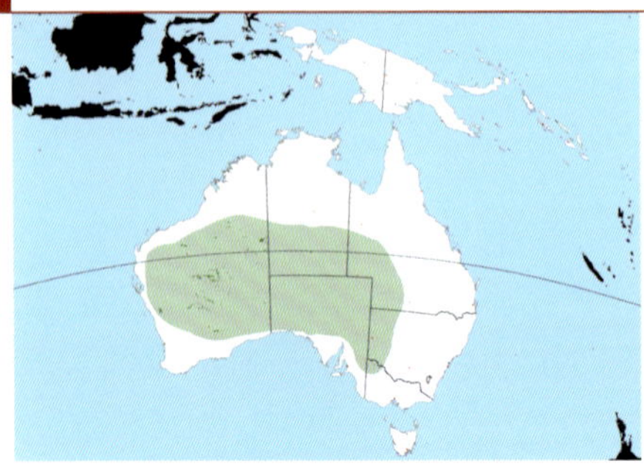

IN A NUTSHELL: A very low, single-layer vegetation dominated by salt-tolerant samphire plants. **Global Habitat Affinities:** NORTH AMERICAN SAGEBRUSH SHRUBLAND; CASPIAN WORMWOOD DESERT. **Continental Habitat Affinities:** SALT PAN. **Species Overlap:** SALT PAN. **Full Bird Assemblage:** habitatsoftheworld.org/Au2F.

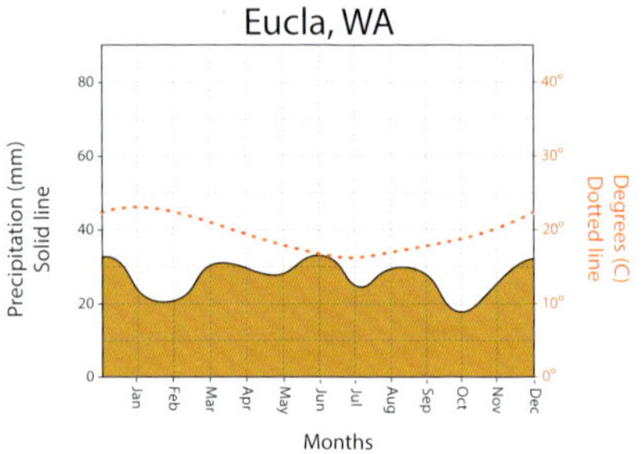

DESCRIPTION: Samphire Flat is a distinctive and ecologically important habitat type in Australia. Samphires are halophytes (salt-tolerant plants) in the family Amaranthaceae with jointed stems and small scale-like leaves. They vary in colour from green to reddish and have several adaptations allowing them to survive in high-salinity environments, such as succulent leaves and stems that store water and excrete excess salt. Samphires play an important role in the ecosystem by helping to stabilise soil, reduce erosion, and provide habitat for wildlife. The diversity of environments in which Samphire Flat is found includes lagoons, clay pans, gypsum lakes, and semi-seasonal wetlands. These habitats occur in regions with disorganised drainage systems, where water flows into salt lakes, creating unique ecological conditions. These areas can range from being seasonally inundated to filling only after extreme rainfall events. The variable conditions contribute to the distinctive halophytic plant community. The samphires found on inland Samphire Flat, primarily in the genus *Tecticornia*, flourish in the challenging conditions found on the margins of salt lakes and saline flats. Some of the more prevalent species include Mungily (*Tecticornia indica*), Grey Samphire (*Tecticornia halocnemoides*), and *Tecticornia disarticulata*.

Samphire plants typically cover up to 30% of Samphire Flat habitat. This vegetation is often found in zones where only the most salt-tolerant plants can survive. Surrounding the samphires, a zone of saltbushes (*Atriplex*, *Maireana*, and *Frankenia* spp.) usually forms a fringe, creating a layered and complex plant community. Some other notable species associated with Samphire Flat include Round-leaved Pigface (*Disphyma crassifolium*), *Sclerolaena deserticola*, and Shrubby Twinleaf (*Roepera aurantiaca*); these plants are also adapted to the saline and often inundated conditions of the habitat. Lake Carnegie (Western Australia) features a rich halophyte community with species such as Black Bluebush (*Maireana pyramidata*) and various annuals. Lake Austin is a gypsum-rich lake south of Cue (Western Australia), characterised by a mosaic of saltbush, bluebush, and samphire vegetation and also home to Helms' Mallow (*Lawrencia helmsii*) of the Malvaceae family.

Samphire Flat is characterised by a single layer of stunted vegetation comprising many salt-tolerant plants that can cope with the highly saline environment. © SHANE KENNEDY, TROPICAL BIRDING TOURS

Coastal Samphire Flat subhabitat and inland Samphire Flat differs in several ways due to the varying conditions and effects they experience. Inland Samphire Flat often forms around salt lakes and ephemeral water bodies where salinity levels can fluctuate dramatically, sometimes becoming extremely saline. Coastal Samphire Flat is influenced by tidal saltwater, leading to more stable salinity levels, and typically has more consistent water availability due to tides, whereas inland flats rely on irregular rainfall and water flows, making them more variable and sometimes dry for extended periods. Coastal areas generally have milder climates, influenced by the ocean, with less temperature variation. Inland areas can experience more extreme temperatures, both hot and cold, and more erratic weather patterns. Coastal Samphire Flat is often more impacted by human activities such as development, tourism, and pollution. While both types of flats support halophytic plants, the species composition can differ. Coastal flats may have a greater diversity of marine-influenced vegetation, whereas inland flats might have species adapted to harsher, more arid conditions. Some plant species typical of Coastal Samphire Flat include Blackseed Glasswort (*Tecticornia pergranulata*), Beaded Samphire (*Salicornia quinqueflora*), and Austral Seablite (*Suaeda australis*), which all thrive with the more consistent salinity and water availability provided by tidal environments.

WILDLIFE: Samphire Flat appears to support few birds, although the critically endangered nocturnal Night Parrot feeds on Samphire Flats near spinifex in c. Australia, and this may be an extremely important habitat for the species. Orange Chat shows some preference for this habitat inland, and Crimson Chat might also be seen. Several raptors can be found in these areas, and

Fat-tailed Dunnart is a nocturnal, mouse-like marsupial that occupies this habitat.
© CHARLEY HESSE, TROPICAL BIRDING TOURS

Brown Falcon, Nankeen Kestrel, and even Swamp and Spotted Harriers may fly over it. Of course you may see an Emu passing through, or some more common open-country species such as Crested Pigeon, Banded Lapwing, Zebra Finch, or Australian Pipit. Mammal-wise, you might see Red Kangaroo, the small nocturnal Fat-tailed Dunnart, or a Dingo if you are lucky.

Lizards are probably the most numerous vertebrates, and some species present in this habitat may include Claypan Dragon (*Ctenophorus salinarum*), Crested Bicycle-Dragon (*Ctenophorus cristatus*), Lozenge-marked Dragon (*Ctenophorus scutulatus*), Midline Knob-tailed Gecko (*Nephrurus vertebralis*), and Common Desert Ctenotus (*Ctenotus leonhardii*).

Coastal Samphire Flat harbours a few more interesting bird species than inland flats. White-fronted Chat has a fairly strong association with this habitat, as does the critically endangered Orange-bellied Parrot on its wintering grounds. Blue-winged Parrot makes some use of the habitat in cold coastal areas such as in Tasmania.

CONSERVATION: Although this habitat does not face threats from clearing, it is susceptible to changes in the hydrology of the ephemeral creeks that drain into it. A more significant recent threat is the discovery that many samphire flats overlie mineral deposits such as lithium and potash. This is regarded as a low-value habitat, and there is little political will to place better environmental protections for it.

DISTRIBUTION: Samphire associations cover huge areas of Western Australia, predominantly in the Murchison and Gascoyne bioregions, with significant presence in the Great Sandy Desert, Carnarvon, and several other regions. The Murchison bioregion, for instance, hosts the largest area of salt lakes in Western Australia, including Lake Barlee, Lake Moore, and Lake Ballard.

Above: **Samphire Flats have a relatively depauperate birdlife. Most of the bird species that occur are widespread (none are restricted to it) and found in a variety of habitats, like this Banded Lapwing.** © SAM WOODS, TROPICAL BIRDING TOURS

Below: **While none of them are restricted to Samphire Flat, a number of chat species occur, such as this White-fronted Chat as well as Crimson and Orange Chats.** © BEN KNOOT

The **Coastal Samphire Flat** subhabitat occurs all around Australia and islands to the north. In the tropics, it is almost always on the inside edge of mangroves and rarely forms areas large enough for a different animal assemblage, so is used by the same animals as surrounding grasslands and mangroves. The habitat becomes much more common in temperate parts of Australia, where it is the dominant estuarine habitat and so is found on most temperate coastlines, in most bays with TIDAL MUDFLATS, and other areas away from rocky shorelines.

WHERE TO SEE: SAMPHIRE FLAT—Lake Ballard, Lake Austin, and Lake Barlee, Western Australia. COASTAL SAMPHIRE FLAT—Boondall Wetlands near Brisbane, Queensland, Australia; Botany Bay, near Sydney, New South Wales, Australia; Bruny Island, Tasmania; Coorong National Park, South Australia.

Australasian Humid Forests Dendrogram (Biome 4)

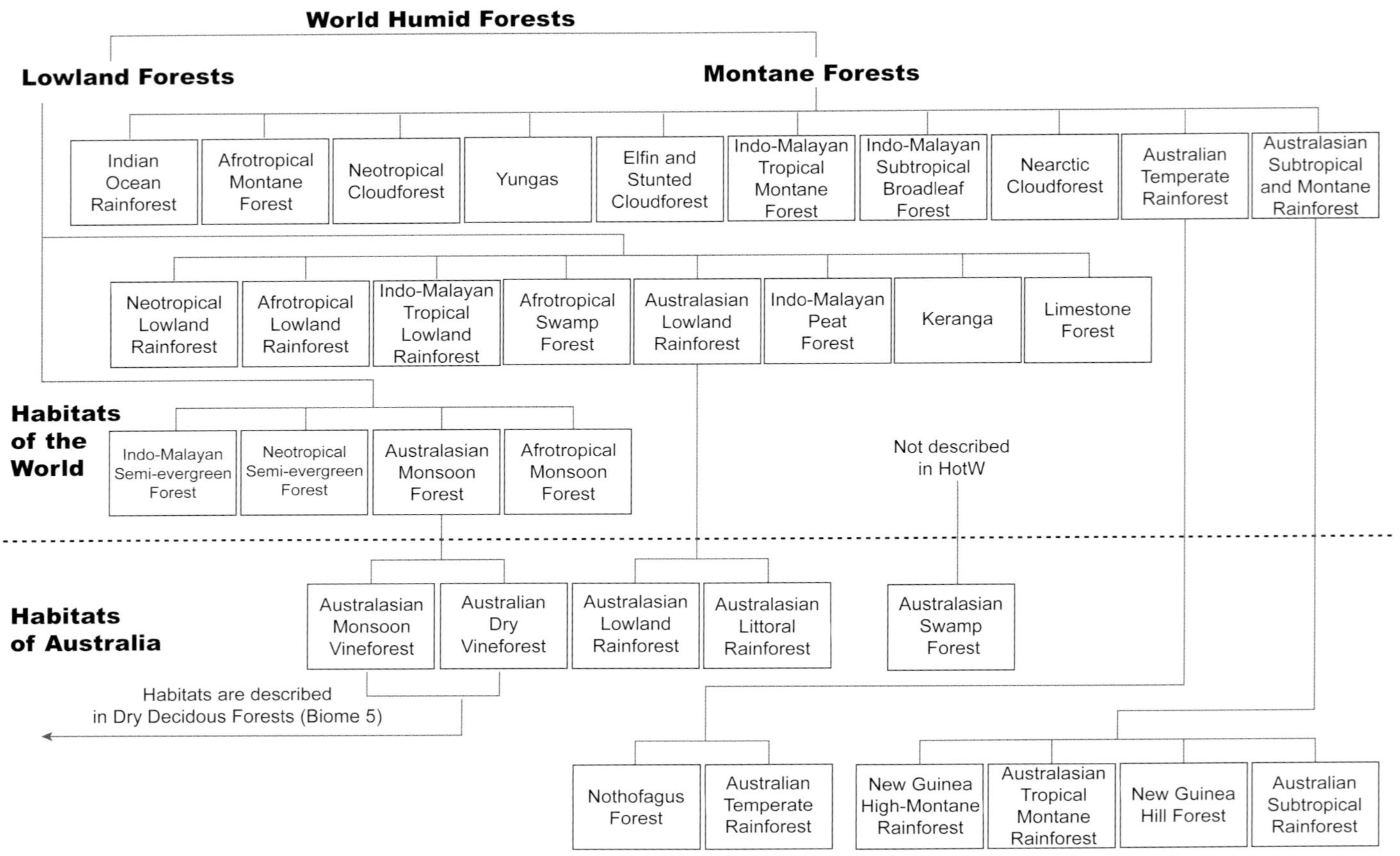

World Humid Forests

Lowland Forests

Montane Forests

Indian Ocean Rainforest
Afrotropical Montane Forest
Neotropical Cloudforest
Yungas
Elfin and Stunted Cloudforest
Indo-Malayan Tropical Montane Forest
Indo-Malayan Subtropical Broadleaf Forest
Nearctic Cloudforest
Australian Temperate Rainforest
Australasian Subtropical and Montane Rainforest

Neotropical Lowland Rainforest
Afrotropical Lowland Rainforest
Indo-Malayan Tropical Lowland Rainforest
Afrotropical Swamp Forest
Australasian Lowland Rainforest
Indo-Malayan Peat Forest
Keranga
Limestone Forest

Habitats of the World

Indo-Malayan Semi-evergreen Forest
Neotropical Semi-evergreen Forest
Australasian Monsoon Forest
Afrotropical Monsoon Forest

Not described in HotW

Habitats of Australia

Australasian Monsoon Vineforest
Australian Dry Vineforest
Australasian Lowland Rainforest
Australasian Littoral Rainforest
Australasian Swamp Forest

Habitats are described in Dry Decidous Forests (Biome 5)

Nothofagus Forest
Australian Temperate Rainforest
New Guinea High-Montane Rainforest
Australasian Tropical Montane Rainforest
New Guinea Hill Forest
Australian Subtropical Rainforest

HUMID BROADLEAF FORESTS

Au4A AUSTRALASIAN LOWLAND RAINFOREST

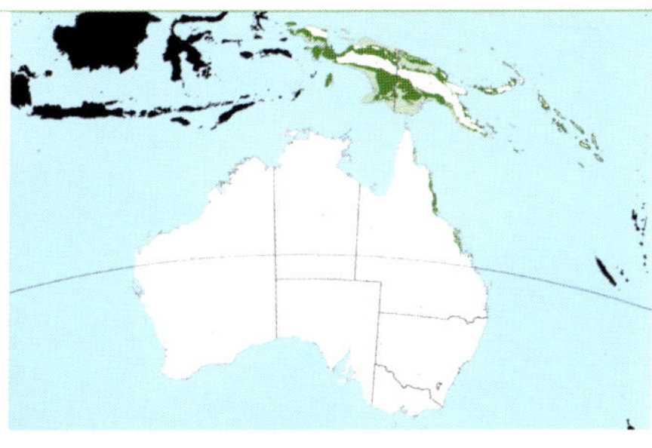

IN A NUTSHELL: Tall, very humid forests found at low elevations. **Global Habitat Affinities:** AMAZON TERRAFIRMA; ASIAN LOWLAND TROPICAL RAINFOREST; AFROTROPICAL LOWLAND RAINFOREST. **Continental Habitat Affinities:** SUBTROPICAL RAINFOREST. **Species Overlap:** SUBTROPICAL RAINFOREST; SWAMP FOREST. **Full Bird Assemblage:** habitatsoftheworld.org/Au4A.

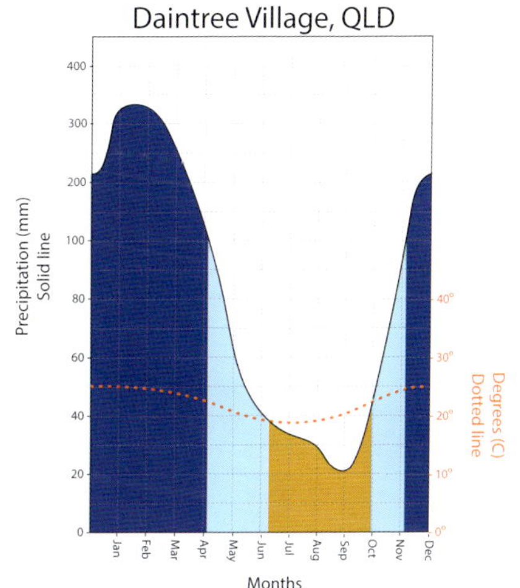

DESCRIPTION: Australasian Lowland Rainforest is the dominant vegetation type in low-lying, wet (but not submerged) tropical environments of New Guinea, surrounding islands, and ne. Australia. It occurs from sea level to about 2000 ft. (600 m) in areas with high annual rainfall of 120+ in. (1300+ mm). However, this habitat extends over a wide latitudinal range, occurring from hot equatorial climates with year-round rainfall (Köppen **Af**) to tropical monsoonal/savanna climates with dry winters and hot, very wet summers (**Am/Awa**).

Much of Australasian Lowland Rainforest occurs more than 1.2 mi. (2 km) from the coast, is greatly reduced by past clearance, and is now categorised as endangered by the Australian federal government. It is characterised by a mega-diverse plant community comprising a large variety of evergreen trees that form a thick canopy (70%+ canopy cover), which blocks out the sun, resulting in a relatively open understorey. The forest canopy here is high, at around 130 ft. (40 m). In light gaps created by treefalls or landslides, there are massive bursts of seedlings of larger trees and early successional trees. These plants compete

Lowland Rainforest has a tall canopy reaching around 130 ft. (40 m).
© IAIN CAMPBELL, TROPICAL BIRDING TOURS/UNSW E&ERC

Australasian Lowland Rainforest occurs in wet, tropical environments below 1000 ft. (300 m) elevation. The high diversity of tree species gives it an unkempt, messy appearance at both ground and canopy level. © IAIN CAMPBELL, TROPICAL BIRDING TOURS/UNSW E&ERC

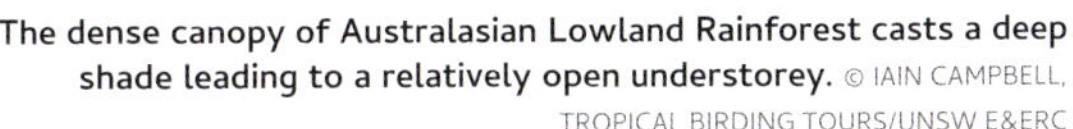

The dense canopy of Australasian Lowland Rainforest casts a deep shade leading to a relatively open understorey. © IAIN CAMPBELL, TROPICAL BIRDING TOURS/UNSW E&ERC

for the new available light and form a different microenvironment that has a very thick undergrowth, until one or two trees win the battle and smother out the others. Stinging trees (*Dendrocnide* spp.) are quite common in such areas. Many trees have buttressed roots, and there is a great variety of vines and rattans but low abundance of *Eucalyptus*, *Melaleuca*, and *Casuarina* spp. Australasian Lowland Rainforest differs from similar habitats in Africa (AFROTROPICAL LOWLAND RAINFOREST) and Asia (ASIAN LOWLAND TROPICAL RAINFOREST) in having figs and sclerophyllous plants (often eucalypts) present within the canopy. It further varies from Asian rainforest in that dipterocarps (Dipterocarpaceae) are not the dominant plant family. The Lowland Rainforests of New Guinea and ne. Australia are remnants of forests that were once more widespread during pluvial periods, when the climate was much wetter. In the lowlands it intergrades with LITTORAL RAINFOREST in a few areas, though most of this habitat is now destroyed.

WILDLIFE: Although Australasian Lowland Rainforest appears similar to ASIAN LOWLAND TROPICAL RAINFOREST, the bird assemblages are very different. Unlike the se. Asian forests, Australasian Lowland Rainforest has only one hornbill species, Blyth's Hornbill, in New Guinea and the Solomons. It also lacks woodpeckers, barbets, and bulbuls; instead, the ecological niche is filled by many large parrot and pigeon species. The paradise-kingfishers fill the niche taken by forest-dwelling

Above: **Southern Cassowary is one of the most iconic species of Lowland Rainforest in the Wet Tropics of ne. Australia. It also inhabits this habitat in New Guinea, though is much harder to see there.** © PABLO CERVANTES, TROPICAL BIRDING TOURS

kingfishers in Asia. Other groups of birds typical of this Australasian forest type are birds-of-paradise, bowerbirds, fig-parrots, fruit-doves, and ground birds like jewel-babblers and pittas, which occupy a similar niche to the Malaysian Rail-babbler in se. Asia or the *Picathartes* rockfowl in Africa.

This habitat is much more extensive in New Guinea, where the many mountain ranges separate forest blocks and bird species, and the New Guinean Lowland Rainforest thus supports many more bird species than its Australian counterpart. Nonetheless, the lowland forests of n. Australia and s. New Guinea share many species, such as Southern Cassowary, Buff-breasted Paradise-Kingfisher, Papuan Pitta, Papuan Eclectus, Palm Cockatoo, White-faced Robin, Frill-necked Monarch, and Magnificent Riflebird.

Australasia does not have native primates (or ungulates), so the rainforest canopy here is populated by marsupials such as possums, spotted cuscuses (*Spilocuscus* spp.), and tree-kangaroos, as well as a large number of fruit bats and smaller bats. The forest-floor niche is dominated by pademelons, bandicoots, and native rodents such as White-

White-faced Robin is usually encountered clasped to the side of a vertical trunk, low to the ground, within the understorey of Lowland Rainforest. © IAIN CAMPBELL, TROPICAL BIRDING TOURS/UNSW E&ERC

Above: **Frill-necked Monarch forages within Lowland Rainforest along tree trunks, in the manner of a nuthatch or sittella. It is restricted to the Cape York Peninsula of n. Queensland.** © IAIN CAMPBELL, TROPICAL BIRDING TOURS/UNSW E&ERC

tailed Giant Rat. Australia's smallest kangaroo, the diurnal Musky Rat-Kangaroo occurs here. A night walk through Lowland Rainforest of ne. Australia might reveal Red-legged Pademelon and bandicoots scurrying through the undergrowth; Black-and white Striped Possum, Green Ringtail Possum, and enigmatic Bennett's and Lumholtz's Tree-Kangaroos in the canopy; and Spectacled and Little Red Flying Foxes and Lesser Long-tongued Nectar Bat flapping around it. New Guinean Quoll, though smaller than a domestic

The far-carrying, high-pitched, two-note whistles of Magnificent Riflebird are a characteristic sound of the Lowland Rainforest on the Cape York Peninsula of ne. Australia and in New Guinea. © IAIN CAMPBELL, TROPICAL BIRDING TOURS/ UNSW E&ERC

Above: **Common Spotted Cuscus is a largely nocturnal, rainforest-dwelling marsupial confined to far ne. Australia and New Guinea.** © JUN MATSUI, SICKLEBILL SAFARIS

cat, is the largest modern mammal predator of these forests in New Guinea. The extraordinary, largely arboreal tree-kangaroos, which have to be seen to be believed, with their thick tails for balance and strong forearms for grip, reach their highest diversity in New Guinea. The eight species in New Guinean Lowland Rainforest are the largest of the mammals found in this habitat.

Herps are well represented in Australasian Lowland Rainforest, where species such as White-lipped Tree Frog (*Nyctimystes infrafrenatus*), Orange-thighed Tree Frog

Green Ringtail Possum is a nocturnal mammal restricted to ne. Queensland, where it occurs in several habitats, including Lowland Rainforest. © SAM WOODS, TROPICAL BIRDING TOURS

(*Ranoidea xanthomera*), and Green-eyed Tree Frog (*Ranoidea serrata*) occur in the canopy. Terrestrial frogs include Northern Barred Frog (*Mixophyes schevilli*), Australian Wood Frog (*Papurana daemeli*), and Fry's Whistling Frog (*Austrochaperina fryi*). Snakes typical of this environment include Southern Green Tree Python (*Morelia viridis*), Australian Scrub Python (*Simalia kinghorni*), and a variety of tree snakes. Some geckos are much more common in rainforest environments than in surrounding eucalypt forests, including Northern Velvet Gecko (*Oedura castelnaui*) and Northern Leaf-tailed Gecko (*Saltuarius cornutus*). Unfortunately, the introduced Cane Toad (*Rhinella marina*) has had a massive impact on this environment in Australia and has devastated populations of the less competitive terrestrial frogs.

Endemism: Because the islands north of Australia are so mountainous, they harbour many distinct areas of endemism—New Guinea alone has over 430 endemic birds, and the Solomon Islands have over 100. The main areas of this habitat are the north and south sides of the main mountain range in New Guinea and surrounding islands. The isolated rainforests of the ne. Australian wet tropics in far n. Queensland and Cape York are also areas of endemism.

Southern Green Tree Python is an arboreal snake found within Lowland Rainforest on the Cape York Peninsula of Australia and on the island of New Guinea.

© IAIN CAMPBELL, TROPICAL BIRDING TOURS/UNSW E&ERC

CONSERVATION: North of Australia, few large areas of Lowland Rainforest are protected by national parks, but the human population is still small in much of this region. Clearing by logging companies and for African Oil Palm plantations poses the greatest threat to these habitats north of Australia. In Australia, the vast majority of this habitat was cleared many decades ago, and the remaining tracts are well protected by the national parks system. In the Iron Range on the Cape York Peninsula (Queensland), large tracts of Lowland Rainforest remain untouched and feel truly wild. Here you can look for birds whose Australian range is limited to tropical Lowland Rainforest, such as Palm Cockatoo, Magnificent Riflebird, White-faced Robin, Northern Scrub-Robin, and Green-backed Honeyeater.

DISTRIBUTION: Tropical rainforest is the dominant lowland habitat of New Guinea, where large areas of it still exist, and New Britain, New Ireland, Bougainville, and most of the Solomon Islands. In Australia it occurs in three areas of Queensland separated by savanna habitat—small areas of Cape York Peninsula; the Wet Tropics, from Cooktown to Townsville; and an outlier near Mackay in c. Queensland.

WHERE TO SEE: Daintree National Park, Queensland, Australia; Kiunga, Papua New Guinea; Nimbokrang, Indonesian New Guinea.

Au4B AUSTRALIAN SUBTROPICAL RAINFOREST

IN A NUTSHELL: Closed-canopy humid forest with many epiphytes and extensive understorey. **Global Habitat Affinities:** ANDEAN CLOUDFOREST; AFRICAN MOIST MONTANE FOREST. **Continental Habitat Affinities:** TROPICAL MONTANE RAINFOREST; TEMPERATE RAINFOREST. **Species Overlap:** LOWLAND RAINFOREST; TEMPERATE RAINFOREST; RAINFOREST WET SCLEROPHYLL FOREST. **Full Bird Assemblage:** habitatsoftheworld.org/Au4B.

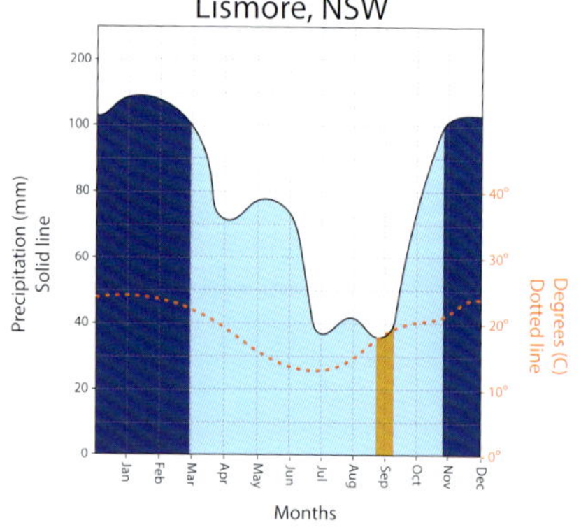

DESCRIPTION: The subtropical forests of Australia, akin to the cloudforests of Africa and South America, are lush and full of epiphytes. They thrive in the cooler and more subtropical parts of e. Australia, from the lowlands to the mountain ranges, and in this regard differ from the cloudforests on other continents, which grow only at higher elevations. The canopies of this evergreen forest are lower than those of the rainforest; subtropical trees rarely grow taller than 100 ft. (33 m) in the lowlands and 80 ft. (25 m) in the highlands, while a LOWLAND RAINFOREST canopy can reach 130 ft. (40 m) high.

In the lowlands, the Subtropical Rainforest canopy is dominated by emergent trees such as Moreton Bay Fig (*Ficus macrophylla*) and canopy species such as White Booyong (*Argyrodendron trifoliolatum*), Giant Water Gum (*Syzygium francisii*), Australian Red Cedar (*Toona ciliata*), Black Bean (*Castanospermum australe*), Native Tamarind (*Diploglottis australis*), White Walnut (*Cryptocarya obovata*), Plum Pine (*Podocarpus elatus*), and Blush Walnut (*Beilschmiedia obtusifolia*). The understorey is dominated by Australian Olive (*Olea paniculata*), Rose Marara (*Pseudoweinmannia lachnocarpa*), and Bolly Gum (*Neolitsea dealbata*). Bangalow Palm (*Archontophoenix cunninghamiana*) is very obvious, especially in forest edges and light gaps.

The forest structure changes slightly above 2000 ft. (600 m), but the wildlife assemblage remains the same at all elevations, so we treat Subtropical Rainforest as one habitat. Here in the ranges, where the slopes can be steep, there are many landslides, and the forest is therefore disjointed, with trees of different ages and heights forming a non-contiguous canopy that lets

The canopy of Subtropical Rainforest reaches only 80 ft. (25 m) tall in the highlands, lower than that of Lowland Rainforest. © IAIN CAMPBELL, TROPICAL BIRDING TOURS/UNSW E&ERC

far more light hit the understorey than in lowland Subtropical Rainforest. Thus, the understorey growth tends to be much thicker, making the upland forest harder to navigate than the lowland forest. The main tree mix here has some very obvious species, such as the emergent conifers Bunya Pine (*Araucaria bidwillii*) and Hoop Pine (*Araucaria cunninghamii*). The angiosperms in the canopy include Black Booyong (*Argyrodendron actinophyllum*), Illawarra Flame Tree (*Brachychiton*

Subtropical Rainforest has a dense, well-vegetated understorey, sometimes making it harder to walk through than Lowland Rainforest, where the ground cover is often more open. © IAIN CAMPBELL, TROPICAL BIRDING TOURS/UNSW E&ERC

acerifolius), Giant Stinging Tree (*Dendrocnide excelsa*) (a tree to be avoided), White Quandong (*Elaeocarpus kirtonii*), Rosewood (*Dysoxylum fraserianum*), Australian Red Cedar, White Beefwood (*Orites excelsus*), and Yellow Carabeen (*Sloanea woollsii*). The understorey has smaller trees, such as Brush Bloodwood (*Baloghia inophylla*), but it is dominated by palms, including Bangalow Palm, Walking Stick Palm (*Linospadix monostachyos*), Alexandra Palm (*Archontophoenix alexandrae*), and Cabbage-tree Palm (*Livistona australis*). Vines are not as common as in Lowland Rainforest, but Wait-a-While (*Calamus muelleri*) is very prevalent; a climbing palm with long, spiny stems, it can reach up to 100 ft. (30 m) in length and extend from the understorey into the subcanopy.

There is a strong relationship between the Subtropical Rainforest and the underlying rock, and much of this habitat is located on basalt, especially basalts in the caldera of the huge shield volcano Mt. Warning (Wollumbin) in New South Wales. We do risk overstating the importance of this relationship, because these rainforests can grow on soils much more depauperate in nutrients than basalts, such as granites, if rainfall is increased enough. A more logical way of expressing the relationship is that in the lowlands of this region, the rainforest mainly occurs on residual soils over basalt and on nutrient-rich alluvial plains, and in the uplands it mainly occurs in areas with significant orographic rainfall, which coincidently often have a basaltic bedrock. These forests form in a warm, humid subtropical climate (Köppen **Cfa**) with hot summers, high rainfall, and no dry season. The average maximum temperatures range from 77 to 86°F (25–30°C), although winter nights can get chilly, as winter minimums average 41–50°F (5–10°C). Rainfall typically ranges from 59 to 79 in. (1500–2000 mm), with the highest rainfall occurring during the summer through most of this habitat, although the difference between summer and winter rainfall totals varies from strong in the north of the range to negligible in the south.

WILDLIFE: The birds found in Subtropical Rainforest that are not expected in TEMPERATE RAINFOREST or LOWLAND RAINFOREST include Marbled Frogmouth (Plumed subsp.), Regent Bowerbird, Australian Logrunner, Albert's Lyrebird, Green Catbird, and Paradise Riflebird. The

The male Regent Bowerbird is one of the most iconic birds of Subtropical Rainforest and an indicator species for the habitat. © PABLO CERVANTES, TROPICAL BIRDING TOURS

Australian Logrunner is a vocal inhabitant of Subtropical Rainforest, most often seen scampering on rocks or logs and foraging on the shady forest floor.

© IAIN CAMPBELL, TROPICAL BIRDING TOURS/UNSW E&ERC

bird assemblage contains many species that are also found in tropical LOWLAND RAINFOREST such as the ground-dwelling and very confiding Australian Brushturkey, and pigeons such as White-headed Pigeon, Superb Fruit-Dove, Brown Cuckoo-Dove, Pacific Emerald Dove, Wompoo Fruit-Dove, Rose-crowned Fruit-Dove, and Topknot Pigeon. Noisy Pitta can be very obvious when calling in spring with its almost constant *Walk-to-work* whistle. Subcanopy species that also occur in LOWLAND RAINFOREST include Rufous Shrikethrush, Australian Rufous Fantail, Black-faced Monarch, Australian Spectacled Monarch, and Pale-yellow Robin, a species that follows birders along the Border Track of Lamington National Park in Queensland.

Birds typical of Subtropical Rainforest yet also occurring in TEMPERATE RAINFOREST include Wonga Pigeon, Superb Fairywren, Eastern Spinebill, White-browed Scrubwren, Rose Robin, Eastern Yellow Robin, Bassian Thrush, and Russet-tailed Thrush.

Mammals abound in Subtropical Rainforest. The small kangaroos Red-necked Pademelon and Red-legged Pademelon are visible during the day, but a night walk in Lamington National Park could yield Common Ringtail Possum, Krefft's Glider, Short-eared Brushtail Possum, Long-nosed Bandicoot, the small marsupial mouse Brown Antechinus, as well as the rodents Fawn-footed Melomys, Australian Swamp Rat, and Australian Bush Rat. Reptiles typical of this habitat include the lizards Land Mullet (*Bellatorias major*), Southern Angle-Headed Dragon (*Lophosaurus spinipes*), Southern Leaf-tailed Gecko (*Saltuarius swaini*), and Orange-tailed Shadeskink (*Saproscincus challenger*). Snakes include the non-venomous Carpet Python (*Morelia spilota*), but most snakes here are highly venomous, including Red-bellied Black Snake (*Pseudechis porphyriacus*), Marsh Snake (*Hemiaspis signata*), Rough-scaled Snake (*Tropidechis carinatus*), and Common Tree Snake (*Dendrelaphis punctulatus*).

Amphibians are particularly prevalent in this habitat and seem more obvious than in surrounding habitats. The forest surrounding O'Reilly's Rainforest Retreat in Lamington National Park hosts, among many others, species such as Fletcher's Frog (*Platyplectrum fletcheri*), Orange-thighed Tree Frog (*Ranoidea xanthomera*), Cascade Stream Frog (*Ranoidea pearsoniana*), Great Barred Frog (*Mixophyes fasciolatus*), Dainty Tree Frog (*Ranoidea gracilenta*), and Fleay's Barred Frog (*Mixophyes fleayi*). Unfortunately, the invasive Cane Toad (*Rhinella marina*) has made it south to this habitat and is on its way to the Temperate Rainforest to the south.

CONSERVATION: Australian Red Cedar, which is also found at lower elevations, is one of the most historically significant trees in Australia, particularly in the Big Scrub region of n. New South Wales. The cedar was highly prized for its rich, durable timber, leading to extensive logging during the 19th and early 20th centuries, where other rainforest trees, which would become valuable

at a later date, were left to rot because the cedar was worth so much more. This wholesale grab for Australian Red Cedar devastated the Big Scrub, which originally covered 185,000 ac. (75,000 ha) and is reduced to less than 1% of its original size.

Most other areas of this habitat were also destroyed, but large patches remained in the steeper terrains of the Border Ranges and other montane areas. Logging of the forest has now ceased, and virtually all remaining examples are under strict protection laws. Climate change and changing fire regimes are a threat, especially to the fringes of the forest and smaller blocks, but overall, what remains of this habitat is better situated than most analogous habitats around the world.

DISTRIBUTION: Subtropical Rainforest habitat occurs from c. Queensland down the eastern ranges to near Sydney in New South Wales. It always occurs to the east of the Great Dividing Range and is replaced by DRY VINEFOREST in more arid regions.

WHERE TO SEE: Lamington National Park, Queensland, Australia; Border Ranges National Park, New South Wales, Australia.

Above: **Superb Fruit-Dove is an inconspicuous canopy resident in this habitat that is more often heard than seen.** © BEN KNOOT

Krefft's Glider is a nocturnal marsupial that spends its time foraging by gliding between trees and drinking sap from the trunks. © SAM WOODS, TROPICAL BIRDING TOURS

Au4C AUSTRALASIAN TROPICAL MONTANE RAINFOREST

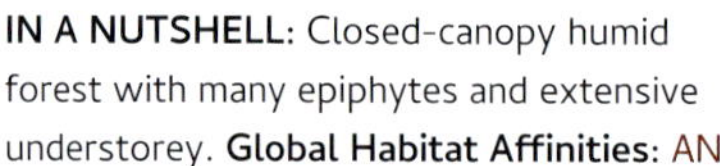

IN A NUTSHELL: Closed-canopy humid forest with many epiphytes and extensive understorey. **Global Habitat Affinities:** ANDEAN CLOUDFOREST; INDIAN OCEAN MONTANE RAINFOREST; HIMALAYAN SUBTROPICAL BROADLEAF FOREST. **Continental Habitat Affinities:** LOWLAND RAINFOREST. **Species Overlap:** LOWLAND RAINFOREST; RAINFOREST WET SCLEROPHYLL FOREST. **Full Bird Assemblage:** habitatsoftheworld.org/Au4C.

DESCRIPTION: Tropical Montane Rainforests of Australasia grow at elevations higher than LOWLAND RAINFOREST. These upland forests have slightly lower tree diversity, more epiphytes, and a much more extensive understorey than lowland rainforests.

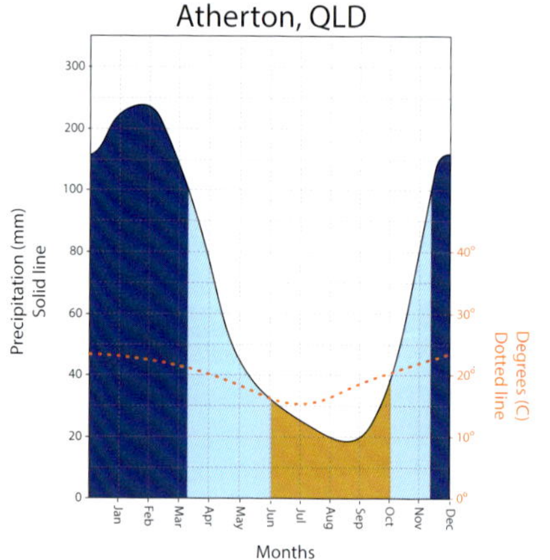

On the edge of the Atherton Tableland in Queensland, Lowland Rainforest merges into this habitat at around 2000 ft. (600 m) elevation. Things are slightly more complicated in New Guinea, where another forest type, NEW GUINEA HILL FOREST, occurs between the Lowland Rainforest and this forest, and merges with this habitat at around 3300 ft. (1000 m).

In n. Australia, Tropical Montane Rainforest reaches to the highest summits of the ranges—there is no tree line. This habitat has a lower canopy than Lowland Rainforest, although it can be as tall as 65–80 ft. (20–25 m), while 30–40 ft. (10–12 m) is more typical at higher elevations. The canopy is characterised by trees that exhibit low branching, in contrast to the elongated, unbranched trunks (boles) typical of canopy trees in Lowland Rainforest. Canopy trees include the conifers Bunya Pine (*Araucaria bidwillii*) and Black Kauri (*Agathis atropurpurea*), as well as a diverse range of angiosperms, including Red Tulip Oak (*Argyrodendron peralatum*), Atherton Oak (*Athertonia diversifolia*), Northern Silky Oak (*Cardwellia sublimis*), Queensland Maple (*Flindersia brayleyana*), Black Bean (*Castanospermum australe*), Rose Maple (*Flindersia laevicarpa*), Giant Water Gum (*Syzygium francisii*), Northern Coachwood (*Ceratopetalum virchowii*), and one of the few acacias in the rainforests, Brown Salwood (*Acacia celsa*).

These forests exhibit features typical of cloud forests around the world, including tree trunks and branches encrusted with mosses and lichens and heavily adorned with epiphytes such as

The forest canopy of Tropical Montane Rainforest is very uneven and shorter than that of Lowland Rainforest. © IAIN CAMPBELL, TROPICAL BIRDING TOURS/UNSW E&ERC

The trees of Tropical Montane Rainforest tend not to have buttressed roots (so common in the lowlands), and the understorey is very messy with much more ground cover than Lowland Rainforest. © IAIN CAMPBELL, TROPICAL BIRDING TOURS/UNSW E&ERC

Golden Bowerbird is a specialist of Australian Tropical Montane Rainforest, most often encountered at one of the few known bowers during the breeding season, when a territorial male tends to the bower frequently, often touching it up with fresh lichen.
© SAM WOODS, TROPICAL BIRDING TOURS

Common Waxflower (*Hoya australis*); Bird's Nest Fern (*Asplenium australasicum*), which can grow to 6 ft. (2 m) in diameter; and Elkhorn Fern (*Platycerium bifurcatum*). The forest floor is much more thickly vegetated than in Lowland Rainforest, full of palm trees such as Bangalow Palm (*Archontophoenix cunninghamiana*), Alexandra Palm (*Archontophoenix alexandrae*), Walking Stick Palm (*Linospadix monostachyos*), and Jaggery Palm (*Caryota urens*).

Although these forests occur in tropical zones, because of their elevation they have a subtropical highland climate (Köppen **Cfb**), characterised by mild temperatures and moderate to high rainfall. The temperatures do not change markedly through the season, varying from 70 to 84°F (21–29°C). The annual rainfall of these regions is generally 50–65 in. (1300–1650 mm), with higher rainfall during the austral summer, but these general rainfall amounts mask the real reason the area is so lush: precipitation changes to 98–118 in. (2500–3000 mm) when cloud cover and orographic rain are taken into account.

Although there is massive overlap of bird and plant species between examples of this forest in Australia and New Guinea, there are some differences in forest structure; in New Guinea these forests have low canopies, at 45–75 ft. (15–25 m), and the undergrowth is very thick. At lower elevations, canopy species such as Papua New Guinea Chinquapin (*Castanopsis acuminatissima*) are dominant, and Hoop Pine (*Araucaria cunninghamii*) and Klinki Pine (*Araucaria hunsteinii*) are the main conifers. Higher up, the forest changes, and beech, podocarp conifers, and myrtles become dominant.

WILDLIFE: The mountain rainforests of New Guinea are extensive and are different enough from the surrounding NEW GUINEA HILL FOREST that many endemic birds and several bird families specific to this habitat have evolved. This is the zone where the island's birds-of-paradise reach their highest diversity, with species such as sicklebills (*Drepanornis* and *Epimachus*) and astrapias. Other birds typical of the New Guinean montane forests include Wattled Ploughbill; Torrent-lark; tiger-parrots; Red-breasted Pygmy-Parrot; lorikeets such as Stella's Lorikeet and the scarce Striated Lorikeet; montane robins such as Subalpine, Blue-grey, and Black-capped Robins; Fan-tailed and Mid-mountain Berrypeckers; Tit Berrypecker; Western and Eastern Crested Berrypeckers; Chestnut Forest Rail; Papuan Whipbird; Rusty Whistler; Black Sittella; Belford's Melidectes; Smoky Honeyeater; and Friendly Fantail.

Bird species limited entirely or primarily to the montane rainforests of n. Queensland, Australia, include Lesser Sooty Owl, Tooth-billed and Golden Bowerbirds, Mountain Thornbill, Atherton Scrubwren, Fernwren, Bridled Honeyeater, Grey-headed Robin, Bower's Shrikethrush, and Chowchilla.

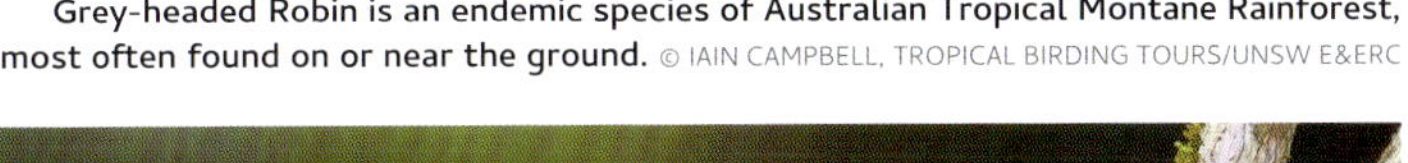

Grey-headed Robin is an endemic species of Australian Tropical Montane Rainforest, most often found on or near the ground. © IAIN CAMPBELL, TROPICAL BIRDING TOURS/UNSW E&ERC

Lumholtz's Tree-Kangaroo is a nocturnal, scarce, and local arboreal kangaroo that is best looked for on an organised night walk with local experts within this habitat. © SAM WOODS, TROPICAL BIRDING TOURS

There are many mammals in this habitat, but they are devilishly hard to see. Target mammals in Australia include Herbert River Ringtail Possum and Lumholtz's Tree-Kangaroo. Those on New Guinea and surrounding islands include Speckled Dasyure, Stein's Cuscus, Mountain Cuscus, Calaby's Pademelon, Dusky Pademelon, pygmy possums, and several species of tree-kangaroos. Reptiles include Amethyst Python (*Simalia amethystina*), Northern Death Adder (*Acanthophis praelongus*), Northern Leaf-tailed Gecko (*Saltuarius cornutus*), and Boyd's Forest Dragon (*Lophosaurus boydii*).

Endemism: The highlands of the islands north of Australia have so many endemic bird areas and centres of plant diversity that almost any mountainous area is part of one. The major montane endemic areas of New Guinea are (from west to east) the mountains of the Vogelkop (or Bird's Head) and Bomberai

Herbert River Ringtail Possum is confined to the highlands of the Wet Tropics in ne. Queensland, where it is most abundant within Australian Tropical Montane Rainforest. © IAIN CAMPBELL, TROPICAL BIRDING TOURS/UNSW E&ERC

Speckled Dasyure is a mouse-like marsupial occupying this habitat on the island of New Guinea. © PHIL GREGORY, SICKLEBILL SAFARIS

Peninsulas including the Fakfak and Kumawa Mountains; the island's main central range (with a significant difference between its eastern and western sides); the Cyclops, Bewani, and Adelbert Mountains; and the mountains of the Huon Peninsula. In Australia the endemic areas are the Atherton Tableland near Cairns (Queensland).

CONSERVATION: Much of the clearing of Tropical Montane Rainforest in Australia happened in the late 19th and early 20th centuries. For the past few decades, Australian montane rainforest has not faced serious clearing pressure, and in many areas substantial tracks of forest have regrown—that is not to say there are not pressures, and urban development is an issue in the Atherton Tableland. To the north of Australia, the situation is dire. Very little of this habitat is protected, the forest continues to be cut with little regard for the consequences, and there are very few protected areas.

DISTRIBUTION: On the islands of New Guinea, New Ireland, and New Britain, Tropical Montane Rainforest habitat is widespread above 3300 ft. (1000 m), reaching up to 13,000 ft. (4000 m) on higher passes. In many areas it is hardly touched, thanks to the remote and incredibly rugged topography. In ne. Queensland, Tropical Montane Rainforest occurs in the cooler upland areas, generally above 2000 ft. (600 m). Farther south, SUBTROPICAL RAINFOREST is generally found at lower elevations from the coast to the lower reaches of the mountains.

WHERE TO SEE: Mt. Hypipamee National Park, Queensland, Australia; Mt. Lewis, Queensland, Australia; Tari and Ambua Lodge area, Papua New Guinea; Kumul Lodge, Papua New Guinea; Keki Lodge, Adelbert Mountains, Papua New Guinea; Mokwam area, Arfak Mountains, Indonesian New Guinea.

Au4D NEW GUINEA HILL FOREST

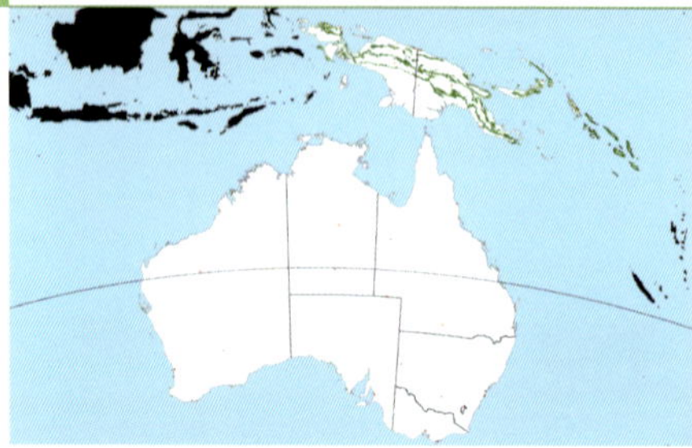

IN A NUTSHELL: Diverse mixed lower-montane humid evergreen forest. **Global habitat affinities:** NEOTROPICAL LOWLAND RAINFOREST; ASIAN LOWLAND TROPICAL RAINFOREST; AFROTROPICAL LOWLAND RAINFOREST. **Continental habitat affinities:** NEW GUINEA HIGH-MONTANE RAINFOREST; LOWLAND RAINFOREST. **Species overlap:** NEW GUINEA HIGH-MONTANE RAINFOREST. **Full Bird Assemblage:** habitatsoftheworld.org/Au4D.

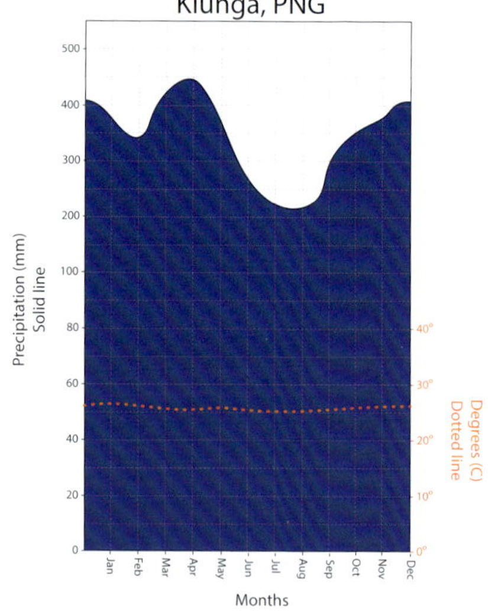

DESCRIPTION: On New Guinean mountainsides, above the LOWLAND RAINFOREST and SWAMP FOREST, the forest has been highly modified by humans and exists as a mosaic of old-growth forest, various ages of regrowth after slash-and-burn agriculture, and small crop gardens. It is very reminiscent of the 'farmbush' HUMID LOWLAND CULTIVATION of the West African rainforests. Some trees are left or planted for their edible fruits, such as the delicious Galip Nut (*Canarium indicum*), Okari Nut (*Terminalia kaernbachii*), Pangi (*Pangium edule*), Betelnut Palm (*Areca catechu*), various pandans (*Pandanus* spp.), and Red Silk Cotton Tree (*Bombax ceiba*) for kapok. Ti (*Cordyline fruticosa*) is used as a boundary marker, and coral trees (*Erythrina* spp.) and African Tulip Tree (*Spathodea campanulata*) are valued for their flowers. Hill Forest generally occurs between 1000 and 3300 ft. (300–1000 m) but can be much lower, as in the Bismarck Archipelago, where it occurs near the coastline. Landslides are frequent in this steep topography, leading to copious secondary regrowth, also seen in volcanic areas and after fires. Hill Forests are usually very rich in species, like the Lowland Rainforest downslope, but can have patches of *Casuarina* groves, especially Papuan Casuarina (*Gymnostoma papuanum*) in recent regrowth where the soils are shallow and sandy and along ridgelines. In older regrowth or in areas

New Guinea Hill Forest has been removed for farming in flat areas and is now found mainly on steep slopes and ridgelines. © JUN MATSUI, SICKLEBILL SAFARIS

of better soils, the casuarinas are quickly replaced by broadleaf rainforest species typical of the Lowland Rainforest such as Moluccan Albizia (*Falcataria falcata*), Fijian Longan (*Pometia pinnata*), and figs (*Ficus* spp.), along with various semi-deciduous broadleaf trees such as Garuga (*Garuga floribunda*), *Brachychiton carruthersii*, Ipil Teak (*Intsia bijuga*), multiple dipterocarps (*Anisoptera* spp.), and *Terminalia* spp. Klinki Pine (*Araucaria hunsteinii*), a regular emergent tree from this forest that resembles the Hoop Pine (*Araucaria cunninghamii*) of mainland Australia, is one of the few Gondwanan conifers that occurs in the Australasian tropics. Bamboos, usually an indicator of human disturbance, are common, with erect, scrambling, and climbing species often dominating the undergrowth. Indigenous gardens with sugarcane and well-drained mounds for sweet potato, yams, and potatoes are cleared in primary forest, often far from villages, creating a patchwork of garden plots and secondary growth. Traditionally, the gardens were left fallow for long periods, allowing secondary growth to become well established and even climax forest to regenerate sometimes, though population pressures are having an adverse effect.

Hill Forest can seem quite thin, with many narrow-trunked trees, reminiscent of the Kerangas forest of Asia. © CHARLEY HESSE, TROPICAL BIRDING TOURS

Although the tree species of New Guinea Hill Forest may be the same as those of Lowland Rainforest, the canopy structure is different in that its height is much lower in this forest, reaching only 60–100 ft. (20–30 m). Other differences are that very few of the trees have buttressed roots, and they tend not to have large girths. Because much of the forest is in some stage of regrowth, many of the canopy trees are of a similar age, and the forest structure lacks the variations of the lower forests. In contrast with the AUSTRALASIAN TROPICAL MONTANE RAINFOREST and NEW GUINEA HIGH-MONTANE RAINFOREST higher on the mountains, palms are still a significant component of both the understorey and canopy. Because this habitat is such a mosaic, sun-loving shrubs and edge plants are common, especially in light gaps, creating a thick understorey that makes it difficult to walk through except on trails. In areas that are older and more established, the canopy filters out the vast majority of the light, making the understorey much more open, easier to navigate, and dominated by saplings of the canopy species.

This forest is especially rich in birds-of-paradise, such as the spectacular Magnificent Bird-of-Paradise. Here a male performs his jaw-dropping display for a female in the Arfak Mountains. © CHARLEY HESSE, TROPICAL BIRDING TOURS

WILDLIFE: Hill Forest is an important habitat in New Guinea, host to many endemic or near-endemic species. These include Magnificent Bird-of-Paradise, Carola's Parotia, Greater Bird-of-Paradise, and the rare and enigmatic Greater Melampitta, restricted to limestone karst formations in the forest. Also occurring are Chestnut-backed Jewel-babbler, Papuan Scrub-Robin, White-rumped Robin, the cryptic and little-known Obscure Berrypecker, Rusty Whistler, the three taxa in the Black-winged Monarch complex (which are likely full species), Goldenface, Wallace's Fairywren, Pale-billed Scrubwren, Olive Flyrobin, and Yellow-legged Flyrobin. Amongst non-passerines are the taxa of the Pheasant Pigeon complex (likely full species), Red-breasted and Brown-headed Paradise-Kingfishers, Yellow-billed Kingfisher (overlapping with LOWLAND RAINFOREST), and parrots, including the rare Striated Lorikeet, Goldie's Lorikeet, Buff-faced Pygmy-Parrot, and, shared with the lowland forests, Pesquet's Parrot (*Psittrichas fulgidus*). In the Hill Forest of the

Great Woodswallow (pictured) is restricted to New Guinea and looks very similar to the much more widespread White-breasted Woodswallow.

© DANIEL LÓPEZ-VELASCO, ORNIS BIRDING EXPEDITIONS

Bismarcks are found Rusty Thicketbird, Golden Monarch, and New Britain Kingfisher, while in the Solomons are Chestnut-bellied Monarch, Oriole Whistler, and Yellow-throated and Solomons White-eyes.

Mammals include Agile Wallaby, Dusky Pademelon, Grey Dorcopsis, Common Spotted Cuscus, and several species of flying foxes (*Pteropus* spp.). Reptiles include Southern Green Tree Python (*Morelia viridis*), Northern Death Adder (*Acanthophis praelongus*), Australasian tree snakes (*Boiga* spp.), Small-eyed Blind Snake (*Ramphotyphlops micrommus*), and Emerald Tree Monitor (*Varanus prasinus*). The frog fauna is large and diverse, especially in marshy areas and around creeks.

CONSERVATION: The vast majority of this habitat has been turned over to subsistence farming, to the degree that it is often hard to discern what is natural old growth and what is secondary or anthropogenic growth. Little of this habitat is protected in national parks, and it continues to be cleared over most of its distribution.

DISTRIBUTION: New Guinea Hill Forest occupies the habitat between LOWLAND RAINFOREST and TROPICAL MONTANE RAINFOREST in the foothills of mountain ranges throughout New Guinea, occurring roughly between 800 and 2600 ft. (250–800 m) but varying with local conditions. The habitat also occurs in the Bismarck Archipelago and Solomon Islands, where it is much closer to the coast.

WHERE TO SEE: Varirata National Park, near Port Moresby, Papua New Guinea; foothills of the Star Mountains, around Tabubil, Papua New Guinea; foothills of the Arfak Mountains, above Manokwari, Indonesian New Guinea; Kukundu and Imbu Rano, Kolombangara, Solomon Islands.

Au4E NEW GUINEA HIGH-MONTANE RAINFOREST

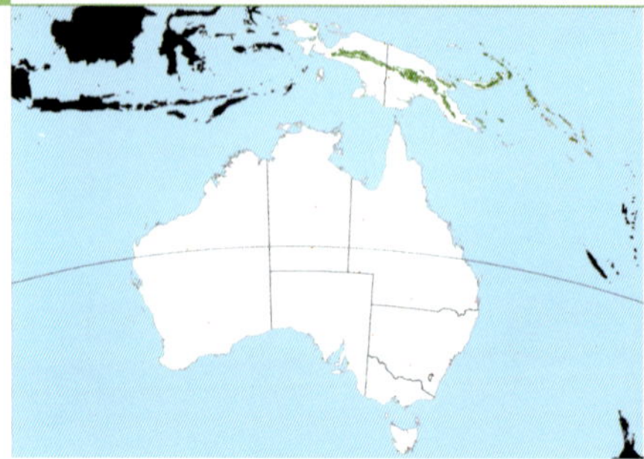

IN A NUTSHELL: Closed-canopy wet montane forest above 6500 ft. (2000 m), with Antarctic beech (*Nothofagus*), podocarps, and oaks, mostly shallow-rooted and with abundant epiphytes, mosses, ferns, and orchids. **Global Habitat affinities:** AFRICAN MOIST MONTANE FOREST; ANDEAN CLOUDFOREST. **Continental Habitat affinities:** TROPICAL MONTANE RAINFOREST. **Species Overlap:** NEW GUINEA HILL FOREST; LOWLAND RAINFOREST; TROPICAL MONTANE RAINFOREST. **Full Bird Assemblage:** habitatsoftheworld.org/Au4E.

DESCRIPTION: This is one of the most distinctive and striking habitats in Australasia, a mountainside forest with a dense, damp, mossy, and shady understorey, a closed canopy, and trees profusely covered with mosses, lichens, and epiphytes. Buttressed trunks are absent, and trees are mostly evergreen, their leaves small and glossy green with waxy cuticles that increase tolerance of variable climate conditions. Trees are shorter than those of lower habitats.

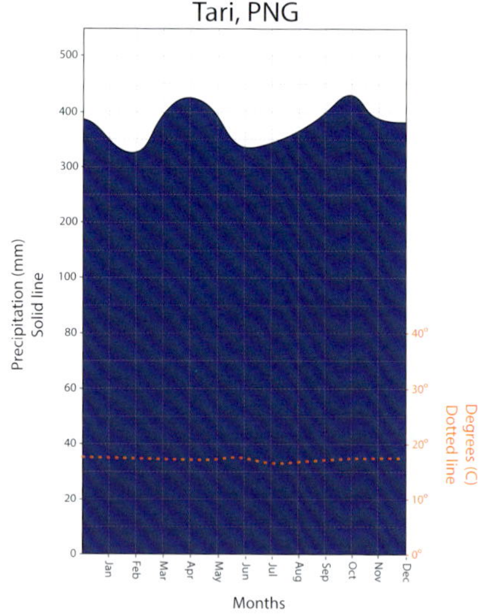

New Guinea High-Montane Rainforests are shady and relatively nutrient-poor, which limits regrowth to shade-tolerant species. With annual rainfall of 6.5 ft. (2 m) up to an incredible 26–33 ft. (8–10+ m) on some high peaks above 7500 ft. (2300 m), it is one of the wettest habitats on earth. Temperatures average 64°F (18°C) in the highlands, generally decreasing with increasing elevation, and frosts are rare below 9200 ft. (2800 m). This habitat is particularly associated with mountains, extinct volcanoes, and craters where orographic rainfall comes into play. It forms a mosaic with AUSTROPARAMO on well-drained sites with deep soils, and with low coarse grasses on wetter sites with poor soils. These grasses are largely replaced above 14,000 ft. (4300 m) by

The trees of High-Montane Rainforest are laden with epiphytes, with some branches being completely covered. © JUN MATSUI, SICKLEBILL SAFARIS

cushion or rosette herbs, mosses, lichens, and ferns, with swamp vegetation of herbs, sedges, mosses, and grasses in shallow boggy depressions.

These forests have slightly lower tree diversity, more epiphytes, and a much more extensive understorey than LOWLAND RAINFOREST. The trees are smaller, from 60–82 ft. (18–25 m) tall at the lower levels to about 20 ft. (6 m) tall at the higher levels, and often stunted or gnarled. The very dense understorey is replete with saplings, roots, and fallen timber, and many tree ferns occupy the shrub layer. Common plants include species of *Castanopsis* (chinquapins, often called 'oaks') at the lower elevations, *Syzygium* (waterberries), *Ilex* (hollies), *Elaeocarpus*, and *Lithocarpus* (stone oaks), and sundry species in the Myrtaceae and Lauraceae families. Conifers include important species of *Dacrycarpus* and *Podocarpus*, whose seeds provide food for the rare Macgregor's Honeyeater, and *Papuacedrus* and *Phyllocladus*, which are widespread as both canopy trees and emergents; all these conifers become more frequent above 7900 ft. (2400 m). Klinki Pine (*Araucaria hunsteinii*), much valued for timber, is another significant conifer at the higher elevations, and can form quite dense stands in certain areas.

Close to the tree line (11,500 ft./3500 m in Papua New Guinea, 13,700 ft./4170 m in Indonesian New Guinea), dominant plants include *Rapanea* spp. and members of the family Ericaceae (heaths) such as *Rhododendron* and various *Dimorphanthera* and *Trochocarpa* spp. Pandans (*Pandanus*) are frequent along edges and creek lines, their fruit being much valued for food by local people. Scrambling bamboo (*Nastus productus*) occurs along forest margins and at treefalls at lower

Arfak Catbird occupies this habitat in the namesake mountains of West Papua, Indonesia, where it can be found foraging within fruiting pandan trees. © CHARLEY HESSE, TROPICAL BIRDING TOURS

levels, important habitat for scrubwrens and Wattled Ploughbill. At the highest elevations, frost hollows, where damp very cold air settles and limits vegetation, seem to be associated with the rare Archbold's Bowerbird. At the highest levels the trees become stunted and dwarfed, often contorted and gnarled and forming a kind of elfin forest, though some emergent conifers are present, and such stands are often small patches in a sea of grass. Drought can have serious effects on these montane forests, and fire is another serious issue during such times. The great drought of 1998 killed hundreds of thousands of trees in the highlands, where they remain today as gaunt skeletons.

WILDLIFE: This mossy forest is an essential and wonderful environment to visit, with many amazing and iconic species. It is prime habitat for endemics and for some of the most extraordinary of all the birds-of-paradise. Key endemics include Feline Owlet-nightjar; New Guinea Eagle; Plum-faced, West Papuan, and Stella's Lorikeets; Fire-maned Bowerbird; Arfak and Huon Catbirds; Arfak, Splendid, and Ribbon-tailed Astrapias; Brown Sicklebill; King-of-Saxony Bird-of-Paradise; and Macgregor's Honeyeater. Other typical species include Painted

The dazzling Splendid Astrapia is one of the most highly sought-after species in this high-elevation habitat. © DANIEL LÓPEZ-VELASCO, ORNIS BIRDING EXPEDITIONS

The gorgeous Painted Tiger-Parrot is an inconspicuous inhabitant of High-Montane Rainforest in both Indonesian New Guinea and Papua New Guinea.
© DANIEL LÓPEZ-VELASCO, ORNIS BIRDING EXPEDITIONS

Tiger-Parrot, Long-bearded and Short-bearded Honeyeaters, Crested and Loria's Satinbirds, Black Sittella, crested berrypeckers, Greater and Lesser Ground-Robins, Papuan Logrunner, Archbold's Bowerbird, Spotted Jewel-babbler, Blue-capped Ifrita, Papuan Scrubwren, Lorentz's and Regent Whistlers, Wattled Ploughbill, the Smoky Honeyeater species complex, Friendly Fantail, and both Forbes's and Chestnut Forest Rails.

Mammals are more limited but include several rarely seen species of tree-kangaroos, plus Mountain Pygmy Possum, *Petaurus* gliders, cuscus species, New Guinean Quoll, Calaby's Pademelon, and various little-known giant naked-tailed rats (*Uromys* spp.) and antechinuses (*Antechinus* spp.). Herps are very limited in this cold, wet environment, but the very large, powerful, and impressive Boelen's Python (*Simalia boeleni*) occurs, as do Papua New Guinea Montane Keelback (*Tropidonophis statisticus*), forest snakes (*Toxicocalamus* spp.), and ground snakes (*Stegonotus* spp.). Frogs include Eastern Mountains Tree Frog (*Litoria dorsivena*) and Montane Pinocchio Frog (*Litoria vivissimia*).

Solomon Islands Upper Montane Cloudforest: In the Solomon Islands, on Guadalcanal, Makira, and Kolombangara, the montane forests between 2600 and 6000 ft. (800–1800 m) form an island subhabitat that holds many rarely seen endemics. Obligate species here include Pale Mountain-Pigeon, Red-breasted Pygmy-Parrot, Shade Warbler, Makira and Guadalcanal Thrushes, Guadalcanal Thicketbird, Solomons Robin, Kolombangara Leaf Warbler (one of the most range-

Greater Ground-Robin is commonly identified by song in this habitat but can be devilishly difficult to see! © DANIEL LÓPEZ-VELASCO, ORNIS BIRDING EXPEDITIONS

restricted species on earth, found only at the highest elevations around the rim of Kolombangara island's central caldera), and Kolombangara White-eye. Bougainville island has its own suite of virtually unknown montane endemics including Bougainville Thicketbird, Bougainville Thrush, Bougainville Fantail, and the mysterious Moustached Kingfisher, this latter species with an equally unknown sibling subspecies on Guadalcanal.

CONSERVATION: Large areas of New Guinea are still covered in this habitat, as it is a steep, difficult terrain, in a remote, wet, and inaccessible region, though some local logging is having an impact. Some national parks in Indonesian New Guinea nominally protect large areas in the Snow and Arfak Mountains.

DISTRIBUTION: The montane areas of the New Guinea cordillera above 6500 ft. (2000 m), with outliers in the Cyclops, Adelbert, and Torricelli Mountains; also on the Melanesian islands of Bougainville, Guadalcanal, Makira, and Kolombangara, where it forms an island montane forest subhabitat extending from c. 2600 to 5900 ft. (800–1800 m).

WHERE TO SEE: Papua New Guinea—Kumul Lodge, Enga Province; Rondon Ridge, Western Highlands; Tari Gap and the Ambua area, Hela Province; Star Mountains of Western Province; Adelbert Mountains, East Sepik and Madang. Indonesian New Guinea—Snow Mountains above Wamena, Highland Papua; Cyclops Mountains, Papua Province; and upper parts of the Arfak Mountains, West Papua Province. Solomon Archipelago—highlands of Bougainville, Papua New Guinea; Guadalcanal, Makira, and Kolombangara, Solomon Islands.

Au4F NOTHOFAGUS FOREST

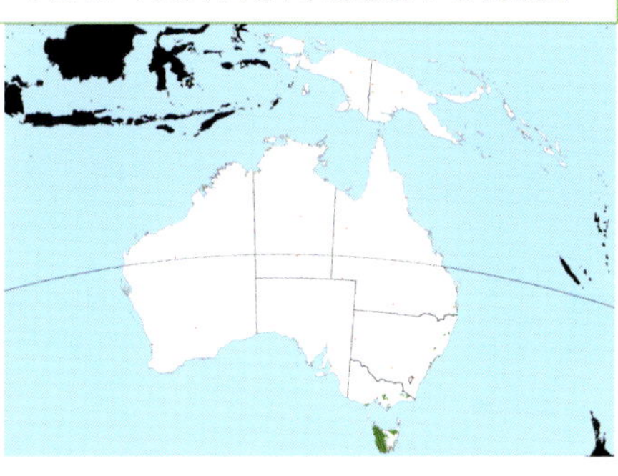

IN A NUTSHELL: Cold, wet broadleaf forest of se. Australia with a closed canopy; dominated by *Nothofagus* beech species, it is of ancient Gondwanan origin. **Global Habitat Affinities:** MAGELLANIC TEMPERATE RAINFOREST; NEW ZEALAND BEECH FORESTS. **Continental Habitat Affinities:** None. **Species Overlap:** TEMPERATE RAINFOREST; SUBTROPICAL RAINFOREST. **Full Bird Assemblage:** habitatsoftheworld.org/Au4F.

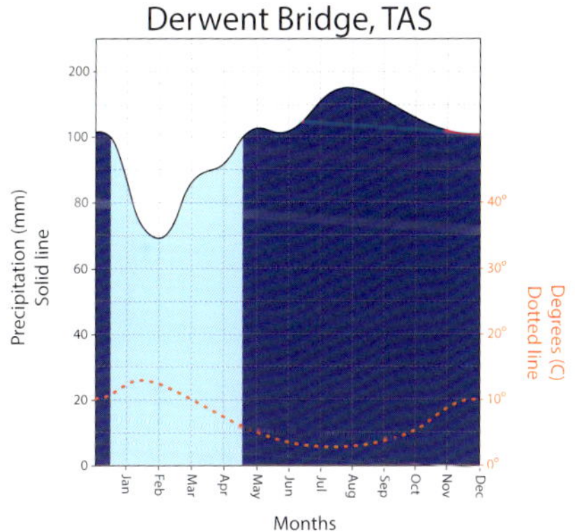

DESCRIPTION: The Nothofagus Forest is extremely distinct from all other wet forests in Australia, as it is the only Australian representative of the temperate deciduous forests biome. This seems incongruous because only a few of the species lose their leaves in winter, but the forest feels very much like EUROPEAN DECIDUOUS RAINFOREST of Turkey and Georgia. Nothofagus Forest is associated with basaltic flows in the very north of its range, but this constraint may not be as important as often described as there are many areas of basaltic flow without this habitat, and some areas of this habitat in Tasmania and Victoria are not restricted to nutrient-rich volcanic soils. Nothofagus Forest is found in areas with cold, but not necessarily freezing, very wet climates such as subpolar oceanic (Köppen **Cfc**) and temperate oceanic (**Cfb**), typically with rainfall between 51 and 83 in. (1300–2100 mm) per year.

It is characterised by lower plant diversity than AUSTRALIAN TEMPERATE RAINFOREST and a simpler, one-layer canopy structure, with canopy heights ranging from as low as 15 ft. (5 m) on exposed ridges, where it gives impressions of the ELFIN FOREST of the Andes, to very tall, up to 130 ft. (40 m), in protected gullies. The tree trunks also differ in nature from those of the other humid forests. These forests lack the buttressed roots of the AUSTRALIAN SUBTROPICAL RAINFOREST, and although some trees are straight-trunked, the *Nothofagus* species often have multiple trunks or large branches emerging only a few feet from the ground and sometimes growing downwards as well. Their root systems and burls can become exposed and covered in moss, giving the forest an otherworldly feel like a scene out of *The Lord of the Rings*.

The Nothofagus Forest floor is dominated by an all-pervading layer of large tree ferns—and occasional visitors like Sam Woods. © IAIN CAMPBELL, TROPICAL BIRDING TOURS/UNSW E&ERC

At the northern limit of this forest in s. Queensland, the canopy trees are dominated by tree species with small leaves, usually less than 2.5 in. (6.5 cm) long, such as Antarctic Beech (*Nothofagus moorei*) and Soft Corkwood (*Caldcluvia paniculosa*). The other main species, such as Yellow Sassafras (*Doryphora sassafras*), Crow's Ash (*Flindersia australis*), and Black Booyong (*Argyrodendron actinophyllum*), have slightly larger leaves, 3–5 in. (7–13 cm) long. Red Carabeen (*Geissois benthamii*) is also a regular component of this forest but has larger leaves, like most trees of the Subtropical Rainforest, and Brown Barrel (*Eucalyptus fastigata*) also occurs, which is unexpected in a rainforest because it is a eucalypt.

In s. New South Wales, Tasmania, and Victoria, Nothofagus Forest is dominated by Myrtle Beech (*Nothofagus cunninghamii*) in lowland areas and Tanglefoot, aka Deciduous Beech (*Nothofagus gunnii*), in the highlands of Tasmania. The well-formed stands of Myrtle Beech in the lowlands are mixed with other trees such as Australian Blackwood (*Acacia melanoxylon*), Southern Sassafras (*Atherosperma moschatum*), and Leatherwood (*Eucryphia lucida*). In Tasmania, the canopy assemblage is joined by the Celerytop Pine (*Phyllocladus aspleniifolius*), a flat-leaved conifer of the Podocarpaceae, another remnant family from the supercontinent Gondwana, when Australia was connected to Antarctica, South America, Africa, India, and proto–New Zealand, and was covered in cold forests of conifers and *Nothofagus*, which survived with up to six months of darkness. Another fascinating feature of Nothofagus Forest is that there is a zone of c. and s. New South Wales where no *Nothofagus* species survive. Their disappearance is a very geologically recent event, as fossils of numerous species have been found in this zone, but the lack of high, extremely wet mountains probably resulted in desiccation of the forest and extinction of these plants during a glacial period.

In the highlands of Tasmania, the forest is dominated by Tanglefoot and has the gnarled stunted appearance of the Elfin Forests of the Andes. This forest is low, with a broken canopy almost always under 33 ft. (10 m) tall, and many of the plants that would occupy the subcanopy in the same forest type downslope become canopy species here. The structure is so different that in other continents, such as Asia, South America, or Africa, it would certainly have many endemic birds and plants, but in Australia, the understorey and ground cover are similar to those of the other examples of the forest, and the birdlife remains the same. This is a prime example where structurally distinct yet floristically similar forests have such similar bird assemblages that they have to be treated as one habitat.

Epiphytes are uncommon in Nothofagus Forests, in contrast to similar-looking forests in the Andes or Himalayas, where epiphytes are such a big part of the temperate humid forests. Vines are also uncommon, although Austral Sarsaparilla (*Smilax australis*) is often present, especially where there are light gaps. Most of the understorey shrubs and subcanopy small trees are similar to those in surrounding RAINFOREST WET SCLEROPHYLL FOREST, such as Tasmanian Laurel (*Anopterus glandulosus*), Prickly Currant Bush (*Coprosma quadrifida*), Rough Tree Fern (*Cyathea australis*), and Soft Tree Fern (*Dicksonia antarctica*), which is usually dense along creeks and varies from sparse to dense in drier parts of the forest. Ferns are omnipresent on the forest floor; Sickle Fern (*Pellaea falcata*) and Gristle Fern (*Oceaniopteris cartilaginea*) are usually present in the northern parts of the range, and Kangaroo Fern (*Microsorum pustulatum*), Veined Bristle Fern (*Crepidomanes venosum*), Austral Filmy Fern (*Hymenophyllum austral*), and Shiny Filmy Fern (*Hymenophyllum flabellatum*) occur in the south of the range. The similarity of the understorey with Rainforest Wet Sclerophyll Forests should not be surprising because *Nothofagus* trees do occur as isolated understorey trees within the colder and wettest types of those forests.

Nothofagus beeches are the most conspicuous tree species. © IAIN CAMPBELL, TROPICAL BIRDING TOURS/UNSW E&ERC

The canopy trees in Nothofagus Forest are very susceptible to fire, and in regions that have had surrounding rainforests cleared and replaced with more flammable eucalypts, the Nothofagus Forest is retreating. Conversely, when fire is completely excluded from an environment, these forests are encroaching on surrounding sclerophyll forests.

WILDLIFE: In Australia, this habitat's only obligate bird species is Rufous Scrub-bird, though Bassian Thrush, Satin Flycatcher, Olive Whistler, Scrubtit, and Pink Robin are all more common in this forest than in surrounding areas. Rufous Scrub-bird is tricky as an indicator species because it occurs only in s. Queensland and n. New South Wales. There are no obligate bird species for this habitat in Victoria or Tasmania. When using bird assemblages to determine habitat, the lack of species rather than the presence of them is a better indicator of the habitat.

Mammals of this habitat in Australia include Parma Wallaby, Red-necked Wallaby, Red-necked and, in Tasmania, Rufous-bellied Pademelons, and Bare-nosed Wombat. Hunters include Spotted-tailed Quoll and, in Tasmania, Eastern Quoll and Tasmanian Devil. Common Ringtail Possum and Greater Glider are in the same family but fill different niches, with the glider being able to glide between trees like flying squirrels of the Northern Hemisphere. Other possums include Common Brushtail Possum and the diminutive Eastern Pygmy Possum. Sugar Glider and Feather-tailed Glider are very small gliding marsupials that are predominantly nectivorous.

Lizards expected in this habitat in Tasmania include Ocellated Coolskink (*Carinascincus ocellatus*), Metallic Coolskink (*Carinascincus metallicus*), Agile Coolskink (*Carinascincus pretiosus*), Heath Coolskink (*Carinascincus orocryptus*), and Blotched Bluetongue (*Tiliqua nigrolutea*). On mainland Australia the lizard assemblage includes Eastern Water Skink (*Eulamprus quoyii*), Cunningham's Skink (*Egernia cunninghami*), Lace Monitor (*Varanus varius*), Australian Water Dragon (*Intellagama lesueurii*), and Wyberba Leaf-tailed Gecko (*Saltuarius wyberba*).

Tiger Snake (*Notechis scutatus*) and Southern Death Adder are found on both the mainland and Tasmania, and other mainland snakes include Carpet Python (*Morelia spilota*), Golden-crowned Snake (*Cacophis squamulosus*), and Eastern Small-eyed Snake (*Cryptophis nigrescens*). Nearly all of these snakes are venomous.

Because this is a very humid environment, amphibians are readily found and include Tasmanian Froglet (*Crinia tasmaniensis*), Common Eastern Froglet (*Crinia signifera*), Southern Smooth Frog (*Geocrinia laevis*), and Brown Tree Frog (*Litoria ewingii*), Northern Stuttering Barred Frog (*Mixophyes balbus*), Glandular Tree Frog (*Ranoidea subglandulosa*), and Red-backed Brood Frog (*Pseudophryne coriacea*).

Olive Whistler is most abundant within the dank understorey of Nothofagus Forest. © SAM WOODS, TROPICAL BIRDING TOURS

Scrubtit is an inconspicuous Tasmanian endemic, best looked for in the fern-dominated understorey of these forests. © BEN KNOOT

Endemism: The endemic Rufous Scrub-bird is found in se. Queensland and ne. New South Wales. Most of the endemic birds of Tasmania use this habitat, though none of them are endemic to it.

CONSERVATION: Nothofagus Forest is well protected because it tends to grow at high elevations in mountain ranges so is not productive farmland. Some forest is cleared for specialised timber, but because the trees are not straight-trunked, they are not cut for regular timber. The vast majority of remaining forest is within protected areas, though patches that occur surrounded by RAINFOREST WET SCLEROPHYLL FOREST in Victoria are vulnerable as this latter forest is still being cut at alarming rates.

DISTRIBUTION: Nothofagus Forest grows down to near sea level in Tasmania but only occurs above 2300 ft. (700 m), and rarely below 3300 ft. (1000 m) in se. Queensland. It is found in Lamington National Park (Queensland) and in e. New South Wales and e. Victoria. It is most common in the western half of Tasmania, where it is the dominant forest type above 2600 ft. (800 m).

WHERE TO SEE: Barrington Tops National Park, New South Wales, Australia; Toolangi State Forest, Victoria, Australia; Mt. Field National Park, Tasmania, Australia.

SIDEBAR — WHAT ARE KEY BIODIVERSITY AREAS, AND WHY DO THEY MATTER?

Key Biodiversity Areas (KBAs) are sites of global significance for the persistence of biodiversity. They contain a globally significant population of one or more species or a globally significant extent of an ecosystem or they have a globally significant area of outstanding ecological integrity. KBAs are identified by 11 quantitative criteria, which makes KBAs comparable between countries within different regions of the world. As a result, KBAs are indicators of the Sustainable Development Goals and the new Biodiversity Plan of the Convention on Biological Diversity being used to track progress by governments in achieving conservation. KBAs are also being used by the private sector to avoid and minimise their impacts on biodiversity. In order to apply the KBA ecosystem criteria, we need a good map of ecosystems that covers their global extent. These maps should be at a relevant scale within a universal ecosystem typology. The Habitats of the World project is facilitating the timely identification, classification, description, and conservation of these KBAs.

Au4G AUSTRALIAN TEMPERATE RAINFOREST

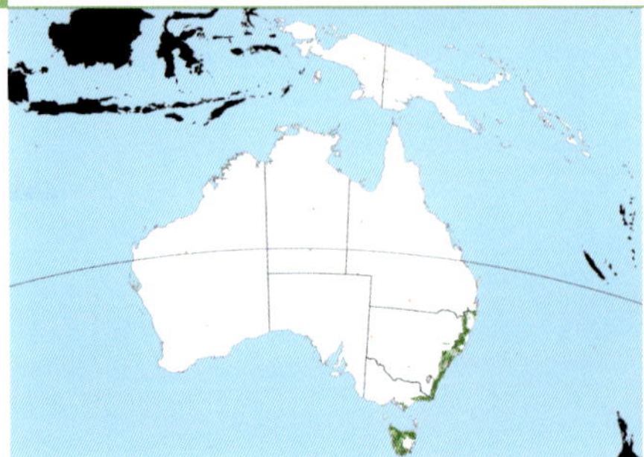

IN A NUTSHELL: Cold, wet, non-sclerophyllous forests of se. Australia whose trees lack buttressed roots and form a closed, broadleaf canopy. **Global Habitat Affinities:** AFRICAN MOIST MONTANE FOREST; NEOTROPICAL TEMPERATE CLOUDFOREST; NEW ZEALAND BEECH FOREST. **Continental Habitat Affinities:** SUBTROPICAL RAINFOREST; NOTHOFAGUS FOREST. **Species Overlap:** SUBTROPICAL RAINFOREST; NOTHOFAGUS FOREST. **Full Bird Assemblage:** habitatsoftheworld.org/Au4G.

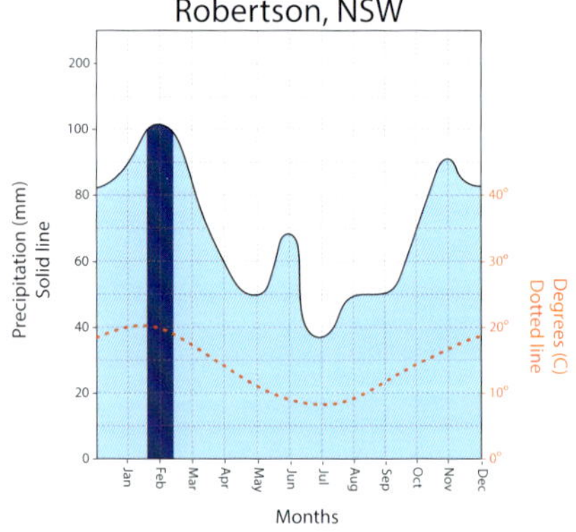

DESCRIPTION: Temperate Rainforests in Australia differ from the surrounding SUBTROPICAL RAINFORESTS in that they look much more uniform, from below and above, having much lower canopy diversity and sometimes even occurring in monotypic stands. Typically, though, Temperate Rainforest is dominated by 5–10 canopy species of broadleaf angiosperms such as Black Olive Berry (*Elaeocarpus holopetalus*), Australian Blackwood (*Acacia melanoxylon*), Lilly Pilly (*Syzygium smithii*), Silver Aspen (*Acronychia wilcoxiana*), and Southern Sassafras (*Atherosperma moschatum*). The canopy is generally 35–65 ft. (11–20 m) tall, and the trees lack large buttressed roots, have more crooked tree trunks often covered in lichen, and ramify (form branches) much closer to the ground. Although this forest lacks the *Araucaria* conifers of the rainforests to the north, it does contain Plum Pine (*Podocarpus elatus*), an indicator of its Gondwanan heritage.

Vines, such as Common Milk Vine (*Leichhardtia rostrata*), and epiphytes occur in the understorey and canopy but are nowhere common. Tree ferns are much more obvious in this habitat than in Subtropical Rainforest, with Soft Tree Fern (*Dicksonia antarctica*) replacing palms as the dominant understorey plant group, and in this respect, the understorey can look similar to that of a RAINFOREST WET SCLEROPHYLL FOREST.

The ecotone (transitional boundary) between Temperate Rainforest and Rainforest Wet Sclerophyll Forest has a mixture of eucalypts and non-eucalypts in the canopy, vines, and a rainforest understorey. © IAIN CAMPBELL, TROPICAL BIRDING TOURS/UNSW E&ERC

The understorey of Temperate Rainforest is far denser than the lower level of the more tropical rainforests. © IAIN CAMPBELL, TROPICAL BIRDING TOURS/UNSW E&ERC

Australian Temperate Rainforest displays a dense, closed canopy.
© IAIN CAMPBELL, TROPICAL BIRDING TOURS/UNSW E&ERC

Where this rainforest blends with Subtropical Rainforest in n. New South Wales and se. Queensland, it tends to develop on the soils derived from nutrient-deficient metamorphic rocks and igneous rocks such as rhyolites rather than the nutrient-rich soils derived from basaltic parent material or alluvium. In the south of its range, it can develop on a wide variety of substrates. When it occurs with NOTHOFAGUS FOREST, it is in the slightly warmer microclimates below the other forest. It can occur as extensive bands of forest but also as small patches within very sheltered areas of Rainforest Wet Sclerophyll Forest, which it will replace if protected from fire.

Generally, this forest type occurs from the humid subtropics to areas of

Superb Lyrebird is one of the most charismatic birds of Temperate Rainforest, known for its extraordinary mimicry, with some individuals famously known for imitations of crying babies, ambulances, and camera shutters!
© JUN MATSUI, SICKLEBILL SAFARIS

temperate oceanic climate (Köppen **Cfa–Cfb**)—generally, climates with rainfall above 40 in. (1000 mm) per year and no very strong dry season.

WILDLIFE: There are no birds restricted to this habitat because it often occurs as a mosaic or mélange within SUBTROPICAL RAINFOREST or RAINFOREST WET SCLEROPHYLL FOREST, with resulting similar bird assemblages. The birds typical of Subtropical Rainforests such as Regent Bowerbird, Albert's Lyrebird, and Marbled Frogmouth extend south to the very northern limit of this habitat and are much less common in it, but others such as Green Catbird, Paradise Riflebird, and Australian Logrunner occur as far south as c. New South Wales. Pilotbird is very indicative of this habitat, and rarely found in others, and is often joined by Superb Lyrebird. Bassian Thrush, Satin Flycatcher, Olive Whistler, Rose Robin, and Pink Robin are all more common in this habitat than in surrounding areas.

Mammals of this habitat in Australia include Common Ringtail Possum, Eastern Pygmy Possum, Eastern Quoll, Swamp Wallaby, and Red-necked and Rufous-bellied Pademelons. Reptiles expected in this habitat include Australian Water Dragon (*Intellagama lesueurii*), Dark-flecked Garden Sunskink (*Lampropholis delicata*), Yellow-bellied Water Skink (*Eulamprus heatwolei*), Eastern Water Skink (*Eulamprus quoyii*), Southern Bar-sided Skink (*Concinnia tenuis*), and Carpet Python (*Morelia spilota*).

CONSERVATION: Much of the clearing of Temperate Rainforest in Australia occurred during the 1800s, and most of the remaining substantial tracts are protected from clear-felling. However, because this habitat often occurs in close proximity to extensive blocks of sclerophyll forests, remnant patches within this mosaic can be destroyed during logging of the eucalypts. Serious urban encroachment is occurring in s. New South Wales, where cities are abutting small patches of this habitat in places such as Nowra and environs.

DISTRIBUTION: These rainforests grow down to sea level in Tasmania but above 3300 ft. (1000 m) in se. Queensland. They are found in isolated pockets in higher elevations of Lamington National Park (Queensland) and e. New South Wales and e. Victoria. The habitat is most common in the western half of Tasmania, where it is the dominant forest type below 2600 ft. (800 m).

WHERE TO SEE: Lamington National Park, Queensland, Australia; Minnamurra Rainforest Centre, New South Wales, Australia; Barrington Tops National Park, New South Wales, Australia; Toolangi State Forest, Victoria, Australia; Fern Gully, Tasmania, Australia; Mt. Field National Park, Tasmania, Australia.

Temperate Rainforest shares many bird species, like the Rose Robin, with Subtropical Rainforest, but no species are restricted to it.

© SAM WOODS, TROPICAL BIRDING TOURS

Au4H AUSTRALASIAN LITTORAL RAINFOREST

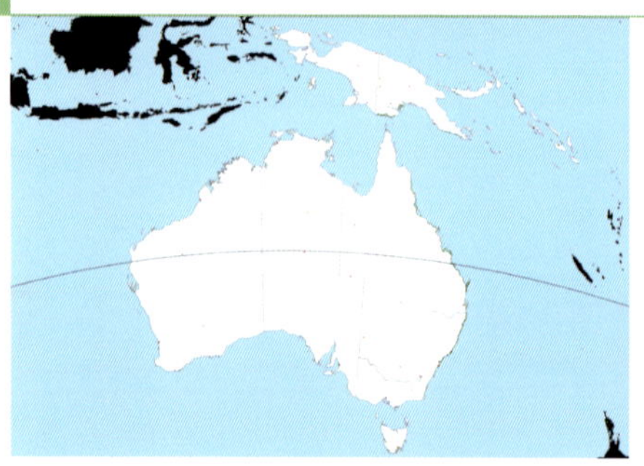

IN A NUTSHELL: Stunted and depauperate humid broadleaf forests found on sandy soils of stabilised dunes and on exposed headlands. **Global Habitat Affinities:** AFRICAN SOUTH COAST FOREST MATRIX; RIPARIAN FOREST. **Continental Habitat Affinities:** MONSOON VINEFOREST; LOWLAND RAINFOREST. **Species Overlap:** LOWLAND RAINFOREST; MONSOON VINEFOREST; TROPICAL HEATHLAND; WALLUM AND AUSBOS. **Full Bird Assemblage:** habitatsoftheworld.org/Au4H.

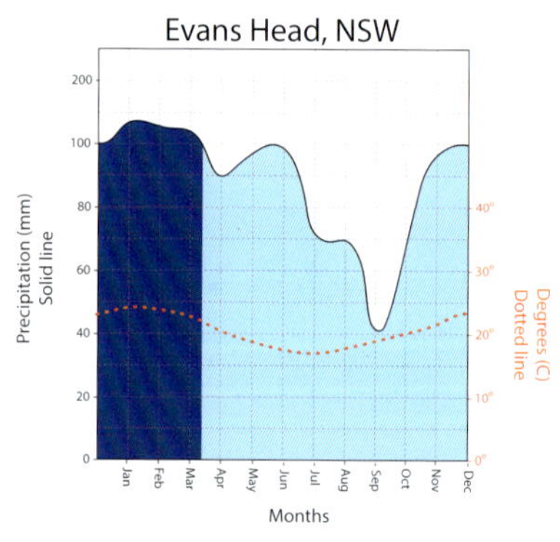

DESCRIPTION: Littoral Rainforests occur on the coast or on small offshore islands, usually on coastal sand deposits, although they can occur on headlands. In general, they are found where the land meets the sea, usually within a few hundred yards (metres) of the shoreline. They are often seen as incongruent, little enclaves of a completely different environment from the surrounding habitats and, as such, are always exciting to spend time exploring. They can be very varied depending on where they occur and can exist as an ecotone between coastal heathlands such as TROPICAL HEATHLAND and surrounding LOWLAND RAINFOREST but also occur in well-watered areas behind beach ridges and as the boundaries between mangroves and surrounding woodlands. The common feature they have is that even when sheltered, they are exposed to strong winds, salt spray, and sandy soils.

The plants change depending on latitude, substrate, and local hydrology, but trees typical of this habitat include Tuckeroo (*Cupaniopsis anacardioides*) and Brush Box (*Lophostemon confertus*). In locations where Littoral Rainforest forms on coastal unconsolidated Quaternary sands, such as swales within a beach dune system, the forest is a mix of plants also found in coastal heathlands that can even form monotypic thickets, such as Broad-leaved Paperbark (*Melaleuca quinquenervia*), Coastal Cypress-Pine (*Callitris columellaris*), Coastal Banksia (*Banksia integrefolia*), Lilly Pilly (*Syzygium smithii*), Tantoon (*Leptospermum polygalifolium*), and Geebung (*Persoonia media*). These plants are joined by Large Mock-Olive (*Notelaea longifolia*), Beach Alectryon (*Alectryon coriaceus*), Cudgerie (*Flindersia schottiana*), Tuckeroo, Beach Acronychia (*Acronychia imperforata*), Burdekin Plum (*Pleiogynium timorense*), and Brush Box, with emergents such as Blush Cudgerie (*Euroschinus falcatus*), *Ficus* trees such as Creek Sandpaper Fig (*Ficus coronata*), Small-leaved

Littoral Rainforest is mainly coastal, usually found on dune swales or on river edges near mangroves. © IAIN CAMPBELL, TROPICAL BIRDING TOURS/UNSW E&ERC

Fig (*Ficus obliqua*), Port Jackson Fig (*Ficus rubiginosa*), and even the conifer Hoop Pine (*Araucaria cunninghamii*).

The closed canopy cover ranges from 15 to 60 ft. (5–20 m) high; typically, there are some emergent melaleucas or eucalypts reaching to 100 ft. (30 m), so that the habitat can sometimes look like a RAINFOREST WET SCLEROPHYLL FOREST or a HEATHY DRY SCLEROPHYLL FOREST from a distance. The typical eucalypts include Tallowwood (*Eucalyptus microcorys*), Carbeen (*Corymbia tessellaris*), Swamp Mahogany (*Eucalyptus robusta*), Blackbutt (*Eucalyptus pilularis*), Forest Red Gum (*Eucalyptus tereticornis*), and Sydney Blue Gum (*Eucalyptus saligna*), while the emergent melaleucas include Weeping Tea Tree (*Melaleuca leucadendra*) and Blue Paperbark (*Melaleuca dealbata*).

The understorey of this rainforest can be much thicker than that of other rainforests, filled with vines such as Austral Sarsaparilla (*Smilax australis*) and Climbing Lily (*Geitonoplesium cymosum*), sometimes approaching heathland in density. Shrubs include Midgen Berry (*Austromyrtus dulcis*) and Native Ginger (*Alpinia caerulea*). Many species of ferns are also present.

When this habitat forms on coastal headlands it tends to look more like an impoverished rainforest than the forests on unconsolidated sands, and it supports a smaller selection of rainforest trees including Hard Quandong (*Elaeocarpus obovata*), Wild Prune (*Sersalisia sericea*), Wild Quince (*Guioa semiglauca*), Yellow Tulipwood (*Drypetes deplanchei*), Brush Box, Coast Canthium (*Cyclophyllum longipetalum*), Three-veined Laurel (*Cryptocarya triplinervis*), Hairy

Alectryon (*Alectryon connatus*), Clustered Persimmon (*Diospyros fasciculosa*), and Tuckeroo. The shrub layer of the headland Littoral Rainforest is much sparser than that of the sandy forests, with shrubs such as Cedar Bay Cherry (*Eugenia reinwardtiana*), Round-leaved Medicosma (*Medicosma obovata*), Chainfruit (*Alyxia ruscifolia*), and Poor-flower Tree (*Memecylon pauciflorum*).

Littoral Rainforest grows over a very wide range of climates from the temperate oceanic climate of s. New South Wales (Köppen **Cfb**) to the monsoonal tropical savanna climate of Madang, Papua New Guinea (Köppen **Aw**), in areas with rainfall as low as 32 in. (800 mm) to as high as 79 in. (2000 mm), and temperatures ranging from winter lows of 46°F (8°C) to highs of 95°F (35°C)—though the vast majority of these forests are found in the subtropical and tropical zones of Australasia. They form on podzols (see appendix, Soil Groups and Habitats) that are much more typical of heathlands but where waterlogging allows for a concentration of both water and nutrients.

WILDLIFE: No species are restricted to this forest, and there is much overlap with nearby habitat types. Orange-footed Megapode and Australian Brushturkey occur, as do Double-eyed Fig-Parrot, Peaceful Dove, Bar-shouldered Dove, Wompoo Fruit-Dove, Rose-crowned Fruit-Dove, Southern Papuan Pitta, Lovely Fairywren, Fairy Gerygone, Brown Honeyeater, Yellow Honeyeater, Mistletoebird, Sahul Sunbird, and the restricted-range Ashy-bellied White-eye off n. Cape York. Black-tailed Whistler, Rufous Shrikethrush, and Hornbill Friarbird (subspecies of Helmeted Friarbird) also occur. In New Guinea, the birdlife includes Orange-bellied Fruit-Dove, Fawn-breasted Bowerbird, Arafura Shrikethrush, Graceful Honeyeater, Helmeted Friarbird, White-shouldered Fairywren, and along the forest edges, Streak-headed and Chestnut-breasted Munias.

CONSERVATION: Littoral Rainforests are naturally highly fragmented, small pockets of forest. Their location in populated areas of Australia is mainly under threat, due less to farming and far more to

Double-eyed Fig-Parrot can be found within Littoral Rainforest where the rainforest meets the sea in ne. Queensland in places like Cairns and Iron Range. © PABLO CERVANTES, TROPICAL BIRDING TOURS

The striking Wompoo Pigeon is a frugivorous species that seeks out fruiting trees within a variety of forest types in Australia and New Guinea. © SAM WOODS, TROPICAL BIRDING TOURS

urban expansion and tourism infrastructure—people just want to live and vacation near the beach. Further fragmentation of these forests reduces their resilience by isolating plant and animal populations. Another major conservation issue is the invasion of non-native species such as Common Lantana (*Lantana camara*) and Bitou Bush (*Osteospermum moniliferum*), which can outcompete native plant species and create a habitat not attractive to most native wildlife.

DISTRIBUTION: This habitat is found around the coasts of New Guinea and its surrounding islands. In Australia, it occurs from Cape York Peninsula, Queensland, to far e. Victoria and is far more common in the north and very limited in s. Australia. It is always found within a few miles (km) of the shoreline.

WHERE TO SEE: Great Sandy National Park, Queensland, Australia; Iluka Nature Reserve, New South Wales, Australia; Madang, Papua New Guinea.

Papuan Pitta migrates into this habitat in extreme ne. Australia from the island of New Guinea. It also occurs in the very similar Lowland Rainforest. © IAIN CAMPBELL, TROPICAL BIRDING TOURS/UNSW E&ERC

Au4l AUSTRALASIAN SWAMP FOREST

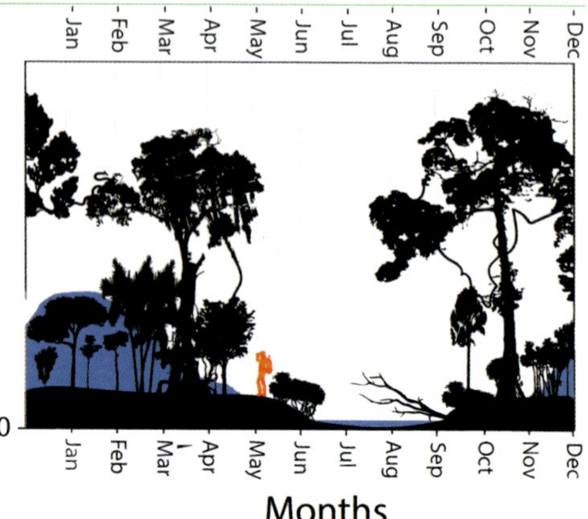

IN A NUTSHELL: Riparian lowland rainforest and *Melaleuca* swamp forest that is flooded for at least part of the year. **Global Habitat Affinities:** IGAPÓ AND VÁRZEA; AFROTROPICAL SWAMP FOREST; PALM SWAMP FOREST. **Continental Habitat Affinities:** LOWLAND RAINFOREST. **Species Overlap:** LOWLAND RAINFOREST; TROPICAL MANGROVE FOREST. **Full Bird Assemblage:** habitatsoftheworld.org/Au4l.

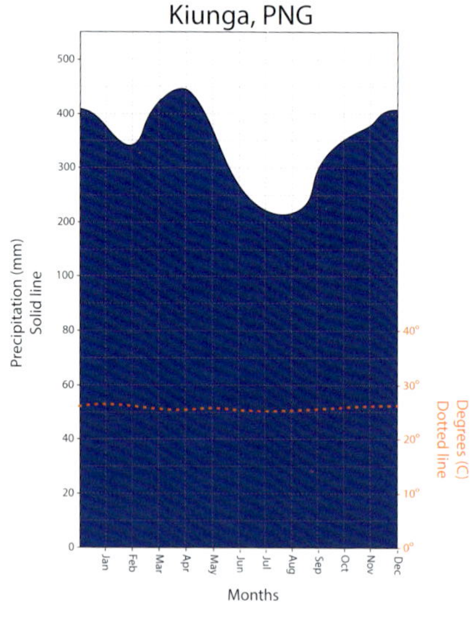

DESCRIPTION: The Australasian equivalent of the SWAMP FOREST of Africa, this habitat consists of riparian forest that, because of geomorphology impeding drainage, produces flooding and creates anaerobic (oxygen-poor) conditions that promote the development of entisols (also called gleysols; see appendix Soil Groups and Habitats), with their characteristic grey, blue, or greenish colour. Australasian Swamp Forest has a profoundly different botanical composition from the typical AUSTRALASIAN LOWLAND RAINFOREST and SUBTROPICAL RAINFOREST that surround it, although in the dry season it has a similar general feeling and wildlife assemblage to the surrounding forests. In the wet season, however, floodwaters turn this forest into an ephemeral wetland, giving it a very different aspect. Typical annual flooding depth is in the range of 12–20 in. (30–50 cm) and lasts for months, although during cyclones or heavy flooding these forests can be covered in over 6 ft. (2 m) of water for weeks at a time.

The canopy of Australasian Swamp Forest is lower than that of rainforest, averaging 50–65 ft. (15–20 m) high, with emergent trees up to 100 ft. (30 m) tall. The most obvious botanical difference between this Swamp Forest and surrounding rainforests is the dominance of *Melaleuca* spp., particularly Broad-leaved Paperbark (*Melaleuca quinquenervia*), Weeping Tea Tree (*Melaleuca leucadendra*), and Cajuputi (*Melaleuca cajuputi*), as well as a profusion of palms, such as Alexandra Palm (*Archontophoenix alexandrae*) and Queensland Fan Palm (*Licuala ramsayi*), in the subcanopy.

The non-melaleuca canopy trees are dominated by species (many with predictable names) such as Swamp Box (*Lophostemon suaveolens*), Swamp Satinash (*Syzygium angophoroides*), Swamp Sheoak (*Casuarina glauca*), Swamp Mahogany (*Eucalyptus robusta*), and Broad-leaved Lilly Pilly (*Syzygium hemilamprum*). Non-palm understorey and subcanopy trees include Tuckeroo (*Cupaniopsis anacardioides*), Pink-flowered Doughwood (*Melicope elleryana*), Umbrella Cheese Tree (*Glochidion sumatranum*), and Cape Nutmeg (*Horsfieldia australiana*). In some Swamp Forests, pandans join the palms as a dominant feature of the understorey, with Thatch Screw-Pine (*Pandanus tectorius*) being the most common species, but Pup Pandan (*Pandanus gemmifer*) is also widespread in these lowland forests. The canopy and understorey have many vines, such as Centipede Tongavine (*Parsonsia straminea*), Hairy Mary (*Calamus australis*), and Vicious Hairy Mary (*Calamus radicalis*), as well as epiphytes such as Bird's Nest Fern (*Asplenium nidus*).

As the ground is saturated for months at a time, the ground-cover plants are far more specialised than the species of most rainforests, and there are many ferns such as Feathered Mosquito Fern (*Azolla pinnata*), Swamp Water Fern (*Blechnum indicum*), Harsh Ground Fern (*Hypolepis muelleri*), and Pouched Coral Fern (*Gleichenia dicarpa*).

These forests generally form in tropical areas with wet tropical climates (Köppen **Af**), although they do grow as far south as subtropical climates (Köppen **Cfa**). They are usually found in hot, very wet climates with annual rainfall above 34 in. (850 mm), up to many feet of rainfall, but the precipitation does not need to be regular, and many Swamp Forests thrive in regions with very monsoonal climates with strong dry seasons but intense wet seasons that turn the forest into a wetland for months at a time. These are all summer wetlands that receive most of their rain

Australasian Swamp Forest has a nearly impenetrable thick and tangled understorey, which is flooded during the wet season. © IAIN CAMPBELL, TROPICAL BIRDING TOURS/UNSW E&ERC

between November and May, although there is often a delay between the rains and the rise in the water table, so the swamps are at their fullest at the end of the wet season and into the early dry season.

A feature that distinguishes these forests from the African Swamp Forest or the south American IGAPÓ AND VÁRZEA is the rarity of aerial roots and stilt roots (reminiscent of mangroves) so prevalent in those forests. Some species of Australasian Swamp Forest such as the Thatch Screw-Pine and Freshwater Mangrove (*Barringtonia acutangula*) do have them, but they are not a major feature.

A fascinating difference between lowlands of Australasia and the Neotropics is that in the brackish-water environment where mangroves meet swamp forest, Australia does not have an extensive equivalent to the saline parts of the PETÉN SWAMP FOREST of Central and South America where rainforest plants grow within the root structure of the mangrove trees. In Australia this niche is occupied by *Melaleuca* spp., particularly Broad-leaved Paperbark and Cajuputi, which grow in brackish and fresh water, so this habitat spans that ecotone. This is important not only in Australasia; this ability to survive in areas with varying salinity and water levels has allowed Broad-leaved Paperbark to become a major pest in the swamps of Florida (USA)—it is hard to compete with a tree that can withstand salinity, flooding, and fire.

WILDLIFE: Because there are so many melaleucas in the canopy and the understorey is dominated by rainforest plants and water-tolerant plants, the bird assemblage of Australasian Swamp Forest is a fascinating mix of rainforest birds, species more typical of savannas, and even mangrove specialists. Fruit-doves are less common in this forest compared with rainforests, and species such as Superb and Wompoo Fruit-Doves are essentially missing from Swamp Forest and replaced by Torresian Imperial-Pigeon, which is very common in this habitat. Other fruit eaters such as Australasian Figbird, Metallic Starling, Green Oriole, and Double-eyed Fig-Parrot are very

In ne. Queensland the Lovely Fairywren (a female is pictured) occurs in understorey thickets in both Lowland Rainforest and nearby Swamp Forest, which have a similar plant composition. © SAM WOODS, TROPICAL BIRDING TOURS

Australian Rufous Fantail is widespread in coastal e. Australia, inhabiting a variety of habitat types, including Swamp Forest. © IAIN CAMPBELL, TROPICAL BIRDING TOURS/UNSW E&ERC

prominent members of the canopy bird assemblage.

Melaleuca-associated honeyeaters such as Brown-backed and Bar-breasted Honeyeaters are common here and are joined by MONSOON VINEFOREST species like Yellow Honeyeater and TROPICAL MANGROVE FOREST species such as Varied Honeyeater and Red-headed Myzomela. Most of the typical rainforest honeyeaters, such as Yellow-spotted and Cryptic Honeyeaters and Helmeted Friarbird, occur here in far fewer numbers than in the rainforests nearby. Understorey species such as Australian Spectacled Monarch, Black-faced Monarch, and Shining Flycatchers are very common, along with other insectivorous birds such as Lovely Fairywren and Australian Rufous Fantail, and many small gleaning species such as Large-billed Gerygone. In the n. Cape York Peninsula around Iron Range, Yellow-billed Kingfisher, Green-backed Honeyeater, Northern Scrub-Robin, and Magnificent Riflebird are all very regularly found in this habitat. New Guinea Swamp Forest has New Guinea Flightless Rail, King Bird-of-Paradise, Frilled Monarch, Fairy Gerygone, Yellow-bellied Gerygone, Papuan Babbler, White-bellied Pitohui, and both Little and Common Paradise-Kingfishers, the Little in the lower stratum.

One of the mammal highlights of a night walk in this forest in n. Queensland is the Striped Possum, an exquisite nocturnal marsupial with distinctive black-and-white stripes down its back. Another marsupial, Northern Brown Bandicoot, remains common in this forest, where it rummages through the undergrowth along with the native rodent White-tailed Giant Rat. Fawn-footed

Melomys is small native rodent that lives in the undergrowth and up into the subcanopy of the Swamp Forest. Spectacled Flying Fox often uses these forests as roosting locations and can congregate in colonies of many thousands of individuals. There are far fewer macropods in this forest than in surrounding woodlands, although Red-legged Pademelon and Swamp Wallaby are regularly found.

Turtles are far more common in these swamps than in surrounding woodlands or forests, and species such as Eastern Short-necked Turtle (*Emydura macquarii*) and Eastern Saw-shelled Turtle (*Myuchelys latisternum*) are regularly seen in the Wet Tropics region. Lizards include large monitors such as Lace Monitor (*Varanus varius*) and small geckos such as the very widespread Mourning Gecko (*Lepidodactylus lugubris*). In n. Queensland, Boyd's Forest Dragon (*Lophosaurus boydii*) is a major attraction in Swamp Forest; a member of the Australasian bearded dragon subfamily, it is a striking lizard with green scales, a spiny crest along its neck, and bold, patterned markings—reminiscent of Green Iguana (*Iguana iguana*). There are many varieties of skinks in this habitat including Closed-litter Rainbow Skink (*Carlia longipes*), Pale-lipped Shadeskink (*Saproscincus basiliscus*), and Northern Red-throated Rainbow Skink (*Carlia crypta*).

As would be expected in a wetlands system, amphibians abound. A typical Swamp Forest in the Wet Tropics of Queensland contains species such as White-lipped Tree Frog (*Nyctimystes infrafrenatus*) and Eastern Dwarf Tree Frog (*Litoria fallax*) in the understorey, while plants closer to the ground and the forest floor are more likely to have Dainty Tree Frog (*Ranoidea gracilenta*), Marbled Frog (*Limnodynastes convexiusculus*), Northern Barred Frog (*Mixophyes schevilli*), Rainforest Stony-creek Frog (*Ranoidea jungguy*), and Eastern Stony-creek Frog (*Ranoidea wilcoxii*). Unfortunately, the forest floor will almost certainly also have many introduced Cane Toads (*Rhinella marina*).

CONSERVATION: Much of this forest has been cleared and the ground drained for agriculture, especially sugarcane farming. The extensive sugarcane fields around Broadwater, New South Wales, and the Edmonton region south of Cairns, Queensland, were once largely Swamp Forest. To the majority of the Australian population, Swamp Forest is not as visually attractive as rainforest or wet sclerophyll forests, which has dire consequences for conservation because people largely don't care about preserving this forest. Clearing and drainage of these forests for farming and now for urban expansion is ongoing. Altered hydrology is a threat because some of the native plants rely on specific water regimes, including seasonal flooding and consistent groundwater levels. Decreased water flow will change the understorey to one more similar to rainforests. There have been some wins for conservation with the creation of Cattana Wetlands near Cairns, but they are few and far between.

DISTRIBUTION: This habitat is found around the coasts of New Guinea and its surrounding islands. In Australia, it occurs from Cape York Peninsula to s. New South Wales in a range of periodically inundated coastal depressions, such as dune swales and estuarine deposits, but also in areas with poor drainage on the ranges along the east coast of Australia.

WHERE TO SEE: Flecker Botanic Gardens, Cairns, Queensland, Australia; Broadwater National Park, Evans Head, New South Wales, Australia; Kiunga area, Papua New Guinea; Veimauri, near Port Moresby, Papua New Guinea; Wasur National Park, South Papua, Indonesian New Guinea.

Opposite: **Night walks in Australasian Swamp Forest can reveal mammals such as Northern Brown Bandicoot, which is abundant in the habitat, and even the stunning Striped Possum (pictured).** © SAM WOODS, TROPICAL BIRDING TOURS

Australasian Dry Deciduous Forests Dendrogram (Biome 5)

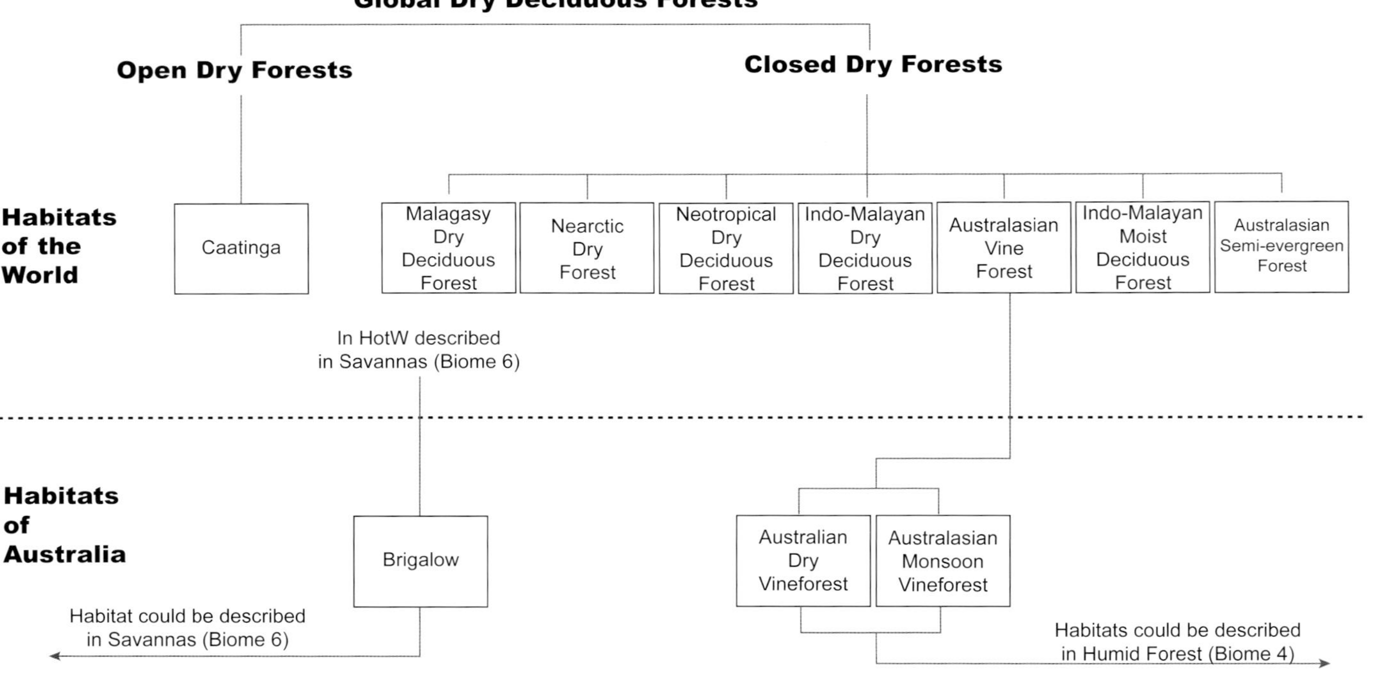

TROPICAL DRY DECIDUOUS FORESTS

Au5A AUSTRALIAN DRY VINEFOREST

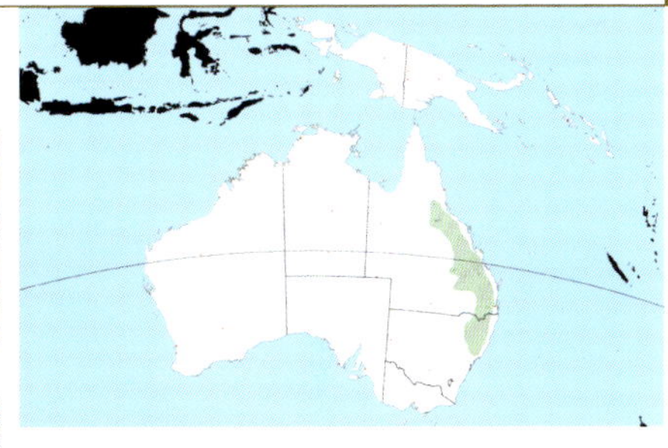

IN A NUTSHELL: Semiarid scrub of subtropical Australia that is a mix of rainforest and dry-deciduous plants. **Global Habitat Affinities:** AGRESTE CAATINGA; DRY DECIDUOUS YUNGAS; INDIAN MOIST DECIDUOUS FOREST. **Continental Habitat Affinities:** MONSOON VINEFOREST. **Species Overlap:** BRIGALOW, MONSOON VINEFOREST; SUBTROPICAL RAINFOREST. **Full Bird Assemblage:** habitatsoftheworld.org/Au5A.

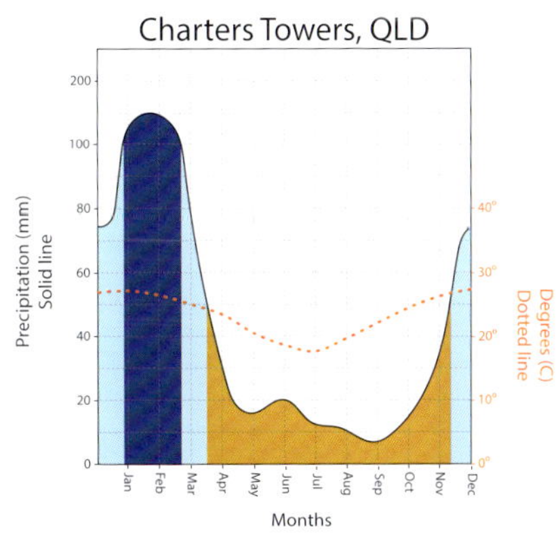

DESCRIPTION: This rainforest-like forest is both a wet and a dry habitat, depending on the season. The forest occurs as a wide variety of dry-deciduous and semi-evergreen 'thickets', 15–60 ft. (5–20 m) in height, with taller emergent trees such as Port Jackson Fig (*Ficus rubiginosa*) and Hoop Pine (*Araucaria cunninghamii*); Brigalow (*Acacia harpophylla*); and eucalypts such as Narrow-leaved Ironbark (*Eucalyptus crebra*), which indicate the surrounding habitats this forest merges with—SUBTROPICAL RAINFOREST, BRIGALOW, and SHRUBBY EUCALYPT SAVANNA, respectively. Many of the other trees are seasonally deciduous, losing leaves in the dry season but forming a very thick canopy and bearing fruit in the wet season, so the canopy looks very open during the dry season but more resembles a rainforest during the wet season when it looks incredibly dense. Some of the most distinctive trees in this vineforest are the bottle trees, such as Broad-leaved Bottle Tree (*Brachychiton australis*) and Queensland Bottle Tree (*Brachychiton rupestris*), which with their pachycaulesque (short, fat) structure look like small versions of the Boab (*Adansonia gregorii*) of nw. Australia, the baobabs of Africa, and the ceibas of South America. Propeller Tree (*Gyrocarpus americanus*) is named for the fascinating structure of its leaf, which looks like a helicopter

An aerial view of Dry Vineforest during the wet season, when the deciduous canopy is leafed out. In the dry season, most of the canopy trees will be leafless. © IAIN CAMPBELL, TROPICAL BIRDING TOURS/UNSW E&ERC

The deciduous understorey of Australian Dry Vineforest changes with the seasons, being more open and easier to walk through during the dry season. © IAIN CAMPBELL, TROPICAL BIRDING TOURS/UNSW E&ERC

The plants of Dry Vineforest are not fire-tolerant and therefore are at risk from fires where overgrazing occurs; the resulting habitat may more closely resemble savanna. © IAIN CAMPBELL, TROPICAL BIRDING TOURS/UNSW E&ERC

rotor. Other canopy trees that occur in this forest include Small-fruited Mock-Olive (*Notelaea microcarpa*), Burdekin Plum (*Pleiogynium timorense*), Crow's Ash (*Flindersia australis*), Scaly Ebony (*Diospyros geminata*), Queensland Ebony (*Diospyros humilis*), Silver Croton (*Croton insularis*), and Narrow-leaf Myrtle (*Backhousia angustifolia*).

The understorey is also deciduous in the dry months, as the name of the habitat may suggest, and is dominated by vines such as Wonga Wonga Vine (*Pandorea pandorana*), Rusty Glossocarya (*Glossocarya hemiderma*), and Tarantula Vine (*Cissus reniformis*). As well as vines, the understorey can have many shrubs and small trees such as Conkerberry (*Carissa ovata*), which also occurs in similar habitats in Asia and Africa, Musk (*Croton phebalioides*), Glasswood, aka Axe Gapper (*Geijera salicifolia*), Straggly Lantern-Bush (*Abutilon oxycarpum*), and, surprisingly, Chainfruit (*Alyxia ruscifolia*), a shrub that is also tolerant of very cold microclimates. Typically, Dry Vineforest has very little native ground cover, but in areas where goats have been allowed to overgraze, introduced grasses and forbs have been able to establish and make the habitat more prone to ground fires.

This habitat is the southern extension of MONSOON VINEFOREST, but here the habitat is no longer driven by the extreme monsoons. This habitat, although still getting more rain in summer than in winter, does not have the extremes of the other habitat and remains a semiarid environment through much of the year. Its climate ranges from dry monsoonal (Köppen **Aw**) to humid subtropical (Köppen **Cfa**), with rainfall varying between 24 and 48 in. (600–1200 mm) per year, increasing from south to north. In drier areas, the habitat tends to grow on landforms and soils that would be conducive to rainforest development if the rainfall were higher, such as nutrient-rich clay soils from sediment or mafic (dark mineral) igneous rocks such as basalt, and in wetter regions it forms on poorer soils developed on nutrient-deficient metamorphic rocks such as gneiss and igneous rocks such as rhyolites. So, as a very general rule, in drier environments better soil is required to sustain this habitat. It is not fire-tolerant and is readily transformed to savannas or temperate woodlands when exposed to increased fire frequency and/or intensity.

WILDLIFE: This forest is as much characterised by absent species as it is by those that occur. In n. Australia, birds such as Fawn-breasted Bowerbird, White-browed Robin, and Yellow-breasted Boatbill are missing from this habitat even though they are indicator species of the nearby MONSOON VINEFOREST. Farther south, in s. Queensland and n. New South Wales, bird species so obvious in the SUBTROPICAL RAINFOREST, such as Green Catbird, Black-faced Monarch, Regent Bowerbird, Australian Logrunner, and Paradise Riflebird, are all conspicuously absent from this habitat. Even the Eastern Whipbird, which is near ubiquitous in the rainforests and wet sclerophyll forests, is absent from this forest. This forest is mainly dominated by bird species more typical of BRIGALOW—such as Fan-tailed Cuckoo, Brown Honeyeater, Rufous Whistler, and Grey Fantail—mixed with Monsoon Vineforest species such as Fairy Gerygone, Varied Triller, Rufous Shrikethrush, Australasian Figbird, and Spangled Drongo, and a few eastern forest species such as Lewin's Honeyeater and Scarlet Myzomela. While birding in this environment does not lead to a large species count, it is always fascinating to know what is missing here from the surrounding environment—biogeography at its most challenging.

The mammals of Dry Vineforest are strongly similar to those of the rainforests, although this forest is markedly depauperate. The assemblage is limited to medium-sized macropods such as Swamp Wallaby, Black-striped Wallaby, and Red-legged Pademelon. In drier periods, more savanna-oriented species such as Agile Wallaby, Euro (a subspecies of Common Wallaroo), and Eastern Grey Kangaroos may use the forest. Common Brushtail Possum and Coppery Brushtail Possum, Short-beaked Echidna, Koala, Platypus, Rufous Bettong, Greater Glider, Sugar Glider, Yellow-bellied Glider, and Northern Brown Bandicoot use the habitat. Macropods using this habitat include Whiptail Wallaby and Herbert's Rock-Wallaby. At the northern extent of this habitat where it merges with tropical rainforests and MONSOON VINEFOREST, the absence of species such as Common Spotted Cuscus, Herbert River Ringtail Possum, and Musky Rat-Kangaroo is notable.

Dry Vineforest is a relatively depauperate bird habitat, mostly sharing a small number of species from Monsoon Vineforest. A few rainforest species also occur here, such as Lewin's Honeyeater. © PABLO CERVANTES, TROPICAL BIRDING TOURS

Dry Vineforest shares many bird species typical of the Monsoon Vineforest found to the north of this habitat, like Australasian Figbird. © SAM WOODS, TROPICAL BIRDING TOURS

The reptile assemblage in these forests reflects a mix of rainforest and savanna species. Lizards include Australian Water Dragon (*Intellagama lesueurii*), Lace Monitor (*Varanus varius*), Copper-tailed Ctenotus (*Ctenotus taeniolatus*), Elegant Snake-eyed Skink (*Cryptoblepharus pulcher*), Eastern Firetail Skink (*Morethia taeniopleura*), Diamond-shielded Sunskink (*Lampropholis adonis*), Major Skink (*Bellatorias frerei*), Dark Bar-sided Skink (*Concinnia martini*), Eastern Stone Gecko (*Diplodactylus vittatus*), Common Prickly Gecko (*Heteronotia binoei*), and Southern Spotted Velvet Gecko (*Oedura tryoni*). The small Ocellated Velvet Gecko (*Oedura monilis*) is closely associated with this habitat through most of its range from n. Queensland to n. New South Wales. Snakes are common in this habitat, including tropical species such as Black-headed Python (*Aspidites melanocephalus*), inland species such as Mulga Snake (*Pseudechis australis*), and typically eastern species such as Robust Blind Snake (*Anilios ligatus*), Eastern Brown Snake (*Pseudonaja textilis*), and Northern Death Adder (*Acanthophis praelongus*).

CONSERVATION: Because this is not a particularly attractive habitat to the general public (regarded as a 'scrub'), Dry Vineforest has been afforded little protection over the decades. What remains now are minuscule patches hardly capable of maintaining their own wildlife assemblages. Because the remnants are surrounded by drier woodlands and fire-prone savannas such as OPEN EUCALYPT SAVANNA, this habitat is under constant threat of being completely wiped out in any one area. The largest remaining block, in Forty Mile Scrub, Queensland, was almost completely destroyed when fire tore through the habitat in 2019. Regrowth is slow, and the large grass component of the regrowth floor suggests that it may be finished off with the next fire. This is one of Australia's more imperilled habitats

DISTRIBUTION: Dry Vineforest is found along the semiarid subtropical eastern seaboard of Australia, just west of the Great Dividing Range. In n. Australia it extends as far north as the southern edge of the Atherton Tableland (Queensland), and in New South Wales it is found around the Warrumbungle mountain range.

WHERE TO SEE: Forty Mile Scrub National Park, Queensland, Australia; Carnarvon Gorge National Park, Queensland, Australia; Mount Kaputar National Park, New South Wales, Australia.

Au5B AUSTRALASIAN MONSOON VINEFOREST

IN A NUTSHELL: The jungle of n. Australia and the islands to the north, with well-defined wet and dry seasons and lots of semi-deciduous trees and shrubs. **Global Habitat Affinities:** SOUTHEAST ASIAN MOIST DECIDUOUS FOREST; AFROTROPICAL MONSOON FOREST; MESOAMERICAN SEMI-EVERGREEN FOREST. **Continental Habitat Affinities:** DRY VINEFOREST; LOWLAND RAINFOREST. **Species Overlap:** LOWLAND RAINFOREST; SWAMP FOREST. **Full Bird Assemblage:** habitatsoftheworld.org/Au5B.

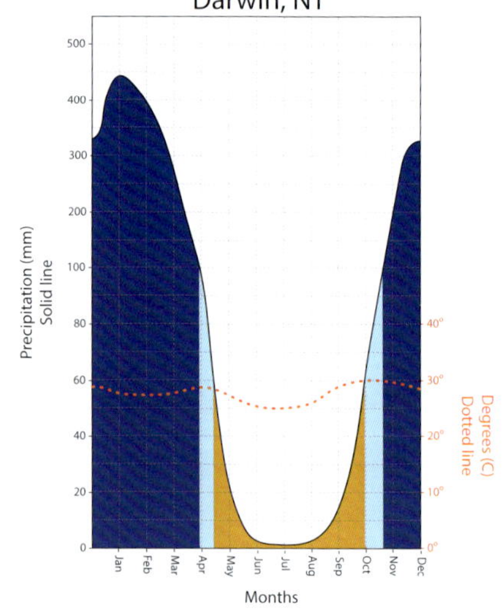

DESCRIPTION: Sprinkled across the tropical north of Australia are patches of semi-deciduous rainforest surrounded by savannas. The habitat is very obvious in the drier areas, such as the Northern Territory, where the boundary with habitats such as TETRODONTA WOODLAND SAVANNA can appear razor-sharp. However, in New Guinea and the Cape York region of n. Queensland, this habitat tends to be an ecotone between the savannas and the LOWLAND RAINFOREST, so the boundary with the savanna is sharp, but the boundary with the rainforest is nebulous and difficult to pinpoint. In the southeast of the habitat's range, where the area is generally drier and the monsoonal influence is not as pronounced, Monsoon Vineforest merges with DRY VINEFOREST; the distinction between the two is not obvious from looking at the vegetation, but the bird and other wildlife assemblages are very obvious, as most of the Monsoon Vineforest bird species have abrupt distribution boundaries around the base of Cape York Peninsula.

This forest could be classified alongside the different Australian rainforests as a version of the humid broadleaf forests, but we have classified it as a version of tropical dry forest because so much of it is deciduous in the dry season. The difference between this forest and true rainforest does not seem to be overall rainfall but rather the duration and intensity of the dry season. Monsoon Vineforest habitat appears very lush in the wet season, when the canopy looks very

Monsoon Vineforest in the wet season, when it is lush and verdant, illustrating the low canopy relative to the similar Lowland Rainforest. © IAIN CAMPBELL, TROPICAL BIRDING TOURS/UNSW E&ERC

similar to that of rainforest, but for several months each year, little or no rain falls (unlike in rainforest), which causes plant stress.

The vineforest canopy typically ranges from 30 to 75 ft. (10–25 m) high, with the occasional emergent tree, and is very irregular, with areas of 90% cover and others with as little as 70% cover. The canopy comprises a mix of deciduous, semi-deciduous, and evergreen trees. Few of the evergreen trees have leaves with 'drip tips', which are common in rainforest, and many are leathery to resist desiccation during the dry season. The vineforest is dominated by species such as Cluster Fig (*Ficus racemosa*), White Fig (*Ficus virens*), Cooktown Ironwood (*Erythrophleum chlorostachys*), Mamajen (*Mimusops elengi*), Red Bush Apple (*Syzygium suborbicular*), Cocky Apple (*Planchonia careya*), and Kakadu Plum (*Terminalia ferdinandiana*).

The understorey in Monsoon Vineforest varies but generally ranges from 6 to 33 ft. (2–10 m) in height. It consists of smaller trees, shrubs, and various vine species that thrive in the shaded conditions created by the dense canopy. The understorey is generally open in the dry season, when it is very easy to walk through the copious dry leaf litter that crackles underfoot, but in the wet season it is a lot more shaded, thickly vegetated, and more difficult to navigate. Vines may not be more common in Monsoon Vineforest than in other rainforests, but they are much more obvious, especially in the undergrowth, where species include Spearbush

The low height of the canopy, the semi-deciduous trees, and a pronounced dry season allow plenty of light to reach the forest floor, resulting in a dense and tangled understorey with extensive vines. © IAIN CAMPBELL, TROPICAL BIRDING TOURS/UNSW E&ERC

In Australia's Kakadu National Park, impressive sandstone escarpments with Rocky Spinifex Desert can be seen towering above the surrounding Monsoon Vineforest. © SAM WOODS, TROPICAL BIRDING TOURS

(*Pandorea doratoxylon*), Snakewood (*Tinospora smilacina*), and Caper Bush (*Capparis spinosa*), which can grow as a vine but also as a shrub. Other shrubs and small trees include the very distinctive Screw Palm (*Pandanus spiralis*), Sea Ebony (*Diospyros maritima*), and Scrub Vitex (*Vitex acuminata*).

Monsoon Vineforest forms primarily in areas with a monsoonal climate (Köppen **Ama**), with hot summers (88–91°F/31–33°C) and hot winters (84–90°F/29–32°C). Most rain falls during the austral summer, approximately November–April. Typical rainfall is 67–83 in. (1700–2100 mm), which is well in the range of rainforest conditions, but the rain is very seasonal, often with less than 0.4 in. (10 mm) during the dry season, and some months with no rain.

These forests tend to form on soils that are generally nutrient-deficient, but soil is

The spectacular Rainbow Pitta is one of the most sought-after bird species in Monsoon Vineforest within Australia's Top End (Northern Territory). © IAIN CAMPBELL, TROPICAL BIRDING TOURS/UNSW E&ERC

not a main determinant of this habitat—the local hydrology and fire regimes set it apart. Monsoon Vineforest can occur along drainage lines and near permanent water, such as Fogg Dam, but also in low-lying depressions that retain water during the wet season. Examples of this are obvious around Weipa, Queensland, where small enclaves of vineforest only a few hundred feet in diameter are surrounded by TETRODONTA WOODLAND SAVANNA in a very flat lateritic bauxite plateau. In other areas such as Nourlangie Rock (Burrungkuy) in Kakadu National Park (Northern Territory), these forests are nestled at the base of impermeable sandstone escarpments that effectively act as funnels, greatly increasing the available water. However, even with this extra water availability, fire is the main determinant because Monsoon Vineforest is not fire-tolerant and is readily transformed to savanna when exposed to increased fire frequency and/or intensity; sitting in depressions or nestled at the base of escarpments protects these forests from being converted to savannas.

WILDLIFE: The bird assemblage of Monsoon Vineforest changes throughout Australia, with some birds being constant, and others restricted to certain regions. In the Northern Territory and far n. Western Australia, birds restricted to this habitat include ground dwellers such as the large mound-nest builder Orange-footed Megapode, plus Pacific Emerald Dove and the brightly coloured Rainbow Pitta. The canopy is full of fruit eaters such as Rose-crowned Fruit-Dove, Green Oriole, Australasian Figbird, and the extremely range-restricted Black-banded Fruit-Dove, which is limited to forests at the base of the Arnhem Land escarpment. In the summer season, Torresian Imperial-Pigeon becomes very common, and Channel-billed Cuckoo migrates from Indonesia. There are many resident insectivores and carnivores such as Little Bronze-Cuckoo, Sahul Brush Cuckoo, Blue-winged Kookaburra, Sahul Cicadabird, Arafura Shrikethrush, and Grey Whistler. Spangled Drongo occurs in a variety of habitats but is ubiquitous in Monsoon Vineforest, where its extremely raucous calls can usually be heard throughout the day.

Where Monsoon Vineforest is close to LOWLAND RAINFOREST it usually has a higher percentage of honeyeaters than rainforest habitats, and these include White-gaped, Rufous-banded, and White-throated Honeyeaters; Dusky and Red-headed Myzomelas; and Silver-crowned Friarbird.

In the Northern Territory, the understorey of Monsoon Vineforest has a different suite of birds, including small species such as Green-backed Gerygone, Large-billed Gerygone, Northern Fantail, Arafura Fantail, and Broad-billed Flycatcher. Medium-sized understorey birds include Arafura Shrikethrush and Buff-sided Robin. Raptors hunting in this forest include Pacific Baza, Grey Goshawk, Brown Goshawk, and Collared Sparrowhawk. Nocturnal birds are not particularly common here, although Large-tailed Nightjar and Rufous Owl are both targets for birders to find.

Monsoon Vineforest in Queensland, and particularly in Cape York Peninsula, has a bird assemblage that is essentially a depauperate version of that of LOWLAND RAINFOREST. Monsoon Vineforest surrounded by rainforest will have a very similar bird assemblage, but in areas to the west of the Lowland Rainforest where Monsoon Vineforest is surrounded by different types of savannas, some indicator rainforest species are notably absent, including Southern Cassowary, Superb Fruit-Dove, Buff-breasted Paradise-Kingfisher, Chestnut-breasted Cuckoo, Papuan Eclectus, Red-cheeked Parrot, Double-eyed Fig-Parrot, Black-eared Catbird, White-faced Robin, Yellow-legged Flyrobin, Frill-necked Monarch, and Northern Scrub-Robin. Other species, however, appear more common in Monsoon Vineforest than in the true rainforests, including Rose-crowned Fruit-Dove, Fawn-breasted Bowerbird, Lovely Fairywren, White-browed Robin, Yellow Honeyeater, Fairy Gerygone, Black-winged Monarch, and Yellow-breasted Boatbill.

Species in Cape York that occur in both Monsoon Vineforest and the other humid forests include ground dwellers such as Australian Brushturkey and Orange-footed Megapode, and the world's largest cockatoo, the massive black Palm Cockatoo. Other canopy birds include the birds-

Rose-crowned Fruit-Dove is particularly fond of this habitat. © JUN MATSUI, SICKLEBILL SAFARIS

of-paradise Trumpet Manucode and Magnificent Riflebird, along with Varied Triller and Sahul Cicadabird. Honeyeaters here include the range-restricted Green-backed and Tawny-breasted Honeyeaters, along with the smaller Graceful Honeyeater, Red-headed Myzomela, and Dusky Myzomela, and the much larger Hornbill subspecies of Helmeted Friarbird. Larger predators that hunt in the understorey include Rufous Shrikethrush and Black Butcherbird.

In New Guinea, no species are endemic to this habitat, and generalists like honeyeaters are widespread, as are Coroneted Fruit-Dove, Dwarf Fruit-Dove, Papuan Babbler, Blue Jewel-babbler, Frilled and Spot-winged Monarchs, Tropical Scrubwren, and Fairy Gerygone, whilst the rare Campbell's Fairywren has been observed in the Middle Fly region of sw. Papua New Guinea.

In Australia, typical reptiles include geckos such as Northern Velvet Gecko (*Oedura castelnaui*) and Common Prickly Gecko (*Heteronotia binoei*), other lizards such as Northern Water Dragon (*Tropicagama temporalis*), Banded Tree Monitor (*Varanus scalaris*), and Top End Dtella (*Gehyra australis*). Some of the snakes include the venomous Rough-scaled Python (*Morelia carinata*) and Common Tree Snake (*Dendrelaphis punctulatus*), and the non-venomous Carpet Python (*Morelia spilota*) and Olive Python (*Liasis olivaceus*). Most mammals are much more catholic in habitat choice, occurring in both this forest and nearby rainforest; examples include Common Brushtail Possum, Rock Ringtail Possum, and Black-footed Tree-Rat.

CONSERVATION: This is a very limited habitat, but where it occurs away from riverine areas, it is prone to clearing. In the Northern Territory, the remaining patches around Darwin are all protected as are those in Kakadu National Park. There is less protection in Cape York Peninsula, and because the small patches that occur around Weipa are the locations of the highest-grade bauxite, they were mined preferentially to the surrounding TETRODONTA WOODLAND SAVANNA. There are no large protected areas of this forest to the north of Australia.

DISTRIBUTION: Throughout its range, Monsoon Vineforest is found mainly in close proximity to the coast, often on sandy soils. Outside of this region, it is the dominant habitat in much of Indonesia's Lesser Sundas and Moluccas, and on small Pacific islands eastwards to New Caledonia. In the MELALEUCA SAVANNA zone of far s. New Guinea, this habitat is found in moist areas where the trees are better protected from fire. Across n. Australia, Monsoon Vineforest may be found along dry creek beds and sheltered gullies, and along edges of sandstone escarpments. There are scattered small patches in e. Australia, including around the Iron Range on Cape York Peninsula and Inskip Point in Queensland.

WHERE TO SEE: East Point, Fogg Dam, and Howard Springs, Northern Territory, Australia; Middle Fly River around Lake Murray, Papua New Guinea.

Buff-sided Robin occupies this habitat in the tropical north of Australia. © IAIN CAMPBELL TROPICAL BIRDING TOURS/UNSW E&ERC

Au5C BRIGALOW

IN A NUTSHELL: A very thick, semiarid, Brigalow-dominated acacia woodland/forest with a mix of eucalypts, casuarinas, and conifers. **Global Habitat Affinities:** INDIAN DRY DECIDUOUS FOREST; MIOMBO. **Continental Habitat Affinities:** MIXED SANDPLAIN WOODLAND (Callitris Woodland subhabitat). **Species Overlap:** GRASSY MULGA; NORTHERN ACACIA SAVANNA; MIXED SANDPLAIN WOODLAND. **Full Bird Assemblage:** habitatsoftheworld.org/Au5C.

One of the most distinctive trees found in Brigalow within a local area of Queensland is the Queensland Bottle Tree, which displays a bulbous, baobab-like trunk and rounded crown. © IAIN CAMPBELL, TROPICAL BIRDING TOURS/UNSW E&ERC

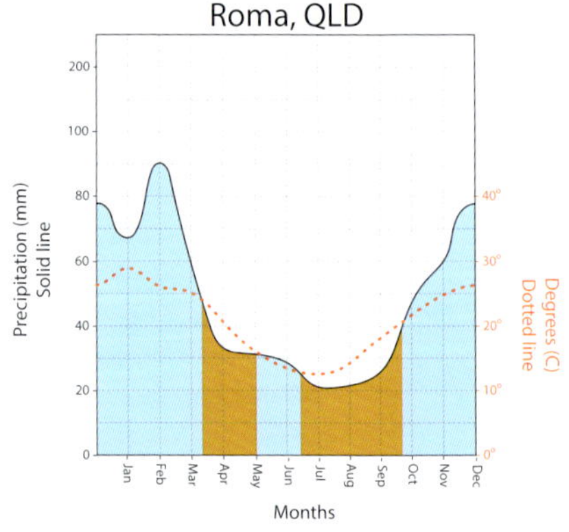

DESCRIPTION: Brigalow is a type of seasonally dry (with summer rain) tropical woodland that forms the ecotone between the AUSTRALIAN DRY VINEFOREST of the eastern ranges and savanna habitats such as OPEN EUCALYPT SAVANNA. In Africa, Asia, and South America, similar environments are covered in types of seasonally dry tropical forest such as ANGOLAN DECIDUOUS FOREST, SAL FOREST, and DRY DECIDUOUS YUNGAS, respectively; however, the canopy of Brigalow woodland is predominantly evergreen. In *Habitats of the World* (the global book of this series), this

Brigalow appears messy. It is acacia-dominated but also contains an assemblage of eucalypts, conifers, and casuarinas. © IAIN CAMPBELL, TROPICAL BIRDING TOURS/UNSW E&ERC

habitat was combined with *Callitris*-dominated MIXED SANDPLAIN WOODLAND because the two types have very similar bird assemblages. However, the more southerly *Callitris* woodlands have a semiarid climate with winter rainfall (Köppen **Bsk**), whereas Brigalow has a semiarid tropical savanna monsoonal climate (Köppen **Awb**) with a hot, moist summer and a very dry, warm winter. It forms more on gilgai soils, which are clays that undergo extensive expansion and contraction when they get wet and dry, making it very difficult for some tree species to grow.

Brigalow woodland can have a very thick canopy, usually 30–75 ft. (10–25 m) high, and could justifiably be regarded as a forest, and it blends into Dry Vineforest in the east of its range. Throughout most of the range, two *Acacia* species, Brigalow (*Acacia harpophylla*) and Gidgee (*Acacia cambagei*), are the most common canopy trees. In the wetter parts of this habitat, where it is tallest and thickest, the *Acacia* canopy is joined by Silver-leaved Ironbark (*Eucalyptus melanophloia*), Bimble Box (*Eucalyptus populnea* subsp. *bimbil*), and Buloke (*Allocasuarina luehmannii*). Walking through this habitat in the lush, wetter areas is difficult because even though the ground can be fairly barren and small shrubs are uncommon, the understorey trees and large shrubs and bushes mentioned above can form a dense thicket; this understorey thicket is usually a mix of younger canopy trees, especially young Bulokes, along with smaller trees and shrubs, including some plants typical of rainforests such as Small-fruited Mock-Olive (*Notelaea microcarpa*), Lamboto (*Psydrax odorata*), Musk (*Croton phebalioides*), and Hedge Saltbush (*Rhagodia spinescens*). Other plants found in Brigalow are more typical of more arid terrains; these include Conkerberry (*Carissa ovata*), Bumble Tree (*Capparis mitchellii*), Barrier Saltbush (*Enchylaena tomentosa*), and Desert Jasmine (*Jasminum lineare*).

The most obvious tree in this woodland is Queensland Bottle Tree (*Brachychiton rupestris*), a distant relative of the baobabs. While not making up a substantial portion of the forest, it is so distinctive, with its pachycaulesque bottle shape, that it stands out. In many areas where the Brigalow woodland has been cleared, these trees have been left, and the devastated landscape has an unfortunate resemblance to cleared areas of Madagascar with standing baobabs or rainforest areas of Africa, Asia, and South America where isolated palms are the only indication of the former magnificence.

Farther inland, where the climate becomes drier and the Brigalow merges with the GRASSY MULGA in the north and MIXED SANDPLAIN WOODLAND in the south, the woodland feels more open, with trees generally below 45 ft. (15m) tall. The Brigalow, Gidgee, and Buloke canopy assemblage is augmented by Pilliga Box (*Eucalyptus pilligaensis*), Bimble Box, and Mulga (*Acacia aneura*). The understorey is much more open than in wetter areas and can even contain chenopods such as Black Cotton Bush (*Maireana decalvans*). Despite being a semiarid habitat, Brigalow woodland was described by early settlers as a form of dry rainforest and referred to as 'scrub', in the same manner they described SUBTROPICAL RAINFOREST and DRY VINEFOREST.

WILDLIFE: The bird assemblage of Brigalow woodland is a fascinating mix of sclerophyll forest species and inland species. Birds that distinguish this habitat include Speckled Warbler, Yellow Thornbill, Striped Honeyeater, Brown-headed Honeyeater, Plum-headed Finch, and Diamond Firetail. Other typical species of this environment are Glossy Black-Cockatoo, Pale-headed Rosella, Rufous Whistler, Blue-faced Honeyeater, and Noisy Friarbird. Turquoise Parrot occurs in the southern edge of this habitat, although it may have been more widespread in the past. Red-capped Robin is more typical of the arid mulga habitats but is also common in this habitat. White-winged Chough and Apostlebird, the only members of the mud-nest-builder family, are common in the more open parts of Brigalow.

Mammals present in this habitat include the endangered Bridled Nail-tail Wallaby and Northern Hairy-nosed Wombat, as well as the more common Whiptail Wallaby, Eastern Grey Kangaroo, and Red-necked Wallaby. Reptiles include Golden-tailed Gecko (*Strophurus taenicauda*), Brigalow Scaly-foot (*Paradelma orientalis*), Southern Death Adder (*Acanthophis antarcticus*), Ornamental Snake (*Denisonia maculata*), and Dunmall's Snake (*Furina dunmalli*).

CONSERVATION: This habitat seemed to escape the decimation suffered by more southerly woodlands until the 1970s, when Queenslanders made up for lost time and cleared vast areas of Brigalow woodland in just a few years, turning it from a very widespread and abundant habitat to a severely threatened one. Very few areas of Brigalow are protected, and even today very recent clearing is evident over much of the habitat's range. In the northern part of its range, areas not cleared for crops have been extensively grazed and altered, and few large stands of Brigalow woodland still exist. The old adage that 'we protect what we love, and we love what we know' comes into play with this habitat, as conservation agencies have locked up good examples of it away from public view, so predictably there is little public appetite to protect it.

DISTRIBUTION: Brigalow habitat is found in e. Australia from south of Townsville,

Speckled Warbler is often abundant within Brigalow. It is an active thornbill species most often seen foraging on or near the ground, sometimes with other thornbills. © BEN KNOOT

Pale-headed Rosella occurs in small groups across a variety of habitats in e. Australia, including Brigalow. © IAIN CAMPBELL, TROPICAL BIRDING TOURS/UNSW E&ERC

Queensland (inland of the Great Dividing Range, west of Brisbane), south to n. New South Wales, where it blends with MIXED SANDPLAIN WOODLAND. This habitat has been extensively cleared in southern areas because it is so productive for agriculture.

WHERE TO SEE: Only minuscule remnants remain of these forests, and unfortunately, most larger patches have inexplicably been made inaccessible by the Queensland National Parks and Wildlife Service. The most accessible location is Southwood National Park, sw. Queensland, Australia.

Blue-faced Honeyeater, a gorgeous species widespread in the north and east sides of Australia, is found in a variety of semiarid habitats, including Brigalow. © SAM WOODS, TROPICAL BIRDING TOURS

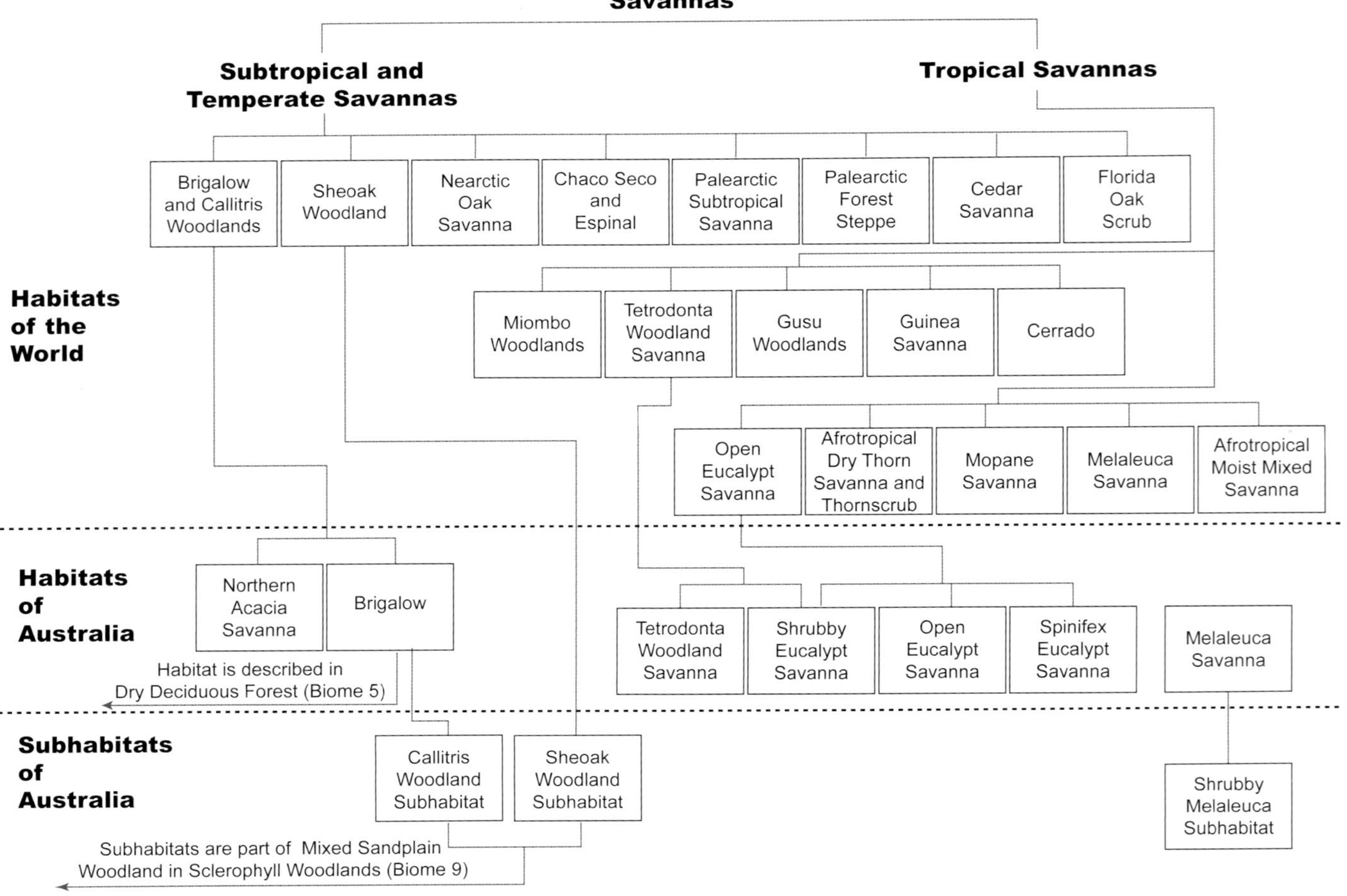

Australasian Savannas Dendrogram (Biome 6)
Savannas
Subtropical and Temperate Savannas
Tropical Savannas
Habitats of the World
Brigalow and Callitris Woodlands
Sheoak Woodland
Nearctic Oak Savanna
Chaco Seco and Espinal
Palearctic Subtropical Savanna
Palearctic Forest Steppe
Cedar Savanna
Florida Oak Scrub
Miombo Woodlands
Tetrodonta Woodland Savanna
Gusu Woodlands
Guinea Savanna
Cerrado
Open Eucalypt Savanna
Afrotropical Dry Thorn Savanna and Thornscrub
Mopane Savanna
Melaleuca Savanna
Afrotropical Moist Mixed Savanna
Habitats of Australia
Northern Acacia Savanna
Brigalow
Habitat is described in Dry Deciduous Forest (Biome 5)
Tetrodonta Woodland Savanna
Shrubby Eucalypt Savanna
Open Eucalypt Savanna
Spinifex Eucalypt Savanna
Melaleuca Savanna
Subhabitats of Australia
Callitris Woodland Subhabitat
Sheoak Woodland Subhabitat
Shrubby Melaleuca Subhabitat
Subhabitats are part of Mixed Sandplain Woodland in Sclerophyll Woodlands (Biome 9)

SAVANNAS

Au6A OPEN EUCALYPT SAVANNA

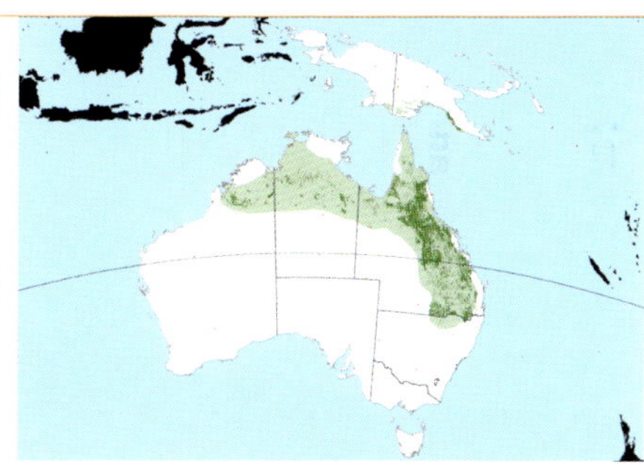

IN A NUTSHELL: A very open tropical savanna with broadly spaced trees, mainly eucalypts, tussock grass cover, and many large termite mounds. **Global Habitat Affinities:** AFROTROPICAL MOIST MIXED SAVANNA; AFRICAN MOPANE; OPEN TREED CERRADO. **Australian Habitat Affinities:** SPINIFEX EUCALYPT SAVANNA. **Species Overlap:** TETRODONTA WOODLAND SAVANNA; SPINIFEX EUCALYPT SAVANNA. **Full Bird Assemblage:** habitatsoftheworld.org/Au6A.

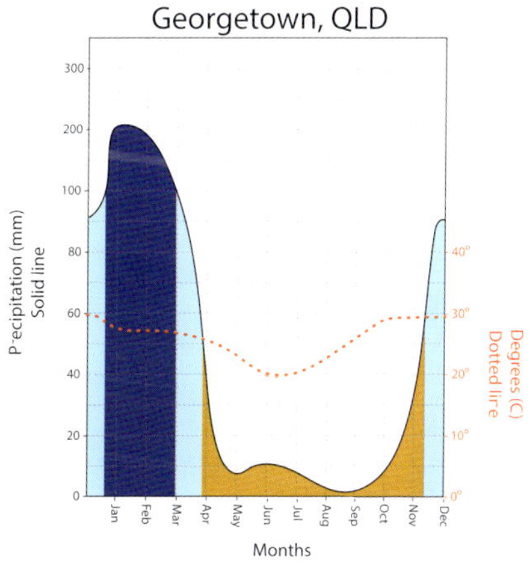

DESCRIPTION: This is the Australasian equivalent of the e. African savannas, and it is one of the images that springs to mind when Australians think of 'the Outback'. In semiarid but well-drained parts of n. Australia and s. New Guinea, where the tropical monsoonal climate is very seasonal, with a hot, wet summer and a very dry, warm winter (Köppen **Awa, Awb**), savannas are the norm. Here the annual rainfall can be as high as 72 in. (1800 mm), which in some environments is enough for rainforest to form; however, most of the rain falls in a few months, so the plants go through many months of water stress, even though most of the trees retain their leaves, rather than dropping them as happens in dry-deciduous forests. In contrast to the flora of many of the better-wooded savannas of Africa or Asia, where there is overlap between the savanna trees and the surrounding dry woodland, the dominant tree species of Australian savannas are restricted to this habitat and not also found in the surrounding deciduous or evergreen forests.

Open Eucalypt Savanna can present a variety of structures, from savanna woodland with an open canopy, similar to TETRODONTA WOODLAND SAVANNA, to treed savanna characterised by trees with crooked trunks scattered randomly across the landscape (with tree cover of 5–30%). Open Eucalypt Savannas transition to either Mitchell grass (*Astrebla* spp.) TROPICAL TUSSOCK GRASSLAND where the soil is very nutrient rich; Tetrodonta Woodland Savanna where the soil is nutrient-poor and the rainfall high; IRONBARK-BOX WOODLAND where the climate becomes temperate; or SPINIFEX EUCALYPT SAVANNA where soils are poor and rainfall lower.

The eucalypt trees (belonging to two genera, *Eucalyptus* and *Corymbia*) in Open Eucalypt Savanna are generally shorter (15–60 ft./5–20 m tall) than those in Tetrodonta Woodland Savanna, and the canopy is rounded and not normally dominated by just one species. Most of the trees are evergreen, though some do lose their leaves during very dry periods. In e. Australia, especially near

Fires are natural, near-annual events in Open Eucalypt Savanna at the onset of the wet season. © IAIN CAMPBELL, TROPICAL BIRDING TOURS/UNSW E&ERC

This one of the most easily identified habitats in Australia, dominated by sparsely distributed *Eucalyptus* and the very similar *Corymbia* trees. © IAIN CAMPBELL, TROPICAL BIRDING TOURS/UNSW E&ERC

In between the widely scattered ironbarks in Open Eucalypt Savanna is a thick layer of grasses. © IAIN CAMPBELL, TROPICAL BIRDING TOURS/UNSW E&ERC

where it merges with Ironbark-Box Woodland, the Open Eucalypt Savanna that develops on sand flats and broad plains often grows taller than 60 ft. (20 m) and tends to be dominated by Poplar Box (*Eucalyptus populnea*), which is a dominant tree of the various temperate eastern woodlands found southwards. The other trees here include Dallachy's Ghost Gum (*Corymbia dallachiana*) and Broad-leaved Poplar Gum (*Eucalyptus platyphylla*). Because these canopy trees have very light-coloured trunks, the savanna here looks very pale; it often has a mid-canopy at around 20 ft. (6 m) of non-eucalypts such as Bastard Sandalwood (*Eremophila mitchellii*). Farther north, these trees have a mid-canopy layer of Doodlallie (*Acacia excelsa*) and Cork-bark Wattle (*Acacia sericophylla*). The other very common form of this habitat in the east, which usually grows on low rises and valley sides, could be described as an 'ironbark savanna' because it is a low, open woodland, most commonly with Narrow-leaved Ironbark (*Eucalyptus crebra*) but also White's Ironbark (*Eucalyptus whitei*) and Cullen's Ironbark (*Eucalyptus culleni*). The ironbarks are joined by Red Bloodwood (*Corymbia erythrophloia*) and Gilbert River Box (*Eucalyptus microneura*). This plant composition gives this version of Open Eucalypt Savanna a very attractive appearance of very dark or black, furrowed trunks that contrast with the warm beige tones of the underlying grasses, reminiscent of the 'cathedral' type of MOPANE from s. Africa.

Farther west the habitat tends to exist as a mosaic with Spinifex Eucalypt Savanna and MELALEUCA SAVANNA. This version of the habitat is lower and more stunted, and non-eucalypt trees have more influence in the canopy, including Jigal Tree (*Lysiphyllum cunninghamii*) and Whitewood (*Atalaya hemiglauca*). The dominant trees remain eucalypts, such as Coolibah (*Eucalyptus microtheca*), Rough-leaf Cabbage Gum (*Corymbia confertiflora*), Weeping Ghost Gum (*Corymbia bella*), and Green-leaf Box (*Eucalyptus chlorophylla*), the last of which is a type of multi-stemmed mallee, similar to the canopy trees of the Spinifex Eucalypt Savanna. Boab (*Adansonia gregorii*) is an iconic tree of Western Australia with its pachycaulesque (very thick, stunted) trunk and sometimes leafless arms. It is related to the kapok (*Ceiba* spp.) trees of South America and in the same genus as the baobabs of Africa.

In all the Australian savannas, the grasses are dominated by C4 tussock grasses, which are tropical grasses that utilise a C4 photosynthesis carbon-fixation process that makes them better

A striking feature of this habitat, massive termite mounds provide nesting sites for birds and prey species for a variety of reptiles. © SAM WOODS, TROPICAL BIRDING TOURS

at dealing with drought, high temperatures, and limited nitrogen or CO_2 than the C3 temperate tussock grasses of s. Australia. The western representatives of this habitat usually have the near-cosmopolitan Tanglehead (*Heteropogon contortus*), Christmas Grass (*Themeda arguens*), and Kangaroo Grass (*Themeda triandra*), all of which occur outside of Australia, suggesting that although the canopy may comprise mainly endemics, the ground layer and wind-dispersed ground cover have close and modern relationships with other tropical grasslands. In the east, the grasses include Pitted Bluegrass (*Bothriochloa decipiens*), Curly Windmill Grass (*Enteropogon acicularis*), and Purple Lovegrass (*Eragrostis lacunaria*), as well as Hoop Mitchell Grass (*Astrebla elymoides*) and Curly Mitchell Grass (*Astrebla lappacea*), which both also occur in the vast Tropical Tussock Grasslands of the Mitchell Plains. Although some patches of spinifex grasses (*Triodia* spp.) do occur, they are too small to carry the specialised birds from the other spinifex-dominated habitats.

Over much of the extent of Open Eucalypt Savanna, the introduced Bufflegrass (*Cenchrus ciliaris*) has become extremely invasive. It is expected to continue spreading and become a dominant member of much of the grass cover in many of Australia's grasslands, grassy woodlands, and savannas.

The most characteristic feature of this environment is near-annual fires towards the start of the wet season. The natural fire regime is augmented by anthropogenic fires, as Aboriginal Australians traditionally regularly burned this environment to maintain the park-like landscape. Modern cattle farmers burn this savanna to stop the encroachment of *Melaleuca* and *Acacia* shrubs. In regions where anthropogenic fire has been limited and fires extinguished, the habitat has changed to SHRUBBY EUCALYPT SAVANNA with a corresponding change of wildlife assemblage. In the wet season, the grasses are very dense, and many areas have ephemeral lakes. Rivers through this habitat often have thick stands of grass that extend out into the dry savanna.

Yellow-tinted Honeyeater occupies this habitat in Australia's tropical north.
© NICK ATHANAS, TROPICAL BIRDING TOURS

WILDLIFE: Wildlife is remarkably similar across the range of this habitat, with animal distribution changing from north to south rather than east to west. Many bird species move over large areas in search of blossoming trees or seeding grasses. Blossom nomads to be expected moving across n. Australia when trees are in bloom include Varied, Red-collared, and Rainbow Lorikeets. There are many honeyeaters in this habitat, including Banded, Yellow-tinted, Rufous-throated, Rufous-banded, and Grey-headed Honeyeaters. Seedeaters feature heavily in the grassy understorey, including a range of finches such as Gouldian, Black-throated, Long-tailed, Masked, and Double-

The gorgeous Gouldian Finch is best sought out at waterholes within this habitat in Australia's Top End (Northern Territory) during the cooler periods of the day.
© IAIN CAMPBELL, TROPICAL BIRDING TOURS/UNSW E&ERC

Waterholes within the tropical Open Eucalypt Savanna are magnets for thirsty birds, particularly finches, such as Gouldian, Long-tailed, Masked, and Double-barred Finches, and in n. Queensland, this Black-throated Finch. © IAIN CAMPBELL, TROPICAL BIRDING TOURS/UNSW E&ERC

barred Finches. Other typical species are Squatter Pigeon, Black-tailed Treecreeper, Great Bowerbird, Australian Bustard, and Australian Pratincole, which prefers recently burned areas. Wetlands and waterholes in Open Eucalypt Savanna become a refuge for many birds, including most seedeaters as well as insectivores and nectivores, and during the dry season, waterholes are the best place to find most bird and mammal species. Around rivers, the range-restricted Purple-crowned Fairywren is a major target for birders.

Both Agile Wallaby and Antilopine Wallaroo inhabit and overlap in this habitat, with the Agile preferring slightly more closed savanna and the Antilopine preferring grassier, more open areas, where it feeds with Northern Nail-tail Wallaby and Euro (a subspecies of Common Wallaroo).

Squatter Pigeon favours this habitat, where it forages inconspicuously in groups on the ground, bursting into flight when disturbed at close quarters. © SAM WOODS, TROPICAL BIRDING TOURS

Smaller mammals include Short-beaked Echidna, Common Brushtail Possum, and Northern Brown Bandicoot. As well as the larger flying foxes, there are numerous small bats in this habitat including the Arnhem Long-eared Bat and Orange Leaf-nosed Bat. This habitat is also one of the best for finding Dingo, a neo-native predator of the smaller marsupials, which although introduced to Australia only around 8000 years ago has replaced the extinct Thylacine (Tasmanian Tiger) to become mainland Australia's apex predator. The main large bats present in this habitat are Black and Little Red Flying Foxes, which, rather than being blossom nomads, concentrate on fruiting trees in the better-watered areas.

Reptiles are common in this environment, where species include Gilbert's Dragon (*Lophognathus gilberti*), Frilled Dragon (*Chlamydosaurus kingii*), Common Prickly Gecko (*Heteronotia binoei*), Northern Marbled Velvet Gecko (*Oedura marmorata*), Straight-browed Ctenotus (*Ctenotus spaldingi*), Bauxite Rainbow Skink (*Carlia amax*), Metallic Snake-eyed Skink (*Cryptoblepharus metallicus*), and the much larger Yellow-spotted Monitor (*Varanus panoptes*). There are numerous larger non-venomous snakes such as Black-headed Python (*Aspidites melanocephalus*), Children's Python (*Antaresia childreni*), Olive Python (*Liasis olivaceus*), and Water Python (*Liasis fuscus*), as well as the venomous Orange-naped Snake (*Furina ornata*), Greater Black Whipsnake (*Demansia papuensis*), Common Keelback (*Tropidonophis mairii*), Brown Tree Snake (*Boiga irregularis*), and Common Tree Snake (*Dendrelaphis punctulatus*). Amphibians feature more in this savanna than in the nearby SPINIFEX EUCALYPT SAVANNA, including species such as Dahl's Aquatic Frog (*Ranoidea dahlii*), Desert Tree Frog (*Litoria rubella*), Ornate Burrowing Frog (*Platyplectrum ornatum*), Australian Green Tree Frog (*Ranoidea caerulea*), and Western Laughing Tree Frog (*Litoria ridibunda*). As with the other savannas, Cane Toad (*Rhinella marina*) has invaded this habitat with all the disastrous consequences for the carnivorous Australian wildlife.

The Frilled Dragon is one of the most dramatic lizards occupying this Outback habitat. © CHARLEY HESSE, TROPICAL BIRDING TOURS

CONSERVATION: Open Eucalypt Savanna suffers from being very widespread and seemingly endless across n. Australia. Farming was mostly limited to very large cattle stations with low stock numbers, but this is changing, and vast areas of this habitat are being clear-felled every year to be replaced by banana, mango, and avocado plantations. Images of tractors pulling chains between them to clear-fell the woodland, and of the burning of it in huge piles, are depressing to see, but because it is ignored by the large southern urban centres, the clearing goes on unabated. Nonetheless, some wonderful projects are being developed by conservation NGOs like Australian Wildlife Conservancy, involving the creation of very large reserves in Cape York Peninsula such as Piccaninny Plains and Brooklyn Station.

DISTRIBUTION: This habitat is widespread across n. Australia from Derby, Western Australia, on the west coast, to the western edge of the Atherton Tableland around Mareeba, Queensland, and down to the New South Wales border in the east. It is the dominant habitat through the northern quarter of the country. This savanna is also extensive along the southern coastal plain of New Guinea, interspersed with patches of monsoon forest along drainage lines and other moister areas. Savannas in the intermontane valleys and along the north coast of New Guinea may have been created by humans.

WHERE TO SEE: Mt. Carbine, Queensland, Australia; Victoria River, Northern Territory, Australia; Port Moresby hinterland and Fly River lowlands, Papua New Guinea.

SIDEBAR 2 THE EXTINCT AUSTRALIAN PLEISTOCENE MEGAFAUNA

Australia once had an extensive Pleistocene megafauna, which became extinct, seemingly due to climate change and anthropogenic causes due to changing fire regimes and hunting. It is theorised that the arrival of Aboriginal people around 65,000 years ago coincided with the disappearance of the megafauna, though dates and overlaps remain contentious. On the southern end of Australia, the Tasmanian megafauna vanished coincident with the arrival of Aboriginal people to the island some 41,000 years ago, with hunting presumed to be a major cause. Some 50 species of marsupial became extinct between 50,000 and 10,000 years ago.

'Imperceptive overkill' is suggested, where anthropogenic pressures slowly and gradually wipe out the vulnerable slow-reproducing megafauna. Such long-gone giant creatures included a sheep-sized echidna; a metre-long (3.3 ft.) type of platypus; *Diprotodon*, the largest known marsupial (10 ft./3 m long), which resembled a giant wombat; and *Procoptodon*, the largest known kangaroo, standing 6–10 ft./2–3 m tall and weighing up to 500 lb. (230 kg). There was also a marsupial 'lion', *Thylacoleo*, an arboreal, almost Fossa-like beast, which died out about 40,000 years ago

Remarkable giant birds, probably mainly herbivorous, included the flightless 'thunder bird' *Dromornis*, of subtropical open woodlands, which at 10 ft. (3 m) tall and weighing up to 1100 lb. (500 kg), was taller than the *Aepyornis* of Madagascar and heavier than the Moa of New Zealand. Another was *Genyornis*, the Mihirung, the last survivor of the family Dromornithidae, extant till about 50,000 years ago. Fragments of burnt eggshells attributed to this species suggest hunting was a factor in its decline; moreover, its habitat was swamps and marshes that were subject to desiccation as the climate became more arid.

Extinct giant creatures, known as Kadimakara after Aboriginal legends, also included reptiles, such as *Megalania*, a huge goanna; and *Wonambi*, a 16–20 ft. (5–6 m) long ambush predator of waterholes. These extinct creatures and others, such as *Diprotodon*, may have been the source of various legends of huge creatures of the Dreamtime—a term encompassing certain traditional Aboriginal beliefs and mythologies.

Au6B SPINIFEX EUCALYPT SAVANNA

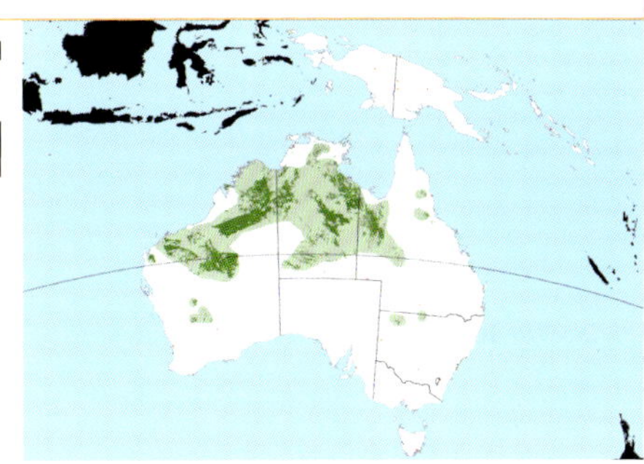

IN A NUTSHELL: A very open, harsh savanna with broadly spaced trees, mainly eucalypts, and a ground cover of *Triodia* spinifex grasses. **Global Habitat Affinities:** AFRICAN MOPANE; SERTÃO CAATINGA. **Continental Habitat Affinities:** OPEN EUCALYPT SAVANNA; SPINIFEX MALLEE; ROCKY SPINIFEX DESERT. **Species Overlap:** OPEN EUCALYPT SAVANNA. **Full Bird Assemblage:** habitatsoftheworld.org/Au6B.

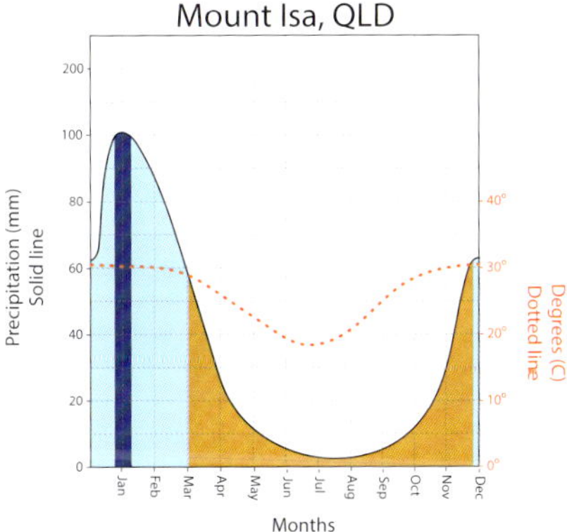

DESCRIPTION: There are a few habitats in the world that are so enigmatic that they defy easy description or classification; this is one of them. Whereas most treed habitats are understandably classified by their canopy trees, in northern inland Australia, it is the type of grass that defines the classification. Seen from above, this savanna looks very similar to MOPANE of Africa or the other open savanna of n. Australia, OPEN EUCALYPT SAVANNA Indeed, Open Eucalypt Savanna and Spinifex Eucalypt Savanna share many of the canopy trees; however, when you attempt to walk through this environment, the differences become jabbingly

At tree level, Spinifex Eucalypt Savanna appears quite similar to Open Eucalypt Savanna, both featuring a widely spaced, eucalypt-dominated canopy.
© GABRIEL CAMPBELL, TROPICAL BIRDING TOURS

Above: **The ground layer is the most significant component of Spinifex Eucalypt Savanna, dominated by *Triodia* (spinifex) grasses, unlike the otherwise similar Open Eucalypt Savanna.** © IAIN CAMPBELL, TROPICAL BIRDING TOURS/UNSW E&ERC

clear. The grasses here are dominated by *Triodia* spp., the peculiar spiky grasses endemic to Australia that easily penetrate clothing and skin, leaving strollers bloodied and without a doubt that they have entered spinifex. If there was a habitat pain index, this would top the scale. The name 'spinifex' creates some confusion because the true *Spinifex* is a genus of grasses found on beaches over much of the world. However, the term 'spinifex' for *Triodia* (and its habitats) has become pervasive in Australia and is now generally accepted.

The canopy of these savannas is extremely open, with the trees rarely interlocking and often standing some 130 ft. (40 m) apart. The eucalypt canopy trees have been classified by some people as mallees, and the habitat has been mapped as an open mallee woodland. This is because many of the eucalypts are mallee-form: multi-stemmed (mainly sprouting from the base) short trees, averaging 20 ft. (6 m) but up to 30 ft. (10 m) tall, which can have large ball roots under the ground called lignotubers. When mallee trees are subjected to fire, the individual stems burn, but the plant can resprout from the lignotuber. If the classification of this habitat were purely structural or even purely floristic, it could justifiably be regarded as a tropical SPINIFEX MALLEE, but the ecosystems are very different. Spinifex Eucalypt Savannas have the classic savanna climate: tropical, with heavy summer rainfall (16–32 in./400–800 mm), hot summers, and warm winters (Köppen **Awa**, **Awb**). Even in their most arid extreme (Köppen **Bwh**), such as around Opalton in w. Queensland, the rainfall is almost entirely related to tropical weather systems. The Spinifex Mallee, in contrast, has a Mediterranean climate (Köppen **Csa**, **Csb**) with cold, wet winters and hot, dry summers. However, it is the animal usage more than anything else that establishes this as a savanna habitat and not a mallee. The wildlife that utilises the canopy trees of this habitat moves freely between Spinifex Eucalypt Savanna and Open Eucalypt Savanna; there is very significant overlap of canopy species between the two habitats, yet there is much less overlap between the two habitats at ground level, with their respective spinifex-grass birds and tussock-grass birds rarely mixing. We reason, therefore, that this is a true savanna, just one with different grasses from all other savannas around the world.

The 'mallee' eucalypts that dominate this system are species such as Blue-leaved Mallee (*Eucalyptus gamophylla*), Sturt Creek Mallee (*Eucalyptus odontocarpa*), Silver Box (*Eucalyptus pruinosa*), Normanton Box (*Eucalyptus normantonensis*), and Cloncurry Box (*Eucalyptus leucophylla*). Other eucalypts are common here, many having a single pachycaulesque (short and very thick) and often very twisted trunk, including Desert Bloodwood (*Corymbia terminalis*), Snappy Gum (*Eucalyptus leucophloia*), and the taller (to 60 ft./18 m) and famously beautiful Ghost Gum (*Corymbia aparrerinja*). Other trees in this environment include Whitewood (*Atalaya hemiglauca*) and Beefwood (*Grevillea striata*), which grows to 50 ft. (15 m) and produces very significant amounts of nectar for blossom nomads. Small groves of Gidgee (*Acacia cambagei*) occur as a mélange within this habitat but have very different

The eucalypts and spinifex grasses of this habitat survive burns at temperatures that kill other grasses, forbs, and saplings of trees like grevilleas. The Spinifex Eucalypt Savanna plants then resprout with the next rains. © IAIN CAMPBELL, TROPICAL BIRDING TOURS/UNSW E&ERC

characteristics and are extremely depauperate in bird species, and thus are treated as a separate habitat, NORTHERN ACACIA SAVANNA.

The very thin shrub layer often has the prickly Conkerberry (*Carissa ovata*) and a suite of senna and *Eremophila* spp., but most of the ground cover is spinifex grasses. The most widespread of these in the north is Soft Spinifex (*Triodia pungens*). Other species include Hard Spinifex (*Triodia basedowii*), Feathertop Spinifex (*Triodia schinzii*), and Giant Grey Spinifex (*Triodia longiceps*). They grow in dense hummocks, most up to 3 ft. (1 m) tall, often expanding outwards in a circular fashion so that while the middle dies, the rings can reach 20 ft. (6 m) in diameter. An individual plant may be able to survive multiple fire cycles and live up to 30 years. The density of spinifex hummocks varies from 5% ground coverage on very rocky areas to 60% coverage, with little ground visible.

This habitat tends to grow in much harsher conditions than the Open Eucalypt Savanna, being found on ridgelines, rocky escarpments, ferricretes, silcretes, lateritic residual plateaus, coarse-grained colluvial fans, and small sand sheets in valley bottoms. The soils are almost always very nutrient-deficient and well drained. In loamy or clayey soils with more available nutrients, the spinifex is replaced by tussock grasses along with *Melaleuca*, *Grevillea*, and *Acacia* shrubs, so the habitat merges into MELALEUCA SAVANNA, Open Eucalypt Savanna, and SPINIFEX MULGA.

A characteristic feature of this environment is the triennial to decennial fires towards the end of the dry season, when lightning strikes are common but the ground is not yet very humid. The natural fire regime is augmented by anthropogenic fires, as Aboriginal Australians regularly burned this environment to maintain the park-like landscape for easier hunting. In the same way that temperate environments often vary drastically in winter and summer, these savannas seem very different during the wet and dry seasons. After a burn-off, the ground is bare, with exposed clay, sand, or many ironstone pisoliths (concentric nodules), and patches of unburnt dry grass scattered across the landscape.

WILDLIFE: As stated above, the canopy bird and other animal assemblages are similar between OPEN EUCALYPT SAVANNA, SHRUBBY EUCALYPT SAVANNA, and Spinifex Eucalypt Savanna; however, the ground and shrub birds are very different in each of these habitats. Many bird species move over large areas in search of blossoming trees. Blossom nomad honeyeaters to be expected when trees are in bloom include Rufous-throated, Yellow-tinted, Grey-fronted, Grey-headed, and White-plumed Honeyeaters. Woodswallows are elegant small birds generally thought of as arboreal species that feed on insects above the canopy, but White-browed and Masked Woodswallows are also blossom nomads that can form flocks of thousands moving huge distances between flowering events. Varied Lorikeet usually replaces Red-collared and Rainbow Lorikeets as the blossom-nomad parrots in this habitat. Other canopy birds to be expected include the large Red-winged Parrot, the diminutive Red-browed Pardalote, Striated Pardalote, and Australia's smallest bird, the Weebill. Black-tailed Treecreeper, White-bellied Cuckooshrike, and White-winged Triller are often seen crossing between canopy trees. Crested Bellbird and Rufous Whistler are both much more often heard than seen, calling while hidden in the canopy and subcanopy.

However, it is the shrub birds and ground birds that are most distinctive in Spinifex Eucalypt Savanna. Grasswrens, a subgroup of the fairywren family, are found mostly in spinifex, chenopod shrubs, or canegrass. In n. Australia, grasswrens are even more habitat faithful, and Carpentarian, Opalton, White-throated, and Black Grasswrens, along with Spinifexbird, are found in Spinifex Eucalypt Savanna but never in Open Eucalypt Savanna. Other ground birds characteristic of this habitat are Spinifex Pigeon, Diamond Dove, Little Buttonquail, Purple-backed Fairywren, Crimson Chat, Pictorella Munia, and Star Finch.

Euro (a subspecies of Common Wallaroo) and Red Kangaroos are the largest of the native herbivores, although they are found in a variety of savanna habitats. Common Rock Rat inhabits areas where the trees thin and the savanna merges into ROCKY SPINIFEX DESERT. Purple-necked

Grey-headed Honeyeater is a blossom nomad that occurs in Spinifex Eucalypt Savanna when there are appropriate flowers in bloom. Nomads like this can be present in large numbers during times of abundant blossoms or completely absent for long periods when no nectar sources are available. © IAIN CAMPBELL, TROPICAL BIRDING TOURS/UNSW E&ERC

The birdlife at ground level is the most specialised in this habitat, comprising spinifex grass specialists like the rare and local Opalton Grasswren. The height of the grasses can often be a limiting factor for grasswrens. © IAIN CAMPBELL, TROPICAL BIRDING TOURS/UNSW E&ERC

Rock-Wallaby, Spectacled Hare-Wallaby, and Allied Rock-Wallaby are all restricted to this habitat, where they spend most of the day hidden in steep gullies within the rocky ridgelines.

There are not as many species of reptiles as one would expect, but in the middle of the day, lizards become obvious, among them Frilled Dragon (*Chlamydosaurus kingii*), Slater's Ring-tailed Dragon (*Ctenophorus slateri*), Horner's Dragon (*Lophognathus horneri*), and Yellow-spotted Monitor (*Varanus panoptes*). Geckos include Gulf Marbled Velvet Gecko (*Oedura bella*), Zigzag Velvet Gecko (*Amalosia rhombifer*), Kristin's Spiny-tailed Gecko (*Strophurus krisalys*), Robust Dtella (*Gehyra robusta*), and Gulf Tree Dtella (*Gehyra lauta*). Snakes include the venomous Orange-naped Snake (*Furina ornata*) and Curl Snake (*Suta suta*). As expected, amphibians are limited in this environment, but Bumpy Rocket Frog (*Litoria inermis*) and Giant Burrowing Frog (*Ranoidea australis*) can sometimes be found.

CONSERVATION: Spinifex Eucalypt Savanna is widespread through semi-desert parts of n. Australia that are very difficult to farm and far from any major urban centres. In other parts of the world, this climate could support goat grazing and farming, but in Australia, the distance from population centres and lack of irrigation mean that this habitat endures less development pressure than other Australian savanna habitats.

DISTRIBUTION: This habitat is widespread across n. Australia, interspersed with OPEN EUCALYPT SAVANNA, from Broome, Western Australia, where it skirts the south of the Kimberley Plateau on the west coast, and across nc. Northern Territory to w. Queensland. It becomes the dominant habitat in the Camooweal to Mt. Isa region of Queensland, which centres on the Mt. Isa Block, a range of extremely old rocks from the Archaean and Proterozoic aeons, some as old as 2.5 billion (yes, billion) years. The habitat continues east to the Winton and Opalton areas of cw. Queensland.

WHERE TO SEE: Lark Quarry, Queensland, Australia; Mt. Isa, Queensland, Australia; Borroloola, Northern Territory, Australia.

The spinifex grasses provide seeds for foraging finches, like these Pictorella Munias (two males and one female). © IAIN CAMPBELL, TROPICAL BIRDING TOURS/UNSW E&ERC

Au6C TETRODONTA WOODLAND SAVANNA

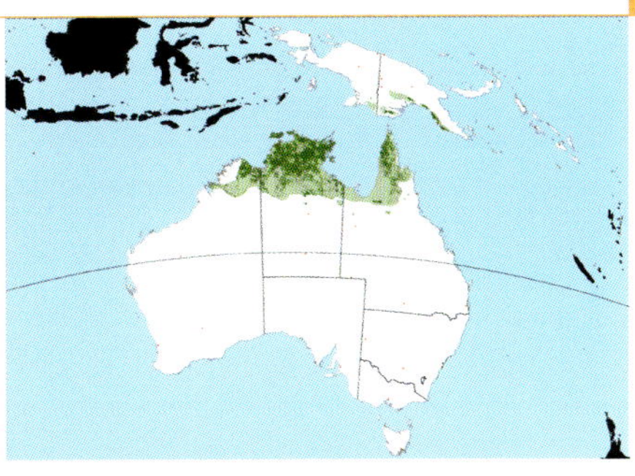

IN A NUTSHELL: Savanna woodland with tall-trunked trees and a very uniform, almost-closed canopy. **Global Habitat Affinities:** MIOMBO; GUSU; TEAK FOREST. **Continental Habitat Affinities:** GRASSY DRY SCLEROPHYLL FOREST; OPEN EUCALYPT SAVANNA. **Species Overlap:** OPEN EUCALYPT SAVANNA. **Full Bird Assemblage:** habitatsoftheworld.org/Au6C.

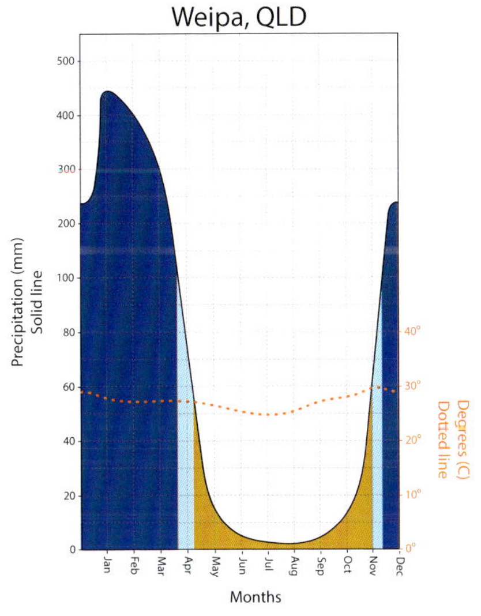

DESCRIPTION: In some vegetation classification systems such as the Australian NVIS-MVS (see Habitat Distribution Maps in the Introduction), this habitat is classified in the same group as dry sclerophyll forests and for good reason. This woodland also has a structure similar to a closed IRONBARK-BOX WOODLAND and a GRASSY DRY SCLEROPHYLL FOREST but is dominated by tropical (C4) grasses and has a very different bird assemblage that is more closely aligned to open savannas than the open forests of the south or east. Tetrodonta Woodland Savanna is very climate- and fire-driven. It receives around 79 in. (2000 mm) annual rainfall. Its range in the w. Cape York region of Queensland is well within the precipitation limits for rainforest, and it is fire that appears to be the limiting factor in the broad, flat areas with little impediments to widespread burns on very regular (<10-year) cycles.

This habitat, which looks like an open forest at a distance, has a canopy height of up to 100 ft. (30 m), although it is usually around 50 ft. (15 m). In some regions, such as on the lateritic bauxite plateau surrounding Weipa, Queensland, the canopy is almost monotypic, mainly Darwin Stringybark (*Eucalyptus tetrodonta*, which gives the habitat its name), with a minor component of Melville Island Bloodwood (*Corymbia nesophila*), Paperbark Gum (*Eucalyptus chartaboma*), and Darwin Woollybutt (*Eucalyptus miniata*), and with Blotchy Bloodwood (*Corymbia stockeri*) as a subcanopy tree. In other areas, especially more eroded places where the kaolinitic saprolite (weathered rock where rock texture is preserved) below the bauxite is exposed or in sandy washouts, the canopy becomes slightly more varied with species such as Clarkson's Bloodwood

The canopy of Tetrodonta Woodland Savanna is nearly closed, unlike that of the similar Open Eucalypt Savanna, which occurs extensively in the same region. © IAIN CAMPBELL, TROPICAL BIRDING TOURS/UNSW E&ERC

The understorey of Tetrodonta Woodland Savanna is open and easy to walk through, with little on the ground aside from grasses and termite mounds. The grasses provide seeds for a variety of finches to feed on. © IAIN CAMPBELL, TROPICAL BIRDING TOURS/UNSW E&ERC

(*Corymbia clarksoniana*) and Cooktown Ironwood (*Erythrophleum chlorostachys*) joining the canopy mix with the dominant Darwin Stringybark.

There is no substantial subcanopy or brushy understorey; most small trees are juvenile versions of the canopy species listed above, augmented by a loose scattering of Soapwood (*Alphitonia pomaderroides*), Cocky Apple (*Planchonia careya*), Hard Cascarilla (*Croton arnhemicus*), and Smooth-leaved Quinine (*Petalostigma banksii*), which usually grow no taller than 25 ft. (8 m).

The ground cover is almost entirely tropical grasses such as Giant Speargrass (*Heteropogon triticeus*), Plume Sorghum (*Sorghum plumosum*), and Silky Browntop (*Eulalia mackinlayi*). These grasses are high and thick in the wet season and into the beginning of the dry season, but by the end of the dry season most of them have burned off, exposing the very round bauxite pisoliths and less rounded ironstone nodules on the savanna floor, and the habitat takes on a park-like feel.

Over the broad region, the fire regime of this habitat has changed, with cool-burning, early wet-season fires becoming more common than the much hotter late-season fires. This has caused a thickening of some forests and an infestation of *Melaleuca* shrubland. In areas with slightly poorer drainage where fire is inhibited, this woodland understorey thickens with rainforest plants, and the woodland reverts to a MONSOON VINEFOREST, so flying over this region you see very small pockmarks of bright green in a sea of olive. On the ground, these Monsoon Vineforest patches can change the soil from ferrosols over the bauxite (aluminium-rich) laterites to gleysols with very high clay content. This feature drives home the questions, if these laterites are millions of years old, how do the surface soils change so much, to what degree is fire the driver of the savanna, and to what degree does the savanna/forest change affect the underlying soil? Stay tuned.

WILDLIFE: In Tetrodonta Woodland Savanna, the largest group of animals by biomass is the termites. They play a very important role in plant breakdown, nutrient cycling, soil mixing (bioturbation), and micro-changes to the water cycle though their mounds. As well as being the primary food source for echidnas, termites are preyed upon by many Australian lizards such as the Frilled Dragon (*Chlamydosaurus kingii*), legless lizards, and geckos. Moreover, termite mounds provide vital nesting locations for species such as Golden-shouldered Parrot and Hooded Parrot. Spinifex Termite (*Nasutitermes triodiae*) mounds can be up to 25 ft.

Termites provide the largest animal biomass in this habitat, and their mounds provide vital nesting habitat for burrowing parrots, like the endangered Golden-shouldered Parrot. © PABLO CERVANTES, TROPICAL BIRDING TOURS

Partridge Pigeon is an inconspicuous terrestrial resident of this habitat, best looked for feeding along road verges at the cooler ends of the day. © SAM WOODS, TROPICAL BIRDING TOURS

(8 m) tall, while magnetic termite (*Amitermes* spp.) mounds are aligned in a southerly direction.

Most of the birds in this habitat are found across n. Australia, such as Weebill; Rufous Whistler, Rufous-banded, Rufous-throated, and Banded Honeyeaters; and Silver-crowned Friarbird. Some species are more restricted, like Partridge Pigeon, Black-tailed Treecreeper, and Northern Shrike-tit in Northern Territory, and Black-backed Butcherbird of Cape York Peninsula. Red Goshawk is a rare, endangered raptor species found in a variety of tropical humid forests, though it appears to live in much higher densities in this habitat, which may be crucial to the species' long-term survival. Many finches occur in this woodland, such as Black-throated, Gouldian, Double-barred, Masked, and Long-tailed Finches, plus Yellow-rumped and Chestnut-breasted Munias (Mannikins), but never in the densities of the OPEN EUCALYPT SAVANNA.

Historical records of the possibly extinct Buff-breasted Buttonquail are centred around Coen, Queensland, in what was an open version of this tropical eucalypt woodland savanna. Over the past 80 years, the understorey has thickened, and this may be a contributing factor to the demise of this species. The restricted-range Hooded Parrot of the Northern Territory and the endangered Golden-shouldered Parrot of Cape York Peninsula both rely on this habitat, and the shift to SHRUBBY EUCALYPT SAVANNA is undoubtedly a cause for concern for the Golden-shouldered Parrot, primarily because it facilitates increased predation from butcherbirds. Other parrots here include Varied and Rainbow Lorikeets, Northern Rosella, and Red-winged Parrot.

Black-tailed Treecreeper is a specialist of this habitat type, usually encountered foraging on the larger branches and trunks of trees. © NICK ATHANAS, TROPICAL BIRDING TOURS

Agile Wallaby is the most common, or at least the most conspicuous, mammal in this environment, outnumbering the Antilopine Wallaroo. Northern Brown Bandicoot moves into this habitat from nearby MONSOON VINEFOREST during the wet season when the grass grows, and terrestrial insects, worms, and seeds become abundant.

Lizards can be conspicuous in Tetrodonta Woodland Savanna, including species such as Chameleon Dragon (*Chelosania brunnea*), Golden-spotted Tree Monitor (*Varanus boehme*),

Northern Rosella occurs within Tetrodonta Woodland Savanna, especially within areas near water in this dry region. © NICK ATHANAS, TROPICAL BIRDING TOURS

Yellow-spotted Monitor, Common Bluetongue (*Tiliqua scincoides*), Six-toothed Rainbow Skink (*Carlia sexdentata*), and Northern Velvet Gecko (*Oedura castelnaui*). Snakes include Common Tree Snake (*Dendrelaphis punctulatus*), Greater Black Whipsnake (*Demansia papuensis*), Spotted Python (*Antaresia maculosa*), Common Keelback (*Tropidonophis mairii*), Brown Tree Snake (*Boiga irregularis*), and the extremely dangerous Coastal Taipan (*Oxyuranus scutellatus*), which is 40 times more venomous than the diamondback rattlesnakes of North America.

During the wet season, besides the ubiquitous invasive Cane Toad (*Rhinella marina*), native frogs such as Small Frog (*Ranoidea manya*), Bridled Rocket Frog (*Litoria nigrofrenata*), Marbled Frog (*Limnodynastes convexiusculus*), Beautiful Tree Frog (*Ranoidea bella*), Cape York Whistling Frog (*Austrochaperina gracilipes*), Ornate Burrowing Frog (*Platyplectrum ornatum*), and Mimic Toadlet (*Uperoleia mimula*) can be found in this habitat. The introduction of the poisonous Cane Toad has had a disastrous effect on this habitat's populations of predatory mammals and reptiles, decimating populations of the Northern Quoll and various monitor lizards.

CONSERVATION: Clearing of Tetrodonta Woodland Savanna is happening at an astounding rate, but it is not getting any real attention in the media. Between 2018 and 2021, approved clearing in the Northern Territory alone increased by 300%, but it is estimated that only 20% of cleared land was approved, so it is a free-for-all with no repercussions for illegal clearing. Areas such as the Lakeland area of Cape York Peninsula that were wild savannas just two decades ago are now major farming districts.

DISTRIBUTION: Tetrodonta Woodland Savanna habitat is widespread in the more humid, tropical bi-seasonal regions of Australia from the Kimberley, Western Australia, across to Cape York Peninsula, Queensland. Extensive stands occur around the town of Weipa in w. Cape York Peninsula. The habitat is found mainly on well-drained, iron-rich, bauxite and lateritic plateaus.

It also occurs as limited stands in New Guinea where it is usually found between MELALEUCA SAVANNA and MONSOON VINEFOREST.

WHERE TO SEE: Weipa, Queensland, Australia; Pine Creek, Northern Territory, Australia; Port Moresby hinterland, Papua New Guinea.

Tetrodonta Woodland Savanna has a diverse reptile fauna, including this Yellow-spotted Monitor, which takes a wide variety of prey, including the abundant termites in this landscape. © IAIN CAMPBELL, TROPICAL BIRDING TOURS/UNSW E&ERC

Au6D SHRUBBY EUCALYPT SAVANNA

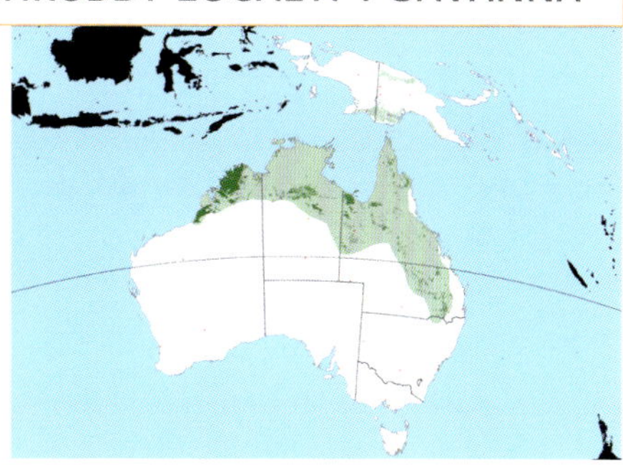

IN A NUTSHELL: A tropical dry woodland/savanna with broadly spaced trees, mainly eucalypts, but with a dense understorey of other plants. **Global Habitat Affinities:** AFROTROPICAL MOIST MIXED SAVANNA; AFRICAN MOPANE; CERRADO SENSU STRICTO. **Continental Habitat Affinities:** OPEN EUCALYPT SAVANNA; MELALEUCA SAVANNA; MIXED SANDPLAIN WOODLAND. **Species Overlap:** TETRODONTA WOODLAND SAVANNA; OPEN EUCALYPT SAVANNA; MELALEUCA SAVANNA. **Full Bird Assemblage:** habitatsoftheworld.org/Au6D.

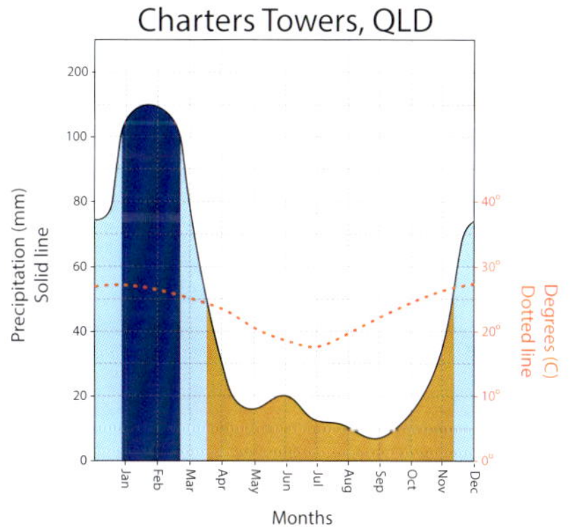

DESCRIPTION: This is a very messy-looking habitat that at a distance resembles a tropical version of MIXED SANDPLAIN WOODLAND, in that it has a canopy of eucalypts along with many other groups of plants. Shrubby Eucalypt Savanna is found in the semiarid to humid parts of n. Australia and s. New Guinea, where the climate is very seasonal, with a hot, wet summer and very dry, warm winter (Köppen **Awa, Awb**). As in OPEN EUCALYPT SAVANNA, the annual rainfall can be as high as 72 in. (1800 mm), which in some environments is enough for rainforest to form; however, because there is a prolonged dry season with resulting plant stress and fires, forest growth is retarded. This forest could understandably be regarded as a tropical dry-deciduous forest, given the thick understorey, and in the absence of anthropogenic influence would likely revert to a forest with limited grass cover. The dominant canopy tree species of Shrubby Eucalypt Savanna are not found in the surrounding evergreen forests, in contrast to the flora of many of the better-wooded savannas of Africa such as GUINEA SAVANNA.

Most of the trees in Shrubby Eucalypt Savanna are evergreen, though some do lose their leaves during very dry periods. The eucalypt trees, of two genera, *Eucalyptus* and *Corymbia*, have a very large height range (15–115 ft./5–35m), yet the bird and other wildlife assemblages do not seem to change as much with canopy height as with the density of the undergrowth. This habitat usually grows on low rises and valley sides as a low, open woodland with eucalypt canopy species such as Darwin Stringybark (*Eucalyptus tetrodonta*), Narrow-leaved Ironbark (*Eucalyptus crebra*), Gilbert River Box (*Eucalyptus microneura*), Desert Bloodwood (*Corymbia terminalis*), and Red

At ground level, Shrubby Eucalypt Savanna has a substantial shrub layer as well as grasses, unlike the similar Open Eucalypt Savanna, which often occurs close by. © IAIN CAMPBELL, TROPICAL BIRDING TOURS/UNSW E&ERC

Shrubby Eucalypt Savanna can be regarded as an ecotone between more open habitats, like Open Eucalypt Savanna and Tetrodonta Eucalypt Savanna, and more closed habitats, such as Heathy Dry Sclerophyll Forest and even Monsoon Vineforest. © IAIN CAMPBELL, TROPICAL BIRDING TOURS/UNSW E&ERC

Bloodwood (*Corymbia erythrophloia*). Compared to Open Eucalypt Savanna, the canopy and subcanopy are much more diverse, with trees such as Beefwood (*Grevillea striata*), Northern Cypress-Pine (*Callitris intratropica*), Black Sheoak (*Allocasuarina littoralis*), Northern Sandalwood (*Santalum lanceolatum*), Jigal Tree (*Lysiphyllum cunninghamii*), and Emu Apple (*Owenia acidula*). Gidgee (*Acacia cambagei*) and Lancewood (*Acacia shirleyi*) are also common in Shrubby Eucalypt Savanna, and when they begin to dominate the canopy, the habitat merges into NORTHERN ACACIA SAVANNA. Whitewood (*Atalaya hemiglauca*), which looks superficially like an acacia, commonly occurs in Shrubby Eucalypt Savanna in most of tropical Australia.

Sometimes thick groves dominated by trees such as Darwin Silky Oak (*Grevillea pteridifolia*), Blue Paperbark (*Melaleuca dealbata*), and Fibre-barked Tea Tree (*Melaleuca stenostachya*) form in the understorey and become dense enough to make walking through the habitat difficult. However, usually the understorey is much more diverse than that of Open Eucalypt Savanna, with small trees and shrubs of a broad mix of species such as Broad-leaved Paperbark (*Melaleuca viridiflora*), Black Sheoak, Brass's Asteromyrtus (*Asteromyrtus brassii*), Torulosa Wattle (*Acacia torulosa*), Townsville Wattle (*Acacia leptostachya*), Lamellar Tea Tree (*Gaudium lamellatum*), Supplejack (*Ventilago viminalis*), and Bush Plum (*Carissa spinarum*). The grasses that grow in shrubby savanna are nearly always the same C4 (tropical) tussock grasses found in Open Eucalypt Savanna or MELALEUCA SAVANNA; however, in a few areas with particularly nutrient-deficient or sandy soil, *Triodia* spinifex grasses may dominate the ground cover.

Fire is a near-annual event in the Australian and New Guinean savannas. In Australia, the natural fire regime is augmented by anthropogenic fires, as Aboriginal peoples traditionally regularly burned this savanna, and modern cattle farmers continue to do so to stop the encroachment of *Melaleuca*, *Grevillea*, and *Acacia* shrubs. Shrubby Eucalypt Savanna usually forms at the expense of Open Eucalypt Savanna where natural and anthropogenic fire has been limited and fires have been extinguished, allowing shrubs to grow and thicken up the understorey. This does not mean that fire is not an important part of the environment but rather that the fires here do not burn enough to stop the formation of the shrubby understorey and the resulting change from an Open Eucalypt Savanna to Shrubby Eucalypt Savanna.

WILDLIFE: Shrubby Eucalypt Savanna may look superficially similar to NORTHERN ACACIA SAVANNA, but it is much more productive for wildlife, being a fascinating mix of OPEN EUCALYPT SAVANNA with some of the more forest-like understorey birds. Because most of the canopy trees are the same as those of other eucalypt-dominated savannas, the forest attracts the same blossom nomads, such as Varied, Red-collared, and Rainbow Lorikeets. The many honeyeaters of this habitat include Yellow, Banded, Yellow-tinted, Rufous-throated, Rufous-banded, and Grey-headed Honeyeaters.

Shrubby Eucalypt Savanna, in common with many other *Eucalyptus*-dominated habitats, boasts a diverse assemblage of nectivorous birds, such as Yellow Honeyeater. © IAIN CAMPBELL, TROPICAL BIRDING TOURS/UNSW E&ERC

Red-backed Fairywren can be found in grassier areas within Shrubby Eucalypt Savanna. © PABLO CERVANTES, TROPICAL BIRDING TOURS

Red-winged Parrot feeds on the seeds of trees, including *Eucalyptus* species, and therefore occurs in this and other eucalypt-dominated habitats. © IAIN CAMPBELL, TROPICAL BIRDING TOURS/UNSW E&ERC

The habitat does lose the typical savanna species such as Gouldian, Long-tailed, Masked, Black-throated, and Star Finches, but these are replaced by finches that prefer a little more cover such as Chestnut-breasted Munia and Double-barred and Plum-headed Finches. This habitat shares many pigeons with the other savannas, and widespread species such as Peaceful Dove and Bar-shouldered Dove are joined here by Partridge Pigeon in the Top End (Northern Territory) and Squatter Pigeon on Cape York Peninsula (Queensland).

Some very open-country savanna species such as Australian Bustard, Brolga, and Australian Pratincole are replaced in this habitat by species such as Pheasant Coucal and Bush Thick-knee. Surprisingly, Emu remains a common species in this thicker habitat. Painted Buttonquail is found here in regions where the possibly extinct Buff-breasted Buttonquail was historically recorded, around Coen, Queensland. Through verbal descriptions from people who have worked in this region for many decades, it appears as though the areas that are now Shrubby Eucalypt Savanna and TETRODONTA WOODLAND SAVANNA were originally Open Eucalypt Savanna, and that this 'thickening' has affected birds such as the buttonquail as well as the critically endangered Golden-shouldered Parrot.

The thicker understorey also favours Sacred and Forest Kingfishers over the Red-backed Kingfisher, which prefers more open habitats. Pale-headed and Northern Rosellas are parrots that prefer the thicker understorey and are much more common in this habitat than in Open Eucalypt Savanna or MELALEUCA SAVANNA, which may be nearby. Other species to be expected in this habitat include Red-backed Fairywren, Red-winged Parrot, Black-chinned Honeyeater, Silver-crowned Friarbird, White-bellied Cuckooshrike, Weebill, and Paperbark Flycatcher.

Agile Wallaby is a widespread macropod that is very common in this habitat, while much more localised species such as Mareeba Rock-Wallaby inhabit this savanna in particularly rocky terrains. Smaller mammals include Short-beaked Echidna, Common Brushtail Possum, Queensland Barred Bandicoot, and Northern Brown Bandicoot. Northern Bettong is a very rare animal that much prefers this habitat over Open Eucalypt Savanna, but it can also be found in some of the northernmost dry sclerophyll forests.

Many of the snakes here are widespread species across n. Australia such as the constrictors Spotted Python (*Antaresia maculosa*), Australian Scrub Python (*Simalia kinghorni*), Black-headed Python (*Aspidites melanocephalus*), and Carpet Python (*Morelia spilota*), and the very dangerous Coastal Taipan (*Oxyuranus scutellatus*). Brown Tree Snake (*Boiga irregularis*) is also common here (and has been introduced to devastating effect to islands in the Pacific). Lizards of Shrubby Eucalypt Savanna include Shaded-litter Rainbow Skink (*Carlia munda*), Frilled Dragon (*Chlamydosaurus kingii*), and Northern Two-Lined Dragon (*Diporiphora bilineata*). The geckos include Dubious Dtella (*Gehyra dubia*), Common Prickly Gecko (*Heteronotia binoei*), and Northern Velvet Gecko (*Oedura castelnaui*).

CONSERVATION: Little attention is paid to this habitat compared to other more 'charismatic' tropical habitats. Shrubby Eucalypt Savanna is under no immediate threat of continental-scale clearing as it generally occurs on areas not conducive to farming; however, large-scale clearing is underway on the lower Cape York Peninsula surrounding Lakeland, Queensland, and clearing seems to be common in the region of Darwin, Northern Territory. This habitat forms at the expense of OPEN EUCALYPT SAVANNA, and it is unclear whether the changing fire regimes and overgrazing may lead to more Shrubby Eucalypt Savanna being created or lost through habitat change.

DISTRIBUTION: This habitat is widespread across n. Australia from Derby, Western Australia, on the west coast, to the western edge of the tropical rainforests on the east coast. It is common between Darwin and Kakadu National Park, Northern Territory. Shrubby Eucalypt Savanna is also extensive along the southern coastal plain of New Guinea, interspersed with OPEN EUCALYPT SAVANNA and patches of MONSOON VINEFOREST along drainage lines and other moister areas. Shrubby savannas in the intermontane valleys and along the north coast of New Guinea may have been created by humans.

WHERE TO SEE: Mareeba Wetlands, Queensland, Australia; Pine Creek, Northern Territory, Australia; Port Moresby hinterland and Fly River lowlands, Papua New Guinea.

The extremely localised Mareeba Rock-Wallaby is found within rockier areas of Shrubby Eucalypt Savanna very close to the town of Mareeba in n. Queensland.
© PABLO CERVANTES, TROPICAL BIRDING TOURS

Au6F NORTHERN ACACIA SAVANNA

IN A NUTSHELL: Acacia woodlands and shrublands of arid and semiarid northern interior Australia. **Global Habitat Affinities:** AFRICAN MOPANE; FLOODED CHACO AND ESPINAL. **Continental Habitat Affinities:** GRASSY MULGA; SPINIFEX MULGA. **Species Overlap:** SHRUBBY EUCALYPT SAVANNA; GRASSY MULGA; SPINIFEX EUCALYPT SAVANNA. **Full Bird Assemblage:** habitatsoftheworld.org/Au6F.

DESCRIPTION: These acacia-dominated woodlands and shrublands are an extension of the broad swath of acacia woodlands, such as SHRUBBY EUCALYPT SAVANNA, BRIGALOW, GRASSY MULGA, and SPINIFEX MULGA, extending through arid and semiarid Australia. The woody plants of Northern Acacia Savanna tend to be in a broom-like or 'whipstick' form and as low as 9 ft. (3 m), rather than the single-trunk trees up to 20 ft. (6 m) tall typical of the other acacia woodlands, but taller versions do occur in patches with nutrient-rich soil. Walking around this habitat is very difficult as so many of the trees have the whipstick form, and even when the trees are single-trunked, the thickest part of the canopy is around head height.

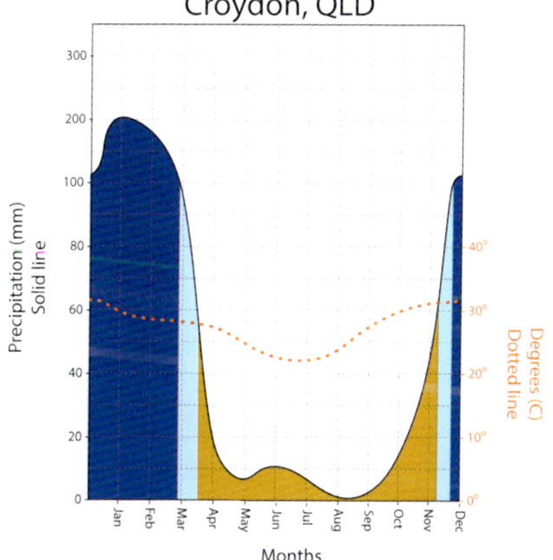

The trees within Northern Acacia Savanna typically display a 'whipstick' form. © IAIN CAMPBELL, TROPICAL BIRDING TOURS/UNSW E&ERC

Above: **Walking through this habitat is often challenging, as the thickest part of the canopy is often at head height!** © IAIN CAMPBELL, TROPICAL BIRDING TOURS/UNSW E&ERC

The savanna contains a mixture of acacias such as Gidgee (*Acacia cambagei*) and Lancewood (*Acacia shirleyi*), along with Torulosa Wattle (*Acacia torulosa*), Townsville Wattle (*Acacia leptostachya*), Pindan Wattle (*Acacia platycarpa*), Julie's Wattle (*Acacia julifera*), Leopardwood (*Flindersia maculosa*), and Archer River Wattle (*Acacia arbiana*). Eucalypts in the mix include Inland Yellowjacket (*Eucalyptus similis*), with distinctive tessellated yellow or yellow-brown bark that occurs from the base of the tree to the outer branches and peels off in white flakes. Other eucalypts are Queensland Peppermint (*Eucalyptus exserta*), Rough-leaved Bloodwood (*Corymbia setosa*), and Brown Bloodwood (*Corymbia trachyphloia*), all occurring as very minor components of the savanna. Large-

The distinctive bark of the Leopardwood, which occurs within Northern Acacia Savanna. © IAIN CAMPBELL, TROPICAL BIRDING TOURS/UNSW E&ERC

leaved Cabbage Gum (*Corymbia grandifolia*) is very interesting because it has lignotubers, like the mallee eucalypt species from farther south, but is also a dry-deciduous tree. Because it can grow to 15 ft. (5 m) tall, it can stand out in these savannas as a tall, white, emergent tree.

This habitat tends not to have a thick, non-acacia shrub layer because the acacias themselves are at shrub height, but it does contain a variety of 'paperbark' melaleucas, such as Fibre-barked Tea Tree (*Melaleuca stenostachya*), Lamellar Tea Tree (*Gaudium lamellatum*), Slender-leaved Starflower (*Calytrix leptophylla*), and Forest Grass Tree (*Xanthorrhoea johnsonii*), a very large representative of a genus of grass trees more typical of HEATHY DRY SCLEROPHYLL. Darwin Silky Oak (*Grevillea pteridifolia*) occurs in stands within a few of these shrublands and is an indication that the habitat is an ecotone with Shrubby Eucalypt Savanna and has a much more diverse bird assemblage; when Darwin Silky Oak flowers, the Northern Acacia Savanna feels completely different, laden with blossom-nomad bird species. Ground cover is much more limited than that of surrounding habitats, with many bare areas between clumps of Soft Spinifex (*Triodia pungens*) or patches of tussock grasses such Northern Wanderrie Grass (*Eriachne obtusa*) and Erect Kerosene Grass (*Aristida holathera*).

This habitat tends to form on lithosols (essentially fragments of bedrock) or other poorly developed soils occurring on outcrops of nutrient-poor metamorphic rocks such as gneiss or quartzites, nutrient-poor igneous rocks such as granites, nutrient-poor sedimentary rocks such as sandstones, or unconsolidated Quaternary sand sheets with very nutrient-deficient sandy soils. As with the vast

The bird community of this habitat is very limited, with a typical morning yielding just a few widespread species, such as this Weebill, Australia's smallest bird at just 3.5 in. (9 cm) long.

© IAIN CAMPBELL, TROPICAL BIRDING TOURS/UNSW E&ERC

The Apostlebird is a widespread species occurring across large swaths of semiarid habitats in e. Australia. © IAIN CAMPBELL, TROPICAL BIRDING TOURS/UNSW E&ERC

Ground Cuckooshrike is a scarce, highly nomadic species found across a wide variety of semiarid and arid habitats in Australia, including Northern Acacia Savanna. It is always a lucky day to see this species, no matter what the habitat is. © SAM WOODS, TROPICAL BIRDING TOURS

majority of habitats in Australia, the age of the rocks on which the soils form is irrelevant, while the chemistry and weathering history of said rocks is of utmost importance. Nearby areas with more nutrient-rich soils or soils with more water-holding capacity are almost always covered in other habitats such as OPEN EUCALYPT SAVANNA, Shrubby Eucalypt Savanna, or Grassy Mulga.

Northern Acacia Savanna has a broad climatic overlap with Open Eucalypt Savanna, sharing a hot monsoonal savanna climate (Köppen **Awa**) of warm, very dry winters and blistering-hot, humid to wet summers, with annual rainfall between 16 and 48 in. (400–1200 mm). The habitat is not as fire-resistant as eucalypt or melaleuca savannas, and that seems to be a limiting factor in the distribution in drier areas, where the drought resistance of the acacia trees would otherwise give this habitat a competitive advantage over the other savannas.

WILDLIFE: Northern Acacia Savanna is remarkable in its low level of bird diversity relative to the very productive savanna habitats such as OPEN EUCALYPT SAVANNA, MELALEUCA SAVANNA, and closely related mulga habitats. The reason for their relative depauperisation is not understood. An hour's birding in mid-morning could easily result in sightings of Weebill, Rufous Whistler, and nothing else, whereas the same effort in a nearby Open Eucalypt Savanna could easily yield 30 species in the same period. If the *Grevillea* or *Melaleuca* trees and shrubs are in flower, blossom nomads such as Varied, Yellow-tinted, and Rufous-throated Honeyeaters enter from surrounding habitats. Apostlebird, Ground Cuckooshrike, and Great Bowerbird feed on the ground. Finches are limited mainly to Double-barred and Zebra Finches, though Pictorella Munia does use this habitat in the drier parts of its range.

Finch diversity in Northern Acacia Savanna is low (compared with Open Eucalypt Savanna), largely limited to the widespread Double-barred Finch (pictured) and Zebra Finch.
© IAIN CAMPBELL, TROPICAL BIRDING TOURS/UNSW E&ERC

Agile Wallaby is the most common of the large macropods, while Common Wallaroo (Euro subsp.), Eastern Grey Kangaroo, and Antilopine Wallaroo all occur in low numbers. Typical reptiles of this habitat include Kristin's Spiny-tailed Gecko (*Strophurus krisalys*), Shaded-litter Rainbow Skink (*Carlia munda*), Common Bluetongue (*Tiliqua scincoides*), and Greater Black Whipsnake (*Demansia papuensis*). Amphibians expected include Ornate Burrowing Frog (*Platyplectrum ornatum*), Short-footed Frog (*Ranoidea brevipes*), and New Holland Frog (*Ranoidea novaehollandiae*).

CONSERVATION: This habitat is found in arid parts of Australia where farming is very difficult, so high-intensity crop cultivation is near impossible. Most farming is limited to low-intensity cattle and sheep grazing, though industrial-scale firewood harvesting is being promoted. Supposedly sustainable harvesting involves cutting only dead limbs for extraction, but this removes the main viable nesting sites for many of the Australian parrot species and many other bird, reptile, and mammal groups.

DISTRIBUTION: Northern Acacia Savanna occurs in a band across c. Australia from the Pilbara region of Western Australia across to s. Cape York Peninsula, Queensland. It generally follows the same range as SPINIFEX MULGA, occurring in soils that are too nutrient-deficient or too sandy for eucalypt savanna development yet not fire-prone.

WHERE TO SEE: Croydon, Queensland, Australia; Daly Waters, Northern Territory, Australia.

The mammal assemblage in Northern Acacia Savanna consists mostly of widespread species like Common Wallaroo. © IAIN CAMPBELL, TROPICAL BIRDING TOURS/UNSW E&ERC

Au6G MELALEUCA SAVANNA

IN A NUTSHELL: A seasonally flooded, fire-prone savanna dominated by melaleuca trees. **Global Habitat Affinities:** WALLACEAN MELALEUCA SAVANNA; very loose association with South American FLOODED CHACO AND ESPINAL. **Continental Habitat Affinities:** None. **Species Overlap:** MONSOON VINEFOREST; OPEN EUCALYPT SAVANNA. **Full Bird Assemblage:** habitatsoftheworld.org/Au6G.

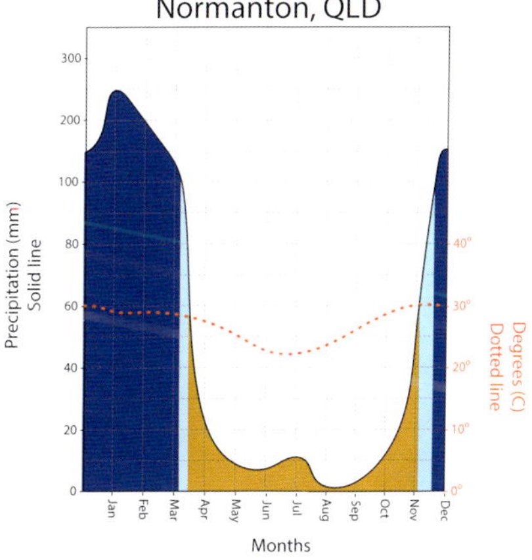

DESCRIPTION: This savanna differs from both the acacia-dominated types such as NORTHERN ACACIA SAVANNA and the eucalypt-dominated types such as OPEN EUCALYPT SAVANNA in that it has to be tolerant of both fire and flooding—thus it replaces the acacias that do not tolerate fire and the eucalypts that prefer better-drained environments. It occurs in the same broad climatic zone as Open Eucalypt Savanna, sharing a tropical savanna climate (Köppen **Aw**) with warm, very dry winters and hot, wet summers reaching up to 113°F (45°C) and receiving most of the annual rainfall of 24–79 in. (600–2000 mm) over a short wet season. However, because it is adapted to areas prone to flooding, it is slightly more azonal than Open Eucalypt Savanna, being less driven by local rain and more by water within a system—and in this regard, it could be classified as a wetland as well as a savanna. This is yet another example of a habitat that can be classified in multiple biomes.

Melaleuca savanna tends to dominate in low-lying areas that are flooded in the wet season and where fires are frequent, though it exists on both broad alluvial plains and drainage depressions on raised palaeo-alluvial plains. The woodland tends to be dominated by two or three species in each location though the mix does change. The higher rises are dominated by Gulbarn (*Melaleuca citrolens*), Broad-leaved Paperbark (*Melaleuca viridiflora*), and Little-leaved Tea Tree (*Melaleuca foliolosa*) with a smattering of other trees such as Silver Oak (*Grevillea parallela*), Jigal Tree (*Lysiphyllum cunninghamii*), and Smooth-leaved Quinine (*Petalostigma banksii*). In the lower areas that are more prone to long periods of standing water, species such as Alice River Bottlebrush (*Melaleuca clarksonii*) become much more common, and Broad-leaved Paperbark dominates the landscape through Cape York Peninsula (Queensland) and s. New Guinea. The Broad-leaved Paperbark, while great for Australasian wildlife, is the curse of Florida (USA), where it is a serious invasive pest.

Melaleuca Savanna is very special in that it can withstand both regular flooding and regular burning. This is also what makes it very invasive in areas such as the Everglades in Florida (USA). © IAIN CAMPBELL, TROPICAL BIRDING TOURS/UNSW E&ERC

Termite mounds are common in many Melaleuca Savanna environments, as here in Lakefield National Park, Queensland. © IAIN CAMPBELL, TROPICAL BIRDING TOURS/UNSW E&ERC

Most of the *Melaleuca* trees have a characteristic papery bark that exfoliates in large sheets, and the trees usually have off-white to cream trunks that are burned black at the base. The height of *Melaleuca* savanna ranges from 10 ft. (3 m) in shrublands to 100 ft. (30 m) in woodlands, with the same species varying in height depending on water conditions. In flood-prone areas, there is little understorey, and the ground can be bare with clay exposed. Away from rivers, the density of trees decreases, transitioning from woodland to very open wooded savanna with a tussock-grass understorey or even to grassland savanna with only two *Melaleuca* trees per acre (around five trees per hectare).

Shrubby Melaleuca subhabitat: On ridgelines, especially lateritic rises with ferricrete or bauxite concentrations, Melaleuca Savanna can become very dense and shrubby, with Fibre-barked Tea Tree, Broad-leaved Paperbark, and Gulbarn forming thickets with shrubby trees such as Silver Oak, Bushman's Clothes Peg (*Grevillea glauca*), Townsville Wattle (*Acacia leptostachya*), and North Coast Wattle (*Acacia leptocarpa*). These thickets can be regarded as an ecotone between Melaleuca Savanna and SHRUBBY EUCALYPT SAVANNA, as these small trees are found as the understorey of the latter habitat where it occurs near Melaleuca Savanna. They contain the canopy bird assemblage of Melaleuca Savanna and the understorey bird assemblage of Shrubby Eucalypt Savanna.

WILDLIFE: These *Melaleuca* stands are prone to mass flowering, and during these times they can be teeming with birds. Nectivorous birds include Red-collared Lorikeet, Bar-breasted Honeyeater, Brown-backed Honeyeater, and Scarlet Myzomela. Most of the Australian raptors use this habitat, and some species such as Black-breasted Kite and Spotted Harrier are more common here than in surrounding habitats. Other birds include Silver-crowned Friarbird, Arafura

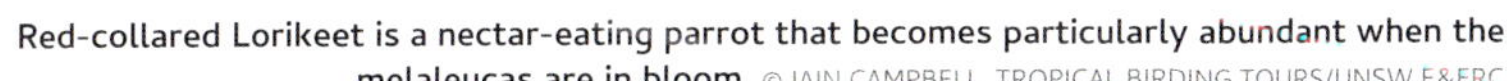

Red-collared Lorikeet is a nectar-eating parrot that becomes particularly abundant when the melaleucas are in bloom. © IAIN CAMPBELL, TROPICAL BIRDING TOURS/UNSW E&ERC

Bar-breasted Honeyeater is a near-obligate species to Melaleuca Savanna.
© NICK ATHANAS, TROPICAL BIRDING TOURS

Shrikethrush, Northern Fantail, and Paperbark Flycatcher. The grassy understorey is the domain of numerous finches such as Double-barred Finch, Chestnut-breasted Munia, White-bellied subspecies of Crimson Finch, and Star Finch. Red-backed Fairywren is by far the most common fairywren through most of this habitat.

In New Guinea, this habitat is very good for Red-capped Flowerpecker, Brown-backed Honeyeater, and in the Trans-Fly region, Noisy Friarbird, and Brown Honeyeater.

Terrestrial mammals, such as the Agile Wallaby, are few, and the dominant groups in n. Australia are flying foxes and other bats, such as Black Flying Fox, Little Red Flying Fox, and Lesser Long-tongued Nectar Bat.

Black-breasted Kite is most abundant in the tropical north of Australia, where Melaleuca Savanna occurs. © IAIN CAMPBELL, TROPICAL BIRDING TOURS/ UNSW E&ERC

Although they are typical of TROPICAL FRESHWATER WETLAND, both Freshwater Crocodile (*Crocodylus johnstoni*) and Saltwater Crocodile (*Crocodylus porosus*) will enter nearby Melaleuca Savanna, so care should be taken walking close to waterways. Larger lizards include Yellow-spotted Monitor (*Varanus panoptes*) and Horner's Dragon (*Lophognathus horneri*), and the many smaller lizards include Metallic Snake-eyed Skink (*Cryptoblepharus metallicus*). The long tussock grasses in the savannas hide many snakes, including Children's Python (*Antaresia childreni*), the very small Spotted Python (*Antaresia maculosa*), Black-headed Python (*Aspidites melanocephalus*), Bird's Head Peninsula Ground Snake (*Stegonotus cucullatus*), and the highly venomous Coastal Taipan (*Oxyuranus scutellatus*). Amphibians include Giant Burrowing Frog (*Ranoidea australis*) and Australian Green Tree Frog (*Ranoidea caerulea*).

CONSERVATION: The Melaleuca Savanna in Australia is pretty well protected because it is of very little economic value and mainly occurs in remote areas. The situation is not so rosy in New Guinea, where the land is cleared for subsistence agriculture in areas with rapid population increase, although it is not cleared for timber. There are no very large established protected areas north of Australia.

DISTRIBUTION: This habitat occurs throughout tropical ne. and nc. Australia and New Guinea. It is widespread in the Trans-Fly region of sc. New Guinea, as well as in n. Australia, especially around the Gulf of Carpentaria coast, and extends through the tropical parts of Australia. There are small patches of *Melaleuca* savanna in coastal areas of s. Queensland and n. New South Wales.

WHERE TO SEE: Lakefield National Park, Queensland, Australia; Fogg Dam, Northern Territory, Australia; Wasur National Park, South Papua, Indonesian New Guinea.

Agile Wallaby occurs widely across much of tropical n. Australia within Melaleuca Savanna as well as neighbouring habitats such as Open Eucalypt Savanna and Tetrodonta Woodland Savanna. © IAIN CAMPBELL, TROPICAL BIRDING TOURS/UNSW E&ERC

Au6H MELALEUCA RIVERINE FOREST

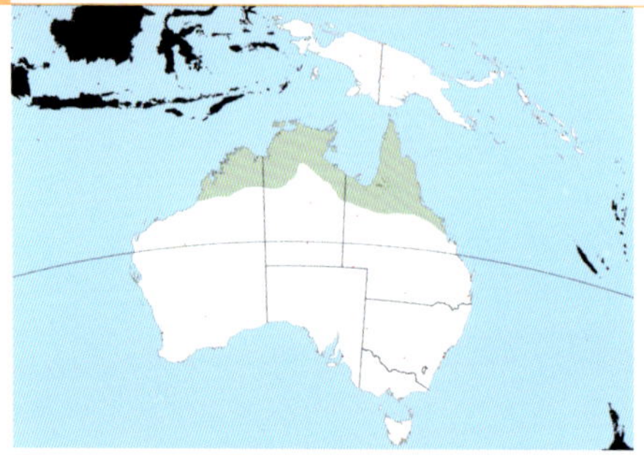

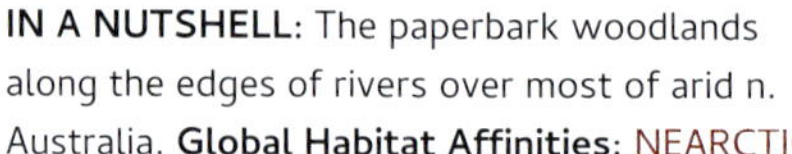

IN A NUTSHELL: The paperbark woodlands along the edges of rivers over most of arid n. Australia. **Global Habitat Affinities:** NEARCTIC WESTERN RIPARIAN WOODLAND; TURANIAN ARID RIPARIAN SCRUB. **Continental Habitat Affinities:** SHEOAK RIPARIAN FOREST; MELALEUCA SAVANNA. **Species Overlap:** MELALEUCA SAVANNA; MONSOON VINEFOREST. **Full Bird Assemblage:** habitatsoftheworld.org/Au6H.

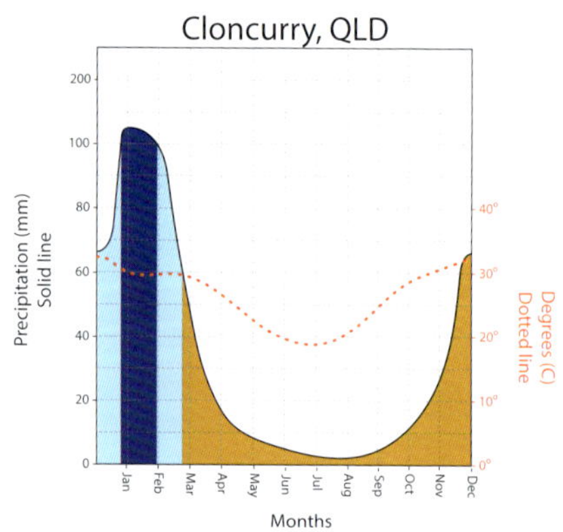

DESCRIPTION: Most people's experience of camping in the Australian savannas in the Top End (Northern Territory) or on the way to Cape York (Queensland) is along riverbeds lined with paperbark trees (*Melaleuca* spp.). These ribbons of water in the otherwise dry environment are overrepresented in people's photographs and memories, though they make up a tiny area of this immense landscape.

Melaleuca Riverine Forest occurs on most of the drainage lines of n. Australia from the rainforest edge to the coast. The forest is somewhat azonal in that it occurs over a range of surrounding habitats from hot monsoonal forests (Köppen **Aw**) to semiarid SPINIFEX EUCALYPT SAVANNA (Köppen **Bsh**). Generally, forests at the river edge are hydromorphic in that they derive their water directly from the river, while surrounding forests are semi-hydromorphic, depending on local rainfall as well as the river water. This relation becomes more intense the more inland the river occurs, so in the driest areas, such as the Spinifex Eucalypt Savanna, the Melaleuca Riverine Forest is completely hydromorphic.

Where Melaleuca Riverine Forest lines rivers surrounded by LOWLAND RAINFOREST or MONSOON VINEFOREST, as in the Wet Tropics or Cape York Peninsula, the habitat is dominated by large paperbarks such as Weeping Tea Tree (*Melaleuca leucadendra*), River Paperbark (*Melaleuca fluviatilis*), Silver-crowned Paperbark (*Melaleuca argentea*), Willow Bottlebrush (*Melaleuca saligna*), and Broad-leaved Paperbark (*Melaleuca viridiflora*). Some of these can be huge, growing to over 120 ft. (40 m), but the closed canopy of these forests is usually between 50 and 100 ft. (15–30 m) high. The canopy also has many rainforest and monsoon forest trees such as White Silky Oak (*Grevillea hilliana*), Northern Olive (*Chionanthus ramiflorus*), Northern Laurel (*Cryptocarya*

In much wetter areas, this forest can begin to look like a melaleuca-dominated Swamp Forest. © IAIN CAMPBELL, TROPICAL BIRDING TOURS/UNSW E&ERC

Overleaf: **In more arid environments, Melaleuca Riverine Forest can take on the appearance of the more open Inland Riverine Woodland.** © IAIN CAMPBELL, TROPICAL BIRDING TOURS/UNSW E&ERC

hypospodia), Blue Quandong (*Elaeocarpus arnhemicus*), Swamp Box (*Lophostemon suaveolens*), Cooktown Ironwood (*Erythrophleum chlorostachys*), Forest Red Gum (*Eucalyptus tereticornis*), and Brown Gardenia (*Atractocarpus fitzalanii*). Golden Penda (*Xanthostemon chrysanthus*), which has been cultivated widely in e. Australia, is joined in the subcanopy by species such as Flaky-barked Satinash (*Syzygium forte*), and Little Gooseberry Tree (*Buchanania arborescens*). Along riverbanks, groves can form of Kanuka Box (*Tristaniopsis exiliflora*), a tree that looks like a eucalypt but with a weeping-willow shape, drooping over the water, its branches even reaching the ground on the opposite side of small creeks. In many regards, this habitat can look very similar to the surrounding Monsoon Vineforest because there are so many vines in the canopy and subcanopy. Ground-cover and shrub layers tend to be poorly developed because the habitat is so prone to monsoonal flooding. In many areas, there is no ground layer or shrub layer at all, and detritus from previous floods is caught up in the lower branches of the trees and understorey, often over 10 ft. (3 m) high. For any tree to establish itself here, it has to grow extremely quickly as a sapling to be large enough to withstand flooding in an almost annual cycle.

The drier examples of Melaleuca Riverine Forest are more often open-canopy woodlands than very closed-canopy forests, but they have many of the same paperbark species as the wetter areas, such as Silver-crowned Paperbark, Weeping Tea Tree, Alice River Bottlebrush (*Melaleuca clarksonii*), Broad-leaved Paperbark, and River Paperbark. The ubiquitous River Red Gum (*Eucalyptus camaldulensis*) of c. Australia joins the canopy assemblage along with Northern Swamp Box (*Lophostemon grandiflorus*), Cluster Fig (*Ficus racemosa*), and Wild Plum (*Xanthostemon umbrosus*). The understorey of these drier examples is usually very open, with few shrubs and a lot of exposed sand. River Red Gum becomes a dominant tree as this habitat extends into drier areas, and when eucalypts become more common than melaleucas the habitat changes into INLAND RIVERINE WOODLAND.

Paperbark Flycatcher of the tropical north of Australia is typically close to water and so is often found within Melaleuca Riverine Forest. © PABLO CERVANTES, TROPICAL BIRDING TOURS

WILDLIFE: The fauna of Melaleuca Riverine Forest is always an amalgamation of the wildlife restricted to the creek and that of the surrounding habitat. This habitat in the Cape York Peninsula contains typical savanna canopy species such as Peaceful Dove, Bar-shouldered Dove, Blue-winged Kookaburra, Red-winged Parrot, Blue-faced Honeyeater, Brown-backed Honeyeater, Rufous-throated Honeyeater, Silver-crowned Friarbird, White-bellied Cuckooshrike, and Paperbark Flycatcher. There will, however, be a sprinkling of typical MONSOON VINEFOREST birds such as Orange-footed Megapode, Torresian Imperial-Pigeon, Papuan Frogmouth, Pacific Baza, Yellow Honeyeater, White-gaped Honeyeater, Helmeted Friarbird, Fairy Gerygone, and even Yellow-breasted Boatbill. Lovely Fairywren, Red-backed Fairywren, Red-browed Firetail, and Double-barred Finch are all species of the understorey of this habitat, with Lovely Fairywren and Red-browed Firetail preferring the thicker viny areas, and Red-backed Fairywren and Double-barred Finch preferring more open and grassier understorey.

Farther inland, where this habitat is surrounded by dry savannas, the bird assemblage is tied more closely to these ribbons of green. The birds expected in this drier type of Melaleuca Riverine Forest include hunters such as Sacred Kingfisher, White-breasted Woodswallow, Northern Fantail, and Buff-sided Robin. Nectivorous birds are a major component of the bird assemblage, including species such as Varied Lorikeet, Red-collared Lorikeet, Yellow Honeyeater, White-gaped Honeyeater, Bar-breasted Honeyeater, and Dusky Myzomela. Purple-crowned Fairywren and Crimson Finch inhabit the thick grasses at the river's edge, and fruit eaters such as Australasian Figbird and Sahul Cicadabird occupy the fruiting trees.

Not many mammals are restricted to this habitat although Black Flying Fox

Buff-sided Robin is generally a secretive bird, but in campgrounds it can become very habituated and confiding. © IAIN CAMPBELL, TROPICAL BIRDING TOURS/UNSW E&ERC

Purple-crowned Fairywren (a male and two females are pictured) inhabits tall stands of grass (mainly canegrass) within Melaleuca Riverine Forest in the tropical north of Australia.

© NICK ATHANAS, TROPICAL BIRDING TOURS

has a preference for it. Reptiles include Common Prickly Gecko (*Heteronotia binoei*), Fine-spotted Mulch Skink (*Glaphyromorphus punctulatus*), Northern Water Dragon (*Tropicagama temporalis*), and Children's Python (*Antaresia childreni*). Among the amphibians are Ornate Burrowing Frog (*Platyplectrum ornatum*), Australian Green Tree Frog (*Ranoidea caerulea*), Striped Rocket Frog (*Litoria nasuta*), Marbled Frog (*Limnodynastes convexiusculus*), and Western Laughing Tree Frog (*Litoria ridibunda*).

CONSERVATION: This habitat is cleared near populated parts of tropical n. Australia for residential areas, but the overall impact has been negligible. It is widespread and of limited use for farming, so most tracts are very secure. It also grows fairly quickly so can colonise areas around dams.

DISTRIBUTION: Melaleuca Riverine Forest is found along most creeks in most monsoonal environments throughout n. Australia, from the Atherton Tableland of ne. Queensland west to the Pilbara of Western Australia. It expands into the arid region as far as Mt. Isa in Queensland. In arid Australia, it merges with INLAND RIVERINE FOREST; in the tropical wet regions, it merges with MONSOON VINEFOREST; and in se. Australia, it merges with SHEOAK RIPARIAN FOREST. *Melaleuca* swamps occur in s. Australia, but they share many of the same species as surrounding casuarinas and other wetland habitats so are treated with the southern extension of SWAMP FOREST.

WHERE TO SEE: Mataranka, Northern Territory, Australia; Yellow Water, Kakadu National Park, Northern Territory, Australia; Cloncurry, Queensland, Australia; Coen, Queensland, Australia.

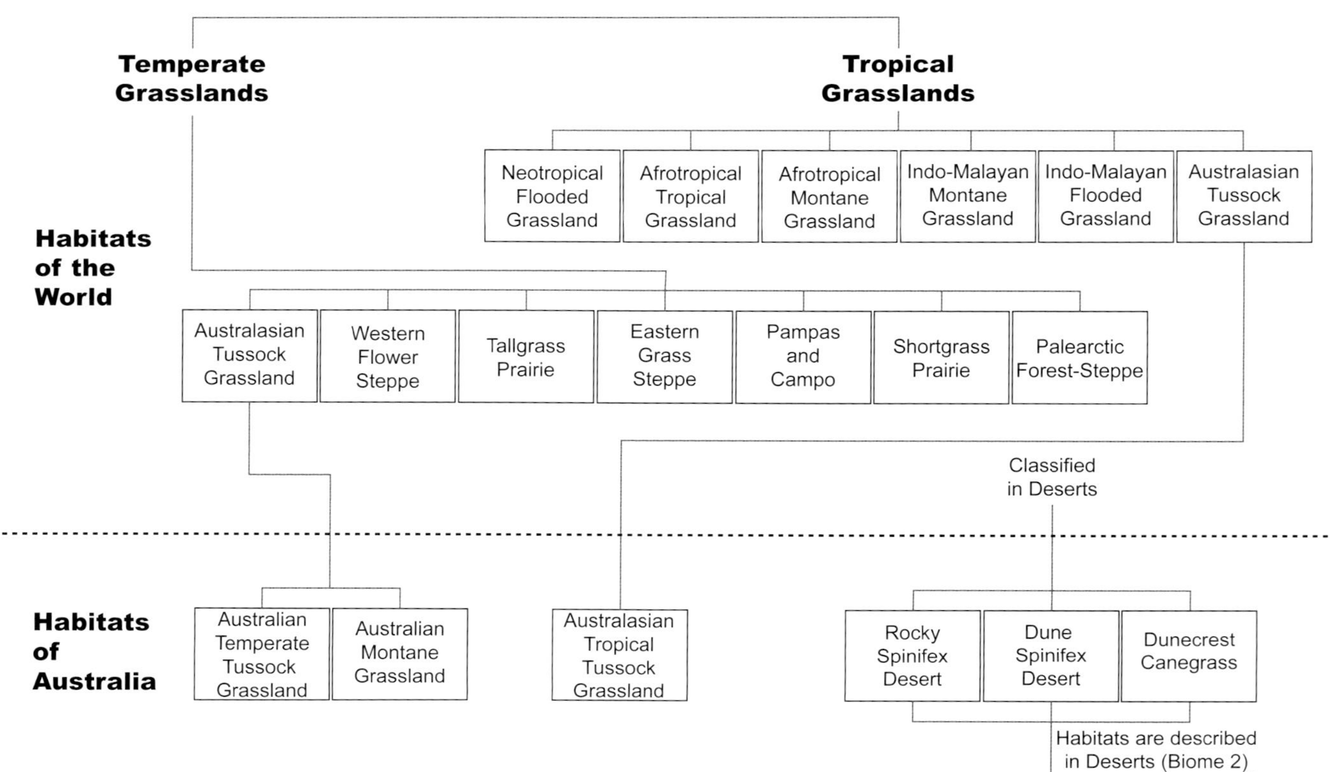
Australian Temperate Tussock Grassland Dendrogram (Biome 7)
Global Grasslands
Temperate Grasslands
Tropical Grasslands
Neotropical Flooded Grassland
Afrotropical Tropical Grassland
Afrotropical Montane Grassland
Indo-Malayan Montane Grassland
Indo-Malayan Flooded Grassland
Australasian Tussock Grassland
Habitats of the World
Australasian Tussock Grassland
Western Flower Steppe
Tallgrass Prairie
Eastern Grass Steppe
Pampas and Campo
Shortgrass Prairie
Palearctic Forest-Steppe
Classified in Deserts
Habitats of Australia
Australian Temperate Tussock Grassland
Australian Montane Grassland
Australasian Tropical Tussock Grassland
Rocky Spinifex Desert
Dune Spinifex Desert
Dunecrest Canegrass
Habitats are described in Deserts (Biome 2)

Au7A TROPICAL TUSSOCK GRASSLAND

IN A NUTSHELL: Almost treeless grassy plains. **Global Habitat Affinities:** AFROTROPICAL GRASSLAND; NEOTROPICAL GRASSLAND; INDIAN TROPICAL GRASSLAND; CHIHUAHUAN DESERT GRASSLAND. **Continental Habitat Affinities:** TEMPERATE TUSSOCK GRASSLAND. **Species Overlap:** OPEN EUCALYPT SAVANNA; GRASSY MULGA; DUNE SPINIFEX DESERT; CHENOPOD SHRUBLAND. **Full Bird Assemblage:** habitatsoftheworld.org/Au7A.

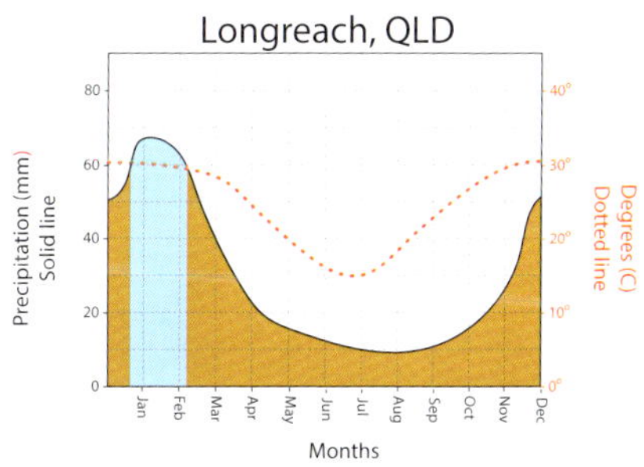

DESCRIPTION: This grassland habitat is the Australian equivalent of the AFROTROPICAL GRASSLAND of Africa, the CHIHUAHUAN DESERT GRASSLAND of North America, or the NEOTROPICAL GRASSLAND of the Grand Sabana in South America. Tropical Tussock Grassland typically grows on massive areas of Cretaceous sediments and alluvial plains in regions with tropical, semiarid savanna climates (Köppen **Bsh**) with summer rainfall.

After the summer rains, the dense, tufted perennial grasses of Tropical Tussock Grassland such as Curly Mitchell Grass (*Astrebla lappacea*), Bull Mitchell Grass (*Astrebla squarrosa*), and Feathertop Wiregrass (*Aristida latifolia*) are found in the lower soils that are prone to occasional waterlogging. In slightly more elevated areas, those grasses are joined by Neverfail Grass

Coastal Tropical Tussock Grassland can tolerate brackish conditions but not as much as Coastal Salt Marsh. © IAIN CAMPBELL, TROPICAL BIRDING TOURS/UNSW E&ERC

It does not rain much in the Mitchell grass plains of Winton, Queensland, but when it does, it can be spectacular. © IAIN CAMPBELL, TROPICAL BIRDING TOURS/UNSW E&ERC

(*Eragrostis setifolia*) and Australian Millet (*Panicum decompositum*), which was a traditional staple grain of Aboriginal Australians. The grasses of this habitat typically grow to 2–3 ft. (60–100 cm) in height, with a crown usually around 2 ft. (60 cm) wide. The tussocks themselves can be close together but are often well spaced, usually about 3 ft. (1 m) apart, so there is often bare earth exposed between grass clumps. Long-lived, with a dual root system for absorbing both smaller rainfalls and deeper subsoil moisture, these grasses can withstand drought and then burst into life after a good rain, giving the landscape the look of a well-planted lawn.

There are often small patches of Queensland Bluebush (*Chenopodium auricomum*) in these grasslands, though rarely growing higher than 5 ft (1.5 m) and not in the thickets that it can form in CHENOPOD SHRUBLAND. The few trees that do grow in these grasslands, which tend to be hundreds of feet apart, can include acacias such as Boree (*Acacia tephrina*), Gidgee (*Acacia cambagei*), and Bastard Mulga (*Acacia sibirica*), as well as Whitewood (*Atalaya hemiglauca*) and Leopardwood (*Flindersia maculosa*), with its very attractive mottled bark.

There is a seemingly esoteric but important distinction between Tropical Tussock Grassland and the tropical grasslands of other continents. Most other

Very large termite mounds can be common in the more humid regions of this habitat but are absent from the more arid terrains. © IAIN CAMPBELL, TROPICAL BIRDING TOURS/UNSW E&ERC

tropical grasslands exist as one type of alternative stable state (ASS) amidst other habitats existing within very similar environmental parameters, yet Tropical Tussock Grassland does not share its very particular environment with other habitats. Some of the other tropical grasslands are pyrrhic, meaning fire is a major determinant in stopping the encroachment of treed savanna or forest; others are trophic, meaning grazing and browsing herbivory from both vertebrates and invertebrates stops the invasion of trees and shrublands. Hysteresis, the lag between when the change (such as a fire) occurs and when the habitat reverts to a pre-fire equilibrium, is important in those other grasslands. By contrast, in Tropical Tussock Grassland, while fire is regular and stops encroachment of small shrubs, it is mainly the soils that keep trees from thriving. They are very clay-rich with significant amounts of smectites (cracking clays) rather than the kaolinites common in most tropical soils. The smectitic clays swell when wet, becoming waterlogged oxygen-poor masses that dry out in blocks with very deep cracks. The regular cracking shears off large lateral roots of trees and shrubs, stopping the roots from taking hold, while grasses, especially Mitchell grasses, have roots that grow though the vertical column, giving them the competitive advantage.

WILDLIFE: It is difficult to describe this habitat without sounding dismissive, as it is so depauperate compared to all those other global grasslands, and anyone expecting lush plains flush with animals will be sorely disappointed. Nonetheless, Tropical Tussock Grassland is an important habitat for Flock Bronzewing, which, along with Letter-winged Kite, has a boom-and-bust life cycle, its numbers fluctuating dramatically. The kite's numbers are dependent on the population of its main food source, the Long-haired Rat. The Flock Bronzewing was once heading towards extinction in the same manner as the North American Passenger Pigeon; flocks of hundreds of thousands of bronzewings in the 1800s were reduced to mere hundreds by the early 1900s. With strict protection, numbers have rebounded, and flocks of thousands are again being reported. Many

Letter-winged Kite forages within remote areas of Tropical Tussock Grassland. However, it is rare, nomadic, and crepuscular in nature, making it notoriously hard to find. © SAM WOODS, TROPICAL BIRDING TOURS

A displaying Australian Bustard is one of the quintessential sights while birding in Australia's Tropical Tussock Grassland. © IAIN CAMPBELL, TROPICAL BIRDING TOURS/UNSW E&ERC

other species of birds use these grasslands, including Australian Bustard, Australian Pratincole, and Inland Dotterel. The very rare Night Parrot is found in some areas, and it has been speculated that it may be found in this habitat and DUNE SPINIFEX DESERT throughout c. Australia.

The star mammal in Tropical Tussock Grassland is Greater Bilby, an odd marsupial that was brought back from near extinction and still requires management in areas where introduced predators have been removed or numbers heavily controlled. Smaller mammals that occur here

Australia's largest marsupial, the Red Kangaroo, inhabits Tropical Tussock Grassland. The largest males are over 5 ft. (1.6 m) tall, with a tail length of nearly 4 ft. (1. 2m), and weigh up to 200 lb. (90 kg). © PABLO CERVANTES, TROPICAL BIRDING TOURS

Spencer's Monitor is found in treeless plains on the Barkly Tableland of the Northern Territory. © CHARLEY HESSE, TROPICAL BIRDING TOURS

include Short-beaked Echidna, Narrow-nosed Planigale, and Stripe-faced Dunnart. Larger grazers such as Red Kangaroo and Common Wallaroo are much more abundant in this habitat than in Dune Spinifex Desert, and these large herbivores provide a food source for carrion eaters such as Dingo, Wedge-tailed Eagle, Black-breasted Kite, and Black Kite.

Numerous lizards occur in Tropical Tussock Grassland, such as the impressive Spencer's Monitor (*Varanus spenceri*) and the smaller Spiny Knob-tailed Gecko (*Nephrurus asper*), Tessellated Gecko (*Diplodactylus tessellatus*), and Common Prickly Gecko (*Heteronotia binoei*). Eyrean Earless Dragon (*Tympanocryptis tetraporophora*) occurs in this habitat but is also widespread in very sparse GIBBER CHENOPODLAND. Eastern Hooded Scaly-Foot (*Pygopus schraderi*), common in these grasslands, at first glance appears to be a snake but is a legless lizard.

There are many snakes in this environment, but rather than pythons, the snake assemblage is dominated by venomous species such as Inland Taipan (*Oxyuranus microlepidotus*), Speckled Brown Snake (*Pseudonaja guttata*), Ingram's Brown Snake (*Pseudonaja ingrami*), Curl Snake (*Suta suta*), De Vis's Banded Snake (*Denisonia devisi*), Eastern Bandy Bandy (*Vermicella annulata*), Eastern Brown Snake (*Pseudonaja textilis*), Collett's Black Snake (*Pseudechis colletti*), and Mulga Snake (*Pseudechis australis*).

CONSERVATION: Because Tropical Tussock Grassland is so much more productive than spinifex for pasture, it has been almost completely exploited for wide-scale cattle grazing. Overall, the habitat seems to be preserved, but overgrazing is a serious issue in drought periods and has caused a reduction in native animal numbers. In the New Guinea highlands, where anthropogenic grasslands are widespread, they are being rapidly converted to farmland with intense crop cultivation and grazing.

DISTRIBUTION: Australasian Tropical Tussock Grassland occurs on more fertile soils than DUNE SPINIFEX DESERT and ROCKY SPINIFEX DESERT, mainly in inland ne. Australia, particularly nw. Queensland, and in s. Northern Territory. Although this habitat is widespread, most of the areas where it occurs are relatively remote, including the Barkly Tableland of s. Northern Territory and the Diamantina region of Queensland. Small patches of grassland occur in the coastal lowlands of New Guinea, and there are extensive stretches of anthropogenic grasslands through the highlands.

WHERE TO SEE: Connells Lagoon, Barkly Tableland, Northern Territory, Australia; Winton, Queensland, Australia.

Au7B TEMPERATE TUSSOCK GRASSLAND

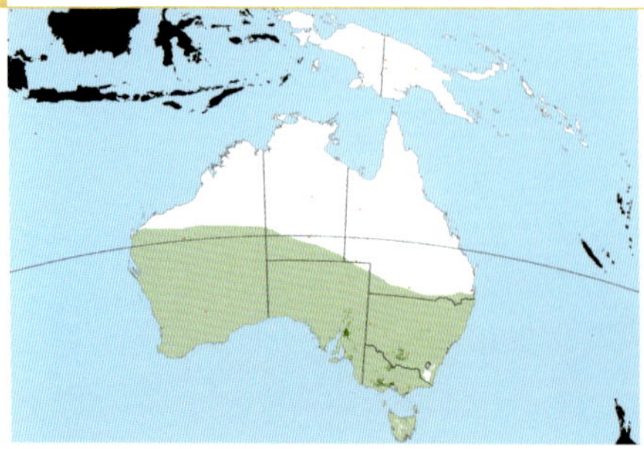

IN A NUTSHELL: The natural, almost treeless grassy plains of s. Australia. **Global Habitat Affinities:** NORTH AMERICAN TALLGRASS PRAIRIE; PAMPAS; KAZAKH FLOWER STEPPE. **Continental Habitat Affinities:** TROPICAL TUSSOCK GRASSLAND; MONTANE GRASSLAND. **Species Overlap:** TROPICAL TUSSOCK GRASSLAND; MONTANE GRASSLAND; OPEN GRAZING LAND. **Full Bird Assemblage:** habitatsoftheworld.org/Au7B.

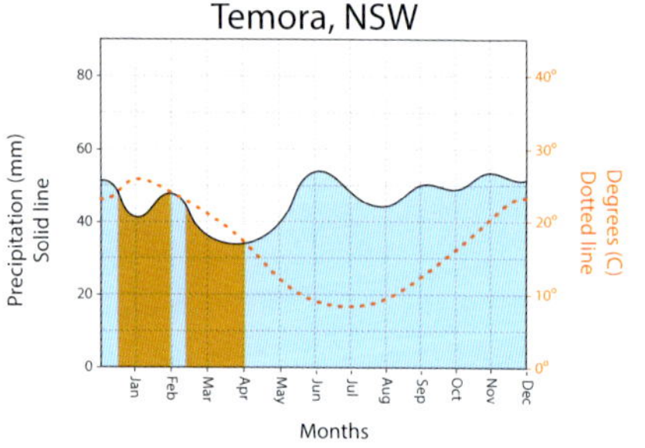

DESCRIPTION: Despite the picture-postcard images of Australia with vast open plains covered in grass, this habitat is, in fact, very endangered, and few of the original grasslands still exist, most having been put under the plough for croplands within decades of Europeans first seeing them. The postcards show rangelands caused by the clearing of woodlands, not the natural tussock grasslands.

In its natural state, Temperate Tussock Grassland habitat is the Australian equivalent of the TALLGRASS PRAIRIE of North America or the PAMPAS of South America. The dense, tufted perennial grasses of Temperate Tussock Grassland grow to 2–3 ft. (60–100 cm) in height, with a crown usually around 2 ft. (60 cm) wide. Their composition varies; C3 (temperate) grasses can nearly completely dominate, or there can be a high forb (flower) component or even very high chenopod component. Some of the grasslands are derived from clearing of IRONBARK-BOX WOODLAND, and the distinction between a pre-European grassland and a post-European derived grassland is very difficult to discern.

The more uniform grassy versions of this habitat are dominated by temperate C3 grasses such as Black Windmill Grass (*Chloris truncata*), Australian Millet (*Panicum decompositum*), Queensland Bluegrass (*Dichanthium sericeum*), Curly Windmill Grass (*Enteropogon ramosus*), Plains Grass (*Austrostipa aristiglumis*), Knotted Corkscrew Grass (*Austrostipa nodosa*), Tall Oat Grass (*Themeda avenacea*), Rough Speargrass (*Austrostipa scabra*), and Leafy Wallaby Grass (*Rytidosperma bipartita*), and sedges such as Purple Nutsedge (*Cyperus rotundus*), a cosmopolitan species also found in Africa, Europe, and Asia. The tussocks themselves are well spaced, usually about 3 ft. (1 m) apart, so there is often bare earth exposed between grass clumps. Unlike many temperate grasslands, where growth is dictated by seasonal cycles, these grasslands can withstand drought and swiftly respond to substantial rainfall, transforming a dry, brown landscape into lush green at any time of year.

Temperate Tussock Grasslands tend to have odd trees dotted throughout, though they can also be vast, open treeless plains. © IAIN CAMPBELL, TROPICAL BIRDING TOURS/UNSW E&ERC

When forbs are present and flowering, the habitat looks much more like Northern Hemisphere steppe habitats such as the KAZAKH FLOWER STEPPE of Kazakhstan or the TALLGRASS PRAIRIE of the United States and Canada, with bursts of mainly blues and yellows across the landscape. Typical species include Woody-root Woodsorrel (*Oxalis perennans*), Tough Scurf-Pea (*Cullen tenax*), Tah-Vine (*Boerhavia domini*), High Sida (*Sida trichopoda*), Corrugated Sida (*Sida corrugate*), Common Woodruff (*Asperula conferta*), Eastern Stork's-Bill (*Erodium crinitum*), Small-flower Goodenia (*Goodenia pusilliflora*), Hoary Sunray (*Leucochrysum molle*), and Tufted Bluebell (*Wahlenbergia capillaris*).

At least some of the chenopod-rich grasslands are anthropogenic, formed by the clearing of Myall (*Acacia melvillei*) from the Chenopod Woodland subhabitat of CHENOPOD SHRUBLAND and the overgrazing of these shrublands. Chenopod shrubs are common in these derived grasslands and in some of the completely natural grasslands, especially on the Hay Plain of New South Wales, where Hairy Bluebush (*Maireana pentagona*) and Bottle Bluebush (*Maireana excavata*), which look like North American sagebrush, occur beside Leafless Bluebush (*Maireana aphylla*), which usually looks dead. Bluebush Daisy (*Cratystylis conocephala*) is a prominent shrub that looks very similar to the bluebushes, with its thick, fluffy bluish leaves, but is a type of aster.

This habitat occurs naturally on very flat areas with loam to clay soils formed on vast alluvial plains. These are often referred to as clay plains, black-soil plains, or gilgai plains. The gilgai soils have smectites (cracking clays), which can absorb a lot of water and therefore expand and contract through the seasons, shearing off tree roots and making it very difficult for trees to establish in this habitat, though a few trees do eke out an existence. On the plains where bluebushes are common, Weeping Myall (*Acacia pendula*) can form groves. Farther to the north and east, trees such as Yellow Box (*Eucalyptus melliodora*), White Box (*Eucalyptus albens*), and Western Rosewood (*Alectryon oleifolius*) skirt the edges of the grassy plains.

WILDLIFE: Temperate Tussock Grasslands host a mass of parrots that nest in other habitats, such as INLAND RIVERINE WOODLAND, but enter this habitat to feed, including Red-rumped Parrot. Ground birds make up a very large component of the bird assemblage of this area. Besides

Many parrots come into this habitat to forage from nearby wooded habitats that have the nesting hollows they require, including the widespread Red-rumped Parrot.
© PABLO CERVANTES, TROPICAL BIRDING TOURS

Some of the most conspicuous birds of Temperate Tussock Grassland are aerial hunters such as Australian Hobby (pictured), Black-shouldered Kite, and Nankeen Kestrel. © BEN KNOOT

the mother of all Australian ground birds, the Emu, there are other obvious species such as Australian Bustard, Masked Lapwing, and Banded Lapwing. The many skulkers include Stubble Quail, Little Buttonquail, Red-chested Buttonquail, the rare Inland Dotterel, and the enigmatic Plains-wanderer, which is in its own monotypic family, somewhat related to buttonquail. Other small insectivorous species that feed close to the ground include Crimson, Orange, and White-fronted Chats, Singing Bushlark, Australian Pipit, and both Rufous and Brown Songlarks.

Birds feeding in or from the air are a notable portion of the bird assemblage, which includes many raptors such as Black-shouldered Kite, Swamp and Spotted Harriers, Nankeen Kestrel, Australian Hobby, and Brown Falcon. Australian Pratincole is a species of shorebird that roosts on the ground but can often be seen in large flocks that look more like terns than shorebirds. Dusky and Black-faced Woodswallows can often be seen hawking over grasslands along with Rainbow Bee-eater, Fairy Martin, and White-backed Swallow. Astoundingly, there are far fewer finches in Temperate Tussock Grassland than in TROPICAL TUSSOCK GRASSLAND, though there does not appear to be an obvious reason for the lack of finches. The only regular finch here is the near-ubiquitous Zebra Finch of c. Australia.

Small mammals are fairly limited in this environment. The Narrow-nosed Planigale is a mouselike marsupial carnivore related to the quolls and Tasmanian Devil. It is tiny, just 3 in. (7.5 cm) long, with a triangular head and thin tail, and is specialised to live in grasslands with chenopods, especially those on cracking clay soils. Other small marsupials include Fat-tailed and Slender-tailed Dunnarts, which also occur in a variety of other, more wooded habitats. The large macropods here include Eastern Grey Kangaroo, Euro (a subspecies of Common Wallaroo), Red Kangaroo, and Western Grey Kangaroo. Southern Hairy-nosed Wombat used to be found in these grasslands, but competition from introduced animals has eradicated it from most of its previous grasslands, and now its population is concentrated more in the CHENOPOD SHRUBLAND of the Nullarbor Plain, a more challenging environment for introduced species. Bats are surprisingly common over Temperate Tussock Grassland at night, including species such as Gould's Wattled Bat, Chocolate Wattled Bat, White-striped Free-tailed Bat, and Inland Broad-nosed Bat, but as expected, there are no fruit-eating bats such as flying foxes.

Venomous snakes are fairly common in the grasslands, including Curl Snake (*Suta suta*), Eastern Brown Snake (*Pseudonaja textilis*), Red-naped Snake (*Furina diadema*), and Prong-snouted Blind Snake (*Anilios bituberculatus*). Constrictor species are not as common, although Carpet Python (*Morelia spilota*) does occur. There are many skink species, such as Southeastern Morethia Skink (*Morethia boulengeri*), Inland Snake-eyed Skink (*Cryptoblepharus australis*), Ragged Snake-eyed Skink (*Cryptoblepharus pannosus*), Wood Mulch Slider (*Lerista muelleri*), and the widespread Shingleback (*Tiliqua rugosa*). Larger lizards include Eastern Bearded Dragon (*Pogona barbata*) and two very large monitors, Lace Monitor (*Varanus varius*) and Sand Goanna (*Varanus gouldii*).

CONSERVATION: Temperate Tussock Grassland habitat has been devastated by farming, and most of what we perceive to be natural grassland is little more than cleared fields and improved pasture. Most of the true grassland has been converted to wheat, sorghum, and cotton cropland, and the grasslands that remain are under intense pressure from introduced species. It is rare to find a grassland that is not infested with weeds such as Wimmera Ryegrass (*Lolium rigidum*) and Wild Oat (*Avena fatua*). Overgrazing by sheep and the introduction of rabbits have also affected the natural grasslands, causing a reduction in the chenopods and forbs in the assemblage and an increase in less-palatable grasses and shrubs. There are no extensive national preserves devoted to the protection of this habitat, and because the habitat looks similar to farmland, conversion of the pitifully small remainder to farmland may pretty much continue unabated.

DISTRIBUTION: Temperate Tussock Grassland once ranged in e. Australia from the Liverpool Plains (New South Wales) and s. Queensland to Adelaide (South Australia) and n. Victoria. In the west they were concentrated around what has become the Western Australian wheat belt. Most of the remaining grasslands are along stock routes and roadside verges.

WHERE TO SEE: Hay Plain, New South Wales, Australia.

Larger macropods such as Western Gray Kangaroo inhabit Temperate Tussock Grassland, often feeding on patches of grass along road verges at night, when they represent a significant danger to passing motorists. © IAIN CAMPBELL, TROPICAL BIRDING TOURS/UNSW E&ERC

Au7C AUSTRALIAN MONTANE GRASSLAND

IN A NUTSHELL: Almost treeless grassy plains of the Australian highlands. **Global Habitat Affinities:** AFRICAN MONTANE GRASSLAND; TUSSOCK PUNA; ASIAN ALPINE MEADOW AND STEPPE. **Continental Habitat Affinities:** TEMPERATE TUSSOCK GRASSLAND. **Species Overlap:** SUBALPINE EUCALYPT WOODLAND; IRONBARK-BOX WOODLAND. **Full Bird Assemblage:** habitatsoftheworld.org/Au7C.

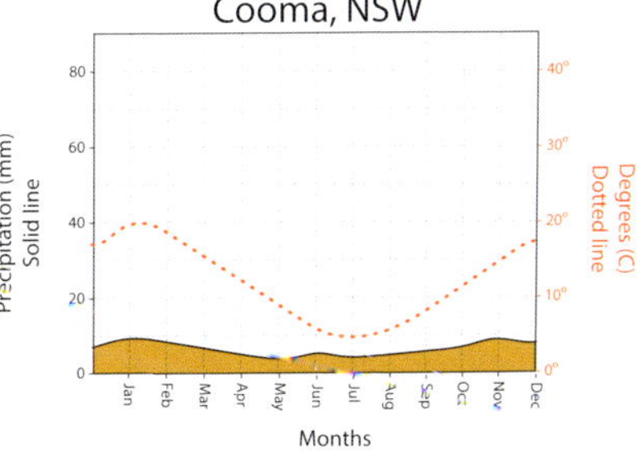

DESCRIPTION: Montane Grassland of Australia is a non-steppe temperate grassland, the equivalent of the Highveld region of South Africa or the grassy areas of the Caucasus. The habitat occurs in two main areas with different climates. On the mainland, Montane Grassland grows between 2000 and 5000 ft. (600–1500 m) elevation on the Great Dividing Range in s. New South Wales and n. Victoria. This region is a rain-shadow area with a cool, dry oceanic climate (Köppen **Cfb**) and annual precipitation around 30 in. (1000 mm). In Tasmania, the grasslands grow much lower, usually between 1000 and 3000 ft. (300–1000 m), in areas with a subpolar oceanic climate (Köppen **Cfc**), cold temperatures, and little water stress, with rainfall of 24 in. (600 mm). The grasslands tend to be found on very fertile soils, often over basalt flows.

In Tasmania they develop as tall grasslands dominated by tussocks of Gunni Poa Grass (*Poa gunnii*), Bog Snow Grass (*Poa costiniana*), Common Tussock Grass (*Poa labillardierei*), and Fine-leaved Snow Grass (*Poa clivicola*), with lower layers and mats of Alpine Wallaby Grass (*Rytidosperma nudiflorum*), and Fan Tuft-Rush (*Oreobolus distichus*), mixed with many small forbs such as Rock Bluebell (*Wahlenbergia saxicola*). There are very widely spaced short subalpine eucalypts such as Tasmanian Snow Gum (*Eucalyptus coccifera*) and Snow Gum (*Eucalyptus pauciflora*), mixed with some much larger, tall-growing trees, such as Cider Gum (*Eucalyptus gunnii*) and Alpine Ash (*Eucalyptus delegatensis*). In Tasmania, Montane Grassland blends into MONTANE HEATHLAND and AUSTRALIAN ALPINE TUNDRA at higher elevations, and to Temperate Heath Thicket (a subhabitat of WALLUM AND AUSBOS) when fire is retarded.

In the Australian mainland highlands, Montane Grasslands form as both glades surrounded by SUBALPINE EUCALYPT WOODLAND and as extensive fields on crests, mid-slopes, and foothills of the rolling plains, on a variety of parent substrates, including residual bedrock, colluvium, and alluvium. The soils that develop are usually high-quality, nutrient-rich chernozem (brown temperate) soils similar to those in the temperate grasslands of North America and Europe. They usually form as tussock grasslands, 1–3 ft. (30–100 cm) tall. Kangaroo Grass (*Themeda*

The distinction between natural Montane Grassland and grazing land is arbitrary in some locations. © GRAHAMEC, CC BY-SA 4.0 <HTTPS://CREATIVECOMMONS.ORG/LICENSES/BY-SA/4.0>, VIA WIKIMEDIA COMMONS

Opposite top: **Brown Quail is found in grasslands, heaths, and grassy areas within woodlands from sea level to the highest grasslands in Australia.** © NICK ATHANAS, TROPICAL BIRDING TOURS

Opposite bottom: **Stubble Quail utilises a variety of open grassland habitats, mostly within the temperate zone.** © SAM WOODS, TROPICAL BIRDING TOURS

triandra) is a common and almost cosmopolitan species, found across Asia, Africa, and the Pacific; fascinatingly, it is a C4 grass, which means that it photosynthesises in a similar way to tropical grasses, rather than the C3 photosynthesis pathway of many temperate grass species of s. Australia. Other grasses to be expected are Common Wallaby Grass (*Rytidosperma caespitosum*), Snow Grass (*Poa sieberiana*), Purple Wiregrass (*Aristida ramosa*), and Common Wheatgrass (*Anthosachne scabra*). There are many small flowers between the tussocks that burst into flower in late spring and early summer.

WILDLIFE: Although these grasslands look similar to MONTANE GRASSLAND of Africa and TUSSOCK PUNA of South America, they are far more depauperate. Some species of resident omnivores eke out a living here, such as Little Raven and Australian Raven, which brave the winters, along with Brown Quail and Galah. Most of the pure 'grassland birds' such as Stubble Quail, Australian Pipit, Willie-wagtail, Australian Magpie, Brown Falcon, Nankeen Kestrel, Black-shouldered Kite, and Flame Robin migrate to these grasslands in summer but return to lower elevations during the colder months. However, most of the birds present in these grasslands are actually found along roadside verges or farm breaks where lines of trees create habitats more like

Raptors such as Black-shouldered Kite (above) and Brown Falcon (below) may nest in neighbouring habitats but hunt within Montane Grassland during the prey-rich breeding season. © PABLO CERVANTES, TROPICAL BIRDING TOURS

SUBALPINE EUCALYPT WOODLAND or GRASSY DRY SCLEROPHYLL FOREST, with corresponding birds such as Yellow-faced, New Holland, and Crescent Honeyeaters, and Eastern Spinebill.

On the mainland, some of the larger macropods move to this habitat in summer months but tend to move into more forested areas in winter. These kangaroo species include Eastern Grey Kangaroo, Swamp Wallaby, and Red-necked Wallaby. In Tasmania, Rufous-bellied Pademelon occurs throughout the MONTANE GRASSLAND, unlike mainland pademelons, which are far more restricted to heavily forested areas. These highlands are one of the best locations for Bare-nosed Wombat and Short-beaked Echidna, as both species fare better in milder temperatures than in the hotter lowland or tropical grasslands.

CONSERVATION: Conservation of this habitat is difficult because the general public sees plenty of modern pasture and thinks that it is natural, so there is little urgency to protect this grassland. Overgrazing by domestic livestock leads to soil compaction, erosion, and the loss of native plant species, which are often replaced by invasive weeds such as Scotch Thistle (*Onopordum acanthium*) and Pilated-leaved Blackberry (*Rubus plicatus*). Fire suppression has altered the natural fire regime critical for maintaining species diversity, leading to woody plant encroachment and a decline in grassland specialists.

DISTRIBUTION: Montane Grassland occurs in the southern highlands of New South Wales and Victoria as far north as Canberra (Australian Capital Territory) as a major system and as very small outliers north to Armidale, New South Wales. It is also found in the Tasmanian highlands.

WHERE TO SEE: Mt. Kosciuszko, New South Wales, Australia; highlands of Tasmania, Australia; Monaro Plains near Cooma, New South Wales, Australia.

Australian Magpie is a widespread pied species where the amount of black varies between races; multiple races can occur in this Australian Montane Grassland

© CHARLEY HESSE, TROPICAL BIRDING TOURS

Australasian Mediterranean Shrublands Dendrogram (Biome 8)

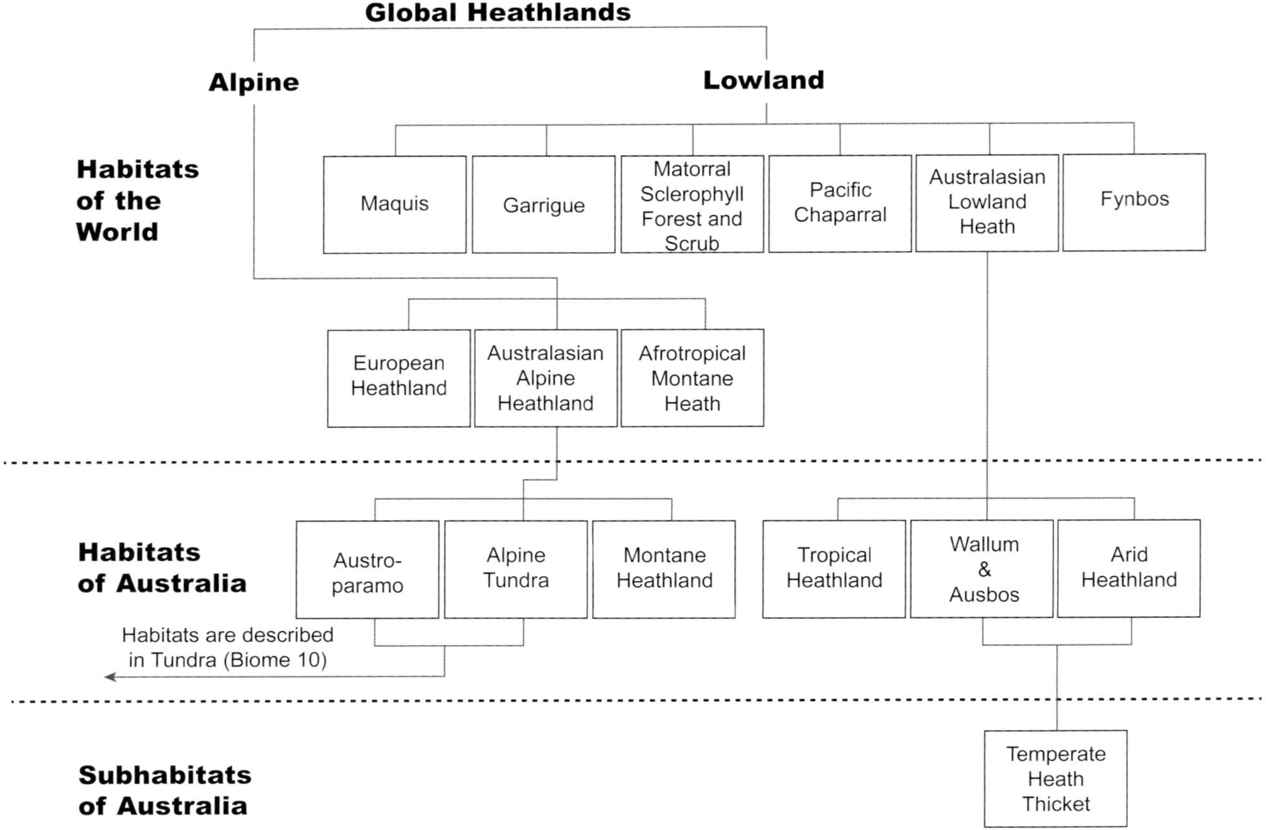

Global Heathlands

Alpine

Lowland

Habitats of the World

Maquis

Garrigue

Matorral Sclerophyll Forest and Scrub

Pacific Chaparral

Australasian Lowland Heath

Fynbos

European Heathland

Australasian Alpine Heathland

Afrotropical Montane Heath

Habitats of Australia

Austro-paramo

Alpine Tundra

Montane Heathland

Tropical Heathland

Wallum & Ausbos

Arid Heathland

Habitats are described in Tundra (Biome 10)

Subhabitats of Australia

Temperate Heath Thicket

MEDITERRANEAN SHRUBLANDS

Au8A WALLUM AND AUSBOS

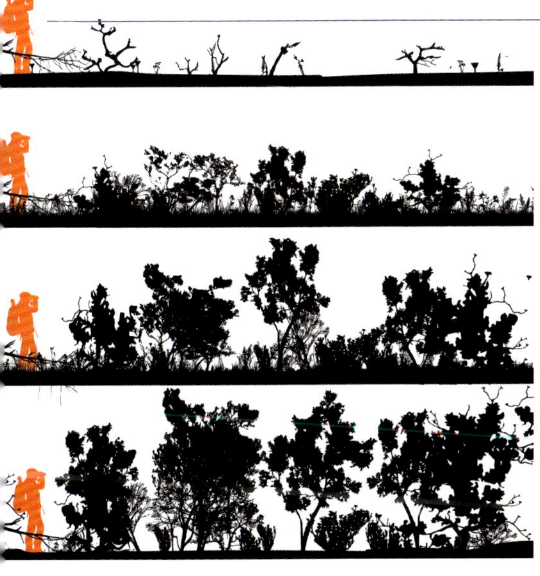

Wallum and Ausbos burn regularly and then regenerate. From top to bottom: recent burn; 5 years post-burn; 10 years post-burn; 15–20 years post-burn.

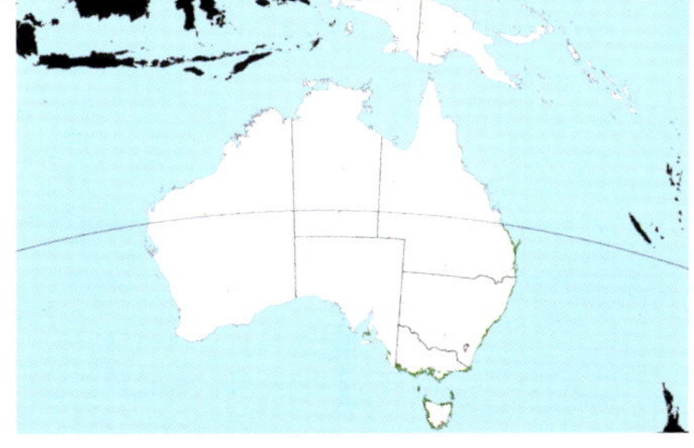

IN A NUTSHELL: Low, sclerophyllous scrub in a winter-rainfall and fire-prone environment. **Global Habitat Affinities:** AFRICAN FYNBOS (Ausbos), AFRICAN STRANDVELD (Wallum). **Continental Habitat Affinities:** KWONGAN HEATHLAND; ARID HEATHLAND; MONTANE HEATHLAND. **Species Overlap:** MONTANE HEATHLAND; HEATHY MALLEE. **Full Bird Assemblage:** habitatsoftheworld.org/Au8A.

DESCRIPTION: Wallum *sensu stricto* is heathland developed on a loose sand substrate in se. Queensland and ne. New South Wales, but we extend the scope here to sandy, humid heathlands around s. Australia. Ausbos is southern coastal heathland developed on a rocky substrate, such as a headland. We have used this name because the habitat is a doppelganger of FYNBOS in South Africa. Wallum and Ausbos are grouped because, although their substrates are different, they have remarkably similar wildlife and act as the same habitat system. They occur in areas with very

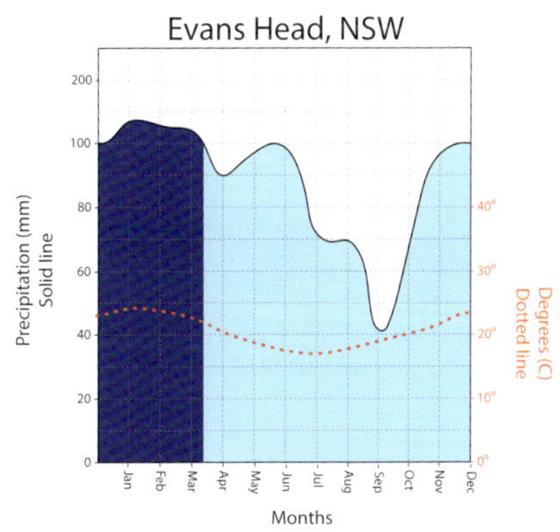

Overleaf: **Ausbos is heathland that grows on headlands, similar to the Fynbos of South Africa.**

© IAIN CAMPBELL, TROPICAL BIRDING TOURS/UNSW E&ERC

Wallum grows on palaeo-sand dunes (pictured here in Evans Head, New South Wales) and is Australia's equivalent of South African Strandveld. © IAIN CAMPBELL, TROPICAL BIRDING TOURS/UNSW E&ERC

shallow, heavily leached, sand-dominated soils formed on either beach sands or quartz-rich rocks such as granites, quartzites, or sandstones, in areas with harsh, often highly saline winds. The resulting soils are very nutrient-deficient with an acidic topsoil similar to the podzols that form under the conifer forests of the Northern Hemisphere. These conditions create an extremely arid microclimate, so the plants that grow here are much hardier than those of surrounding environments. This habitat is typically found in areas with a Mediterranean-type climate (Köppen **Csa**, **Csb**) with warm to mild, dry summers and mild, wet winters. Wallum also occurs in the parts of Queensland with a subtropical climate (Köppen **Cfa**) with warm, wet summers, mild, wet winters, and no dry season.

In general appearance and structure, Wallum and Ausbos are uniform across Australia. The floral makeup of any small area is successional and in constant flux due to regular fires. Many plant species in this region have evolved not only to withstand fire but to depend on it for their reproductive cycles. Several species have seeds that require the intense heat of a fire to germinate, a process known as pyriscence. Fire also reduces the dominance of one species, and a lack of fire can lead to overgrowth of the larger banksias (*Banksia* spp.), melaleucas (*Melaleuca* spp.), and sheoaks (*Casuarina* and *Allocasuarina* spp.) and change the habitat to **Temperate Heath Thicket** (see below), a subhabitat of Wallum and Ausbos with a corresponding decrease in biodiversity.

When areas are freshly burned, the heathland growth is very short (1–2 ft./30–60 cm tall) and made up of many species of wildflowers and other forbs. It reaches maximum floral diversity around four years after burning, when the heathland has many more species; Zigzag Bog-Rush (*Schoenus brevifolius*), Wallum Boronia (*Boronia falcifolia*), Thyme Honey-Myrtle (*Melaleuca thymifolia*), Wallum Hakea (*Hakea actites*), and Swamp Grass Tree (*Xanthorrhoea fulva*) grow low to the ground, while Shrubby Baeckea (*Baeckea frutescens*) will reach up to 15 ft. (5 m). Dominant banksia species include the low Swamp Banksia (*Banksia robur*), which usually tops out at only 6 ft. (2 m). At this stage, the habitat is easy to walk through. After about five years post-fire, the herbaceous growth is gradually replaced by shrubs, typically *Banksia* spp., such as Old Man

Banksia (*Banksia serrata*) and Heath-leaved Banksia (*Banksia ericifolia*), which will continue to grow into a thicket; *Melaleuca* spp. such as Prickly-leaved Paperbark (*Melaleuca nodosa*); and many others including Prickly Broom-Heath (*Monotoca scoparia*) and Black Sheoak (*Allocasuarina littoralis*). These shrubs are normally very thick and difficult to walk through, forming a canopy around 6 ft. (2 m) high, from which emerge a few small, mallee-form (with many thin trunks branching out of one large root ball in a whipstick fashion) eucalypts, such as Coast Mallee Ash (*Eucalyptus obstans*) and Yellow-topped Mallee Ash (*Eucalyptus luehmanniana*). The vegetation at this stage, with a profusion of highly productive flowers around head height, is very attractive to wildlife. After about 20 years, most species of *Banksia*, *Grevillea*, and *Hakea* have been outcompeted by a few larger banksias, melaleucas, sheoaks, and tea trees, and the habitat turns to Temperate Heath Thicket, which is nowhere near as productive as earlier successions.

Temperate Heath Thicket is a subhabitat of Wallum and Ausbos (which are heavily regulated by fire) that develops in the absence of fire over extended periods. Without periodic burns, the heaths grow taller, and the highly diverse low shrubland is replaced by dense, closed-canopy thickets with much less diversity, usually dominated by a few species of large shrubs or small trees. Although it is part of the same broader Wallum–Ausbos system, this subhabitat feels remarkably different from the diverse shrublands, as if something got out of hand, and all but the hardiest plants have been removed, and those sometimes occur in monotypic thickets. Groves of *Banksia* trees such as Old Man Banksia (*Banksia serrata*), Wallum Banksia (*Banksia aemula*), and Heath-leaved Banksia (*Banksia ericifolia*) are up to 20 ft. (6 m) tall and typically impenetrable. The tea-tree thickets are usually around 16 ft. (5 m) tall and have slightly more open canopies, but because the trunks are much thinner, more trees are packed into each square yard. They are dominated by species such as Coast Tea Tree (*Gaudium laevigatum*), Paperbark Tea Tree (*Gaudium trinervium*), and Prickly-leaved Paperbark (*Melaleuca nodosa*). Stands of Black Sheoak (*Allocasuarina littoralis*) and Scrub Sheoak (*Allocasuarina distyla*), which can look like dense juniper groves from the Northern Hemisphere, form in slightly more saline areas. Eucalypts, some mallee-form, such as Broad-leaved White Mahogany (*Eucalyptus latisinensis*), can grow through the canopy to become emergent. The sheoak thickets tend to have graminoid (grass and grasslike) ground cover, but the other thickets have a shrub layer of plants like Sweet Wattle (*Acacia suaveolens*), Fern-leaved Banksia (*Banksia oblongifolia*), Tantoon (*Leptospermum polygalifolium*), Wedding Bush (*Ricinocarpos pinifolius*), and Common Aotus (*Aotus ericoides*). The canopy of the thickets can become infested with native creepers and vines, and introduced *Lantana* can form thickets within the habitat.

In s. Australia, the habitat is less likely to have a monotypic canopy and more likely to have Long-leaved Wattle (*Acacia longifolia*) as the main tree, with a subcanopy of Coast Beard-Heath (*Leucopogon parviflorus*) and Silver Banksia

Red Wattlebird is a vociferous large honeyeater that congregates around blossoms in this s. Australian habitat. © IAIN CAMPBELL, TROPICAL BIRDING TOURS/UNSW E&ERC

(*Banksia marginata*) as well as Drooping Sheoak (*Allocasuarina verticillata*) and Common Boobialla (*Myoporum insulare*). Counterintuitively, while this subhabitat forms from the gradual replacement of many species by a few when not burnt over a long period, at an extreme, Temperate Heath Thicket can merge into a humid habitat, LITTORAL RAINFOREST, which again has much more biodiversity than the thicket. At this extreme, the canopy is dominated by Coastal Banksia (*Banksia integrifolia*), which can grow to a massive 75 ft. (25 m), with an understorey of Coast Tea Tree, Sweet Pittosporum (*Pittosporum undulatum*), and Tuckeroo (*Cupaniopsis anacardioides*). The thickets develop from Wallum more than from Ausbos, where the swales between beach palaeo-dunes accumulate water and help retard fire. On Ausbos, very old heath is likely to have emergent mallee-form eucalypts rather than thickets of them.

WILDLIFE: Because this is a successional habitat that changes markedly from immediately post-fire through to the point at which it changes to Temperate Heath Thicket, the bird assemblage also changes over time. The birds that occur in early to mid-succession, when plant growth is less than 5 ft. (1.5 m) high and most diverse, are the shy and difficult-to-see indicator species such as Southern Emuwren and Chestnut-rumped Heathwren, along with Brown Quail. One of the main target birds for nature observers in e. Australia, the semi-nocturnal Ground Parrot, is best found flying across heathland at dusk.

When the heath is taller but still very diverse, Eastern Bristlebird occurs and is a strong indicator of this habitat. Nectivorous honeyeaters become the dominant canopy birds across the range of the habitat, and depending on location, the heathlands hold species such as Eastern Spinebill; Red and Little Wattlebirds; Tawny-crowned, New Holland, White-eared, and White-cheeked Honeyeaters; and Noisy Friarbird. The year-round profusion of flowers allows for this diversity of resident honeyeaters and sets this bird assemblage apart from that of any other habitat.

Fairywrens are common and conspicuous birds of the Wallum and Ausbos, with

New Holland Honeyeater is a common heathland species, particularly in se. Australia. © IAIN CAMPBELL, TROPICAL BIRDING TOURS/ UNSW E&ERC

Superb Fairywren, an abundant and widespread species in e. Australia, is particularly conspicuous in this habitat. © SAM WOODS, TROPICAL BIRDING TOURS

Variegated Fairywren and Red-backed Fairywren being dominant in more northerly areas of the east coast, and Superb Fairywren filling the niche in the southern heathlands and Tasmania. Finches, as a group, are not well represented in this habitat, but Beautiful Firetail is a stunning species found primarily in Wallum and Ausbos, and Red-browed Firetail is regularly found here. Other species of this habitat include Fan-tailed Cuckoo, Yellow-tailed Black-Cockatoo, Brown Thornbill, White-browed Scrubwren, Eastern Whipbird, Golden Whistler, and Dusky Woodswallow. In Tasmania, Scarlet Robin, Flame Robin, and Tasmanian Scrubwren join the bird assemblage.

Mammals abound but are mostly nocturnal species that are not easily seen. A night walk around Curra Moors, Royal National Park (New South Wales), could turn up Common Ringtail Possum, Australian Swamp Rat, both Sugar Glider and Feather-tailed Glider, and the Brown Antechinus—a carnivorous and arboreal marsupial mouse. Swamp Wallaby and Red-necked Wallaby are regular macropods on the mainland; in Tasmania, Rufous-bellied Pademelon and Eastern Grey Kangaroo become far more obvious. Both Short-beaked Echidna and Bare-nosed Wombat occur in mainland Wallum and Ausbos, and are joined in Tasmania by Tasmanian Devil, Spotted-tailed Quoll, Southern Brown Bandicoot, and Eastern Barred Bandicoot.

On mainland Australia, Lace Monitor (*Varanus varius*) and Heath Monitor (*Varanus rosenbergi*) are the larger lizards to be expected, while the smaller lizards include Jacky Dragon (*Amphibolurus muricatus*), Eastern Water Dragon (*Intellagama lesueurii* subsp. *lesueurii*), Broad-tailed Gecko (*Phyllurus platurus*), and Cunningham's Skink (*Egernia cunninghami*). In Tasmania the heaths also contain Blotched Bluetongue (*Tiliqua nigrolutea*), White's Skink (*Liopholis whitii*), and the gorgeous Ocellated Coolskink (*Carinascincus ocellatus*). As in the KWONGAN HEATHLAND of Western Australia, snakes are very obvious in this habitat. Highly venomous species such as Red-bellied Black Snake (*Pseudechis porphyriacus*), Southern Death Adder (*Acanthophis antarcticus*), Eastern Brown Snake (*Pseudonaja textilis*), and Broad-headed Snake (*Hoplocephalus bungaroides*) are common in New South Wales; and in Tasmania, Tiger Snake (*Notechis scutatus*) can be very common in these heathlands along with Lowlands Copperhead (*Austrelaps superbus*).

There is much overlap in wildlife between Wallum and Ausbos and the **Temperate Heath Thicket** subhabitat. The bird assemblage differs in the ground birds rather than canopy species; Southern Emuwren, Chestnut-rumped Heathwren, and Ground Parrot are some birds typical of Wallum and Ausbos that are not to be expected in these thickets. Most of the species that feed in the canopy of Wallum and Ausbos, such as Red and Little Wattlebirds and Tawny-crowned, New

Holland, and White-cheeked Honeyeaters, visit Temperate Heath Thicket when it is in flower, but because it lacks the plant diversity of the shorter heaths, flowering is less regular, and the blossom nomads may be absent for significant amounts of time. This subhabitat also has some very strong indicator species, such as Eastern Bristlebird and Grey Shrikethrush. Some birds more typical of rainforests become more likely in the taller thickets, such as White-browed Scrubwren, Eastern Spinebill, Lewin's Honeyeater, and Golden Whistler. At the northern extent of this habitat, near Inskip Point in se. Queensland, this habitat has become one of the last refuges for the vulnerable Black-breasted Buttonquail, a bird much more typical of SUBTROPICAL RAINFOREST.

CONSERVATION: Some large swaths of this habitat are protected in areas such as Broadwater, Bundjalung, and Royal National Parks in New South Wales. However, because this is the dominant habitat along the east and south coasts of Australia, it is under clearing pressure for tourism and urban development.

DISTRIBUTION: Variations of Wallum and Ausbos and Temperate Heath Thicket are found from c. Queensland to Tasmania and South Australia. The habitat blends into MONTANE HEATHLAND with elevation and into ARID HEATHLAND along the Nullarbor Plain.

WHERE TO SEE: Broadwater National Park, near Evans Head, New South Wales, Australia; The Neck, Bruny Island, Tasmania, Australia.

Swamp Wallaby occurs in Wallum and Ausbos heathland habitat on mainland Australia.
© IAIN CAMPBELL, TROPICAL BIRDING TOURS/UNSW E&ERC

Au8B ARID HEATHLAND

IN A NUTSHELL: Low, sclerophyllous scrub in an arid, winter-rainfall, and fire-prone environment. **Global Habitat Affinities:** AFRICAN FYNBOS; AFRICAN STRANDVELD; EUROPEAN GARRIGUE. **Continental Habitat Affinities:** WALLUM AND AUSBOS; KWONGAN HEATHLAND; MONTANE HEATHLAND. **Species Overlap:** KWONGAN HEATHLAND; MONTANE HEATHLAND; HEATHY MALLEE. **Full Bird Assemblage:** habitatsoftheworld.org/Au8B.

DESCRIPTION: Arid Heathland is similar to WALLUM AND AUSBOS in that all are low heathlands, but it is much drier and tends to have scattered tall *Acacia*, *Callitris*, and *Melaleuca* shrubs. The canopy can range from a single layer just 1 ft. (30 cm) tall to an open canopy 13 ft. (4 m) tall with a shrub layer to around 6 ft. (2 m). This habitat is one of the most floristically diverse on the planet; with approximately 8000 plant species, it rivals the very similar FYNBOS and STRANDVELD habitats of

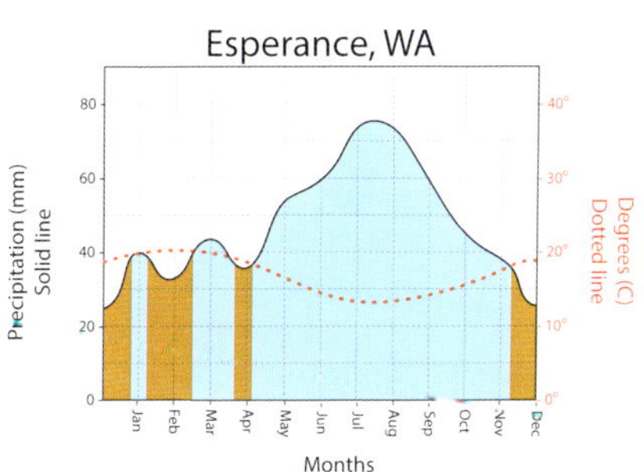

Patches of low Arid Heathland grow between groves of Heathy Mallee in nw. Victoria.
© IAIN CAMPBELL, TROPICAL BIRDING TOURS/UNSW E&ERC

Arid Heathland forms a ring around Wilpena Pound in the Flinders Ranges, South Australia. © IAIN CAMPBELL, TROPICAL BIRDING TOURS/UNSW E&ERC

South Africa, which host 9000 plant species. Although an immense number of wildflowers occur in Arid Heathland, there are some taller canopy species, which tend to be fairly constant through the habitat's range. In the west of Australia, what distinguishes Arid Heathland from the more humid heathlands is the prominence of small trees such as Bruce Cypress-Pine (*Callitris arenaria*), Red Toothbrushes (*Grevillea hookeriana*), Compass Bush (*Allocasuarina pinaster*), Shrubby Sheoak (*Allocasuarina campestris*), One-sided Bottlebrush (*Melaleuca quadrifida*), and Graceful Honey-Myrtle (*Melaleuca radula*).

Candlestick Banksia (*Banksia attenuata*), a very conspicuous species that is prominent in KWONGAN HEATHLAND, is also found through much of the Arid Heathland of Western Australia. Other banksias include Desert Banksia (*Banksia ornata*), Firewood Banksia (*Banksia menziesii*), Sceptre Banksia (*Banksia sceptrum*), and Acorn Banksia (*Banksia prionotes*). Also numerous are dryandra *Banksia* spp. (which until recently were placed in a separate genus), distinguished from the other banksias by deeply lobed, leathery leaves and woody cones with large, prominent bracts. Dryandra species are generally found in the drier and harsher regions of sw. Australia and therefore play a much more dominant role in Arid Heathland than in the wetter heaths.

Most of the short Arid Heathlands get taller and thicker with time after fire and eventually change to **Temperate Heath Thicket** (covered as a subhabitat in the Wallum and Ausbos account). However, within Arid Heathland habitat are smaller patches of permanent, very low heathland that attain an alternative stable state (ASS), in which they don't become taller, regardless of time since the last fire. These patches are dominated by short plants, most reaching 3 ft. (1 m) tall, such as Pink Dryandra (*Banksia carlinoides*), Prickly Dryandra (*Banksia armata*), Cushion Fanflower (*Scaevola crassifolia*), Ribbed Hakea (*Hakea costata*), Champion Bay Poison (*Gastrolobium* *oxylobioides*), and Yellow Featherflower (*Verticordia chrysantha*), with occasional emergents such as Sandplain Woody Pear (*Xylomelum angustifolium*).

In the north, Arid Heathlands become much more desert-like before merging into NORTHERN ACACIA SAVANNA. In these northernmost heaths, the banksias and hakeas are replaced by acacias such as Summer-scented Wattle (*Acacia rostellifera*), melaleucas such as Claw Flower (*Melaleuca chrysantherea*), grevilleas such as Lace Net Grevillea (*Grevillea stenomera*), sheoaks such as Dwarf Sheoak (*Allocasuarina humilis*), eremophilas such as Wedge-leaf Desert Fuchsia (*Eremophila cuneifolia*), and sennas (aka cassias) such as Silver Senna (*Senna artemisioides*).

Arid Heathland generally forms in drier regions than KWONGAN HEATHLAND, WALLUM AND AUSBOS, and TROPICAL HEATHLAND, in climates ranging from semiarid, Mediterranean type with hot, dry summers and moist winters (Köppen **Csb**) to semiarid and hot (Köppen **Bsh**). Rainfall ranges from 10 to 35 in. (250–900 mm), and most of the rainfall occurs in the austral winter (June–August), with almost no rain falling over the summer months. Summer temperatures average up to 95°F (35°C) and rise well above 104°F (40°C) in heat waves, and the dry summer months are brutal for most plants. This habitat forms over a variety of nutrient-poor substrates, such as calcareous sands on the coastlines of the Great Australian Bight (South Australia to Western Australia); and siliceous sand deposits in Victoria in the southeast and coastal areas north of Perth in Western Australia. It is most widely distributed in c. Western Australia, where it also grows on highly inert lateritic soils. These are some of the oldest soils on the planet—developed by hundreds of

Arid Heathland occurs down to the coast in dry regions such as the western coastline of the Eyre Peninsula, South Australia. © IAIN CAMPBELL, TROPICAL BIRDING TOURS/UNSW E&ERC

The gorgeous Western Spinebill occurs in this habitat in sw. Australia. © KEITH BARNES, TROPICAL BIRDING TOURS

thousands of years of leaching of nutrients, leaving quartz sands and iron/aluminium oxyhydroxide concretions called pisoliths—which also makes them some of the most nutrient-deficient soils.

WILDLIFE: The bird assemblage of Arid Heathland changes much less than that of the KWONGAN HEATHLAND or WALLUM AND AUSBOS over time after fire. The exact reason for this is unknown, but one possibility is that the climate of this heathland is just so much harsher at the best of times that most of the birds and other wildlife have to be more adaptable to minor changes. The bird assemblage you see when the heath is 3 ft. (1 m) tall is not going to be markedly different from when the heathland doubles in height. Missing from this habitat are many birds typical of the temperate, more coastal heathlands, including Eastern Spinebill, Striated Fieldwren, Noisy Scrub-bird, Southern Emuwren, Rufous Bristlebird, Western Bristlebird, and both Red-eared and Beautiful Firetails. Species that seem to be much more common in Arid Heathland than other heathlands include Western Fieldwren and Rufous Fieldwren. Other ground birds and shrubland birds that occur here include quail, such as Brown Quail and Stubble Quail; ground-feeding warblers, such as White-browed Scrubwren and Spotted Scrubwren; and pigeons such as Common Bronzewing and Brush Bronzewing.

The honeyeater assemblage is a mix of coastal and inland species such as Western Spinebill, New Holland Honeyeater, Western Wattlebird, Red Wattlebird, White-fronted Honeyeater, and Singing Honeyeater. Tawny-crowned Honeyeater is interesting in that it is very confined to WALLUM AND AUSBOS on the east coast, but it follows this habitat well inland in nw. Victoria and inland Western Australia. Superb Fairywren and Red-winged Fairywren, both found in the wetter heathlands and missing from this habitat, are replaced here by Blue-breasted, Splendid, and Purple-backed Fairywrens. This low-heath habitat is a prime hunting ground for Spotted Harrier and Swamp Harrier, both of which soar slowly over grasslands and shrublands, along with other

Tawny-crowned Honeyeater occurs in Arid Heathland throughout southern Australia. © SAM WOODS, TROPICAL BIRDING TOURS

raptors such as Brown Falcon and Black-shouldered Kite.

Arid Heathland is great for small mammals and is the stronghold for Silky Mouse, a gorgeous little rodent that has a strong association with Desert Banksia. Western Pygmy Possum is found in a variety of open habitats through semiarid s. Australia but seems to have a strong affinity for Arid Heathland. Other typical mammals include a suite of generalist macropods such as Western Grey Kangaroo, Swamp Wallaby, Red-necked Wallaby, and Red Kangaroo.

Typical reptiles include dragons such as Painted Dragon (*Ctenophorus pictus*), Mallee Tree Dragon (*Amphibolurus norrisi*), Eastern Bearded Dragon (*Pogona barbata*), Spotted Military Dragon (*Ctenophorus maculatus*), Long-nosed Dragon (*Gowidon longirostris*), Western Netted Dragon (*Ctenophorus reticulatus*), and the much larger Heath Monitor (*Varanus rosenbergi*). Geckos are a prominent group of reptiles here, with a range of species including Soft Spiny-tailed Gecko (*Strophurus spinigerus*), Southern Marbled Gecko (*Christinus marmoratus*), White-spotted Ground Gecko (*Lucasium alboguttatum*), Ornate Stone Gecko (*Diplodactylus ornatus*), Western Tree Dtella (*Gehyra variegata*), and Common Prickly Gecko (*Heteronotia binoei*).

Skinks include widespread generalists such as Dark-flecked Garden Sunskink (*Lampropholis delicata*), and Eastern Striped Skink (*Ctenotus orientalis*), along with the widespread but habitat-restricted Shrubland Morethia Skink (*Morethia obscura*), which prefers this heathland along with the drier mallee habitats. Snakes in this habitat include Southwestern Carpet Python (*Morelia imbricata*), Bardick (*Echiopsis curta*), Dugite (*Pseudonaja affinis*), Crowned Snake (*Elapognathus coronatus*), and Tiger Snake (*Notechis scutatus*).

CONSERVATION: The areas where this habitat forms, in semiarid and arid landscapes with nutrient-deficient soils, are not very attractive to farming. Although a satellite map will show large areas of intact Arid Heathland in s. Western Australia and nw. Victoria, conservation is still an issue, as some of these areas, with irrigation and fertilisers, could be turned over to intensive cultivation of arid-land shrubs such as Australian Sandalwood (*Santalum spicatum*).

DISTRIBUTION: This habitat skirts the drier side of KWONGAN HEATHLAND in Western Australia and Victoria, where it typically merges into HEATHY MALLEE or CHENOPOD SHRUBLAND. Found from w. Victoria, sw. New South Wales, and the Eyre Peninsula of South Australia through the Great Australian Bight, it reaches the west coast north of Perth. It is much more common in s. Australia than in the north, although patches of heathland are scattered throughout dry tropical Australia.

WHERE TO SEE: Fitzgerald River National Park, Western Australia; Lake Logue Nature Reserve, Western Australia; Little Desert National Park, Victoria, Australia.

Au8C TROPICAL HEATHLAND

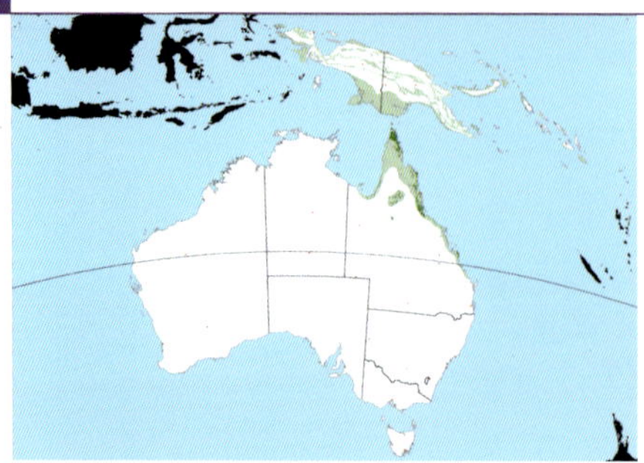

IN A NUTSHELL: Tropical low, sclerophyllous scrub in a fire-prone environment. **Global Habitat Affinities:** AFRICAN FYNBOS. **Continental Habitat Affinities:** MONTANE HEATHLAND. **Species Overlap:** MONTANE HEATHLAND; SHRUBBY EUCALYPT SAVANNA. **Full Bird Assemblage:** habitatsoftheworld.org/Au8C.

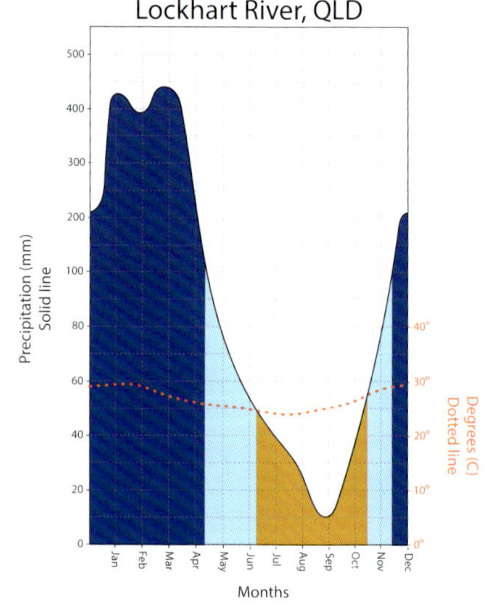

DESCRIPTION: Its lack of a typical heathland bird assemblage distinguishes this habitat from MONTANE HEATHLAND and WALLUM AND AUSBOS. In another obvious contrast, those two habitats have Mediterranean-type climates (Köppen **Csa**, **Csb**), while Tropical Heathland is typically found in areas with prominent summer rainfall, in rainforest (Köppen **Af**) and monsoon (Köppen **Aw**) climates with average year-round highs of 77–88°F (25–31°C) and annual rainfall ranging between 33 and 94 in. (830–2380 mm). It occurs in tropical areas with very shallow, heavily leached, sand-dominated soils. It is formed on either quartz-rich rocks such as granites and sandstones or, more rarely, beach sands. The resulting soils are very nutrient-deficient, with an acidic topsoil that creates an arid microclimate even in areas with extremely high rainfall, so the plants that grow here are much hardier than those of surrounding environments. In an apparent contradiction, the soils that create the arid conditions can be waterlogged.

The floristic composition of any given small area is inherently successional and perpetually dynamic due to the regular occurrence of fire. Numerous plant species within this habitat have evolved not only to endure fire but also to rely on it for their reproductive processes. Specifically, several species possess seeds that necessitate the intense heat of a fire to initiate germination, a phenomenon termed pyriscence. Additionally, fire serves to mitigate the predominance of certain species, and the absence of fire can result in the proliferation of *Melaleuca* spp. and rainforest plants, in some instances transforming the habitat into a MONSOON VINEFOREST thicket.

On ridgelines and escarpments where fire promotes this heathland over Monsoon Vineforest, the heath is a tall shrubland, up to 12 ft. (3 m), dominated by melaleucas such as Broad-leaved Paperbark (*Melaleuca viridiflora*) and Fibre-barked Tea Tree (*Melaleuca stenostachya*), which

While Tropical Heathland can look very similar to Ausbos from s. Australia, it lacks almost all the characteristic bird species or guilds.

© IAIN CAMPBELL, TROPICAL BIRDING TOURS/UNSW E&ERC

can also occur in the surrounding MELALEUCA SAVANNA and SHRUBBY EUCALYPT SAVANNA. The melaleucas are usually accompanied by plants such as Tropical Banksia (*Banksia dentata*), Brass's Wattle (*Acacia brassii*), Darwin Silky Oak (*Grevillea pteridifolia*), Forest Grass Tree (*Xanthorrhoea johnsonii*), Winged Boronia (*Boronia alulata*), Broad-leaved Native Cherry (*Exocarpos latifolius*), Native Cherry (*Shonia tristigma*), Purple-stemmed Turkey Bush (*Leptospermum purpurascens*), Broombush (*Jacksonia thesioides*), and Liniment Tree (*Asteromyrtus symphyocarpa*). The occasional Yellow Box Penda (*Welchiodendron longivalve*) and Blotchy Bloodwood (*Corymbia stockeri*) can occur as scraggly emergents up to 45 ft. (15m) tall. In waterlogged areas, Common Swamp Pitcher Plant (*Nepenthes mirabilis*) can be very common, accompanied by other carnivorous plants such as Fan-Leaved Sundew (*Drosera petiolaris*) and Tropical Sundew (*Drosera burmanni*).

In the sandier substrates such as palaeo-sand dunes, the habitat looks more like the WALLUM of temperate Australia, with low groves of Darwin Silky Oak becoming more common, along with Myrtle Tea Tree (*Neofabricia myrtifolia*), Roepera (*Neoroepera banksii*), Buettner's Labichea (*Labichea buettneriana*), Winged Boronia, and Banks' Guinea Flower (*Hibbertia banksii*), with Black Sheoak (*Allocasuarina littoralis*) and Tropical Banksia as emergents.

WILDLIFE: None of the typical heathland birds, such as the emuwrens, heathwrens, bristlebirds, whipbirds, ground parrots, or firetails, are present in Tropical Heathland. Even fairywrens—ubiquitous in heathlands around Australia—are missing here, though Lovely Fairywren is found in LOWLAND RAINFOREST and MONSOON VINEFOREST surrounding this habitat. The lack of endemic bird species or typical heathland birds is truly mystifying. The only bird species close to being

Fire is very important for Tropical Heathland, though the fires are usually localised so there is a mosaic of heaths in different stages of regrowth.
© IAIN CAMPBELL, TROPICAL BIRDING TOURS/UNSW E&ERC

As incongruous as it seems, Tropical Heathland with melaleucas can merge into Monsoon Vineforest on Cape York Peninsula, Queensland.
© IAIN CAMPBELL, TROPICAL BIRDING TOURS/UNSW E&ERC

In Australia, Tropical Heathland and White-streaked Honeyeater are both restricted to the Cape York Peninsula. The honeyeater also moves from this into surrounding habitats.
© LAURIE ROSS, TRACKS BIRDING

endemic is White-streaked Honeyeater, which breeds in the Tropical Heathland of Cape York Peninsula (Queensland) yet disperses into surrounding thicker forests during the dry season. A visit to this habitat in the dry season is likely to be very dull for a birder, as just a few species, such as Yellow-spotted Honeyeater, Graceful Honeyeater, Dusky Myzomela, Brown Honeyeater, Helmeted Friarbird, and Noisy Friarbird, eke out an existence with the few plants flowering at this time of year.

Among the heathlands, Tropical Heathland is also conspicuous in its lack of pygmy possums; this group of small marsupials is prevalent in the heathlands across s. Australia but absent here. Long-tailed Pygmy Possum is rare here but common in surrounding rainforest and eucalypt forest. Chestnut Dunnart, a small carnivorous marsupial mouse, is the only species restricted to this heath, while Eastern Chestnut Mouse is also found in WALLUM and MONTANE HEATHLAND as far south as c. New South Wales. Some species expected in Tropical Heathland but not restricted to it include Cape York Rat, White-tailed Giant Rat, Cape York Melomys, and Long-nosed Bandicoot.

While Tropical Heathland has a few more habitat-restricted reptiles than birds, the habitat is still depauperate in obligate, strong indicator species. Some, such as Crevice Rainbow Skink (*Lygisaurus rimula*), are restricted to Cape York Peninsula, while many of the Australian species, such as Black-tailed Bar-lipped Skink (*Glaphyromorphus nigricaudis*), Cape York Mulch Skink (*Glaphyromorphus crassicauda*), and Shrub Whiptail-Skink (*Emoia longicauda*), also occur in New Guinea. Generalist reptiles found here and across a variety of habitats in tropical Australia include Six-toothed Rainbow Skink (*Carlia sexdentata*) and Macleay's Water Snake (*Pseudoferania polylepis*). Most of the reptile species occurring in e. Australia are found down the eastern seaboard in a variety of habitats; some of these include Major Skink (*Bellatorias frerei*), Zigzag Velvet Gecko (*Amalosia rhombifer*), Black-headed Python (*Aspidites melanocephalus*), Striped Snake-eyed Skink (*Cryptoblepharus virgatus*), and Black-striped Snake (*Cryptophis nigrostriatus*).

CONSERVATION: The few heathlands on the coasts are under intense pressure for development, but most of this habitat is found on ridgelines far from habitation. Because this habitat develops on nutrient-poor soils, there is little threat of clearing for cropland.

DISTRIBUTION: Tropical Heathland occurs from c. coastal Queensland (Rockhampton) to New Guinea. In its sandy form, it is widespread around the coastal areas of Cape York Peninsula. Heathlands that form on residual rocks are restricted to mountains, where they grow on exposed ridges and headlands.

WHERE TO SEE: Mt. Tozer, Iron Range, Queensland, Australia.

Au8D KWONGAN HEATHLAND

IN A NUTSHELL: Low, sclerophyllous scrub in a winter-rainfall and fire-prone environment. **Global Habitat Affinities:** AFRICAN FYNBOS; AFRICAN STRANDVELD. **Continental Habitat Affinities:** ARID HEATHLAND; MONTANE HEATHLAND. **Species Overlap:** MONTANE HEATHLAND; HEATHY MALLEE. **Full Bird Assemblage:** habitatsoftheworld.org/Au8D.

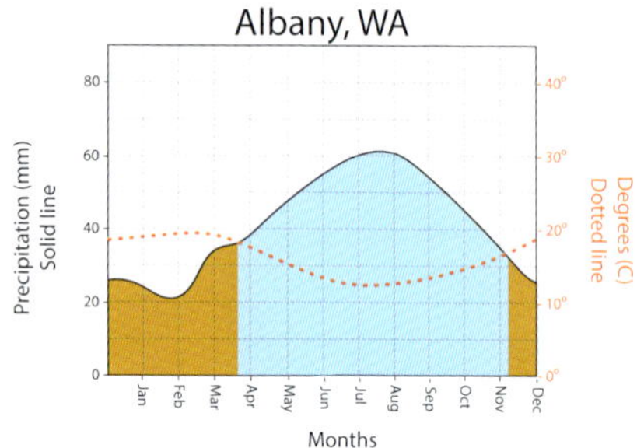

DESCRIPTION: Kwongan is a moist heathland of extreme sw. Western Australia. The word 'Kwongan' is derived from an Aboriginal language and has been used for multiple open woodlands and heathlands of Western Australia, but 'Kwongan Heathland' is used for the wetter heathlands with distinct plant, bird, and other wildlife assemblages that differ from those of the drier ARID HEATHLAND and WESTERN EUCALYPT WOODLAND.

Kwongan Heathland exhibits remarkable similarities to the WALLUM AND AUSBOS habitats

The small area of this photo has hundreds of plant species, the majority of which are endemic to sw. Western Australia. © IAIN CAMPBELL, TROPICAL BIRDING TOURS/UNSW E&ERC

Candlestick Banksia is a prominent member of the Kwongan Heathland flora around Cheynes Beach in sw. Western Australia. © SAM WOODS, TROPICAL BIRDING TOURS

of e. Australia. It develops in regions with very shallow, heavily leached, sand-dominated soils derived from beach sands or quartz-rich rocks such as granites, quartzites, or sandstones. These areas are often subjected to harsh, highly saline winds, resulting in very nutrient-deficient soils with acidic topsoil, similar to podzols found under Northern Hemisphere conifer forests. These conditions create an extremely arid microclimate, resulting in the development of sclerophyllous shrublands dominated by hardy plant species. What makes this even more fascinating is that these harsh conditions have allowed an astonishingly high number of highly range-restricted endemic plants. With around 8000 plant species, the floral biodiversity of Kwongan Heathland is matched by that of the FYNBOS habitat of the Cape Floral Province of South Africa.

This habitat is typically found in regions with a Mediterranean-type climate (Köppen **Csb**), characterised by warm to mild, dry summers and wet, mild winters. The floral composition of these areas is highly dynamic due to the influence of regular fires. Many plant species in this region have evolved to not only withstand fire but to depend on it for their reproductive cycles (pyriscence). Fire also helps to maintain species diversity by preventing the dominance of a few species; without fire, larger *Banksia* spp., *Melaleuca* spp., and *Casuarina* and *Allocasuarina* spp. (sheoaks) can overgrow, converting the habitat to **Temperate Heath Thicket** (covered as a subhabitat in Wallum and Ausbos), which is much less biodiverse.

After a major fire, Kwongan Heathland is characterised by short vegetation, 1–3 ft. (30–90 cm) high, dominated by a diverse array of wildflowers, forbs, and shrubs, including Coastal Jugflower (*Adenanthos cuneatus*), as well as fire-resistant grass trees such as Baarl (*Xanthorrhoea platyphylla*) and Bullanock (*Kingia australis*), which stand out amidst the smaller regrowth. Floral diversity peaks at three to five years post-fire, when species such as Scallop Hakea

(*Hakea cucullata*), Harsh Hakea (*Hakea prostrata*), Pincushion Hakea (*Hakea laurina*), Coast Honey-Myrtle (*Melaleuca systena*), and Grey Honey-Myrtle (*Melaleuca incana*) flourish. Banksias are represented by species like the low Prostrate Banksia (*Banksia gardneri*), Creeping Banksia (*Banksia repens*), Great Banksia (*Banksia grandis*), and Baxter's Banksia (*Banksia baxteri*), which typically grows to 6 ft. (2 m) tall. At this stage, the habitat is relatively open and easy to traverse.

Approximately five years post-fire, herbaceous growth is gradually replaced by shrubs, typically banksias such as Great Banksia, Scarlet Banksia (*Banksia coccinea*), Candlestick Banksia (*Banksia attenuata*), and Firewood Banksia (*Banksia menziesii*), along with melaleucas such as Moonah (*Melaleuca preissiana*), Swamp Paperbark (*Melaleuca rhaphiophylla*), and Chenille Honey-Myrtle (*Melaleuca huegelii*). These shrubs form dense thickets with a canopy height around 6 ft. (2 m), from which emerge a few small, mallee-form eucalypts, such as Bell-fruited Mallee (*Eucalyptus preissiana*) and Spider Gum (*Eucalyptus conferruminata*). This stage, characterised by a profusion of flowers at head height, is highly attractive to wildlife.

After approximately 20 years, monotypic groves of larger banksias and melaleucas, such as One-sided Bottlebrush (*Melaleuca quadrifida*), sheoaks like Western Sheoak (*Allocasuarina fraseriana*) and Rock Sheoak (*Allocasuarina huegeliana*), and acacias such as Golden Wattle (*Acacia pycnantha*) outcompete most species of *Banksia*, *Grevillea*, and *Hakea*. This shift leads to the formation of a thicket that is less productive and biodiverse than earlier successional stages.

WILDLIFE: The floral biodiversity is so extreme that one would reasonably expect a similar level of biodiversity and endemism with birdlife, but this is hardly the case. The birdlife is mostly shared with surrounding habitats, such as HEATHY MALLEE and JARRAH-MARRI FOREST, and most of the species have massive ranges, well above the 19,300 sq. mi. (50,000 km^2) used as the mark of a restricted-range species.

Because this is a successional habitat that changes markedly from newly post-fire to the point at which it changes to **Temperate Heath Thicket**, the bird assemblage also changes over time. The birds that occur in early to mid-succession, when it is less than 5 ft. (1.5 m) high and most diverse, are shy and difficult-to-see indicator species such as Southern Emuwren, along with Brown Quail. The western subspecies of the Ground Parrot used to be regular here but is now critically endangered, with possibly fewer than 100 individuals clinging to existence. At this very low, open stage of growth, Elegant Parrot uses this habitat, and Rock Parrot visits from the nearby coastline. Fairywrens are common and conspicuous birds of Kwongan Heathland, Red-winged Fairywren being the dominant species here and in nearby KARRI FOREST. Splendid Fairywren occurs in fewer locations but is far more conspicuous when present. Blue-breasted Fairywren occurs but is far more regular in the drier ARID HEATHLAND and HEATHY

Kwongan Heathland is the primary habitat for the notoriously shy Western Whipbird, which on calm, sunny days may occasionally emerge into the open. © SAM WOODS, TROPICAL BIRDING TOURS

The shy Western Bristlebird is an obligate of this habitat in sw. Australia. © SAM WOODS, TROPICAL BIRDING TOURS

MALLEE habitats. Finches, as a group, are not well represented in this habitat, but Red-eared Firetail is a stunning species that can be obvious at times, perching on power lines and vocalising.

When the heath is taller but still very diverse, some of the other obligate species are Western Whipbird, Western Bristlebird, and Noisy Scrub-bird, an endangered species from Western Australia whose only relative (in its family) is a species from the vastly different NOTHOFAGUS FOREST of e. Australia. Nectivorous honeyeaters like Western Spinebill, Red and Western Wattlebirds, and Tawny-crowned, White-eared, New Holland, and White-cheeked Honeyeaters are the dominant canopy species. The year-round profusion of flowers allows for this diversity of resident honeyeaters and sets this bird assemblage apart from that of any other habitat.

White-eared Honeyeater is a widespread species through the heath habitats of s. Australia. © KEN BEHRENS, TROPICAL BIRDING TOURS

The tiny Honey Possum is a significant pollinator in Kwongan Heathland, where it can be seen extracting nectar from flowering plants like banksias during their vibrant blooming periods. © KEITH BARNES, TROPICAL BIRDING TOURS

Common species that occur here include Red-capped Parrot, Australian Ringneck, Western Rosella, Spotted Scrubwren, Western subspecies of Golden Whistler, Dusky Woodswallow, Grey Currawong, and White-breasted Robin. Mammals abound but are mostly nocturnal species that are not easily seen. A night walk around Two Peoples Bay in Western Australia could turn up Honey Possum, Western Pygmy Possum, Southern Brown Bandicoot, and the newly rediscovered Gilbert's Potoroo. The diurnal kangaroos include Quokka and Western Grey Kangaroo.

Reptiles are frequently found in this type of habitat. Heath Monitor (*Varanus rosenbergi*), which measures up to 5 ft. (1.5 m) long, is the largest of the lizards found here. Smaller lizards include Shingleback (*Tiliqua rugosa*), King's Skink (*Egernia kingii*), and Bull Skink (*Liopholis multiscutata*). Southwestern Carpet Python (*Morelia imbricata*) is fairly common and is more readily seen than the highly venomous species such as Tiger Snake (*Notechis scutatus*), Bardick (*Echiopsis curta*), and Crowned Snake (*Elapognathus coronatus*). In short, it is an extremely bad idea to wander off the track in this heathland without sturdy footwear.

CONSERVATION: The biggest conservation issue with Kwongan Heathland is habitat loss and fragmentation caused by urban expansion and coastal development. The area around Two Peoples Bay was slated for development when the Noisy Scrub-bird was discovered and the land preserved. Much of the remaining Kwongan Heathland is in protected areas, but the coastal sites remain under intense development pressure. As coastal regions become more desirable for housing and tourism, large tracts of native heathland are being replaced by residential areas, roads, and infrastructure, leading to the isolation of remaining patches and the disruption of ecological connectivity.

DISTRIBUTION: Variations of Kwongan Heathland are found around far sw. Western Australia. It blends into ARID HEATHLAND along the Nullarbor Plain east of Esperance and north of Perth.

WHERE TO SEE: Two Peoples Bay, Western Australia; Cheynes Beach, Western Australia.

Au8F MONTANE HEATHLAND

IN A NUTSHELL: Low, sclerophyllous scrub in a winter-rainfall, fire-prone environment. **Global Habitat Affinities:** AFRICAN FYNBOS; CHILEAN SCLEROPHYLL SCRUB; EUROPEAN MAQUIS. **Continental Habitat Affinities:** TROPICAL HEATHLAND; WALLUM AND AUSBOS. **Species Overlap:** TROPICAL HEATHLAND; HEATHY MALLEE. **Full Bird Assemblage:** habitatsoftheworld.org/Au8F.

DESCRIPTION: This habitat occurs in areas with nutrient-poor soils that are very shallow, heavily leached, and sand-dominated, and in areas with harsh, desiccating winds and that are prone to fire. These conditions create an extremely arid microclimate, even in some environments that can be waterlogged for part of the year, so the plants that grow here are much hardier than those of surrounding environments.

The habitat forms on ridgelines and mountaintop rock outcrops where boulders are common, although in some large level areas, the topography can have a flat, moorland appearance. It usually

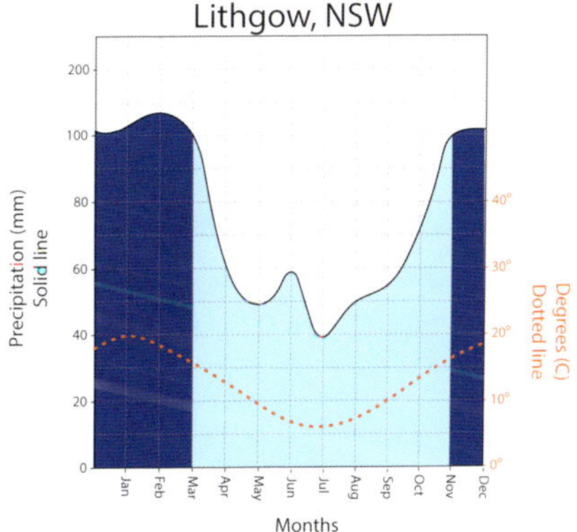

If unburnt for many years, the heathland thickens into a near-impenetrable thicket, and both plant and animal species diversity decreases. © IAIN CAMPBELL TROPICAL BIRDING TOURS/UNSW E&ERC

Barren Grounds Nature Reserve in New South Wales has fields of very low heathland supporting groves of eucalypts with mallee-form growth. © IAIN CAMPBELL, TROPICAL BIRDING TOURS/UNSW E&ERC

occurs between 1600 and 4300 ft. (500–1300 m) and is found on many of the coastal ranges in areas with a temperate oceanic climate (Köppen **Cfb**) but does extend into more subtropical areas. In the higher mountain ranges, it can occur very close to wet forests such as RAINFOREST WET SCLEROPHYLL FOREST or SUBTROPICAL RAINFOREST. In some areas, a fascinating ecotone forms between Montane Heathland and rainforest. Here, the heathlands are constantly subjected to very strong winds, but in some very protected tiny gullies, the waterlogged soils develop a lot of organic matter and promote the growth of rainforest ground-cover plants more typical of the surrounding wet forests.

One of the biggest issues with vegetation classification throughout the world is the classification of vegetation types based on the age of underlying rock parent material. This case provides a prime example. Montane Heathland is common on Permian sandstones (formed 260 MYA), but the age of the rock is irrelevant, and there is no correlation between age of rock type and type of heathland. Quartz-rich sandstone promotes formation of nutrient-poor sandy soils in which this habitat develops; however, Montane Heathland also forms on other sandstones of various ages, from Ordovician (485 MYA) to Triassic (201 MYA), as well as nutrient-poor shales, and felsic (silica-rich) igneous rocks such as granite and felsic metamorphic rocks such as gneiss. As a general rule, the more nutrient-rich or clay-rich the soils, or the more protected the location, the lower the rainfall needed to change this habitat into one of the taller forests such as HEATHY DRY SCLEROPHYLL FOREST.

In both general appearance and structure, Montane Heathlands are very varied, yet all follow a similar pattern of succession because the floral makeup of any small area changes due to fire and is in constant flux. As a rule, they attain their floristic and vegetation structure after about five years post-fire, but different forms of the heathland can exist in an alternative stable state and will not change with time. When areas are freshly burned, the heath cover is very short (1–2 ft./30–60 cm tall) and made up of many species of wildflowers and other forbs, reaching maximum floral diversity around four years after burning. At this stage, the habitat is easy to walk through. Emergents such as Blue-leaved Stringybark (*Eucalyptus agglomerata*), Silvertop Ash (*Eucalyptus sieberi*), and Oyster Bay Cypress-Pine (*Callitris rhomboidea*) can rarely surpass 100 ft. (30 m) here but don't grow in close proximity, so do not form a canopy over the lower shrubs. A decade after burning, the habitat is a closed heathland, and although the canopy is usually lower than 10 ft. (3 m), it sometimes reaches 16 ft. (5 m). Montane Heathland is dominated by thick canopy shrubs such as Small-leaf Tea Tree (*Leptospermum parvifolium*), Paperbark Tea Tree (*Gaudium trinervium*), Spidery Tea Tree (*Leptospermum arachnoides*), Common Fringe-Myrtle (*Calytrix tetragona*), Stiff-leaf Wattle (*Acacia obtusifolia*), Finger Hakea (*Hakea dactyloides*), and Conestick (*Petrophile pulchella*).

Banksias are not as prevalent as in the lowland WALLUM AND AUSBOS, but Heath-leaved Banksia (*Banksia ericifolia*) and Sword-leaved Banksia (*Banksia penicillata*) are both common. While Montane Heathland is not a sclerophyll woodland, small eucalypts also feature as major components of many of these heathlands and can form groves with typical species such as Narrow-leaved Snappy Gum (*Eucalyptus racemosa*), Brittle Gum (*Eucalyptus mannifera*), and Narrow-leaved Stringybark (*Eucalyptus sparsifolia*). Mallees are semiarid eucalypt woodlands (see SPINIFEX MALLEE for full explanation); some areas of Montane Heathland form a very mallee-like tall shrubland dominated by mallee-form (multi-stemmed) eucalypts such as Faulconbridge Mallee Ash (*Eucalyptus burgessiana*) and Blue Mountains Mallee Ash (*Eucalyptus stricta*), but even this form of the habitat is not a mallee and maintains the same broad wildlife assemblage as other examples of Montane Heathland.

The understorey and shrub layers of Montane Heathland are dominated by stunted or young versions of canopy plants such as Paperbark Tea Tree and Heath-leaved Banksia. Other subshrubs, growing only to 6 ft. (2 m), are plants like Blunt Beard-Heath (*Leucopogon muticus*), Daphne Heath (*Brachyloma daphnoides*), Swamp Banksia (*Banksia paludosa*), and Hairpin Banksia (*Banksia spinulosa*). Broad-leaved Drumsticks (*Isopogon anemonifolius*) has lignotubers (root balls), which make it especially resistant to fire, and the plants therefore live for many decades through multiple fire cycles. *Allocasuarina* spp. are usually a minor component of most heathlands, though Dwarf Sheoak (*Allocasuarina nana*) and Scrub Sheoak (*Allocasuarina distyla*) are found in many of the heaths. The ground cover of Montane Heathland is similar to that of Heathy Dry Sclerophyll Forest in that it is dominated by sedges such Chaffy Scale-Rush (*Lepyrodia scariosa*), Sticky Saw Sedge (*Lepidosperma viscidum*), Hairy Bog-Rush (*Schoenus villosus*), and various forbs growing between rocks. Sometimes the large Forest Grass Tree (*Xanthorrhoea johnsonii*) grows to heights of 15 ft. (5 m), and after strong fires which most other plants have died, the highly fire-resistant grass-tree stumps remain, dotting the landscape, soon to resprout with new growth.

WILDLIFE: Montane Heathland undergoes significant stages from recently burned to heathlands up to 10 years old, resulting in corresponding shifts in the bird assemblage over time. In the early to mid-successional stages, when the vegetation is less than 5 ft. (1.5 m) high and at its most diverse, or when the habitat remains stunted as moorland, the indicator species Southern Emuwren and the endangered Ground Parrot can be observed, both of which are also found in WALLUM AND AUSBOS habitats. When the heathland matures to approximately 6 ft. (2 m) in height, it becomes a prime habitat for Beautiful Firetail, the very rare Eastern Bristlebird, and the highly localised Rockwarbler.

Nectivorous species comprise a higher portion of the bird assemblage of Montane Heathland than nearby habitats such as TEMPERATE RAINFOREST. At least some plants are in flower throughout the year here, but there are also mass blooming events when resident nectivorous honeyeaters such as Eastern Spinebill, Lewin's Honeyeater, Little Wattlebird, New Holland Honeyeater, and White-cheeked Honeyeater are accompanied by blossom nomads such as Yellow-faced Honeyeater, Crescent Honeyeater, and White-naped Honeyeater. The blooming of the heathland brings in a mix of species from a variety of habitats that would not normally be seen feeding together such as Scarlet Myzomela, more typical of the much taller wet sclerophyll forests, and White-eared Honeyeater, more typical of open mallee woodlands.

Cockatoos such as Yellow-tailed Black-Cockatoo and Gang-gang Cockatoo are very conspicuous as they fly over the Montane Heathlands; they do drop into the emergent eucalypts but generally do not spend much time in the majority of the low heath. Cuckoo species are not as common in this habitat as in surrounding forest, but Fan-tailed Cuckoo is a prominent species here that nest-parasitises many of the smaller species. Superb Fairywren is the only fairywren found in this habitat in Tasmania, but on the mainland Variegated Fairywren also occurs, with the two species parsing into microhabitats, the Superb preferring the taller heath and the Variegated the sparser and shorter groves. Other skulkers in the low heath include the often heard but seldom seen Chestnut-rumped Heathwren, Striated Fieldwren, White-browed Scrubwren, and Tasmanian Scrubwren.

The elegant Southern Emuwren is an unobtrusive resident of Montane Heathland, making it a major highlight whenever it is seen well. © NICK ATHANAS, TROPICAL BIRDING TOURS

Chestnut-rumped Heathwren is a shy species of the thicker groves within the montane heathland
© KEN BEHRENS, TROPICAL BIRDING TOURS

As with most of the e. Australian habitats, the mammals here tend to be generalists such as Bare-nosed Wombat, Sugar Glider, Australian Swamp Rat, Mainland Dusky Antechinus, Brown Antechinus, Spotted-tailed Quoll, Short-beaked Echidna, and the rare Long-nosed Potoroo. The heathlands do have some more specialised species such as Australian Bush Rat, Agile Antechinus, and Eastern Pygmy Possum. This habitat is not very attractive to most of the larger macropods, with the most common wallaby on the mainland being Swamp Wallaby. That species does not occur in Tasmania, where the niche is filled by Bennett's Wallaby, a Tasmanian subspecies of Red-necked Wallaby.

There are many snakes in this habitat; Red-bellied Black Snake (*Pseudechis porphyriacus*) is common on the mainland, Highlands Copperhead (*Austrelaps ramsayi*) is also present, and Tiger Snake (*Notechis scutatus*) is seemingly ubiquitous throughout this habitat. Other reptile species occurring here include Eastern Three-lined Skink (*Acritoscincus duperreyi*), Yellow-bellied Water Skink (*Eulamprus heatwolei*), Black Rock Skink (*Egernia saxatilis*), Eastern Water Skink (*Eulamprus quoyii*), and White's Skink (*Liopholis whitii*). Amphibians associated with these heathlands include Haswell's Froglet (*Paracrinia haswelli*), Common Eastern Froglet (*Crinia signifera*), and Southern Heath Frog (*Litoria watsoni*).

CONSERVATION: Montane Heathland forms on soils generally too poor to farm, does not contain trees viable for logging, and is dominated by ground cover non-palatable for grazing. These factors, combined with the good fortune of being located in scenically attractive regions like the Blue Mountains of New South Wales, mean it has been spared the widespread destruction of surrounding forest habitats and is now largely locked up in national parks. Some unprotected areas have been cleared for pine plantations, but this is a limited threat. Changing fire regimes, with areas close to urban areas not being burnt or being burnt too frequently, may become a threat to the biodiversity and balance between fire-resistant and fire-imperilled plants.

DISTRIBUTION: Montane Heathland occurs from se. Queensland through the coastal ranges and the Great Dividing Range of New South Wales to Victoria. It is common in Tasmania, where it generally occurs above 1600 ft. (500 m) but does grow at lower elevations.

WHERE TO SEE: Barren Grounds Nature Reserve, New South Wales, Australia; Blue Mountains, New South Wales, Australia, Mt. Nelson, Tasmania, Australia.

Australasian Sclerophyll Woodlands and Forests Dendrogram (Biome 9)

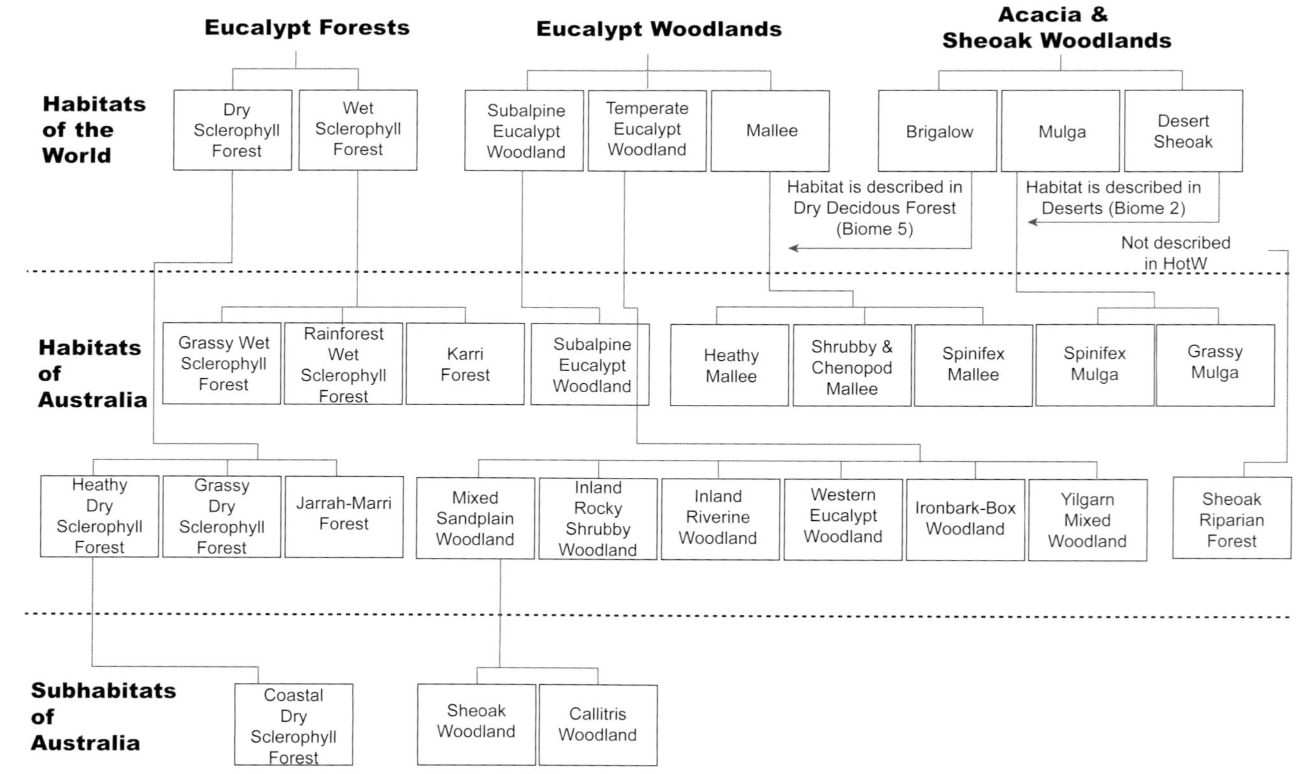

SCLEROPHYLL WOODLANDS AND FORESTS

Au9A GRASSY WET SCLEROPHYLL FOREST

IN A NUTSHELL: A tall moist forest with a eucalypt canopy and an open grassy understorey. **Global Habitat Affinities:** Fills niche of semi-evergreen forests but not related to others globally. **Continental Habitat Affinities:** KARRI FOREST; RAINFOREST WET SCLEROPHYLL FOREST. **Species Overlap:** AUSTRALIAN SUBTROPICAL RAINFOREST; TROPICAL MONTANE RAINFOREST; RAINFOREST WET SCLEROPHYLL FOREST; GRASSY DRY SCLEROPHYLL FOREST. **Full Bird Assemblage:** habitatsoftheworld.org/Au9A.

DESCRIPTION: In these tall to extremely tall eucalypt forests, Mountain Ash (*Eucalyptus regnans*) has reached the dazzling height of 374 ft. (114 m), although the canopy is usually in the range of 165 ft. (50 m). The trees are almost always straight-trunked and only start branching three-quarters of the way up the bole; the crowns are usually small and open, so although this is regarded as a closed forest, an immense amount of light penetrates to the ground compared with the nearby rainforests. Because this forest spans from Cape York Peninsula, Queensland, with a tropical, wet-year-round climate (Köppen **Af**), to Tasmania, with a cold and wet-year-round

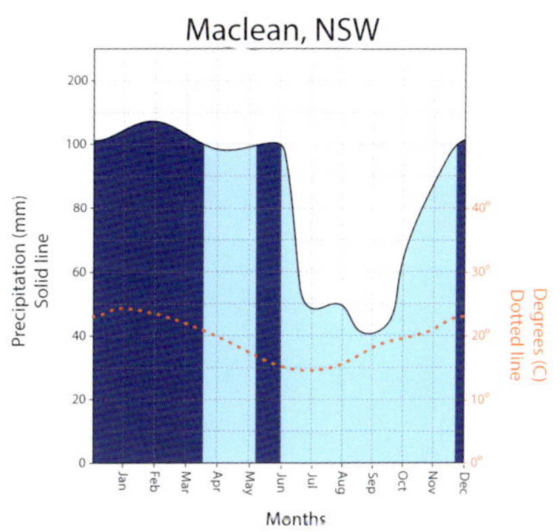

The understorey of Grassy Wet Sclerophyll Forest is much more open than that of Rainforest Wet Sclerophyll Forest, allowing enough light to reach the ground to promote thick grass cover. © IAIN CAMPBELL, TROPICAL BIRDING TOURS/UNSW E&ERC

climate (Köppen **Cfb**), the dominant eucalypt species predictably change depending on the region, from Flooded Gum (*Eucalyptus grandis*) in n. Australia, to Blackbutt (*Eucalyptus pilularis*) on the mid-eastern coast, to Mountain Ash and Tasmanian Blue Gum (*Eucalyptus globulus*) in the south. Other eucalypts that make up a significant proportion of the canopy in different areas include Errinundra Shining Gum (*Eucalyptus denticulata*), Alpine Ash (*Eucalyptus delegatensis*), Grey Gum (*Eucalyptus punctata*), Bangalay (*Eucalyptus botryoides*), Tallowwood (*Eucalyptus microcorys*), and Red Mahogany (*Eucalyptus resinifera*). These eucalypts are distinct from many in that they generally do not contain lignotubers, so they are not quite as resistant towards fire as the species in more open eucalypt woodlands. Other 'gums' that co-occupy the high canopy include Spotted Gum (*Corymbia maculata*), which looks very similar to the eucalypts and until recently was regarded as one, and Pink Bloodwood (*Corymbia intermedia*), which is also very common in GRASSY DRY SCLEROPHYLL FOREST. Other tree species typical of this forest tend to be a bit shorter and form a subcanopy rather than an understorey; they include Rough-barked Apple (*Angophora floribunda*), Grey Myrtle (*Backhousia myrtifolia*), Turpentine Tree (*Syncarpia glomulifera*), and Smudgee (*Angophora woodsiana*).

The lower stratum (layer) is usually a sparse cover of smaller trees. In the southern forests, the beautiful Soft Tree Fern (*Dicksonia antarctica*) is often present in the shrub and lower tree level and can form groves, giving the forest an awe-inspiring structure with a carpet of tree ferns and then a huge gap with no other trees until the base of the eucalypt canopy, more than 100 ft. (30 m) above. In n. Australia, the much less obtrusive Rebecca Tree Fern (*Cyathea rebeccae*) does not form groves but spreads gloriously in light gaps, and in se. Queensland, Rough Tree Fern (*Cyathea australis*) fills this niche, along with Cabbage-tree Palm (*Livistona australis*). Other small trees at the base of this forest include numerous wattles, such as Mabels's Wattle (*Acacia mabellae*), and plants such as Lilly Pilly (*Syzygium smithii*), Blueberry Ash (*Elaeocarpus reticulatus*), Variable Muttonwood (*Myrsine variabilis*), and Large Mock-Olive (*Notelaea longifolia*). Climbers such as Five-leaved Water Vine (*Apocissus hypoglauca*) are often present in the lower strata. The ground cover is dominated by a variety of grasses, forbs, and ferns such as Austral Bracken (*Pteridium esculentum*), Prickly Rasp Fern (*Blechnum neohollandicum*), and Common Ground Fern (*Calochlaena dubia*), along with graminoids (grasslike plants) such as the Variable Sword-Sedge (*Lepidosperma laterale*).

This forest is a very moist, yet fire-dependent habitat where low-intensity forest fires usually occur every 4–8 years and higher-intensity fires every 10–15 years. If fires do not occur for a couple of decades, the light-dependent, non-rainforest plants will be smothered by plants more suited to rainforest like Lilly Pilly, and the understorey will change into a forest more like RAINFOREST WET SCLEROPHYLL FOREST. We can think of this habitat as the intermediary between Grassy Dry Sclerophyll Forest and Rainforest Wet Sclerophyll Forest, with the different forest types in a mosaic or mélange determined by fire frequency and the protection from fire, but when fire is irregular, boundaries are nebulous.

WILDLIFE: The canopy of this forest is very similar to that of RAINFOREST WET SCLEROPHYLL FOREST, so the canopy bird species are typical of that habitat and include parrots such as Crimson Rosella, Australian King-Parrot, Swift Parrot, Rainbow

Swift Parrots migrate from mainland Australia into Grassy Wet Sclerophyll Forest in Tasmania for the breeding season, when they congregate at blooming eucalyptus trees, such as Tasmanian Blue Gum. © BEN KNOOT

When eucalypts are blossoming within Grassy Wet Sclerophyll Forest, Yellow-tufted Honeyeaters can become especially conspicuous, noisy, and aggressive around these nectar sources. © SAM WOODS, TROPICAL BIRDING TOURS

Lorikeet; Red-browed Treecreeper; and a swath of honeyeaters, such as Eastern Spinebill, Bell Miner, Scarlet Myzomela, and Lewin's, Yellow-tufted, White-throated, and White-naped Honeyeaters. In Tasmania, they are joined by Black-headed and Strong-billed Honeyeaters. Both Striated and Spotted Pardalotes occur in this forest in far greater numbers than in nearby rainforests, as does Eastern Shrike-tit. This forest has a larger variety of robins than most habitats, with both rainforest and open-country species including Rose, Eastern Yellow, Pink, Scarlet, and Pale-yellow Robins, and in Tasmania, Dusky Robin. Raptors are dominated by canopy-hunting species such as Grey Goshawk, Pacific Baza, Brown Goshawk, and Collared Sparrowhawk.

As would be expected, Rainforest Wet Sclerophyll Forest and this Grassy Wet Sclerophyll Forest overlap greatly in arboreal mammals and share several marsupial flyers, reminiscent of the Northern Hemisphere flying squirrels, such as Greater Glider, Yellow-bellied Glider, Feather-tailed Glider, and Sugar Glider. Also in the canopy are the large Common Ringtail Possum, Common Brushtail Possum, and Mountain Brushtail Possum, as well as Koala—which used to be nearly ubiquitous in the sclerophyll forests but sadly has been declining in numbers.

The forest-floor mammal assemblage is very different, with this habitat lacking rainforest understorey mammals such as Red-legged Pademelon and Musky Rat-Kangaroo and instead having more of the larger macropods such as Eastern Grey Kangaroo, Swamp Wallaby, and Red-necked Wallaby. The medium-sized Spotted-tailed Quoll, Long-nosed Bandicoot, and Southern Brown Bandicoot all use this forest but are very catholic in their habitat choices, so can be found in both more open forests and more closed forests than this habitat. The very small marsupial carnivores expected here include White-footed Dunnart, Brush-tailed Phascogale, and

The monotonous call of the Spotted Pardalote is one of the most characteristic sounds of Grassy Wet Sclerophyll Forest in Australia. © ANDRES VASQUEZ, TROPICAL BIRDING TOURS

Tasmanian Dusky Antechinus. Until recently, Eastern Barred Bandicoot and Eastern Quoll were both widespread on the mainland. Both are now extinct on the mainland but still hang on in this habitat in Tasmania.

While the open forest canopy and understorey do not have as many reptiles as the rainforests, skinks still seem very common in this habitat, especially coolskinks such as Metallic Coolskink (*Carinascincus metallicus*) and Southern Forest Coolskink (*Carinascincus coventryi*). Other types of skinks here include Southern Grass Skink (*Pseudemoia entrecasteauxii*), McCoy's Skink (*Anepischetosia maccoyi*), and Trunk-climbing Skink. Blotched Bluetongue (*Tiliqua nigrolutea*) is rather common in this habitat. Snakes are obvious here, nearly all of them venomous, with species such as Tiger Snake (*Notechis scutatus*) and Red-bellied Black Snake (*Pseudechis porphyriacus*) common in the south along with Lowlands Copperhead (*Austrelaps superbus*), which is highly venomous and extremely dangerous (much more so than the unrelated North American Copperhead).

Koalas are most abundant in either type of wet sclerophyll forest in Australia, although populations have undergone dramatic declines in recent years. © BEN KNOOT

CONSERVATION: Grassy Wet Sclerophyll Forest is highly productive for high-quality timber, and although the habitat has some nominal protection, and commercial logging was supposed to cease, old-growth forests are still being clear-felled in places such as Victoria.

DISTRIBUTION: In the tropics of e. Australia, Grassy Wet Sclerophyll Forests occur patchily along the western margins of rainforests. In the subtropics, they are a buffer between higher-elevation rainforests and RAINFOREST WET SCLEROPHYLL FOREST and GRASSY DRY SCLEROPHYLL FOREST. In temperate areas, such as the coastal ranges of New South Wales and the Otway Ranges of Victoria, these forests are more extensive, forming large stands.

WHERE TO SEE: Eden, New South Wales, Australia; Bruny Island, Tasmania, Australia; Millaa Millaa Falls, Queensland, Australia.

Au9B RAINFOREST WET SCLEROPHYLL FOREST

IN A NUTSHELL: A forest with a eucalypt canopy and an understorey of plants usually associated with rainforest. **Global Habitat Affinities:** Fills the niche of semi-evergreen forests but not related to others globally. **Continental Habitat Affinities:** KARRI FOREST; GRASSY WET SCLEROPHYLL FOREST. **Species Overlap:** AUSTRALIAN SUBTROPICAL RAINFOREST; TROPICAL MONTANE RAINFOREST; GRASSY WET SCLEROPHYLL FOREST; GRASSY DRY SCLEROPHYLL FOREST. **Full Bird Assemblage:** habitatsoftheworld.org/Au9B.

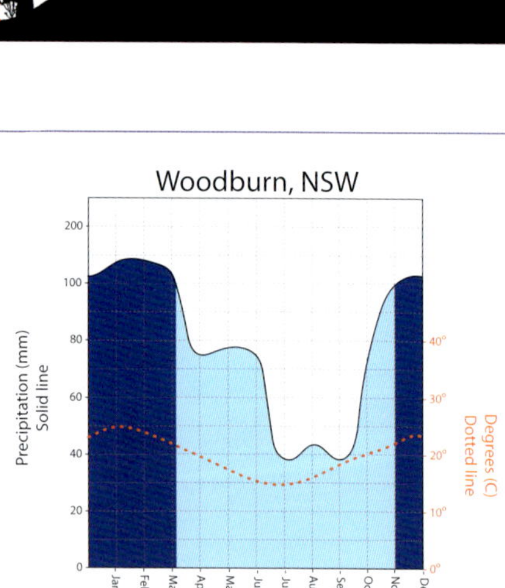

DESCRIPTION: This habitat is called Rainforest Wet Sclerophyll Forest because the canopy is a eucalypt-dominated sclerophyll forest, and the understorey is a rainforest-like, broadleaf evergreen mash-up, which is very different from all the other types of sclerophyll forest. These wet sclerophyll forests form in high-rainfall, high-fertility areas. They are the tallest forests in Australia and among the tallest in the world, their canopies reaching 180 ft. (55 m), with some emergent trees to 260 ft. (80 m) and a living Mountain Ash (*Eucalyptus regnans*) measuring 330 ft. (100.5 m). In Victoria and Tasmania, the forest can have a wide variety of canopy heights, with the very tallest in fertile lowland areas and much shorter forests in subalpine regions.

Because this forest spans 40 degrees of latitude down Australia's eastern coast, from a tropical and wet-year-round climate (Köppen **Af**) to a cold and wet-year-round climate (Köppen **Cfb**), the dominant eucalypt species predictably changes. In far n. Queensland, the canopy is dominated by the smooth-barked and pink-toned Flooded Gum (*Eucalyptus grandis*), with occasional non-eucalypts such as Turpentine Tree (*Syncarpia glomulifera*). Farther to the south, in se. Queensland and New South Wales, the smooth-barked Sydney Blue Gum (*Eucalyptus saligna*), Dunn's White Gum (*Eucalyptus dunnii*), Broad-leaved Stringybark (*Eucalyptus acmenoides*), and Tallowwood

The canopy of Rainforest Wet Sclerophyll Forest can be very uniform when it is monotypic and the trees are of a similar age. © IAIN CAMPBELL, TROPICAL BIRDING TOURS/UNSW E&ERC

The understorey of these forests usually has many rainforest shrubs and small trees. © IAIN CAMPBELL, TROPICAL BIRDING TOURS/UNSW E&ERC

The broadleaf evergreen plants of the understorey support an assemblage of birds shared with rainforests, like Eastern Yellow Robin. © PABLO CERVANTES, TROPICAL BIRDING TOURS

(*Eucalyptus microcorys*) are the most prominent trees. Alpine Ash (*Eucalyptus delegatensis*), Tasmanian Blue Gum (*Eucalyptus globulus*), and the tallest of them all, the Mountain Ash, all have the same, very clean, smooth feel as the Karri trees (*Eucalyptus diversicolor*) of Western Australia.

Although the forest canopy may look dense from a distance, and the canopy trees almost always form a closed, interlocking canopy, the eucalypt leaves are small, and large amounts of light penetrate the upper canopy, allowing a subcanopy and understorey to develop of rainforest trees such as Jackwood (*Cryptocarya glaucescens*) and Rose Walnut (*Endiandra discolor*) in the north, and Musk Daisy-Bush (*Olearia argophylla*), New Zealand Hazel (*Pomaderris apetala*), and Tasmanian Blanketleaf (*Bedfordia salicina*) in the south; in the coldest areas, the subcanopy is dominated by Myrtle Beech (*Nothofagus cunninghamii*) and the conifer Celerytop Pine (*Phyllocladus aspleniifolius*), and the forest can form a mélange with NOTHOFAGUS FOREST. The very dense understorey of rainforest-type plants makes walking through this habitat very difficult, and wandering is near impossible.

The boundary between Rainforest Wet Sclerophyll Forest and the various rainforests is often sharp but at times can be very nebulous, with the habitats merging where the increased soil fertility and moisture availability promote rainforest formation. We can think of this habitat as the intermediary between the various rainforest habitats and GRASSY WET SCLEROPHYLL FOREST, where the different forest types are in a mosaic or mélange, and the boundaries are determined by fire frequency and protection from fire. An intense fire can instantly kill rainforest subcanopy and understorey plants and promote the growth of the eucalypts, changing the Rainforest Wet

The rainforest component of the Rainforest Wet Sclerophyll Forest understorey is an important factor for Pink Robins, which are absent from Grassy Wet Sclerophyll Forest. © BEN KNOOT

Sclerophyll Forest to a Grassy Wet Sclerophyll Rainforest; there is a hysteresis (delayed effect) where Grassy Wet Sclerophyll Forest will return very slowly to Rainforest Wet Sclerophyll Forest and even to rainforest if fire is stopped for many decades.

WILDLIFE: This is the tale of two habitats in one. The similarity of the understorey to the various rainforest habitats, both physically and in terms of plant species composition, leads to significant overlap in bird species. Birds of the understorey include Superb Lyrebird; Crescent Honeyeater; Eastern Spinebill; Satin Flycatcher; Pilotbird; Eastern Yellow Robin; Pink Robin; Yellow-throated, Large-billed, White-browed, and Tasmanian Scrubwrens; Scrubtit; Tasmanian Thornbill; Eastern Whipbird; and Satin

In Australia, the explosive, whip-cracking duet of the Eastern Whipbird is often heard emanating from the rainforest understorey of this habitat. © IAIN CAMPBELL, TROPICAL BIRDING TOURS/UNSW E&ERC

Black-headed Honeyeater is a Tasmanian endemic that is a common inhabitant of Rainforest Wet Sclerophyll Forest.
© IAIN CAMPBELL, TROPICAL BIRDING TOURS/UNSW E&ERC

Bowerbird. In contrast, the canopy is very similar to that of GRASSY DRY SCLEROPHYLL FOREST, so the canopy bird species are typical of that habitat and include Crimson Rosella, Australian King-Parrot, Rainbow Lorikeet, Red-browed Treecreeper, and a swath of honeyeaters such as Yellow-faced Honeyeater, Black-headed Honeyeater, Bell Miner, Scarlet Myzomela, and White-naped Honeyeater.

Besides the rainforest mammals that occur in the wet sclerophyll understorey, like Red-legged Pademelon, this habitat holds some habitat-restricted mammals, such as Northern Bettong,

In e. Australia, the distinctive, descending call of Scarlet Myzomela can reveal the presence of blooming flowers in the canopy of eucalypt-dominated forests like these.
© IAIN CAMPBELL, TROPICAL BIRDING TOURS/UNSW E&ERC

Red-necked Pademelon inhabits the dark, rainforest-like floor of these forests.
© SAM WOODS, TROPICAL BIRDING TOURS

Yellow-bellied Glider, Parma Wallaby, Squirrel Glider, and Australian Swamp Rat. Around Sydney, wet sclerophyll forest is home to Eastern Grey Kangaroo, Swamp Wallaby, Common Ringtail Possum, Common Brushtail Possum, and Eastern Pygmy Possum, along with the occasional Feather-tailed Glider. Koala was once a common mammal of wet sclerophyll forests but has suffered significant population declines due to habitat fragmentation. Reptiles typical of this habitat, although rare, include Pale-headed Snake (*Hoplocephalus bitorquatus*), Broad-headed Snake (*Hoplocephalus bungaroides*), and Heath Monitor (*Varanus rosenbergi*).

CONSERVATION: Where this forest occurs as a mosaic or mélange with one of the rainforest types such as SUBTROPICAL RAINFOREST, TROPICAL MONTANE RAINFOREST, or TEMPERATE RAINFOREST, it is well protected. However, the nominal protections for examples of this forest that occur away from the rainforests are far weaker, and logging of these magnificent forests continues. The forestry departments are shrewd and leave a façade of good habitat along public roads, but viewed from above, the destruction is obvious.

DISTRIBUTION: In the tropics of e. Australia, wet sclerophyll forests occur patchily along the western margins of rainforests. In the subtropics, they are a buffer between higher-elevation rainforests and HEATHY DRY SCLEROPHYLL FOREST. In temperate areas, such as the Blue Mountains of New South Wales and the Otway Ranges of Victoria, these forests are more extensive, forming large stands.

WHERE TO SEE: Blue Mountains (e.g., Mt. Wilson, Wollemi National Park), New South Wales, Australia; Bruny Island, Tasmania, Australia; Millaa Millaa Falls, Queensland, Australia.

Au9C KARRI FOREST

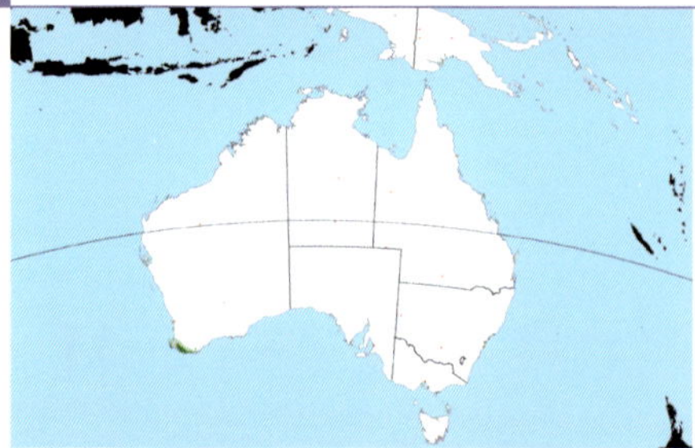

IN A NUTSHELL: A Western Australian forest with a eucalypt canopy and an understorey of plants usually associated with rainforest. **Global Habitat Affinities:** Fills the niche of semi-evergreen forests but not related to others globally. **Continental Habitat Affinities:** GRASSY WET SCLEROPHYLL FOREST; RAINFOREST WET SCLEROPHYLL FOREST. **Species Overlap:** JARRAH-MARRI FOREST, KWONGAN HEATHLAND. **Full Bird Assemblage:** habitatsoftheworld.org/Au9C.

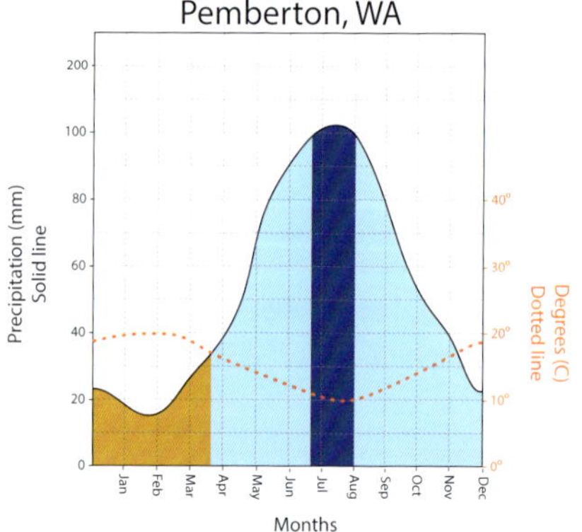

DESCRIPTION: In the extreme southwest of Australia, the northern edge of the winds from the Southern Ocean frontal system meets the warm waters of the Leeuwin Current to create a mild, wet, Mediterranean-type climate (Köppen **Csb**), with rainy winters and relatively dry summers, that contrasts sharply with the much more arid conditions immediately to the north and east. The forests are named after the dominant tree, the magnificent Karri (*Eucalyptus diversicolor*), which grows over 230 ft. (70 m) tall.

Karri Forest is one of the most spectacular environments in the world. The Karri's cream-coloured, very smooth boles can soar 130 ft. (40 m) without branches, giving the impression of marble columns; where other forests can be described as 'cathedral', the Karri Forest has the aura of the Parthenon. The canopy height is usually over 165 ft. (50 m), and while the quintessential examples of this habitat are monotypic, it also occurs with a spattering of other eucalypts, such as Marri (*Corymbia calophylla*), Jarrah (*Eucalyptus marginata*), Rate's Tingle (*Eucalyptus brevistylis*), and Red Tingle (*Eucalyptus jacksonii*); the accompanying canopy trees, however, usually reach just 100–165 ft. (30–50 m), so they can appear as an extremely tall subcanopy. The canopy is classified as closed because the branches from canopy trees touch each other, but the leaves of the eucalypt trees are very small, so a lot of light penetrates the canopy to the forest understorey.

The mid-canopy and understorey of the very tall Karri Forest can be quite open.
© IAIN CAMPBELL, TROPICAL BIRDING TOURS/UNSW E&ERC

Karri trees have a very similar feel to the Mountain Ash (*Eucalyptus regnans*) of RAINFOREST WET SCLEROPHYLL FOREST of e. Australia, but the forest's understorey assemblage does not look like the rainforest understorey but instead is very similar to that of GRASSY WET SCLEROPHYLL FOREST of e. Australia. The Karri Forest understorey is composed of a thick layer of plants that also occur in more open areas, such as Karri Hazel (*Trymalium spatulatum*), Karri Sheoak (*Allocasuarina decussata*), Karri Wattle (*Acacia pentadenia*), Karri Oak (*Chorilaena quercifolia*), Karri Bluebush (*Hovea elliptica*), Swan River Peppermint (*Agonis flexuosa*), numerous *Banksia* spp., and a cycad called Zamia Palm (*Macrozamia riedlei*).

The Karri Forest often occurs as a mosaic with the much more widespread JARRAH-MARRI FOREST, and where they occur together, the Karri Forest grows on nutrient-rich loam soils, while the Jarrah-Marri Forest tends to be on the comparatively nutrient-deficient podzols and the extremely nutrient-deficient lateritic regosols.

WILDLIFE: Karri Forest does not have any obligate bird species and shares many of its canopy birds with the JARRAH-MARRI FOREST. The canopy bird assemblage is very similar in the two habitats, and nectivorous species such as the regional endemic Gilbert's Honeyeater, Red Wattlebird, New Holland Honeyeater, and Purple-crowned Lorikeet are common in both. Insectivorous canopy species include the subspecies of Australian Ringneck called the 'Twenty-eight Parrot', Fan-tailed Cuckoo, Red-capped Parrot, the diminutive Spotted and Striated Pardalotes, and the endemic Western Whistler (subspecies of Golden Whistler) and Western Shrike-tit.

Many of the canopy bird species of this habitat are shared with Jarrah-Marri Forests, such as Gilbert's Honeyeater. © SAM WOODS, TROPICAL BIRDING TOURS

In the understorey, the differences between this habitat and the more open forests and woodlands become apparent. The Red-winged Fairywren is an indicator species of this forest, living in small family groups in the thick understorey. Other understorey and ground birds expected include Common Bronzewing, Rufous Treecreeper, White-breasted Robin, and Spotted Scrubwren.

Mammals of these forests include Western Grey Kangaroo, Western Ringtail Possum, Western Brush Wallaby, Quenda, Yellow-footed Antechinus, Common Brushtail Possum, and Australian Bush Rat. Snakes include the venomous Dugite (*Pseudonaja affinis*), found regularly in the Pemberton area where extensive Karri Forest remains, though it is

The giant Karri Forest is home to the handsome Red-capped Parrot and other regional specialties of Western Australia. © IAIN CAMPBELL, TROPICAL BIRDING TOURS/UNSW E&ERC

'Twenty-eight Parrot' is a local form of Australian Ringneck, restricted to the sw. corner of Australia, where it occurs in Karri Forest.
© SHANE KENNEDY, TROPICAL BIRDING TOURS

not specific to Karri Forest and is also found in a variety of disturbed habitats. Other reptiles in these forests include Southwestern Crevice Skink (*Egernia napoleonis*), Lowlands Earless Skink (*Hemiergis peronii*), Common Southwest Ctenotus (*Ctenotus labillardieri*), Western Three-lined Skink (*Acritoscincus trilineatus*), and King's Skink (*Egernia kingii*).

CONSERVATION: About half of the original Karri Forests have been cleared or significantly altered since European arrival. Industrial logging of old-growth forests was banned in 2024, but small-scale cutting is still permitted, and extensive Karri plantations are being developed. Overall, the remaining forests are well protected.

DISTRIBUTION: This forest is restricted to the extreme southwest of Western Australia from Cape Naturaliste to Denmark. An eastern outlier of this habitat in the Porongurup Range occurs as a mélange with JARRAH-MARRI FOREST.

WHERE TO SEE: Warren National Park, Western Australia; Pemberton area, Western Australia.

Au9D GRASSY DRY SCLEROPHYLL FOREST

IN A NUTSHELL: Eucalypt forest that has an open canopy and a grassy understorey with occasional *Casuarina* and *Acacia* spp. **Global Habitat Affinities:** None. **Continental Habitat Affinities:** HEATHY DRY SCLEROPHYLL FOREST; JARRAH-MARRI FOREST. **Species Overlap:** HEATHY DRY SCLEROPHYLL FOREST; JARRAH-MARRI FOREST; IRONBARK-BOX WOODLAND; GRASSY WET SCLEROPHYLL FOREST. **Full Bird Assemblage:** habitatsoftheworld.org/Au9D.

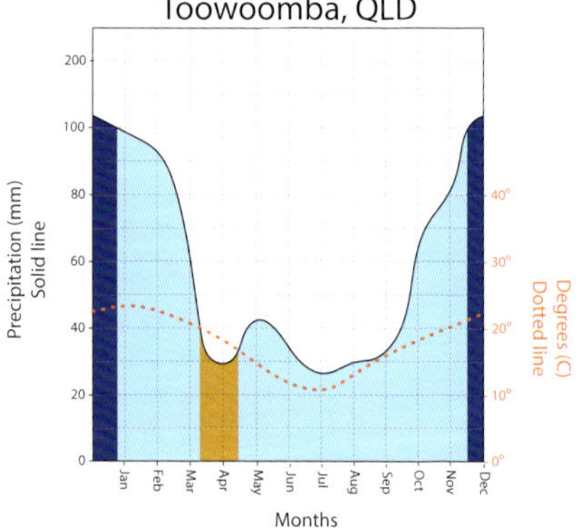

DESCRIPTION: This is the lusher, more productive sister habitat of the HEATHY DRY SCLEROPHYLL FOREST; it forms along the eastern seaboard of Australia and Tasmania on more nutrient-rich soils and, because of this soil's potential, has been more extensively cleared. Grassy Dry Sclerophyll Forest is a tall to very tall, open eucalypt forest with a sparse mid-stratum of *Allocasuarina* spp. and broadleaf, non-sclerophyll small trees and shrubs.

The semi-canopy, where the trees touch but there is not much inter-tree branch mixing, is made of eucalypts shared with either GRASSY WET SCLEROPHYLL FOREST or IRONBARK-BOX WOODLAND. These include stringybarks such as Thin-leaved Stringybark (*Eucalyptus eugenioides*) and Tindal's Stringybark (*Eucalyptus tindaliae*); gums such as Forest Red Gum (*Eucalyptus tereticornis*), Manna Gum (*Eucalyptus viminalis*), and Cabbage Gum (*Eucalyptus amplifolia*); and ironbarks such as Narrow-leaved Ironbark (*Eucalyptus crebra*) and Northern Grey Ironbark (*Eucalyptus siderophloia*). Other typical canopy trees include Pink Bloodwood (*Corymbia intermedia*), Dallachy's Ghost Gum (*Corymbia dallachiana*), Swamp Box (*Lophostemon suaveolens*), and Broad-leaved Apple (*Angophora subvelutina*), which usually grows as a subcanopy tree that is almost as high as the other trees but rarely exceeds 60 ft. (20 m). Most of the canopy is taller than the apple, with the average canopy reaching 60–120 ft. (20–40 m), while many individual trees grow to 165 ft. (50 m). Although a wide variety of shapes are possible, the canopy trees typically grow

Grassy Dry Sclerophyll, such as this example in Lamington National Park, Queensland, can occur extremely close to rainforest yet is composed of grasses and grass trees.
© IAIN CAMPBELL, TROPICAL BIRDING TOURS/UNSW E&ERC

While Grassy Dry Sclerophyll Forest can be very tall, the trees are spaced widely enough to allow a lot of light to reach the forest floor; in slightly moister areas, this promotes shrubs more typical of Rainforest Wet Sclerophyll Forest, as shown here. © IAIN CAMPBELL, TROPICAL BIRDING TOURS/UNSW E&ERC

Grassy Dry Sclerophyll can occur in drier areas more typical of Heathy Dry Sclerophyll but is usually on more productive soils, so is in greater danger of clearance for farming. © IAIN CAMPBELL, TROPICAL BIRDING TOURS/UNSW E&ERC

with a straight trunk that remains unbranched for two-thirds of its height and a crown that spreads to about half the tree height. This can give the forest a very planned, cathedral-like appearance, similar to the KARRI FOREST of Western Australia. Rainforest trees are occasionally present in the canopy, especially when this forest abuts the rainforests or is separated from them by only a very narrow band (an ecotone) of RAINFOREST WET SCLEROPHYLL FOREST.

The understorey is usually sparse to semi-dense, with a small tree layer, 12–45 ft. (4–15 m) tall, that commonly includes Forest Sheoak (*Allocasuarina torulosa*), Cocky Apple (*Planchonia careya*), Red Ash (*Alphitonia excelsa*), and acacias such as Lightwood (*Acacia implexa*), which can form monotypic groves. The lower layers very frequently include Coffee Bush (*Breynia oblongifolia*), Badu Island Cycad (*Cycas badensis*), and Winged Broom-Pea (*Jacksonia scoparia*), along with acacias such as Curracabah (*Acacia concurrens*). In some areas, grass trees such as Queensland Grass Tree (*Xanthorrhoea glauca*) can be quite distinctive, especially after a fire, when most other shrubs have died and the branches of this plant have burnt back, but trunks remain and can be well over 6 ft (2m) tall. The ground cover is made up of various grass and sedge species and in some places can be thick enough to appear as a rich grassland.

This habitat forms on a variety of nutrient-neutral soils; these are less rich than soils formed on alluvial plains and on basalt, which tend to promote rainforest or Rainforest Wet Sclerophyll Forest, but more nutrient-rich than the depauperate soils that form on quartzites or sandstones, which promote the growth of Heathy Dry Sclerophyll Forest. Grassy Dry Sclerophyll Forest occurs in a wide range of rainfall conditions from semiarid (20 in./500 mm annual rainfall) to very humid (50 in./1300 mm). While these forests are found from Cape York Peninsula, Queensland, to Tasmania, they are most common in a humid, subtropical climate (Köppen **Cfa**) and at elevations of 2600–4000 ft. (800–1200 m).

The boundary between this forest and the various rainforests can be razor sharp on ranges, which suggests that fire is a main determinant of the forest type there. In other areas, wet sclerophyll forests occur between the two, and the canopy trees merge gradually between this habitat and the wetter forests, suggesting that fire is determining the understorey assemblage, which is constantly in flux while the canopy species survive the numerous fire cycles.

WILDLIFE: In the eastern or southern portions of its range, Grassy Dry Sclerophyll Forest shares its bird assemblage with HEATHY DRY SCLEROPHYLL FOREST, adjoining IRONBARK-BOX WOODLAND, or GRASSY WET SCLEROPHYLL FOREST. In these forests, the canopy species include nectivorous parrots such as Little Lorikeet, Scaly-breasted Lorikeet, and Rainbow Lorikeet, as well as the blossom-nomad honeyeaters such as Yellow-faced, White-throated, and White-naped Honeyeaters and Scarlet Myzomela. Other honeyeaters, such as the Yellow-tufted Honeyeater, occur in gullies within this habitat, sharing them with the extremely aggressive Bell Miner, which is a communal species that feeds on aphids and whose feeding patterns have been linked to infestations and resulting dieback within dry sclerophyll forests.

Red-browed and White-throated Treecreepers appear sympatric in this habitat, although the White-throated has a much broader habitat range and is also found in the surrounding rainforests. Spotted Quail-thrush is a bird more typical of dryer eucalypt forests and woodlands but can be

In e. Australia, Red-browed Treecreeper occupies Grassy Dry Sclerophyll Forest, particularly in hilly areas. © SAM WOODS, TROPICAL BIRDING TOURS

Forty-spotted Pardalote is an endangered Australian songbird that occurs in Grassy Dry Sclerophyll Forest in very specific coastal areas of Tasmania that are dominated by Manna Gum. © BEN KNOOT

found remarkably close to the rainforest in this habitat, such as at Duck Creek Road in Lamington National Park, Queensland.

Spotted, Forty-spotted, and Striated Pardalotes are small passerines especially numerous in Grassy Dry Sclerophyll Forest, usually gleaning in the canopy with thornbills such as Brown Thornbill. Yellow Thornbill and Striated Thornbill are both common in this forest especially where there are groves of sheoaks. Scarlet Robin is a regular species in this forest in Tasmania, though it prefers more open habitats on mainland Australia.

Most of the mammals here, such as Short-beaked Echidna, are generalists that also occupy the surrounding forests, but the Koala is a notable exception, occurring in this forest but almost never found in nearby rainforests. In the Grassy Dry Sclerophyll Forest, the Koala shares the canopy with other nocturnal mammals such as Common Brushtail Possum, Squirrel Glider, Sugar Glider, and Greater Glider, a large relative of the ringtail possums that soars like a flying squirrel of the Northern Hemisphere. The larger macropods are, for the most part, absent from this habitat, but Whiptail Wallaby and

In se. Australia, the open understorey of Grassy Dry Sclerophyll Forest is inhabited by the spectacular Scarlet Robin. © IAIN CAMPBELL, TROPICAL BIRDING TOURS/UNSW E&ERC

Red-necked Wallaby are more common. The very small marsupials to be expected here include the shrew-like Yellow-footed Antechinus and Slender-tailed Dunnart, which is a relative of the quolls and Tasmanian Devil. Southern Bettong, Eastern Barred Bandicoot, and Long-nosed Bandicoot are all possible in this habitat in Tasmania.

There are far fewer reptiles in Grassy Dry Sclerophyll Forest than in surrounding rainforests, but it has plenty of snakes, such as Red-bellied Black Snake (*Pseudechis porphyriacus*), Tiger Snake (*Notechis scutatus*), Carpet Python (*Morelia spilota*), Common Tree Snake (*Dendrelaphis punctulatus*), and Eastern Brown Snake (*Pseudonaja textilis*).

Lizards here include the very large Lace Monitor (*Varanus varius*) and Eastern Bearded Dragon (*Pogona barbata*), together with arboreal skinks and geckos such as Clouded Velvet Gecko (*Amalosia jacovae*) and Eastern Stone Gecko (*Diplodactylus vittatus*). The widespread Common Bluetongue (*Tiliqua scincoides*) is found here with its similar-looking cousin, the Pink-tongued Skink (*Cyclodomorphus gerrardii*). In addition to tongue colour, the Pink-tongued Skink differs in being a slug and snail specialist, rather than an opportunistic feeder, and is usually located rummaging through the leaf litter. Frogs that inhabit this forest include Great Barred Frog (*Mixophyes fasciolatus*), Northern Banjo Frog (*Limnodynastes terraereginae*), Tyler's Laughing Tree Frog (*Litoria tyleri*), Peron's Laughing Tree Frog (*Litoria peronii*), and Australian Green Tree Frog (*Ranoidea caerulea*).

CONSERVATION: This forest, with its tall, straight trees forming on good soil, has been hard hit by clearing, far more so than the closely associated HEATHY DRY SCLEROPHYLL FOREST. Much of the remaining Grassy Dry Sclerophyll Forest is protected within forest reserves, although logging continues, particularly in Victoria. This is a very fire-dominated habitat, and a change in the fire regime that limits the occurrence of fire can cause an infestation of acacias in the understorey and change it to a thicket with emergents. Over-burning kills some of the canopy tree saplings, especially the non-eucalypts. Overgrazing of the grasses and seedlings causes sheoaks to become more prevalent and also promotes an invasion of cypress-pines (*Callitris* spp.), which do not normally live in this habitat.

DISTRIBUTION: This forest is found from Queensland to South Australia and Tasmania. It is found mainly on the coastal ranges but does occur in the high ranges as well. In Tasmania, it is more common around the eastern and northern parts of the island and is very limited in the southwest.

WHERE TO SEE: Duck Creek Road, Lamington National Park, Queensland, Australia; w. Australian Capital Territory.

Some of the few large mammals found in Grassy Dry Sclerophyll Forest in Australia include the handsome Whiptail Wallaby (pictured) and the robust Red-necked Wallaby. © SAM WOODS, TROPICAL BIRDING TOURS

Au9E HEATHY DRY SCLEROPHYLL FOREST

IN A NUTSHELL: Eucalypt forest that has an open canopy and usually has an understorey with casuarinas and acacias and a shrub layer dominated by heath plants such as banksias and hakeas. **Global Habitat Affinities:** None. **Continental Habitat Affinities:** GRASSY DRY SCLEROPHYLL FOREST; JARRAH-MARRI FOREST. **Species Overlap:** GRASSY DRY SCLEROPHYLL FOREST; WESTERN EUCALYPT WOODLAND; IRONBARK WOODLAND; GRASSY WET SCLEROPHYLL FOREST. **Full Bird Assemblage:** habitatsoftheworld.org/Au9E.

DESCRIPTION: This is the most-extensive remaining forest type in moist temperate regions of se. Australia, covering much of the Blue Mountains of New South Wales and parts of the Great Dividing Range of New South Wales and s. Queensland. Although many images of Australia's early colonial history show pioneers in this environment, it has been saved the fate of IRONBARK-BOX WOODLAND and GRASSY DRY SCLEROPHYLL FOREST. It remains widespread because it forms in very rocky and mountainous areas with shallow, much poorer soils than the rangelands and is therefore less desirable for farming. This is a fire-dependent habitat, and most of the understorey shrubs are adapted to regenerate after fire, while most canopy trees rapidly regrow leaves. The forest occurs over a very wide latitudinal range, with corresponding climates ranging from monsoonal (Köppen **Aw**) in ne. Queensland to temperate (Köppen **Cfb**) in Tasmania, but generally humid, with rainfall between 24 and 63 in. (600–1600 mm). As a rule, the warmer the environment, the greater the rainfall required to keep this habitat from changing to a savanna; and the colder the environment, the lesser the rainfall needed to keep the habitat from reverting to RAINFOREST WET SCLEROPHYLL FOREST, GRASSY WET SCLEROPHYLL FOREST, or TEMPERATE RAINFOREST.

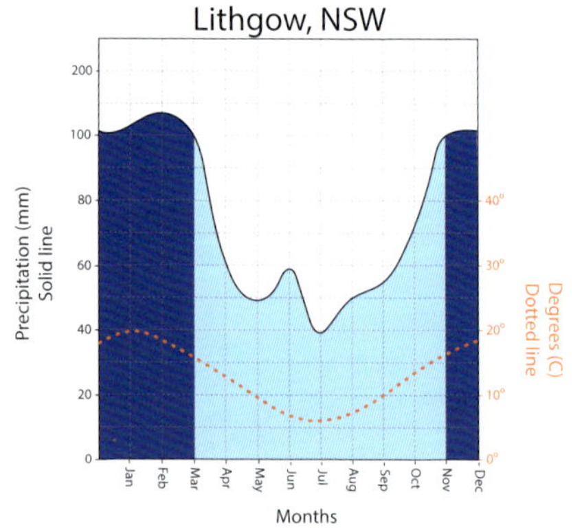

This forest type can be regarded as an ecotone between Grassy Wet Sclerophyll Forest and WALLUM AND AUSBOS heathlands of the coast and Ironbark-Box Woodland or MIXED SANDPLAIN WOODLAND of semiarid e. Australia. This forest, therefore, displays a wide variety of structures,

This habitat often forms in very rocky terrain where the soils are sandy and poorly drained.
© IAIN CAMPBELL, TROPICAL BIRDING TOURS/UNSW E&ERC

The undergrowth composition of Heathy Dry Sclerophyll Forest ranges from thick heathland to open sclerophyllous shrubs, as depicted here. © IAIN CAMPBELL, TROPICAL BIRDING TOURS/UNSW E&ERC

from short, open-canopied forest that could be regarded as a woodland to near-closed-canopy forest of trees reaching 80 ft. (25 m). In areas with particularly harsh environments, the canopy is dominated by trees such as Faulconbridge Mallee Ash (*Eucalyptus burgessiana*) and Blue Mountains Mallee Ash (*Eucalyptus stricta*). These trees have a mallee growth form with multiple narrow trunks forming from a gnarled lignotuber (root ball) at or just beneath the ground, and although the habitat is sometimes referred to as mallee, it has no wildlife association with arid habitats like HEATHY MALLEE or SPINIFEX MALLEE.

Heathy Dry Sclerophyll Forest surrounds Sydney (New South Wales), which is built on Sydney sandstone, a quartzitic sandstone that produces particularly nutrient-deficient, very sandy soils (podzols). Most areas are exposed to wind and regular fire, so only Ausbos heathland can grow, but in slightly more favourable areas, Heathy Dry Sclerophyll with a canopy of Narrow-leaved Snappy Gum (*Eucalyptus racemosa*), Narrow-leaved Stringybark (*Eucalyptus sparsifolia*), and White Stringybark (*Eucalyptus globoidea*) can take hold. The understorey flora ranges from shrubs of head height to small trees 15 ft. (5 m) high and is dominated by plants associated with the surrounding heathlands, such as Hairpin Banksia (*Banksia spinulosa*), Finger Hakea (*Hakea dactyloides*), and Broad-leaved Drumsticks (*Isopogon anemonifolius*). Grasses are not prominent in this habitat, and instead the ground is covered by small shrubs such as Wreath Bush-Pea (*Pultenaea tuberculata*). On the western edge of the coastal plain, on the lower slopes of the Blue

The mixed nature of the canopy is evident from a bird's-eye view, with the acacias, eucalypts, and cypress-pines all having very different canopy structures. © IAIN CAMPBELL, TROPICAL BIRDING TOURS/UNSW E&ERC

Mountains, taller trees such as Sydney Peppermint (*Eucalyptus piperita*) and Narrow-leaved Stringybark become common, with the mallee-form Faulconbridge Mallee Ash and Blue Mountains Mallee Ash as a lower canopy. The lower canopy also contains heathland plants growing as small trees, to 50 ft. (15 m), such as Old Man Banksia (*Banksia serrata*).

Much farther inland, in places such as the Warrumbungles (New South Wales), this habitat starts to blend with Ironbark-Box Woodland or the Mixed Sandplain Woodland. In these areas, Heathy Dry Sclerophyll is an open forest dominated by eucalypts such as White Box (*Eucalyptus albens*), Long-leaved Box (*Eucalyptus goniocalyx*), Bundy (*Eucalyptus nortonii*), Yellow Box (*Eucalyptus melliodora*), Red Stringybark (*Eucalyptus macrorhyncha*), and Narrow-leaved Ironbark (*Eucalyptus crebra*). Numerous canopy plants here are more typical of Mixed Sandplain Woodland, including Black Cypress-Pine (*Callitris endlicheri*), White Cypress-Pine (*Callitris glaucophylla*), and Rough-barked Apple (*Angophora floribunda*).

The heathy understorey in the more westerly forests of New South Wales is usually closed and difficult to walk through, with many short wattles that branch out near head height such as Lightwood (*Acacia implexa*), Western Silver Wattle (*Acacia decora*), Tableland Wattle (*Acacia caesiella*), and Deane's Wattle (*Acacia deanei*). Other shrubs expected in this community include Rosemary Cassinia (*Cassinia quinquefaria*), *Cassinia leptocephala*, Australian Blackthorn (*Bursaria spinosa*), and the globally distributed Akeake (*Dodonaea viscosa*).

In the western plains of New South Wales, the Heathy Dry Sclerophyll merges into Mixed Sandplain Woodland, forming a broad ecotone that is difficult to classify. © IAIN CAMPBELL, TROPICAL BIRDING TOURS/UNSW E&ERC.

WILDLIFE: From se. Queensland to Victoria, the bird assemblage of Heathy Dry Sclerophyll Forest is shared with GRASSY DRY SCLEROPHYLL FOREST, adjoining temperate IRONBARK-BOX WOODLAND, or nearby GRASSY WET SCLEROPHYLL FOREST. In these forests, the canopy species include Scaly-breasted Lorikeet, Little Lorikeet, Eastern Shrike-tit, Red-browed Treecreeper, White-naped Honeyeater, and White-throated Treecreeper. This habitat is a very important feeding area for the critically endangered Regent Honeyeater. This spectacular black, yellow, and white honeyeater nests in SHEOAK RIPARIAN FOREST but uses this habitat preferentially when not breeding. Striated, Spotted, and Forty-spotted Pardalotes all occur in this habitat. Dusky Robin, Yellow-throated Honeyeater, and Black-headed Honeyeater are all common in Tasmanian Heathy Dry Sclerophyll Forest. The undergrowth of this habitat on the mainland is a favourite haunt of Purple-backed Fairywren, Spotted Quail-thrush, White-browed Scrubwren, Striated Thornbill, and Painted Buttonquail.

On the western edge of this habitat in South Australia, the bird assemblage has a lot of overlap with the GRASSY DRY SCLEROPHYLL FOREST, with species such as Common Bronzewing, Turquoise Parrot, Australian Ringneck, the 'orange' (Adelaide) subspecies of Crimson Rosella, Spiny-cheeked Honeyeater, Singing Honeyeater, White-plumed Honeyeater, Brown-headed

Eastern Shrike-tit occupies the canopy of Heathy Dry Sclerophyll Forest in e. Australia, particularly favouring gum trees with long strips of peeling bark.
© IAIN CAMPBELL, TROPICAL BIRDING TOURS/UNSW E&ERC

Scaly-breasted Lorikeet is a nomadic e. Australian parrot that in times of plentiful nectar can be found in this habitat. © IAIN CAMPBELL, TROPICAL BIRDING TOURS/UNSW E&ERC

Honeyeater, Striped Honeyeater, Little Friarbird, Noisy Friarbird, Yellow Thornbill, Inland Thornbill, White-winged Chough, Apostlebird, and Double-barred Finch.

Most Australian mammals are nocturnal as are the vast majority found in this dry sclerophyll habitat, including Eastern Barred Bandicoot, Rufous Bettong, Common Brushtail Possum, Eastern Pygmy Possum, Yellow-footed Antechinus, Spotted-tailed Quoll, Southern Brown Bandicoot, Squirrel Glider, and Sugar Glider. Larger ground grazers here include Eastern Grey Kangaroo, Red-necked Wallaby, Common Wallaroo, Swamp Wallaby, Black-striped Wallaby, Whiptail Wallaby, and Brush-tailed Rock-Wallaby. Short-beaked Echidna, Koala, and Bare-nosed Wombat are also regularly encountered in this habitat.

Many reptiles are found in these forests, and notable species include Zigzag Velvet Gecko (*Amalosia rhombifer*), Border Thick-tailed Gecko (*Uvidicolus sphyrurus*), Jacky Dragon (*Amphibolurus muricatus*), Eastern Bearded Dragon (*Pogona barbata*), Lace Monitor (*Varanus varius*), and Copper-tailed Ctenotus (*Ctenotus taeniolatus*). Widespread snakes include Broad-headed Snake (*Hoplocephalus bungaroides*) and Eastern Brown Snake (*Pseudonaja textilis*), while Red-bellied Black Snake (*Pseudechis porphyriacus*) occurs in s. Australian Heathy Dry Sclerophyll Forest.

CONSERVATION: Heathy Dry Sclerophyll Forest is usually much better protected than other forest types in Australia in part due to its location on land that is unattractive for farming; it also occurs on some of the continent's most iconic, and therefore better protected, landscapes. However, many finer-detailed state maps reveal units of Heathy Dry Sclerophyll Forest that are under threat from urban expansion.

Spotted Quail-thrush inhabits this forest but is generally extremely difficult to track down (except when singing), as it spends much time concealed on the ground. © SAM WOODS, TROPICAL BIRDING TOURS/UNSW E&ERC

DISTRIBUTION: Heathy Dry Sclerophyll Forest occurs widely in e. Australia, from the west of the Atherton Tableland (Queensland) through Capertee Valley and Hunter Valley (New South Wales) to much of e. Victoria, se. South Australia, and Tasmania.

WHERE TO SEE: Capertee Valley, New South Wales, Australia; Lamington National Park, Queensland, Australia.

Eastern Barred Bandicoot occupies this habitat in se. Australia. © CHARLEY HESSE, TROPICAL BIRDING TOURS

Au9F JARRAH-MARRI FOREST

The understory of the forest is almost completely removed during large fires (above left), and it may take a few years for the shrub layer to return (below left).

IN A NUTSHELL: Eucalypt forest of Western Australia that has an open canopy of Jarrah and Marri trees over a shrubby understorey and significant amounts of grass. **Global Habitat Affinities:** None. **Continental Habitat Affinities:** HEATHY DRY SCLEROPHYLL FOREST; GRASSY DRY SCLEROPHYLL FOREST. **Species Overlap:** KARRI FOREST; WESTERN EUCALYPT WOODLAND. **Full Bird Assemblage:** habitatsoftheworld.org/Au9F.

DESCRIPTION: Dominated by Jarrah and Marri trees, this habitat is the western equivalent of the HEATHY DRY SCLEROPHYLL FOREST and GRASSY DRY SCLEROPHYLL FOREST of e. Australia and contains elements of both, with both heathy and grassy elements. It is not, however, divided into healthy and grassy versions because the understorey is less relevant to the bird assemblage, and the vast majority of these forests contain both grassy and heathy patches. In the wetter areas, Jarrah-Marri Forest is replaced by KARRI FOREST, while in the drier areas, it gradually merges over a broad boundary and wide ecotone with WESTERN EUCALYPT WOODLAND.

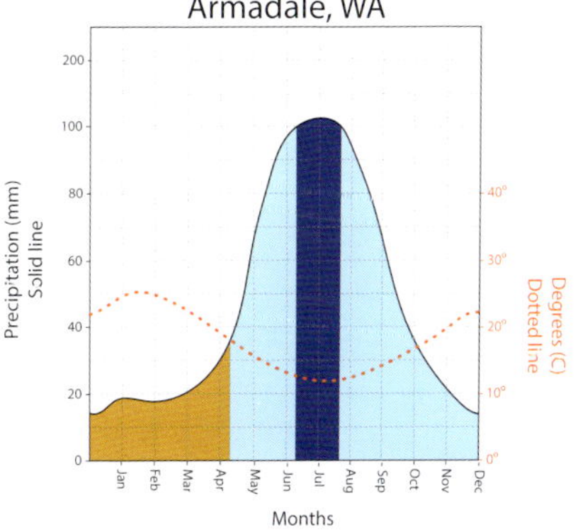

These dry sclerophyll forests vary greatly in canopy height, from 30 to 90 ft. (10–30 m), and density, from quite open to closed, though most commonly they have a mid-dense canopy with the crowns of the trees touching. The individual tree boles are not particularly straight, and there is widespread branching at lower levels in the canopy. The canopy is dominated by Jarrah (*Eucalyptus marginata*) or Marri (*Corymbia calophylla*), and most of the forests have a mixture of the two. Other trees found in the canopy are typically eucalypts such as Flat-topped Yate (*Eucalyptus occidentalis*), Yarri (*Eucalyptus patens*), Redheart (*Eucalyptus decipiens*), and Mountain Marri (*Corymbia haematoxylon*), which was also regarded as a eucalypt before the *Corymbia* genus was created in 1995. The drooping Western Sheoak

The Jarrah-Marri Forest is more open and shorter than the sympatric Karri Forest.
© IAIN CAMPBELL, TROPICAL BIRDING TOURS/UNSW E&ERC

The understorey of the Jarrah-Marri Forest is usually heathy, and this habitat can be considered the w. Australian equivalent of the Heathy Dry Sclerophyll Forest of e. Australia.
© IAIN CAMPBELL, TROPICAL BIRDING TOURS/UNSW E&ERC

(*Allocasuarina fraseriana*) also features in the canopy assemblage of most of these forests, though it feels misplaced amid the more upright, dense-canopied Jarrah trees.

Jarrah-Marri Forest occurs mainly on soils that are fairly impoverished, growing on either coastal sands with very sandy soils or ancient lateritic plateaus where the soils are so leached of nutrients that all that remains is highly inert sand and a mix of iron (ferricrete) and aluminium (bauxite) concretions called pisoliths, which contain almost no nutrients of value to growing trees. When the forest grows on the sands it looks very much like Heathy Dry Sclerophyll Forest with an incredible assortment of banksias, such as Great Banksia (*Banksia grandis*) in the subcanopy and much smaller Couch Honeypot (*Banksia dallanneyi*), Parrot Bush (*Banksia sessilis*), and Prickly Dryandra (*Banksia armata*) in the shrub layer. The plant diversity of the understorey is extremely high, with grass trees such as Balga (*Xanthorrhoea preissii*); nectar-producing plants such as Fuchsia Grevillea (*Grevillea bipinnatifida*), Honey Bush (*Hakea lissocarpha*), and One-sided Bottlebrush (*Melaleuca quadrifida*); and orchids such as Winter Donkey Orchid (*Diuris brumalis*)

On the lateritic plateau, the Jarrah-Marri Forest has a shrubbier feel than the coastal forests, with understorey plants such as Great Banksia, River Banksia (*Banksia seminuda*), Bullich (*Eucalyptus megacarpa*), Western Sheoak (*Allocasuarina fraseriana*), Snottygobble (*Persoonia longifolia*), and the cycad Zamia Palm (*Macrozamia riedlei*).

This is a fire-dependent habitat, and most of the understorey shrubs are adapted to regenerate after fire, while most canopy trees rapidly experience epicormic regrowth, where dormant buds, located beneath the bark along the trunk and branches, activate and sprout new shoots after the fire. It results in 'fluffy'-looking trees with leaves sprouting along the trunks. Once branches have established a new canopy, the emergency epicormic leaves along the trunk and branches die, and the trees look normal again.

These forests form in a semiarid Mediterranean climate (Köppen **Csa**) with hot, dry summers and mild, moist winters. The average summer high temperature in January is around 75°F (24°C), and the average winter low in July is around 39°F (4°C). Most of the annual rainfall of around 21 in. (540 mm) occurs in June and July. Summers are very dry, with less than 1 in. (25 mm) of rain in any month.

WILDLIFE: Birds in sw. Western Australia are far more generalist than in e. Australia, and the three forest/woodland habitats (Jarrah-Marri Forest, KARRI FOREST, and WESTERN EUCALYPT WOODLAND) have no strictly obligate (found in only one habitat) or endemic species. Many of the widespread open forest and woodland birds of e. Australia can be

Epicormic regrowth along the trees' trunks and large branches is very common in the Jarrah-Marri Forest and allows for rapid regrowth and photosynthesis after fire without the growth of twigs.

© IAIN CAMPBELL, TROPICAL BIRDING TOURS/UNSW E&ERC

Blue-breasted Fairywren occurs in sections of Jarrah-Marri Forest that have a shrubby understorey.
© SAM WOODS, TROPICAL BIRDING TOURS

found in this forest, such as Common Bronzewing, Fan-tailed Cuckoo, Spotted Pardalote, Grey Shrikethrush, Rufous Whistler, Grey Fantail, and Mistletoebird. There is more overlap with KWONGAN HEATHLAND and even WALLUM AND AUSBOS than with the eastern forests, with species such as Red Wattlebird, New Holland Honeyeater, and White-cheeked Honeyeaters common.

Numerous western species found in these forests have sister species in the eastern forests that essentially fill the same niche, although the species here tend to be more generalist, such as Blue-breasted Fairywren; Western Spinebill, a sister species to Eastern Spinebill; Western Wattlebird, a split from Little Wattlebird; Gilbert's Honeyeater, a sister to White-naped Honeyeater; Spotted Scrubwren, a sister to White-browed Scrubwren; Western subspecies of Golden Whistler; and Western Yellow Robin, a sister to Eastern Yellow Robin. Other western songbirds found here include Red-winged Fairywren, Western Thornbill, and White-breasted Whistler. Parrots feature strongly in this environment, which hosts many species more typical of open temperate eucalypt woodlands such as Regent Parrot and the very distinctive subspecies of Australian Ringneck called 'Twenty-eight Parrot', as well as more forest-oriented species such as Western Rosella and the stunning Red-capped Parrot.

The black-cockatoos are of far more importance in these forests than in the east. Both of the white-tailed species, Carnaby's Black-Cockatoo and Baudin's Black-Cockatoo, occur here, with the Baudin's having a strong association with Marri trees. The Red-tailed Black-Cockatoo also occurs in this forest yet is largely absent from the two dry sclerophyll forests of se. Australia.

The vast majority of mammals found in the Jarrah-Marri Forest are nocturnal, such as the critically endangered Woylie (Western Bandicoot) and Quenda (Western Brown Bandicoot), which are both small to medium-sized carnivorous marsupials with pointed snouts and hunched backs. They look like small wallabies but run instead of hop. Western Quoll (aka Chuditch) is the largest native carnivore in Western Australia. Brown with white spots on its back and about the size of a domestic cat, it has become very endangered through competition with the introduced cat and is now mainly restricted to reserves with predator-proof enclosures. Common Brushtail Possum and Western Ringtail Possum are omnivores that occur widely through this habitat. Red-tailed Phascogale is a very small arboreal carnivore with a long nose and large ears; it resembles the nectivorous Honey Possum but has a much more frenzied breeding season, wherein all males die after their first mating as a result of stress-related diseases.

Numbat, Australia's answer to the Aardvark of Africa or the tamanduas of South America, is a small, termite-eating marsupial restricted to sw. Australia, distinctive with its reddish-brown fur, white stripes on its back, and bushy tail. It is not strictly nocturnal, so it can be found in early morning, later afternoon, and on very overcast days wandering the dirt roads through this woodland. Short-beaked Echidna also feeds on termites in these forests but is far more catholic in habitat choices and is found over most of Australia.

Larger ground grazers here include Western Grey Kangaroo and Euro (subspecies of Common Wallaroo). There are numerous smaller macropods, such as Tammar Wallaby and Western Brush Wallaby, a gorgeous species with a black face that contrasts starkly with its grey-brown body. Black-flanked Rock-Wallaby used to be widespread but was wiped out by foxes and cats, and the population exists only in enclosures. Quokka still exists in this habitat but is far easier to see on Rottnest Island (offshore from Perth), where it has become completely habituated to the throngs of tourists that visit the island.

Many reptiles are found in these forests; notable species include Heath Monitor (*Varanus rosenbergi*) and geckos such as the Western Tree Dtella (*Gehyra variegata*), Southern Marbled Gecko (*Christinus marmoratus*), Thick-tailed Barking Gecko (*Underwoodisaurus milii*), and Speckled Stone Gecko (*Diplodactylus lateroides*). Skinks include the Southwestern Crevice Skink (*Egernia napoleonis*), King's Skink (*Egernia kingii*), and the Lowlands Earless Skink (*Hemiergis peronii*). Snakes include the very widespread Tiger Snake (*Notechis scutatus*) and Southern Death Adder (*Acanthophis antarcticus*), along with more localised Dugite (*Pseudonaja affinis*) and Gould's Hooded Snake (*Suta gouldii*).

CONSERVATION: Much of the original Jarrah-Marri Forests were removed in the early days of European settlement. The large remaining tracts are almost all on lateritic escarpments east of Perth that have incredibly nutrient-deficient soils for farming, though the logging of the existing forests continues. There are many reserves in this region along with the establishment of predator-free enclosures for the reintroduction of endangered marsupials.

DISTRIBUTION: These forests are concentrated in sw. Western Australia, from Albany on the south coast around to Perth on the west coast. They are replaced in the wettest areas by KARRI FOREST and in drier areas by WESTERN EUCALYPT WOODLAND. There is an outlier of this woodland in Stirling Range and Porongurup National Parks.

WHERE TO SEE: Porongurup National Park, Western Australia; Jarrahdale State Forest, Western Australia; Tone-Perup Nature Reserve, Western Australia.

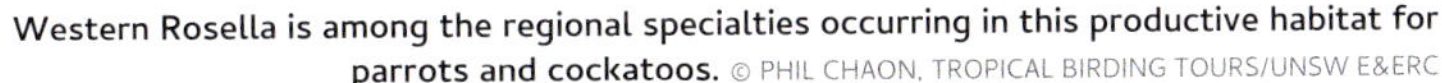

Western Rosella is among the regional specialties occurring in this productive habitat for parrots and cockatoos. © PHIL CHAON, TROPICAL BIRDING TOURS/UNSW E&ERC

Au9G IRONBARK-BOX WOODLAND

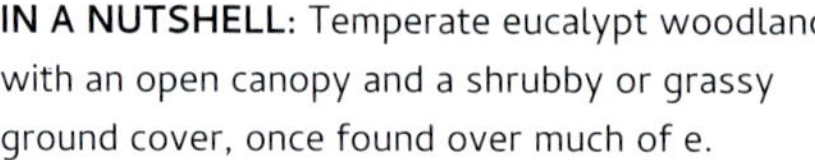

IN A NUTSHELL: Temperate eucalypt woodland with an open canopy and a shrubby or grassy ground cover, once found over much of e. Australia. **Global Habitat Affinities:** CHILEAN SCLEROPHYLL SCRUB. **Continental Habitat Affinities:** WESTERN EUCALYPT WOODLAND. **Species Overlap:** HEATHY DRY SCLEROPHYLL FOREST; GRASSY DRY SCLEROPHYLL FOREST; HEATHY MALLEE; INLAND RIVERINE WOODLAND; MIXED SANDPLAIN WOODLAND. **Full Bird Assemblage:** habitatsoftheworld.org/Au9G.

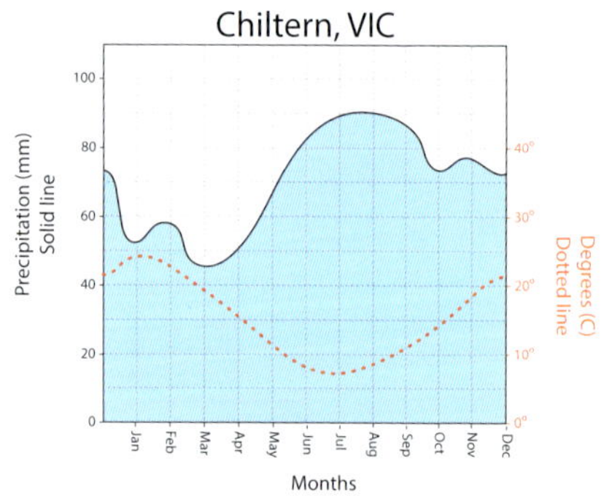

DESCRIPTION: Although the name suggests Ironbark-Box Woodland is limited to a few types of eucalypts, this habitat encompasses a variety of eucalypt woodlands and open forests that were once very extensive across the fertile valleys and rolling hills of temperate e. Australia. Because the woodlands were open with a lot of grass as ground cover, they were easily converted to farmland, and when European settlers ventured inland from Sydney and Melbourne in the early 1800s, they destroyed the Ironbark-Box Woodlands within decades. It is now possible to drive 1000 mi. (1600 km) from Brisbane (Queensland) to Melbourne (Victoria) through endless farmland and hardly pass a block of forest that is large enough to sustain a full natural bird and mammal assemblage; one of the dullest drives on the planet is made all the more depressing because when intact, these Ironbark-Box Woodlands are so impressive, bursting with a huge variety of wildlife.

These woodlands mainly span the humid–semiarid boundary in climates (Koppen **Cfb** and **Cfa**) characterised by mild temperatures, no dry season, and moderate rainfall of 19–27.5 in. (480–700 mm), spread throughout the year, with summers ranging from mild to hot. In the southern reaches, there is more rainfall in winter than summer, while in the north, there is more rainfall in summer.

The woodlands form over a variety of nutrient-rich soils, including those developed in alluvial floodplains of major river systems and loam to clay soils developed on residual parent material of basalts and shales. In wetter and cooler areas, this habitat can even form over felsic (quartz-rich) granitic batholiths (huge intrusions of rock spanning thousands of acres/hectares), though they tend to be replaced here by GRASSY DRY SCLEROPHYLL FOREST. In drier areas where the soils are nutrient-deficient, the habit merges into MIXED SANDPLAIN WOODLAND. Some of these

The temperate Ironbark-Box Woodlands are usually open with a pronounced grass ground cover. Younger groves like this can have the height of a mature forest, but the trees are much narrower than old-growth trees. © IAIN CAMPBELL, TROPICAL BIRDING TOURS/UNSW E&ERC

Even in areas where the Ironbark-Box Woodland remains uncut, the habitat undergoes intense grazing pressure from sheep farming. The bark of White Box is shown. © IAIN CAMPBELL, TROPICAL BIRDING TOURS/UNSW E&ERC

woodlands can look remarkably similar to the OPEN EUCALYPT SAVANNA of tropical and subtropical n. Australia and could reasonably be classified as a temperate savanna. However, the grass species here use C3 photosynthesis and thrive in cooler, wetter environments, while proper savannas are, by definition, dominated by C4 grasses that use a different photosynthesis process, making them better adapted to hot, dry conditions. Grass type may seem irrelevant, but many birds in Australia have a distribution that matches the types of grass present in the open woodland environment.

Because the Ironbark-Box Woodland block extends from e. South Australia north to s. Queensland, a range of species dominates the canopy. In the southwestern part of the habitat's range, Mugga Ironbark (*Eucalyptus sideroxylon*), Western Grey Box (*Eucalyptus microcarpa*), Yellow Box (*Eucalyptus melliodora*), and Yellow Gum (*Eucalyptus leucoxylon*) form a woodland with a canopy that ranges from 45 to 75 ft. (15–25 m) in height, with some emergents reaching 90 ft. (30 m). Where the woodlands are more open, the trees tend to be bent and branch out close to the ground, reminiscent of English Oak (*Quercus robur*) from Europe or White Oak (*Quercus alba*) from North America. However, when the trees are more closely spaced, they tend to form straighter boles and only start to branch above 20 ft. (6.5 m). The denser Ironbark-Box Woodlands also have more White Cypress-Pine (*Callitris glaucophylla*) and Buloke (*Allocasuarina luehmannii*) in the canopy.

Farther east towards se. Queensland, the woodland is often dominated by Grey Box (*Eucalyptus moluccana*) and White Box (*Eucalyptus albens*) but also contains trees such as Silver-leaved Ironbark (*Eucalyptus melanophloia*), which extends north-northwest into the OPEN EUCALYPT SAVANNA, along with non-eucalypt species such as Kurrajong (*Brachychiton populneus*) and Weeping Myall (*Acacia pendula*). In recently disturbed areas, White Cypress-Pine can form groves and may be a sign of habitat degradation through overgrazing. Tumbledown Red Gum (*Eucalyptus dealbata*) can be prevalent in the eastern woodlands, even forming monotypic stands, but usually grows as a subcanopy tree rarely reaching more than 45 ft. (15 m).

Although the Grey Box community of w. New South Wales is highly threatened and purportedly protected, clearing and burning continue. © IAIN CAMPBELL, TROPICAL BIRDING TOURS/UNSW E&ERC

The shrub layer of Ironbark-Box Woodland is generally sparse, though some disturbed areas can form, comprising groves of Golden Wattle (*Acacia pycnantha*), Gold-dust Wattle (*Acacia acinacea*), and Spreading Wattle (*Acacia genistifolia*), which can reach 25 ft. (8 m) and splash the subcanopy with yellow during flowering. Other shrubs expected in the westerly woodlands include Drooping Cassinia (*Cassinia arcuata*) and Australian Blackthorn (*Bursaria spinosa*), forming an understorey 12 ft. (4 m) tall, and Twiggy Bush-Pea (*Pultenaea largiflorens*) and Cranberry Heath (*Styphelia humifusa*), prominent shrubs reaching around 2 ft. (60 cm). In the easterly Ironbark-Box Woodland, although understorey shrubs are absent or very sparse, fast-growing Lightwood (*Acacia implexa*) can form a subcanopy up to 45 ft. (15 m) high. Galvanised Burr (*Sclerolaena birchii*) and Black Roly-poly (*Sclerolaena muricata*) can form dense patches, 3 ft. (1 m) in height, in areas with nutrient-deficient or sandy soil. The many grasses in this habitat include temperate and localised species such as Rough Speargrass (*Austrostipa scabra*) and Tall Oat Grass (*Themeda avenacea*) as well as the very widespread Kangaroo Grass (*Themeda australis*), a C4 grass found through most of Africa and Asia. Forbs are common and highly localised, though some species such as Corrugated Sida (*Sida corrugata*) are common throughout this habitat.

WILDLIFE: Mass blooming of eucalypts in Ironbark-Box Woodland can be spectacular, and during these events the canopy can be a donnybrook of blossom nomads frantically feeding. Nectivorous parrots such as the common Rainbow Lorikeet and Musk Lorikeet fight with the much rarer Little Lorikeet and the critically endangered Swift Parrot for prime spots, with groups constantly flying out of the trees and making forced re-entry. Honeyeaters are also in the mix, with substantial numbers of Fuscous, Brown-headed, White-plumed, Black-chinned, and Yellow-faced Honeyeaters following the blossoms. When there is a mass blooming, species such as Painted Honeyeater seem to come out of nowhere. The rarest of the Australian honeyeaters, the Regent Honeyeater, used to appear regularly in this habitat but is now critically endangered and rarely seen. It uses the SHEOAK RIPARIAN FOREST to breed but spends most of its time away from the nest feeding in this woodland.

Horsfield's Bronze-Cuckoo and Shining Bronze-Cuckoo are both canopy insectivores and nest parasites, having unsuspecting much smaller birds raise their young. Horsfield's Bronze-Cuckoo lays its eggs in the nests of understorey species such as Superb Fairywren, Variegated Fairywren, and Speckled Warbler, whereas Shining Bronze-Cuckoo prefers to nest-predate other canopy species such as Brown Thornbill, Striated Thornbill, and Western Gerygone. Understorey hunters of this forest such as Sacred Kingfisher, Hooded Robin, Red-capped Robin, Scarlet Robin, and wintering Flame Robin tend to sit waiting on low branches, scanning for prey. Other species prefer to glean branches methodically, searching for insects, such as Eastern Shrike-tit, Varied Sittella, Spotted Pardalote, and Striated Pardalote.

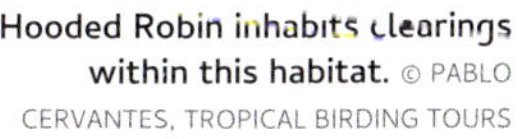

Hooded Robin inhabits clearings within this habitat. © PABLO CERVANTES, TROPICAL BIRDING TOURS

The rich assemblage of ground-foraging parrots found in Ironbark-Box Woodland includes the striking Eastern Rosella. © IAIN CAMPBELL, TROPICAL BIRDING TOURS/UNSW E&ERC

The open nature of these woodlands is conducive to raptors, with ambush hunters such as Brown Goshawk and Collared Sparrowhawk weaving through the understorey and the larger soaring raptors such as Little Eagle and Wedge-tailed Eagle scanning for prey from overhead.

Ground-feeding parrots are an important part of the bird assemblage, and species such as Elegant Parrot, Australian Ringneck, Eastern Rosella, Red-rumped Parrot, and Blue-winged Parrot are among the targets for birders. Turquoise Parrot and Superb Parrot are spectacular species strongly associated with these woodlands, but unfortunately populations of both have declined due to habitat destruction.

Mammals are particularly rich, with tiny marsupial predators such as Yellow-footed Antechinus and Brush-tailed Phascogale thriving along with larger species such as omnivorous Common Brushtail Possum and herbivorous Common Ringtail Possum. Greater Glider is an herbivorous species of ringtail possum that has adapted to gliding in much the same manner as Northern Hemisphere flying squirrels. Sugar Glider and Squirrel Glider are very small; female Sugar Glider weighs just 4 oz. (115 grams) and measures 9.5 in. (24 cm) from nose to tail tip. Koala was once very common in this habitat, but its numbers have drastically decreased in recent years. Larger macropods include Swamp Wallaby and Eastern Grey Kangaroo. Short-beaked Echidna and Bare-nosed Wombat are both regularly found in decent-sized patches of remaining habitat. Platypus is found on the clean rivers that drain the less disturbed blocks of this forest (and many other forested habitats).

Reptiles expected in Ironbark-Box Woodland include the large Lace Monitor (*Varanus varius*) and Eastern Bearded Dragon (*Pogona barbata*), and the smaller Eastern Three-toed Earless Skink (*Hemiergis talbingoensis*), Southern Rainbow Skink (*Carlia tetradactyla*), Pale-flecked Garden Sunskink (*Lampropholis guichenoti*), Southeastern Morethia Skink (*Morethia boulengeri*), Robust Ctenotus (*Ctenotus*

Platypus is one of the most iconic mammals found within Ironbark-Box Woodland. © CHARLEY HESSE, TROPICAL BIRDING TOURS

Bare-nosed Wombat is an inconspicuous inhabitant of this woodland, its presence often betrayed by its giant ground burrows. © SAM WOODS, TROPICAL BIRDING TOURS

robustus), and Copper-tailed Ctenotus (*Ctenotus taeniolatus*). Regular snakes include Red-bellied Black Snake (*Pseudechis porphyriacus*), Eastern Brown Snake (*Pseudonaja textilis*), and Dwyer's Snake (*Suta dwyeri*).

CONSERVATION: If you see a vegetation map of Australia and notice the huge white patch in the southeast of the continent marked 'No Native Vegetation', that is pretty much the extent of what was the once-immense Ironbark-Box Woodland. The only truly comparable level of destruction worldwide is the area that used to be the semi-evergreen Mata Atlantica (Atlantic Forest) of se. Brazil. Larger areas of Ironbark-Box Woodland remnants, thankfully, are protected in national parks. Slivers of ecosystems, such as the Grey Box woodland reserves of se. Australia, are purportedly strictly protected, but as of April 2024, Grey Box woodland was still being clear-felled in the Lake Cargelligo region of New South Wales. Where tourist brochures show the vast farmland with happy-faced farmers, we naturalists see a lost world.

DISTRIBUTION: These woodlands characterise the regions in se. Australia between the dry sclerophyll forests and subalpine woodlands of coastal regions and the truly arid habitats of the interior such as MIXED SANDPLAIN WOODLAND. They can be found from the outskirts of Adelaide in South Australia to the Toowoomba area of se. Queensland. Much of what is now suburban Melbourne used to be this temperate woodland. Ironbark-Box Woodland is also found in ne. Tasmania.

WHERE TO SEE: Chiltern area, Victoria; Dalyenong Nature Conservation Reserve, Victoria; Junee area, New South Wales, Australia.

Au9H INLAND RIVERINE WOODLAND

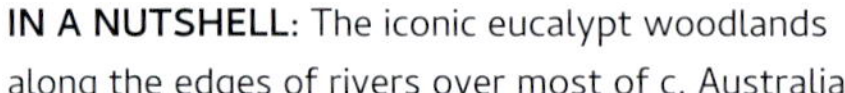

IN A NUTSHELL: The iconic eucalypt woodlands along the edges of rivers over most of c. Australia.
Global Habitat Affinities: NEARCTIC WESTERN RIPARIAN WOODLAND; TURANIAN ARID RIPARIAN SCRUB.
Continental Habitat Affinities: MELALEUCA RIVERINE FOREST; IRONBARK-BOX WOODLAND. **Species Overlap:** IRONBARK-BOX WOODLAND; MELALEUCA RIVERINE FOREST. **Full Bird Assemblage:** habitatsoftheworld.org/Au9

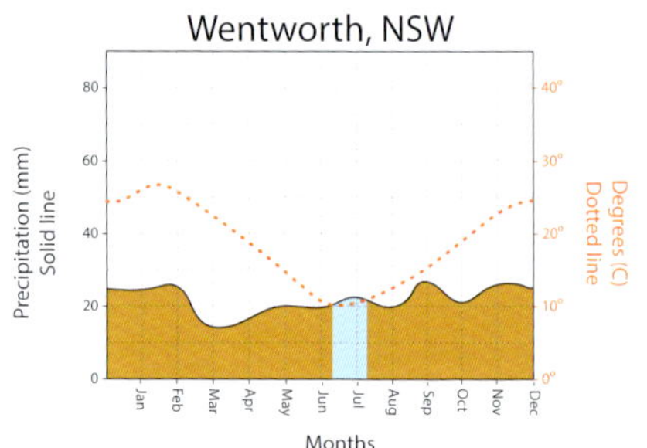

DESCRIPTION: When people think of inland Australia, the image of eucalypt-lined creeks winding through the desert comes to mind. Inland Riverine Woodland is the habitat that lines the greatest rivers—the Darling, Murray, Murrumbidgee, and Lachlan—of arid and semiarid e. Australia from the western slopes of the Great Dividing Range to South Australia. It also occurs throughout c. Australia, where some of the great rivers don't even make it to the coast—for example, Cooper Creek, rising in Queensland, drains into Lake Eyre

River Red Gums can form a ribbon along dry ephemeral rivers surrounded by desert habitat. This riverbed in South Australia was a raging torrent a week after this photo taken. © IAIN CAMPBELL, TROPICAL BIRDING TOURS/UNSW E&ERC

in ne. South Australia. Collectively, the central basins of Australia are roughly the same size as the Amazon Basin, though the rivers produce only around 1/300th of the Amazon's water discharge, as very little rain falls over their length. These rivers are slivers of green in a mass of brown, which makes them even more fascinating. In Western Australia, the rivers lined with this habitat are small, and most even ephemeral.

Generally, the eucalypt groves along the banks derive their water directly from the river and can thrive even on poor sandy soils, while trees farther away grow only where there are nutrient-rich clay soils, which hold water for longer. Dominated by relatively few species, Inland Riverine Woodlands occur in swaths that range from tens of feet wide where the banks are steepest to tens of miles wide where the alluvial plains are very flat.

The dominant tree is almost always River Red Gum (*Eucalyptus camaldulensis*) along with Coolabah (*Eucalyptus coolabah*), which shades many a billabong (the Australian word for an oxbow lake). Other trees that are typical of this habitat include Carbeen (*Corymbia tessellaris*), Black Box (*Eucalyptus largiflorens*), Yellow Box (*Eucalyptus melliodora*), and Poplar Box (*Eucalyptus populnea*), all of which can extend much farther away from rivers than River Red Gum and may merge with other eucalypt woodlands. River Sheoak (*Casuarina cunninghamiana*) occurs in limited numbers and at the eastern edge of this habitat becomes a major component of the forest where it changes to SHEOAK RIPARIAN FOREST. In the north of this habitat, *Melaleuca* spp. become more dominant, and the habitat merges with MELALEUCA RIVERINE FOREST.

In some riverine forests, such as along the Murrumbidgee River in s. New South Wales, the trees can form substantial forests with a closed canopy reaching 100 ft. (33 m), and with a lush grass layer after flooding, they resemble a GRASSY DRY SCLEROPHYLL FOREST. Usually though,

Opposite: **Much of the Inland Riverine Woodland that occurs on flat fertile plains has been removed for farming. What remains is largely concentrated in narrow reserves along river edges, such as this example on the Murrumbidgee River, New South Wales.** © IAIN CAMPBELL, TROPICAL BIRDING TOURS/UNSW E&ERC

life is much tougher for these forests, and the trees grow to only 60 ft. (20 m), although they can still be large and single-stemmed, with huge boles, some taking on a pachycaulesque appearance. A feature that can astound visitors is the number of cavities in a single tree. When branches fall from River Red Gums, the vestiges of the branches usually hollow out, making the trees extremely important for nesting wildlife. Except after flooding, the ground layer is sparse, with little grass and relatively few shrubs. The farther inland the river extends, the more that Lignum (*Duma florulenta*) becomes a dominant feature of the understorey, spreading into the clay plains where trees can no longer grow.

This forest can be viewed as an ephemeral wetland that requires very periodic flooding to survive. The habitat can also be viewed as azonal in that it occurs over a range of climates from summer-rain, semiarid (Köppen **Bsh**) to very arid (Köppen **Bwh**) to wet-winter/dry-summer Mediterranean-type (Köppen **Csa**) conditions. An increase of the water levels of mere tens of feet that would be of minimal impact in less flat parts of the world cause flooding over massive areas in this environment. The floodwaters move very slowly, so people in the lower reaches of these drainage systems can have weeks of warning of impending major flooding. Many of the habitat's plants propagate after flooding, and the rare but severe floods often wipe out much of the understorey, meaning the canopy of River Red Gums can be hundreds of years old while the shrub layer may have a uniform age of rarely more than a few decades.

WILDLIFE: Over much of c. Australia, Inland Riverine Woodlands, harbouring the only large trees for hundreds of miles, provide the majority of nesting sites for much of the wildlife. These

White-plumed Honeyeater is particularly abundant in riparian woodlands.
© PABLO CERVANTES, TROPICAL BIRDING TOURS

ribbons of forest extend wooded habitats from woodlands and savannas into the arid interior, and along these ribbons the woodland and savanna birds extend their ranges into the deserts. White-plumed Honeyeater is most common in this habitat, where it occurs along with other honeyeaters such as Brown and Blue-faced Honeyeaters. Australia is often referred to as the land of parrots, and without these trees for nesting holes, many of them could not survive and feed in the surrounding more arid habitats. Some species, such as the Superb Parrot and the Yellow subspecies of Crimson Rosella, are closely associated with this habitat throughout the year, although most of the parrots also venture into other habitats when not breeding. In the nesting season in the Murray area, which hosts various species as many birds share holes, you might expect to find Galah, Sulphur-crested Cockatoo, Crimson Rosella, Eastern Rosella, and Red-rumped Parrot. To the north around Cooper Creek in far sw. Queensland, this parrot assemblage would be joined by Red-winged Parrot, Bourke's Parrot, Australian Ringneck, Greater Bluebonnet, and thousands upon thousands of Budgerigars. With this many parrots, it is no surprise that raptors concentrate in these areas as well; Brown Goshawk, Australian Hobby, Brown Falcon, and the very rare Grey Falcon all hunt birds here.

The abundance of tree hollows makes Inland Riverine Woodland an important habitat for nesting parrots. Superb Parrot is the poster child for this habitat in se. Australia. © BEN KNOOT

Although this is a riverine environment, fish-eating kingfishers such as the Azure Kingfisher are found only on the eastern edge of this habitat's range; elsewhere they are replaced by Sacred and Red-backed Kingfishers, generalists that feed more on insects and reptiles. Although waterbirds and marshland birds don't feed in these woodlands, some nest in trees along the river edge, which are often filled with Australasian Darter and Little Black, Little Pied, and Great Cormorants.

Mammals typical of less arid regions extend into the drier parts of Australia along these river-fringing woodlands. Species found in this habitat west of the bulk of their range include Koala, Swamp Wallaby, Common Ringtail Possum, Common Brushtail Possum, and even Rakali, an aquatic rodent. Short-beaked Echidna, Eastern Grey Kangaroo, and Red Kangaroo all occur in Inland Riverine Woodland, sometimes erupting into near-plague proportions.

Lizards include Eastern Bearded Dragon (*Pogona barbata*), Lace Monitor (*Varanus varius*), Sand Goanna (*Varanus gouldii*), Eastern Tree Dtella (*Gehyra versicolor*), Robust Ctenotus (*Ctenotus robustus*), Southern Marbled Gecko (*Christinus marmoratus*), and Thick-tailed Barking Gecko

Inland Riverine Woodland is used by a variety of cavity nesters, such as Sacred Kingfisher.
© IAIN CAMPBELL, TROPICAL BIRDING TOURS/UNSW E&ERC

(*Underwoodisaurus milii*). Snakes include Carpet Python (*Morelia spilota*), Red-bellied Black Snake (*Pseudechis porphyriacus*), and Eastern Brown Snake (*Pseudonaja textilis*).

As expected, amphibians are much more common in these woodlands than in the surrounding arid lands, and species include Spotted Marsh Frog (*Limnodynastes tasmaniensis*), Peron's Laughing Tree Frog (*Litoria peronii*), Giant Banjo Frog (*Limnodynastes interioris*), and Barking Frog (*Limnodynastes fletcheri*).

CONSERVATION: Many of the forests along Australia's biggest rivers were removed for farming when Europeans first arrived in Australia's interior. The towns that grew along the rivers were built from these trees. Much of what is left of the River Red Gum forests is supposedly protected from further logging, but clearing of the box woodlands farther from the river continues for crop cultivation.

DISTRIBUTION: Inland Riverine Woodland is found throughout most of arid and semiarid Australia from the western slopes of the Great Dividing Range in the east through the central deserts of Australia in ribbons following the inland rivers to c. Western Australia.

Au9I SHEOAK RIPARIAN FOREST

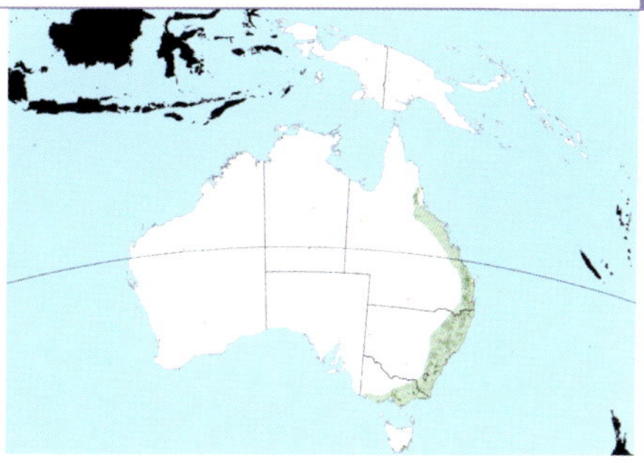

IN A NUTSHELL: Casuarina-dominated forest fringing rivers throughout the ranges of e. Australia. **Global Habitat Affinities:** Eastern Riparian Woodland subhabitat of NEARCTIC TEMPERATE DECIDUOUS FOREST; MEDITERRANEAN RIPARIAN FOREST. **Continental Habitat Affinities:** Sheoak Woodland subhabitat of MIXED SANDPLAIN WOODLAND. **Species Overlap:** IRONBARK-BOX WOODLAND; GRASSY DRY SCLEROPHYLL FOREST; HEATHY DRY SCLEROPHYLL FOREST. **Full Bird Assemblage:** habitatsoftheworld.org/Au9I.

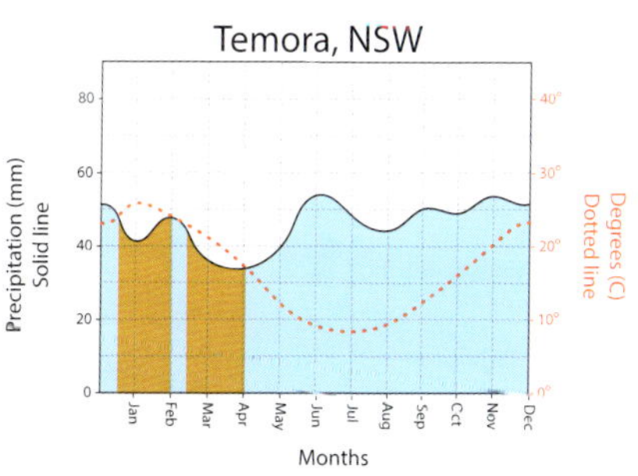

DESCRIPTION: Sheoak Riparian Forest is a habitat of very limited extent spread over a vast area of e. Australia along the creeks of the Great Dividing Range, and exists as a mélange within the surrounding habitats, sharing the wildlife that passes through. Care should be taken not to confuse this habitat with thicker patches of sheoaks within WALLUM AND AUSBOS; upon initial impression, they are similar, but Sheoak Riparian Forest is associated with different dry sclerophyll forests, not heathlands or wetlands.

This is an azonal habitat with regards to temperature, found from n. Queensland to Victoria, in climates ranging from tropical, with a hot, wet summer and cool, dry winter (Köppen **Aw**), to temperate continental, with a warm summer and cool winter (Köppen **Cfb**). The rainfall range is fairly narrow, from 40 in. (1000 mm) per year in the northern forests to 21 in. (540 mm) in the south, whereas the average minimum temperature ranges from a mild 64°F (18°C) in the north to 32°F (0°C) in the south.

Sheoak Riparian Forest tends to form on sandy lithosols on the edge of gullies and on sandy alluvial soils on the gully floor; on wider valley floors, this habitat is replaced by GRASSY DRY SCLEROPHYLL FOREST or HEATHY DRY SCLEROPHYLL FOREST, and where the soils are nutrient-rich, the casuarinas are replaced by eucalypts forming temperate IRONBARK-BOX WOODLAND. In contrast to INLAND RIVERINE WOODLAND and MELALEUCA RIVERINE FOREST, which are both hydromorphic, obtaining most of their moisture through the river systems on which they grow,

Sheoak Riparian Forest forms distinct ribbons through other habitats such as Heathy Dry Sclerophyll Forest. © IAIN CAMPBELL, TROPICAL BIRDING TOURS/UNSW E&ERC

Sheoak Riparian Forest is also heavily influenced by local rainfall so is semi-hydromorphic; this may seem an esoteric distinction, but it means that where Inland Riverine Woodland and Melaleuca Riverine Forest can have extremely sharp boundaries with their surrounding habitats, Sheoak Riparian Forest usually merges, with a nebulous ecotone, into surrounding habitats such as HEATHY DRY SCLEROPHYLL FOREST. On the western edge of the habitat range, it merges with and is replaced by Inland Riverine Woodland, whereas in the north of Australia, melaleucas become more dominant and the habitat merges with Melaleuca Riverine Forest.

The structure of Sheoak Riparian Forest varies from the odd casuarina along the edge of a creek to closed-canopy forests hundreds of yards (metres) wide. The canopy, which tends to be around 60–90 ft. (20–30 m) in height, is dominated by River Sheoak (*Casuarina cunninghamiana*), with its long spiny leaves that look like the quills of a Southern Cassowary; eucalypts such as Forest Red Gum (*Eucalyptus tereticornis*), Yellow Box (*E. melliodora*), or River Red Gum (*E. camaldulensis*); and Rough-barked Apple (*Angophora floribunda*). Black Tea Tree (*Melaleuca bracteata*) also occurs in the canopy, and the subcanopy is dominated by other melaleucas such as River Paperbark (*Melaleuca fluviatilis*) and Weeping Tea Tree (*Melaleuca leucadendra*). One of the most important members of the plant assemblage for birds is Needle-leaf Mistletoe, aka Sheoak Mistletoe (*Amyema cambagei*); this parasite is commonly found growing on River Sheoak and has a leaf structure that mimics the host, but it has flowers that produce prolific amounts of nectar when they bloom between winter and early summer. This habitat usually has a dense shrubby layer around 6–20 ft. (2–6 m) tall with species such as Grey Myrtle (*Backhousia myrtifolia*),

Regent Honeyeater is an endangered bird that spends most of its time in open eucalypt forests and woodlands but uses this habitat to breed. Almost all wild individuals are banded. © ROB HYNSON

Lightwood (*Acacia implexa*), Tree Violet (*Melicytus dentatus*), Australian Blackthorn (*Bursaria spinosa*), Sweet Bursaria (*Bursaria spinosa* subsp. *spinosa*), and many tea-tree species such as Tantoon (*Leptospermum polygalifolium*). In the western part of the range, the shrub layer can be sparser and contain chenopods such as Berry Saltbush (*Atriplex semibaccata*) along with other dryland shrubs such as River Bottlebrush (*Callistemon sieberi*). Because the creeks have intermittent but very severe flash flooding, the ground layer is often composed of alluvial gravels and sands devoid of vegetation. In areas where there is some soil development, grasses, many forbs, and very small shrubs form a ground cover.

WILDLIFE: For the most part, this habitat occurs as a mélange with surrounding habitats, so the wildlife assemblage usually mirrors those habitats. However, the Regent Honeyeater is a critically endangered bird that mainly lives in HEATHY DRY SCLEROPHYLL FOREST and GRASSY DRY SCLEROPHYLL FOREST but has a very strong preference to nest in Sheoak Riparian Forest. The Regent Honeyeater's nesting usually coincides with the blooming of Needle-leaf Mistletoe, though the birds need to augment their diet by feeding on surrounding trees from the nearby sclerophyll forests, especially Mugga Ironbark (*Eucalyptus sideroxylon*). Yellow Thornbill

Yellow Thornbill feeds on *Casuarina* and *Allocasuarina* trees so is very often found in this habitat. © JUN MATSUI, SICKLEBILL SAFARIS

Glossy Black-Cockatoo feeds almost exclusively on the cones of a handful of casuarina tree species, which are found within Sheoak Riparian Forest. © SAM WOODS, TROPICAL BIRDING TOURS

also shows a strong preference for this habitat over surrounding forests, and Yellow-tufted and White-cheeked Honeyeaters are also present. Through most of its distribution, the endangered Glossy Black-Cockatoo shows a preference for this habitat and can often be heard crunching on *Casuarina* seedpods.

CONSERVATION: Given the importance of this habitat for the nesting success and long-term survival of the Regent Honeyeater, it is astonishing that it is not regarded as a critical ecosystem worthy of strict protection in regions where the honeyeater could nest, but there is no more protection in New South Wales than there is of the much more common HEATHY DRY SCLEROPHYLL FOREST.

DISTRIBUTION: Sheoak Riparian Forest occurs in e. Australia from the western edge of the Atherton Tableland near Cairns, Queensland, south to n. Victoria. It is most widespread on the western slope of the Great Dividing Range but exists on some coastal drainage rivers, especially in the Hunter River valley and Blue Mountains of New South Wales.

WHERE TO SEE: Capertee Valley, New South Wales; Ravenshoe, Queensland, Australia.

Au9J SUBALPINE EUCALYPT WOODLAND

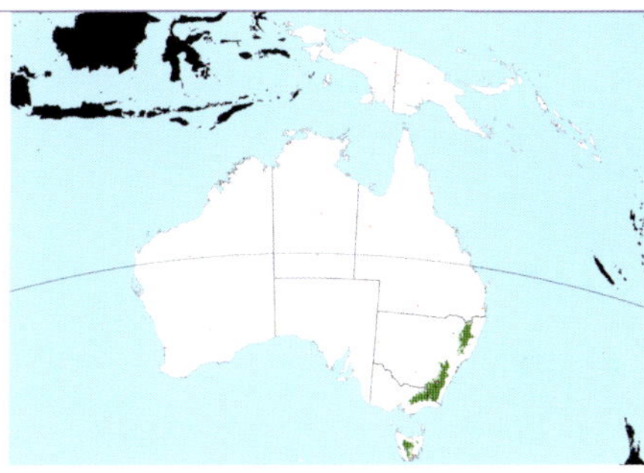

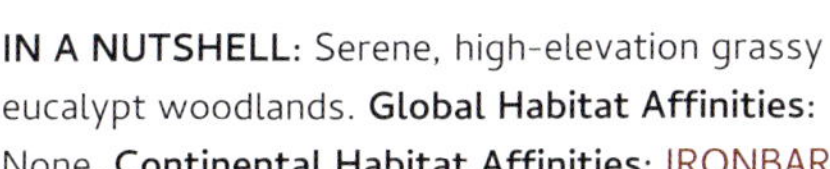

IN A NUTSHELL: Serene, high-elevation grassy eucalypt woodlands. **Global Habitat Affinities:** None. **Continental Habitat Affinities:** IRONBARK-BOX WOODLAND; GRASSY WET SCLEROPHYLL FOREST. **Species Overlap:** MONTANE HEATHLAND; IRONBARK-BOX WOODLAND; GRASSY WET SCLEROPHYLL FOREST. **Full Bird Assemblage:** habitatsoftheworld.org/Au9J.

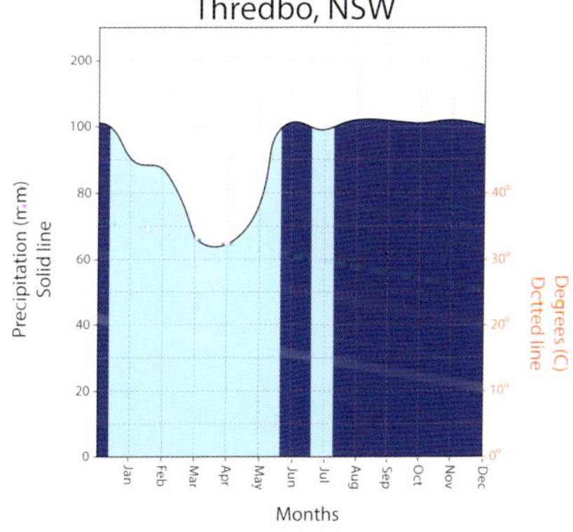

DESCRIPTION: Standing in Subalpine Eucalypt Woodland near the tree line of the Snowy Mountains (New South Wales) or highland Tasmania, you may be enveloped by a sense of tranquillity amidst the raw natural beauty. This habitat is at the higher end of the forest zone and differs from any other Australian habitat. Because it remains evergreen through the winter, it is also unlike most other temperate broadleaf habitats around the world. The forest can form as low as 1000 ft. (300 m) in Tasmania but much higher farther north, such as in New South Wales, where it forms at around 3000–6000 ft. (1000–1850 m). Temperature is a major driver of these woodlands, and the higher examples survive in areas with as many as 120 days of frost per year. The climate is generally oceanic continental (Köppen **Cfb**), although Subalpine Eucalypt Woodlands occur in a wide precipitation range, from semiarid conditions

Expanses of this habitat can be accessed in Kosciuszko National Park, New South Wales. © INNA OSMOLOVSKY/UNSW E&ERC

Snowfall is common in Subalpine Eucalypt Woodland through the winter months, and the intricate colours of Snow Gum bark are even more stunning against the white backdrop than shown here. © INNA OSMOLOVSKY/UNSW E&ERC

with a rainfall of 27 in. (600 mm) to extremely wet environments receiving 83 in. (2100 mm) per year.

The structure of Subalpine Eucalypt Woodland varies from open grassy forest to open grassy woodland, generally with a mid-dense to open crown cover. Some are tall open forests of Brown Barrel (*Eucalyptus fastigata*) and Mountain Gum (*Eucalyptus dalrympleana*), growing to 150 ft. (45 m), with a subcanopy of Snow Gum (*Eucalyptus pauciflora*), while others are shorter open woodlands of Snow Gum joined by Black Sallee (*Eucalyptus stellulata*), Ribbon Gum (*Eucalyptus rubida*), and Jounama Snow Gum (*Eucalyptus debeuzevillei*). At the extremes of the tree line, Snow Gum and Black Sallee, with their smooth, multicolour bark, can take on a twisted, pachycaulesque shape (reminiscent of the high pines of the Rocky Mountains of North America) and may become wind-sheared, leaning leeward, away from the dominant wind direction, and taking on a lopsided, krummholz form. The small tree and shrub understorey can be dominated by acacias such as Silver Wattle (*Acacia dealbata*) and Australian Blackwood (*Acacia melanoxylon*) and other sclerophyllous shrubs such as Small-fruit Hakea (*Hakea macrocarpa*), Lance Beard-Heath (*Leucopogon lanceolatus*), and Mountain Beard-Heath (*Acrothamnus hookeri*). In some locations this subalpine woodland merges into the surrounding MONTANE HEATHLAND and has a grass- and forb-rich ground cover, rather than a heath cover, dominated by grasses such as *Poa* species. Snow Grass (*Poa sieberiana*), near ubiquitous in this habitat, is joined by many other 'snow grasses' as well as ferns such as Austral Bracken (*Pteridium esculentum*).

The trees of Subalpine Eucalypt Woodland can be stunted and resemble mallees, with multiple branches rising from a common point low in the trunk, or they can be single-trunked. © INNA OSMOLOVSKY/UNSW E&ERC

WILDLIFE: Subalpine Eucalypt Woodlands do not hold many special bird species and are best viewed as a depauperate version of lower-elevation IRONBARK-BOX WOODLAND. From a bird assemblage perspective, this habitat may be classified as a combination of a few high-elevation woodland species and a limited number of ALPINE TUNDRA birds. The only real indicator species in these woodlands is the Gang-gang Cockatoo of se. Australia. It is surprising that the extensive uplands of Tasmania do not really have any special birds—only Scrubtit might be a candidate for classification as a subalpine bird, and that is a stretch.

Australian Subalpine Eucalypt Woodlands play a different role in bird migration than subalpine habitats in the Northern Hemisphere,

The unobtrusive Gang-gang Cockatoo is an indicator species for Subalpine Eucalypt Woodland in se. Australia. © SAM WOODS, TROPICAL BIRDING TOURS

In Tasmania, the dazzling Flame Robin migrates up into Subalpine Eucalypt Woodland to breed. © IAIN CAMPBELL, TROPICAL BIRDING TOURS/UNSW E&ERC

where NORTH AMERICAN HIGH-ELEVATION PINE WOODLANDS are visited by Neotropical migrants from Central and South America, and EUROPEAN MONTANE SPRUCE-FIR FOREST is visited by sub-Saharan migrants from tropical Africa. Here, in stark contrast, the summer migrants are mainly short-distance, north–south migrants from other parts of Australia or local migrants from lower elevations, arriving for the summer months when the snow melts and most plants bloom.

These local movers and some longer-distance migrant honeyeaters are very important in this habitat, though on the mainland some nectivorous species are resident and do overwinter here, such as Yellow-faced, Brown-headed, White-eared, and Crescent Honeyeaters, plus Red Wattlebird and Eastern Spinebill. In Tasmania, local elevational migrants include Crescent

Honeyeater and Yellow Wattlebird, and rarely Strong-billed Honeyeater and New Holland Honeyeater, the last of which avoids this habitat on mainland Australia. Black-headed Honeyeater is a Tasmanian endemic species that has displayed an interesting elevational movement, having been recorded in this habitat more often in winter than in summer, for no obvious reason.

It is not only blossom nomads that visit Subalpine Eucalypt Woodlands in summer. There are many raptors, including Black-shouldered Kite, Wedge-tailed Eagle, Swamp Harrier, Collared Sparrowhawk, Australian Hobby, and Brown Falcon. In Tasmania, Flame Robin arrives in a huge influx, becoming one of the most common insectivores in the habitat, and although some Olive Whistlers overwinter, their numbers are augmented by local elevational migrants and some birds crossing the Bass Strait from mainland Australia to breed here. Many species avoid this habitat in Tasmania in the winter months, but some resident species include Yellow-tailed Black-Cockatoo, Sulphur-crested Cockatoo, Green Rosella, Superb Fairywren, Tasmanian Scrubwren, Scrubtit, Tasmanian Thornbill, Yellow-throated Honeyeater, Olive Whistler, and Black Currawong. On the mainland, overwintering species include Yellow-tailed Black-Cockatoo, Crimson Rosella, Superb Lyrebird, White-throated Treecreeper, White-browed Scrubwren, Brown Thornbill, Striated Thornbill, Grey Shrikethrush, Pied Currawong, Grey Currawong, and Little Raven.

Mammals present in both the mainland and Tasmania may include Short-beaked Echidna, Bare-nosed Wombat, Red-necked Wallaby, Common Brushtail Possum, and Common Ringtail Possum. Rufous-bellied Pademelon and Tasmanian Dusky Antechinus may join them in Tasmania. Reptiles present in Tasmania may include Ocellated Coolskink (*Carinascincus ocellatus*), Metallic Coolskink (*Carinascincus metallicus*), Boulder Coolskink (*Carinascincus microlepidotus*), and Tiger Snake (*Notechis scutatus*). Mainland Subalpine Eucalypt Woodland may have Southern Grass Skink (*Pseudemoia entrecasteauxii*), Tussock Skink (*Pseudemoia pagenstecheri*), Southern Water Skink (*Eulamprus tympanum*), and Highlands Copperhead (*Austrelaps ramsayi*). The habitat's amphibians include Southern Brood Frog (*Pseudophryne semimarmorata*) on Tasmania and Common Eastern Froglet (*Crinia signifera*) on the mainland.

CONSERVATION: Subalpine Eucalypt Woodland faces significant conservation issues. Being at the upper edge of the forest zone, it is threatened by rising temperatures and increased frequency and intensity of bushfires, consequences of climate change. Most of these woodlands have been cleared since European colonisation, and most of those remaining have been infested with invasive weeds, such as Sheep Sorrel (*Acetosella vulgaris*), White Clover (*Trifolium repens*), and Spear Thistle (*Cirsium vulgare*), planted to create 'improved' pastures. Feral animals such as the Brumby (wild horse) pose a threat to the habitat, but eradication is difficult because they are so charismatic.

DISTRIBUTION: In mainland Australia, this habitat is limited, occurring along the Great Dividing Range and in the Snowy Mountains of New South Wales. It is very widespread through the highlands of Tasmania and even close to the coast near Hobart at Mt. Wellington.

WHERE TO SEE: Mt. Kosciuszko, New South Wales, Australia; Mt. Buffalo, Victoria, Australia; Mt. Wellington, Tasmania, Australia.

Au9K INLAND ROCKY SHRUBBY WOODLAND

IN A NUTSHELL: A scrubby mallee-form woodland formed on outcrops and ridgelines with a mix of cypress-pines, wattles, and sheoaks. **Global Habitat Affinities:** CARRASCO CAATINGA; EAST DECCAN EVERGREEN SCRUB. **Continental Habitat Affinities:** MIXED SANDPLAIN WOODLAND; HEATHY DRY SCLEROPHYLL FOREST. **Species Overlap:** MIXED SANDPLAIN WOODLAND; HEATHY DRY SCLEROPHYLL FOREST; SHRUBBY AND CHENOPOD MALLEE. **Full Bird Assemblage:** habitatsoftheworld.org/Au9K.

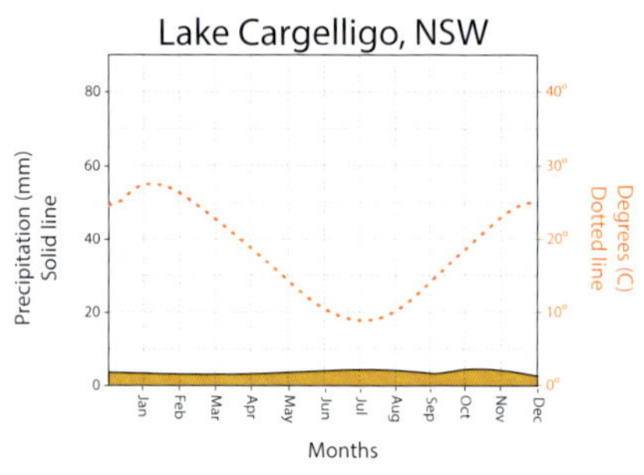

DESCRIPTION: This habitat comprises the woodlands and shrublands that form on the rocky outcrops and ridgelines in the semiarid temperate parts of Australia. There is a fair amount of variety among them, and they are under-visited habitat because no specific bird or mammal species are restricted to them. They tend to form on felsic (lighter-colour) rocks that contain minerals such as quartz, feldspar, and mica. These rocks include igneous rocks such as granite and granodiorite, highly siliceous metamorphic rocks such as gneiss or quartzite, or sedimentary rocks such as quartzitic sandstone. The reason for this association between vegetation and rock type is twofold: first, these rocks are the most resistant to chemical and mechanical weathering; second, these rocks are felsic, so usually are high in silica and aluminium, with significant amounts of potassium and sodium, while the less resistant mafic (dark-mineral) rocks such as basalt tend to be rich in magnesium, iron, and calcium and have a lower silica content and therefore are dominated by minerals such as pyroxene, olivine, and plagioclase feldspar. So, when soils develop on the basalts or on alluvial clays, they promote other habitats such as MIXED SANDPLAIN WOODLAND, GRASSY MULGA, or IRONBARK-BOX WOODLAND rather than this Inland Rocky Shrubby Woodland.

The woodland can be closed to open and is always shrubby; the tree assemblage changes with lithology (rock type) and soil type, although it is almost always a matrix of eucalypts, *Acacia* spp., and *Callitris* spp. in varying percentages. On the ridgetops, the soils are generally poorly sorted, well-drained, sandy lithosols, with very little soil-profile development and lacking the nutrients required by most plants. The resulting habitat is stunted, with a canopy rarely exceeding 30 ft. (10 m) tall, dominated by species such as Grey Mallee (*Eucalyptus morrisii*), Dwyer's Red Gum (*Eucalyptus dwyeri*), Gum Coolabah (*Eucalyptus intertexta*), Black Cypress-Pine (*Callitris endlicheri*), and less often White Cypress-Pine (*Callitris glaucophylla*). Mulga (*Acacia aneura*) and

Inland Rocky Shrubby Woodland is often in dramatic locations on the sides and tops of rocky ridges. © IAIN CAMPBELL, TROPICAL BIRDING TOURS/UNSW E&ERC

Currawang (*Acacia doratoxylon*) occur in areas with slightly higher iron content in the soil, such as zones with relict lateritic pisolites or zones of relatively recent ferricrete formation.

The understorey and shrub layers are usually limited on the ridgetops and dominated by acacias such as Stringybark Wattle (*Acacia linearifolia*), Dead Finish (*Acacia tetragonophylla*), Streaked Wattle (*Acacia lineata*), and Prickly Wattle (*Acacia paradoxa*). Drooping Sheoak (*Allocasuarina verticillata*), Crimson Turkey Bush (*Eremophila latrobei*), and Seven Dwarfs Grevillea (*Grevillea floribunda*) can form thickets that make walking through the woodland difficult. Much of the ground is either bare rock outcrop or strewn with large boulders, so it is surprising that spinifex grasses (*Triodia* spp.) are rare here; they are replaced by bunchgrasses such as *Austrostipa densiflora*, Bristly Wallaby Grass (*Rytidosperma setaceum*), and various three-awns and wiregrasses (*Aristida* spp.).

On the sides of the hills, the canopy can comprise taller thickets (reaching 40 ft./12 m) of Black Cypress-Pine (*Callitris endlicheri*), White Cypress-Pine (*Callitris glaucophylla*), Mugga Ironbark (*Eucalyptus sideroxylon*), Tumbledown Red Gum (*Eucalyptus dealbata*), Kurrajong (*Brachychiton populneus*), and Currawang (*Acacia doratoxylon*), and the habitat can start to resemble a HEATHY DRY SCLEROPHYLL FOREST. The understorey on these slopes ranges from very sparse to very thick with patches of young cypress-pines forming dense, almost impenetrable thickets where overgrazing has occurred. Where the cypress-pines are not concentrated, the other small trees and shrubs include Drooping Sheoak and the same ridgetop acacias described earlier. The smaller shrubs include Crimson Turkey Bush (*Eremophila latrobei*), Cough Bush (*Cassinia laevis*), Pinkwood (*Beyeria viscosa*), and Gaping Mint-Bush (*Prostanthera ringens*).

Summers in these semiarid woodlands (Köppen **Bsh**) are hot, with maximum temperatures sometimes surpassing 100°F (38°C). Winter maximum temperatures typically range from 57 to 68°F (14–20°C), with nighttime temperatures dropping to near freezing 32°F (0°C). Most of this habitat straddles the winter-rain/summer-rain boundary, so rainfall is fairly evenly distributed throughout the year. The annual rainfall ranges between 12 and 24 in. (300–600 mm), with the northern areas getting more rain in summer, and the south more rain in winter.

WILDLIFE: Because this habitat has no obligate bird species, it is relatively under-birded, and that is a shame, because it has a fascinating bird assemblage that is a mix of species from very different habitats. It seems incongruous to have ground birds of mallee habitats, such as Shy Heathwren, along with ground birds more typical of BRIGALOW, such as Speckled Warbler. Nectivorous birds feature heavily, with inland honeyeaters such as Spiny-cheeked Honeyeater; more coastal species such as Red Wattlebird, White-plumed Honeyeater, Brown-headed Honeyeater, and Striped Honeyeater; and honeyeaters more typical of the mallee habitats such as Yellow-plumed and

The cypress-pines within Inland Rocky Shrubby Woodland hold a diverse mix of thornbill species, including Chestnut-rumped Thornbill. © IAIN CAMPBELL, TROPICAL BIRDING TOURS/UNSW E&ERC

White-eared Honeyeaters. Thornbills are very well represented, with Weebill, Inland Thornbill, Chestnut-rumped Thornbill, and Buff-rumped Thornbill all found throughout the habitat, and Yellow Thornbill concentrated in the cypress-pines. White-browed, Masked, and Black-faced Woodswallows can often be seen overhead. Robins are not well represented, as nearby species such as Hooded Robin, Scarlet Robin, and Flame Robin avoid this habitat and instead are replaced by Eastern Yellow Robin, more typical of more easterly habitats, and Red-capped Robin, more typical of mulga habitats. Other insectivorous birds expected here include Spotted Pardalote, Striated Pardalote, Western Gerygone, Rufous Whistler, and Jacky-winter. Parrots are not as common as in surrounding IRONBARK-BOX WOODLAND, but Turquoise Parrot can be surprisingly numerous in this habitat.

Mammals are mainly generalists in this part of the country and move from these woodlands in very dry periods to habitats such as MIXED SANDPLAIN WOODLAND, which may have more available water. Among the typical macropods that commonly occur here are Eastern Grey Kangaroo, Swamp Wallaby, and Common Wallaroo, while Western Grey Kangaroo and Red Kangaroo are less abundant.

Lizards of the Inland Rocky Shrubby Woodlands include widespread species with

This habitat could be viewed as a temperate, heathy analogy of the Rocky Spinifex Desert and Spinifex Eucalypt Savanna habitats that occur atop sandstone escarpments of tropical Australia. © GABRIEL CAMPBELL, TROPICAL BIRDING TOURS

When extensive blooms are present, flocks of White-browed Woodswallows move into the area, sometimes mixed in with Masked Woodswallows. © SAM WOODS, TROPICAL BIRDING TOURS

catholic habitat choices such as Lace Monitor (*Varanus varius*), Sand Goanna (*Varanus gouldii*), Nobbi Dragon (*Diporiphora nobbi*), Eastern Bearded Dragon (*Pogona barbata*), and Tree Skink (*Egernia striolata*), and more habitat-restricted species such as Robust Ctenotus (*Ctenotus robustus*), Southeastern Morethia Skink (*Morethia boulengeri*), Thick-tailed Barking Gecko (*Underwoodisaurus milii*), and Eastern Stone Gecko (*Diplodactylus vittatus*). Snakes expected include Carpet Python (*Morelia spilota*), Yellow-faced Whipsnake (*Demansia psammophis*), and Shield-snouted Brown Snake (*Pseudonaja aspidorhyncha*). Amphibians are not common in this very dry habitat, but some species are common along creek lines such as Giant Banjo Frog (*Limnodynastes interioris*), Barking Frog (*Limnodynastes fletcheri*), and Spotted Marsh Frog (*Limnodynastes tasmaniensis*).

CONSERVATION: Because Inland Rocky Shrubby Woodland forms on such poor soils in rugged terrain, it has been spared the clearing that has devastated IRONBARK-BOX WOODLAND. However, it does suffer from overgrazing, especially from wild goats, and the goat numbers can at times appear inconceivably large. Changes to the understorey have already occurred, and without some measures, many plants in the woodlands will be replaced by less palatable shrubs and trees such as Black Cypress-Pine.

DISTRIBUTION: Inland Rocky Shrubby Woodland is concentrated in w. New South Wales, although it occurs from s. Queensland south to w. Victoria in locations such as the Grampians region.

WHERE TO SEE: Gundabooka National Park, New South Wales, Australia; Cocoparra National Park, New South Wales, Australia.

Although the Euro (a subspecies of Common Wallaroo) is one of a group of macropods found in a variety of habitats through c. Australia, it is the dominant kangaroo in this habitat. © IAIN CAMPBELL, TROPICAL BIRDING TOURS/UNSW E&ERC

Au9L MIXED SANDPLAIN WOODLAND

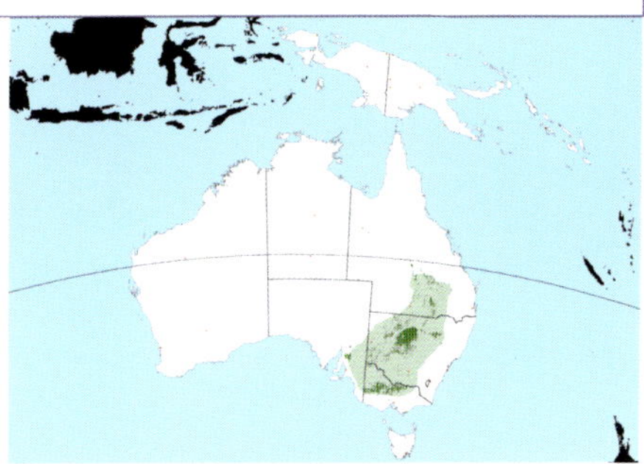

IN A NUTSHELL: The mixed eucalypt, cypress-pine, sheoak, and acacia woodlands of semiarid Australia. **Global Habitat Affinities:** AFRICAN MOPANE; DRY CHACO; CASPIAN RIPARIAN SCRUB. **Continental Habitat Affinities:** YILGARN MIXED WOODLAND; INLAND ROCKY SHRUBBY WOODLAND; BRIGALOW. **Species Overlap:** INLAND ROCKY SHRUBBY WOODLAND; BRIGALOW; GRASSY MULGA; and HEATHY DRY SCLEROPHYLL FOREST. **Full Bird Assemblage:** habitatsoftheworld.org/Au9L.

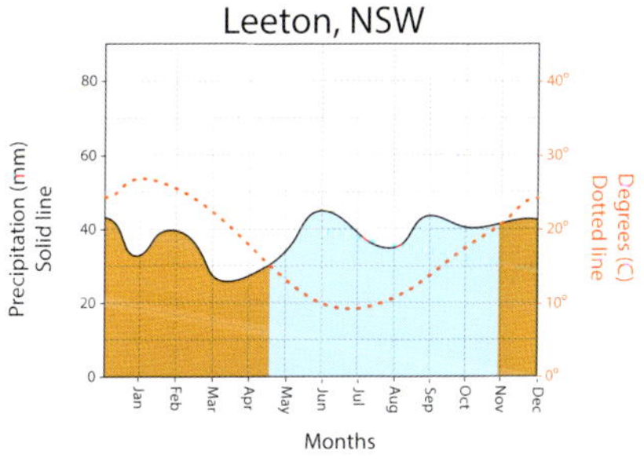

DESCRIPTION: These are mixed semiarid woodlands with a matrix of eucalypt, *Acacia*, *Callitris*, *Casuarina*, and *Allocasuarina* spp. in varying percentages. The habitat always looks messy and irregular with pronounced variations in canopy height, thickness, and species makeup over very small areas.

The woodland can be closed to open with a canopy ranging from 30 to 75 ft. (10–25 m) tall and dominated by species such as Bimble Box (*Eucalyptus populnea* subsp. *bimbil*), Pilliga Box (*Eucalyptus pilligaensis*), Gum Coolabah (*Eucalyptus intertexta*), Silver-leaved Ironbark (*Eucalyptus melanophloia*), and White Cypress-Pine (*Callitris glaucophylla*). The subcanopy is much more varied, with acacias such as Mulga (*Acacia aneura*) and Doodlallie (*Acacia excelsa*), as well as Buloke (*Allocasuarina luehmannii*), Wilga (*Geijera parviflora*), and Whitewood (*Atalaya hemiglauca*). *Eremophila* spp., which are incredibly important plants for blossom nomads, also feature strongly in the understorey, with large shrubs and small trees such as Bastard Sandalwood (*Eremophila mitchellii*), Tar Bush (*Eremophila glabra*), and Weeping Emu Bush (*Eremophila longifolia*) all attracting birds when in bloom.

Chenopods, such as Small-leaf Bluebush (*Maireana microphylla*), Cotton Bush (*Ptilotus obovatus*), Galvanised Burr (*Sclerolaena birchii*), and Spear-fruit Copperburr (*Sclerolaena patenticuspis*), are often a dominant component of the shrub layer and ground cover. This shrub layer can be so dense that walking through the woodland is difficult, or it can be very sparse, with many grasses and forbs covering the ground. When cleared or overgrazed, the regrowth may result in a thickening of plant growth and an intense concentration of White Cypress-Pine (eventually becoming Callitris Woodland subhabitat; see below), at the expense of other plants in the understorey, which severely reduces the woodland's biodiversity.

From the air, the bare areas between trees are clearly visible in Mixed Sandplain Woodland. In dry years, these can be devoid of grasses or forbs. © GABRIEL CAMPBELL, TROPICAL BIRDING TOURS

This semiarid habitat (Köppen **Bsh**) straddles the winter-rain/summer-rain boundary, so the annual rainfall of 12–24 in. (300–600 mm) is somewhat evenly distributed throughout the year, but there is a slight peak during late summer in northerly areas and in the winter months in southerly areas. Rain in the north is concentrated in summer thunderstorms, while in the south it is in slow-

moving drizzle over days. Summers are very hot, with maximums usually exceeding 95°F (35°C) and occasionally surpassing 104°F (40°C). Winter maximum temperatures typically range from 59 to 68°F (15–20°C), while nighttime temperatures can drop to around 41°F (5°C).

Mixed Sandplain Woodlands are concentrated on the sandy or loamy soils formed on broad alluvial and colluvial plains in a matrix with other habitats, depending on local soils and landforms. Nearby areas with very poor, sandy soils tend to have mallee habitats such as SPINIFEX MALLEE; the rocky outcrops tend to have INLAND ROCKY SHRUBBY WOODLAND; clay-rich soils have

Callitris (or Cypress-Pine) Woodlands are examples of Mixed Sandplain Woodland dominated by stands of *Callitris* spp. with a minor eucalypt component.
© IAIN CAMPBELL, TROPICAL BIRDING TOURS/UNSW E&ERC

GRASSY MULGA; and the gilgai soils have CHENOPOD SHRUBLAND.

Sheoak Woodland is a subhabitat of Mixed Sandplain Woodland that is dominated by *Allocasuarina* and *Casuarina* spp. (sheoaks), with only a minor presence of other species. In e. Australia, the dominant sheoak is Belah (*Casuarina cristata*), which forms low woodlands, 30–60 ft. (10–20 m) tall, occasionally with Kurrajong (*Brachychiton populneus*), Western Rosewood (*Alectryon oleifolius*), and White Cypress-Pine. In the Eyre Peninsula of South Australia, the subhabitat is dominated by Drooping Sheoak (*Allocasuarina verticillata*). The understorey is very similar to that of the typical Mixed Sandplain Woodland, with Mulga and Wilga, but tends to have many more chenopods such as Small-leaf Bluebush, Galvanised Burr, and the chenopod-like Bluebush Daisy (*Cratystylis conocephala*).

The **Callitris Woodland** subhabitat, dominated by White Cypress-Pine, can occur from infiltrations of other habitats after clearing or overgrazing, especially by goats, but under 'natural' conditions it occurs as open woodland that ranges from 30 to 75 ft. (10–25 m) in height. It often has a minor component of Buloke, Gum Coolabah, Bimble Box, Western Grey Box (*Eucalyptus macrocarpa*), and Kurrajong. Glossy-leaved Red Mallee (*Eucalyptus oleosa*) is regularly found in the woodland from extreme sw. New South Wales to South Australia. Bootlace Oak (*Hakea chordophylla*), Silver Senna (*Senna artemisioides*), and Australian Blackthorn (*Bursaria spinosa*) are

The woodlands usually have a mix of eucalypts and sheoaks but also contain many acacias.
© IAIN CAMPBELL, TROPICAL BIRDING TOURS/UNSW E&ERC

Callitris Woodland can form extensive stands, such as in the basin of Wilpena Pound, South Australia. © GABRIEL CAMPBELL, TROPICAL BIRDING TOURS

typical understorey shrubs. As with the Sheoak Woodland subhabitat, this woodland tends to form on slightly more nutrient-rich soils than the typical Mixed Sandplain Woodland.

WILDLIFE: Like the plant assemblage of Mixed Sandplain Woodland, the bird assemblage is a mixture of species from more humid regions and c. Australia, representing a variety of guilds (groups of bird species that feed in a similar way). The mix of eucalypt canopy trees and *Eremophila* understorey means that there are many nectivores and blossom nomads, including inland species such as Painted Honeyeater, Spiny-cheeked Honeyeater, Singing Honeyeater, Black Honeyeater, Striped Honeyeater, Masked Woodswallow, and White-browed Woodswallow, along with more coastal species such as Brown-headed Honeyeater and Little Friarbird.

Because Mixed Sandplain Woodlands have so many *Acacia*, *Callitris*, and *Allocasuarina* trees and shrubs, the bird assemblage also contains many insectivores, such as Black-eared Cuckoo, Horsfield's Bronze-Cuckoo, Pallid Cuckoo, Striated Pardalote, Weebill, Yellow Thornbill, Varied Sittella, Crested Bellbird, Rufous Whistler, Restless Flycatcher, and Red-capped Robin. Hooded Robin has had a recent massive population crash through most of its range, but the numbers in this habitat seem to be stable. There are also many insectivorous bird species in the shrubby understorey, such as White-browed Treecreeper, Brown Treecreeper, Chestnut-rumped Thornbill, Inland Thornbill, and Buff-rumped Thornbill. Three special Australian families found here are the gregarious babblers represented by

Painted Honeyeater is a blossom nomad that moves into habitats like Mixed Sandplain Woodland when there is an abundance of blooming flowers. © SAM WOODS, TROPICAL BIRDING TOURS

The combination of nectar-rich eucalyptus trees in the canopy and *Eremophila* bushes in the understorey makes Mixed Sandplain Woodland an excellent environment for nectivorous birds such as Striped Honeyeater. © BEN KNOOT

White-browed Babbler and Chestnut-crowned Babbler; the mud-nest builders, comprising the gregarious Apostlebird and White-winged Chough; and the fairywrens, with Purple-backed Fairywren and the absolutely exquisite, electric-blue Splendid Fairywren. Seed-eating and ground-feeding guilds are dominated by pigeons and parrots such as Common Bronzewing, Crested Pigeon, Peaceful Dove, Turquoise Parrot, Australian Ringneck, and Mulga Parrot.

The numerous bats found in this habitat include Little Broad-nosed Bat, Lesser Long-eared Bat, White-striped Free-tailed Bat, and Bristle-faced Free-tailed Bat, but they are unlikely to be stumbled upon serendipitously. Other nocturnal mammals include two small carnivorous marsupial mice, Fat-tailed Dunnart and Kultarr. This is the zone where Western Grey Kangaroo and Eastern Grey Kangaroo overlap, with the number changing in favour of the Western Grey Kangaroo west of Cobar, New South Wales. Red Kangaroo occurs in low numbers in this habitat but is sometimes found in areas with a chenopod understorey. Short-beaked Echidna is common.

Reptiles seem much more obvious in Mixed Sandplain Woodland, where the mixture of semiarid species includes the larger Lace Monitor (*Varanus varius*) and Sand Goanna (*Varanus gouldii*) and the smaller Central Bearded Dragon (*Pogona vitticeps*), Eastern Bearded Dragon (*Pogona barbata*), Nobbi Dragon (*Diporiphora nobbi*), Burns's Dragon (*Amphibolurus burnsi*), and Central Netted Dragon (*Ctenophorus nuchalis*). Shingleback (*Tiliqua rugosa*) is also found. Smaller lizards such as geckos are prevalent but much harder to find, being strictly nocturnal; they include Inland Marbled Velvet Gecko (*Oedura cincta*), Eastern Spiny-tailed Gecko (*Strophurus williamsi*), Eastern Stone Gecko (*Diplodactylus vittatus*), and Common Prickly Gecko (*Heteronotia binoei*). Surprisingly, some species that are much more typical of humid forests, such as Eastern Tree Dtella (*Gehyra versicolor*), can also be found in this habitat, though not in the nearby mallee areas.

There are the typical highly venomous snakes such as Shield-snouted Brown Snake (*Pseudonaja aspidorhyncha*), Ringed Brown Snake (*Pseudonaja modesta*), Blue-

White-browed Babbler is a highly social species that roams the understorey of Mixed Sandplain Woodland in noisy groups. © IAIN CAMPBELL, TROPICAL BIRDING TOURS/ UNSW E&ERC

There is plentiful food in Mixed Sandplain Woodland for ground-feeding, seed-eating birds such as Turquoise Parrot. © BEN KNOOT

bellied Black Snake (*Pseudechis guttatus*), and Mulga Snake (*Pseudechis australis*), as well as the less venomous but still dangerous Curl Snake (*Suta suta*). Despite the semiarid nature of Mixed Sandplain Woodlands, amphibians are notably common; species such as Desert Tree Frog (*Litoria rubella*), Desert Froglet (*Crinia deserticola*), Crucifix Spadefoot Frog (*Notaden bennettii*), Peron's Laughing Tree Frog (*Litoria peronii*), Broad-palmed Rocket Frog (*Litoria latopalmata*), and Ornate Burrowing Frog (*Platyplectrum ornatum*) are present.

The subhabitats **Callitris Woodland** and **Sheoak Woodland** have a very similar mammal assemblage, with species such as Yellow-footed Rock-Wallaby in the Wilpena Pound area (South Australia), along with more widespread species such as Western Grey Kangaroo, Red Kangaroo, Common Wallaroo, Short-beaked Echidna, and Common Brushtail Possum. Reptiles found in the Sheoak Woodland include Swift Rock Dragon (*Ctenophorus modestus*), Flinders Ranges Rock Skink (*Liopholis personata*), Thick-tailed Barking Gecko (*Underwoodisaurus milii*), Ranges Stone Gecko (*Diplodactylus furcosus*), Shingleback, Southeastern Morethia Skink (*Morethia boulengeri*), Tree Skink (*Egernia striolata*), Sand Goanna, and Carpet Python (*Morelia spilota*).

CONSERVATION: Because the typical Mixed Sandplain Woodland forms on such poor soils in semiarid regions, and because it generally has poor wood for intense forestry, it has been spared the widespread clearing of habitats such as GRASSY MULGA, BRIGALOW, and IRONBARK-BOX WOODLAND. However, these woodlands have been seriously overgrazed, and fire has been retarded, resulting in a thickening of the woodland in some locations, forming a 'scrub' dominated by dense stands of young White Cypress-Pine. Because the Sheoak Woodland subhabitat often forms on nutrient-rich soils, it has been cleared far more often, and the previously extensive Sheoak Woodlands of South Australia have been utterly destroyed.

DISTRIBUTION: Mixed Sandplain Woodlands are concentrated in wc. New South Wales, although they occur from s. Queensland down to n. and w. Victoria and se. SA. The Sheoak and Callitris subhabitats occur in pockets throughout that area, such as in Binya and Back Yamma State Forests in New South Wales, but both are more prevalent in South Australia, with Callitris Woodland forming forests in Wilpena Pound (east of the Flinders Ranges) while pathetically small remnants of Sheoak Woodland remain on the Eyre Peninsula. There is also Callitris Woodland east of the wheat belt in Western Australia, but it is an outlier with a bird assemblage very similar to the surrounding WESTERN EUCALYPT WOODLAND and is included in that habitat.

WHERE TO SEE: MIXED SANDPLAIN WOODLAND (typical)—Toorale National Park, New South Wales, and environs of Cobar, New South Wales, Australia; CALLITRIS WOODLAND—Wilpena Pound, South Australia, and Binya State Forest, New South Wales, Australia; SHEOAK WOODLAND—Binya State Forest and Back Yamma State Forest, New South Wales, Australia, and Eyre Peninsula, South Australia.

Au9M HEATHY MALLEE

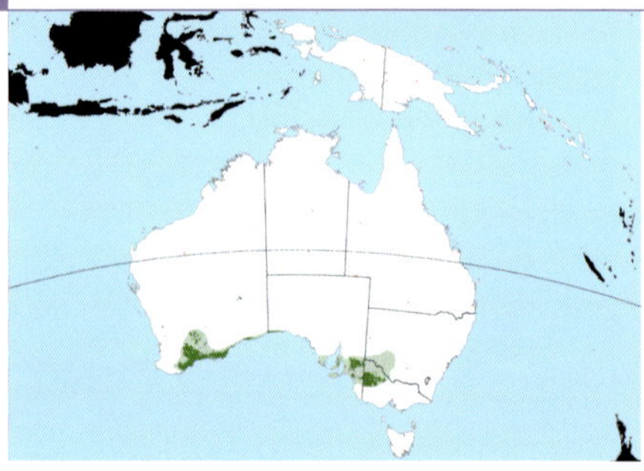

IN A NUTSHELL: A combination of heathy understorey, with plants of the family Proteaceae, and a low, dry, uniform woodland of mallee-form eucalypts (with most branches sprouting from the tree base). **Global Habitat Affinities:** SERTÃO CAATINGA. **Continental Habitat Affinities:** SHRUBBY AND CHENOPOD MALLEE; ARID HEATHLAND. **Species Overlap:** SHRUBBY AND CHENOPOD MALLEE; SPINIFEX MALLEE; ARID HEATHLAND; WESTERN EUCALYPT WOODLAND; WALLUM AND AUSBOS. **Full Bird Assemblage:** habitatsoftheworld.org/Au9M.

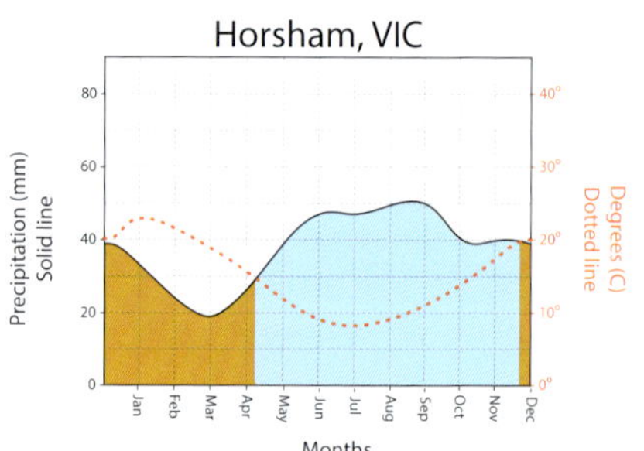

DESCRIPTION: The other two mallee habitats described in this book (SHRUBBY AND CHENOPOD MALLEE and SPINIFEX MALLEE) are distinctly Australian habitats and will feel alien to anyone visiting for the first time. Heathy Mallee, however, could easily be regarded as a broad, nebulous ecotone between these mallees and Australian heathland habitats such as WALLUM AND AUSBOS, of which there are global analogies, such as the AFRICAN FYNBOS for Ausbos and AFRICAN

The understorey of Heathy Mallee contains very few eucalypts and is dominated by heathland plants. © IAIN CAMPBELL, TROPICAL BIRDING TOURS/UNSW E&ERC

Heathy Mallee can merge with Arid Heathland in a mélange or nebulous boundary with a broad ecotone. Here, with many of the heathland plants in an open mallee canopy, the distinction between the two habitats is difficult to discern. © IAIN CAMPBELL, TROPICAL BIRDING TOURS/UNSW E&ERC

STRANDVELD for Wallum; because this ecotone is so widespread and contains distinctive wildlife, it is treated as a distinct habitat, Heathy Mallee.

The canopy is eucalypt-dominated low woodland, mainly from 9–12 ft. (3–4 m) up to 20 ft. (6 m) tall, with the canopy coverage varying from 10 to 50% and lacking a secondary tree layer. While eucalypt canopy species overlap among the mallee habitat types, Heathy Mallee is dominated by species such as Yellow Mallee (*Eucalyptus incrassata*), Slender-leaf Mallee (*Eucalyptus leptophylla*), and Dumosa Mallee (*Eucalyptus dumosa*), along with Yellow Gum (*Eucalyptus leucoxylon*) and Desert Stringybark (*Eucalyptus arenacea*). The canopy can also have species such as the conifer Scrub Cypress-Pine (*Callitris verrucosa*) and an angiosperm that looks like a conifer, Dwarf Sheoak (*Allocasuarina pusilla*), as well as Silver Banksia (*Banksia marginata*), which can grow very low to the ground as a shrub or grow taller than the eucalypt species as an emergent tree.

In contrast with Spinifex Mallee, this habitat has a very dense understorey of heath-like plants that interlock to form a dense mid-canopy that is very difficult to walk through, and if the limited mallee canopy were to be removed, the habitat would look very much like an ARID HEATHLAND. The mid-canopy in this habitat, at 3–10 ft. (1–3 m), is dominated by plants such as Mallee Tea Tree (*Leptospermum coriaceum*), Common Fringe-Myrtle (*Calytrix tetragona*), Desert Hakea (*Hakea mitchellii*), and Broom Baeckea (*Hysterobaeckea behrii*), and it can be overrun in places with climbers associated with wetter regions, such as Slender Dodder-Laurel (*Cassytha glabella*). Ground cover is fairly sparse, with a few *Triodia* spinifex plants, but is more likely to be dominated by low shrubs such as Desert Baeckea (*Rinzia orientalis*) along with ephemerals that sprout only in wetter years.

Mallees have lignotuber root balls that can be over 9 ft. (3 m) in diameter, sinker roots that can penetrate the soil down to 80 ft. (25 m), and lateral roots. The root system enables the plant not only to tap into deeper water tables but to store water and starch in the lignotuber, which allows it to quickly resprout after periods of fire when all branches have been killed. This means that although the aboveground part of the tree may be young, the plant itself may be hundreds of years old. Even though Heathy Mallee and Shrubby and Chenopod Mallee both have similar mallee canopy trees, fire is more important to this habitat because many of the understorey Proteaceae spp. here, such as the banksias, require fire to seed.

Heathy Mallee forms over a wide range of landscapes and soils but is generally associated with nutrient-poor soils formed from stabilised palaeo–sand dunes, uniform aeolian (air-transported) sands, or well-sorted but nutrient-poor alluvium. At a local scale, where the soil is extremely nutrient-deficient, even the hardiest of heathy understorey plants have difficulty surviving, and the habitat is replaced by Spinifex Mallee. Heathy Mallee is found in harsh semiarid environments where annual rainfall is around 10 in. (250 mm) and falls mainly in the winter. This dry hot-summer/wetter cold-winter climate is classified as Mediterranean/semiarid (Koppen **Csa–Bsk**). In hotter areas to the north, this habitat is replaced by Spinifex Mallee.

WILDLIFE: Birding in all mallee habitats can be extremely varied because many of the characteristic species are blossom nomads, which are found in the area only when their food plants are in bloom, such as Purple-crowned and Musk Lorikeets, Masked and White-browed Woodswallows, and White-fronted, Purple-gaped, Yellow-plumed, and Black Honeyeaters. Heathy Mallee differs from other mallees in having many tree and shrubs in its subcanopy and understorey that also produce prolific amounts of nectar, so the blossom-nomad guild is augmented by a series of nectivorous and resident honeyeater species more typical of WALLUM AND AUSBOS, such as

Purple-gaped Honeyeater is found in most of the different mallee woodlands from s. Australia. © IAIN CAMPBELL, TROPICAL BIRDING TOURS/UNSW E&ERC

Regent Parrot frequently forages within areas of Heathy Mallee.
© IAIN CAMPBELL, TROPICAL BIRDING TOURS/UNSW E&ERC

Eastern Spinebill, Little and Red Wattlebirds, and White-plumed, Tawny-crowned, New Holland, White-eared, White-naped, Brown-headed, and Black-chinned Honeyeaters. On those occasions when the mallee eucalypts and the subcanopy trees are both in bloom, the birding can be intense with phenomenal amounts of activity.

Bird activity is not limited to the canopy here, and many species with other feeding preferences use this habitat. Common Bronzewing is a large ground pigeon that occurs in a wide variety of mallees and other woodlands, but in the Heathy Mallee it is joined by the much more restricted Brush Bronzewing. Little and Painted Buttonquails and Blue-winged and Red-rumped Parrots are ground birds that are generally uncommon but are widespread here. The spectacular Regent Parrot is a major target of birders visiting this habitat. Purple-backed Fairywren may be found throughout the range of Heathy Mallee, while Blue-breasted Fairywren is limited to the western portion and Superb Fairywren to the eastern. Shy Heathwren can occur in this habitat in low numbers in e. Australia but is far less common than either Rufous Fieldwren in the east or Western Fieldwren in the west. Southern Whiteface, a tiny bird that feeds on the ground, is joined there by a suite of thornbills, including Yellow-rumped, Slender-billed, and Chestnut-rumped Thornbills, as well as White-fronted Chat. Other thornbills in the area that feed more in the shrubs and canopy include Buff-rumped, Striated, Inland, and Brown Thornbills. In areas with more *Casuarina* and *Allocasuarina* trees, Yellow Thornbill can be locally common.

Other widespread canopy and subcanopy species include Horsfield's Bronze-Cuckoo, Masked and Black-faced Woodswallows, White-winged Triller, Crested Bellbird, Spotted and Striated Pardalotes, Weebill, and a suite of robins including Red-capped, Flame, Scarlet, and Western Yellow Robins. Jacky-winter seems ubiquitous in this habitat. Open-country raptors are more common in this type of mallee, and Nankeen Kestrel, Brown Falcon, and even the much rarer Black Falcon are regulars here. Little Eagles soar overhead, Spotted Harriers cruise low over the more open areas, and Brown Goshawks hunt from within the canopy.

Mallee areas are great places to go herping as they host numerous species of geckos, such as Thick-tailed Barking Gecko (*Underwoodisaurus milii*) and Beaded Gecko (*Lucasium damaeum*), many legless lizards, and Burton's Snake-Lizard (*Lialis burtonis*). Notable skinks include Western Bluetongue (*Tiliqua occipitalis*) and Shingleback (*Tiliqua rugosa*). Large mammals include Red Kangaroo, Western Grey Kangaroo, Bare-nosed Wombat, and in a few locations, Southern Hairy-nosed Wombat.

CONSERVATION: Heathy Mallee forms on better soils than SPINIFEX MALLEE but on poorer soils than SHRUBBY AND CHENOPOD MALLEE. In the mallee regions of Victoria and South Australia, this habitat has been better protected than the latter but cleared more than the former. The protections of this habitat on private land are negligible, and widespread clearing still occurs, but vast areas are protected in some very large national parks.

DISTRIBUTION: Heathy Mallee woodland occurs through the southern part of semiarid s. Australia. A large portion of the original mallee cover has been cleared, though because Heathy Mallee forms in areas with poorer soils than SHRUBBY AND CHENOPOD MALLEE, it has been spared some of the clearing. Some large tracts occur in Little Desert National Park (Victoria); however, much of this habitat exists as long strips of woodland between roads and grainfields.

WHERE TO SEE: Little Desert National Park, Victoria, Australia; Stirling Range National Park, Western Australia.

Western Fieldwren (pictured) inhabits Heathy Mallee in Western Australia but is replaced by Rufous Fieldwren in this habitat in the east. © IAIN CAMPBELL, TROPICAL BIRDING TOURS/UNSW E&ERC

Au9N SHRUBBY AND CHENOPOD MALLEE

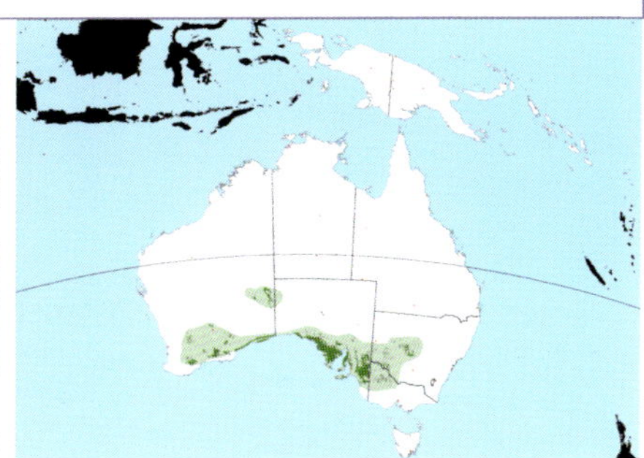

IN A NUTSHELL: A dense mallee habitat composed of eucalypt trees in a characteristic whipstick form (with most branches sprouting from the plant base) and a grassy or shrubby understorey with chenopods such as saltbushes. **Global Habitat Affinities:** None. **Continental Habitat Affinities:** SPINIFEX MALLEE; HEATHY MALLEE. **Species Overlap:** HEATHY MALLEE; SPINIFEX MALLEE; WESTERN EUCALYPT WOODLAND; CHENOPOD SHRUBLAND. **Full Bird Assemblage:** habitatsoftheworld.org/Au9N.

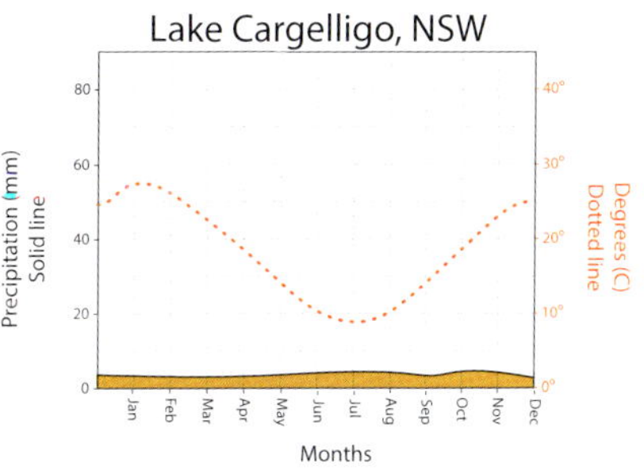

DESCRIPTION: Mallee habitats are extremely difficult for visitors to visualise. When travelling through w. New South Wales or rural South Australia, you may find yourself wondering, 'Am I in mallee yet?'—but if you need to ask that question, you probably are not. It is so different from any other habitat type that when you encounter it, you will know. Shrubby and Chenopod Mallee comprises a range of microhabitats that have fairly uniform canopies dominated by mallee eucalypts and understoreys of either arid-adapted shrubby plants, grasses other than spinifex, or chenopod shrubs. The mallee-form, of many equal-sized branches sprouting from a large root ball (lignotuber), is found in some non-mallee habitats, but the mallee habitats are those woodlands with the canopy made up almost exclusively of eucalypts with this growth form.

In Shrubby and Chenopod Mallee, the canopy can be as low as 9 ft. (3 m) in open mallee shrubland; up to 20 ft. (6 m) in tall, open mallee woodland; and in some cases, up to 24 ft. (8 m) in closed woodland. Some eucalypts, such as Dumosa Mallee (*Eucalyptus dumosa*), Bull Mallee (*Eucalyptus behriana*), Red Mallee (*Eucalyptus socialis*), and Yorrell (*Eucalyptus gracilis*), are found in all types of mallee habitats in both the dense 'whipstick' form and the taller 'bull' mallee-form. A single plant may change form, starting regrowth after a major fire in the whipstick form with many shoots and changing over time as some of the branches become dominant. Glossy-leaved Red Mallee (*Eucalyptus oleosa*) is limited to the habitat's more nutrient-rich soils and tends to be less hardy than the other mallee species, although it grows large. While the vast majority of canopy species are eucalypts, the conifers White Cypress-Pine (*Callitris glaucophylla*), Slender Cypress-Pine (*Callitris gracilis*), and Scrub Cypress-Pine (*Callitris verrucosa*) can be found in some areas. Another group of canopy trees that can survive in this habitat are the sheoaks, such as Buloke (*Allocasuarina luehmannii*). At first impression, sheoaks look remarkably similar to the cypress-

In some areas, such as Little Desert National Park in Victoria (pictured), there can be a nebulous ecotone between Shrubby and Chenopod Mallee and the scrubbier Heathy Mallee.
© IAIN CAMPBELL, TROPICAL BIRDING TOURS/UNSW E&ERC

pines mentioned, but they are angiosperms (flowering plants) with minute flowers and tiny, scale-like leaves arranged on branchlets that resemble pine needles.

In the tallest mallee stands, the species of chenopods (succulent, salt-tolerant plants) or chenopod-like plants that dominate the understorey are species that also occur outside of the mallee in CHENOPOD SHRUBLAND. The typical chenopods include Cottony Saltbush (*Chenopodium curvispicatum*), Frosted Goosefruit (*Chenopodium desertorum*), Mallee Saltbush (*Atriplex stipitata*), Rosy Bluebush (*Maireana erioclada*), Erect Mallee Bluebush (*Maireana pentatropis*), Pearl Bluebush (*Maireana sedifolia*), Cannonball Burr (*Dissocarpus paradoxus*), and Slit-Wing Bluebush (*Maireana georgei*). Bluebush Daisy (*Cratystylis conocephala*), though not a chenopod, looks remarkably similar and is often mistaken for a bluebush. Other plants growing among the chenopods include acacias such as Mulga (*Acacia aneura*) as well as a host of species from other inland groups.

In the more stunted mallee woodlands, 9–12 ft. (3–4 m) tall, the eucalypts with their dense whipstick forms can almost have a broom-head habit. Here the canopy eucalypts (as short as they are) such as White Mallee and Red Mallee are joined by others such as Green Mallee (*Eucalyptus viridis*) and Blue-leaved Mallee (*Eucalyptus polybractea*), along with tea trees such as Broombush (*Melaleuca uncinata*) and Rosy Paperbark (*Melaleuca diosmatifolia*), and a suite of acacias such as Umbrella Wattle (*Acacia oswaldii*), Myall (*Acacia melvillei*), and Haviland's Wattle (*Acacia havilandiorum*). The understorey is full of other shrubs adapted to semiarid and arid conditions and capable of living in this harsh environment; a typical suite of plants from this habitat in se. Australia includes Seven Dwarfs Grevillea (*Grevillea floribunda*), Tar Bush (*Eremophila glabra*), Silver Senna (*Senna artemisioides*), and the very cosmopolitan Akeake (*Dodonaea viscosa*), which is found in many semiarid temperate parts of the world. Most of these plants can exist as low, near-prostrate shrubs surrounded by bare ground and also as bushes that reach into the subcanopy. The shrub layers are thickest when the canopy height is limited to 8 ft. (2.5 m) and thin out when the canopy shrubs grow higher than this, after which forbs and grasses start to become more prevalent as

Shrubby and Chenopod Mallee forms on areas with more nutrient- and clay-rich soils than the other mallees and has a mixture of chenopods and chenopod-like plants such as Bluebush Daisy. This soil type also means that it is in greater danger of being cleared for farming. © IAIN CAMPBELL, TROPICAL BIRDING TOURS/UNSW E&ERC

ground cover, and areas left unburnt for decades may develop large amounts of leaf litter on the ground, similar to SPINIFEX MALLEE.

In contrast to Spinifex Mallee, which forms mainly on simple lithosols (immature soils) formed over palaeo-sand dunes, this habitat is more common in inter-dune plains and swales with calcareous, sandy-loam or loamy-clay soils. Calcrete (a chemically deposited calcium-carbonate rock) often forms a few feet below the soil surface, and calcareous nodules are common at the surface; this is in contrast with Heathy Mallee, where ironstone nodules are more common, and Spinifex Mallee, where silcrete (silica) concretions are more likely.

Shrubby and Chenopod Mallee habitat usually occurs in regions with semiarid or Mediterranean (Köppen **Bsk**, **Csa**) climates receiving less than 12 in. (300 mm) of annual rainfall, which occurs in the austral winter, with mild to hot summers and mild winters.

WILDLIFE: Malleefowl and Southern Scrub-Robin are both iconic ground birds of the mallee habitats. Malleefowl is the world's only temperate or arid-land representative of the megapodes—birds that build mounds of rotting vegetation in which they lay their eggs, allowing the heat generated from decomposition to incubate them. Southern Scrub-Robin is the temperate and arid counterpart to Northern Scrub-Robin of Cape York Peninsula (Queensland). It is furtive yet very vocal—easy to locate by ear but difficult to set eyes on. Shrubby and Chenopod Mallee is much richer in bird species than Spinifex Mallee because it has many of the same canopy tree species but also many chenopod, *Callitris*, *Allocasuarina*, *Grevillea*, and *Melaleuca* plants, which promote greater diversity of the bird assemblage, and species such as Shy Heathwren and White-browed Babbler are widespread here. Because this habitat spans most of the south of the continent, it has both western and eastern endemic species, such as Blue-breasted Fairywren, Spotted Scrubwren,

Malleefowl is the most iconic of all mallee birds, though it is typically scarce and hard to find almost everywhere it occurs. © SAM WOODS, TROPICAL BIRDING TOURS

Copperback Quail-thrush, and Western Whipbird in the west; and Red-lored Whistler and Black-eared Miner in the east. Red-lored Whistler is a vulnerable species; its habitat requirements are poorly understood as it has very localised, small, and disjunct populations in both this habitat and Spinifex Mallee. The endangered Black-eared Miner is threatened by the encroachment of and interbreeding with the much more widespread Yellow-throated Miner.

The different mallees have very similar canopy-bird assemblages with many blossom nomads, species that can move vast distances in search of flowering plants but are distinct from migratory birds, which travel set routes with the seasons. Blossom nomads of this habitat include Purple-crowned Lorikeet and Purple-gaped, Spiny-cheeked, White-fronted, Black, and White-eared Honeyeaters. An interesting feature of Yellow-plumed Honeyeater is that it is a very strong indicator of mallee habitats in e. Australia, but in the western part of the continent it is far more catholic in its habitat requirements and is also common in WESTERN EUCALYPT WOODLAND. Other mallee canopy species in this habitat include Western

If there are flowers in bloom within the mallee, nectar nomads may be seen, such as White-fronted Honeyeater. © BEN KNOOT

Gerygone, western subspecies of Golden Whistler, Rufous Whistler, Gilbert's Whistler, and Grey Currawong.

Other widespread ground and shrub birds that are also relatively common in Shrubby and Chenopod Mallee include Emu, Spotted Nightjar (a nocturnal bird that roosts and nests on the ground but feeds overhead), White-fronted Chat, Yellow-rumped and Chestnut-rumped Thornbills, and Purple-backed Fairywren. Widespread canopy and subcanopy species include Australian Owlet-nightjar, Australian Ringneck, Horsfield's Bronze-Cuckoo, Masked and Black-faced Woodswallows, Singing Honeyeater, Southern Whiteface, Crested Bellbird, Spotted and Striated Pardalotes, Weebill, Red-capped Robin, Western Yellow Robin, and Brown Treecreeper, an understorey species that often feeds on the ground.

Western Grey Kangaroo is common through this habitat. Smaller mammals include the carnivorous marsupials Spinifex Mulgara and Slender-tailed Dunnart. Mitchell's Hopping Mouse, a rodent well adapted to the sandy soils of the mallee, fills the same niche as the gerbils of the cold deserts of c. Asia.

In this habitat, any area of sand in the early morning will reveal the abundance of nocturnal reptiles. Larger species of lizards include Sand Goanna (*Varanus gouldii*) and Lace Monitor (*Varanus varius*). Smaller lizards include Shingleback (*Tiliqua rugosa*), Painted Dragon (*Ctenophorus pictus*), Nobbi Dragon (*Diporiphora nobbi*), and Broad-banded Sand-Swimmer (*Eremiascincus richardsonii*). Geckos include Southern Spiny-tailed Gecko (*Strophurus intermedius*), Thick-tailed Barking Gecko (*Underwoodisaurus milii*), and Eastern Beaked Gecko (*Rhynchoedura ormsbyi*). Despite the very arid environment, there are numerous amphibians, including Desert Tree Frog (*Litoria rubella*), Desert Trilling Frog (*Neobatrachus sudelli*), Giant Banjo Frog (*Limnodynastes interioris*), and Wrinkled Toadlet (*Uperoleia rugosa*).

CONSERVATION: Of the mallee types, Shrubby and Chenopod Mallee has been the most cleared and exploited because it forms on better soils than SPINIFEX MALLEE or HEATHY MALLEE, and significant areas have been clear-felled for grazing or crops. Unlike the clearing of some temperate eucalypt woodlands, which are thinned but with some trees left, clearing this habitat is done with bulldozers and chains, leaving only ribbons of trees along fence lines and roadsides.

DISTRIBUTION: Shrubby and Chenopod Mallee is found across s. Australia from the goldfields of Western Australia to Round Hill, New South Wales, with a few outliers as far as West Wyalong, New South Wales. It generally skirts the southern edge of CHENOPOD SHRUBLAND habitat and reaches the southern coast in some locations.

WHERE TO SEE: Round Hill, New South Wales, Australia; Wyperfeld National Park, Victoria, Australia; Gluepot Reserve, South Australia.

Shingleback is a medium-sized skink resembling an Australian version of the North American Gila Monster. © IAIN CAMPBELL, TROPICAL BIRDING TOURS/UNSW E&ERC

Au9O SPINIFEX MALLEE

IN A NUTSHELL: A low, dry, uniform woodland of mallee-form eucalypts—with most branches sprouting from the tree bases and with sparse undergrowth dominated by spinifex grasses. **Global Habitat Affinities:** SERTÃO CAATINGA. **Continental Habitat Affinities:** SHRUBBY AND CHENOPOD MALLEE; HEATHY MALLEE. **Species Overlap:** SHRUBBY AND CHENOPOD MALLEE; HEATHY MALLEE; ARID HEATHLAND; WESTERN EUCALYPT WOODLAND. **Full Bird Assemblage:** habitatsoftheworld.org/Au9O.

DESCRIPTION: Spinifex Mallee is one of the most quintessentially Australian habitats and absolutely foreign to anyone who has not visited Australia. Mallee is both a growth form and a habitat. The mallee growth form has multiple narrow trunks growing from a gnarled lignotuber (root ball) at or just beneath ground level. This growth form, which looks similar to anthropogenic coppicing, is not restricted to mallee habitats and can be found in a variety of eucalypts throughout Australia

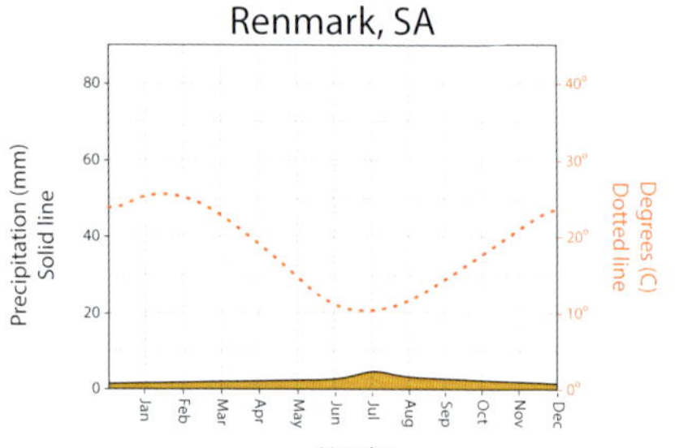

The ground cover of Spinifex Mallee is much more open than other mallee habitats, leaving many areas of bare sand. © IAIN CAMPBELL, TROPICAL BIRDING TOURS/UNSW E&ERC

This is a fire-prone environment, and while the trunks and branches can be completely destroyed, the mallee trees recover by resprouting from the lignotuber (root ball).
© IAIN CAMPBELL, TROPICAL BIRDING TOURS/UNSW E&ERC

Spinifex grasses grow in large hummocks in which the older part at the centre of the plant eventually dies, leaving a ring of younger growth. The plants last many decades, through multiple fire events burning the grass back to the roots. © GABRIEL CAMPBELL, TROPICAL BIRDING TOUR

in heathlands and even savannas. The three mallee habitats, however, are distinctive scrubby woodlands dominated by several species of eucalypt with the distinctive 'whipstick' mallee growth form. Spinifex Mallee is less determined by the eucalypt canopy than by the open understorey, dominated by various species of *Triodia* (spinifex grasses) as ground cover. The canopy reaches 12–24 ft. (4–8 m), and its density varies from interlocking to 20% coverage. However, because the eucalypt leaves are so small and sparse, significant light penetrates the canopy even when it is completely interlocking. The dominant mallee eucalypts are Dumosa Mallee (*Eucalyptus dumosa*), Glossy-leaved Red Mallee (*Eucalyptus oleosa*), Yorrell (*Eucalyptus gracilis*), Grey Mallee (*Eucalyptus morrisii*), Fruit-ridged Mallee (*Eucalyptus angulosa*), and Soap Mallee (*Eucalyptus diversifolia*). Non-eucalypt canopy species are not common in Spinifex Mallee, but the very hardy Scrub Cypress-Pine (*Callitris verrucosa*) and Wilga (*Geijera parviflora*) do occur. Even though the canopy is so open, it does not lead to a thick understorey, as would be expected; the generally sparse shrub layers are dominated by Spine Bush (*Acacia colletioides*), Comb Grevillea (*Grevillea huegelii*), Tar Bush (*Eremophila glabra*), Showy Daisy-Bush (*Olearia pimeleoides*), and Erect Mallee Bluebush (*Maireana pentatropis*).

The ground cover is dominated by *Triodia* grasses, called spinifex in Australia—and not to be confused with the true *Spinifex*, a genus of beach grasses found over much of the world. The main spinifex species in the mallee districts of s. Australia is Porcupine Grass (*Triodia scariosa*). Spinifex is usually widely spaced and has a curious and unique growth form, occurring in large, low hummocks, usually less than 5 ft. (1.5 m) tall, with each stem growing from the same node as the root, so that the stems have independent sources for nutrients. The stems of spinifex become infused with silica at the tips, making the plants very rigid. As the spinifex ages, the centre dies, but the hummock ring continues to grow and can reach 15 ft. (5 m) wide. After rains, and if there has not been a fire for some decades, the spinifex grasses risk getting smothered by other grasses and ephemeral or perennial forbs such as Balcada Grass (*Austrostipa nitida*), Fuzz-Weed (*Vittadinia cuneata*), Blue Mallee Flower (*Halgania cyanea*), and Wiry Podolepis (*Podolepis capillaris*). The survival strategy for the spinifex is to have mass seedings during good seasons, but for the seeds to have delayed sprouting. In periods of intense fire, some of the original spinifex grasses can be burned back to the base and resprout, though the seeds may survive the fire and sprout with the next rain.

The climate that promotes this habitat is harsh and semiarid with a hot summer and wetter cold winter (Köppen **Bsk**). In hotter, less fire-prone areas to the north, this habitat is replaced by SPINIFEX MULGA. Spinifex Mallee is often surrounded by the other two mallee habitats, SHRUBBY AND CHENOPOD MALLEE and HEATHY MALLEE, which both occur on better soils. In contrast, this habitat dominates harsher environments of calcareous brown-red sands or loamy sands from stabilised linear palaeo–sand dunes.

WILDLIFE: Because the understorey is so open and different from that of SHRUBBY AND CHENOPOD MALLEE and HEATHY MALLEE, the understorey birds are quite different. What immediately sets Spinifex Mallee apart is its pair of obligate ground birds: Mallee Emuwren and Murray Mallee subspecies of Striated Grasswren. While there are stands of this habitat in New South Wales and Western Australia without these species, these birds are extremely specific to this habitat. Mallee Emuwren is endangered and restricted to nw. Victoria and far e. South Australia. Other understorey species that seem more common in this mallee than surrounding eucalypt or acacia woodlands include Black-throated and White-bellied subspp. of Western Whipbird, Southern Scrub-Robin, Hooded Robin, and White-browed Babbler.

Spinifex Mallee shares many of its canopy species with Heathy Mallee and Shrubby and Chenopod Mallee, including Purple-crowned Lorikeet and a suite of honeyeaters including Pied,

Mallee Emuwren is restricted to this habitat, where it inhabits the spinifex ground layer that sets this habitat apart from other types of mallee. © IAIN CAMPBELL, TROPICAL BIRDING TOURS/ UNSW E&ERC

Purple-gaped, Yellow-plumed, Spiny-cheeked, White-fronted, Black, Brown-headed, Striped, and White-eared Honeyeaters. This is because many of these birds are blossom nomads, species that follow the plant blooms and will move vast distances in search of them (distinct from migratory birds, which have set routes with the seasons). This phenomenon highlights one of the stark differences between Australia's semiarid sclerophyll woodlands and other arid and semiarid habits around the world: most environments are predictable in terms of the bird assemblage from year to year, in that the species are seasonal, whereas sclerophyll woodlands such as mallees, mulgas, and arid heathlands can be absolutely packed with canopy nectar feeders one year and amazingly empty another.

Parrots and cockatoos are canopy breeders as well as ground feeders, and although none are strictly limited to this habitat, the relative abundance of the occurring species is a characteristic of this habitat, as is the near absence of Little Corella and Sulphur-crested Cockatoo, both almost ubiquitous elsewhere. The species to expect here include Pink Cockatoo, Regent Parrot, Australian Ringneck, and Red-rumped Parrot. The very rare and spectacular Scarlet-chested Parrot nests in this habitat, though it tends to move into CHENOPOD SHRUBLAND when not breeding.

Other mallee species in this habitat include Pallid Cuckoo; Horsfield's Bronze-Cuckoo; White-browed Treecreeper; Chestnut and Copperback Quail-thrushes (which also feed on the ground); Yellow-throated Miner, which is interbreeding with the endangered Black-eared Miner; Western Gerygone; Western subspecies of Golden Whistler; Rufous, and Gilbert's Whistlers; and both Spotted and Striated Pardalotes. Chestnut-crowned Babbler, Red-capped Robin, and Jacky-winter occur here but are nowhere near as common as they are in surrounding SPINIFEX MULGA where the habitats merge in a mosaic. Red-lored Whistler is a vulnerable mid-canopy insectivore; its distribution and habitat requirements are poorly understood though it may be often overlooked.

The terrestrial Chestnut Quail-thrush can be found in various types of mallee. © IAIN CAMPBELL, TROPICAL BIRDING TOURS/UNSW E&ERC

Malleefowl, the world's only arid megapode (mound-building bird), and Emu, Australia's only arid land ratite (member of the bird group that includes ostriches, kiwis, cassowaries, and rheas), both occur in this habitat. They are more visible here due to the open nature of the woodland although they may not be any more common than in the other mallee habitats.

Large mammals include Red, Eastern Grey, and Western Grey Kangaroos, Bare-nosed Wombat, and, in a few locations, Southern Hairy-nosed Wombat. Short-beaked Echidna may not be especially common here but is very obvious and can often be found on the sides of the sandy roads going through the mallee. Arboreal mammals do not feature greatly in Spinifex Mallee, but Common Brushtail Possum, Western Pygmy Possum, and Little Pygmy Possum can all be found, if at low densities. There are some fascinating ground-dwelling carnivores, such as Mallee Ningaui, which looks like a very long-nosed house mouse, and the diminutive Mitchell's Hopping Mouse, which looks very much like a gerbil from the Arabian deserts.

Mallee areas are great places to go herping, hosting numerous species of geckos, such as Eastern Tree Dtella (*Gehyra versicolor*), Thick-tailed Barking Gecko (*Underwoodisaurus milii*), Southern Spiny-tailed Gecko (*Strophurus intermedius*), and Beaded Gecko (*Lucasium damaeum*). Larger lizards include Sand Goanna (*Varanus gouldii*) and Lace Monitor (*Varanus varius*), as well as dragons such as Southern Mallee Dragon (*Ctenophorus tuniluki*), Central Bearded Dragon (*Pogona vitticeps*), and Nobbi Dragon (*Diporiphora nobbi*). There are many species of legless lizards, as well as Burton's Snake-Lizard (*Lialis burtonis*). Notable skinks include Western Bluetongue (*Tiliqua occipitalis*) and the flat Shingleback, aka Stumpy-tailed Lizard (*Tiliqua rugosa*), Ragged Snake-eyed Skink (*Cryptoblepharus pannosus*), Southeastern Morethia Skink (*Morethia boulengeri*), and Desert Skink (*Liopholis inornata*). Snakes include the venomous Shield-snouted Brown Snake (*Pseudonaja aspidorhyncha*) and Eastern Brown Snake (*Pseudonaja textilis*).

CONSERVATION: A large portion of the original mallee cover has been cleared, but because Spinifex Mallee develops in drier, hotter areas with poorer soils than Shrubby and Chenopod Mallee, this habitat has been spared some of the clearing. Many narrow corridors of Spinifex Mallee exist, and long strips of the habitat follow roads in many areas.

DISTRIBUTION: Spinifex Mallee occurs as small patches of woodland through much of semiarid s. Australia from the Stirling Ranges in Western Australia to Round Hill in New South Wales. The largest patches are just north of the Nullarbor Plain in New South Wales and in the eastern part of the Yilgarn Block in Western Australia.

WHERE TO SEE: Hattah-Kulkyne National Park, Victoria, Australia; Round Hill Nature Reserve, New South Wales, Australia; Gluepot Reserve, South Australia; Stirling Range National Park, Western Australia.

Au9P WESTERN EUCALYPT WOODLAND

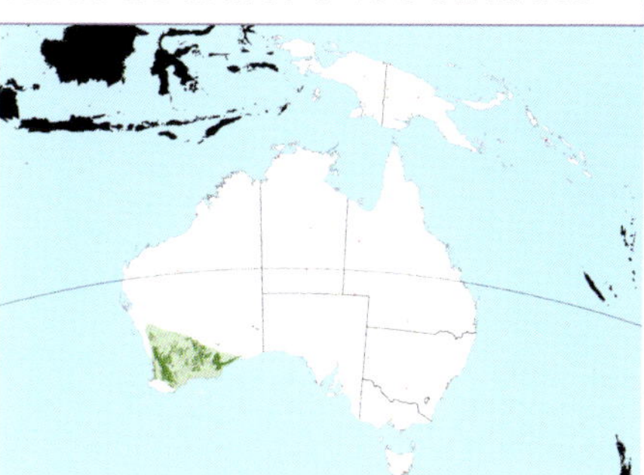

IN A NUTSHELL: A eucalypt woodland with an open canopy and a shrubby or grassy ground cover found in sw. Australia. **Global Habitat Affinities:** CHILEAN SCLEROPHYLL SCRUB. **Continental Habitat Affinities:** IRONBARK-BOX WOODLAND. **Species Overlap:** JARRAH-MARRI FOREST; HEATHY MALLEE; SHRUBBY AND CHENOPOD MALLEE. **Full Bird Assemblage:** habitatsoftheworld.org/Au9P.

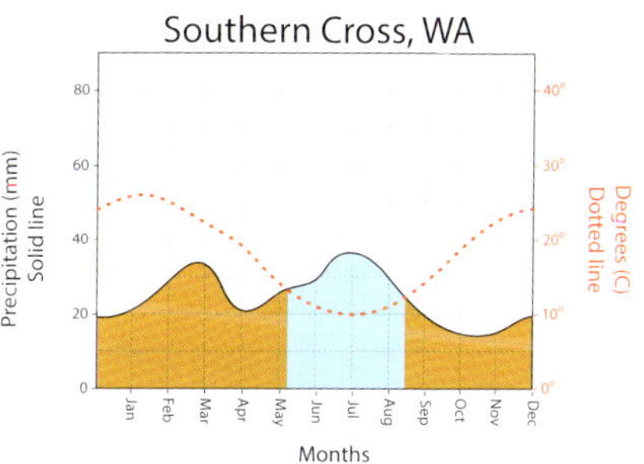

DESCRIPTION: This habitat of sw. Western Australia encompasses a variety of eucalypt woodlands with different canopy trees that, although individually distinctive, form a fairly uniform block of habitat with very similar wildlife assemblages. While some small areas of Western Eucalypt Woodland may be more open on the ground, such as the Dryandra Woodland, and other areas may be denser, such as the Coolgardie Woodlands, the habitat as a whole remains pretty

The canopy trees in this woodland can often be monotypic, as in this Wandoo stand in Dryandra Woodland National Park, Western Australia. © IAIN CAMPBELL, TROPICAL BIRDING TOURS/UNSW E&ERC

The grassy ground cover in this woodland has made it easily converted to grazing land or cleared for crop growing, leaving only a very small percentage of the original habitat intact.
© IAIN CAMPBELL, TROPICAL BIRDING TOURS/UNSW E&ERC

distinctive. Much of this habitat has been razed for farming in the w. Australian wheat belt, so the most extensive remaining stands are examples of the western and eastern fringes of what was once a massive area of temperate eucalypt woodland.

One of most common trees in the region is the Wandoo (*Eucalyptus wandoo*), remaining in extensive stands in the western part of the habitat's range. Here it forms an open eucalypt woodland with a canopy 30–90 ft. (10–30 m) high that ranges from almost closed, with the trees nearly touching, to widely spaced, with less than 50% of the ground in shade. The Wandoo tree rarely grows straight, and this habitat is characterised by bent trees or trees that branch at around head height. The Wandoo is joined in the canopy by other eucalypts such as Powderbark Wandoo (*Eucalyptus accedens*), Brown Mallet (*Eucalyptus astringens*), and Salmon White Gum (*Eucalyptus lane-poolei*). Jarrah (*Eucalyptus marginata*) and Marri (*Corymbia calophylla*) also occur, and on the western edge of this habitat, where they begin to dominate the canopy, an ecotone forms with JARRAH-MARRI FOREST. The understorey of the western examples of Western Eucalypt Woodland is fairly open with widely spaced small trees such Rock Sheoak (*Allocasuarina huegeliana*); Golden Dryandra (*Banksia nobilis*), which grows to about 12 ft. (4m) high; and Prickly Dryandra (*Banksia armata*) and Round-fruit Banksia (*Banksia sphaerocarpa*), which are both smaller shrubs that flower prolifically. Other shrubs expected here are Bitter Quandong (*Santalum murrayanum*) and Harsh Hakea (*Hakea prostrata*). Flowers and low shrubs are a strong part of the ground cover, while grasses make up a much smaller part of the plant assemblage here than in the equivalent IRONBARK-BOX WOODLAND of e. Australia.

Father east this woodland has a much shrubbier appearance and looks much more like a cross between a mallee and a short dry sclerophyll forest. Here, York Gum (*Eucalyptus loxophleba*), Salmon Gum (*Eucalyptus salmonophloia*), Red Morrell (*Eucalyptus longicornis*), Coral Gum (*Eucalyptus torquata*), and Goldfields Blackbutt (*Eucalyptus lesouefii*) form canopies 30–60 ft. (10–20 m) high with some emergent trees reaching 100 ft. (33 m). Some of the trees, such as Gimlet (*Eucalyptus salubris*), have a vague mallee appearance, with multiple trunks sprouting very low to the ground. However, they do not form lignotubers (root balls), are not as fire- or drought-resistant as mallee species, and are referred to as 'mallets'. The understorey in the easterly portion of the habitat is a mash-up of eucalypts, including small trees such as Silver-topped Gimlet (*Eucalyptus campaspe*) and Cleland's Blackbutt (*Eucalyptus clelandiorum*), along with a wide variety of other small trees such as Raspberry Jam Tree (*Acacia acuminata*), the microphyllous (tiny-leaved) Rock Sheoak (*Allocasuarina huegeliana*), Water Bush (*Grevillea nematophylla*), and many melaleuca species such as One-sided Bottlebrush (*Melaleuca quadrifida*) and Granite Bottlebrush (*Melaleuca elliptica*).

The understorey of the habitat changes much more than the canopy, and where the soils are calcareous and more saline, this habitat contains many plants that also occur in CHENOPOD SHRUBLAND such as Old Man Saltbush (*Atriplex nummularia*), Cottony Saltbush (*Chenopodium curvispicatum*), Barrier Saltbush (*Enchylaena tomentosa*), and Berry Saltbush (*Atriplex semibaccata*), along with bluebushes such as Pearl Bluebush (*Maireana sedifolia*) and Short-leaf Bluebush (*Maireana brevifolia*).

WILDLIFE: Many of the canopy bird species that use this habitat are blossom nomads, which will move towards the coast or inland along with the flowering of eucalypts and/or the emergence of insects associated with those flowerings. Birds that can be expected to turn up at the onset of a mass flowering event include Purple-crowned Lorikeet, Tawny-crowned Honeyeater, Spiny-cheeked Honeyeater, Yellow-plumed Honeyeater, Brown Honeyeater, White-eared Honeyeater, Gilbert's Honeyeater, and Brown-headed Honeyeater. New Holland Honeyeater and White-cheeked Honeyeater both occur and tend to be more territorial and move less than the other honeyeaters. Small canopy predators include the rare Western Shrike-tit, Spotted Pardalote, Striated Pardalote, and Australia's smallest bird, the Weebill, which weighs in at a mighty 0.21 oz. (6 g) and measures 3.5 in. (9 cm) long. Raptors seem very obvious in this open habitat, and the vast majority of Australia's diurnal raptors occur here, including Black-shouldered Kite, Square-tailed Kite, Little Eagle, Wedge-tailed Eagle, Brown Goshawk, and Collared Sparrowhawk.

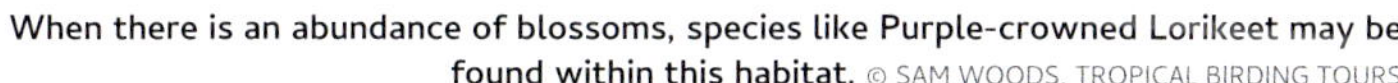

When there is an abundance of blossoms, species like Purple-crowned Lorikeet may be found within this habitat. © SAM WOODS, TROPICAL BIRDING TOURS

Spiny-cheeked Honeyeater is one of many nectivorous species found in Western Eucalypt Woodland in Western Australia. © PABLO CERVANTES, TROPICAL BIRDING TOURS

Areas with a more open understorey tend to attract insectivorous species such as Rufous Treecreeper, Yellow-rumped Thornbill, Restless Flycatcher, Scarlet Robin, Jacky-winter, Hooded Robin, and Western Yellow Robin. In areas where the understorey is thicker, birds that tend to skulk are more prevalent, such as Blue-breasted Fairywren, Splendid Fairywren, Spotted Scrubwren, Red-capped Robin, and Western Yellow Robin. As in the IRONBARK-BOX WOODLAND of e. Australia, parrots are an important part of the bird assemblage; Regent Parrot, Elegant Parrot, Australian Ringneck, Western Rosella, and Red-capped Parrot all occur in this habitat.

Some mammals common in Western Eucalypt Woodland are Short-beaked Echidna, Western Grey Kangaroo, and Common Brushtail Possum; some less common macropods are Western Brush Wallaby and Tammar Wallaby; and some other exciting species include Yellow-footed Antechinus, the endangered Numbat, and the critically endangered Woylie.

In the east of its range, Yellow-plumed Honeyeater is a mallee specialist, while in the west it is a eucalypt woodland generalist. © IAIN CAMPBELL, TROPICAL BIRDING TOURS/UNSW E&ERC

Common reptiles include Shingleback (*Tiliqua rugosa*), Sand Goanna (*Varanus gouldii*), Buchanan's Snake-eyed Skink (*Cryptoblepharus buchananii*), and Southwestern Carpet Python (*Morelia imbricata*); less common species are Southwestern Clawless Gecko (*Crenadactylus ocellatus*), Reticulated Velvet Gecko (*Hesperoedura reticulata*), Dwarf Bearded Dragon (*Pogona minor*), and King's Skink (*Egernia kingii*). Some amphibians present are

Western Spotted Frog (*Heleioporus albopunctatus*), Humming Frog (*Neobatrachus pelobatoides*), and Bleating Froglet (*Crinia pseudinsignifera*).

CONSERVATION: This habitat took the brunt of clearing for the wheat fields of Western Australia and has been almost completely removed. The remains are small remnants and a series of human-maintained forest corridors along country roads. Although fragmented, these remnants form the backdrop to the iconic 'country' of Western Australia.

DISTRIBUTION: Western Eucalypt Woodlands characterise the regions in sw. Australia between the JARRAH-MARRI FOREST of coastal areas and ranges and the truly arid habitats of the interior such as SHRUBBY AND CHENOPOD MALLEE and CHENOPOD SHRUBLAND. To the north, it merges into GRASSY MULGA.

WHERE TO SEE: Dryandra Woodland National Park, Western Australia.

Though once much more catholic in habitat choice, the endangered Numbat is found mainly in Western Eucalypt Woodland. © KEITH BARNES, TROPICAL BIRDING TOURS

Au9Q GRASSY MULGA

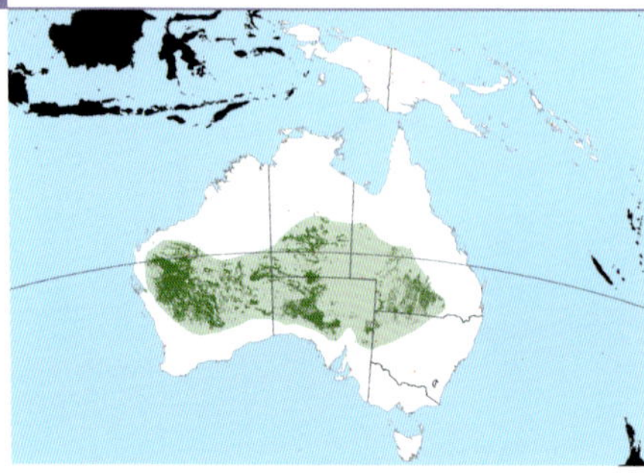

IN A NUTSHELL: Open acacia woodlands and shrublands of interior Australia, dominated by Mulga (*Acacia aneura*), with a grassy or sclerophyllous ground cover. **Global Habitat Affinities:** DRY CHACO; AFRICAN MOPANE. **Continental Habitat Affinities:** SPINIFEX MULGA. **Species Overlap:** IRONBARK-BOX WOODLAND; BRIGALOW. **Full Bird Assemblage:** habitatsoftheworld.org/Au9Q.

DESCRIPTION: Mulga, a widespread and common woodland, can be described as the non-fire-resistant, more drought-resistant, acacia-dominated sister habitat to the fire-resistant, eucalypt-dominated mallee habitats. It gets its name from its dominant tree, Mulga (*Acacia aneura*), which usually grows as a single-trunked tree, although it can occur in shrub form. It is highly likely that the tree currently described as Mulga comprises

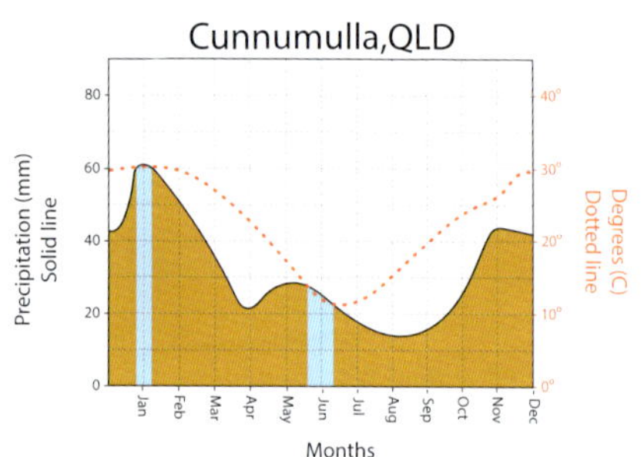

The ground between trees in Grassy Mulga is bare most of the time but can fill with forbs and grasses after good rains. © IAIN CAMPBELL, TROPICAL BIRDING TOURS/UNSW E&ERC

Grassy Mulga is dominated by the Mulga tree but also contains other acacias.
© IAIN CAMPBELL, TROPICAL BIRDING TOURS/UNSW E&ERC

multiple, closely related species. Mulga forms a fairly uniform canopy in any one location, although the height of the canopy varies substantially through the wide climatic belt in which the species occurs. The species is well adapted to dry conditions, and instead of true leaves, it has elongated, leaf-shaped phyllodes (expanded leaf stems). The phyllodes point upwards in a manner similar to the joint-firs (*Ephedra* spp.) of Asia, and as water falls onto the phyllodes, it is channelled from the twigs to the branches and closer to the base of the trunk, therefore concentrating the amount of water available to the tree's roots at the expense of surrounding vegetation. The trees have deep taproots as well as an extensive shallow root system within the top 12 in. (30 cm) of the soil.

Grassy Mulga tends to form on clay pans but also grows on top of lateritic plateaus, especially in Western Australia, where the soils may be sandier than the soils in the east, but the ferricrete or lateritic pans at a few feet (1 m) below the soil can impede drainage and allow the Mulga trees to attain water.

Over most of c. Australia, Grassy Mulga woodlands are around 20 ft. (6 m) high and contain Mulga mixed with other acacias such as Sandhill Wattle (*Acacia ligulata*), Horse Mulga (*Acacia ramulosa*), Gidgee (*Acacia cambagei*), and Nelia (*Acacia loderi*), along with Western Rosewood (*Alectryon oleifolius*), and Emu Apple (*Owenia acidula*). Mallee eucalypt species also occur in this habitat, such as Glossy-leaved Red Mallee (*Eucalyptus oleosa*) and York Gum (*Eucalyptus loxophleba*), although they tend to occur where there is slightly more water in the system, as they are less resistant to drought than Mulga. The shrub layer, which may be up to 9 ft. (3 m) tall but is usually 4–6 ft. (1.5–2 m), is dominated by chenopods such as Black Bluebush (*Maireana pyramidata*) and other shrubs such as Barrier Saltbush (*Enchylaena tomentosa*), *Sclerolaena* spp., and Hedge Saltbush (*Rhagodia spinescens*).

In very dry regions with nutrient-deficient soils, Grassy Mulga is closely associated with SPINIFEX MULGA; the main difference is that the Spinifex Mulga occurs on sandier soils and has a ground cover of spinifex grasses (*Triodia* spp.) rather than tussock grasses or chenopods. In the dry regions, Grassy Mulga tends to take hold on small, low, recent dunes formed over clay pans. It is an open shrubland, 12 ft. (4m) high, with a canopy assemblage including Thargo Wattle (*Acacia ammophila*), Supplejack (*Ventilago viminalis*), Snakewood (*Acacia eremaea*), Whitewood (*Atalaya hemiglauca*), Gundabluie (*Acacia victoriae*), and Silver Needlewood (*Hakea leucoptera*); emergent trees can include Belah (*Casuarina cristata*) and Silver-leaved Ironbark (*Eucalyptus melanophloia*). A subcanopy or low shrub layer may include Akeake (*Dodonaea viscosa*), Turpentine Bush (*Eremophila sturtii*), Honeysuckle Grevillea (*Grevillea juncifolia*), Charleville Turkey Bush (*Eremophila gilesii*), Dead Finish (*Acacia tetragonophylla*), and Northern Sandalwood (*Santalum lanceolatum*). The ground layer is dominated by tussock grasses and forbs.

In areas with higher rainfall and/or nutrient-rich soils, Grassy Mulga can form as a closed woodland that merges into BRIGALOW habitat. Its canopy, up to 45 ft. (15 m) in height, comprises Kariku Sheoak (*Casuarina pauper*), Gidgee (*Acacia cambagei*), Poplar Box (*Eucalyptus populnea*), Brigalow (*Acacia harpophylla*), and Turpentine Bush (*Eremophila sturtii*). The shrub layer can be very thick and include Bastard Sandalwood (*Eremophila mitchellii*), Charleville Turkey Bush (*Eremophila gilesii*), and Wilga (*Geijera parviflora*). The ground cover is a mix of tussock grasses, such as Kangaroo Grass (*Themeda australis*), Mitchell Mulga Grass (*Thyridolepis mitchelliana*), Neverfail Grass (*Eragrostis setifolia*), and Lemon Grass (*Cymbopogon ambiguus*), and many forbs.

To the north of the mulga belt (the broad swath of Spinifex Mulga and Grassy Mulga across Australia) the canopy is dominated by Lancewood (*Acacia shirleyi*) and Gidgee, and the habitat merges with NORTHERN ACACIA SAVANNA. At this northern edge of the habitat, the acacias grow closer together and can take on whipstick or a broom-head form, and walking through the woodland becomes difficult.

WILDLIFE: Many of the bird and mammal species found in Grassy Mulga range widely, from one side of Australia to the other, and also occur in SPINIFEX MULGA, SHRUBBY AND CHENOPOD MALLEE, and IRONBARK-BOX WOODLAND. Birds that are widespread in Grassy Mulga woodlands of c. Australia include White-browed Treecreeper, Bourke's Parrot, Mulga Parrot, Spiny-cheeked Honeyeater, Chestnut-breasted Quail-thrush, and Splendid Fairywren. Hall's Babbler is restricted to dense woodlands, while Grey Honeyeater and Slaty-backed Thornbill prefer shorter, shrubbier areas of Grassy Mulga. Spotted Bowerbird, Western Bowerbird, Splendid Fairywren, Painted Honeyeater, Chestnut-breasted Quail-thrush, Inland Thornbill, Red-backed Kingfisher, Red-capped Robin,

The ground-feeding Bourke's Parrot is an indicator species for Grassy Mulga. © IAIN CAMPBELL, TROPICAL BIRDING TOURS/UNSW E&ERC

The skulking Chestnut-breasted Quail-thrush is a major attraction for naturalists visiting the mulga areas of sw. Queensland and nw. New South Wales. © JUN MATSUI, SICKLEBILL SAFARIS

Splendid Fairywren is a spectacular species that occurs in Grassy Mulga, particularly in areas where there is a thicker understorey. © IAIN CAMPBELL, TROPICAL BIRDING TOURS/UNSW E&ERC

Red-capped Robin is a stunning widespread species that is regularly encountered in Grassy Mulga. © IAIN CAMPBELL, TROPICAL BIRDING TOURS/UNSW E&ERC

Crested Bellbird, Spiny-cheeked Honeyeater, and Pink Cockatoo are also found throughout Grassy Mulga.

Grassy Mulga is one of the preferred habitats of the larger macropods, and Red, Western Grey, and Eastern Grey Kangaroos and Common Wallaroo are all found here in good numbers. Arboreal mammals are far fewer in number; the most common species is the Common Brushtail Possum. Geckos feature heavily in Grassy Mulga woodlands, including velvet geckos (*Oedura* spp.), Box-patterned Ground Gecko (*Lucasium steindachneri*), Variable Fat-tailed Gecko (*Diplodactylus conspicillatus*), Western Beaked Gecko (*Rhynchoedura ornata*), and spiny-tailed geckos (*Strophurus* spp.). A large number of other lizards live here, including Yakka Skink (*Egernia rugosa*). Snakes typical of this environment include Mulga Snake (*Pseudechis australis*), Red-naped Snake (*Furina diadema*), Dwyer's Snake (*Suta dwyeri*), De Vis's Banded Snake (*Denisonia devisi*), Ringed Brown Snake (*Pseudonaja modesta*), and Yellow-naped Snake (*Furina barnardi*).

CONSERVATION: Huge areas of Grassy Mulga have been destroyed in this millennium. It is seen as 'scrub' to be cleared and farmed, and there is no comprehensive conservation program for this habitat. The biggest and most effective conservation projects are being undertaken by conservation NGOs such as the Australian Wildlife Conservancy, which manages the Bowra Sanctuary in Queensland.

DISTRIBUTION: Grassy Mulga woodland habitat is widespread and often encountered across Australia's arid interior, extending from just north of Kalgoorlie, Western Australia, to east of Cunnamulla, sw. Queensland.

WHERE TO SEE: Bowra Sanctuary, Queensland, Australia; Eulo Bore, Queensland, Australia.

Au9R SPINIFEX MULGA

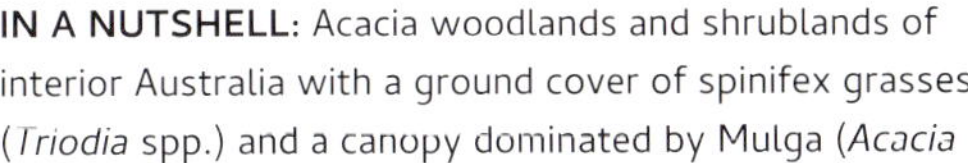

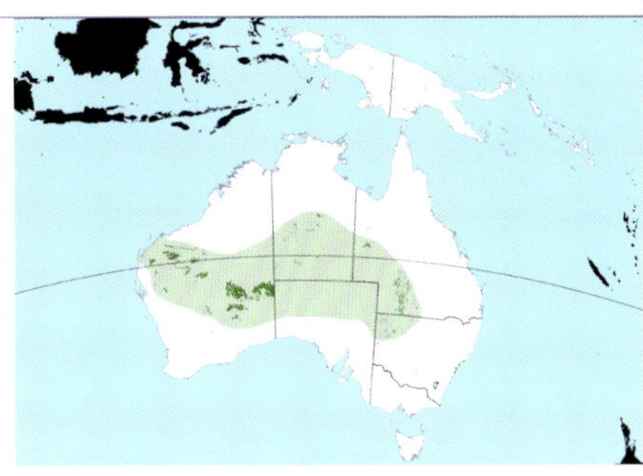

IN A NUTSHELL: Acacia woodlands and shrublands of interior Australia with a ground cover of spinifex grasses (*Triodia* spp.) and a canopy dominated by Mulga (*Acacia aneura*). **Global Habitat Affinities:** AFRICAN MOPANE; DECCAN THORNSCRUB. **Continental Habitat Affinities:** GRASSY MULGA; SPINIFEX EUCALYPT SAVANNA. **Species Overlap:** ROCKY SPINIFEX DESERT; GRASSY MULGA; SPINIFEX EUCALYPT SAVANNA. **Full Bird Assemblage:** habitatsoftheworld.org/Au9R.

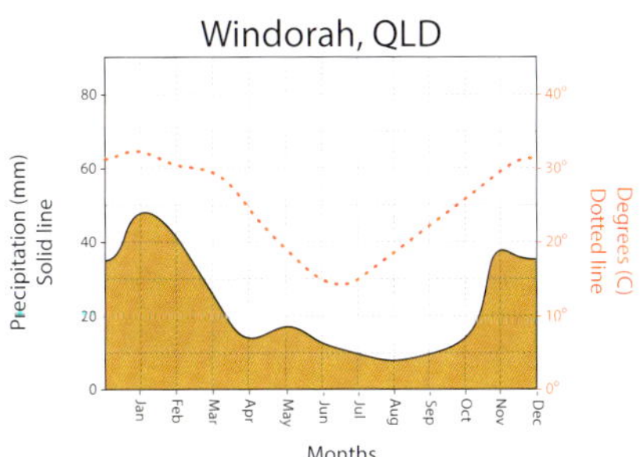

DESCRIPTION: The two mulga habitats, which cover much of c. Australia, are drought-resistant, acacia-dominated sister habitats to the fire-resistant eucalypt-dominated mallee habitats. There is a constant battle in the desert between the mallees and the mulgas. In zones where they are in direct competition, the battle is determined by what nature brings first: if an extreme drought comes along, the mallees will die and the mulgas survive;

Spinifex Mulga has far fewer shrubs than Grassy Mulga and is dominated by spiky spinifex grasses that can make walking through it less than fun. © IAIN CAMPBELL, TROPICAL BIRDING TOURS/UNSW E&ERC

Spinifex Mulga often occurs in a mosaic with Rocky Spinifex Desert and Spinifex Eucalypt Savanna. © GABRIEL CAMPBELL, TROPICAL BIRDING TOURS

however, if an extreme fire sweeps through, the mulgas will die and the mallees survive.

Spinifex Mulga is a woodland named for its dominant ground cover, spinifex grasses (*Triodia* spp.), and its dominant canopy species, Mulga (*Acacia aneura*). *Triodia* 'spinifex' grasses are peculiar spiky grasses endemic to Australia and not to be confused with the true *Spinifex*, a genus of grasses found on beaches over much of the world. The main species of Spinifex Mulga are Weeping Spinifex (*Triodia brizoides*), Soft Spinifex (*Triodia pungens*), and Giant Grey Spinifex (*Triodia longiceps*), although there are many more in tropical environments. It may seem counterintuitive to distinguish Spinifex Mulga and GRASSY MULGA on the basis of a grass, but spinifex is a hummock grass and appears very different from the tussock grasses of Grassy Mulga. Spinifex grass plants are usually widely spaced and have a curious and unique growth form of large, low hummocks, usually less than 5 ft. (1.5 m) across, with each stem growing from the same node as the root, so that the stems have independent sources for nutrients. As the spinifex ages, the centre dies, but the outer ring continues to grow, so that rings often reach 15 ft. (5 m) wide.

The canopy species are usually single-trunked trees up to 20 ft. (6 m) tall, although they can occur in shrub form as low as 9 ft. (3 m). They form a fairly uniform canopy in any one location, although the height of the canopy varies substantially through the wide climatic belt in which Spinifex Mulga occurs, with shorter canopies in drier areas. Spinifex Mulga is generally more open than Grassy Mulga, and the trees rarely form a closed canopy. Mulga (*Acacia aneura*) is the dominant canopy species, but the canopy is much more varied than that of Grassy Mulga. A variety of acacia species are in the mix, and sometimes other species are the dominant trees, and Mulga is a minor component of the canopy. Even this is open to debate, as it is highly likely that multiple, very closely related species make up what is currently described as Mulga. The other acacias include those that dominate the NORTHERN ACACIA SAVANNA such as Gidgee (*Acacia cambagei*), Lancewood (*Acacia shirleyi*), Georgina Gidgee (*Acacia georginae*), Bendee (*Acacia catenulata*), and Doodlallie (*Acacia excelsa*). These trees are well adapted to dry conditions, and instead of leaves, they have elongated, leaf-shaped phyllodes (modified leaf stems serving the functions of leaves). The phyllodes point upwards in a manner similar to the joint-firs (*Ephedra* spp.) of Asia, and as water falls onto the phyllodes, it is channelled from the twigs to the branches and closer to the base of the trunk, therefore concentrating the amount of water available to the tree's roots at the expense of surrounding vegetation. The trees have an extensive shallow root system within the top 12 in. (30 cm) of the soil as well as deep taproots. The *Acacia* canopy species are joined by species of other genera such as Whitewood (*Atalaya hemiglauca*), Red Lancewood (*Archidendropsis basaltica*), and the very beautiful Leopardwood (*Flindersia maculosa*), its bark mottled with hues of red and yellow. Eucalypts, such as Mountain Yapunyah (*Eucalyptus thozetiana*), also occur in this habitat, especially where it begins to merge with SPINIFEX EUCALYPT SAVANNA.

The shrub layer also differs from that of Grassy Mulga, in that chenopods and forbs are much rarer in this habitat, replaced by shrubs such as Crimson Turkey Bush (*Eremophila latrobei*), Silver Senna (*Senna artemisioides*), and Pigface Hemichroa (*Hemichroa mesembryanthema*). There is usually Warrior Bush (*Apophyllum anomalum*), which looks remarkably similar to Firebush (*Leptadenia pyrotechnica*) of the Middle East, in that the plant can give the impression of a fluffy Sasquatch.

Spinifex Mulga occupies slightly drier regions than Grassy Mulga and has a hot desert climate (Köppen **Bwh**) with annual rainfall of around 13 in. (320 mm), most of which falls in the austral summer months. Summers are very hot with average summer daytime temperatures as high as 100°F (38°C), while winters are as hot as 75°F (25°C).

Where the two mulga habitats occur in close proximity, Grassy Mulga forms on loamy or clay-rich soils in swales on vast alluvial or colluvial plains. In contrast, Spinifex Mulga takes hold on some of the most inert, nutrient-deficient soils in c. Australia. It mainly forms on lateritic surfaces, in soils from which almost all nutrients have been removed over millions of years of chemical weathering, resulting in sands with many ironstone nodules and inert kaolin clays deep in the soil profile. It can also occur at sides and bases of escarpments (called breakaways) around these plateaus, but even here, the soils are very nutrient-poor, making growing difficult for the vast majority of grasses, forbs, and chenopods.

To the north of the Spinifex Mulga, the canopy is dominated by Lancewood and Gidgee, and the habitat merges with Northern Acacia Savanna. At this northern edge of the habitat, the acacias grow closer together and can take on a whipstick or broom-head form, and walking through the woodland becomes difficult. When eucalypts become common in the canopy, but the spinifex-dominated ground cover remains, this habitat merges with Spinifex Eucalypt Savanna.

WILDLIFE: Many of the bird and mammal species found here range widely from one side of Australia to the other and overlap extensively among this habitat, GRASSY MULGA, ROCKY SPINIFEX DESERT, and SPINIFEX EUCALYPT SAVANNA.

Ground birds (or at least birds that feed in the ground cover) are more typical of Spinifex Eucalypt Savanna, but Opalton Grasswren and Spinifexbird both occur in Spinifex Mulga. Parrots are notably less prevalent in this habitat than in Grassy Mulga. Birds that are widespread

The canopy plants and birds are similar in Grassy Mulga and Spinifex Mulga. Crested Bellbird can be found widely in both types.

© IAIN CAMPBELL, TROPICAL BIRDING TOURS/UNSW E&ERC

Hall's Babbler, a mulga specialist, occurs in groups within both types of this habitat. © IAIN CAMPBELL, TROPICAL BIRDING TOURS/UNSW E&ERC

through the Spinifex Mulga woodland of c. Australia include White-browed Treecreeper, Spiny-cheeked Honeyeater, Crested Bellbird, Chestnut-breasted Quail-thrush, Splendid Fairywren, Grey Honeyeater, and Slaty-backed Thornbill. Hall's Babbler is a mulga woodland endemic from sc. Queensland and, while more extensive in Grassy Mulga, does occur in Spinifex Mulga within the bird's range.

Long-haired Rat is a species with huge population fluctuations. While it is predominantly an inhabitant of more open terrain, it occurs in Spinifex Mulga after an eruption in numbers prompts it to wander into surrounding habitats. Kultarr, a small marsupial, and Spinifex Hopping Mouse, a small rodent, resemble the jerboas of Asian cold deserts. They are found in spinifex-dominated areas including Spinifex Mulga, although the Kultarr generally stays on the edge of this habitat while the mouse can be found well into large mulga stands. Other small mammals expected in this habitat are Stripe-faced Dunnart and Desert Mouse.

Lizards of Spinifex Mulga include Leopard Ctenotus (*Ctenotus pantherinus*), Red-sided Ctenotus (*Ctenotus pulchellus*), Kristin's Spiny-tailed Gecko (*Strophurus krisalys*), and Slater's Ring-tailed Dragon (*Ctenophorus slateri*). A variety of snakes occur in this habitat throughout c. Australia including Red-naped Snake (*Furina diadema*).

CONSERVATION: Like Grassy Mulga, this habitat has been destroyed in large areas in this millennium; Spinifex Mulga is also regarded as 'scrub' to be cleared and farmed, but because the soil on which this habitat grows is not as fertile as those under Grassy Mulga, it is less desirable for farming than this sister habitat. More Spinifex Mulga is protected in national parks than Grassy Mulga; a cynical conservationist could easily argue that the Australian government seems more inclined to protect the less productive habitats over land that can be easily destroyed for farming.

DISTRIBUTION: Spinifex Mulga is found from sw. Queensland (around Winton) through c. Australia to Western Australia. It largely overlaps with GRASSY MULGA, though is replaced by that habitat in semiarid e. Australia and by SPINIFEX EUCALYPT SAVANNA and NORTHERN ACACIA SAVANNA to the north.

WHERE TO SEE: Bladensburg National Park, Queensland, Australia; Lark Quarry, Queensland, Australia; Laverton, Western Australia.

Au9S YILGARN MIXED WOODLAND

IN A NUTSHELL: The mixed eucalypt, cypress-pine, sheoak, and acacia woodlands of semiarid Western Australia. **Global Habitat Affinities:** NEARCTIC WESTERN RIPARIAN WOODLAND; TURANIAN ARID RIPARIAN SCRUB. **Continental Habitat Affinities:** MIXED SANDPLAIN WOODLAND. **Species Overlap:** WESTERN EUCALYPT WOODLAND; JARRAH-MARRI FOREST; HEATHY MALLEE. **Full Bird Assemblage:** habitatsoftheworld.org/Au9S.

DESCRIPTION: This is a Western Australian mixed, semiarid woodland with a matrix of *Eucalyptus*, *Acacia*, *Banksia*, *Melaleuca*, *Callitris*, and *Allocasuarina* spp. in varying proportions. The habitat exhibits significant structural heterogeneity over a small area, with pronounced variations in canopy height, density, and species composition, giving it a messy but very interesting look.

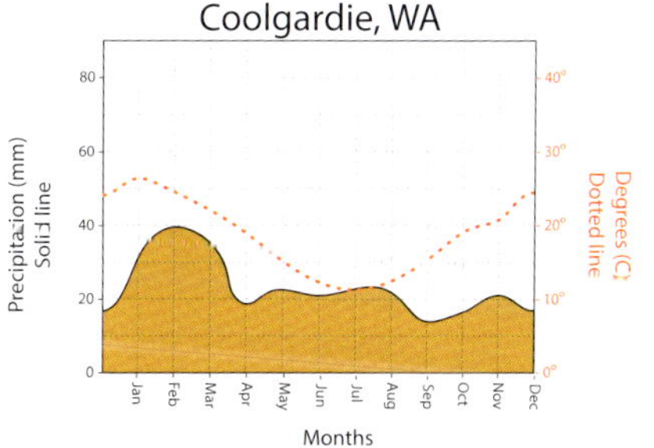

The woodland can be semi-open to open with a canopy in the range of 40–80 ft. (12–25m) in height when dominated by species such as York Gum (*Eucalyptus loxophleba*) and Salmon Gum (*Eucalyptus salmonophloia*); and 33–60 ft. (10–18 m) in the more arid east where dominated by Coral Gum (*Eucalyptus torquata*), Redwood (*Eucalyptus transcontinentalis*), Goldfields Blackbutt (*Eucalyptus lesouefii*), Silver-topped Gimlet (*Eucalyptus Campaspe*), and Merrit (*Eucalyptus flocktoniae*). The thick subcanopy is usually 15–25 ft. (5–8 m) tall and much more varied, with Rock Sheoak (*Allocasuarina huegeliana*) as well as acacias such as Prain's Wattle (*Acacia prainii*), Raspberry Jam Tree (*Acacia acuminata*), Dead Finish (*Acacia tetragonophylla*), and Tan Wattle (*Acacia hemiteles*). Melaleucas such as One-sided Bottlebrush (*Melaleuca quadrifida*) feature in the understorey, along with groves of the gymnosperm *Callitris*, such as Scrubby Cypress-Pine (*Callitris canescens*), and more inland plants such as Desert Quandong (*Santalum acuminatum*). Parasitic mistletoes such as Wireleaf Mistletoe (*Amyema preissii*), which grows mainly on wattles (*Acacia* spp.), are obvious in the canopy.

The understorey plants vary, depending on soil type, from arid heathland-type shrubs to succulent chenopods. The heathland-type understorey plants include Brilliant Hopbush (*Dodonaea microzyga*) and Bottlebrush Grevillea (*Grevillea paradoxa*). *Eremophila* spp., which are incredibly important plants for blossom nomads, also feature strongly in the understorey; large shrubs and small trees, such as Silver Emu Bush (*Eremophila scoparia*), Slender Fuchsia Bush (*Eremophila decipiens*), and Narrow-leaved Emu Bush (*Eremophila alternifolia*), all attract birds when in bloom.

Yilgarn Mixed Woodland is made up of eucalypts more typical of mallee habitats and acacias more typical of mulga habitats. © GABRIEL CAMPBELL, TROPICAL BIRDING TOURS

This woodland is the Western Australian equivalent of Mixed Sandplain Woodland of the southeast, and as in that habitat, small monotypic groves of *Casuarina* and *Allocasuarina* can occur locally. © IAIN CAMPBELL, TROPICAL BIRDING TOURS/UNSW E&ERC

The canopy of Yilgarn Mixed Woodland is very open and stunted, allowing a lot of light to reach the ground. The ground cover is usually dominated by chenopods in clay-rich soils (pictured) and spinifex in sand-rich soils. © IAIN CAMPBELL, TROPICAL BIRDING TOURS/UNSW E&ERC

Chenopods frequently dominate the shrub layer and ground cover, with notable species including Bladder Saltbush (*Atriplex vesicaria*), Grey Copperburr (*Sclerolaena diacantha*), and Pearl Bluebush (*Maireana sedifolia*). The density of this shrub layer can vary significantly, ranging from nearly impenetrable thickets to sparsely populated areas interspersed with various grasses and forbs. In instances of land clearance or overgrazing, subsequent regrowth often leads to a 'thickening' phenomenon, characterised by a proliferation of *Callitris*, *Melaleuca*, and *Allocasuarina* spp. This regrowth dynamic results in reduced understorey plant diversity and a consequent decline in overall woodland biodiversity.

This semiarid habitat (Köppen **Bsh**) spans the winter-rain/summer-rain boundary and receives less precipitation than the similar MIXED SANDPLAIN WOODLAND. The annual rainfall of 9–12 in. (230–310 mm) is relatively evenly distribution throughout the year—however, there is a slight peak in late summer in the northerly areas and a peak during the winter months in the southerly areas. Summers are very hot, with maximum temperatures usually exceeding 95°F (35°C) and occasionally reaching 113°F (45°C). Winter maximum temperatures are typically in the range of 59–68°F (15–20°C), while nighttime temperatures drop to around 41°F (5°C) and can occasionally reach freezing.

Yilgarn Mixed Woodlands are concentrated on the sandy or loamy soils formed on the rocks of the Yilgarn Block, which are billions of years old. The rocks that characterise this area have been extremely weathered over tens of millions of years. Prolonged weathering of the parent rock under palaeo-conditions of high rainfall and temperature (savanna climates) leached away soluble minerals leaving clays (saprolite) that retain just the texture of the original rock. Insoluble

Grey Butcherbird is a widespread species of coastal and semiarid parts of Australia, where its distinctive song can be heard in small country towns. © IAIN CAMPBELL, TROPICAL BIRDING TOURS/ UNSW E&ERC

oxides of iron and aluminium concentrate on the surface as laterites of ironstone nodules and bauxite pisoliths. These soils are incredibly inert and nutrient-deficient, making growth difficult for most plant species.

WILDLIFE: A fascinating feature of Australian biogeography is that birds in w. Australia appear to be much more generalist than those in the east, so there is much more species overlap between habitats. The reasons for this are not understood, but one possibility is that during the much drier ice ages, the w. Australian species all took refuge in a small pocket of the extreme southwest, whereas in e. Australia, there were far more options and fewer bottlenecks. Another reason could be that the much more varied landscape of e. Australia allows for far more differentiation and specialisation. The nectivorous bird assemblage found in habitats throughout w. Australia is fascinating in that it contains species such as Yellow-plumed, White-fronted, Tawny-crowned, and White-eared Honeyeaters, which are more confined to mallee or heathland habitats in the east. Other typical nectivorous birds and blossom nomads of this habitat include Purple-crowned Lorikeet; Spiny-cheeked, Singing, and Black Honeyeaters; plus Masked and White-browed Woodswallows.

Because Yilgarn Mixed Woodlands have so many *Acacia*, *Allocasuarina*, and *Melaleuca* trees and shrubs, the canopy bird assemblage also contains many insectivorous bird species such as Black-eared Cuckoo, Grey Shrikethrush, Horsfield's Bronze-Cuckoo, Pallid Cuckoo, White-winged Triller, Striated Pardalote, Weebill, Varied Sittella, Crested Bellbird, Rufous Whistler, and Red-capped Robin. There are also many insectivorous bird species in the shrubby understorey, such as Brown Treecreeper, Western Fieldwren, the gregarious White-browed Babbler, and Yellow-rumped, Western, and Inland Thornbills, the last of which is far more common in the west than the east. Fairywrens are a prominent feature of these woodlands, and Blue-breasted Fairywren and the exquisite electric-blue Splendid Fairywren are very common in much of this habitat. Interestingly, the latter is much more confiding in Western Australia than its eastern subspecies is in MIXED SANDPLAIN WOODLAND. Seed-eating and ground-feeding guilds are dominated by pigeons and parrots such as Common Bronzewing, Crested Pigeon, Peaceful Dove, Australian Ringneck, and Mulga Parrot.

The carnivorous mammals of semiarid Western Australia have seriously declined. Numbat used to occur here but has been extirpated. Western Quoll was also once widespread here, but few modern sightings have been recorded. Visitors to these woodlands can expect to find Common

Wallaroo, Western Grey Kangaroo, and Short-beaked Echidna. The semiarid nature of this zone is evident in the presence of smaller species such as Mitchell's Hopping Mouse, which normally occurs in more arid regions, and Western Pygmy Possum, which is more widespread in wetter heathlands than this habitat.

Reptiles are much more obvious in Yilgarn Mixed Woodland, which hosts a mix of semiarid species such as the large Sand Goanna (*Varanus gouldii*) and the smaller Central Bearded Dragon (*Pogona vitticeps*), Shingleback (*Tiliqua rugosa*), and Ornate Crevice-Dragon (*Ctenophorus ornatus*), which is particularly common around granitic outcrops. Smaller lizards include Goldfields Pebble Dragon (*Tympanocryptis pseudopsephos*), a strange-looking lizard that resembles both a rock and a Cane Toad with a rat tail, and Crested Bicycle-Dragon (*Ctenophorus cristatus*). Geckos are prevalent but much harder to find, as species such as Thick-tailed Barking Gecko (*Underwoodisaurus milii*) and Common Prickly Gecko (*Heteronotia binoei*) are strictly nocturnal. There are the typical highly venomous snakes, such as Mulga Snake (*Pseudechis australis*), Western Brown Snake (*Pseudonaja mengdeni*), and Gould's Hooded Snake (*Suta gouldii*), as well as the less venomous but still dangerous Southern Desert Banded Snake (*Simoselaps bertholdi*).

CONSERVATION: Because Yilgarn Mixed Woodland forms on such poor soils in semiarid regions, it is of limited value for widespread crop farming and has not been devastated like the WESTERN EUCALYPT WOODLAND of the Avon wheat belt. In some locations, where Yilgarn Mixed Woodland is dominated by dense stands of *Callitris* and *Allocasuarina*, it has been seriously overgrazed and fire has been retarded, resulting in the thickening of the woodland to 'scrub'.

DISTRIBUTION: Yilgarn Mixed Woodland occurs in Western Australia from the edge of the Yilgarn Block near Southern Cross (at the edge of the wheat belt) east to Kalgoorlie and south to just beyond Norseman. The boundary between this habitat and WESTERN EUCALYPT WOODLAND can be easily seen on satellite imagery as the boundary between the agricultural region and the mining region.

WHERE TO SEE: Goldfields Woodlands National Park, Western Australia; Dundas Nature Reserve, Western Australia.

Varied Sittella has many subspecies that were once regarded as separate species. The Black-capped subspecies (pictured) of sw. Australia is regularly found in Yilgarn Mixed Woodland. © IAIN CAMPBELL, TROPICAL BIRDING TOURS/UNSW E&ERC

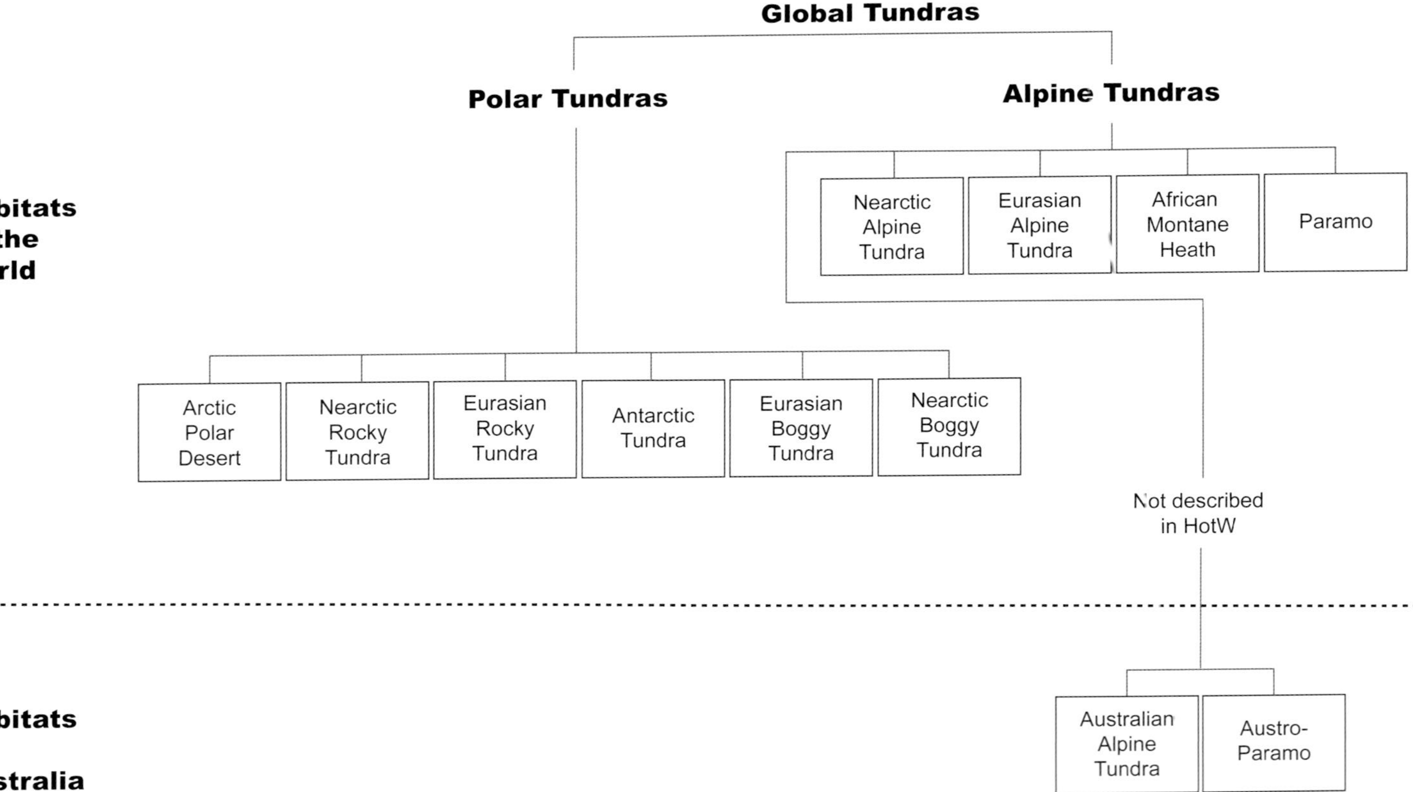
Australasian Tundras Dendrogram (Biome 10)
Global Tundras
Polar Tundras
Alpine Tundras
Habitats of the World
Nearctic Alpine Tundra
Eurasian Alpine Tundra
African Montane Heath
Paramo
Arctic Polar Desert
Nearctic Rocky Tundra
Eurasian Rocky Tundra
Antarctic Tundra
Eurasian Boggy Tundra
Nearctic Boggy Tundra
Not described in HotW
Habitats of Australia
Australian Alpine Tundra
Austro-Paramo

Au10A AUSTRALIAN ALPINE TUNDRA

IN A NUTSHELL: Low sclerophyllous scrublands and forb fields in alpine areas that are very exposed to strong winds and can have infertile soils. **Global Habitat Affinities:** NEARCTIC ALPINE TUNDRA; EUROPEAN ALPINE TUNDRA; ASIAN ALPINE TUNDRA. **Continental Habitat Affinities:** AUSTROPARAMO; SUBALPINE EUCALYPT WOODLAND. **Species Overlap:** MONTANE HEATHLAND; MONTANE GRASSLAND; SUBALPINE EUCALYPT WOODLAND. **Full Bird Assemblage:** habitatsoftheworld.org/Au10A.

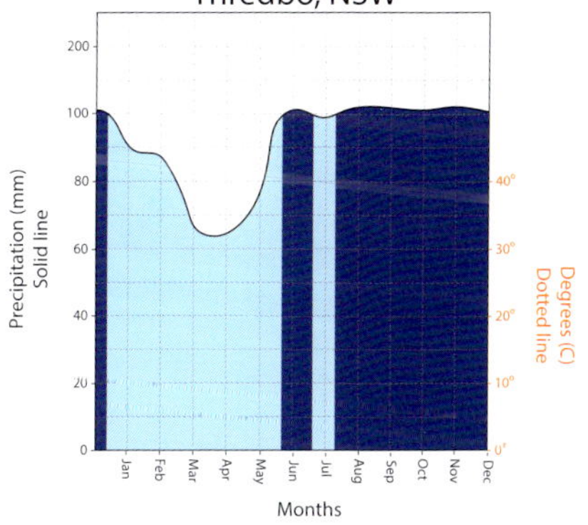

DESCRIPTION: This alpine habitat is a scattered mosaic of low, grassy heathland or forb field on slopes and treeless plains, comprising small plants that manage to survive in extremely cold, windy, and dry conditions, often growing in infertile soil or rock fields. Australian Alpine Tundra is subject to extremes in temperature and water availability but does not have the extended periods of midwinter darkness and midsummer sunshine experienced by Arctic tundra. Plants in Australia have very little in common with those of the Northern Hemisphere tundra, and Australian Alpine Tundra is botanically more diverse than its northern counterparts.

This habitat occurs at the highest elevations, above 5300 ft. (1600 m) in New South Wales and Victoria, and over 3000 ft. (1000 m) in the highlands of Tasmania, and as such it has a temperate oceanic climate (Köppen **Cfb**) with mild, relatively wet summers, year-round precipitation with snowfall in winter, and the warmest month below 72°F (22°C). Precipitation varies substantially but is generally 55–98 in. (1400–2500 mm) per annum in the Snowy Mountains (New South Wales) and 47–75 in. (1200–1900 mm) in Tasmania. The soils associated with Alpine Tundra are very immature lithosols with chemistry that is often unrelated to the underlying substrate. The limited humic (organic) layers lie directly over seeming fresh rock and are derived from the extremely slow decomposition of organic material rather than the weathering of the underlying rock. In these frigid environments, weathering is more mechanical, with breakdown through frost wedging rather than chemical decomposition of minerals, thus resulting in little clay development in the soil profile.

Their name conjures up images of dramatic landscapes, as in Europe's Alps, but the Australian Alps are much more subdued, more rounded hills than towering peaks.

© INNA OSMOLOVSKY, UNSW E&ERC

This is a complex mosaic of microhabitats with wet bogs, protected groves of shrubby heathlands, exposed grasslands and herb fields, and above those feldmark, a microhabitat reminiscent of ARCTIC CRYPTIC TUNDRA, where little grows. Because most wildlife in these zones lives in a broad range of these microhabitats, they are treated here as one large habitat, Australian Alpine Tundra. Small-leaved shrubs, herbs, and tussock grasses dominate the vegetation, which is usually less than 6 ft. (2 m) tall. The dominant shrubs are Coral Heath (*Epacris microphylla*), Yellow Kunzea (*Kunzea ericifolia*), Common Oxylobium (*Oxylobium ellipticum*), Alpine Grevillea (*Grevillea australis*), and Mountain Grevillea (*Grevillea victoriae*); the *Grevillea* spp. are important because they can flower even when almost completely covered in snow. In snow crannies (areas protected from desiccating winds by snow), Mountain Plum

Some areas of Australian Alpine Tundra can be shrubby and look remarkably like Nearctic Rocky Tundra around Nome in Alaska.

© INNA OSMOLOVSKY, UNSW E&ERC

Pine (*Podocarpus lawrencei*) can form small groves with forbs such as snow daisies (*Celmisia* spp.) and billy buttons (*Craspedia* spp.). Areas with poorer drainage have cushion bogs and grass bogs that resemble the ANDEAN CUSHION PARAMO of South America, with species such as New Zealand Sphagnum (*Sphagnum cristatum*) growing with Wire Rush (*Empodisma minus*) and Pineapple Grass (*Astelia alpina*), along with sedges such as Asian Shortstem Sedge (*Carex breviculmis*) and wetland heath plants such as Swamp Heath (*Epacris paludosa*). Generally, it is easy to move through this environment, though the ground is often soft and uneven underfoot.

Species richness decreases with elevation, and on the ridgelines of the Snowy Mountains and the higher areas of Tasmania where the vegetation is exposed to severe frosts, the coldest temperatures, and desiccating high winds, the makeup of the tundra changes to feldmark. This is a zone of few dwarf shrubs such as Rock Heath (*Epacris petrophila*) and Spreading Coprosma (*Coprosma pumila*), generally growing less than 12 in. (30 cm) tall, mixed with cushion-forming Cushion Cupflower (*Colobanthus pulvinatus*) or prostrate plant species and bare rock.

The lower edges of these alpine heathlands have low trees, 10 ft. (3m tall), which are not stunted, windswept versions of larger trees but often their smaller close relatives that are better suited to this environment.

WILDLIFE: Although the alpine heathlands in Australia are floristically rich, they do not hold many special bird species and are best viewed as a depauperate version of lower-elevation heath thickets. From a bird assemblage perspective, this habitat attracts a few high-elevation woodland species and a limited number of heathland birds. Most of the species that occur here avoid the winter months, and only species like Tasmanian Nativehen, Green Rosella, Tasmanian Scrubwren, Striated Fieldwren, Black Currawong, and Forest Raven winter in this environment in Tasmania, and White-browed Scrubwren, Grey Currawong, and Australian and Little Ravens on the mainland. Even these wintering birds will move downslope if the snowfalls become too heavy, often forming wintering flocks until they can move back upslope.

The role Australian Alpine Tundra plays in bird migration is very different from that of the Northern Hemisphere analogous habitats, which are visited mainly by long-distance migrants; for example, in NEARCTIC ALPINE TUNDRA, the visitors are Neotropical migrants from Central and South America, while EUROPEAN ALPINE TUNDRA is visited by sub-Saharan migrants from tropical Africa. In stark contrast, the nectar-feeding birds here are mainly north–south migrants from other parts of Australia or local elevational migrants such as Red Wattlebird, Eastern Spinebill, and White-eared, Yellow-faced, and Crescent Honeyeaters. In Tasmania, Crescent Honeyeater is joined by New Holland Honeyeater, and where there are groves of eucalypts in the snow crannies, Yellow-throated Honeyeater occurs. It is interesting that New Holland Honeyeater makes it to the alpine zone in Tasmania yet is predominantly a lowland heath species on mainland Australia.

Striated Fieldwren is a hardy indicator species for Australian Alpine Tundra, remaining there year-round unlike many other inhabitants. © BEN KNOOT

Crescent Honeyeater breeds in Australian Alpine Tundra, though it descends into lower-elevation habitats during the harsher winter months.
© IAIN CAMPBELL, TROPICAL BIRDING TOURS/UNSW E&ERC

Other species that can be found in this habitat after the spring melt include Brush Bronzewing, Fan-tailed Cuckoo, Yellow-rumped Thornbill, Scrubtit, Olive Whistler, Flame and Scarlet Robins, Jacky-winter, Singing Bushlark, and Australian Pipit.

Alpine mammals include macropods, such as Eastern Grey Kangaroo, Rufous-bellied Pademelon, and Red-necked Wallaby; possums such as Mountain Brushtail Possum and Common Brushtail Possum; and small mice such as Broad-toothed Mouse. The larger Bare-nosed Wombat is commonly seen, even during the day, though it tends to be more nocturnal in other habitats. The near-ubiquitous Short-beaked Echidna remains fairly common in Australian Alpine Tundra.

There are a surprising number of reptiles despite the harsh winter conditions of this habitat. Typical reptiles of the mainland tundra include Alpine Water Skink (*Eulamprus kosciuskoi*), Jacky Dragon (*Amphibolurus muricatus*), Robust Ctenotus (*Ctenotus robustus*), Blotched Bluetongue (*Tiliqua nigrolutea*), Tussock Skink (*Pseudemoia pagenstecheri*), Southern Water Skink (*Eulamprus tympanum*), Cunningham's Skink (*Egernia cunninghami*), and Southern Grass Skink (*Pseudemoia entrecasteauxii*). In Tasmania the typical assemblage includes Alpine Coolskink (*Carinascincus greeni*), Metallic Coolskink (*Carinascincus metallicus*), Southern Grass Skink, and Tiger Snake (*Notechis scutatus*).

CONSERVATION: The main threat to Australian Alpine Tundra is climate change, with observed warming trends leading to upslope shifts of over 30% of the plants. The reduced snow persistence, important for frost-dependent species, is leading to invasion of introduced species. Wild horses cause degradation of the tundra through trampling and soil erosion, though because they are charismatic, there is public pressure not to remove them from this fragile habitat.

DISTRIBUTION: In mainland Australia, this habitat is limited, occurring along the Great Dividing Range and in the Snowy Mountains of New South Wales and Victoria. It is much more widespread through the highlands of Tasmania.

WHERE TO SEE: Mt. Kosciuszko, New South Wales, Australia; Mt. Buffalo, Victoria, Australia; Mt. Wellington, Tasmania, Australia.

Au10B AUSTROPARAMO

IN A NUTSHELL: Low, sclerophyllous scrublands with infertile soil found above the tree line and exposed to strong winds. **Global Habitat Affinities:** AFROPARAMO; KINABALU PARAMO. **Continental Habitat Affinities:** AUSTRALIAN ALPINE TUNDRA. **Species Overlap:** NEW GUINEA HIGH-MONTANE RAINFOREST. **Full Bird Assemblage:** habitatsoftheworld.org/Au10B.

DESCRIPTION: Austroparamo is the Australasian equivalent of the PARAMO of South America or the AFROPARAMO of Africa. Found above 9000 ft. (3000 m) on the island of New Guinea, this habitat looks superficially similar to NEARCTIC ALPINE TUNDRA or AUSTRALIAN ALPINE TUNDRA, with small plants that manage to survive in extremely cold and windy conditions, often growing in infertile soil or on rock fields. However, these tropical, alpine heathlands are similar to Paramo and Afroparamo in that they are subject to extremes in temperature and water availability but do not undergo the many months of darkness and months of continuous sunshine experienced by Arctic tundra.

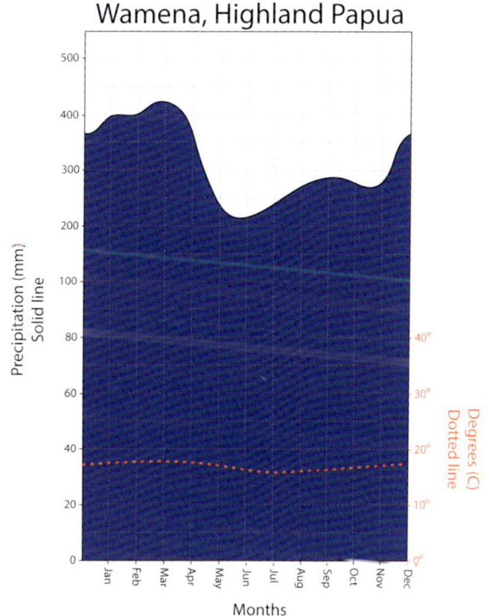

Precipitation in the Austroparamo is not high, with annual amounts in the range of 28–80 in. (700–2000 mm), but because the habitat is so high, cold, and covered in mist, overall moisture is abundant, and this a very humid habitat. Soils are almost always acidic, nutrient-deficient, and sandy, with very little relationship to the underlying rock type. Because of the very cold climate, chemical weathering is so weak here that the soils form from organic material, rather than underlying rock. Over most of the area, nighttime temperatures drop to near or below freezing, but temperatures can rise to around 65–70°F (18–21°C) during the middle of the day.

Austroparamo is a series of hills, mires, bogs, and marshes, and generally has a very boggy feel to it, with highly irregular drainage patterns. The plants in New Guinea have very little in common with those of the Northern Hemisphere tundra, and Austroparamo is far more floristically rich than its northern counterparts, supporting a mixture of endemic shrubs, grasses, and mosses. In wetter areas, the landscape is dominated by cushion plants and flowers such as Large New Guinea Carrot (*Anisotome latifolia*) and Papuan Buttercup (*Ranunculus perindutus*), plants with a rosette

The tree line in New Guinea varies greatly in elevation and aspect. Here in Tari Gap, Papua New Guinea, the Austroparamo occurs in small patches below the tree line as well as large blankets above it. © JUN MATSUI, SICKLEBILL SAFARIS

form such as New Guinea Astelia (*Astelia papuana*), dwarf shrubs, horsetails, mosses, and tussock grasses. Orchids can survive here, including New Guinea Dendrobium (*Dendrobium cuthbertsonii*). In snow crannies and other protected areas, the trees more prominent in the NEW GUINEA HIGH-MONTANE RAINFOREST below, such as Macgregor's Rhododendron (*Rhododendron macgregoriae*), occur in dwarf forms. Areas with poorer drainage have cushion bogs and grass bogs that resemble the wet Paramo of the n. Andes. Generally, it is easy to move through this environment, although the ground is often uneven underfoot. Species richness decreases with elevation, and at the upper limit, the ground is covered by cushion plants and bare rock.

The elevation of the tree line in the New Guinea highlands is influenced primarily by temperature and moisture availability. Fire retardation may result in the expansion of New Guinea High-Montane Rainforest into Austroparamo. With rising global temperatures due to climate change, areas previously too cold for tree growth now support such vegetation. This change can significantly alter the composition and dynamics of the mountain ecosystems, impacting both the biodiversity and the local animal communities that depend on these ecosystems.

WILDLIFE: The Austroparamo heathlands of New Guinea, sometimes referred to as subalpine shrublands, are less diverse than habitats at lower elevations but have a very distinct avifauna,

Snow Mountain Quail is a large quail that lives on the highest mountains of New Guinea. © DANIEL LÓPEZ-VELASCO, ORNIS BIRDING EXPEDITIONS

comprising mainly such groups as honeyeaters, robins, and munias. These heaths adjoin grasslands where local species like Snow Mountain Quail (Snow Mountains, Indonesian New Guinea) and Alpine Munia (se. Papua New Guinea) occur, as well as the more widespread Alpine Pipit and Papuan Harrier. In the skies overhead, the wide-ranging Mountain Swiftlet is seen regularly, while shrubbery

Snow Mountain Munia (pictured) of w. New Guinea is sometimes considered conspecific with Alpine Munia of e. New Guinea. © DANIEL LÓPEZ-VELASCO, ORNIS BIRDING EXPEDITIONS

When most people think of pipits, they imagine vast grasslands, savannas, and deserts. The Alpine Pipit, however, prefers the Austroparamo in the mountains of New Guinea.
© KEN BEHRENS, TROPICAL BIRDING TOURS

is home to Brown Quail, Archbold's Nightjar, Painted Tiger-Parrot, and a series of high-living honeyeaters: Grey-streaked, Orange-cheeked, Long-bearded, Short-bearded, and Sooty Honeyeaters. Robins are less conspicuous, but Subalpine and Snow Mountain Robins occur in the highlands of New Guinea along with finches such as the wide-ranging Mountain Firetail and the more local Snow Mountain Munia. The most striking of all the inhabitants of this habitat are Eastern and Western Crested Berrypeckers, members of an endemic New Guinean family. None of the heath species appear to be restricted to the habitat, except perhaps the grassland species (Snow Mountain Quail, Alpine Pipit); most others range into the nearby grasslands or the upper montane forest edge.

Mammals that occur in this habitat include Eastern Long-beaked Echidna, Long-tailed Pygmy Possum, and Subalpine Woolly Rat; while Calaby's Pademelon, Long-tailed and Raffray's Bandicoots, Habbema and Speckled Dasyures, and Coppery Ringtail Possum occur in nearby subalpine grasslands.

CONSERVATION: Austroparamo is a very fragile habitat that takes a long time to stabilise, is extremely slow-growing, and has very long-lived vegetation. Once it has been overgrazed or cleared, leaving the landscape in an impoverished state, regeneration requires an incredibly long time. Few areas are protected, and rapid population growth is now placing pressure on this environment in what were, until recently, remote areas. Climate change will cause the rise of some plant species to the detriment of others, though the type of habitat that develops cannot be predicted.

DISTRIBUTION: Austroparamo is widely distributed but very localised in the highest elevations of the New Guinea highlands in both Indonesia and Papua New Guinea.

WHERE TO SEE: Snow Mountains, Central Papua, Indonesian New Guinea; Mt. Albert Edward and Mt. Victoria, Central Province, Papua New Guinea.

Au11A AUSTRALASIAN TROPICAL FRESHWATER WETLAND

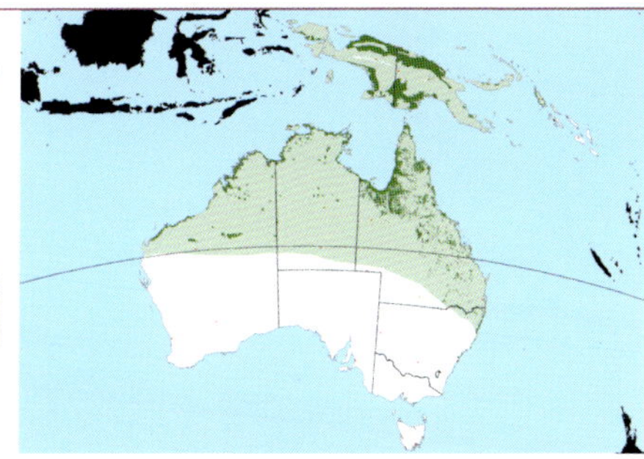

IN A NUTSHELL: Habitat that is permanently or seasonally flooded with shallow fresh water and vegetated mostly by hydrophilic reeds, shrubs, and floating plants. **Global Habitat Affinities:** AFROTROPICAL SHALLOW FRESHWATER MARSH; ASIAN TROPICAL WETLAND; NEOTROPICAL TROPICAL WETLAND. **Continental Habitat Affinities:** TEMPERATE WETLAND. **Species Overlap:** TEMPERATE WETLAND. **Full Bird Assemblage:** habitatsoftheworld.org/Au11A.

DESCRIPTION: Tropical Freshwater Wetlands are expanses of water that exist as part of river floodplains, billabongs (oxbow lakes), or even man-made structures such as dams. They encompass a species-rich mosaic of microhabitats—swamp savanna, open marsh, herbaceous swamp, flooded grassland. There is a lot of complexity within wetland habitats, but the most striking difference is between those that are permanently flooded with deeper water and those that are areas of shallower water. These wetlands can be as deep as 26 ft. (8 m) in billabongs and dams or extremely shallow on floodplains with large swaths of exposed mud. Because most Tropical Freshwater Wetlands are in areas of monsoonal climate, they change dramatically through the year. Some of the shallow wetlands are ephemeral, filling up during the wet season (December–April), when the water can rise 15 ft. (5 m), and then drying out over the rest of the year, perhaps completely, before the rain arrives again.

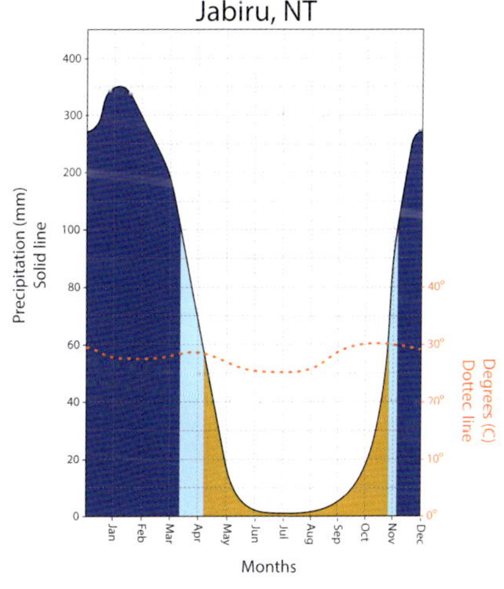

Mats of floating vegetation are a feature of these tropical wetlands, particularly in shallow areas. The wetlands are sometimes bordered by reeds or exposed mudflats in shallow areas and by *Pandanus* (screw-pine) where there are steeper banks. Floating plants tend to grow in slow-flowing areas with deeper water and sometimes blanket huge areas. Water lilies are often a major component and at times can cover a whole body of water. Common species include the Australia native Blue Water Lily (*Nymphaea violacea*). The flora of shallow marshes is much shorter and more uniform in stature than that of deeper areas and is often dominated by grasses and sedges.

Tropical Freshwater Wetlands can be ephemeral or permanent, such as Cattana Wetlands (pictured), near Cairns, Queensland. © GABRIEL CAMPBELL, TROPICAL BIRDING TOURS

Comb-crested Jacana utilises its long toes to traverse the floating vegetation that is a distinctive characteristic of Australasian Tropical Freshwater Wetlands. © SHANE KENNEDY, TROPICAL BIRDING TOURS

This is partly because these plants are more resistant to fires that can sweep in from neighbouring grasslands and affect ephemeral swamps that dry out during the dry season. These shallow marshes can transition into grassland, but their wet drainage lines usually remain even in the heart of the dry season. Common sedges include fringe rushes (*Fimbristylis* spp.) and spikerushes (*Eleocharis* spp.), and common grasses are Tanglehead (*Heteropogon contortus*) and Ditch Millet (*Paspalum scrobiculatum*).

WILDLIFE: Wetlands are great places for birdwatching and, unlike many other habitats, can be productive at any time of day. The water-lily habitat is important for birds like Comb-crested Jacana and Green Pygmy-Goose and may also support massive congregations of Magpie Geese and whistling-ducks. At the end of the dry season, these wetlands may hold thousands of birds, including Radjah Shelduck; Black-necked Stork; Magpie Goose; Cotton and Green Pygmy-Geese; Plumed and Wandering Whistling-Ducks; Australasian Darter; Pied and Little Pied Cormorants; Glossy, Australian, and Straw-necked Ibises; Royal and Yellow-billed Spoonbills; Pied and Pacific Herons; Australasian Swamphen; and White-browed Crake. Masses of shorebirds can also be found, including Black-fronted and Red-kneed Dotterels and Australian Pratincole; these Australian resident species undergo local movements and are seen mostly in the far north from June to November. Boreal migrant shorebirds that breed in Siberia and other parts of n. Asia include Marsh, Wood, and Sharp-tailed Sandpipers, Red-necked Stint and Common Greenshank; they are seen mostly from September to April, but in some places like Kakadu National Park, Northern Territory, the numbers are greatly concentrated during migration in spring and autumn (fall), especially from September to November, when they are more readily seen on the exposed mud. After the onset of the rains, higher water levels make many waterbirds less visible and in some areas limit access due to flooded roads. In the dry season, these wetlands are also an important refuge for land birds such as pigeons, parrots, and finches, which come to drink. Paperbark and Shining Flycatchers can be found in the bordering trees, and Golden-headed Cisticola, Australian Reed Warbler, and Crimson Finch in the surrounding long grass. Azure and Little Kingfishers fish from overhangs around the edges.

The water itself does not hold many mammals compared

The majestic Black-necked Stork is confined largely to wetlands in tropical areas.
© IAIN CAMPBELL, TROPICAL BIRDING TOURS/UNSW E&ERC

Noisy groups of Magpie Geese are often the most conspicuous inhabitants of Australasian Tropical Freshwater Wetlands, sometimes numbering in the thousands. © SHANE KENNEDY, TROPICAL BIRDING TOURS

with TEMPERATE WETLANDS, but Agile Wallaby and Antilopine Wallaroo can often be found around wetland edges. Although not a native species, the domestic Water Buffalo is found feral in n. Australia and makes use of this habitat, impacting the ecosystem by trampling and eating vegetation, causing erosion, and competing with native species for resources. Efforts are made to manage their populations to mitigate these impacts.

Two of Australia's most sought-after reptiles, the monstrous and exceptionally aggressive Saltwater Crocodile (*Crocodylus porosus*) and the much smaller and more passive Freshwater Crocodile (*Crocodylus johnstoni*), live in tropical wetlands. Northern Snake-necked Turtle (*Chelodina rugosa*) and Northern Australian Snapping Turtle (*Elseya dentata*) compete with Mertens's Water Monitor (*Varanus mertensi*) for basking positions on the water's edge, although the arrival of the Cane Toad (*Rhinella marina*) has resulted in a serious population decline of the water monitor. Common Keelback (*Tropidonophis mairii*), a snake that does not suffer from the Cane Toad's toxin, can be found in good numbers around tropical wetlands, along with Water Python (*Liasis fuscus*) and Common Tree Snake (*Dendrelaphis punctulatus*), which hunts in brush overhanging the water's edge.

CONSERVATION: Tropical Freshwater Wetlands in New Guinea and the Solomons have no significant protection and are being drained and converted to cultivation at an alarming rate. Tropical wetlands in Australia are better protected but are still at risk from invasive species, such as Para Grass (*Urochloa mutica*) from Africa and Olive Hymenachne (*Hymenachne amplexicaulis*) from Central America, that outcompete native grasses. Widespread overgrazing by cattle and feral buffalo destroy the edges of the wetlands, though many cattle farm dams are de facto wetlands that protect local wildlife. Along the east coast of Australia, development pressure, originally from sugarcane farms and now urban encroachment, has led to removal of most Tropical Freshwater Wetlands.

Plumed Whistling-Duck (pictured) enters the water much less often than Wandering or Spotted Whistling-Ducks. © NICK ATHANAS, TROPICAL BIRDING TOURS

DISTRIBUTION: Tropical wetlands are found across far n. and e. Australia in areas with a monsoonal climate, in the lowlands of New Guinea, and on some of the Solomon Islands. The wetlands of New Guinea's Sepik region and elsewhere on the island's northern slope are less monsoon-dependent and savanna-oriented, being surrounded by rainforest and swamp forest, while those of the island's Trans-Fly region in the south are surrounded by savanna and closely associated with the wetlands of mainland Australia. The most famous wetland in Australia is the enormous Yellow Water in Kakadu National Park. A Yellow Water cruise offers one of the best opportunities in the world for waterbird photography from a boat. In ne. Queensland, Lake Mitchell and the Mareeba wetlands on the Atherton Tableland are good examples of tropical wetlands. Smaller ephemeral wetlands can be found anywhere in tropical Australasia and are usually great places for birdwatching.

WHERE TO SEE: Hasties Swamp National Park, Atherton, Queensland, Australia; Yellow Water, Kakadu National Park, Northern Territory, Australia; Wasur National Park, South Papua, Indonesian New Guinea.

The elegant Pied Heron is one of the only Australian herons confined to tropical wetlands. © IAIN CAMPBELL, TROPICAL BIRDING TOURS/UNSW E&ERC

Au11B AUSTRALIAN TEMPERATE WETLAND

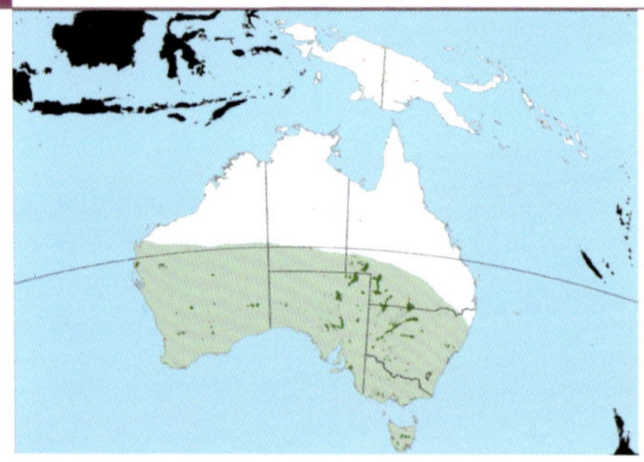

IN A NUTSHELL: Wetlands of s. Australia that are permanently waterlogged or temporarily flooded with fresh water and are vegetated by temperate, hydrophilic reeds, rushes, and sedges. **Global Habitat Affinities:** ASIAN TEMPERATE WETLAND; SOUTH AFRICAN TEMPERATE WETLAND. **Continental Habitat Affinities:** TROPICAL FRESHWATER WETLAND. **Species Overlap:** TROPICAL FRESHWATER WETLAND. **Full Bird Assemblage:** habitatsoftheworld.org/Au11B.

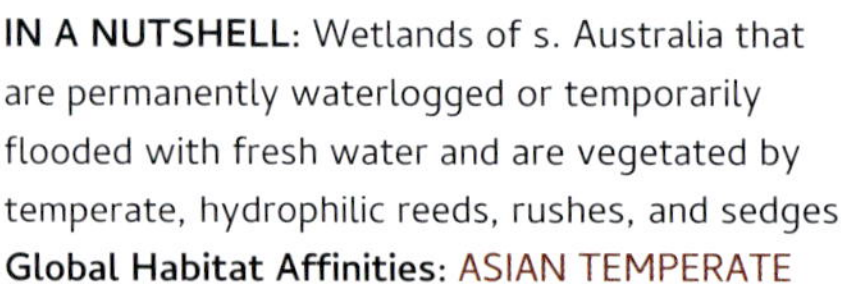

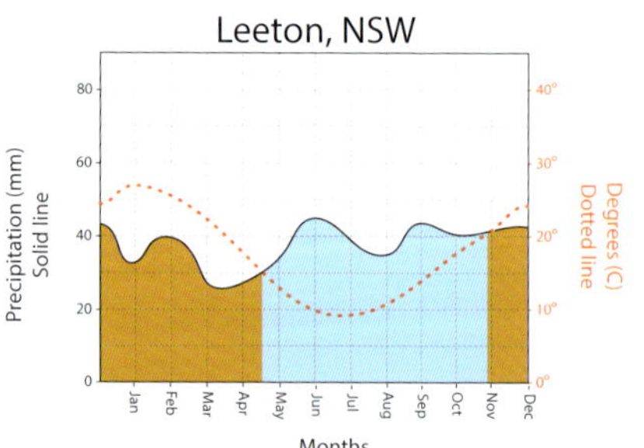

DESCRIPTION: Wetlands can consist of permanent depressions, river floodplains, oxbow lakes (billabongs), human-made lakes, sewage works, and the ephemeral lakes of desert regions. Temperate Wetlands generally lack the mats of floating vegetation that characterise the TROPICAL FRESHWATER WETLANDS of the north, and they attract a very different suite of animals. All Australian temperate freshwater wetlands are subject to the vagaries of climate, and while most are permanent, they still experience fluctuations in water levels, filling up after rain and slowly evaporating during times of drought. The lakes of far inland Australia, like Lake Eyre, are empty most of the time and may fill up only every few years. Although primarily saltwater lakes at low water levels, they take on characteristics of freshwater lakes at high water levels after heavy rains. More permanent but shallow lakes can be thickly vegetated with cumbungi, or cattails (*Typha* spp.), which provide thick cover for shyer animal species. Some other typical temperate freshwater hydrophilic plant species include Common Reed (*Phragmites australis*) and twigrushes (*Machaerina* spp.). Some wetlands include flooded woodland, and often there are stands of dead trees with many tree cavities. Since these are surrounded by water, limiting access by land predators (mainly mammals), they are havens for hole-nesting birds such as parrots.

WILDLIFE: Bird populations in temperate wetlands fluctuate along with water levels, and while some species stay on, others are nomadic in nature, roaming great distances. Therefore, some species may be present at certain sites year-round for years at a time, but they may also be absent

Bird numbers fluctuate greatly in Temperate Wetlands such as Fivebough Swamp in New South Wales. In times of drought, these permanent wetlands become a refuge for species from vast areas of c. Australia where most wetlands are ephemeral. © GABRIEL CAMPBELL, TROPICAL BIRDING TOURS

for similar periods in response to changing water availability. Sporadically flooded wetlands are important nesting areas for birds such as Australian Pelican and Banded Stilt. Permanent lakes attract secretive species like Australian, Spotless, and Baillon's Crakes; Black-tailed Nativehen; and Australasian Bittern. In more coastal areas, the open waters are often permanent and attract species like Black Swan, and Hardhead, Pink-eared, Blue-billed, and Musk Ducks. The reedy edges are home to passerines such as Australian Reed Warbler and Little Grassbird. The exceedingly rare, crepuscular Australian Painted-Snipe breeds in ephemeral freshwater wetlands and continues to decline due to changes in land use and the loss of these temporary water regimes. The rare Australasian Bittern prefers tall, dense rushes, reeds, and sedges interspersed with pools.

Freshwater wetlands comprise a couple of very different subhabitats, the vegetated edges of the wetlands and the open water. The open water of **Deepwater Lakes and Dams** holds a particular set of birds, which can include the stiff-tailed Blue-billed Duck, which is almost always seen out on the open water, where it dives down to catch aquatic invertebrates. Great Crested, Hoary-headed, and Australasian Grebes feed in a similar way and are also usually seen out on the open water. The unusual Musk Duck also dives down to catch aquatic invertebrates but is less tied to the open water and also likes areas with dense aquatic vegetation.

Black Swan can be numerous, sometimes numbering in the hundreds, in Temperate Wetlands of se. Australia. © IAIN CAMPBELL, TROPICAL BIRDING TOURS/UNSW E&ERC

Pink-eared Duck is a gorgeous duck of s. Australia that somewhat resembles a shoveler.
© SHANE KENNEDY, TROPICAL BIRDING TOURS

Several freshwater turtles found in Temperate Wetland include Eastern Snake-necked Turtle (*Chelodina longicollis*), Southwestern Snake-necked Turtle (*Chelodina oblonga*), Eastern Short-necked Turtle (*Emydura macquarii*), and Broad-shelled Turtle (*Chelodina expansa*), one of the longest-lived freshwater turtles in the world. Tiger Snake (*Notechis scutatus*), Eastern Brown Snake (*Pseudonaja textilis*), and Red-bellied Black Snake (*Pseudechis porphyriacus*) are often found around temperate freshwater wetlands.

CONSERVATION: Although there are plenty of protected temperate freshwater wetlands in Australia, a number of animal species with very specific habitat requirements have been affected by habitat loss or degradation. In many populated areas where remaining wetlands are nominally protected, the hydrology is often changed so much that most of the species requiring vegetated edges are displaced, and only a few animal species remain. The situation is much better in inland Australia where there are serious efforts to preserve the massive wetlands in areas such as Macquarie Marshes, New South Wales.

DISTRIBUTION: Temperate Wetlands in s. Australia are widespread, and most cities and small towns have a sewage pond or town weir that holds some wetland birds. Some good examples of accessible permanent wetlands with a nice diversity of species are Fivebough Wetlands, near Leeton, New South Wales; Gum Swamp, near Forbes, New South Wales; Werribee Sewage Plant, near Melbourne, Victoria; and Herdsman Lake, Perth, Western Australia. Ephemeral wetlands can occur throughout the temperate areas of Australia and are always worth a quick stop to check out what you might find.

WHERE TO SEE: Fivebough Wetlands, Leeton, New South Wales, Australia; Werribee Sewage Plant, Melbourne, Victoria, Australia.

Little Grassbird is a vocal inhabitant of well-vegetated fringes of Temperate Wetlands.
© IAIN CAMPBELL, TROPICAL BIRDING TOURS/UNSW E&ERC

Au11C LIGNUM SWAMP

IN A NUTSHELL: Lignum thickets in wetlands of s. inland Australia. **Global Habitat Affinities:** NORTH AFRICAN TEMPERATE WETLAND. **Continental Habitat Affinities:** TEMPERATE WETLAND. **Species Overlap:** TEMPERATE WETLAND. **Full Bird Assemblage:** habitatsoftheworld.org/Au11C.

DESCRIPTION: Lignum (*Duma florulenta*) grows in permanent braided channels, brackish ephemeral swamps, and clay pans on floodplains in inland areas that are otherwise dominated by CHENOPOD SHRUBLAND and GIBBER CHENOPODLAND. In less arid and less saline areas of s. Australia, TEMPERATE WETLAND dominated by cumbungi, or cattails (*Typha* spp.), replaces this habitat. Although Lignum extends over much of s. Australia and is a minor component of other temperate wetlands, and even colonises some dams and boreholes, the wetland is designated Lignum Swamp when Lignum is the dominant plant.

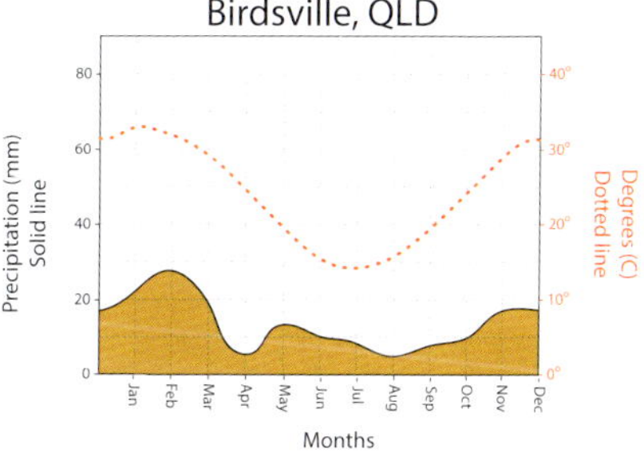

Lignum Swamps blend into the surrounding gibber plains in the areas where flooding is very ephemeral. © GABRIEL CAMPBELL, TROPICAL BIRDING TOURS

Previous page: **Where water stays longer along creek beds, Lignum can grow well above head height and become impenetrable. Birding is mainly done from the edges of the thickets.** © IAIN CAMPBELL, TROPICAL BIRDING TOURS/UNSW E&ERC

Lignum grows as a perennial, open to closed thicket shrubland, up to 7 ft. (2.5 m) tall. Its tangle of thin, intertwined branchlets makes each bush near impenetrable, forming dense thickets to the exclusion of other species. After significant rains, or flooding from rains that fall hundreds of miles upstream, new leaves grow, and the lignum clumps change from dull grey-green to a vibrant olive-green. The plant is semi-deciduous—the leaves proliferate on new branchlets but soon die, and the leafless twigs then continue to undertake photosynthesis. Because this habitat grows in similar climates (Köppen **Bsk**, **Bwk**) to CHENOPOD SHRUBLAND, it is predictable that other plants that grow within these shrublands are predominantly chenopods, such as Queensland Bluebush (*Chenopodium auricomum*), Nitre Goosefoot (*Chenopodium nitrariaceum*), and Leafless Bluebush (*Maireana aphylla*), and chenopod-like shrubs such as Black Roly-poly (*Sclerolaena muricata*). Some small shrublike trees can grow in this habitat, including Shoestring Acacia (*Acacia stenophylla*), Gundabluie (*Acacia victoriae*), Bignonia Emu Bush (*Eremophila bignoniiflora*), and even the large Coolabah (*Eucalyptus coolabah*), which can grow to 60 ft. (20 m) in height.

In wet periods, amphibious plants grow in the marsh, and in dry years, the large gaps between thickets are either bare, cracking clays or sparsely covered with plants such as Yellow Pea Bush (*Sesbania cannabina*) and Indian Jointvetch (*Aeschynomene indica*). Lignum Swamp is not fire-tolerant and is easily destroyed by fires spreading from surrounding grasslands and shrublands, which may be a significant factor in this habitat being very limited in spinifex-dominated environments.

WILDLIFE: Small passerines are limited in Lignum Swamp, but Grey Grasswren is found only in these tangles and is an obligate species to this habitat. Purple-backed Fairywren also occurs here,

The elusive Grey Grasswren is a highly specialised species as it is the only Australian songbird confined to Lignum Swamp. © PETE MORRIS

Black-tailed Nativehen is an eruptive species that in good years breeds in c. Australia; the birds then disperse to coastal areas after breeding. © SAM WOODS, TROPICAL BIRDING TOURS

and White-winged Fairywren is fairly common on the edges of these wetland thickets. Chirruping Wedgebill is a skulker that is found in the chenopod shrubs within the swamps. Waterbird populations in Lignum Swamps fluctuate along with water levels, and while some species stay on, others are nomadic in nature, roaming great distances. Therefore, some species may be present at certain sites year-round for years at a time and then absent for similar periods in response to changing water availability. Black-tailed Nativehen is usually present even when water levels are very low. Australian Painted-Snipe and Freckled Duck both breed in the swamps in good years.

Mammals are not common in this habitat, although the native Long-haired Rat and small marsupial Fat-tailed Dunnart can be found. Reptiles found around Lignum may include Painted Dragon (*Ctenophorus pictus*), Ribbon Ctenotus (*Ctenotus taeniatus*), Sand Goanna (*Varanus gouldii*), and Shield-snouted Brown Snake (*Pseudonaja aspidorhyncha*).

CONSERVATION: Lignum swamps are highly sensitive to changes in hydrology and land use. There has been an estimated 75% decline in lignum cover in some regions, threatening the Grey Grasswren, which depends on dense lignum for nesting. Additional pressures include overgrazing by livestock and feral animals, and invasive weeds. On the edges of the main range of this habitat, potential river regulation disrupts the natural flood cycles essential for lignum regeneration. However, the great news for Lignum Swamp conservation is the creation of the vast Narriearra Caryapundy Swamp National Park in far nw. New South Wales, which protects a large percentage of the Grey Grasswren population as well as many of the other species that rely on this habitat for episodic breeding.

DISTRIBUTION: Although the Lignum shrub is widespread throughout semiarid s. Australia, Lignum Swamp is limited to nw. New South Wales, sw. Queensland, and ne. South Australia, mainly through the Channel Country and Bulloo Overflow. A depauperate version also occurs in nw. Victoria, though the bird assemblage here is the same as in surrounding WETLANDS.

WHERE TO SEE: Goyder Lagoon, Birdsville Track, South Australia; Bulloo Overflow, sw. Queensland, Australia; Narriearra Caryapundy Swamp National Park, nw. New South Wales, Australia.

Au11D MONTANE BOG AND FEN

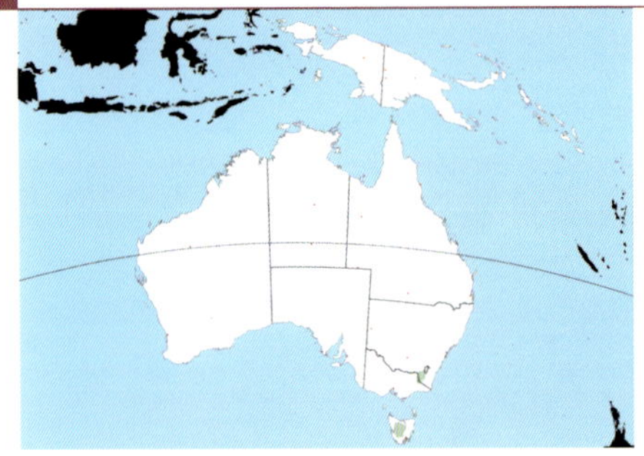

IN A NUTSHELL: Waterlogged montane areas that accumulate peat deposits and contain mosses, grasses, and sedges, plus shrubs and even stunted trees. **Global Habitat Affinities:** ASIAN FRESHWATER SWAMP FOREST. **Continental Habitat Affinities:** COASTAL SALT MARSH; TEMPERATE WETLAND. **Species Overlap:** TEMPERATE WETLAND. **Full Bird Assemblage:** habitatsoftheworld.org/Au11D.

DESCRIPTION: Bogs are wetland areas that accumulate peat, a deposit of dead plant material, often mosses, primarily *Sphagnum*. They receive all their water through precipitation and tend to be acidic, nutrient-poor, and waterlogged. Vegetation in bogs, in addition to mosses, includes shrubs and sometimes stunted trees. Fens are similar to bogs but are usually less acidic and receive nutrients from groundwater as well as rainwater. They have a higher diversity of plant life, including grasses, sedges, wildflowers, and sometimes shrubs and trees. Fens are also peat-forming but tend to be more nutrient-rich than bogs. Moss-derived peat deposits in bogs and fens can be shallow or up to 6.5 ft. (2 m) deep and play an important role in carbon storage. They generally form above 2000 ft. (600 m) elevation in areas with impeded drainage, such as along shelves or drainage lines. The peats are generally acidic (pH 3.5–4.5) but the pH is higher when they occur above limestone.

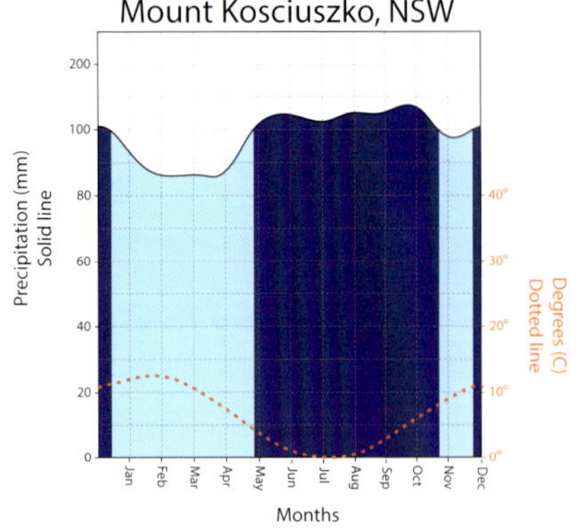

WILDLIFE: Treeless sphagnum bogs in Tasmania have a fairly limited bird assemblage, including Tasmanian Nativehen, Striated Fieldwren, and Australian Pipit. In bogs and fens with a few shrubs and stunted trees, you might start seeing species such as Tasmanian Scrubwren, Pink Robin, Tasmanian Thornbill, and Scrubtit. Some mammals that might be found in Tasmanian bogs include Bare-nosed Wombat, Rufous-bellied Pademelon, Red-necked Wallaby, and Short-beaked Echidna. Reptiles may include several coolskinks (genus *Carinascincus*), such as Metallic Coolskink (*C. metallicus*), Alpine Coolskink (*C. greeni*), Ocellated Coolskink (*C. ocellatus*), and Agile Coolskink (*C. pretiosus*). One might also spot one or two snake species, such as Tiger Snake (*Notechis scutatus*) and White-lipped Snake (*Drysdalia coronoides*), and amphibians such as Tasmanian Froglet (*Crinia tasmaniensis*).

In the *Sphagnum* bogs of the Australian Alps in Victoria and New South Wales, the bird assemblage is also limited to just a few species, including Flame Robin and Australian Pipit. Unfortunately, invasive mammals such as European Rabbit, Brown Hare, and Red Fox are more likely to be seen, but some native species like Short-beaked Echidna, Australian Bush Rat and Broad-toothed Mouse are also present. Reptiles that occur in bogs and fens in the Australian

Alps include Southern Grass Skink (*Pseudemoia entrecasteauxii*), Tussock Skink (*Pseudemoia pagenstecheri*), Southern Water Skink (*Eulamprus tympanum*), and Highlands Copperhead (*Austrelaps ramsayi*); amphibians include Common Eastern Froglet (*Crinia signifera*).

CONSERVATION: Much of the Montane Bog and Fen is protected in large national parks such as Kosciuszko; however, historical grazing and current feral herbivores such as horses and deer have caused widespread trampling, erosion, and vegetation loss, leading to altered water dynamics. Climate change is resulting in increased temperatures and reduced snow cover. Recent bushfires burned large areas of alpine peatlands, causing severe structural damage and hindering peat accumulation and regeneration.

DISTRIBUTION: Bogs and fens are generally found in highland and subalpine regions, particularly in c., ne., and nw. Tasmania, and the Australian Alps of Victoria, New South Wales, and Australian Capital Territory. Small patches of bog and fen habitat exist in the high mountains of New Guinea, though they are generally treated as part of the AUSTROPARAMO, as the wildlife assemblage is very similar to that of the surrounding cushion plants.

WHERE TO SEE: Cradle Mountain–Lake St. Clair National Park, Tasmania, Australia; Alpine National Park, Victoria, Australia; Kosciuszko National Park, New South Wales, Australia; Namadgi National Park, Australian Capital Territory.

Wetlands in Australia's alpine areas are often surrounded by rafts of vegetation and spongy mosses. JJ HARRISON (HTTPS://WWW.JJHARRISON.COM.AU/), CC BY-SA 3.0 (HTTPS://CREATIVECOMMONS.ORG/LICENSES/BY-SA/3.0), VIA WIKIMEDIA COMMONS

Au12A AUSTRALASIAN TROPICAL MANGROVE FOREST

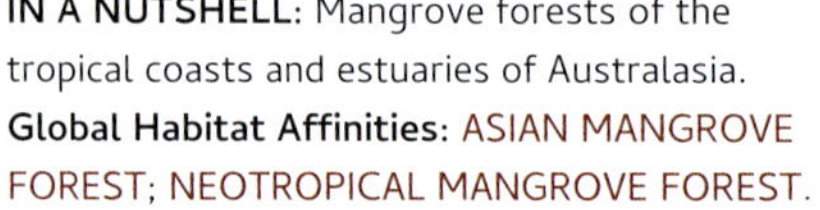

IN A NUTSHELL: Mangrove forests of the tropical coasts and estuaries of Australasia. **Global Habitat Affinities:** ASIAN MANGROVE FOREST; NEOTROPICAL MANGROVE FOREST. **Continental Habitat Affinities:** TEMPERATE MANGROVE. **Species Overlap:** LOWLAND RAINFOREST; TEMPERATE MANGROVE. **Full Bird Assemblage:** habitatsoftheworld.org/Au12A.

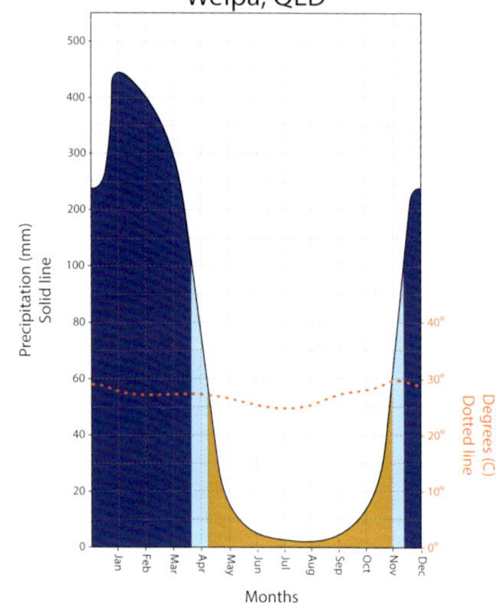

DESCRIPTION: Mangrove forests comprise trees adapted to grow in a flooded saline environment. Most grow in intertidal conditions, often in large inlets and tidal river systems, though some freshwater species do exist. Within this habitat there are microhabitats, with fringe mangroves on the ocean side, and forests in the more protected areas.

On the ocean side, mangrove stands are protected from the sea by smaller fringe mangroves (described below), and the trees become larger in the more protected zones, so when seen from above, the canopy looks like ribbons of different-height mangroves. Within each zone, the canopy is remarkably uniform and often monospecific, as though all the trees in each zone are the same age, which is often the case. Generally, mangroves closer to the ocean and those on the land side of the system are limited to 12–20 ft. (4–6 m), but the very established and protected forests have canopies to 60 ft. (20 m) with emergent trees reaching 90 ft. (30 m). Some large *Avicennia* mangrove trees have straight trunks going directly into the mud, and the forest looks like a uniform rainforest emerging from a muddy substrate. However, most *Rhizophora* species have spiderlike prop roots that branch from the bottom quarter

Towards the land-side edge of a mangrove stand, the canopy becomes very messy, with trees of very different canopy heights often interspersed with nearby Monsoon Vineforest trees. © IAIN CAMPBELL, TROPICAL BIRDING TOURS/UNSW E&ERC

of the trees and give the mangrove forests an eerie feel. When the tide is in, canoeing through these forests with the spider roots is very difficult, as the roots are so interlocked as to form an almost impenetrable barrier. Even when the mud is dry, walking through *Rhizophora* mangroves is extremely difficult; however, walking through Grey Mangrove (*Avicennia marina*) woodlands is much easier.

With over 40 species of mangroves in Australia, it may seem surprising that only one is endemic, restricted to the Northern Territory. However, the widespread distribution of mangroves is understandable when we consider their dispersal technique. There are 45 species in New Guinea, 39 in Queensland, 6 in far n. New South Wales, and 1 in s. New South Wales–South Australia. Species diversity is highest in the tropics, where diverse mangrove forests also support several non-mangrove salt-tolerant plants, such as Mangrove Palm (*Nypa fruticans*) and Mangrove Lily (*Crinum pedunculatum*). The ubiquitous mangrove species for the region is Grey Mangrove, which occurs from Africa to New Zealand and is the only species in the TEMPERATE MANGROVE to the south of this habitat. Spotted Mangrove (*Rhizophora stylosa*), Red Mangrove (*Rhizophora mangle*), and Looking-glass Mangrove (*Heritiera littoralis*) are often emergent trees, while Grey Mangrove, Orange Mangrove (*Bruguiera gymnorhiza*), and Reflexed Orange Mangrove (*Bruguiera cylindrica*) dominate the canopy.

The canopy is closed, and the limited understorey comprises young plants, mainly of the canopy species. Usually the mud is open, and there is little ground cover, although in less inundated areas, Sea Celery (*Apium prostratum*), Mangrove Fern (*Acrostichum speciosum*), and Streaked Arrow Grass (*Triglochin striata*) can grow. In the south of the range around the Queensland–New South Wales border, where far fewer mangrove species exist, the forests are dominated by Grey Mangrove, River Mangrove (*Aegiceras corniculatum*), Milky Mangrove (*Excoecaria agallocha*), and Orange Mangrove. When these last species peter out and the thicket is limited to Grey Mangrove, the habitat is classified as Temperate Mangrove.

Mangroves tend to be tropical, but survival in this extremely harsh environment requires unusual adaptations such as viviparous seeds, which germinate while still attached to the parent tree, in contrast to the typical model of seed dormancy. The seedlings, which can be shaped like large daggers, have a well-developed root and shoot system before they detach. Mangroves that disperse widely use hydrochory, whereby buoyant and water-resistant seeds or seedlings are released into the water and carried by currents to new locations, allowing colonisation of newly exposed mudflats. Although mangroves are salt-tolerant plants, salinity does limit their growth, and they rarely survive in water with saline levels above 70 ppt (parts per thousand). This is not usually an issue though, as most seawater is only around 35 ppt. Temperature is more of a limiting

In well-established groves, the trees grow in more monotypic stands, sometimes with spiderlike prop roots, giving the understorey a very uniform appearance.

© GABRIEL CAMPBELL, TROPICAL BIRDING TOURS

factor, as mangroves are globally restricted to tropical and subtropical zones, and very few examples exist in temperate regions.

In Mexico to South America, PETÉN SWAMP FOREST is a hybrid of mangrove and swamp forest. While a hybrid mangrove–swamp forest does not occur in Australia and New Guinea, an ecotone of mangroves and AUSTRALASIAN SWAMP FOREST that resembles Petén can form in areas where mangroves are less frequently inundated. These are closed mangrove forests of Orange Mangrove and Smallflower Bruguiera (*Bruguiera parviflora*), which both can grow taller than 100 ft. (30 m), merging with large melaleuca trees such as Cajuputi (*Melaleuca cajuputi*), smaller trees like Mangrove Palm (*Nypa fruticans*), Sea Hibiscus (*Hibiscus tiliaceus*) in the understorey, and Mangrove Fern (*Acrostichum speciosum*) and Mangrove Lily (*Crinum pedunculatum*) as

ground cover. These mangrove forests can also have epiphytes such as orchids from surrounding rainforests growing on trunks and branches. In the most developed of these forests, where they meet LOWLAND RAINFOREST, the change from mangrove forest to rainforest can be imperceptible when seen from the air, and it is only on the ground that the boundaries are obvious. There is considerable structural variation, both within and between species of mangroves, and different species tend to grow in slightly different conditions.

Fringe mangroves are the shorter mangroves that grow on the oceanside of the forests and endure more tidal and wave action than stands closer inland. Fringe mangrove shrubs and trees are more resistant to salt water and tend to be more stunted than more protected stands. Vegetation is generally 5–10 ft. (1.5–3 m) tall and thicker than the protected stands. These stands gradually extend into either SANDY BEACH or TIDAL MUDFLAT on the shoreline. Fringe mangroves contain Grey Mangrove, Spotted Mangrove, White-flowered Black Mangrove (*Lumnitzera racemosa*), Rib-fruited Mangrove (*Bruguiera exaristata*), and Shrubby Mangrove (*Aegialitis annulata*).

WILDLIFE: Mangroves in Australasia, more so than any other part of the world, hold many species that are not found in other habitats. Because of the large extent of mangroves around the Australian coast, most mangrove birds are not considered range-restricted species, because the criteria for this designation require they be found in an area smaller than 19,300 sq. mi. (50,000 km^2). However, if the criteria took into account just how narrow the band of mangroves really is over the vast distances in which the habitat occurs, many of the Australian mangrove species would be regarded as range-restricted. In n. Australia, bird species strongly associated with mangroves include Chestnut Rail, White-breasted Whistler, Black-tailed Whistler, Mangrove Robin, Dusky Gerygone, Red-headed Myzomela, Australian Yellow White-eye, and Mangrove Fantail. Farther south, the mangrove stands of se. Queensland hold Mangrove Honeyeater and Mangrove Gerygone.

From New Guinea to the Solomon Islands, the equatorial and tropical mangrove forests form an important habitat for a very distinctive bird assemblage. The most obvious group is the kingfishers, with Beach Kingfisher and Torresian Kingfisher having strong associations with mangroves, though the Little and Yellow-billed Kingfishers also occur in the surrounding SWAMP FOREST and LOWLAND RAINFOREST. Feeding on the mud at the base of the mangroves are more terrestrial species, such as Chestnut Rail and Red-billed Brushturkey, as well as roosting Beach Thick-knee. Although the canopies do have passerines, such as White-bellied Pitohui, Island Whistler, Olive-crowned Flowerpecker, Glossy-mantled Manucode, Brown-backed Honeyeater, and Black Thicket-Fantail, these mangrove forests are richest in parrots, such as Red Lory and Brown Lory, as well as pigeons, such Blue-capped, Wallace's, and Orange-fronted Fruit-Doves, and Collared

Australasian Tropical Mangrove Forest is home to a number of mangrove specialists, such as Black-tailed Whistler. © NICK ATHANAS, TROPICAL BIRDING TOURS

Australia's smallest kingfisher, the Little Kingfisher, is most abundant in tropical mangroves. © IAIN CAMPBELL, TROPICAL BIRDING TOURS/UNSW E&ERC

and Yellowish Imperial-Pigeons. Even within a mangrove area, the distribution of some species of birds is highly stratified. For example, in Broome, Western Australia, the White-breasted Whistler prefers the fringe mangroves closer to the water's edge, while the sympatric Black-tailed Whistler prefers taller mangrove forests farther inland.

Very few mammals are restricted to n. Australian mangroves, but Water Mouse is confined to this woodland from Northern Territory to se. Queensland. Due to the inaccessibility of this habitat to terrestrial mammal predators, bats such as Black and Spectacled Flying Foxes use mangroves

Beach Thick-knees may be seen foraging for crabs at the edge of mangrove stands. © SAM WOODS, TROPICAL BIRDING TOURS

Saltwater Crocodiles inhabit mangroves, so swimming in these areas is best avoided!
© IAIN CAMPBELL, TROPICAL BIRDING TOURS/UNSW E&ERC

as roosting sites around n. Australia. Grey-headed Flying Fox also uses these mangroves as roosting sites.

Snakes present include White-bellied Mangrove Snake (*Fordonia leucobalia*), Little File Snake (*Acrochordus granulatus*), Common Keelback (*Tropidonophis mairii*), Yellow-bellied Sea Snake (*Hydrophis platurus*), Children's Python (*Antaresia childreni*), and Greater Black Whipsnake (*Demansia papuensis*). The most notable reptile of the northern mangroves as far south as c. Queensland is Saltwater Crocodile (*Crocodylus porosus*), the apex predator of this environment. Lizards include Horner's Dragon (*Lophognathus horneri*), Gilbert's Dragon (*Lophognathus gilberti*), Northern Water Dragon (*Tropicagama temporalis*), Mangrove Monitor (*Varanus indicus*), Yellow-spotted Monitor (*Varanus panoptes*), Burton's Snake-Lizard (*Lialis burtonis*), Shaded-litter Rainbow Skink (*Carlia munda*), Striped Snake-eyed Skink (*Cryptoblepharus virgatus*), and Dubious Dtella (*Gehyra dubia*). Some amphibians found around mangroves include Australian Green Tree Frog (*Ranoidea caerulea*) and Northern Laughing Tree Frog (*Litoria rothii*).

CONSERVATION: Tropical Mangrove Forest is an undervalued habitat, especially given its importance as a nursery for the species that sustain much of the commercial fishing industry. The forests are being converted to shrimp farms in Indonesia and degraded by urban development in Papua New Guinea and the Solomon Islands. They are much better protected in Australia because they are often in areas with little human habitation. While most of the remaining stands are protected, many areas on the east coast of Australia fell to development long ago. With growing population pressure in the Cairns area of Queensland, constant development proposals are being submitted to reclaim these forests, and the long-term survival of the surrounding mangroves is uncertain.

DISTRIBUTION: Large mangrove forests exist on the Fly and Kikori Rivers of New Guinea, and most of New Britain and the Solomon Islands are ringed with mangrove forests. In Australia, these mangroves range from nw. Western Australia around the northern coast of Australia to the Queensland–New South Wales border. They usually form a small fringe along calm parts of the coast where mud can accumulate and along the estuaries of rivers where they can form large stands. Extensive mangrove forest systems can be found in Australia around Cairns airport, Queensland; Darwin, Northern Territory; and Broome, Western Australia. Stands of Grey Mangrove are found around Brisbane airport, Queensland, and Ballina, New South Wales.

WHERE TO SEE: Jack Barnes Mangrove Boardwalk, Cairns, Queensland, Australia; Boondall Wetlands, Brisbane, Queensland, Australia; Sorong, Southwest Papua, Indonesian New Guinea.

Au12B AUSTRALIAN TEMPERATE MANGROVE

IN A NUTSHELL: Simple mangrove shrublands along the s. Australian coastline. **Global Habitat Affinities:** ASIAN MANGROVE FOREST. **Continental Habitat Affinities:** TROPICAL MANGROVE FOREST. **Species Overlap:** SUBTROPICAL RAINFOREST; TROPICAL MANGROVE FOREST. **Full Bird Assemblage:** habitatsoftheworld.org/Au12B.

DESCRIPTION: Temperate Mangrove is saline and tidally flooded but floristically is a much simpler habitat than TROPICAL MANGROVE FOREST. Here, the mangroves are dominated by Grey Mangrove (*Avicennia marina*), joined by River Mangrove (*Aegiceras corniculatum*), over most of the New South Wales coast, and the very occasional Spotted Mangrove (*Rhizophora stylosa*) in far n. New South Wales. In Victoria and South Australia, the mangroves are monotypic stands of Grey Mangrove, fringed by Swamp Sheoak (*Casuarina glauca*) and Narrow-leaved Paperbark (*Melaleuca linariifolia*). Where tidal flooding of the mud floor is not a daily occurrence, plants of COASTAL SALT MARSH and SAMPHIRE FLAT, such as Beaded Samphire (*Sarcocornia quinqueflora*) and Seashore Dropseed (*Sporobolus virginicus*), can establish on the mud banks.

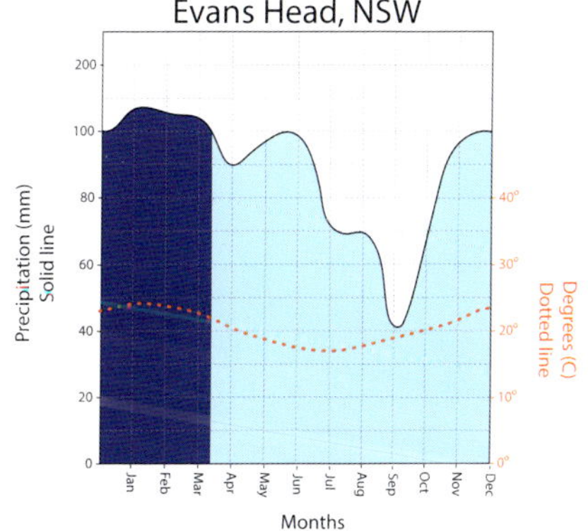

This habitat almost always fringes estuaries; on the inland side, the structure is shrubland to open forest, and even open to dense forest, with a canopy height up to 30 ft. (10 m), of Grey Mangrove with scattered smaller River Mangroves in the canopy and as a subcanopy. Very few other trees grow within these groves. These stands are almost always fringed by monotypic stands of Grey Mangrove shrubs on the ocean side where tidal and wave action are most intense. In the south of the habitat range, the structure is always as a low shrubland, around 6–9 ft. (2–3 m) in height. On the drier and more protected inland side of estuaries, this habitat often merges with Temperate Heath Thicket (a subhabitat of WALLUM AND AUSBOS), COASTAL SALT MARSH, or SAMPHIRE FLAT, though sometimes it blends with LITTORAL RAINFOREST in n. New South Wales.

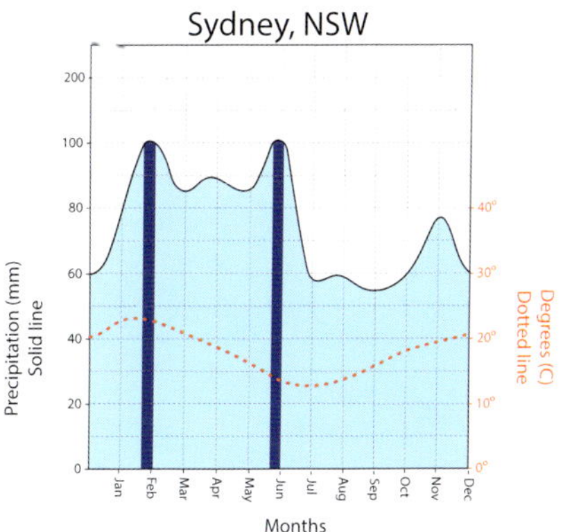

Temperate Mangroves are nearly always monotypic stands of very low trees.
© GABRIEL CAMPBELL, TROPICAL BIRDING TOURS

Temperate Mangrove occurs over a variety of climates from humid subtropical (Köppen **Cfa**) to dry Mediterranean (Köppen **Csa**). Although this habitat is regulated by other factors, such as the salinity of the water, the role the temperature plays is evident by the gradual change in growth form from trees in subtropical n. New South Wales to shrubs in s. New South Wales.

WILDLIFE: Temperate Mangroves are more defined by what is lacking in them than by what occurs within the habitat. The only mangrove specialist bird that occurs in these stands is the Mangrove Gerygone, which extends over much of the n. Australian coastline down to s. New South Wales. Torresian Kingfisher and Mangrove Honeyeater, two bird species that occur in TROPICAL MANGROVE FOREST, reach their distribution limit near this habitat in northernmost New South Wales and thus are regarded as 'negative' indicators of this habitat (i.e., those birds should not be here, and if they are, the habitat is Tropical Mangrove Forest). Birds you would expect in Temperate Mangrove habitat in n. New South Wales include Leaden Flycatcher, Brown Honeyeater, Black-faced Cuckooshrike, Australasian Figbird , Olive-backed Oriole, and Spangled Drongo. Magpie-lark preferentially nests in mangrove stands, and these birds lay deep-red eggs, in contrast to the off-cream eggs of birds of this species living outside the mangroves. In South Australia, the mangroves become extremely depauperate, with no birds specific to this habitat. The birds that use it are predominantly herons, such as White-faced Heron and Great Egret, feeding on the mudflats. Canopy birds such as Black-faced Cuckooshrike are few and incidental, as are birds from surrounding heathlands such as Grey Fantail, Inland Thornbill, and, where samphire plants exist as a ground cover, White-fronted Chat.

Mammals are not common in Temperate Mangrove. Indo-Pacific Bottlenose Dolphin can enter the mangroves, and both Long-nosed Fur Seal and Australian Sea Lion live nearby. The only resident mammal is the rodent Rakali, though it has very wide habitat choices and may be found in most freshwater and estuarine environments. It is sometimes called the Australian Otter because it has partly webbed hind feet and water-repellent fur, much like a North American Common Muskrat.

Mangrove Gerygone is one of the few mangrove specialist species that extend into Temperate Mangrove. © JUN MATSUI, SICKLEBILL SAFARIS

As would be expected, the fish known as mudskippers (genus *Periophthalmus*) are common here. Among turtles, both Southern Slider (*Lerista dorsalis*) and Eastern Short-necked Turtle (*Emydura macquarii*) are regularly recorded. Other reptiles include Lowlands Earless Skink (*Hemiergis peronii*), Eastern Water Skink (*Eulamprus quoyii*), Southern Marbled Gecko (*Christinus marmoratus*), and Southern Spiny-tailed Gecko (*Strophurus intermedius*). In addition, Shingleback (*Tiliqua rugosa*), Eastern Bearded Dragon (*Pogona barbata*), and Common Bluetongue (*Tiliqua scincoides*) can all occur on the mangrove fringes where the habitat blends with other habitats such as SAMPHIRE FLAT and WALLUM.

CONSERVATION: Temperate mangroves usually occur around areas with huge development pressure for urban encroachment, land reclamation, and industrial infrastructure expansion such as port development. Things as seemingly innocuous as river dredging or breakwater construction can drastically impact the mangrove ecosystems.

DISTRIBUTION: Extensive Temperate Mangrove forest systems can be found around coastal se. Australia, from Tweed Heads in n. New South Wales to Ceduna in South Australia. In Western Australia, they occur from Geraldton to near Perth. They are always within the tidal zone, so rarely more than 20 mi. (32 km) inland.

WHERE TO SEE: Evans Head, New South Wales, Australia; Badu Mangroves, Homebush Bay, Sydney, New South Wales, Australia; Barker Inlet–St. Kilda Aquatic Reserve, Adelaide, South Australia.

Australian Temperate Mangroves are largely inhabited by widespread species like Magpie-lark and hold almost no mangrove specialty birds (unlike Tropical Mangrove Forests). © SAM WOODS, TROPICAL BIRDING TOURS

Au12C AUSTRALASIAN SANDY BEACH

IN A NUTSHELL: The typical sandy beaches in Australasia. **Global Habitat Affinities:** ASIAN TROPICAL SANDY BEACH. **Continental Habitat Affinities:** SANDY CAY. **Species Overlap:** TIDAL MUDFLAT. **Full Bird Assemblage:** habitatsoftheworld.org/Au12C.

DESCRIPTION: Most of coastal s. Australia is dominated by erosional headlands and rocky coastlines interspersed with depositional sandy beaches. Many areas have been developed, but there are still thousands of miles of undeveloped coastline. The sandy beaches are often not simply one beach with a foredune but a series of relict dunes paralleling the beach and representing palaeo-shorelines, often containing saline lagoons that are used by wetland birds and shorebirds. In s. Australia, the slope of the beach changes markedly, from very flat through the summer months to much steeper during the winter months, when rougher seas remove much of the sand that was deposited in the warmer season.

A few hardy plants grow above the high-tide line, including grasses like Beach Spinifex (*Spinifex sericeus*), creepers like Beach Morning Glory (*Ipomoea pes-caprae*), and succulents like the colourful Australian Pigface (*Carpobrotus rossii*). Farther back, small woody shrubs and stunted trees, including Beach Sheoak (*Casuarina equisetifolia*), can take hold, and the habitat merges into WALLUM in the east and KWONGAN HEATHLAND in the west.

Beaches like this are typical of much of the temperate Australian coastline.
© IAIN CAMPBELL, TROPICAL BIRDING TOURS/UNSW E&ERC

Pied Oystercatcher generally favours sandy beaches, although it may also inhabit rocky coastlines along with Sooty Oystercatcher. © PABLO CERVANTES, TROPICAL BIRDING TOURS

WILDLIFE: Beaches are generally a poor habitat for wildlife and tend to be the domain of shorebirds and marine species. Sandy beaches provide habitat for Pied Oystercatcher; Hooded Plover; most tern species, including Great Crested, Caspian, and Fairy Terns; and gulls such as Silver, Pacific, and Kelp Gulls. Most shorebirds prefer TIDAL MUDFLAT due to the greater abundance of food, although some migrant species like Sanderling tend to prefer Sandy Beach. Penguins, including Little Penguin, come ashore to Australian beaches late in the afternoon and nest in dunes. This habitat gives its name to the Beach Thick-knee, which searches for its food, crabs, along sandy beaches as well as on mudflats. White-bellied Sea-Eagle and Osprey can also be seen flying along sandy beaches searching for fish.

In Australasia, the richest shoreline habitats are in the south, where the cold waters bring in abundant nutrients, and Common Bottlenose Dolphins are often seen close to the shoreline. Other marine mammals that frequent these shores include Australian Sea Lion and Long-nosed and Brown Fur Seals. Non-marine mammals are rare in this habitat, though Dingoes can sometimes be found on remote beaches of the Australian mainland.

Australasian sandy beaches provide important breeding habitat for Green Sea Turtle (*Chelonia mydas*), Loggerhead Sea Turtle (*Caretta caretta*), and Hawksbill Sea Turtle (*Eretmochelys imbricata*), which are all globally threatened species adversely affected by beach development.

CONSERVATION: Vast stretches of the n. Australian coastline are barely touched by humans, and the beach wildlife is left undisturbed. In the south of Australia there is a greater human

Hooded Plover breeds on sandy beaches in s. Australia, where it is susceptible to disturbance by visiting tourists or irresponsible local dog walkers. © SAM WOODS, TROPICAL BIRDING TOURS

Great Crested Terns often roost in mixed-tern flocks on sandy beaches. © IAIN CAMPBELL, TROPICAL BIRDING TOURS/UNSW E&ERC

population density, and species such as Hooded Plover and Fairy Tern have difficulty breeding because of constant disturbance on their nesting beaches. Even areas of supposed protection, such as blocked-off beaches, are repeatedly disturbed by dog walkers and beachgoers. Between Brisbane, Queensland, and Perth, Western Australia, urban development is a constant pressure as this shoreline is absolute prime real estate, and only those beaches preserved in national parks are safe from development in the long term. In New Guinea and the Solomon Islands, it is open season for development, and there is little protection from destruction of the coastline.

DISTRIBUTION: This habitat is found all around Australia, New Guinea, and the Solomon Islands, although it is more prominent in temperate areas.

WHERE TO SEE: Bruny Island, Tasmania, Australia; Evans Head, New South Wales, Australia; Kangaroo Island, South Australia; Cheynes Beach, Western Australia.

Mixed flocks of terns and gulls in s. Australia may hold the giant Pacific Gull, one of the world's largest gull species. © PABLO CERVANTES, TROPICAL BIRDING TOURS

Au12D AUSTRALASIAN SANDY CAY

IN A NUTSHELL: In the waters off n. Australia and the islands to the north and east, bare or sparsely vegetated sandy cays form over coral reefs. **Global Habitat Affinities:** ASIAN OFFSHORE TROPICAL CAY AND ISLANDS. **Continental Habitat Affinities:** SANDY BEACH. **Species Overlap:** SANDY BEACH. **Full Bird Assemblage:** habitatsoftheworld.org/Au12D.

DESCRIPTION: In shallow tropical seas, large coral barrier-reef systems can develop. In some localities within these large systems, the material derived from the breakdown of coral becomes concentrated to form sandy islets known as cays. At first, coral debris gets swept over the coral platform and can be kept there by the convergence of waves. This accumulates and becomes cemented into beach rock by the action of algae. Cays often extend perpendicular to prevailing winds, but they can be altered and even destroyed by the action of tropical cyclones. Many of these small islands are covered at high tide, but on some, wind can raise the dunes high enough to support sparse vegetation. Usually, the vegetation is hardy grasses such as Pacific Island Thintail (*Lepturus repens*) and Beach Spinifex (*Spinifex sericeus*). Other herbaceous cover includes Sea Purslane (*Sesuvium portulacastrum*), Beach Moonflower (*Ipomoea violacea*), and some low shrubs such as Beach Sunflower (*Wollastonia uniflora*). On some islands, small, stunted trees such as Grand Devil's-Claws (*Pisonia grandis*) can also develop into thickets. Nutrients fertilizing the vegetation come from seabird droppings.

WILDLIFE: These remote cays are very important for tropical seabirds, as they provide predator-free breeding areas. Some species are widespread and catholic in their nesting sites, breeding on

Most Australasian Sandy Cays have a small bit of vegetation but are otherwise bare sand. Thousands of seabirds nest and many other species roost on Michaelmas Cay, near Cairns, Queensland (pictured), and other cays in the region. © IAIN CAMPBELL, TROPICAL BIRDING TOURS/UNSW E&ERC

nearly all the sandy cays. Species breeding on the more open, sandy, and sparsely grass-dominated islands include Brown and Black Noddies, Brown Booby, and Great Crested, Lesser Crested, Little, Bridled, Roseate, Black-naped, and Sooty Terns. Other species, like Red-footed Booby and Lesser and Great Frigatebirds, require trees for nesting, while burrow-nesting species like shearwaters and petrels nest on the larger islands that have significant ground cover. These seabirds are joined by less-pelagic species such as Pacific Reef-Heron and nonbreeding, migrant shorebirds such as Ruddy Turnstone and Sanderling.

CONSERVATION: The vast majority of the bird breeding colonies in Australia are well protected from development. Even popular sites that have hundreds of visitors a day, such as Michaelmas Cay, restrict the visitors to a small section of the island to protect the nesting seabirds. Some cays such as Heron Island were developed before extensive protections existed but are responsibly managing tourist resorts and nesting seabird colonies. The greatest risk to the low cays in Australia may be sea-level rise and increased cyclone activity due to climate change. The case is not so rosy in Indonesia, Papua New Guinea, or the Solomon Islands, where there is very little protection from tourist-resort development or overfishing.

DISTRIBUTION: These coral reefs and corresponding coral cays surround n. and ne. Australia (with the exception of the Gulf of Carpentaria), New Guinea, the Solomons, and other islands of the sw. Pacific, wherever the seas are shallow enough to support reef growth. The biggest swath of these habitats is in the Great Barrier Reef, which extends down the e. Australian coast from n. Cape York Peninsula south to c. Queensland. The reef system is very accessible, with numerous tourist resorts strung along its entire length. The most accessible sandy cay is Michaelmas Cay, a 4.4 ac. (1.8 ha) island, about 20 mi. (30 km) offshore from the coastal city of Cairns. Widely considered the premier cay for visiting birders, it can hold up to 200,000 breeding seabirds and has been designated a Key Biodiversity Area (KBA) by Birdlife International.

WHERE TO SEE: Michaelmas Cay, Queensland, Australia; Green Island, Queensland, Australia.

Australasian Sandy Cays provide critical nesting sites for seabirds, such as Brown Booby, which favour these as they are free of ground predators. © IAIN CAMPBELL, TROPICAL BIRDING TOURS/UNSW E&ERC

Au12E AUSTRALIAN SALT PAN

IN A NUTSHELL: Sparsely vegetated or unvegetated habitat on highly alkaline soils, usually evaporation pans. **Global Habitat Affinities:** AFRICAN SALT PANS AND LAKES; ASIAN SALT PAN. **Continental Habitat Affinities:** COASTAL SALT MARSH; TIDAL MUDFLAT. **Species Overlap:** TIDAL MUDFLAT; COASTAL SALT MARSH; TEMPERATE WETLAND. **Full Bird Assemblage:** habitatsoftheworld.org/Au12E.

DESCRIPTION: Most Australians know Lake Eyre as a massive area of South Australia that floods. It is, in fact, the continent's largest salt pan, a flat expanse of land covered with salt crusts or salt crystals, typically found in arid or semiarid regions where evaporation rates exceed precipitation. These saline environments often result from the evaporation of water from inland lakes or other water bodies, leaving behind concentrated deposits of common salts such as halite, gypsum, and calcite, and, less commonly, thenardite and epsomite.

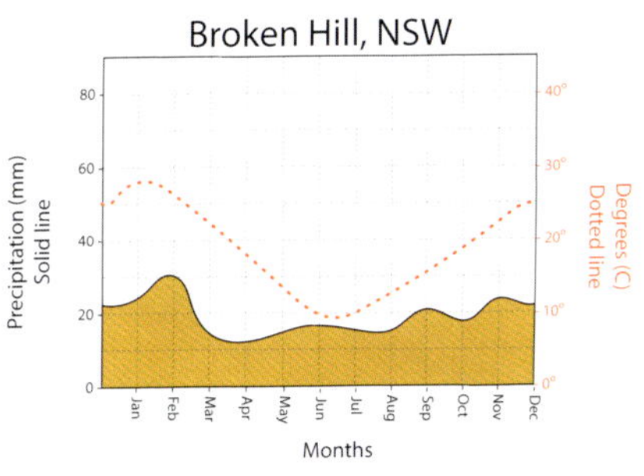

Flooding is a natural and recurring phenomenon in inland Australia, where some areas experience long periods of drought followed by intense rainfall events. Flooding events are

When dry, Salt Pans are incredibly desolate places. © GABRIEL CAMPBELL, TROPICAL BIRDING TOURS

Banded Stilt is equally at home in Salt Pans as in freshwater marshes. © ALAN MCBRIDE

irregular and sporadic but usually occur every few years, though they can be decadal. The timing and magnitude of flooding can also be influenced by climate phenomena such as El Niño and La Niña. Salt Pan habitat can change from dry, barren pans almost devoid of life to large water bodies full of birds. These areas tend to have highly saline and alkaline soils (solonchaks), often rich in sodium carbonate, with poor drainage, which are easily flooded after rain. The pans can be found near the coast or inland, and coastal Salt Pans can also form when seawater is trapped in coastal lagoons; in coastal regions they receive water on a daily tidal cycle or fortnightly spring-tide cycle. Inland salt pans attain their water from rains in very distant areas. In Western Australia, both Lake Hillier, on Middle Island in the Recherche Archipelago, and Hutt Lagoon, on the west-central coast, are known as the 'pink lake' for their hue, caused by hypersalinity and the resulting high concentrations of the alga *Dunaliella salina*, which produces carotenoid pigments, particularly beta-carotene, a substance also found in carrots. The resulting colour looks utterly unnatural (so much so that a onetime client of one of the authors absolutely refused to believe that it was anything except pollution from a mine's tailings dam).

Salt Pan is a hostile environment in which very few plants will grow, and those that do tend to be salt-tolerant plants (halophytes), predominantly chenopods but also some grasses. On the coast flats the plant assemblage includes chenopods such as Beaded Samphire (*Salicornia quinqueflora*) and Mungily (*Tecticornia indica*), and the common grass Seashore Dropseed (*Sporobolus virginicus*).

Although dry pans are virtually barren, algae will grow and small shrimp quickly hatch after a pan is flooded, providing a source of food for the ecosystem. Despite their inhospitable appearance, these lakes can be highly productive, with high rates of photosynthesis enabled by the huge amount of dissolved carbon dioxide. Flooded Salt Pans rapidly become wetlands bustling with large bird populations.

The coastal examples of this habitat are azonal, occurring throughout the coastline of Australia, though with a strong preference for the cooler and drier southern climate (Köppen **Bwk**). The inland Salt Pan habitats are mainly in the harshest, hottest, and driest climatic environments of Australia, where rain may not fall for a year and summer temperatures can approach 120°F (50°C) (Köppen **Bwh**), as well as colder Australian deserts (Köppen **Bwk**).

Artificial salt pans are known as saltworks or salt farms. At these locations, salt water is pumped into pools and allowed to evaporate, leaving behind salt crusts, which are harvested. These commercial salt pans can replicate the conditions of natural ones and be highly attractive to waterbirds.

WILDLIFE: Birds are the most abundant and conspicuous form of wildlife in Australian Salt Pans and salt lakes. When Salt Pan floods, huge numbers of birds flock inland to take advantage of the food source. How these species are able to predict habitat conditions so far away is still a bit of a mystery. Some species of birds that breed on Salt Pans include Australian Pelican, Black Swan, Grey Teal, Australasian and Hoary-headed Grebes, Banded and Pied Stilts, Red-necked Avocet, Red-capped Plover, Black-fronted Dotterel, Silver Gull, and Caspian and Whiskered Terns.

Lake Eyre Dragon (*Ctenophorus maculosus*) and Eyre Basin Beaked Gecko (*Rhynchoedura eyrensis*) are both lizards adapted to the saline conditions of the salt lakes. Other species that live here but are also adapted to other desert environments include Desert Skink (*Liopholis inornata*), Painted Dragon (*Ctenophorus pictus*), Sand Goanna (*Varanus gouldii*), and Centralian Bluetongue (*Tiliqua multifasciata*). The Perentie (*Varanus giganteus*) is Australia's largest lizard, reaching just over 8 ft. (2.5 m) long, and along with Dingo is the apex predator here, though it is seldom found well into the salt lake environment and hunts on the fringes.

CONSERVATION: Coastal Salt Pans face urban encroachment though many are protected in reserves. The Salt Pans in c. Australia face far fewer pressures due to their remoteness and extreme environment, making them a very marginal environment for farming. Those pans in areas such as along the Murray-Darling basin face threats from flow-alteration regimes, which effect the flooding cycle of the pans.

DISTRIBUTION: Salt Pan habitat is found in arid and semiarid regions of Australia; natural salt pans and lakes of various sizes can be found both inland and along the coast, and Australia has some of the largest salt lakes in the world. Salt Pan is found mainly in Western and South Australia but also in some areas of the Murray-Darling river system of New South Wales, and arid parts of Queensland and Northern Territory. As salt water needs to be pumped in, artificial saltworks are usually situated close to the coast. The relatively few examples of these are also mainly in Western and South Australia, although access to these sites is usually restricted.

WHERE TO SEE: NATURAL SALT PAN—Lake Ballard, Western Australia; Lake Eyre, South Australia; Lake Amadeus, Northern Territory, Australia; ARTIFICIAL SALTWORKS—Shark Bay, Western Australia; Mulgundawa (southeast of Adelaide), South Australia.

Au12F AUSTRALIAN COASTAL SALT MARSH

IN A NUTSHELL: Coastal areas that support low, salt-tolerant marsh vegetation. **Global Habitat Affinities:** NEARCTIC SALT MARSH; EUROPEAN COASTAL SALT MARSH; AFRICAN SALT MARSH. **Continental Habitat Affinities:** TIDAL MUDFLAT. **Species Overlap:** TIDAL MUDFLAT. **Full Bird Assemblage:** habitatsoftheworld.org/Au12F.

DESCRIPTION: Coastal Salt Marshes are formed by the gradual buildup of sediments by the tides. They form mainly in sheltered spots such as bays and estuaries, where wave action is lessened, and are generally found in the intertidal zone but sometimes grow above the normal high-tide line. Whereas TIDAL MUDFLAT is basically an unvegetated habitat, Coastal Salt Marsh is a low habitat of halophytic (salt-tolerant) plants.

Few plants can grow in Australian Coastal Salt Marsh, but those that do have adaptations to tolerate high salinity levels and fluctuating water levels characteristic of the habitat. These plants fall into two major groups: grasses, rushes, and sedges; and succulents. Some typical grasses are Common Reed (*Phragmites australis*) and Seashore Dropseed (*Sporobolus virginicus*); rushes include Sea Rush (*Juncus kraussii*); and sedges include Slender Club-Rush (*Isolepis cernua*). Succulents such as Beaded Samphire (*Salicornia quinqueflora*) and Batis (*Batis argillicola*) are often found in the most highly saline parts of the salt marsh. In the tropics, salt marshes are much less common than they are in temperate regions. The occasional tropical marshes usually contain succulent species rather than grasses.

Coastal Salt Marshes occur over much of Australia but are much more common in s. Australia, where they replace mangroves as the dominant habitat along estuaries.
© IAIN CAMPBELL, TROPICAL BIRDING TOURS/UNSW E&ERC

The Hunter River estuary region of New South Wales is renowned for its wetlands, many of which are Coastal Salt Marsh. © ALAN MCBRIDE

WILDLIFE: In Coastal Salt Marsh, as in TIDAL MUDFLAT, the regularly exposed silts and clays have large numbers of small organisms, including clams, Australian Ghost Shrimp (*Trypaea australiensis*), and worms. Crabs are also common. However, the most noticeable animals in this habitat are birds. Salt marshes are important roosting and feeding areas for many shorebirds and wading birds. They provide a refuge for shorebirds at high tide when Tidal Mudflats are submerged, and large numbers may gather to wait for the next low tide. As they do on mudflats, shorebirds choose the water depth that best suits their leg and bill lengths, with longer-legged species sorting themselves in the deeper marsh pools. The vast majority of species are migratory waders that breed in Siberia or Alaska and are therefore present only during the austral summer (October–March), but some species are resident. Coastal Salt Marshes can provide good viewing opportunities, because the birds are usually closer than when they are observed out on the mudflats.

Australian Pelican nests in inland Australia as well as on extensive areas of Coastal Salt Marsh. © IAIN CAMPBELL, TROPICAL BIRDING TOURS/ UNSW E&ERC

Some shorebirds likely to be encountered in Australian Coastal Salt Marsh include Whimbrel, Far Eastern Curlew, Bar-tailed and Black-tailed Godwits, Great and Red Knots, Sharp-tailed and Curlew Sandpipers, Red-necked Stint, and Common Greenshank. Various ducks may be attracted to pools, such as Australian Shelduck, Pacific Black Duck, and Grey Teal. Other common waterbirds found may include Australian Pelican, White-faced Heron, Royal Spoonbill, and Australian Ibis. Gull-billed Terns can be seen taking flying insects over salt marshes. Shy species take advantage of the vegetative cover, including Australasian Swamphen and especially Lewin's Rail, which has a preference for salt marshes. Grass and reed beds are also inhabited by several passerine species like Golden-headed Cisticola, Striated Fieldwren, Australian Reed Warbler, and Little and Tawny Grassbirds.

CONSERVATION: In the south of Australia, these salt marshes are often near population centres, so there is urban development pressure. They are less disturbed than nearby SANDY BEACH, however, because they are not an inviting environment for most people to visit, being smelly and mosquito-ridden—and this is great for the wildlife.

DISTRIBUTION: Coastal Salt Marsh is found along Australia's more temperate shorelines and is most prevalent around estuaries and sheltered bays. Primarily a temperate and subtropical habitat, it is largely, but not completely, replaced in a similar ecological niche by mangroves in the tropics. As such, salt marshes are common along the southern coasts of Australia, with fewer farther north. They usually occur just inland from TIDAL MUDFLATS, in slightly more sheltered but still highly saline areas. In the subtropics, they can be found alongside mangroves.

WHERE TO SEE: Moreton Bay Marine Park, Queensland, Australia; Hunter River Estuary, New South Wales; Western Port, Victoria, Australia; Coorong National Park, South Australia.

Lewin's Rail is a very cryptic species that is far more often heard than seen. © ALAN MCBRIDE

Au12G AUSTRALASIAN TIDAL MUDFLAT

IN A NUTSHELL: The muddy areas that are periodically exposed either through fluctuating tidal waters or movement of water by wind. **Global Habitat Affinities:** NEOTROPICAL TIDAL MUDFLAT; ASIAN TIDAL MUDFLAT. **Continental Habitat Affinities:** SANDY BEACH. **Species Overlap:** SANDY BEACH; COASTAL SALT MARSH. **Full Bird Assemblage:** habitatsoftheworld.org/Au12G.

DESCRIPTION: Tidal Mudflats are usually exposed layers of estuarine sands, silts, and clays, and are found in bays and lagoons, on shallow, mud-dominated beaches, and along edges of slow-flowing rivers. These soils are much richer than the nutrient-poor substrates of sandy and rocky coastlines found away from estuaries and support a bounty of invertebrates. In Tidal Mudflats, the sediment is deposited in the intertidal zone, where the swaths of mud are exposed and submerged twice a day. In other very shallow areas, wind can cause significant water-level change, and the silts are exposed or submerged based on wind direction. At depth, the muds are anaerobic, due to the small sediment size, so only a very specialised assemblage of animals is able to exist just below the mud surface. The regularly exposed silts and clays are extremely bioturbated by massive numbers of small organisms. Few plants can grow in these harsh environments, but the mudflats

Around tropical Australia and New Guinea, the Tidal Mudflats are often bound by mangroves, and the habitats share the bird assemblages. © KEN BEHRENS, TROPICAL BIRDING TOURS

Curlew Sandpiper breeds over a wide longitudinal range in the very north of mainland Asia, preferring Eurasian Boggy Tundra. In Australia it is restricted to Tidal Mudflats, rarely leaving for drier or sandier habitats. © JUN MATSUI, SICKLEBILL SAFARIS

are ringed by mangroves in tropical and subtropical areas. Walking on the dryer or sandy edges of these flats is easy, but care is required as some areas have very soft mud and are difficult to navigate. Other, rarer areas have thixotropic quicksand where one can sink thigh-deep into the mud and get caught in the incoming tide. There have been incidents of people dying whilst out collecting molluscs such as mussels, oysters, and pipis on Tidal Mudflats.

WILDLIFE: Tidal Mudflats are important roosting and feeding areas for many shorebirds. The vast majority of species are migratory waders that breed in Siberia or Alaska and are therefore present only during the austral summer (October–March). However, some species are resident, such as Beach Thick-knee, Pied Oystercatcher, and Red-capped Plover. Mudflats also provide important resting and feeding areas for herons, egrets, ibises, terns, and gulls. Tidal flats vary in structure, and some species prefer flats with a sandy substrate (e.g., Sanderling, and Siberian and Greater Sand-Plovers), while others prefer the muddy substrates of estuaries. Different shorebirds also feed in different areas of the flats, with the species segregating on the shoreline in accordance with their leg and bill structures, which dictate the depth of water in which they can feed. It can be difficult to see shorebirds at low tide, as they are often quite a distance away. The best viewing opportunities are generally as the tide comes in and forces the birds up the shore. Once the tide has covered the feeding areas, the birds will travel to high-tide roosts, where thousands of waders may gather to wait for the next low tide. This can be the best opportunity to view and photograph them, when the many birds in one place allow direct comparisons of different species.

Some nonbreeding migrant shorebirds are more concentrated on the northern side of Australia, such as Asian Dowitcher, Grey-tailed Tattler, and the critically endangered Nordmann's Greenshank, while others are spread around the whole coastline, such as Great and Red Knots, Broad-billed Sandpiper, Bar-tailed Godwit, and Red-necked Stint. Some species of migrant shorebirds, including Great Knot and Far Eastern Curlew, are considered globally threatened, and their wintering grounds in Australasia are of vital conservation importance.

This habitat is rather poor in mammals, although at high tide various species of dolphins and eared seals can be found searching for fish. Dugongs (and sea turtles) also make some use of sea-grass meadows nearby. Several fish species are found along the water's edge at tidal mudflats, but no group characterises them quite like the mudskippers (*Periophthalmus* spp.), fish that actually come out of the water and have specialised respiratory adaptations that allow them to move between land and water. The Tidal Mudflats are important for many invertebrates, which spend time both under the mud and feeding on the exposed flats when the waters recede, including Australian Ghost Shrimp (*Trypaea australiensis*), crabs such as Light-blue Soldier Crab (*Mictyris longicarpus*), clams, and worms.

Great Knot is an Asian migrant species that nests in Asian Alpine Tundra and Asian Tundra Taiga. In Australia it prefers less-disturbed Tidal Mudflats but has become habituated to people on the Cairns Esplanade. © JUN MATSUI, SICKLEBILL SAFARIS

CONSERVATION: Tidal Mudflats are not an attractive environment to people without a love of nature, so there is rarely an uproar when these important feeding areas are reclaimed (i.e., destroyed) for development. Even the most famous shorebird site in Queensland, the Cairns Esplanade, which is known around the world, is under constant threat of being turned into a beach for tourists. There are massive areas of Tidal Mudflats around the Gulf of Carpentaria and along the north coast of Western Australia, but they lack formal protection. This habitat has no protection in the populated areas north of Australia and is overexploited for invertebrates, netted for fishing, and reclaimed for development.

DISTRIBUTION: Tidal Mudflats are found throughout Australasian coastal regions. They are most prevalent around estuaries, sheltered bays, and, in Australia, beaches in the north of the country where the seas are calm.

WHERE TO SEE: Roebuck Bay near Broome, Western Australia; Lee Point near Darwin, Northern Territory, Australia; Cairns Esplanade, Queensland, Australia; Richmond River estuary, Ballina, New South Wales, Australia; Port Phillip Bay, Victoria, Australia; Wasur National Park, South Papua, Indonesian New Guinea; Biak Island, Papua, Indonesian New Guinea.

Au12H AUSTRALASIAN ROCKY HEADLAND

IN A NUTSHELL: Rocky coastal areas, lacking vegetation or sparsely vegetated with marine algae near rock pools, varying from low rocky beach to towering cliffs. **Global Habitat Affinities:** NEOTROPICAL ROCKY COASTLINE. **Continental Habitat Affinities:** None. **Species Overlap:** TIDAL MUDFLAT. **Full Bird Assemblage:** habitatsoftheworld.org/Au12H.

DESCRIPTION: In Australia, rocky formations are one of the commonest types of coastlines, and these are interspersed with depositional sandy beaches. The geological origins of these various rocky shorelines are diverse. Headlands are typically composed of more resistant materials than surrounding ones, but this difference is relative, even between two hard rocks—one will weather and erode faster than the other. Similarly, coastlines with weak limestone cliffs may be only marginally more resistant to erosion than adjacent shales. For material to become a headland, it must better withstand the relentless mechanical action of waves and the chemical attack of salt compared to surrounding rocks.

In regions with flat or gently tilted sedimentary rocks, headlands tend to be flat, and bays are wide. When rocks are intruded by volcanic materials or are steeply tilted, such as vertical sedimentary formations, differential weathering and erosion are more pronounced, creating rugged coastlines with numerous bays and islands. Various geomorphological features arising from this erosion are crucial for vegetation and wildlife.

The most prominent rocky headlands are sea cliffs, formed by wave action. Steep cliffs are most pronounced where there is layering or jointing, such as with columnar basalts or schists, and are less likely to form in homogeneous rocks like granite, which tends to produce more rounded headlands. Erosion at the base of cliffs can form sea caves, which may eventually break through headlands to create natural arches. When these arches collapse, they leave isolated pillars of rock known as sea stacks. These rugged, isolated formations often become predator-free zones, providing prime nesting sites for species such as gulls and gannets.

The boundary between the Great Australian Bight and the Nullarbor Plain is stark and barren Rocky Headland. © SHANE KENNEDY, TROPICAL BIRDING TOURS

Islets along the rocky coastline become a haven for nesting seabirds and pinnipeds.
© IAIN CAMPBELL, TROPICAL BIRDING TOURS/UNSW E&ERC

There are not many plants that can survive in this harsh environment with its salt spray and rocky soil. Most of the plants are widespread beach-adapted species, although there are a few plants specialised to cliff niches. Some plants often found along rocky coastlines include Coastal Rosemary (*Westringia fruticosa*), Coastal Banksia (*Banksia integrifolia*), and Coast Tea Tree (*Gaudium laevigatum*). Many plants of the rocky shore are seaweeds, which are algae. Farther back from shore, lichens can also be found. Rock pools hold various marine algae, anemones, and small fish.

WILDLIFE: Rocky coastal habitats are generally wildlife-poor and tend to be the domain of shorebirds and marine species. Compared to Tidal Mudflats, rocky shorelines are relatively poor in shorebirds, but they are the favoured habitat of the nonbreeding migrants Ruddy Turnstone and Whimbrel, and in Australia are key for the Sooty Oystercatcher, which feeds on bivalves like mussels along the marine ecotone. Australian Rocky Headlands are also the preferred habitat of Black-faced Cormorant. Coastal cliffs in some locations (such as Point Danger, Victoria) provide breeding habitat for Australasian Gannet, although it usually nests on rocky islands offshore. Some other birds that make use of sea cliffs include Peregrine Falcon, White-bellied Sea-Eagle, and Osprey. One interesting species found on headlands is the New South Wales endemic

Rockwarbler, which is found on rocky outcrops on the coast as well as high plateaus inland. Around the southern coasts the Rock Parrot often feeds on the headlands.

Mammals that occur along rocky shores in this region include Brown and Long-nosed Fur Seals and the endangered Australian Sea Lion in s. Australia.

CONSERVATION: The rocky headlands of e. Australia are under development pressure for tourism and urban development, but the vast majority of the northern, western, and southern coastlines are very remote and not yet under development pressure.

DISTRIBUTION: Rocky Headlands are found all around Australia, New Guinea, and the Solomon Islands, although they are more prominent in temperate areas of mainland Australia. Headlands popular for land-based sea-watching include Magic Point in Sydney, New South Wales; Bass Point near Shellharbour, New South Wales; Cape Nelson near Portland, Victoria; Eaglehawk Neck and Bruny Island, Tasmania; and Cape Naturaliste near Albany, Western Australia.

WHERE TO SEE: Bruny Island, Tasmania, Australia; Bass Point, New South Wales, Australia; Evans Head, New South Wales, Australia; Twelve Apostles, Victoria, Australia.

Rocky crevices provide nesting sites for Rock Parrot in s. Australia.
© SAM WOODS, TROPICAL BIRDING TOURS

Au12l AUSTRALASIAN TROPICAL PELAGIC WATERS

IN A NUTSHELL: The coastal, continental, and deep-sea waters throughout the tropical and subtropical areas of the region. **Global Habitat Affinities:** AFRICAN PELAGIC WATERS; ASIAN TROPICAL PELAGIC WATERS. **Continental Habitat Affinities:** TEMPERATE PELAGIC WATERS. **Species Overlap:** TEMPERATE PELAGIC WATERS. **Full Bird Assemblage:** habitatsoftheworld.org/Au12l.

DESCRIPTION: In many tropical and subtropical areas of Australasia, the edge of the continental shelf, where the ocean rapidly becomes much deeper, is usually far offshore, and most of the seas are shallow, such as the Gulf of Carpentaria and most of the other waters between n. Australia and the island of New Guinea. In fact, these land areas were joined during past times of low water levels. These seawaters lack upwellings of nutrient-rich, colder water from deeper layers and therefore are far less productive for oceanic life than TEMPERATE PELAGIC WATERS. The edge of the continental shelf gets closer to the Australian coast in the far southeastern reaches of Tropical Pelagic Waters, at Brisbane, Queensland. There are some steep, deepwater trenches in the region east of New Guinea—for example, south of New Britain (Bismarck Archipelago) and Bougainville (Solomon Islands archipelago) in the Solomon Sea; and south of the e. Solomon islands arching down to the northern tip of Vanuatu.

The South Equatorial Current (SEC), which brings warm water from east to west across the Pacific Ocean, meets the Australian landmass on the coast of Queensland. This splits into the East Australian Current (EAC), heading south, and the weaker Hiri Current, heading north into the Coral Sea. The SEC also passes along the north side of New Guinea, and the Indonesian Throughflow

Tropical Pelagic Waters are home to Great Frigatebird, a kleptoparasite that steals prey from other seabirds. © IAIN CAMPBELL, TROPICAL BIRDING TOURS/UNSW E&ERC

flows down through the Banda Sea and joins with the Holloway Current between Australia and New Guinea to meet the Indian Ocean. One more important current is the Eastern Gyre, which circles around an area of deep water in the e. Indian Ocean. When these currents pass the edge of the continental shelf, this increases the upwelling of nutrient-rich deep water to the surface.

WILDLIFE: Australasian Tropical Pelagic Waters lack the diverse pelagic bird and cetacean fauna seen farther south. Terns, noddies, frigatebirds, tropicbirds, and boobies predominate in these waters, and some species, such as White and Black-naped Terns, Great and Lesser Frigatebirds, Brown and Red-footed Boobies, and White-tailed and Red-tailed Tropicbirds are particularly tied

White-tailed Tropicbird is more common in the west than in the east of Australia. © ROB HYNSON

Tahiti Petrel breeds outside the area but visits Australasian Tropical Pelagic Waters in summer. © ROB HYNSON

to it. Although tubenoses (albatrosses, petrels, shearwaters, and storm-petrels) do occur in this habitat, they are found at much lower densities than in AUSTRALIAN TEMPERATE PELAGIC WATERS. Among the more widely distributed species found here are Wedge-tailed and Streaked Shearwaters, and Wilson's Storm-Petrel. Some species occurring here are also found in Polynesia, like Tahiti Petrel, while others, such as Beck's Petrel, Providence Petrel, and Heinroth's Shearwater, are largely restricted to this region and breed here. Off nw. Australia, Bulwer's and Jouanin's Petrels occur, as do Matsudaira's and Swinhoe's Storm-Petrels; the ranges of some of these extend through the Banda Sea in Indonesia. A small, outlying breeding population of Herald Petrels occurs on Raine Island in the n. Great Barrier Reef. Seasonality is important to pelagic bird movements, and sightings are concentrated in April–May and October.

As many bird species require updrafts produced from waves to fly and feed, but sea mammals are less visible in the waves,

Providence Petrel breeds high on the forested mountains of Lord Howe Island in the Tasman Sea and regularly appears off Australia's eastern coast. © ROB HYNSON

in general, the calmer the sea, the duller the birding and the better the cetacean-watching. The commonest marine mammals found in subtropical and tropical Australasian waters include Humpback and Common Minke Whales, Spinner Dolphin, Indo-Pacific and Common Bottlenose Dolphins, and Dugong. Less-common species include Melon-headed, Blue, Bryde's, and Sperm Whales; False Killer Whale; Short-finned Pilot Whale; and Australian Snubfin, Pantropical Spotted, and Risso's Dolphins. Australian Snubfin Dolphin is one of the only marine mammals restricted to this region.

CONSERVATION: Overfishing is a serious problem in the tropical oceans around Australia, New Guinea, and the Solomon Islands. Climate change is not only causing coral bleaching in the nearby reef systems; it is also increasing temperatures in the deeper water and causing dead zones, where very little life exists. Most of this region has no protection, and even those areas with nominal protection are under threat from offshore drilling and deep-sea mining.

DISTRIBUTION: This habitat spans from the Indian Ocean in the west, across the northern side of the Australian landmass to the southwestern parts of the Pacific Ocean in the east. This includes the Timor, Arafura, and Coral Seas, the island of New Guinea, and the Solomon Islands. Although Brisbane falls south of the Tropic of Capricorn, its subtropical pelagic waters are included here.

WHERE TO SEE: Pelagic boat trips out of Brisbane, Queensland, Australia; and Broome, Western Australia. Some pelagic expedition ships pass through this region and are the best way to see the majority of the pelagic bird species.

SIDEBAR SEAMOUNTS OF EASTERN AUSTRALIA

The seamounts off e. Australia are underwater mountains rising from depths of around 13,000 ft. (4000 m) to about 1000 ft. (300 m) below the surface. These submerged peaks are hotspots of marine productivity, driven by upwellings where ocean currents, regardless of direction, bring nutrient-rich waters to the surface. This process fuels plankton growth, attracting marine life and seabirds, creating vital feeding grounds in the otherwise vast and barren deep ocean.

Over the past decade, these seamounts have become a focal point for pelagic birdwatching, particularly due to their importance for rare seabirds. Among the most notable is the New Caledonian Storm-Petrel, a species rediscovered south of New Caledonia in 2008. Since 2010, it has been observed on multi-day pelagic trips to the seamounts, particularly from February to April, when conditions are ideal. On one of these, 10–15 individuals were seen on a single trip—highlighting the seamounts as a key habitat.

In addition to the New Caledonian Storm Petrel, the seamounts host other rare seabirds scarcely seen elsewhere in Australian waters. The 'Magnificent Petrel' (dark morph of the Collared Petrel) has been recorded in Australia only at these seamounts, while the Band-rumped Storm-Petrel and Polynesian Storm-Petrel also occur predominantly here. White-bellied Storm-Petrels are expected during the summer months, though sightings remain rare on shorter pelagic trips.

In contrast to the continental shelf, where productivity depends on eastward currents, the isolated nature of the seamounts ensures consistent upwellings regardless of current direction. These 'islands of productivity' serve as critical foraging areas for seabirds, underscoring their ecological importance. For birdwatchers and researchers, the seamounts offer unique opportunities to observe some of the world's rarest and most elusive seabird species.

Au12J AUSTRALIAN TEMPERATE PELAGIC WATERS

IN A NUTSHELL: The deep waters lying off the continental shelf in the temperate areas of Australia. **Global Habitat Affinities:** AFRICAN PELAGIC WATERS; SOUTH AMERICAN TEMPERATE PELAGIC WATERS. **Continental Habitat Affinities:** TROPICAL PELAGIC WATERS. **Species Overlap:** TROPICAL PELAGIC WATERS. **Full Bird Assemblage:** habitatsoftheworld.org/Au12J.

DESCRIPTION: Australian Temperate Pelagic Waters span from the southeast portion of the Indian Ocean to the sw. Pacific Ocean. In these southern, temperate areas, the edge of the continental

Pintado Petrel is a regular feature on springtime pelagic trips out of Wollongong, south of Sydney. © ROB HYNSONV

shelf, where the ocean rapidly becomes much deeper, is closer to shore than it is farther north. At the continental break (where the shelf ends), upwellings of nutrient-rich, colder waters produce substantial concentrations of sea life, from microscopic organisms right up the food chain to large pelagic fish. The waters over the break are always more productive than the shallow waters coastward and the very deep ocean seaward and therefore the best place for seeing oceanic wildlife. In addition to these cold-water upwellings, the presence of marine life is also affected by major ocean currents. The East Australian Current (EAC) flows southwards along Australia's east coast, while the Leeuwin Current flows southwards along the west coast. Although warm currents typically have lower nutrient concentrations than cold currents, the EAC and Leeuwin Current are exceptions, due to specific oceanographic processes. By the time these warm currents have reached temperate zones, they have accumulated nutrients from deeper ocean layers farther north.

WILDLIFE: Australia has a diverse pelagic bird and cetacean fauna and has some of the best seabird-viewing areas of the world. Australian Temperate Pelagic Waters attract a great diversity of pelagic birds, including shearwaters, petrels, storm-petrels, prions, albatrosses, and gannets. In general, the pelagic waters of the Pacific Ocean have a more diverse seabird assemblage than those of the Indian Ocean, which basically hold a subset of the former. Seasonality is very important to pelagic bird movements: generally, the austral winter (June–August) is best for prions such as Fairy, Antarctic, and Slender-billed Prions; albatrosses such as Antipodean Albatross, Indian Yellow-nosed, Buller's, White-capped, and Black-browed Albatrosses; and some of the more southerly breeding petrel species such as Southern and Northern Giant-Petrels, Blue Petrel, Pintado Petrel, and Providence Petrel.

The austral spring and summer (September–February) are better for groups such as shearwaters such as Flesh-footed, Wedge-tailed, Sooty, and Short-tailed Shearwaters; northern petrels such as Wilson's Storm-Petrel, Grey-faced Petrel, White-necked Petrel, and Gould's Petrel; and tropical-breeding species such as Red-tailed and White-tailed Tropicbirds and Red-footed and Brown Boobies.

The jaegers (skuas) familiar to Northern Hemisphere birders, such as the Long-tailed, Parasitic, and Pomarine Jaegers, which all breed on northern tundras such as NEARCTIC ROCKY TUNDRA and EUROPEAN ROCKY TUNDRA, all appear in Australian Temperate Pelagic Waters in the boreal winter, while Brown Skua and South Polar Skua, which breed in subantarctic waters, come to Australian waters in the austral winter.

Most of the terns, such as Brown, Black, and Grey

The region's greatest diversity of seabirds is found within Temperate Pelagic Waters. All the Australian albatrosses occur south of the tropics, and Antipodean Albatross is a regular winter visitor to the southern continental shelf. © ROB HYNSON

Blue Petrel is a circumpolar species breeding as far away as South Georgia Island in the South Atlantic and feeding in Australian waters. © ROB HYNSON

Noddies, and White, Sooty, and Bridled Terns, are summer visitors from tropical areas; or are long-distance migrants from the temperate Northern Hemisphere, such as Arctic Tern and Common Tern. White-fronted Tern is a nonbreeding winter visitor from New Zealand, while Great Crested, Fairy, and Little Terns can breed in Australian temperate waters. The three Australian-breeding gull species are all from this region: Silver Gull is familiar to Australians who have tried to eat chips on the beach; Pacific Gull is restricted mainly to Tasmanian waters; and Kelp Gull is found through most Southern Hemisphere pelagic waters. Pelagic birding trips can be worthwhile at any time of year, but in general, the calmer the sea, the duller the birding and the better the cetacean-watching, as many bird species require updrafts produced from waves to fly and feed.

The cetaceans found in the pelagic waters of the region include Humpback, Southern Right, Sperm, Long-finned Pilot, and Blue Whales; Indo-Pacific Bottlenose, Common Bottlenose, Common, and Risso's Dolphins; and Orca. The best months for whale-watching depend on location and species. Many whales breed in Antarctic waters farther south in the austral summer. Southern Right Whale spends the austral winter months in s. Australian waters. Many Humpback Whales winter farther north but are often seen migrating along the coasts.

CONSERVATION: Longline fishing poses serious conservation issues in Australian Temperate Pelagic Waters due to its high bycatch rates, threats to non-target species, and impact on vulnerable marine ecosystems. Dragnet fishing disturbs the seafloor and also has massive bycatch implications. Although things have improved dramatically since one of the authors grew up in a commercial fishing town, seabird numbers are still affected by bycatch. Moreover, climate change is inducing rapid warming of marine waters, especially in the Tasman Sea, causing southward shifts in species distributions.

DISTRIBUTION: Australian Temperate Pelagic Waters are found from the Indian Ocean to the Pacific Ocean around the southern side of the Australian landmass. Along the southwest and southeast coasts of Australia, the edge of the continental shelf is closer to shore than farther north, but this is not the case in the c. Great Australian Bight or between Victoria and Tasmania, where the seas are shallow. Around most of s. Australia, regardless of the width of the continental shelf, the shelf break (the edge of the shelf) and continental slope are very steep, dropping to the deep and flat abyssal plain. Most Australian pelagic boat tours depart from southern ports and take a few hours to get out to the continental break. Whale-watching trips are also popular but tend not to go out as far.

WHERE TO SEE: Regular pelagic boat trips leave from Sydney and Wollongong, New South Wales, Australia; Eaglehawk Neck, Tasmania, Australia; Portland, Victoria, Australia; and Albany and Perth, Western Australia.

POST-COLONIAL ANTHROPOGENIC HABITATS

Au13A AUSTRALASIAN CROPLAND

IN A NUTSHELL: The farmland that has replaced the original habitats with crops. **Global Habitat Affinities:** ASIAN TEMPERATE CROPLAND; SOUTH AFRICAN TEMPERATE CULTIVATION. **Continental Habitat Affinities:** None. **Species Overlap:** Surrounding habitats when small corridors are preserved.

DESCRIPTION: Most large-scale crop farming in Australia's temperate zones is seed monocultures, including wheat, barley, and hops. Wheat farming is common throughout s. Australia and is the most important crop in mallee areas. This farming has drastically altered massive tracts of natural habitat throughout inland se. and sw. Australia. This has resulted in severe fragmentation of habitats such as the various mallee woodlands and mulga woodlands in

Wheat fields have replaced much of the original semiarid forest and woodlands of temperate Australia. © GABRIEL CAMPBELL, TROPICAL BIRDING TOURS

Though the woodlands have gone, some cockatoos have adapted to the new opportunities that crop farming brings. © SAM WOODS, TROPICAL BIRDING TOURS

New South Wales, Victoria, and Western Australia. In the Brigalow Belt of nc. New South Wales and sc. Queensland, the native BRIGALOW habitat has also been converted into wheat and barley. While the vast majority of bird species have lost within this equation, the new croplands and permanent water sources have benefitted others. Species that have adapted well include larks, some raptors, and many parrot species. Conversely, species such as Malleefowl, Gilbert's Whistler, and Turquoise and Superb Parrots (among others) have lost much of their range to the expansion of these agricultural operations. Sulphur-crested Cockatoo and Little Corella are major pest species of croplands. With current laws, it is illegal to trap and sell cockatoos in the pet trade, but it is legal to kill birds in the thousands as crop pests!

Rice is also grown in Australia, where Japonica is the most common variety grown. In New South Wales, rice is typically planted around October, and its growth can extend until December. This timing allows the rice crops to take advantage of the warmer temperatures, longer daylight hours, and higher rainfall. Rice cultivation on the island of New Guinea is not as extensive as in some other parts of the world, and rice is not a staple crop for the majority of the population. There has, however, been an increase in rice farming by Javan immigrants in Indonesian New Guinea, leading to deforestation.

WILDLIFE: Country roads of inland Australia in the wheat belts have become established strongholds of birds such as Rufous and Brown Songlarks, Singing Bushlark, Nankeen Kestrel, Black-shouldered Kite, and a host of parrot species, including Australian Ringneck, Greater Bluebonnet, and Red-rumped Parrot. Superb Parrots move from riverine forests into seed monocultures at harvest time. Parrot flocks concentrate along railway lines to feed on harvested grain falling from the uncovered carriages at certain times of year. This is considered acceptable loss, and it is a great time for birders to view large numbers of parrots. One particularly good place to observe this phenomenon is the area between Junee and Coolamon in New South Wales. In Western Australia, Carnaby's Black-Cockatoo enters cropland.

Despite their limited extent in Australia, rice fields have an outsized conservation importance for the threatened Australasian Bittern. Possibly a third of Australia's bitterns utilise the Riverina rice-growing area in New South Wales, where the paddy fields mimic a natural wetland. The change away from permanent ponds to grow rice has affected birds as the flooded season is insufficient for successful breeding. Conservationists are trying to encourage farmers to keep their paddy fields flooded for longer.

Red-rumped Parrot is a very common bird of the wheat and barley fields of e. Australia. © PABLO CERVANTES, TROPICAL BIRDING TOURS

DISTRIBUTION/WHERE TO SEE: Cropland is found through most of the humid and semiarid regions of Australia and is really only missing from the desert areas of c. Australia. The savanna areas have not yet been converted to cropland, though OPEN EUCALYPT SAVANNA is being cleared at an alarming rate, so this anthropogenic habitat is expanding. Some major areas for seed monocultures are around Perth, Western Australia; w. New South Wales, Australia; and the Eyre Peninsula, South Australia. Rice cultivation takes place in certain regions of Australia, particularly in the Riverina region of New South Wales, which is known for its fertile land and suitable climate for rice farming.

Carnaby's Black-Cockatoo uses croplands for feeding, though the lack of large trees with nesting holes is a major conservation problem for this species. © SHANE KENNEDY, TROPICAL BIRDING TOURS

Au13B AUSTRALASIAN BANANAS AND SUGARCANE

IN A NUTSHELL: Tropical plantations that have replaced the original habitats. **Global Habitat Affinities:** AFRICAN SAVANNA CULTIVATION; AFRICAN HUMID LOWLAND CULTIVATION. **Continental Habitat Affinities:** OPEN EUCALYPT SAVANNA (for sugarcane). **Species Overlap:** Surrounding habitats when small corridors are preserved.

DESCRIPTION: Sugarcane farming in Australia began in the nineteenth century and has grown into a significant industry as the country has become one of the world's top sugar producers. Roughly 1 million acres (400,000 ha) are devoted to sugarcane production, valued at about AU$2 billion and playing a vital role in the region's economy. Sugarcane thrives in the low, flat areas of Queensland and n. New South Wales with their subtropical to tropical climate, high rainfall, and fertile soils. Sugarcane is a very different habitat where it replaces forest but is not so different from native savanna habitats such as those around Mareeba in n. Queensland. Sugarcane farming is also significant on the island of New Guinea, especially in Papua New Guinea, although not to the extent as in Australia, either in area or economic value.

Vast areas that were Open Eucalypt Savanna a few years ago have been converted to bananas, and the widespread clearing of the savanna continues unabated.
© GABRIEL CAMPBELL, TROPICAL BIRDING TOURS

Sugarcane fields mimic native grasslands, so they retain some of the species original to the natural habitat. © GABRIEL CAMPBELL, TROPICAL BIRDING TOURS

Banana farming also began in Australia in the nineteenth century and has grown into a major industry, almost meeting domestic consumption. Currently 25,000 ac. (10,000 ha) are devoted to banana farming, and the industry is valued at around AU$600 million annually. Banana plantations are mainly in Queensland, which provides the ideal climate with warm temperatures and high humidity. Banana farming is also important on New Guinea, where the crop is grown mainly on smallholdings. It provides an important source of income for local people, and as a staple food, the banana is also important for local food security.

WILDLIFE: Sugarcane can be good habitat for Pheasant Coucal and also several species of waxbills, including Chestnut-breasted Munia and Crimson Finch. On the island of New Guinea, White-shouldered Fairywren is often found in this habitat. In Australia, sugarcane is now usually cut raw, and not burnt first, although it is still sometimes burnt for nostalgic reasons. Burning attracts Whistling and Square-tailed Kites and Eastern Cattle-Egrets to feed on animals trying to escape the fire. Some reptiles of sugarcane fields include Eastern Brown Snake (*Pseudonaja textilis*) and Red-bellied Black Snake (*Pseudechis porphyriacus*). One of the most harmful introductions of a non-native species in Australia was that of the Cane Toad (*Rhinella marina*), introduced in 1935 to control the Greyback Cane Beetle (*Dermolepida albohirtum*), which was causing significant damage to sugarcane crops. The toad not only was ineffective in controlling the beetle but became invasive, spreading rapidly and causing untold harm to native wildlife, which are poisoned by the toad's toxic secretions when they attempt to eat it.

Crimson Finch was originally found in grass stands around Tropical Freshwater Wetlands or river edges. It is now seen mainly in cane fields, including those in suburban Cairns, Queensland. © ANDRES VASQUEZ, TROPICAL BIRDING TOURS

Banana plantations are not particularly good for native wildlife, although this is also dependent on management practices. Areas keeping some surrounding native habitat will retain more wildlife. Various snakes and lizards may be found in plantations, preying on insects and other small animals—depending on the extent of agricultural chemicals used.

DISTRIBUTION/WHERE TO SEE: Sugarcane farming is a significant agricultural industry in Australia, particularly in the northern regions where the climate and fertile soils are conducive to its cultivation. Some of the most important areas of sugarcane farming include the Burdekin and Herbert River regions of Queensland. While not as prominent as Queensland, New South Wales also has some important sugarcane farming regions, including the Richmond and Clarence River valleys, particularly around the town of Broadwater. The Northern Territory has a smaller but growing sugarcane industry located primarily in the Darwin region. The Ord River Irrigation Area in Western Australia is another region where sugarcane is grown. Irrigation from the river allows for the cultivation of crops like sugarcane in an otherwise arid region. Some important areas for sugarcane production in Papua New Guinea include the area around the Ramu and Markham River valleys and some parts of Western Province.

Bananas are grown in certain elevated areas of n. New South Wales and Queensland. Some important areas for banana farming in Queensland are around Mareeba, Innisfail, and Tully. In New South Wales, it is concentrated in the Coffs Harbour region. Banana farming occurs widely on New Guinea, especially in the lowlands, which have warm temperatures and high humidity, and usually around human habitation on smallholdings. Some highland areas with suitable microclimates and good soil also have some banana farming on a smaller scale.

Au13C AUSTRALIAN OPEN GRAZING LAND

IN A NUTSHELL: Farmland that has altered the original habitats and is used for open-range cattle grazing. **Global Habitat Affinities:** AFRICAN GRAZING LAND; ASIAN GRAZING LAND; NEOTROPICAL GRAZING LAND. **Continental Habitat Affinities:** INTENSIVE PASTURE. **Species Overlap:** Surrounding habitats, especially open woodlands and savannas.

DESCRIPTION: Grazing lands can be of two types: INTENSIVE PASTURE, referring to dairy farms, horse pasture, and intensive sheep farming (widespread in s. Australia); and Open Grazing Land, used for less intensive open-range sheep or cattle grazing, usually for cattle raised for meat, which often occurs in more tropical areas where it is not so different from the natural savanna environments. Clearing of the originally forested regions of New Guinea and elsewhere in the sw. Pacific for pig and goat grazing, coconut plantations, and cassava fields has resulted in more of a polyculture environment. Widespread beef-cattle grazing occurs in the savanna and open woodland parts of lowland New Guinea and has occurred in some form across nearly the whole of the Australian continent, even the arid inland. The intensity of this grazing depends on the suitability of local conditions. While the effect has not been significant in some inland areas where grazing is light due to lack of nutrients, such as in DUNE SPINIFEX DESERT and ROCKY SPINIFEX DESERT habitats, more productive areas, such as Mitchell grass expanses in TROPICAL TUSSOCK GRASSLAND and most of e. Australia, have been more heavily impacted.

In inland and tropical Australia, much of the beef-cattle grazing occurs in unfenced private concessions with open-range, low-density operations (reminiscent of the vast ranches of the American Southwest), and the original savanna or woodland is intact or only slightly disturbed here. These private holdings appear much wilder and less obviously human-modified than the landscape of the coastal and temperate regions, which has undergone dramatic and conspicuous modification. In many areas of n. Australia, the distinction between Open Grazing Land and OPEN EUCALYPT SAVANNA or MELALEUCA SAVANNA is extremely nebulous in the wetter years, when grass is in abundance, and becomes clear only in periods of drought, when the more natural savannas retain ground cover while the overgrazed patches become dust bowls.

Sheep grazing in semiarid lands often leads to overgrazing, as has occurred in Australia's original Chenopod Shrubland, which has been greatly altered. GABRIEL CAMPBELL, TROPICAL BIRDING TOURS

Some Open Grazing Land can blend in with surrounding natural habitat and appear very much like habitats such as Open Eucalypt Savanna. © GABRIEL CAMPBELL, TROPICAL BIRDING TOURS

As cattle are not native to Australia, and the native mammals produced only hard, dry pellets, there were no native insects that could effectively recycle cattle dung. Dung would therefore accumulate, attracting huge numbers of flies. To help combat this influx, many species of dung beetles were introduced as part of the Australian Dung Beetle Project from the 1960s onwards, and these are present to this day. Grazing cattle, especially in the dry interior of Australia, has required the use of artificial water sources. The subsequent increase in the availability of water has also led to elevated kangaroo populations, which in turn can have other deleterious effects on the environment, like the over-utilisation of food resources.

WILDLIFE: Open-range cattle grazing is so widespread and takes place on such a wide variety of habitats that it is hard to generalise about the wildlife. As a rule, areas devoted to cattle grazing will have an overall lower diversity than the habitat in its natural state. It will hold a subset of the natural community unless it is so altered as to become suitable to species that wouldn't normally be found there.

In n. Australia, the bores and dams associated with cattle farms can be highly productive for birds, which gather to drink in significant numbers, especially in late afternoon and at dusk. Indeed, this can be one of the best ways to find many northern birds. Examples are Cockatiel, Gouldian Finch, as well as other finches, and a variety of honeyeaters. One species that has benefitted from the increase in cattle farming is, of course, Eastern Cattle-Egret. This bird forages around cattle, sometimes perches on them, feeding on insects that have been disturbed and even cattle ticks. Agile Wallaby and Antilopine Wallaroo occur in low-intensity grazing lands, as do Sand Goanna (*Varanus gouldii*) and Frilled Dragon (*Chlamydosaurus kingii*).

DISTRIBUTION/WHERE TO SEE: Open-range cattle grazing takes place throughout the Australian interior. Some of the more important areas include the Barkly Tableland of Northern Territory, the Channel Country of sw. Queensland and nw. New South Wales, the Gulf of Carpentaria coastline of Queensland, the Kimberley and Pilbara regions of Western Australia, and the Flinders Ranges and Nullarbor Plain of South Australia. Most intense sheep farming in Australia is on TEMPERATE TUSSOCK GRASSLANDS of w. New South Wales and inland Western Australia, where comparatively little of the original habitats remains. Large-area, low-intensity sheep ranging, however, is most common in chenopod-dominated regions that were originally CHENOPOD SHRUBLAND and GIBBER CHENOPODLAND, where little 'improved' pastures are required for grazing. In these areas where the ranchers care for the land and do not overgraze, the distinction between pasture and the original shrublands can be difficult to discern.

Au13D AUSTRALASIAN INTENSIVE PASTURE

IN A NUTSHELL: Farmland that has replaced the original habitats and is used for intensive grazing of livestock. **Global Habitat Affinities:** AFRICAN GRAZING LAND; ASIAN GRAZING LAND; NEOTROPICAL GRAZING LAND. **Continental Habitat Affinities:** OPEN GRAZING LAND. **Species Overlap:** Surrounding habitats when small corridors are preserved.

DESCRIPTION: Intensive Pasture, referring to grazing lands used by dairy farms and small-scale, paddock-based sheep farms (widespread in s. Australia), undergoes more intensive use and is more often fenced than OPEN GRAZING LAND, which is usually for meat and often occurs in more tropical areas. Intensive Pasture is found in high-moisture areas and is usually enclosed in fencing. Conversion to Intensive Pasture radically alters the original habitats—the clear-felling of the original forest of e. and sw. Australia for use as dairy-cattle grazing lands has resulted in the typical Western European image of cleared fields with hedgerows and an occasional stand of trees for shade.

Most grass species used in Intensive Pasture are not native to Australia (largely originating in Europe and Africa) and have been carefully selected for their suitability. Tall Fescue (*Festuca arundinacea*), Cocksfoot (*Dactylis glomerata*), and Phalaris (*Phalaris aquatica*) are tolerant of dry conditions and provide high-quality forage. Other species like Ryegrass (*Lolium perenne*) and

Intensive Pasture is grazing land where the animals are confined to very small areas, and the grassland has little to do with the original or surrounding vegetation.
© CHARLEY HESSE, TROPICAL BIRDING TOURS

Kikuyu Grass (*Pennisetum clandestinum*) also have high nutritional value and productivity and can withstand heavy grazing.

WILDLIFE: Southern pasture lands provide habitat for common, open-country birds like Emu, Masked Lapwing, Australian Magpie, Magpie-lark, and Brown and Rufous Songlarks. Parrot species are particularly visible, and Sulphur-crested Cockatoo, Galah, Little and Long-billed Corellas, and Eastern Rosella are readily seen. Other more exciting species are occasionally seen, like Banded Lapwing, buttonquail spp., and even Plains-wanderer in some specific areas of New South Wales and Victoria.

Some of the larger kangaroos, such as Eastern Grey, Western Grey, and Red Kangaroos, have thrived in these southern grazing lands and should be easily spotted if you are within their range. Other nocturnal mammals such as wombats and echidnas can also be found in pastures. Although Bare-nosed Wombat has a preference for native grasses, it will also consume non-native grass species found in Intensive Pasture. Short-beaked Echidna feeds on ants and termites found in pasturelands. Some reptile species found in Intensive Pasture may include Shingleback (*Tiliqua rugosa*), Common Bluetongue (*Tiliqua scincoides*), Eastern Brown Snake (*Pseudonaja textilis*), Tiger Snake (*Notechis scutatus*), and Eastern Bandy Bandy (*Vermicella annulata*).

DISTRIBUTION/WHERE TO SEE: Intensive dairy farming in Australia is limited mainly to areas with reliable rainfall and fertile soils, but infrastructure supporting production and processing is also a determining factor. Victoria is particularly important for dairy farming, with some significant areas in Gippsland, Warrnambool, and the Otway region, and also areas near the New South Wales border and the Mount Gambier area of South Australia. Intensive sheep farming is concentrated in the Western Slopes region of New South Wales (i.e., the Great Dividing Range), where large swaths of natural open woodlands, mallee woodlands, and scrublands have been cleared. Here, however, much more of the original vegetation is left in corridors than in dairy farms in coastal areas of Australia.

Galah is a species of cockatoo that can be an incredibly common species in farmland throughout Australia, and is abundant even on intensive pasture.
© PABLO CERVANTES, TROPICAL BIRDING TOURS

Au13E AUSTRALASIAN URBAN ENVIRONMENTS

IN A NUTSHELL: Areas of human habitation. **Global Habitat Affinities:** ASIAN CITIES; NORTH AMERICAN URBAN AND SUBURBAN ENVIRONMENTS. **Continental Habitat Affinities:** Affinities with surrounding habitats. **Species Overlap:** Surrounding habitats.

DESCRIPTION: Urban areas in Australia contain a variety of land uses, from the concrete urban sprawl of large cities to green parks to leafy suburban residential areas. These areas provide more than just human habitation and service industries, and large cities like Sydney, Melbourne, Brisbane, and Adelaide hold a remarkable array of wildlife. Green spaces enhance the quality of urban life, giving city-dwellers exposure to nature (sometimes their only exposure), and also play a role in preserving Australia's unique natural heritage. The blend of natural habitats within cities provides sanctuary for numerous species of birds, mammals, reptiles, and plants. From the lush expanses of Sydney's Royal Botanic Garden to the green corridors of Melbourne, urban Australia is alive with nature.

Urban areas in Australia often support a rich variety of native plants. Sydney's Royal Botanic Garden is a showcase of Australian flora, featuring iconic species such as the Wollemi Pine (*Wollemia nobilis*), one of the world's most ancient and rarest trees. The gardens also host the native Gymea Lily (*Doryanthes excelsa*), known for its tall flowering stalks and vibrant red blooms. In Melbourne, parks and gardens are often home to native tree species like River Red Gum (*Eucalyptus camaldulensis*) and various other *Eucalyptus* spp., which provide habitat and food for urban wildlife. Adelaide Botanic Garden features an impressive collection of native plants, including the striking kangaroo paws (*Anigozanthos* spp.), with their unique, claw-shaped flowers.

Compared with most cities around the world, Sydney is remarkably well treed. From the balcony that affords this city view, a fanatical birder has logged a remarkable 50 species. © CHRIS GLADWIN

How much nature thrives alongside human populations depends very much on town planning. Many Australian towns and cities have done a good job of creating green spaces and have nature in abundance. Trees and other greenery help filter out pollutants, and being surrounded by them is also beneficial for the psychological well-being of citizens. People don't always go to the trouble of planting native species, but urban parks and woodlots still attract a variety of birds and other animals. Most cities nowadays have parks, which are popular places for walking, jogging, picnics, dates, or just hanging out with friends and family. Water features are often part of such parks, along with grassy lawns and trees for shade. With a bit of careful planning, such places can become real oases for wildlife, and animals usually become very used to human presence, making them great subjects for amateur nature photography. Their presence can be used to educate and nurture an interest in wildlife for people who don't have the opportunity to visit wild areas. Many birding clubs offer monthly guided walks in city parks to encourage people to take up the hobby.

WILDLIFE: More than almost anywhere else in the world, Australian cities hold a dazzling array of native wildlife. They are home to a wide variety of bird species that have adapted to urban environments. Pied Currawong, Noisy Miner, and Australian Ibis are ubiquitous in the cities of e. Australia. In many towns and cities, you can spot the colourful Rainbow Lorikeet flying over, and Sulphur-crested Cockatoos are often seen perched on city trees and even balconies, opening garbage cans, and using drinking fountains. Australian Magpie, with its distinctive black and white plumage and melodic song, is a common sight in parks and gardens. Urban wetlands, like those in Melbourne's Royal Park, attract waterfowl such as Pacific Black Duck and White-faced Heron.

While less visible than birds, urban mammals are also present. The charismatic Koala is readily found in some of Brisbane's urban parks. Common Brushtail Possum, often active at night, is frequently seen in city parks and gardens and sometimes found exploring suburban backyards. In Perth, you might encounter the Quenda (also known as the Western Brown Bandicoot), which has adapted to living in the green spaces within the city. Bats play a significant role in urban ecosystems. Grey-headed Flying Fox, a large fruit bat, roosts in colonies in places like Sydney's Royal Botanic Garden, contributing to pollination and seed dispersal.

Reptiles too have found niches within urban areas. Australian Water Dragon (*Intellagama lesueurii*), often seen basking near water bodies in Brisbane's South Bank Parklands, is a striking lizard that has adapted well to city life. In warmer regions like Darwin, Frilled Dragon (*Chlamydosaurus kingii*) can sometimes be seen in gardens and parks. Eastern Water Skink (*Eulamprus quoyii*) and

Pied Currawong is a major nest predator of smaller native bird species in the urban landscape.
© SAM WOODS, TROPICAL BIRDING TOURS

Noisy Miners gather in groups and regularly harass other species until they abandon territories. © SHANE KENNEDY, TROPICAL BIRDING TOURS

Elegant Snake-eyed Skink (*Cryptoblepharus pulcher*) are also commonly seen around Sydney and Brisbane; and Southern Marbled Gecko (*Christinus marmoratus*) and Common Bluetongue (*Tiliqua scincoides*) around Melbourne and Adelaide.

DISTRIBUTION/WHERE TO SEE: Urban areas are found throughout Australia, but the main centres of human habitation are concentrated along the coast. Some of the best areas for urban wildlife-watching are the parks and botanical gardens in the larger cities such as Royal Botanic Garden, Sydney, New South Wales, Australia; Royal Park, Melbourne, Victoria, Australia; South Bank Parklands, Brisbane, Queensland, Australia; Adelaide Botanic Garden, South Australia.

Australian Ibis (pictured) is now so ubiquitous in Australian cities that it is nicknamed 'Bin Chicken'. It is fascinating that this bird's use of urban habitats is now being copied by other species such as Straw-necked Ibis. © SHANE KENNEDY, TROPICAL BIRDING TOURS

Au13F AUSTRALASIAN TREE PLANTATIONS

IN A NUTSHELL: Monoculture tree plantations, mostly of various *Pinus* and *Eucalyptus* species. **Global Habitat Affinities:** NORTH AMERICAN TREE PLANTATIONS; AFRICAN TREE PLANTATIONS. **Continental Habitat Affinities:** None. **Species Overlap:** GRASSY DRY SCLEROPHYLL FOREST.

DESCRIPTION: The main tree species grown commercially in plantations in Australia are eucalypts and pines. The net worth of the industry is almost US$3 billion, and it employs over 50,000 people, contributing considerably to the country's economy and local employment. The common species used are Tasmanian Blue Gum (*Eucalyptus globulus*), Shining Gum (*Eucalyptus nitens*), and Monterey Pine (*Pinus radiata*). They are usually grown in same-age monocultures that can blanket large areas. These species have been selected due to their fast growth rates and suitability to particular climates and soils. Tasmanian Blue and Shining Gums can attain heights of 100–150 ft. (30–50 m), usually within 10–15 years, before they are harvested. Monterey Pine grows to about 60 ft. (20 m) and is typically harvested at 20–30 years of age. These growth rates are affected by climate, soil quality, and management practices. Plantations have an unsurprisingly unnatural feel, due to the trees being planted in rows and, after a few years of growth, their having little to no understorey, making them easy to walk through. From a distance, eucalyptus plantations may resemble GRASSY DRY SCLEROPHYLL FOREST, but they differ in all the trees being the same age

Tree plantations can be of non-native species such as pines or natives such as eucalypts and melaleucas. Even with native trees such as Tasmanian Blue Gum (pictured), when planted in monocultures such as this, these woodlots are essentially biological deserts.
© IAIN CAMPBELL, TROPICAL BIRDING TOURS/UNSW E&ERC

and the lack of understorey herbs, shrubs, or epiphytes, leading to a comparatively sterile environment. Both pine and gum trees are essential products in Australia's timber and paper industries. Pine trees are used mainly for structural timber in construction but also for chipboard and plywood. Eucalyptus trees are used mainly for paper and pulp production but also for construction timber and furniture. Eucalyptus oil is also extracted and has various medicinal and industrial uses.

Yellow-tailed Black-Cockatoo is one of the few species that has adapted to take advantage of introduced conifer plantations. © PABLO CERVANTES, TROPICAL BIRDING TOURS

WILDLIFE: As commercial eucalyptus plantations usually contain single-species stands of trees that are the same age, even if they are tree species native to the area, these forests lack habitat diversity and might contain only a small subset of native species, usually fairly generalist ones. Some birds that can be found in commercial eucalyptus or pine plantations may include Yellow-tailed Black-Cockatoo, Sulphur-crested Cockatoo, and Red-rumped Parrot. Eucalyptus trees can produce large amounts of nectar, and several species of nectar-feeding birds may be attracted during flowering, including Rainbow Lorikeet, Eastern Spinebill, and Black-chinned and White plumed Honeyeaters. In Tasmanian eucalyptus plantations, Black-headed and Yellow-throated Honeyeaters may be found. Commercial pine forests are even worse, as pines are not even native to Australia, and will generally hold very few animal species. Some species that may persist in pine plantations include birds such as Eastern Rosella and Red-rumped Parrot, mammals such as Sugar Glider and Common Brushtail Possum, and various common butterflies and beetles.

DISTRIBUTION/WHERE TO SEE: Roughly 4.8 million acres (1.95 million ha) of commercial tree plantations cover Australia, largely eucalyptus and pine plantations, pine being slightly more abundant than eucalyptus. Some important regions for these plantations include sw. Western Australia, which has a suitable Mediterranean climate for eucalyptus plantations; the Gippsland region of Victoria, which has suitable rainfall and soil conditions for both eucalyptus and pine; n. New South Wales, which has a subtropical climate beneficial for both eucalyptus and pine; se. Queensland, which has a warm climate and reliable rainfall supporting rapid tree growth; and finally Tasmania, which has a favourable climate and rich soils particularly good for growing eucalyptus species.

APPENDIX

SOIL GROUPS AND HABITATS

There are numerous soil classification systems, all with different names for the various soil types. The global soil reference is the World Reference Base for Soil Resources (WRB). The American system is the USDA's Soil Taxonomy, which might be better described as 'Soil Typology', because although it is hierarchical, it does not have an evolutionary direction, and soils can change from one type to another. The Australian reference is the Australian Soil Classification (ARC). In this book, we usually use the USDA system and clarify it with more specific names such as 'laterite' (a type of ferralsol) when needed. Although a direct walk-through between the soil systems is difficult, in part because the WRB system has 32 types and the USDA 12 types, we can do a rough comparison with biomes, ASC order, USDA order, and their WRB equivalents where they exist (see table).

The soils in the 'order' level of the USDA classification are as follows:

Alfisols are moderately leached soils that have a subsurface horizon of clay accumulation. They are fertile and in the Australasia region found mainly in temperate forests such as NOTHOFAGUS FOREST.

Andisols are formed in volcanic ash and other volcanic materials. They chemically weather very quickly in tropical humid terrains so are very fertile and generally retain water well; for these reasons, they tend to promote growth of rainforests such as AUSTRALASIAN TROPICAL MONTANE RAINFOREST.

Aridisols are dry soils typical of both hot deserts such as the DUNE SPINIFEX DESERT and cold deserts such as GIBBER CHENOPODLAND. They often show evidence of soil horizon development but have limited organic matter due to limited vegetation cover.

Entisols are young soils with little or no horizon development. They are commonly found in areas of recent sediment deposition, colluvial slopes, and alluvial plains after massive flooding. In waterlogged areas, when they have a mid-grey colour through leaching and anaerobic conditions, they can be called 'gleysols', though this is not part of the USDA soil typology. They will form into one of the other soil groups and generally do not determine vegetation type.

Gelisols are the soils that develop close to the surface in alpine regions. Decomposition is so slow, they usually develop organic-rich surface horizons. Because chemical weathering of the underlying rock is so limited, they are minimally affected by the chemistry of the inorganic matter. They are typical of AUSTRALIAN ALPINE TUNDRA.

Histosols are soils found in areas of impeded drainage and seasonal or permanent flooding. They have little soil development and are usually composed of organic materials and can form peat. They are found mainly in marshes or flooded forests such as AUSTRALASIAN SWAMP FOREST.

Inceptisols are a slightly more developed version of entisols, with minimal horizon development. They are widespread, can be found in a variety of environments, and don't really have a strong relationship with any vegetation type.

Mollisols are soils rich in organic matter that have a thick, dark surface horizon. They are mainly associated with temperate grasslands such as AUSTRALIAN MONTANE GRASSLAND.

Oxisols are the highly weathered tropical soils found in tropical humid environments with fairly uniform rainfall. They are characterised by low fertility due to intense leaching over time but can be fertile if formed on mafic (iron and magnesium) igneous rocks such as basalt. Typical habitats are Australian AUSTRALASIAN LOWLAND RAINFOREST.

Podzols (often called **podosol** in Australia and **spodosol** in the US) are acidic soils under heathlands in cool, moist environments, such as WALLUM AND AUSBOS. The intense leaching of nutrients caused by the highly acidic waters removes organic material and most minerals from the surface, leaving it white-coloured, and deposits them in a dark iron- and organic-rich horizon within 6 ft. (2 m) of the surface.

Ultisols are widespread in tropical Australia. They are highly weathered, with a subsurface horizon of clay accumulation, and usually have a very high iron and aluminium-oxide concentration at the soil surface. Because they form in environments with strong seasonal rainfall (monsoonal regions) and fluctuating water tables, they promote the development of TETRODONTA WOODLAND SAVANNA.

Vertisols are clayey soils that swell when wet and shrink when dry, causing deep cracks during dry periods and sometimes making it difficult for large trees to grow. In Australia, they are strongly associated with tussock grasslands, but they can underlie a variety of other grasslands or low scrub habitats.

It is generally understood that soil is determined by underlying geology and hydrology, and that it greatly influences vegetation type. Changes in hydrology affect the soil type; typical examples

BIOME	Aus. ASC	USDA Group	WORLD WRB
Conifer Forests		Spodosol	Podzol
Deserts and Arid Scrubs	Kandosol Calcarosol Rudosol	Aridisol	Durisol Regosol
Temperate Deciduous Forests	Kurosol	Alfisol Spodosol	Luvisol Podzol
Tropical Humid Forests	Ferrosol Podosol	Oxisol Andisol	Ferralsol Andosol
Dry Deciduous Forests	Ferrosol Inceptisol Tenosol	Oxisol Incepitsol	Ferralsol Cambisol
Savannas	Kurosol Kandosol Rudisol Tenosol	Ultisol Entisol	Acrisol Leptosol
Grasslands and Steppes	Ferrosol Vertisol	Mollisol Vertisol Alfisol	Chernozem Vertisol
Mediterranean Shrublands	Podosol Kurosol	Spodosol Ultisol	Podzol Acrisol
Sclerophyll Woodlands	Kandosol Dermosol Tenosol	Aridisol Inceptisol Entisol	Arisol Acrisol Cambisol Arenosol
Tundras	Rudisol Kurosol	Entisol Gelisol Ultisol	Regosol Calisol Cryosol
Freshwater Wetlands	Organisol	Histosol	Histosol Gleysol
Salt-Dominated Habitats	Calcarosol Sodosol Hydrosol	Aridisol Natric Alfisol Aridisol	Calcisol Solonetz Solonchak

would be the impeding of drainage over a mollisol in the grasslands and the resulting formation of a histosol, or the drying of a humid region and the underlying soil becoming more desiccated and changing from an oxisol (where the iron minerals are usually oxyhydroxides like goethite) to a type of ultisol called ferralsol or laterite (where the iron minerals are oxides such as hematite).

Vegetation can also influence soil type, such as when desertification occurs or, as is well documented in Europe, when TEMPERATE DECIDUOUS FOREST is replaced by plantations of spruce or pine, and the increase in acidity of the waters percolating from the decomposing conifer needles changes the soils from alfisols to podzols.

COMMON CANOPY LEAF TYPES AND THE FORESTS WHERE YOU MAY FIND THEM

This table presents the most common leaf types used in describing different types of forest canopy and some of the habitats where they are prominent. This does not take into account the many types of leaves of understorey plants such as grasses, sedges, ferns, and euphorbias.

PLANT GROUP	LEAF SHAPE	LEAF NAME	HABITATS
GYMNOSPERMS		**Conifer Lobe** Flat, lobed, evergreen.	Temperate forests, mixed conifer/broadleaf forests
		Conifer Needle Thin linear leaves. Usually evergreen.	Boreal conifer forests, dry conifer forests
ANGIOSPERMS		**Deciduous Broadleaf** Broad, thin leaves that grow quickly and last one season.	Temperate deciduous forests, wet/dry deciduous forests
		Evergreen Broadleaf Broad, thin, often with drip tips. They last a long time.	Rainforests, cloud forests
		Sclerophyllous Evergreen Thick, leathery leaves that resist transpiration and fires.	Eucalypt forests, sclerophyll forests, heathlands, Maquis, fynbos, mallee, Mulga, matorral, cerrado
		Microphyllous Small leaves that resist transpiration.	Acacia savanna, thornscrub, Chaco seco, desert scrubs

INDEX

Note: Common names of species are indexed, unless there is no common name in which case the scientific name is indexed.

Habitats are worded **in full** in the index beginning with the word Australasian, or Australian, where relevant. The words 'Australasian or Australian' has been dropped from references to habitats within the *actual* text e.g. 'Lowland Rainforest' refers to *Australasian* Lowland Rainforest (*see page* 9).

Page numbers in **bold** indicate photographs.

Species mentioned in passing *without* further information have not been indexed. The Introduction, and geographical/geological/climatic features have not been indexed. The emphasis of the index is on species and the habitat types.

acacias and *Acacia* spp.
- Arid Heathland 201, 203
- Brigalow 129
- Grassy Mulga 306, 307, 308
- Heathy Dry Sclerophyll Forest 245
- Inland Rocky Shrubby Woodland 274, 275
- Lignum Swamp 340
- Mixed Sandplain Woodland 279, **282**
- Northern Acacia Savanna 159, **159**, 160, **160**, 161
- Open Eucalypt Savanna 135
- Spinifex Mulga 312, 313
- Tropical Tussock Grassland 178
- Yilgarn Mixed Woodland 315, **316**

Acronychia, Beach 106
Adder
- Northern Death 86, 91, 121
- Southern Death 100, 130, 199, 253

African Fynbos 193, 201, 206, 210, 211, 215, 286
African Grazing Land 385, 387
African Humid Lowland Cultivation 382
African Moist Montane Forest 76, 92, 102
African Montane Grassland 187
African Mopane 133, 141, 153, 159, 279, 306, 311
African Pelagic Waters 372, 376
African Salt Marsh 362
African Salt Pans and Lakes 359
African Savanna Cultivation 382
African South Coast Forest Matrix 106
African Strandveld 193, 201, 210, 286–87
African Tree Plantations 392
Afroparamo 325, **326**
Afrotropical Grassland 177
Afrotropical Lowland Rainforest 69, 71, 88
Afrotropical Moist Mixed Savanna 133, 153
Afrotropical Monsoon Forest 122
Afrotropical Shallow Freshwater Marsh 329
Afrotropical Swamp Forest 110
Agreste Caatinga 117
Akeake 245, 292, 308
Albatross 377
- Antipodean 377, **377**

Albizia, Moluccan 89
Alectryon
- Beach 106
- Hairy 107–8

algae 361, 368, 370
Allocasuarina 33, 196, 211, 217, 236, 279, 282, 293, 315, **316**, 319
Alpine Tundra, Australian 31, 187, 271, 320, 321–24, **322**, 325
Amazon Terrafirma 69
Andean Cloudforest 76, 82, 92
Andean Cushion Paramo 323
Angolan Deciduous Forest 128
Antechinus
- Agile 219
- Brown 79, 199, 219
- Fat-tailed False 52
- Mainland Dusky 219
- Tasmanian Dusky 225, 273
- Yellow-footed 234, 241, 247, 258, 304

Aotus, Common 197
Apostlebird 130, **162**, 163, 247, 284
Apple
- Broad-leaved 236
- Cocky 123, 149, 238
- Emu 155, 307
- Red Bush 123
- Rough-barked 222, 245, 266

Arctic Cryptic Tundra 322
Arid Heathland 34, 192, 193, 200, **201**, 201–5, **202**, **203**, 210, 212, 214, 286, 287, 296, 299
- Temperate Heath Thicket (subhabitat) 192, 202

Aristida grasses 51
Artificial Saltworks 361
Ash
- Alpine 187, 222, 228
- Blue Mountains Mallee 217, 243, 245
- Blueberry 223
- Coast Mallee 197
- Crow's 98, 119
- Faulconbridge Mallee 217, 243, 245
- Mountain 221, 222, 226, 228
- Red 238
- Silvertop 217
- Yellow-topped Mallee 197

Asian Alpine Meadow and Steppe 187
Asian Alpine Tundra 321
Asian Cities 389
Asian Flower Steppe 60
Asian Freshwater Swamp Forest 342
Asian Grazing Land 385, 387
Asian Lowland Tropical Rainforest 69, 71, 88
Asian Mangrove Forest 344, 351
Asian Offshore Tropical Cay and Islands 357
Asian Salt Pan 359
Asian Temperate Cropland 379
Asian Temperate Wetland 334
Asian Tidal Mudflat 365
Asian Tropical Pelagic Waters 372
Asian Tropical Sandy Beach 354
Asian Tropical Wetland 329
Aspen, Silver 102
Astelia, New Guinea 326
Asteromyrtus, Brass's 155
Astrapia
- Arfak 94
- Ribbon-tailed 94
- Splendid 94, **94**

Ausbos 193, **194**, **195**, 198, 286
- *see also* Wallum and Ausbos

Australasian Bananas and Sugarcane **382**, 382–84, **383**
Australasian Cropland **379**, 379–81, **380**
Australasian Intensive Pasture 385, **387**, 387–88
Australasian Littoral Rainforest 68, 71, 106–9, **107**, 198, 351
Australasian Lowland Rainforest 17, 28, 38, 68, 69–75, **70**, **71**, 76, 78, 79, 82, 88, 90, 91, 92, 93, 106, 110, 122, 125, 170, 207, 344, 348
Australasian Monsoon Vineforest 17, 38, 68, 106, 113, 116, 117, 119, 120, 122–27, **123**, **124**, 149, 150, 152, 158, 165, 170, 174, 175, 206, 207, **208**, 209
Australasian Rocky Headland 30, 38, **368–69**, 368–71, **370–71**
Australasian Sandy Beach 38, 348, **354**, 354–56, 357, 364, 365

Australasian Sandy Cay 28, 354, **357**, 357–58
Australasian Swamp Forest 29, 38, 68, 69, 88, 110–15, **111**, 122, 175, 347, 348
Australasian Tidal Mudflat 67, 348, 354, 355, 359, 362, 363, 364, **365**, 365–67, 368
Australasian Tree Plantations **392**, 392–93
Australasian Tropical Freshwater Wetland 35, 169, 329–33, **330**, 334
Australasian Tropical Mangrove Forest 29, 38, 110, 113, 344–50, **345**, **346–47**, 351, 352
Australasian Tropical Montane Rainforest 29, 39, 68, 76, 82–87, **83**, 90, 91, 92, 221, 226, 231
Australasian Tropical Pelagic Waters 372–375, 376
Australasian Urban Environments **389**, 389–91
Australia, habitats 27–39
  Desert Outback 27, 36–37, **36–37**
  Savanna North 27, 35–36
  Semiarid Eastern 27, 31–33
  Southwest 27, 33–34
  Temperate Southeast 27, 30–31
  Tropical and Subtropical Northeast 27, 28–29
Australian Alpine Tundra 31, 187, 271, 320, 321–24, **322**, 325
Australian Coastal Salt Marsh 342, 351, 359, **362**, 362–64, **363**, 365
Australian Dry Vineforest 33, 68, 81, 116, 117–21, **118**, **119**, 122, 128, 130
Australian Montane Grassland 176, 182, 187–91, **188**, 189, 321
Australian Open Grazing Land 182, **385**, 385–86, **386**, 387
Australian Salt Pan 36, 64, **359**, 359–61
Australian Subtropical Rainforest 29, 30, 68, 69, 76–81, **77**, 87, 97, 102, 105, 110, 117, 120, 130, 200, 216, 221, 226, 231, 351
Australian Temperate Mangrove 30, 344, 345, 351–53, **352**
Australian Temperate Pelagic Waters 372, 374, 376–78
Australian Temperate Rainforest 17, 30, 31, 68, 76, 78, 79, 97, 102–5, **103**, **104**, 218, 231, 242
Australian Temperate Wetland 329, 332, 334–36, **335**, 337, 341, 342, 359
  Deepwater Lakes and Dams 335
Austroparamo 39, 92, 320, 321, 325–28, **326**, 343
Austrostipa densiflora 275
Avicennia mangrove trees 344, 345
Avocet, Red-necked 361
Axe Gapper (Glasswood) 119
Ayers Rock (Uluru) 36, 42, **42–43**

Baarl 211
Babbler
  Chestnut-crowned 284, 299
  Hall's 308, 314, **314**
  Papuan 113, 127
  White-browed 283–84, **284**, 293, 298, 318
Baeckea
  Alpine 342
  Broom 287
  Desert 287
  Shrubby 196
Balga 251
bamboos 89, 93
Bananas, farming 382, **382**, 383, 384
Bandicoot
  Eastern Barred 199, 225, 241, 247, **248**
  Long-nosed 79, 209, 224, 241
  Long-tailed 328
  Northern Brown 113, 114, 120, 139, 150, 157
  Queensland Barred 157
  Raffray's 328
  Southern Brown 199, 214, 224, 247
  Western (Woylie) 252, 304
  Western Brown (Quenda) 234, 252, 390
bandicoots 72
Bandy Bandy, Eastern 181, 388
Bangalay 222
Banksia
  Acorn 202
  Baxter's 212
  Candlestick 202, **211**, 212
  Coastal 106, 198, 370
  Creeping 212
  Desert 202, 205
  Fern-leaved 197
  Firewood 202, 212
  Great 212, 251
  Hairpin 217, 244
  Heath-leaved 197, 217
  Old Man 196–97, 245
  Prostrate 212
  River 251
  Round-fruit 302
  Scarlet 212
  Sceptre 202
  Silver 197, 287
  Swamp 196, 217
  Sword-leaved 217
  Tropical 207
  Wallum 197
Banksia and banksias 196, 197, 202, 211, 212, 233, 251, 315
Bardick 205, 214
Bat
  Arnhem Long-eared 139
  Bristle-faced Free-tailed 284
  Lesser Long-eared 284
  Lesser Long-tongued Nectar 73, 168
  Little Broad-nosed 284
  Orange Leaf-nosed 139
  White-striped Free-tailed 185, 284
Batis 362
bats 72, 185, 390
Baza, Pacific 125, 174, 224
Bean, Black 76, 82
Beard-Heath
  Blunt 217
  Coast 197
  Lance 270
  Mountain 270
Beech
  Antarctic 98
  Deciduous 98
  Myrtle 98, 228
  Nothofagus 97, 98, **99**
Bee-eater, Rainbow 44, **45**, 185
Beefwood 143, 155
  White 78
Beetle, Greyback Cane 383
beetles, dung 386
Belah 282, 308
Bellbird, Crested 144, 283, 289, 295, 310, **313**, 314, 318
Bendee 312
Berry, Midgen 107
Berrypecker
  Eastern Crested 85, 95, 328
  Fan-tailed 85
  Mid-mountain 85
  Obscure 90
  Tit 85
  Western Crested 85, 95, 328
Bettong
  Northern 157, 230
  Rufous 120, 247
  Southern 241
Bicycle-Dragon, Crested 66, 319
Big Red (sand dune) 46, **47**
Bilby, Greater 43, 180
biomes 19–20, 27
Birdflower, Green 46
Bird-of-Paradise
  Greater 90
  King 113

King-of-Saxony 94
Magnificent 90, **90**
Wilson's **39**
birds-of-paradise 29, 72, 85, 125
Birdsville/Birdsville Track 36, 46, 48
Bitou Bush 109
Bittern, Australasian 335, 381
Blackberry, Pilated-leaved 191
Blackbutt 107, 222
Cleland's 303
Goldfields 302, 315
Black-Cockatoo
Baudin's 252
Carnaby's 252, 381, **381**
Glossy 130, 268, **268**
Red-tailed 252
Yellow-tailed 199, 218, 273, 393, **393**
Blackthorn, Australian 245, 257, 267, 282
Blackwood, Australian 98, 102, 270
Blanketleaf, Tasmanian 228
Bloodwood
Blotchy 147, 207
Brown 160
Brush 78
Clarkson's 147
Desert 143, 153
Melville Island 147
Pink 222, 236
Red 135, 155
Rough-leaved 160
Sandhill 42
blossom nomads (nectivorous birds) 44, 44, 57, 137, 144, **145**, 155, 161, 167, 174, 198, 213, 218, 257, 288, 294, 299, 303, 318
Bluebell, Rock 187
Bluebonnet
Greater 263, 380
Naretha 57
Bluebush
Black 55, 64, 307
Bottle 183
Erect Mallee 292, 298
Hairy 183
Karri 233
Leafless 183, 340
Low 60
Pearl 55, 60, 292, 303, 317
Queensland 178, 340
Rosy 55, 292
Short-leaf 303
Slit-Wing 292
Small-leaf 279, 202
Bluegrass
Pitted 136
Queensland 182
Bluetongue
Blotched 100, 199, 225, 324
Centralian 361
Common 151, 164, 241, 353, 388, 391
Saltbush Slender 58, 62
Western 290, 300
Boab 117, 135
Boatbill, Yellow-breasted 125, 174
Bog-Rush
Hairy 217
Zigzag 196
bogs 342
Boobialla, Common 198
Booby
Brown 358, **358**, 373, 377
Red-footed 358, 373, 377
Booyong
Black 77, 98
White 76
Boree 178
Boronia
Wallum 196
Winged 207
Bottle Tree
Broad-leaved 117
Queensland 117, **128**, 129
Bottlebrush
Alice River 165, 171
Granite 303
One-sided 202, 212, 251, 303, 315
River 267
Willow 170
Bougainville island 96
Bowerbird
Archbold's 94, 95
Fawn-breasted 108, 125
Fire-maned 94
Golden **84**, 85
Great 138, 163
Regent 78, **78**, 105
Satin 229–30
Spotted 308
Tooth-billed 85
Western 308
bowerbirds 72
Box
Bimble 129, 130, 279, 282
Black 261
Brush 106, 107
Cloncurry 143
Gilbert River 135, 153
Green-leaf 135
Grey 256, **256**
Kanuka 171
Long-leaved 245
Normanton 143
Northern Swamp 171
Pilliga 130, 279
Poplar 135, 261, 308
Silver 143
Swamp 111, 171, 236
Western Grey 256, 282
White 183, 245, 256
Yellow 183, 245, 256, 261, 266
Boxthorn, Australian 56
Brachychiton carruthersii 89
Bracken, Austral 223, 270
Brigalow (*Acacia harpophylla*) 117, 129, 130, 308
Brigalow (habitat) 32, 33, 116, 117, 120, **128**, 128–31, **129**, 159, 276, 279, 285, 306, 308, 380
Brigalow Belt 32
Bristlebird
Eastern 198, 200, 217
Western 213, **213**
Bronze-Cuckoo
Horsfield's 257, 283, 289, 295, 299, 318
Little 125
Shining 257
Bronzewing
Brush 204, 289, 324
Common 204, 234, 246, 252, 284, 289, 318
Flock 48, 179
Broombush 207, 292
Broom-Heath, Prickly 197
Broom-Pea, Winged 238
Brown Barrel 98, 270
Browntop, Silky 149
Bruguiera, Smallflower 347
Brumby (wild horse) 273
Brush Cuckoo, Sahul 125
Brushturkey
Australian 79, 108, 125
Red-billed 348
Budgerigar 44, 263
Buffalo, Water 332
Bufflegrass 136
Bulanock 211
Bullich 251
Buloke 129, 130, 256, 279, 282, 291
Bumble Tree 129
Bundy 245
Burr
Cannonball 292
Galvanised 56, 257, 279, 282
Giant Red 56
Bursaria, Sweet 267
Bush Apple, Red 123
Bushlark, Singing 185, 324, 380
Bushman's Clothes Peg 167

Bush-Pea
  Twiggy 257
  Wreath 244
Bustard, Australian 138, 180, **180**, 185
Butcherbird
  Black 127
  Black-backed 150
  Grey **318**
Buttercup, Papuan 325
Buttonquail
  Black-breasted 200
  Buff-breasted 150, 157
  Little 56, 144, 185, 289
  Painted 157, 246, 289
  Red-chested 185
buttonquails 388

Cajuputi 110, 112, 347
Callitris 19, 33, 129, 274, 279, **282**, 293, 315, 319
Callitris Woodland (Mixed Sandplain Woodland subhabitat) 13, 132, 220, 282, **282**, **283**, 285
Camel, Dromedary 45, 48
Canegrass, Sandhill 43, 46, 48
Canthium, Coast 107
Caper Bush 124
Carabeen
  Red 98
  Yellow 78
Carbeen 107, 261
Carrasco Caatinga 274
Carrot, Large New Guinea 325
Cascarilla, Hard 149
Caspian Riparian Scrub 279
Caspian Wormwood Desert 64
Cassinia
  Drooping 257
  Rosemary 245
Cassinia leptocephala 245
Cassowary, Southern 29, 72, **72**, 125
Casuarina 33, 71, 88, 196, 211, 279, 282, **316**
Casuarina, Papuan 88
Catbird
  Arfak 94, **94**
  Black-eared 125
  Green 78, 105
  Huon 94
cats, feral 43, 45, 48, 58
cattails (*Typha* spp.) 334, 337
cattle 385, 386, **386**, 387
Cattle-Egret, Eastern 383, 386
Cay, Australian Sandy 28, 354, **357**, 357–58
cays 357, 358
Cedar, Australian Red 76, 78, 80–81
Celery, Sea 345
Central Middle Eastern Reg Desert 60
Cerrado Sensu Stricto 153
Chainfruit 108, 119
Champion Bay Poison 202
Chat
  Crimson 48, 65, 67, 144, 185
  Orange 48, 56, **57**, 62, 65, 67, 185
  White-fronted 62, 66, **67**, 185, 289, 295, 352
Cheese Tree, Umbrella 111
Chenopod Mallee. *See* Shrubby and Chenopod Mallee
Chenopod Shrubland 36, 40, **54**, 54–59, **55**, **57**, **58**, 60, 177, 178, 183, 185, 205, 282, 291, 292, 295, 299, 303, 305, 337, 340, 386
Chenopod Woodland 55, **56–57**, 58
chenopods 55, 56, **56**, 57, 60, 62, 183, 279, 282, 291, 292, **293**, 307, 317, 340
Cherry
  Broad-leaved Native 207
  Cedar Bay 108
  Native 207
Chihuahuan Desert Grassland 177
Chilean Sclerophyll Scrub 215, 254, 301
Chinquapin, Papua New Guinea 85
chinquapins (*Castanopsis*) 93
Chough, White-winged 130, 247, 284
Chowchilla 85
Chuditch (Western Quoll) 252, 318
Cicadabird, Sahul 125, 127, 174
Cisticola, Golden-headed 331, 364
Claw Flower 203
climate change 81, 273, 324, 326, 328, 342, 343, 358, 375, 378
Clover, White 273
Club-Rush, Slender 362
Coachwood, Northern 82
Coastal Salt Marsh 342, 351, 359, **362**, 362–64, **363**, 365
Coastal Tropical Tussock Grassland **177**
Cockatiel 386
Cockatoo
  Gang-gang 218, 271, **271**
  Palm 72, 75, 125
  Pink 299, 310
  Sulphur-crested 263, 273, 299, 380, 388, 390, 393
cockatoos 299
Cocksfoot 387
Coffee Bush 238
Compass Bush 202
Conestick 217
Conkerberry 119, 129, 144
Coober Pedy 60, 63
Coolabah 60, 261, 340
  Gum 274, 279, 282
Coolibah 135
Coolskink
  Agile 100, 342
  Alpine 324, 342
  Boulder 273
  Heath 100
  Metallic 100, 225, 273, 324, 342
  Ocellated 100, 199, 273, 342
  Southern Forest 225
Copperburr
  Grey 317
  Spear-fruit 279
Copperhead
  Highlands 219, 273, 343
  Lowlands 199, 225
Coprosma, Spreading 323
coral trees 88
Coral-Fern, Alpine 342
Cord-Rush, Mountain 342
Corella
  Little 299, 380, 388
  Long-billed 388
Corkwood, Soft 98
Cormorant
  Black-faced 370
  Great 263
  Little Black 263
  Little Pied 263, 331
  Pied 331
Corymbia 134, **134**, 135, 144, 147, 153, 160
Cotton Bush 279
  Black 130
Cotton Tree, Red Silk 88
Coucal, Pheasant 157, 383
Couch Honeypot 251
Cough Bush 276
Crab, Light-blue Soldier 367
Crake
  Australian 335
  Baillon's 335
  Spotless 335
  White-browed 331
Crevice-Dragon, Ornate 319
Crocodile
  Freshwater 169, 332
  Saltwater 169, 332, 350, **350**
Cropland, Australasian 186, **379**, 379–81, **380**
Croton, Silver 119
Ctenotus
  Common Desert 66
  Common Southwest 235
  Copper-tailed 121, 247, 259
  Leopard 314

Red-sided 314
Ribbon 48, 341
Robust 258, 263, 278, 324
Straight-browed 139
Wedgesnout 48
Cuckoo
Black-eared 283, 318
Channel-billed 125
Chestnut-breasted 125
Fan-tailed 120, 199, 218, 233, 252, 324
Pallid 283, 299, 318
Sahul Brush 125
Cuckoo-Dove, Brown 79
Cuckooshrike
Black-faced 57, 352
Ground **162**, 163
White-bellied 144, 157, 174
Cudgerie 106
Blush 106
cumbungi (cattails) 334, 337
Cupflower, Cushion 323
Curlew, Far Eastern 364, 367
Curracabah 238
Currant Bush, Prickly 99
Currawang (*Acacia doratoxylon*) 275
Currawong
Black 273, 323
Grey 214, 273, 295, 323
Pied 273, 390, **390**
Cuscus
Common Spotted **74**, 91, 120
Mountain 86
Stein's 86
cuscuses 95
spotted (*Spilocuscus* spp.) 72
Cycad, Badu Island 238
Cypress-Pine
Black 245, 274, 275, 278
Bruce 202
Coastal 106
Northern 155
Oyster Bay 217
Scrub 287, 291, 298
Scrubby 315
Slender 291
White 245, 256, 274, 275, 279, 282, 285, 291
cypress-pines 33, 241, **277**

Dacrycarpus 93
Daisy
Bluebush 55, **56**, 183, 282, 292, 293, **293**
Poached-egg 55
Daisy-Bush
Musk 228
Showy 55, 298
Darter, Australasian 263, 331
Dasyure
Habbema 328
Speckled 86, **87**, 328
Dead Finish (*Acacia tetragonophylla*) 275, 308, 315
Deccan Thornscrub 311
Deepwater Lakes and Dams 335
Dendrobium, New Guinea 326
Deserts 19, 40–67
Caspian Wormwood 64
Central Middle Eastern Reg 60
Dune Spinifex *see* Dune Spinifex Desert
Rocky Spinifex *see* Rocky Spinifex Desert
Saharan Erg 46
Saharan Reg 60
Devil, Thorny (lizard) 44
Devil's-Claws, Grand 357
Dingo 52, 58, 62, 66, 139, 181, 355, 361
Dodder-Laurel, Slender 287
Dolphin
Australian Snubfin 375
Common 378
Common Bottlenose 355, 375, 378
Indo-Pacific Bottlenose 352, 375, 378
Pantropical Spotted 375
Risso's 375, 378
Spinner 375
Doodlallie 135, 279, 312
Dorcopsis, Grey 91
Dotterel
Black-fronted 331, 361
Inland 56, 62, **63**, 180, 185
Red-kneed 331
Doughwood, Pink-flowered 111
Dove
Bar-shouldered 108, 157, 174
Diamond 44, 48, 144
Pacific Emerald 79, 125
Peaceful 48, 108, 157, 174, 284, 318
Dowitcher, Asian 367
Dragon
Australian Water 100, 105, 121, 390
Boyd's Forest 86, 115
Burns's 284
Canegrass Two-lined 48
Central Bearded 48, 53, 58, **58**, 284, 300, 319
Central Netted 44, 48, 284
Chameleon 150
Claypan 58, 62, 66
Dwarf Bearded 304
Eastern Bearded 185, 205, 241, 247, 258, 263, 278, 284, 353
Eastern Water 199
Eyrean Earless 181
Frilled 139, **139**, 146, 149, 157, 386, 390
Gibber 62
Gibber Earless 58, 62
Gilbert's 139, 350
Goldfields Pebble 62, 319
Horner's 146, 169, 350
Jacky 199, 247, 324
Lake Eyre 361
Long-nosed 44, 53, 205
Lozenge-marked 66
Mallee Tree 205
Military 44
Nobbi 278, 284, 295, 300
Northern Two-Lined 157
Northern Water 127, 175, 350
Nullarbor Earless 58, 62
Painted 48, 205, 295, 341, 361
Slater's Ring-tailed 53, 146, 314
Southern Angle-headed 79
Southern Mallee 300
Spotted Military 205
Swift Rock 285
Western Netted 205
Drongo, Spangled 120, 125, 352
Dropseed, Seashore 351, 360, 362
Drumsticks, Broad-leaved 217, 244
Dry Chaco 279, 306
Dry Deciduous Yungas 117, 128
Dry Vineforest *see* Australian Dry Vineforest
Dryandra 202
Golden 302
Pink 202
Prickly 202, 251, 302
Dryandra Woodland National Park 34, **301**
Dtella
Dubious 157, 350
Eastern Tree 48, 62, 263, 284, 300
Gulf Tree 146
Robust 146
Tope End 127
Western Tree 205, 253
Duck
Blue-billed 335
Freckled 341
Hardhead 335
Musk 335
Pacific Black 364, 390
Pink-eared 335, **336**
Dugite 205, 234–35, 253
Dugong 367, 375

Dunaliella salina 360
Dune Spinifex Desert 36, 40, 41–45, **42**, **43**, 46, 48, 49, 51, 60, 177, 180, 181, 385
Dunecrest Canegrass 17, 36, 40, 41, 43, 46–48, **47**, **48**
dung beetles 386
Dunnart
Chestnut 209
Fat-tailed 66, **66**, 185, 284, 341
Slender-tailed 185, 241, 295
Stripe-faced 181, 314
White-footed 224

Eagle
Little 258, 289, 303
New Guinea 94
Wedge-tailed 44, 57, 181, 258, 273, 303
East Australian Current (EAC) 372, 377
East Deccan Evergreen Scrub 274
Ebony
Queensland 119
Scaly 119
Sea 124
Echidna
Eastern Long-beaked 328
Short-beaked 120, 139, 157, 181, 191, 199, 219, 240, 247, 252, 258, 263, 273, 284, 285, 300, 304, 319, 324, 342, 388
Eclectus, Papuan 72, 125
ecosystem 8, 12
ecotones 14–15, **103**, 106, 154, 242, 286, **287**
Egret, Great 352
Elaeocarpus 93
Elfin Forest 97, 99
Emu **31**, 66, 157, 185, 295, 300, 388
Emu Bush
Bignonia 340
Narrow-leaved 315
Silver 315
Emuwren
Mallee 298, **299**
Rufous-crowned **50**, 52
Southern 198, 199, 212, 217, **218**
epicormic regrowth 251, **251**
epiphytes 76, 82, 93, **93**, 99, 348
Eremophila 51, 279, 283, **284**, 315
Ericaceae, species 93
eucalypts, found in
Australasian Littoral Rainforest 107
Australasian Urban Environments 389
Australian Dry Vineforest 117
Grassy Dry Sclerophyll Forest 236
Grassy Wet Sclerophyll Forest 221, 222
Heathy Dry Sclerophyll Forest 243, 244, 245
Heathy Mallee 33, 287
Inland Riverine Woodland 260, 261, **261**
Ironbark-Box Woodland 254, 256
Jarrah-Marri Forest 249–50
Karri Forest 34, 232
mallee-form *see* mallee-form
Mixed Sandplain Woodland 279, **282**
Montane Heathland 217
Northern Acacia Savanna 160, 161
Open Eucalypt Savanna 134, **134**, 135
Rainforest Wet Sclerophyll Forest 226
Rocky Spinifex Desert 50
Shrubby and Chenopod Mallee 33, 291, 292
Spinifex Eucalypt Savanna **141**, 143
Spinifex Mallee 298
Tree Plantations 392, **392**, 393
Wallum and Ausbos 197
Western Eucalypt Woodland 301, 302, 303
Yilgarn Mixed Woodland 34
see also Gum; *specific eucalypt habitats*
Eucalyptus 71, 134, **134**, 135, 153, 222, 315
Euro (Common Wallaroo subspecies) 58, 62, 120, 138, 144, 185, 253, **278**
European Alpine Tundra 321, 323
European Coastal Salt Marsh 362
European Deciduous Rainforest 97
European Garrigue 201
European Maquis 215
European Montane Spruce-Fir Forest 272
European Rocky Tundra 377
extinct Australian Pleistocene megafauna 140

Fairywren
Blue-breasted 204, 212, 252, **252**, 289, 293, 304, 318
Campbell's 127
Lovely 108, **112**, 113, 125, 174, 207
Purple-backed 44, 48, 144, 204, 246, 284, 289, 295, 340
Purple-crowned 138, 174, **175**
Red-backed **156**, 157, 168, 174, 199
Red-winged 204, 212, 234, 252
Splendid 204, 212, 284, 304, 308, **309**, 314, 318
Superb 199, **199**, 204, 218, 257, 273, 289
Variegated 199, 218, 257
Wallace's 90
White-shouldered 108, 383
White-winged 48, 57, 341
Falcon
Black 289
Brown 44, 57, 66, 185, 189, **190**, 205, 263, 273, 289
Grey 52, 263
Peregrine 370
Fanflower, Cushion 202
Fantail
Arafura 125
Australian Rufous 79, 113, **113**
Bougainville 96
Friendly 85, 95
Grey 120, 252, 352
Mangrove 348
Northern 125, 168, 174
Featherflower, Yellow 203
Feathergrass, Tall 55
fens 342
Fern
Austral Filmy 99
Bird's Nest 84, 111
Common Ground 223
Elkhorn 84
Feathered Mosquito 111
Gristle 99
Harsh Ground 111
Kangaroo 99
Mangrove 345, 347
Pouched Coral 111
Prickly Rasp 223
Shiny Filmy 99
Sickle 99
Swamp Water 111
Tree *see* Tree Fern
Veined Bristle 99
ferns 99
Fernwren 85
Fescue, Tall 387
Fieldwren
Rufous 204, 289, 290
Striated 218, 323, **323**, 342, 364
Western 204, 289, **290**, 318
Fig
Cluster 123, 171
Creek Sandpaper 106
Moreton Bay 76
Port Jackson 107, 117
Small-leaved 106–7
White 123
Figbird, Australasian 113, 120, **121**, 125, 174, 352

Fly-Parrot, Double-eyed 108, **108**, 113, 125
fig-parrots 72
Finch
  Black-throated 137, **138**, 150
  Crimson 174, 331, 383, **384**
    White-bellied subspecies 168
  Double-barred 137–38, 150, 157, 163, **163**, 168, 174, 247
  Gouldian 137, **137**, 150, 386
  Long-tailed 137, 150
  Masked 137, 150
  Plum-headed 130, 157
  Star 144, 168
  Zebra 44, **44**, 66, 163, 185
fire(s)
  anthropogenic 136, 144, 155
  Australian Dry Vineforest 119, 121
  Dunecrest Canegrass 47
  Grassy Dry Sclerophyll Forest 238, 239, 241
  Grassy Wet Sclerophyll Forest 223
  Heathy Dry Sclerophyll Forest 242
  Heathy Mallee 288
  Ironbark-Box Woodland **256**
  Jarrah-Marri Forest 251
  Kwongan Heathland 211
  Lignum Swamp 340
  Montane Heathland 216–17
  Nothofagus Forest 100
  Open Eucalypt Savanna **134**, 136
  Rainforest Wet Sclerophyll Forest and 228
  Rocky Spinifex Desert 51
  Shrubby Eucalypt Savanna 153, 155
  Spinifex Eucalypt Savanna **142**, 143, 144
  Spinifex Mallee **297**, 298
  Tetrodonta Woodland Savanna 149
  Tropical Heathland 206, **208**
  Tropical Tussock Grassland 179
  Wallum and Ausbos 193, 196, 197
Firetail
  Beautiful 199, 217
  Diamond 130
  Mountain 328
  Painted 52
  Red-browed 174, 199
  Red-eared 213
Flame Tree, Illawarra 77
floating vegetation 329, **330**
Flooded Chaco and Espinal 159, 165
flooding
  Australian Salt Pans 359–60, 361
  Inland Riverine Woodland 261, 262
  Melaleuca Riverine Forest 171
  Melaleuca Savanna 165, 166, 167
Flowerpecker
  Olive-crowned 348
  Red-capped 168
Flycatcher
  Broad-billed 125
  Leaden 352
  Paperbark 157, 168, 174, 331
  Restless 283, 304
  Satin 100, 105, 229
  Shining 113, 331
Flying Fox
  Black 139, 168, 174, 349
  Grey-headed 350, 390
  Little Red 73, 139, 168
  Spectacled 73, 115, 349
flying foxes 91, 139
Flyrobin
  Olive 90
  Yellow-legged 90, **125**
forbs 46, 47, 51, 60, 182, 183, 187, 257, 323
forests *see specific types*
Fox, Red 342
Freshwater habitats 20, 329–43
  Australasian Tropical Freshwater Wetland 35, 329–33, **330**, 334
  Australian Temperate Wetland 332, 334–36, **335**, 337, 341, 342, 359
  Lignum Swamp 36, **337**, 337–41, **338–39**
  Montane Bog and Fen 342–43, **343**
Friarbird
  Helmeted 108, 113, 127, 174, 209
  Hornbill 108
  Little 247, 283
  Noisy 130, 168, 198, 209, 247
  Silver-crowned 125, 150, 157, 167, 174
Frigatebird
  Great 358, **372**
  Lesser 358, 373
Fringe-Myrtle, Common 217, 287
Frog
  Australian Wood 75
  Barking 264, 278
  Bridled Rocket 151
  Broad-palmed Rocket 285
  Bumpy Rocket 146
  Cape York Whistling 151
  Cascade Stream 80
  Crucifix Spadefoot 285
  Dahl's Aquatic 139
  Desert Spadefoot 44
  Desert Trilling 295
  Eastern Stony-creek 115
  Fleay's Barred 80
  Fletcher's 80
  Fry's Whistling 75
  Giant Banjo 264, 278, 295
  Giant Burrowing 146, 169
  Great Barred 80, 241
  Humming 305
  Marbled 115, 151, 175
  Montane Pinocchio 95
  New Holland 164
  Northern Banjo 241
  Northern Barred 75, 115
  Northern Stuttering Barred 100
  Ornate Burrowing 139, 151, 164, 175, 285
  Rainforest Stony-creek 115
  Red-backed Brood 100
  Short-footed 164
  Small 151
  Southern Brood 273
  Southern Heath 219
  Southern Smooth 100
  Spotted Marsh 264, 278
  Striped Rocket 175
  Tree *see* Tree Frog
  Western Spotted 304–5
Froglet
  Bleating 305
  Common Eastern 100, 219, 343
  Desert 285
  Eastern 273
  Haswell's 219
  Tasmanian 100, 342
Frogmouth
  Marbled 78, 105
  Papuan 174
Fruit-Dove
  Black-banded 125
  Blue-capped 348
  Coroneted 127
  Dwarf 127
  Orange-bellied 108
  Orange-fronted 348
  Rose-crowned 79, 108, 125, **126**
  Superb 79, **80–81**, 112, 125
  Wallace's 348
  Wompoo 79, 108, 112
fruit-doves 72
Fuchsia, Wedge-leaf Desert 203
Fuchsia Bush, Slender 315
Fuzz-Weed 298
Fynbos, African 193, 201, 206, 210, 211, 215, 286

Galah 189, 263, 388, **388**
Galip Nut 88
Gannet, Australasian 370
Gardenia, Brown 171
Garuga 89

Gecko
  Beaded 290, 300
  Border Thick-tailed 247
  Box-patterned Ground 310
  Broad-tailed 199
  Central Clawless 53
  Centralian Rough Knob-tailed 53
  Clouded Velvet 241
  Common Prickly 121, 127, 139, 157, 175, 181, 205, 284, 319
  Eastern Beaked 295
  Eastern Spiny-tailed 284
  Eastern Stone 121, 241, 278, 284
  Eyre Basin Beaked 361
  Gibber 62
  Golden-tailed 130
  Gulf Marbled Velvet 146
  Inland Marbled Velvet 284
  Kristin's Spiny-tailed 146, 164, 314
  Midline Knob-tailed 66
  Mourning 115
  Northern Leaf-tailed 75, 86
  Northern Marbled Velvet 139
  Northern Spiny-tailed 44
  Northern Velvet 75, 127, 151, 157
  Ocellated Velvet 121
  Ornate Stone 205
  Ranges Stone 285
  Reticulated Velvet 304
  Smooth Knob-tailed 44
  Soft Spiny-tailed 205
  Southern Leaf-tailed 79
  Southern Marbled 205, 253, 263, 353, 391
  Southern Spiny-tailed 295, 300, 353
  Southern Spotted Velvet 121
  Southwestern Clawless 304
  Speckled Stone 253
  Spiny Knob-tailed 181
  Tessellated 181
  Thick-tailed Barking 253, 263, 278, 285, 290, 295, 300, 319
  Variable Fat-tailed 310
  Western Beaked 310
  White-spotted Ground 205
  Wyberba Leaf-tailed 100
  Zigzag Velvet 146, 209, 247
geckos (velvet or spiny-tailed) 310
Geebung 106
Gerygone
  Dusky 348
  Fairy 108, 113, 120, 125, 127, 174
  Green-backed 125
  Large-billed 113, 125
  Mangrove 348, 352, **353**
  Western 257, 277, 294–95, 299
  Yellow-bellied 113
Giant Rat, White-tailed 72–73
Giant-Petrel, Northern and Southern 377
Gibber Chenopodland 17, 36, 40, 48, 54, 56, 60–63, **61**, **63**, 181, 337, 386
Gibberbird 62, **62**
gibbers 60, **61**
Gidgee 129, 130, 143, 155, 160, 178, 307, 308, 312
  Georgina 312
Gimlet 302
  Silver-topped 303, 315
Ginger, Native 107
Glasswood (Axe Gapper) 119
Glasswort, Blackseed 65
Glider
  Feather-tailed 100, 199, 224, 231
  Greater 100, 120, 224, 240, 258
  Krefft's 79, **81**
  Squirrel 231, 240, 247, 258
  Sugar 100, 120, 199, 219, 224, 240, 247, 258, 393
  Yellow-bellied 120, 224, 231
Glossocarya, Rusty 119
Goanna, Sand 44, 62, 185, 263, 278, 284, 285, 295, 300, 304, 319, 341, 361, 386
goats 119, 278, 282
Godwit
  Bar-tailed 364, 367
  Black-tailed 364
Goldenface 90
Goose, Magpie 331, **332**
Gooseberry Tree, Little 171
Goosefoot, Nitre 340
Goosefruit, Frosted 292
Goshawk
  Brown 125, 224, 258, 263, 289, 303
  Grey 125, 224
  Red 150
Grass
  Alpine Wallaby 187
  Balcada 298
  Black Windmill 182
  Bog Snow 187
  Bristly Wallaby 275
  Bull Mitchell 177
  Button 342
  Christmas 136
  Common Tussock 187
  Common Wallaby 188
  Curly Mitchell 136, 177
  Curly Windmill 136, 182
  Cutting 342
  Erect Kerosene 46, 161
  Fine-leaved Snow 187
    Hoop Mitchell 136
  Kangaroo 136, 187, 257, 308
  Kikuyu 388
  Knotted Corkscrew 182
  Leafy Wallaby 182
  Lemon 308
  Mitchell 133, **178**, 179, 385
  Mitchell Mulga 308
  Neverfail 177, 308
  Northern Wanderrie 161
  Para 332
  Pineapple 323
  Plains 182
  Poa Gunnii 187
  Porcupine 50, 298
  Pretty Wanderrie 60
  Red Spathe 51
  Roebourne Plains 60
  Snow 188, 270
  Streaked Arrow 345
  Tall Oat 182, 257
  Woollybutt 46
grass(es)
  C3 136, 182, 188, 255
  C4 135–36, 155, 188, 255, 257
Grass Tree
  Forest 161, 207, 217
  Queensland 238
  Swamp 196
Grassbird
  Little 335, **336**, 364
  Tawny 364
Grasslands 20, 176, 177–91
  African Montane 187
  Afrotropical 177
  Australian Montane 176, 182, 187–91, **188**, 189, 321
  Chihuahuan Desert 177
  Indian Tropical 177
  Neotropical 177
  Temperate Tussock 56, 176, 177, 182–86, **183**, 187, 386
  Tropical Tussock *see* Tropical Tussock Grassland
Grasswren
  Black 52, 144
  Carpentarian 144
  Eyrean 47–48, **48**
  Grey 340, **340**, 341
  Opalton 52, 144, **145**, 313
  Pilbara 52
  Sandhill 43
  Striated, Murray Mallee subspecies 298
  Thick-billed 56
  White-throated 144
grasswrens 144

- Grassy Dry Sclerophyll Forest 29, 31, 32, 147, 191, 220, 221, 222, 225, 226, 230, 236–41, **237**, **238**, 242, 246, 249, 254, 261, 265, 267, 392
- Grassy Mulga 17, 33, 34, 54, 56, 58, 128, 130, 159, 177, 220, 274, 279, 282, 285, 305, **306**, 306–10, **307**, 311, 312, 313, 314
- Grassy Wet Sclerophyll Forest 30, 220, 221–25, **222**, 226, 228–29, 232, 233, 236, 239, 242, 246, 269
- Great Barrier Reef 28, 358
- Great Sandy Desert 41
- Grebe
  - Australasian 335, 361
  - Great Crested 335
  - Hoary-headed 335, 361
- Greenshank
  - Common 331, 364
  - Nordmann's 367
- Grevillea
  - Alpine 322
  - Bottlebrush 315
  - Comb 298
  - Fuchsia 251
  - Honeysuckle 308
  - Lace Net 203
  - Mountain 322
  - Sandhill 46
  - Seven Dwarfs 275, 292
- *Grevillea* 57, 197, 212, 293
- Ground-Robin
  - Greater 95, **96**
  - Lesser 95
- Guinea Flower, Banks' 207
- Guinea Savanna 153
- Gulbarn 165, 167
- Gull
  - Kelp 355, 378
  - Pacific 355, **356**, 378
  - Silver 355, 361, 378
- Gum
  - Bolly 76
  - Brittle 217
  - Broad-leaved Poplar 135
  - Cabbage 236
  - Cider 187
  - Coral 302, 315
  - Dallachy's Ghost 135, 236
  - Dunn's White 226
  - Dwyer's Red 274
  - Errinundra Shining 222
  - Flooded 222, 226
  - Forest Red 107, 171, 236, 260
  - Ghost 143
  - Giant Water 76, 82
  - Grey 222
  - Jounama Snow 270
  - Large-leaved Cabbage 160–61
  - Manna 236
  - Mountain 270
  - Narrow-leaved Snappy 217, 244
  - Paperbark 147
  - Ribbon 270
  - River Red 60, 171, 261, **261**, 262, 264, 266, 389
  - Rough-leaf Cabbage 135
  - Salmon 302, 315
  - Salmon White 302
  - Shining 392
  - Snappy 50, 143
  - Snow 187, 270, **270**
  - Spider 212
  - Spotted 222
  - Sydney Blue 107, 226
  - Tasmanian Blue 222, **223**, 228, 392, **392**
  - Tasmanian Snow 187
  - Tumbledown Red 256, 275
  - Weeping Ghost 135
  - Yellow 256, 287
  - York 302, 307, 315
- Gundabluie 308, 340
- Gusu 147

- habitat niche 28, 30, 32, 33, 36, 37, 38
- Hairy Mary, and Vicious Hairy Mary 111
- Hakea
  - Desert 287
  - Finger 217, 244
  - Harsh 212, 302
  - Pincushion 212
  - Ribbed 202
  - Scallop 211
  - Small-fruit 270
  - Wallum 196
- *Hakea* 197, 211
- halophytes 64, 65, 360
- Hare, Brown 342
- Hare-Wallaby
  - Rufous 43
  - Spectacled 146
- Harrier
  - Papuan 327
  - Spotted 66, 167, 185, 204, 289
  - Swamp 66, 185, 204, 273
- Hazel
  - Karri 233
  - New Zealand 228
- Heath
  - Alpine 342
  - Candle 342
  - Coral 322
  - Cranberry 257
  - Daphne 217
  - Rock 323
  - Swamp 323
- heathland *see* Mediterranean Shrublands
- Heathwren
  - Chestnut-rumped 198, 199, 218, **219**
  - Shy 276, 289
- Heathy Dry Sclerophyll Forest 30, 31, 34, 107, 161, 216, 217, 220, 231, 236, 239, 241, 242–48, **243**, **244–45**, 249, 254, 265, 266, 267, 268, 274, 275, 279
  - Coastal (subhabitat) 220
- Heathy Mallee 17, 33, 34, 193, 201, **201**, 205, 210, 212–13, 215, 220, 243, 254, **286**, 286–90, **287**, 291, **292**, 295, 296, 298, 301, 315
- Hemichroa, Pigface 313
- Heron
  - Pacific 331
  - Pied 331, **333**
  - White-faced 352, 364, 390
- Hibiscus, Sea 347
- Himalayan Subtropical Broadleaf Forest 82
- Hobby, Australian 185, **185**, 263, 273
- Honey Bush 251
- Honeyeater
  - Banded 137, 150, 155
  - Bar-breasted 113, 167, **168**, 174
  - Black 283, 288, 294, 299, 318
  - Black-chinned 157, 257, 289, 393
  - Black-headed 224, 230, **230**, 246, 273, 393
  - Blue-faced 130, **131**, 174, 263
  - Bridled 85
  - Brown 108, 120, 168, 209, 263, 303, 352
  - Brown-backed 113, 167, 168, 174, 348
  - Brown-headed 130, 246–47, 257, 272, 276, 283, 289, 299, 303
  - Crescent 191, 218, 229, 272–73, 323, **324**
  - Cryptic 113
  - Fuscous 257
  - Gilbert's 233, **234**, 252, 303
  - Graceful 108, 127, 209
  - Green-backed 75, 113, 127
  - Grey 308, 314
  - Grey-fronted 144
  - Grey-headed 44, 137, 144, **145**, 155
  - Grey-streaked 328
  - Lewin's 120, **120**, 200, 218, 224
  - Long-bearded 95, 328
  - Macgregor's 93, 94
  - Macleay's **29**
  - Mangrove 348, 352

Honeyeater *continued*
New Holland 191, 198, **198**, 199–200, 204, 213, 218, 233, 252, 273, 289, 303, 323
Orange-cheeked 328
Painted 257, 283, **283**, 308
Pied 44, 298
Purple-gaped 288, **288**, 294, 299
Regent 246, 257, 267, **267**
Rufous-banded 125, 137, 150, 155
Rufous-throated 137, 144, 150, 155, 163, 174
Short-bearded 95, 328
Singing 44, 57, 204, 246, 283, 295, 318
Smoky, species complex 85, 95
Sooty 328
Spiny-cheeked 57, 246, 276, 283, 294, 299, 303, **304**, 308, 310, 314, 318
Striped 130, 247, 276, 283, **284**, 299
Strong-billed 224, 273
Tawny-breasted 127
Tawny-crowned 198, 199, 204, **205**, 213, 289, 303, 318
Varied 113, 163
White-cheeked 198, 200, 213, 218, 252, 268, 303
White-eared 198, 213, **213**, 218, 272, 277, 289, 294, 299, 303, 318, 323
White-fronted 204, 288, 294, 299, 318
White-gaped 125, 174
White-naped 218, 224, 230, 239, 246, 289
White-plumed 44, 144, 246, 257, **262**, 263, 276, 289, 393
White-streaked 209, **209**
White-throated 125, 224, 239
Yellow 108, 113, 125, 155, **155**, 174
Yellow-faced 191, 218, 230, 239, 257, 272, 323
Yellow-plumed 276–77, 288, 294, 299, 303, **304**, 318
Yellow-spotted 113, 209
Yellow-throated 246, 273, 323, 393
Yellow-tinted 137, **137**, 144, 155, 163
Yellow-tufted 224, **224**, 239, 268
Honey-Myrtle
Chenille 212
Coast 212
Graceful 202
Grey 212
Thyme 196
Hopbush, Brilliant 315
Hornbill, Blyth's 71
Humid Broadleaf Forests 19, 68, 69–115
see also specific forest types (see contents page)
Humid Lowland Cultivation 88
Hunter River estuary **363**
Hymenachne, Olive 332
hysteresis 179, 229

Ibis
Australian 331, 364, 390, **391**
Glossy 331
Straw-necked 331, 391
Ifrita, Blue-capped 95
Igapó and Várzea 110, 112
Iguana, Green 115
Ilex 93
Imperial-Pigeon
Collared 348
Torresian 112, 125, 174
Yellowish 349
Indian Dry Deciduous Forest 128
Indian Moist Deciduous Forest 117
Indian Ocean Montane Rainforest 82
Indian Tropical Grassland 177
Indonesian New Guinea 8, 38
Inland Riverine Woodland 171, 175, 183, 220, 254, **260**, 260–64, **261**, 265
Inland Rocky Shrubby Woodland 220, 274–78, **275**, **276–77**, 279, 281
Intensive Pasture, Australasian 385, **387**, 387–88
invasive amphibians (Cane Toad) 75, 80, 115, 139, 151, 332, 383
invasive mammals 342
invasive plants 109, 136, 165, 191, 273, 332
Ironbark
Cullen's 135
Mugga 256, 267, 275
Narrow-leaved 117, 135, 153, 236, 245
Northern Grey 236
Silver-leaved 129, 256, 279, 308
White's 135
Ironbark-Box Woodland 33, 133, 135, 147, 182, 187, 220, 236, 239, 242, 246, 254–59, **255**, **256**, 260, 265, 269, 271, 274, 277, 278, 285, 302, 304, 306, 308
Ironwood, Cooktown 123, 149, 171

Jacana, Comb-crested **330**, 331
Jackwood 228
Jacky-winter 277, 289, 299, 304, 324
jaegers (skuas) 377
Jarrah (*Eucalyptus marginata*) 232, 249, 301
Jarrah-Marri Forest 34, 212, 220, 232, 233, 235, 236, 242, 249–53, **250**, **251**, 301, 302, 305, 315
Jasmine, Desert 129
Jewel-babbler
Blue 127
Chestnut-backed 90
Spotted 95
jewel-babblers 72
Jigal Tree 135, 155, 165
Jointvetch, Indian 340
Jugflower, Coastal 211

Kakadu National Park 35, **124**, 125, 333
Kangaroo
Eastern Grey 120, 130, 164, 185, 191, 199, 224, 231, 247, 258, 263, 277, 284, 300, 310, 324, 388
Red 52, 58, 62, 66, 144, **180**, 181, 185, 205, 263, 277, 284, 285, 290, 300, 310, 388
Western Grey 185, **186**, 205, 214, 234, 253, 277, 284, 285, 290, 295, 300, 304, 310, 319, 388
Karri (*Eucalyptus diversicolor*) 228, 232
Karri Forest 34, 212, 220, 221, 226, 232–35, **233**, 238, 249, 251, 253
Kauri, Black 82
Kazakh Flower Steppe 182, 183
Keelback
Common 139, 151, 332, 350
Montane 95
Kestrel, Nankeen 57, 66, 185, 189, 289, 380
Key Biodiversity Areas (KBAs) 101
Kinabalu Paramo 325
Kingfisher
Azure 263, 331
Beach 348
Forest 157
Little 331, 348, **349**
Moustached 96
New Britain 91
Red-backed 157, 263, 308
Sacred 157, 174, 257, 263, **264**
Torresian 348, 352
Yellow-billed 90, 113, 348
King-Parrot, Australian 223, 230
Kite
Black 181
Black-breasted 44, 167, **168**, 181
Black-shouldered 57, 185, 189, **190**, 205, 273, 303, 380
Letter-winged 179, **179**
Square-tailed 303, 383
Whistling 383
Knot
Great 364, 367, **367**
Red 364, 367
Koala 120, 224, **225**, 231, 240, 247, 258, 263, 390

Kookaburra, Blue-winged 125, 174
Kultarr 62, 284, 314
Kunzea, Yellow 322
Kurrajong 256, 275, 282
Kwongan Heathland 34, 193, 199, 201, 202, 203, 204, 205, **210**, 210–14, **211**, 232, 252, 354

Labichea, Buettner's 207
Lake Austin 64
Lake Carnegie 64
Lake Eyre 260, 334, 359
Lamboto 129
Lamington National Park (Queensland) 29, 79, 80, 81, 101, 240
Lancewood 155, 160, 308, 312, 313
  Red 313
Lantana 197
  Common 109
Lantern-Bush, Straggly 119
Lapwing
  Banded 56, **67**, 185, 388
  Masked 185, 388
Laurel
  Northern 170
  Tasmanian 99
  Three-veined 107
Leaf Warbler, Kolombangara 95–96
Leatherwood 98
Leopardwood 160, **160**, 178, 313
Lightwood 238, 245, 257, 267
lignotuber 143, 161, 217, 243, 287, 291, 296, **297**
Lignum (*Duma florulenta*) 262, 337, **338–39**, 340
Lignum Swamp 36, **337**, 337–41, **338–39**
Lilly Pilly 102, 106, 223
  Broad-leaved 111
Lily
  Climbing 107
  Gymea 389
  Mangrove 345, 347
Liniment Tree 207
Lithocarpus 93
Littoral Rainforest *see* Australasian Littoral Rainforest
Lizard, Stumpy-tailed *see* Shingleback
logging 80–81, 105, 140, 231, 253
Logrunner
  Australian 78, **79**, 105
  Papuan 95
Longan, Fijian 89
Lorikeet
  Goldie's 90
  Little 239, 246, 257
  Musk 257, 288
  Plum-faced 94
  Purple-crowned 233, 288, 294, 298, 303, **303**, 318
  Rainbow 137, 144, 150, 155, 223–24, 230, 239, 257, 390, 393
  Red-collared 137, 144, 155, 167, **167**, 174
  Scaly-breasted 239, 246, **247**
  Stella's 85, 94
  Striated 85, 90
  Varied 137, 144, 150, 155, 174
  West Papuan 94
Lory
  Brown 348
  Red 348
Lovegrass, Purple 136
Lowland Rainforests *see* Australasian Lowland Rainforest
Lyrebird
  Albert's 78, 105
  Superb **104**, 105, 229, 273

Magellanic Temperate Rainforest 97
Magpie, Australian 189, **191**, 388, 390
Magpie-lark 352, **353**, 388
Mahogany
  Broad-leaved White 197
  Red 222
  Swamp 107, 111
Maireana 51
Mallee 287
  Bell-fruited 212
  Blue-leaved 50, 143, 292
  Bull 291
  Dumosa 287, 291, 298
  Finke River 50
  Fruit-ridged 298
  Glossy-leaved Red 282, 291, 298, 307
  Green 292
  Grey 274, 298
  Kingsmill's 50
  Red 291, 292
  Slender-leaf 287
  Soap 298
  Sturt Creek 143
  White 292
  Yellow 287
Mallee Flower, Blue 298
mallee habitats 33, 217, 291, 296
  Heathy *see* Heathy Mallee
  Shrubby and Chenopod *see* Shrubby and Chenopod Mallee
  Spinifex *see* Spinifex Mallee
mallee-form 33, 50, 143, 197, **216**, 217, 274, 286, 291, 296
  'whipstick' 298
Malleefowl 293, **294**, 300, 380
Mallet, Brown 302
'mallets', description 302
Mallow, Helms' 64
Mamajen 123
Mangrove
  Freshwater 112
  Grey 345, 348, 351
  Looking-glass 345
  Milky 345
  Orange 345, 347
  Red 345
  Reflexed Orange 345
  Rib-fruited 348
  River 345, 351
  Shrubby 348
  Spotted 345, 348, 351
  White-flowered Black 348
Mangrove Forest 344
  Asian 344, 351
  Australasian Tropical 29, 38, 110, 113, 344–50, **345**, **346–47**, 351, 352
  Australian Temperate (forest/shrubland) 30, 344, 345, 351–53, **352**
  Neotropical 344
mangroves 344, 345–46
  fringe 348
  roots 346, **346–47**
Mania (Mannikins)
  Chestnut-breasted 150
  Yellow-rumped 150
Manucode
  Glossy-mantled 348
  Trumpet 127
Maple
  Queensland 82
  Rose 82
Marara, Rose 76
Marri 232, 249, 302
  Mountain 250
Martin, Fairy 185
Medicosma, Round-leaved 108
Mediterranean Riparian Forest 265
Mediterranean Shrublands 20, 192, 193–219
  Arid *see* Arid Heathland
  Kwongan *see* Kwongan Heathland
  Montane *see* Montane Heathland
  Tropical 106, 192, 203, 206–9, **208**, 215
  Wallum and Ausbos *see* Wallum and Ausbos
Megapode, Orange-footed 108, 125, 174
Melaleuca and melaleucas 71, 107, 110, 112, 136, 149, 161, 165, 167, 170, 196, 197, 203, 206, **208**, 211, 212, 261, 293, 315, 347

Melaleuca Riverine Forest 170–75, **171**, **172–74**, 260, 261, 265, 266
Melaleuca Savanna 11, 35, 38, 127, 132, 135, 144, 152, 153, 155, 157, 163, 165–69, **166**, 170, 207, 385
  Shrubby Melaleuca (subhabitat) 132, 167
Melampitta, Greater 90
Melidectes, Belford's 85
Melomys
  Cape York 209
  Fawn-footed 79, 115
Merrit 315
Mesoamerican Semi-evergreen Forest 122
Michaelmas Cay 28, **357**, 358
migration, of birds 272, 323, 331, 366, 378
Millet
  Australian 178, 182
  Ditch 331
mimicry, bird 104
Miner
  Bell 224, 230, 239
  Black-eared 294, 299
  Noisy 390, **391**
  Yellow-throated 294, 299
Mint-Bush
  Alpine 342
  Gaping 276
Miombo 128, 147
Mistletoe
  Needle-leaf (Sheoak) 266, 267
  Wireleaf 315
Mistletoebird 108, 252
Mixed Sandplain Woodland 17, 33, 128, 129, 130, 131, 153, 220, 242, **245**, 254, 259, 265, 274, 277, 279–85, **280–81**, **282**, 315, 317, 318
  Callitris Woodland (subhabitat) 13, 220, 282, **282**, **283**, 285
  Sheoak Woodland (subhabitat) 13, 132, 220, 282, **282**, 285
Mock-Olive
  Large 106, 223
  Small-fruited 119, 129
Monarch
  Australian Spectacled 79, 113
  Black-faced 79, 113
  Black-winged 90, 125
  Chestnut-bellied 91
  Frilled 113, 127
  Frill-necked 72, **73**, 125
  Golden 91
  Spot-winged 127
Monitor
  Black-headed 53
  Heath 199, 205, 214, 231, 253
  Lace 100, 115, 121, 185, 199, 241, 247, 258, 263, 278, 284, 295, 300
  Mangrove 350
  Mertens's Water 332
  Rusty Desert 44
  Short-tailed 44
  Spencer's 181, **181**
  Tree *see* Tree Monitor
  Yellow-spotted 139, 146, 151, **152**, 169, 350
Monsoon Vineforest *see* Australasian Monsoon Vineforest
Montane Bog and Fen 342–43, **343**
Montane Grassland, Australian 176, 182, 187–91, **188**, 189, 321
Montane Heathland 30, 31, 187, 192, 193, 200, 201, 206, 210, **215**, 215–19, **216**, 269, 270, 321
Montane Rainforest *see* Australasian Tropical Montane Rainforest
Moonah 212
Moonflower, Beach 357
Mopane 135, 141
Morning Glory, Beach 354
Morrell, Red 302
Mountain-Pigeon, Pale 95
Mouse
  Broad-toothed 324, 342
  Desert 314
  Dusky Hopping 48
  Eastern Chestnut 209
  Mitchell's Hopping 295, 300, 319
  Silky 205
  Spinifex Hopping 314
  Water 349
mudskippers 353, 367
Mulga
  Bastard 60, 178
  Horse 307
Mulga (*Acacia aneura*) 43, 55, 60, 130, 274, 279, 282, 292, 306–7, 312
Mulga (habitats)
  Grassy *see* Grassy Mulga
  Spinifex *see* Spinifex Mulga
Mulgara
  Crest-tailed 48
  Spinifex 295
Mullet (lizard), Land 79
Mungily 64, 360
Munia
  Alpine 327
  Chestnut-breasted 108, 157, 168, 383
  Pictorella 144, **146**, 163
  Snow Mountain **327**, 328
  Streak-headed 108
Musk 119, 129
Muttonwood, Variable 223
Myall 183, 292
  Weeping 183, 256
  Western 55
Myrtle
  Grey 222, 266
  Narrow-leaf 119
Myzomela
  Dusky 125, 127, 174, 209
  Red-headed 113, 125, 127, 348
  Scarlet 120, 167, 218, 224, 230, **230**, 239

Namib Sand Desert 46
Nativehen
  Black-tailed 335, 341, **341**
  Tasmanian 323, 342
Natural Salt Pan 361
Nearctic Alpine Tundra 321, 323, 325
Nearctic Rocky Tundra 322, 377
Nearctic Salt Marsh 362
Nearctic Temperate Deciduous Forest 265
Nearctic Western Riparian Woodland 170, 260, 315
nectivorous birds *see* blossom nomads
Needlewood, Silver 308
Nelia 307
Neotropical Grassland 177
Neotropical Grazing Land 385, 387
Neotropical Lowland Rainforest 88
Neotropical Mangrove Forest 344
Neotropical Rocky Coastline 368
Neotropical Temperate Cloudforest 102
Neotropical Tidal Mudflat 365
Neotropical Tropical Wetland 329
New Guinea 8, 38
  east (Papua New Guinea) 8, 38, **326**
  endemic birds 75, 94
  habitats 38–39, 332, 333
  west (Indonesian New Guinea) 8, 38
New Guinea High-Montane Rainforest 39, 68, 88, 90, 92–96, **93**, 325, 326
New Guinea Hill Forest 39, 68, 82, 85, 88–91, **89**, 92
New Guinea Swamp Forest 113
New Guinean Lowland Rainforest 71, 72, 74
New Zealand Beech Forest 97, 102
Nightjar
  Archbold's 328
  Large-tailed 125
  Spotted 295
Ningaui, Mallee 300
Noddy
  Black 358, 377
  Brown 358, 377
  Grey 377–78

North African Temperate Wetland 337
North American High-Elevation Pine Woodlands 272
North American Sagebrush Shrubland 54, 64
North American Tallgrass Prairie 182
North American Tree Plantations 392
North American Urban and Suburban Environments 389
Northern Acacia Savanna 41, 50, 128, 132, 144, 155, **159**, 159–64, **160**, 165, 203, 308, 312, 314
Northern Islands, habitats 38–39
Nothofagus 97, 98, **99**
Nothofagus Forest 17, 31, 68, 97–101, **98**, **99**, 102, 104, 213, 228
Nullarbor Plain 54, **54**, **55**, 58
Numbat 252, 304, **305**, 318
Nutmeg, Cape 111
Nutsedge, Purple 182

Oak
  Atherton 82
  Bootlace 282
  Darwin Silky 155, 161, 207
  Ironbark-Box Woodland tree similarity 256
  Karri 233
  Northern Silky 82
  Red Tulip 82
  Silver 165, 167
  White Silky 170
Oat, Wild 186
Oil Palm, African 75
Okari Nut 88
Olive
  Australian 76
  Northern 170
Olive Berry, Black 102
Open Eucalypt Savanna 32, 35, 38, 121, 128, 132, 133–40, **134**, **135**, 141, 144, 146, 147, 150, 153, 155, 157, 158, 163, 165, 177, 255, 256, 381, 382, 385, **386**
Open Grazing Land, Australian 182, **385**, 385–86, **386**, 387
Open Treed Cerrado 133
orchids 251, 326
Oriole
  Green 113, 125
  Olive-backed 352
Osprey 355, 370
Otter, Australian 352
Outback, Australia 27, 36–37, **37**, 133
overgrazing 56, 119, 157, 181, 186, 191, 241, 278, 282, 285, 341, 385
Owl
  Lesser Sooty 85
  Rufous 125
Owlet-nightjar
  Australian 57, 295
  Feline 94
Oxylobium, Common 322
Oystercatcher
  Pied 355, **355**, 366
  Sooty 370

Pademelon
  Calaby's 86, 95, 328
  Dusky 86, 91
  Red-legged 73, 79, 115, 120, 230
  Red-necked 79, 100, 105, **231**
  Rufous-bellied 100, 105, 191, 199, 273, 324, 342
pademelons 72
Painted-Snipe, Australian 335, 341
Palm
  Alexandra 78, 84, 110
  Bangalow 76, 78, 84
  Betelnut 88
  Cabbage-Tree 78, 223
  Jaggery 84
  Mangrove 345, 347
  Queensland Fan 110
  Screw 124
  Walking Stick 78, 84
  Zamia 233, 251
Palm Swamp Forest 110
Pampas 182
pandans, and *Pandanus* 88, 93, 111, 329
Pangi 88
Paperbark
  Blue 107, 155
  Broad-leaved 106, 110, 112, 155, 165, 167, 170, 171, 206
  Narrow-leaved 351
  Prickly-leaved 197
  River 170, 171, 266
  Rosy 292
  Silver-crowned 170, 171
  Swamp 212
Papua New Guinea 8, 38, **326**
Papuacedrus 93
Paradise-Kingfisher
  Brown-headed 90
  Buff-breasted 72, 125
  Common 113
  Little 113
  Red-breasted 90
paradise-kingfishers 71–72
Paramo 325
Pardalote
  Forty-spotted 240, **240**, 246
  Red-browed 144
  Spotted 224, **224**, 233, 240, 246, 252, 257, 277, 289, 295, 299, 303
  Striated 144, 224, 233, 240, 246, 257, 277, 283, 289, 295, 299, 303, 318
Parotia, Carola's 90
Parrot
  Blue-winged 66, 258, 289
  Bourke's 263, 308, **308**
  Elegant 212, 258, 304
  Golden-shouldered 149, **149**, 150, 157
  Ground 198, 199, 212, 217
  Hooded **35**, 149, 150
  Mulga 44, 57, 284, 308, 318
  Night 52, 62, 65, 180
  Orange-bellied 66
  Pesquet's 90
  Princess 43
  Red-capped 214, 233, **234**, 252, 304
  Red-cheeked 125
  Red-rumped 183, **184**, 258, 263, 289, 299, 380, **381**, 393
  Red-winged 144, 150, **156**, 157, 174, 263
  Regent 252, 289, **289**, 299, 304
  Rock 212, 371, **371**
  Scarlet-chested 43, **43**, 57, 299
  Superb 258, 263, **263**, 380
  Swift 223, **223**, 257
  Turquoise 130, 246, 258, 277, 284, **285**, 380
  'Twenty-eight' (Australian Ringneck subspecies) 233, **235**, 252
Parrot Bush 251
parrots 299
Pea
  Bluebush 46
  Sturt's Desert 55
Pea Bush, Yellow 340
Pear, Sandplain Woody 203
peat 342
Pelagic Waters
  Temperate, Australian 372, 374, 376–78
  Tropical, Australasian 372–375, 376
Pelican, Australian 335, 361, 364, **364**
Penda
  Golden 171
  Yellow Box 207
Penguin, Little 355
Peppermint
  Queensland 160
  Swan River 233
  Sydney 245
Perentie 53, 361

Persimmon, Clustered 108
Petaurus gliders 95
Petén Swamp Forest 112, 347
Petrel
  Beck's 374
  Blue 377, **378**
  Bulwer's 374
  Gould's 377
  Grey-faced 377
  Herald 374
  Jouanin's 374
  'Magnificent' 375
  Pintado 376, 377
  Providence 374, **374**, 377
  Tahiti 374, **374**
  White-necked 377
Phalaris 387
Phascogale
  Brush-tailed 224, 258
  Red-tailed 252
Pheasant Pigeon complex 90
Phyllocladus 93
Picathartes 72
Pigeon
  Crested 44, 48, 66, 284, 318
  Partridge 150, **150**, 157
  Spinifex 52, **52**, 144
  Squatter 138, **138**, 157
  Topknot 79
  White-headed 79
  Wompoo **109**
Pigface
  Australian 354
  Round-leaved 56, 64
Pilotbird 105, 229
Pine
  Bunya 77, 82
  Celerytop 98, 228
  Hoop 77, 85, 89, 107, 117
  Klinki 85, 89, 93
  Monterey 392
  Mountain Plum 322–23
  Plum 76, 102
  Wollemi 389
pine trees, plantations 392, 393
'pink lake' 360
Pinkwood 276
Pinocchio Frog, Montane 95
Pipit
  Alpine 327, 328, **328**
  Australian 66, 185, 189, 324, 342
Pitcher Plant, Common Swamp 207
Pitohui, White-bellied 113, 348
Pitta
  Noisy 79
  Papuan 72, **109**
  Rainbow **124**, 125
  Southern Papuan 108
pittas 72
Pittosporum, Sweet 198
Plains-wanderer 56, **59**, 62, 185, 388
Planigale, Narrow-nosed 181, 185
Platypus 120, 258, **258**
Plectrachne 49
Pleistocene megafauna 140
Ploughbill, Wattled 85, 94, 95
Plover
  Hooded 355, **355**, 356
  Red-capped 361, 366
Plum
  Burdekin 106, 119
  Bush 155
  Kakadu 123
  Wild 171
Poa spp. 270
Podocarpus 93
Podolepis, Wiry 298
Poor-flower Tree 108
Possum
  Black-and-white Striped 73
  Common Brushtail 100, 120, 139, 157, 224, 231, 234, 240, 247, 252, 258, 263, 273, 285, 300, 304, 310, 324, 390, 393
  Common Ringtail 79, 100, 105, 199, 224, 231, 258, 263, 273
  Coppery Brushtail 120
  Coppery Ringtail 328
  Eastern Pygmy 100, 105, 219, 231, 247
  Green Ringtail 73, **74**
  Herbert River Ringtail 86, **86**, 120
  Honey 214, **214**
  Little Pygmy 300
  Long-tailed Pygmy 209, 328
  Mountain Brushtail 224, 324
  Mountain Pygmy 95
  Short-eared Brushtail 79
  Striped 113, **114**
  Western Pygmy 205, 214, 300, 319
  Western Ringtail 234, 252
possums 72, 86
Post-Colonial Anthropogenic Habitats 20, 379–93
  see also specific habitats (see contents page)
Potoroo
  Gilbert's 214
  Long-nosed 219
Pratincole, Australian 56, 138, 180, 185, 331
prions 377
Propeller Tree 117
Prune, Wild 107
pseudo-chenopods (e.g. Bluebush Daisy) 55, **56**
Pup Pandan 111
Purslane, Sea 357
Pygmy-Goose
  Cotton 331
  Green 331
Pygmy-Parrot
  Buff-faced 90
  Red-breasted 85, 95
pyriscence 196, 206, 211
Python
  Amethyst 86
  Australian Scrub 75, 157
  Black-headed 121, 139, 157, 169, 209
  Boelen's 95
  Carpet 79, 100, 105, 127, 157, 185, 241, 264, 278, 285
  Centralian Carpet 53
  Children's 139, 169, 175, 350
  Mulga 121
  Olive 127, 139
  Robust Blind 121
  Rough-scaled 127
  Southern Green Tree 75, **75**, 91
  Southwestern Carpet 205, 214, 304
  Spotted 151, 157, 169
  Water 139, 332

Quail
  Brown 189, **189**, 198, 204, 212, 328
  Snow Mountain 327, **327**
  Stubble 185, 189, **189**, 204
Quail-thrush
  Chestnut 299, **300**
  Chestnut-breasted 308, **309**, 314
  Cinnamon 48, 56, 62
  Copperback 294, 299
  Nullarbor 54, 56
  Spotted 239–40, 246, **248**
Quandong
  Bitter 302
  Blue 171
  Desert 315
  Hard 107
  White 78
Quenda (Western Brown Bandicoot) 234, 252, 390
Quince, Wild 107
Quinine, Smooth-leaved 149, 165
Quokka **34**, 214, 253
Quoll
  Eastern 100, 105, 225
  New Guinean 73–74, 95
  Spotted-tailed 100, 199, 219, 224, 247
  Western (Chuditch) 252, 318

Rabbit, European 43, 342
Rail
  Chestnut 348
  Chestnut Forest 85, 95
  Forbes's Forest 95
  Lewin's 364, **364**
  New Guinea Flightless 113
Rail-babbler, Malaysian 72
Rainforest Wet Sclerophyll Forest 29, 30, 31, 76, 82, 99, 101, 102, **103**, 105, 107, 216, 220, 221, 223, 224, 225, 226–31, **227**, 232, 233, 238, 242
rainforests *see specific rainforests*
Rakali 263, 352
Raspberry Jam Tree 303, 315
Rat
  Australian Bush 79, 219, 234, 342
  Australian Swamp 79, 199, 219, 231
  Cape York 209
  Common Rock 144
  Long-haired 62, 179, 314, 341
  Subalpine Woolly 328
  White-tailed Giant 115, 209
Rat-Kangaroo, Musky 73, 120
rats, giant naked-tailed 95
Raven
  Australian 189, 323
  Forest 323
  Little 189, 273, 323
Redheart 250
Redthroat 56
Redwood 315
Reed, Common 334, 362
Reef-Heron, Pacific 358
reptiles, extinct, Pleistocene 140
Rhizophora mangrove species 345
Rhododendron, Macgregor's 326
rice cultivation 380, 381
Riflebird
  Magnificent 72, **73**, 75, 113, 127
  Paradise 78, 105
Ringneck, Australian 214, 246, 258, 263, 284, 295, 299, 304, 318, 380
  'Twenty-eight Parrot' (subspecies) 233, **235**, 252
Riparian Forest 106
  Mediterranean 265
  Sheoak *see* Sheoak Riparian Forest
Robin
  Black-capped 85
  Blue-grey 85
  Buff-sided 125, **127**, 174, **174**
  Dusky 224, 246
  Eastern Yellow 224, **228**, 229, 277
  Flame 189, 199, 257, **272**, 273, 277, 289, 324, 342
  Grey-headed 85, **85**
  Hooded 257, **257**, 277, 283, 298, 304
  Mangrove 348
  Pale-yellow 79, 224
  Pink 100, 105, 224, 229, **229**, 342
  Red-capped 130, 257, 277, 283, 289, 295, 299, 304, 308, **310**, 318
  Rose 105, **105**, 224
  Scarlet 199, 224, 240, **240**, 257, 277, 289, 304, 324
  Snow Mountain 328
  Solomons 95
  Subalpine 85, 328
  Western Yellow 252, 289, 295, 304
  White-breasted 214, 234
  White-browed 125
  White-faced 72, **72**, 75, 125
  White-rumped 90
Rock-Pigeon
  Chestnut-quilled **51**, 52
  White-quilled 52
rock-wallabies 52
Rock-Wallaby
  Allied 146
  Black-flanked 253
  Brush-tailed 247
  Herbert's 120
  Mareeba 157, **158**
  Purple-necked 144, 146
  Yellow-footed 52, **53**, 285
Rockwarbler 217, 371
Rocky Headland, Australasian 30, 38, **368–69**, 368–71, **370–71**
Rocky Spinifex Desert 17, 36, 40, 41, 42, **49**, 49–53, 60, **124**, 141, 144, 181, 311, 312, 313, 385
Roepera 207
Roly-poly, Black 257, 340
Rosella
  Crimson 223, 230, 263, 273
    'orange' (Adelaide) subspecies 246
    Yellow subspecies 263
  Eastern 258, **258**, 263, 388, 393
  Green 273, 323
  Northern 150, **151**, 157
  Pale-headed 130, **131**, 157
  Western 214, 252, **253**, 304
Rosemary, Coastal 370
Rosewood 78
  Western 183, 282, 307
Royal Botanic Garden, Sydney 389
Rush
  Sea 362
  Wire 323, 342
Ryegrass 387
  Wimmera 186
Saharan Erg Desert 46
Saharan Reg Desert 60
Sal Forest 128
Saline Habitats 20, 344–78
  Australasian Rocky Headland 30, 38, **368–69**, 368–71, **370–71**
  Australasian Sandy Beach 38, 348, **354**, 354–56, 357, 364, 365
  Australasian Sandy Cay 28, 354, **357**, 357–58
  Australasian Tidal Mudflat *see* Australasian Tidal Mudflat
  Australasian Tropical Mangrove Forest *see* Australasian Tropical Mangrove Forest
  Australasian Tropical Pelagic Waters 372–375, 376
  Australian Coastal Salt Marsh 342, 351, 359, **362**, 362–64, **363**, 365
  Australian Salt Pan 36, 64, **359**, 359–61
  Australian Temperate Mangrove 30, 344, 345, 351–53, **352**
  Australian Temperate Pelagic Waters 372, 374, 376–78
Sallee, Black 270
Salt Marsh
  African 362
  Australian Coastal 342, 351, 359, **362**, 362–64, **363**, 365
  European Coastal 362
  Nearctic 362
Salt Pan, Australian 36, 64, **359**, 359–61
salt pans, artificial (saltworks) 361
Saltbush
  Barrier 129, 303, 307
  Berry 55, 267, 303
  Bladder 55, 56, 60, 317
  Cottony 292, 303
  Hedge 60, 129, 307
  Mallee 292
  Old Man 55, 56, 303
  Pop 60
  Toothed 55
saltbushes 54, 64
Salwood, Brown 82
Samphire
  Beaded 65, 351, 360, 362
  Grey 64
Samphire Flat 40, 64–67, **65**, **67**, 351, 353
  Coastal 65, 66, 67, **67**
  Inland 65, 66
samphires 64
sand dunes 46, **47**
Sandalwood
  Australian 205
  Bastard 135, 279, 308

Sandalwood *continued*
Northern 155, 308
Sanderling 355, 358, 366
Sandpiper
Broad-billed 367
Curlew 364, **366**
Marsh 331
Sharp-tailed 331, 364
Wood 331
Sand-Plover
Greater 366
Siberian 366
Sand-Swimmer, Broad-banded 295
Sandy Beach, Australasian 38, 348, **354**, 354–56, 357, 364, 365
Sandy Cay, Australasian 28, 354, **357**, 357–58
Sarsaparilla, Austral 99, 107
Sassafras
Southern 98, 102
Yellow 98
Satinash
Flaky-barked 171
Swamp 111
Satinbird
Crested 95
Loria's 95
Savannas 20, 132, 133–75
Afrotropical Moist Mixed 133, 153
Guinea 153
Melaleuca *see* Melaleuca Savanna
Melaleuca Riverine Forest *see* Melaleuca Riverine Forest
Northern Acacia *see* Northern Acacia Savanna
Open Eucalypt *see* Open Eucalypt Savanna
Shrubby Eucalypt *see* Shrubby Eucalypt Savanna
Spinifex Eucalypt *see* Spinifex Eucalypt Savanna
Tetrodonta Woodland *see* Tetrodonta Woodland Savanna
Wallacean Melaleuca 165
Scale-Rush, Chaffy 217
Scaly-foot
Brigalow 130
Eastern Hooded 181
Sclerolaena spp. 64, 307
Sclerophyll Woodlands and Forests 20, 220, 221–319, 298
see also specific habitats (see contents page)
Scoparia 342
Screw-Pine 329
Thatch 111, 112
Scrub-bird
Noisy 125, 213, 214
Rufous 100, 101
Scrub-Robin
Northern 75, 113
Papuan 90
Southern 293, 298
Scrubtit 100, **101**, 229, 271, 273, 324, 342
Scrubwren
Atherton 85
Large-billed 229
Pale-billed 90
Papuan 95
Spotted 204, 214, 234, 252, 293, 304
Tasmanian 199, 218, 229, 273, 323, 342
Tropical 127
White-browed 199, 200, 204, 218, 229, 246, 273, 323
Yellow-throated 229
scrubwrens 94
sea cliffs, sea caves 369
Sea Lion, Australian 352, 355, 371
Sea Turtle
Green 355
Hawksbill 355
Loggerhead 355
Seablite, Austral 65
Sea-Eagle, White-bellied 355, 370
Seal
Brown Fur 355, 371
Long-nosed Fur 352, 355, 371
seamounts, Eastern Australia 375
Sedge
Asian Shortstem 323
Sticky Saw 217
sedges 331, 362
Senna, Silver 51, 203, 282, 292, 313
Sertão Caatinga 141, 286, 296
Shadeskink
Orange-tailed 79
Pale-lipped 115
Shearwater
Flesh-footed 377
Heinroth's 374
Short-tailed 377
Sooty 377
Streaked 374
Wedge-tailed 374, 377
sheep farming 255, 385, **385**, 386, 387, **387**
Shelduck
Australian 364
Radjah 331
Sheoak
Beach 354
Black 155, 197, 207
Desert 36, 42, 55
Drooping 198, 275, 282
Dwarf 203, 217, 287
Forest 238
Kariku 43, 55, 60, 308
Karri 233
River 261, 266
Rock 212, 302, 303, 315
Scrub 197, 217
Shrubby 202
Swamp 111, 351
Western 212, 250–51
Sheoak Riparian Forest 170, 175, 220, 246, 257, 261, 265–68, **266**
Sheoak Woodland (Mixed Sandplain Woodland subhabitat) 13, 132, 220, 282, **282**, 285
sheoaks 33, 34, 196, 282, **282**, 291
Shingleback 185, 214, 284, 285, 290, 295, **295**, 300, 304, 319, 353, 388
Shrikethrush
Arafura 108, 125, 167–68
Bower's 85
Grey 200, 252, 273, 318
Rufous 79, 108, 120, 127
Shrike-tit
Eastern 224, 246, **246**, 257
Northern 150
Western 233, 303
Shrimp, Australian Ghost 363, 367
Shrubby and Chenopod Mallee 17, 33, 34, 56, 220, 274, 286, 290, 291–95, **292**, **293**, 296, 298, 301, 305, 308
Shrubby Eucalypt Savanna 117, 132, 136, 144, 150, 153–58, **154**, 159, 167, 206, 207
Shrubby Woodland, Inland Rocky 220, 274–78, **275**, **276–77**, 279, 281
Shrublands
Chenopod *see* Chenopod Shrubland
Mediterranean *see* Mediterranean Shrublands
Sicklebill, Brown 94
sicklebills 85
Sida, Corrugated 257
Simpson Desert 36, 46, **47**
Sittella
Black 85, 95
Varied 257, 283, 318, **319**
Black-capped subspecies **319**
Skink
Alpine Water 324
Bauxite Rainbow 139
Black Rock 219
Black-tailed Bar-lipped 209
Buchanan's Snake-eyed 304

Bull 214
Cape York Mulch 209
Closed-litter Rainbow 115
Crevice Rainbow 209
Cunningham's 100, 199, 324
Dark Bar-sided 121
Dark-flecked Garden Sun- 205
Desert 300, 361
Eastern Firetail 121
Eastern Striped 205
Eastern Three-lined 219
Eastern Three-toed Earless 258
Eastern Water 100, 105, 219, 353, 390
Elegant Snake-eyed 121, 391
Fine-spotted Mulch- 175
Flinders Ranges Rock 285
Inland Snake-eyed 185
King's 214, 235, 253, 304
Lowlands Earless 235, 253, 353
Major 121, 209
McCoy's 225
Metallic Snake-eyed 139, 169
Northern Red-throated Rainbow 115
Pink-tongued 241
Ragged Snake-eyed 185, 300
Shaded-litter Rainbow 157, 164, 350
Shrubland Morethia 205
Six-toothed Rainbow 151, 209
Southeastern Morethia 185, 258, 278, 285, 300
Southern Bar-sided 105
Southern Grass 225, 273, 324, 343
Southern Rainbow 258
Southern Water 273, 324, 343
Southwestern Crevice- 235, 253
Striped Snake-eyed 209, 350
Tree 278, 285
Trunk-climbing 225
Tussock 273, 324, 343
Western Three-lined 235
White's 199, 219
Yakka 310
Yellow-bellied Water 105, 219
Skua
Brown 377
South Polar 377
Slider
Southern 353
Wood Mulch- 185
Smudgee 222
Snake
Bird's Head Peninsula Ground 169
Black-striped 209
Blue-bellied Black 284–85
Broad-headed 199, 231, 247
Brown Tree 139, 151, 157
Collett's Black 181
Common Tree 79, 127, 139, 150, 241, 332
Crowned 205, 214
Curl 53, 146, 181, 185, 285
De Vis's Banded 181, 310
Dunmall's 130
Dwyer's 259, 310
Eastern Brown 121, 181, 185, 199, 241, 247, 259, 264, 300, 336, 383, 388
Eastern Small-eyed 100
Golden-crowned 100
Gould's Hooded 253, 319
Ingram's Brown 181
Little File 350
Macleay's Water 209
Marsh 79
Mulga 44, 53, 181, 285, 310, 319
Narrow-banded Shovel-nosed 44
Northern Desert Banded 44
Orange-naped 139, 146
Ornamental 130
Pale-headed 231
Prong-snouted Blind 185
Red-bellied Black 79, 199, 219, 225, 241, 247, 259, 264, 336, 383
Red-naped 185, 310, 314
Ringed Brown 44, 284, 310
Robust Blind 121
Rough-scaled 79
Shield-snouted Brown 62, 278, 284, 300, 341
Small-eyed Blind 91
Southern Desert Banded 319
Speckled Brown 181
Tiger 100, 199, 205, 214, 219, 225, 241, 253, 273, 324, 336, 342, 388
Western Brown 44, 319
White-bellied Mangrove 350
White-lipped 342
Yellow-bellied Sea 350
Yellow-naped 310
Snake-Lizard, Burton's 290, 300, 350
snakes, forest and ground 95
Snakewood 124, 308
Snottygobble 251
Soapwood 149
Solomon Islands 8, 38–39
endemic birds 75
Upper Montane Cloudforest 95–96
Songlark
Brown 56, 185, 380, 388
Rufous 185, 380, 388
Sorghum, Plume 149
Sorrel, Sheep 273
South African Temperate Cultivation 379
South African Temperate Wetland 334
South American Temperate Pelagic Waters 376
South Equatorial Current (SEC) 372–73
Southeast Asian Moist Deciduous Forest 122
Sparrowhawk, Collared 125, 224, 258, 273, 303
Spearbush 123–24
Speargrass
Giant 149
Rough 182, 257
Sphagnum, New Zealand 323, 342
Sphagnum bogs 342, 342
Sphagnum spp. 342
Spine Bush 298
Spinebill
Eastern 191, 198, 200, 218, 224, 229, 272, 289, 323, 393
Western 204, **204**, 213, 252
Spinifex 41, 143, 298, 312
spinifex (grass, *Triodia* spp.) 33, 35, 39, 41, 42, **42**, 43, 46, 49, 136, **142**, 143, 287, **297**, 298, 307, 312
competitive strategy, with seeds 51
hummocks, growth form of 42, **42**, 46, 49, **50**, 51, 144, **297**, 298, 312
Spinifex (*Triodia* spp.)
Feathertop 42, 47, 144
Giant Grey 50, 144, 312
Hard 42, 43, 46, 47, 144
Limestone 50
Soft 42, 50, 144, 161, 312
Weeping 50, 312
Spinifex, Beach (*Spinifex sericeus*) 354, 357
Spinifex Eucalypt Savanna 11, 35, 36, 49, 132, 133, 135, **141**, 141–46, **142**, **143**, 159, 170, 311, 312, 313, 314
Spinifex Mallee 17, 33, 141, 143, 217, 220, 243, 281, 286, 288, 290, 291, 293, 295, **296**, 296–300, **297**
Spinifex Mulga 36, 43, 144, 159, 164, 220, 298, 299, 306, 307, 308, **311**, 311–14, **312**
Spinifexbird 52, 144, 313
Spoonbill
Royal 331, 364
Yellow-billed 331
Starflower, Slender-leaved 161
Starling, Metallic 113
Stilt
Banded 335, **360**, 361
Pied 361
Stinging Tree, Giant 78
Stinging trees (*Dendrocnide* spp.) 71

Stint, Red-necked 331, 364, 367
Stork, Black-necked 331, **331**
Storm-Petrel
Band-rumped 375
Matsudaira's 374
New Caledonian 375
Polynesian 375
Swinhoe's 374
White-bellied 375
Wilson's 374, 377
Streptoglossa, Fragrant 51
Stringybark
Blue-leaved 217
Broad-leaved 226
Darwin 147, 149, 153
Desert 287
Narrow-leaved 217, 244, 245
Red 245
Thin-leaved 236
Tindal's 236
White 244
Subalpine Eucalypt Woodland 31, 187, 191, 220, **269**, 269–73, **270**, **271**, 321, **322**
Subtropical Rainforest *see* Australian Subtropical Rainforest
Succulent Karoo 36, 54
Succulent Puna 54
sugarcane fields/farming 115, 382, 383, **383**, 384
Sugarwood 55
Sunbird, Sahul 108
Sundew
Fan-leaved 207
Tropical 207
Sunflower, Beach 357
Sunray
Common White 60
Pygmy 55
Sunskink
Dark-flecked Garden 105
Diamond-shielded 121
Pale-flecked Garden 258
Supplejack 155, 308
Swallow, White-backed 44, 185
Swamp Forest
Afrotropical 110
Asian Freshwater 342
Australasian *see* Australasian Swamp Forest
New Guinea 113
Palm 110
Petén 112, 347
Swamphen, Australasian 331, 364
Swan, Black 335, **335**, 361
Swiftlet, Mountain 327
Sword-Sedge, Variable 223
Syzygium 93

Taipan
Coastal 151, 157, 169
Inland 181
Tallgrass Prairie 182, 183
Tallowwood 107, 222, 226
Tamarind, Native 76
Tanglefoot 98, 99
Tanglehead 136, 331
Tantoon 106, 197, 267
Tar Bush 279, 292, 298
Tasmania 100, 101
habitats 31, 98, 99, 187, 191, 246, 269, 272–73, 323, 342, 343
Tasmanian Devil 100, 199, 241
Tattler, Grey-tailed 367
Tea Tree
Black 266
Coast 197, 198, 370
Fibre-barked 155, 161, 167, 206
Lamellar 155, 161
Little-leaved 165
Mallee 287
Myrtle 207
Paperbark 197, 217
Small-leaf 217
Spidery 217
Weeping 107, 110, 170, 171, 266
Teak, Ipil 89
Teak Forest 147
Teal, Grey 361, 364
Tecticornia spp. 64
Temperate Heath Thicket 192, 196, 197, 199–200, 202, 211, 212, 351
Temperate Mangrove, Australian 30, 344, 345, 351–53, **352**
Temperate Pelagic Waters *see* Australian Temperate Pelagic Waters
Temperate Rainforest *see* Australian Temperate Rainforest
Temperate Tussock Grassland 56, 176, 177, 182–86, **183**, 187, 386
Temperate Wetland *see* Australian Temperate Wetland
Terminalia spp. 89
Termite, Spinifex, mounds 149
termites 43, 51, 149
mounds **136**, 149–50, **166**, **178**
Tern
Arctic 378
Black-naped 358, 373
Bridled 358, 378
Caspian 355, 361
Common 378
Fairy 355, 356, 378
Great Crested 355, **356**, 358, 378
Gull-billed 364
Lesser Crested 358
Little 358, 378
Roseate 358
Sooty 358, 378
Whiskered 361
White 373, 378
White-fronted 378
Tetrodonta Woodland Savanna 17, 28, 35, 38, 122, 125, 127, 132, 133, 134, 147–52, **148–49**, 153, 157
Thicketbird
Bougainville 96
Guadalcanal 95
Rusty 91
Thicket-Fantail, Black 348
Thick-knee
Beach 348, **349**, 355, 366
Bush 157
Thintail, Pacific Island 357
Thistle
Scotch 191
Spear 273
Thorn, Umbrella 42
Thornbill
Brown 199, 240, 257, 273, 289
Buff-rumped 277, 283, 289
Chestnut-rumped 277, **277**, 283, 289, 295
Inland 247, 277, 283, 289, 308, 318, 352
Mountain 85
Slaty-backed 308, 314
Slender-billed 289
Striated 240, 246, 257, 273, 289
Tasmanian 229, 273, 342
Western 252, 318
Yellow 13, 130, 240, 247, **267**, 267–68, 277, 283, 289
Yellow-rumped 44, 289, 295, 304, 318, 324
Thrush
Bassian 100, 105
Bougainville 96
Guadalcanal 95
Makira 95
Ti (*Cordyline fruticosa*) 88
Tidal Mudflat, Australasian *see* Australasian Tidal Mudflat
Tiger-Parrot, Painted 94–95, **95**, 328
tiger-parrots 85
Tingle
Rate's 232
Red 232
Toad, Cane 75, 80, 115, 139, 151, 332, 383

Toadlet
Mimic 151
Wrinkled 295
Tongavine, Centipede 111
Toothbrush, Red 202
Torrent-lark 85
Tree Fern
Rebecca 222–23
Rough 99, 223
Soft 99, 102, 222
tree ferns **98**
Tree Frog
Australian Green 139, 169, 175, 241, 350
Beautiful 151
Brown 100
Dainty 80, 115
Desert 139, 285, 295
Eastern Dwarf 115
Eastern Mountains 95
Glandular 100
Green-eyed 75
Northern Laughing 350
Orange-thighed 74, 80
Peron's Laughing 241, 264, 285
Tyler's Laughing 241
Western Laughing 139, 175
White-lipped 74, 115
Tree Monitor
Banded 127
Emerald 91
Golden-spotted 150
Tree Plantations, Australasian **392**, 392–93
Tree Snake
Brown 139, 151
Common 79, 79 , 127, 139, 150, 241, 332
tree snakes 91
Treecreeper
Black-tailed 138, 144, 150, **150**
Brown 283, 295, 318
Red-browed 224, 230, 239, **239**, 246
Rufous 234, 304
White-browed 283, 299, 308, 314
White-throated 239, 246, 273
Tree-Kangaroo
Bennett's 73
Lumholtz's 73, 86, **86**
tree-kangaroos 29, 72, 74, 95
Triller
Varied 120, 127
White-winged 144, 289, 318
Triodia see spinifex (grass, *Triodia* spp.)
Tropical Dry Deciduous Forests 19, 116, 117–31
Australasian Monsoon Vineforest *see* Australasian Monsoon Vineforest
Australian Dry Vineforest *see* Australian Dry Vineforest
Brigalow *see* Brigalow (habitat)
Tropical Freshwater Wetland *see* Australasian Tropical Freshwater Wetland
Tropical Heathland 106, 192, 203, 206–9, **208**, 215
Tropical Mangrove Forest *see* Australasian Tropical Mangrove Forest
Tropical Montane Rainforest *see* Australasian Tropical Montane Rainforest
Tropical Pelagic Waters *see* Australasian Tropical Pelagic Waters
Tropical Tussock Grassland 32, 39, 41, 46, 49, 133, 176, **177**, 177–81, **178**, **179**, 182, 185, 385
Coastal **177**
Tropicbird
Red-tailed 373, 377
White-tailed 373, **373**, 377
Tuckeroo 106, 108, 111, 198
Tuft-Rush, Fan 187
Tulip Tree, African 88
Tulipwood, Yellow 107
Tundra 20, 320, 321–28
Arctic Cryptic 322
Asian Alpine 321
Australian Alpine 31, 187, 271, 320, 321–24, **322**, 325
Austroparamo 39, 92, 320, 321, 325–28, **326**, 343
European Alpine 321, 323
European Rocky 377
Nearctic Alpine 321, 323, 325
Nearctic Rocky 322, 377
Turanian Arid Riparian Scrub 170, 260, 315
Turkey Bush
Charleville 308
Crimson 275, 276, 313
Purple-stemmed 207
Turnstone, Ruddy 358, 370
Turpentine Bush 308
Turpentine Tree 222, 226
Turtle
Broad-shelled 336
Eastern Saw-shelled 115
Eastern Short-necked 115, 336, 353
Eastern Snake-necked 336
Northern Australian Snapping 332
Northern Snake-necked 332
Sea *see* Sea Turtle
Southwestern Snake-necked 336
turtles **115**, 353
Tussock Puna 187, 189
twigrushes 334
Twinleaf, Shrubby 64

Uluru (Ayers Rock) 36, 42, **42–43**
UNESCO World Heritage Site 28, 35
Upper Montane Cloudforest, Solomon Islands 95–96
Urban Environment, Australasian **389**, 389–91

Vine
Common Milk 102
Five-leaved Water 223
Tarantula 119
Wonga Wonga 119
vines 78, 99, 102, 107, 111, 119, 123, **123**, 171
Violet, Tree 267
Vitex, Scrub 124

Wait-a-While 78
Wallaby
Agile 91, 120, 138, 150, 157, 164, 168, **169**, 332, 386
Bennett's 219
Black-striped 120, 247
Bridled Nail-tail 130
Northern Nail-tail 138
Parma 100, 231
Red-necked 100, 130, 191, 199, 205, 219, 224, 241, 247, 273, 324, 342
Swamp 105, 115, 120, 191, 199, **200**, 205, 219, 224, 231, 247, 258, 263, 277
Tammar 253, 304
Western Brush 234, 253, 304
Whiptail 120, 130, 240, **241**, 247
Wallacean Melaleuca Savanna 165
Wallaroo
Antilopine 138, 150, 164, 332, 386
Common 52, 164, **164**, 181, 247, 277, 285, 310, 318–19
Euro subspecies *see* Euro
Wallum 193, 196, **196**, 207, 209, 287, 353, 354
Wallum and Ausbos 30, 31, 106, 187, 192, 193–200, **194**, **195**, **196**, 201, 203, 204, 206, 210, 215, 217, 242, 252, 265, 286, 288
Temperate Heath Thicket (subhabitat) 192, 196, 197, 199–200, 202, 211, 212, 351
Walnut
Blush 76
Rose 228
White 76
Wandoo 302
Powderbark 302

Warbler
- Australian Reed 331, 335, 364
- Kolombangara Leaf 95–96
- Shade 95
- Speckled 130, **130**, 257, 276

Warrior Bush 313
Water Bush 303
Water Lily, Blue 329
waterlogging/waterlogged soils 108, 179, 207, 215, 216
Wattle
- Archer River 160
- Brass's 207
- Cork-bark 135
- Deane's 245
- Gold-dust 257
- Golden 212, 257
- Haviland's 292
- Julie's 160
- Karri 233
- Long-leaved 197
- Mabels's 223
- North Coast 167
- Pindan 50, 160
- Prain's 315
- Prickly 275
- Sandhill 46, 307
- Silver 270
- Spreading 257
- Stiff-leaf 217
- Streaked 275
- Stringybark 275
- Summer-scented 203
- Sweet 197
- Tableland 245
- Tan 315
- Thargo 307–8
- Torulosa 155, 160
- Townsville 155, 160, 167
- Umbrella 292
- Western Silver 245

Wattlebird
- Little 198, 199, 218, 289
- Red **197**, 198, 199, 204, 213, 233, 252, 272, 276, 289, 323
- Western 204, 213, 252
- Yellow 273

Waxflower, Common 84
Wedding Bush 197
Wedgebill, Chirruping 341
Weebill 144, 150, 157, **161**, 163, 277, 283, 289, 295, 303, 318
Weeping Emu Bush 279
Western Eucalypt Woodland 34, 210, 220, 242, 249, 251, 253, 254, 285, 286, 291, 294, 296, **301**, 301–5, **302**, 315, 319
Whale
- Blue 375, 378
- Bryde's 375
- Common Minke 375
- False Killer 375
- Humpback 375, 378
- Long-finned Pilot 378
- Melon-headed 375
- Short-finned Pilot 375
- Southern Right 378
- Sperm 375

whales 375, 378
wheat fields **379**
Wheatgrass, Common 188
Whimbrel 364, 370
Whipbird
- Eastern 120, 199, 229, **229**
- Papuan 85
- Western **212**, 213, 294, 298
  - Black-throated (subspecies) 298
  - White-bellied (subspecies) 298

Whipsnake
- Central 53
- Greater Black 139, 151, 164, 350
- Yellow-faced 278

Whiptail-Skink, Shrub 209
Whistler
- Black-tailed 108, 348, **348**, 349
- Gilbert's 295, 299, 380
- Golden 199, 200, 295
  - Western subspecies 214, 233, 252, 299
- Grey 125
- Island 348
- Lorentz's 95
- Olive 100, **100**, 105, 273, 324
- Oriole 91
- Red-lored 294, 299
- Regent 95
- Rufous 120, 130, 144, 150, 163, 252, 277, 283, 295, 299, 318
- Rusty 85, 90
- White-breasted 252, 348, 349

Whistling-Duck
- Plumed 331, **333**
- Wandering 331, 333

White Box **255**
White-eye
- Ashy-bellied 108
- Australian Yellow 348
- Kolombangara 96
- Solomons 91
- Yellow-throated 91

Whiteface
- Banded 56
- Chestnut-breasted 56, 62
- Southern 44, 289, 295

Whitewood 135, 143, 155, 178, 279, 308, 313
Wilga 279, 282, 298, 308
Willie-wagtail 189
Willow, Weeping 42
Wiregrass
- Feathertop 60, 177
- Purple 188

Wombat
- Bare-nosed 100, 191, 199, 219, 247, 258, **259**, 273, 290, 300, 324, 342, 388
- Northern Hairy-nosed 130
- Southern Hairy-nosed 185, 290, 300

Woodlands *see specific woodlands/forests*
Woodswallow 144
- Black-faced 57, 185, 277, 289, 295
- Dusky 57, 185, 199, 214
- Great **91**
- Masked 144, 277, 278, 283, 288, 289, 295, 318
- White-breasted 174
- White-browed 144, 277, 278, 283, 288, 318

Woollybutt, Darwin 147
Woylie (Western Bandicoot) 252, 304

Yapunyah, Mountain 313
Yarri 250
Yate, Flat-topped 250
Yellow Water, Kakadu National Park 333
Yellowheads, Erect 60
Yellowjacket, Inland 160
Yilgarn Mixed Woodland 34, 220, 279, 315–19, **316**, **317**
Yorrell 291, 298